GEEK GIRL

HOLLY SMALE

HarperCollins *Children's Books*

First published in paperback in Great Britain
by HarperCollins *Children's Books* in 2013
HarperCollins *Children's Books* is a division of HarperCollins*Publishers* Ltd,
77-85 Fulham Palace Road, Hammersmith, London, W6 8JB.

The HarperCollins website address is: www.harpercollins.co.uk

23

ISBN 978-0-00-748944-2

Printed and bound in England by Clays Ltd, St Ives plc

geek/gi:k/h noun informal, chiefly N. Amer.

1 an unfashionable or socially inept person.

2 an obsessive enthusiast.

3 a person who feels the need to look up the word 'geek' in the dictionary.

DERIVATIVES ***geeky*** adjective.

ORIGIN from the related English dialect word *geck* 'fool'.

1

My name is Harriet Manners, and I am a geek.

I know I'm a geek because I've just looked it up in the *Oxford English Dictionary*. I drew a little tick next to all the symptoms I recognise, and I appear to have them all. Which – and I should be perfectly honest here – hasn't come as an enormous surprise. The fact that I have an *Oxford English Dictionary* on my bedside table anyway should have been one clue. That I keep a Natural History Museum pencil and ruler next to it so that I can neatly underline interesting entries should have been another.

Oh, and then there's the word **GEEK**, drawn in red marker pen on the outside pocket of my school satchel. That was done yesterday.

I didn't do it, obviously. If I *did* decide to deface my own property, I'd choose a poignant line from a really good book, or an interesting fact not many people know. And I definitely wouldn't do it in red. I'd do it in black, or blue, or perhaps green. I'm not a big fan of the colour red, even if it *is* the longest wavelength of light discernible by the human eye.

To be absolutely candid with you, I don't actually know *who* decided to write on my bag – although I have my suspicions – but I can tell you that their writing is almost illegible. They clearly weren't listening during our English lesson last week when we were told that handwriting is a very important Expression of the Self. Which is quite lucky because if I can just find a similar shade of pen, I might be able to slip in the letter *R* in between *G* and *E*. I can pretend that it's a reference to my interest in ancient history and feta cheese.

I prefer Cheddar, but nobody has to know that.

Anyway, the point is: as my satchel, the anonymous vandal and the *Oxford English Dictionary* appear to agree with each other, I can only conclude that I am, in fact, a geek.

Did you know that in the old days the word 'geek' was used to describe a carnival performer who bit the head off a live chicken or snake or bat as part of their stage act?

Exactly. Only a geek would know a thing like that.

I think it's what they call ironic.

2

Now that you know who I am, you're going to want to know where I am and what I'm doing, right? Character, action and location: that's what makes a story. I read it in a book called *What Makes a Story*, written by a man who hasn't got any stories at the moment, but knows exactly how he'll tell them when he eventually does.

So.

It's currently December, I'm in bed – tucked under about fourteen covers – and I'm not doing anything at all apart from getting warmer by the second. In fact, I don't want to alarm you or anything, but I think I might be really sick. My hands are clammy, my stomach's churning and I'm *significantly* paler than I was ten minutes ago. Plus, there's what can only be described as a sort of… *rash* on my face. Little red spots scattered at totally random and not at *all* symmetrical points on my cheeks and forehead. With a big one on my chin. And one just next to my left ear.

I take another look in the little hand-held mirror on my bedside table, and then sigh as loudly as I can. There's no doubt about it: I'm clearly very ill. It would be wrong to risk spreading this dangerous infection to other, possibly less hardy, immune systems. I shall just have to battle through this illness alone.

All day. Without going anywhere at all.

Sniffling, I shuffle under my duvets a little further and look at my clock on the opposite wall (it's very clever: all the numbers are painted at the bottom as if they've just fallen down, although this does mean that when I'm in a hurry, I have to sort of guess what the time is). Then I close my eyes and mentally count:

10, 9, 8, *7, 6, 5, 4, 3, 2…*

At which point, absolutely on cue as always, the door opens and the room explodes: hair and handbag and coat and arms everywhere. Like a sort of girl bomb. And there, as if by very punctual magic, is Nat.

Nat – for the record – is my Best Friend, and we are so utterly in tune that it's like we have one brain, divided into two pieces at birth. Or (more likely) two brains, entwined shortly afterwards. Although we didn't meet until we were five years old, so obviously I'm speaking *metaphorically* or we'd both be dead.

What I'm trying to say is: we're close. We're

harmonised. We're one and the same. We're like a perfect stream of consciousness, with never a cross word between us. We work with perfect, unquestioning synergy. Like two dolphins that jump at exactly the same time and pass the ball to each other at Sea World.

Anyway. Nat takes one step into the room, looks at me, and then stops and puts her hands on her hips.

"Good morning," I croak from under the covers, and then I start coughing violently. Human coughs release air at roughly 60mph, and without being vain, I'd like to think that mine reaches 65mph or 70mph minimum.

"Don't even *think* about it," Nat snaps.

I stop coughing and look at her with my roundest, most confused eyes. "Hmmm?" I say innocently. And then I start coughing again.

"I mean it. Don't even think about thinking about it."

I have *no* idea what she's talking about. The fever must be making my brain swell.

"Nat," I say feebly, closing my eyes and pressing my hand against my head. I'm a shell of the person I used to be. A husk. "I have bad news." I open one eye and take a peek round the room. Nat still has her hands on her hips.

"Let me guess," she says in a dry voice. "You're sick."

I give a weak but courageous smile: the sort Jane gives Lizzie in *Pride and Prejudice* when she's bedridden with a really bad cold, but is being very brave about it. "You know me so well," I say affectionately. "It's like we have one mind, Nat."

"And you're out of it if you think I'm not about to drag you out of bed by your feet." Nat takes a few steps towards me. "Also, I want my lipstick back," she adds.

I clear my throat. "Lipstick?"

"The one you've dotted all over your face."

I open my mouth and then shut it again. "It's not lipstick," I say in a small voice. "It's a dangerous infection."

"Then your dangerous infection is glittery, Harriet, and just so happens to match my new shoes perfectly."

I shift a little bit further down the bed so that only my eyes are visible. "Infections are very advanced these days," I say with as much dignity as I can muster. "They are sometimes extremely light-reflective."

"Featuring small flecks of gold?"

I raise my chin defiantly. "Sometimes."

Nat's nose twitches and she rolls her eyes. "Right.

And your face is producing white talcum powder, is it?"

I sniff quickly. Oh, *sugar cookies.* "It's important to keep sick people dry," I say as airily as I can. "Dampness can allow bacteria to develop."

Nat sighs again. "Get out of bed, Harriet."

"But—"

"Get out of bed."

"Nat, I…"

"Out. Now."

I look down at the duvets in a panic. "But I'm not ready! I'm in my pyjamas!" I'm going to give it one last desperate shot. "Nat," I say, changing tack and using my most serious, profound voice. "You don't understand. How will you feel if you're wrong? How will you *live* with yourself? I might be *dying*."

"Actually, you're right," Nat agrees, taking another two steps towards me. "You are. I'm literally seconds away from killing you, Harriet Manners. And if that happens, I'll live with myself just fine. Now get out of bed, you little faker."

And, before I can protect myself, Nat lunges suddenly towards me and tugs the covers away.

There's a long silence.

"Oh, *Harriet*," Nat eventually says in a sad and

simultaneously triumphant voice.

Because I'm lying in bed, fully dressed, with my shoes on. And in one hand is a box of talcum powder; in the other is a bright red lipstick.

3

OK, so I lied a little bit.

Twice, actually.

Nat and I are not in perfect harmony at all. We're definitely close, and we definitely spend all of our time together, and we definitely adore each other very much, but there are *moments* now we've almost grown up where our interests and passions divide a teensy bit.

Or – you know – a lot.

It doesn't stop us being inseparable, obviously. We're Best Friends because we frequently make each other laugh, so much so that I once made orange juice come out of her nose (on to her mum's white rug – we stopped laughing pretty shortly afterwards). And also because I remember when she peed on the ballet-room floor, aged six, and she is the only person in the entire world who knows I still have a dinosaur poster taped to the inside of my wardrobe.

But over the last few years, there have definitely been *minuscule* points where our desires and needs have… conflicted a little bit. Which is why I *may* have said I was a little bit sicker than I actually felt this morning, which was: not much.

Or at all, actually. I feel great.

And why Nat is a bit snappy with me as we run towards the school coach as fast as my legs will carry me.

"You know," Nat sighs as she waits for me to catch up for the twelfth time. "I watched that *stupid* documentary on the Russian Revolution for you last week, and it was about four hundred hours long. The least you can do is participate in an Educational Opportunity to See Textiles from an Intimate and Consumer Perspective with me."

"*Shopping*," I puff, holding my sides together so they don't fall apart. "It's called shopping."

"That's not what's written on the leaflet. It's a school trip: there has to be *something* educational about it."

"No," I huff. "There isn't." Nat pauses again so that I can try and catch up. "It's just shopping."

To be fair, I think I have a point. We're going to The Clothes Show Live, in Birmingham. So-called – presumably – because they show clothes to you. Live. In Birmingham. And let you buy them. And take them home with you afterwards.

Which is otherwise known as *shopping*.

"It'll be fun," Nat says from a few metres ahead of me. "They've got everything there, Harriet. Everything anyone could possibly ever want."

"Really?" I say in the most sarcastic voice I can find, considering that I'm now running so fast that my breath is starting to squeak. "Do they have a triceratops skull?"

"...No."

"Do they have a life-size model of the first airborne plane?"

"...Probably not."

"And do they have a John Donne manuscript, with little white gloves so that you can actually touch it?"

Nat thinks about it. "I think it's unlikely they have that," she admits.

"Then they don't have *everything* I want, do they?"

We reach the coach steps and I can barely breathe. I don't understand it: we've both run the same distance, and we've both expended the same energy. I'm an entire centimetre shorter than Nat so I have less mass to move, at the same speed (on average). We both have exactly the same amount of PE lessons. And yet – despite the laws of physics – I'm huffing and purple, and Nat's only slightly glowing and still capable of breathing out of her nose.

Sometimes science makes no sense at all.

Nat starts rapping in a panic on the bus door. We're late – thanks to my excellent acting skills – and it looks like the class might be about to leave without us. "Harriet," Nat snaps, turning to look at me as the doors start making sucking noises, as if they're kissing. "Tsar Nicholas II was overthrown by Lenin in 1917."

I blink in surprise. "Yes," I say. "He was."

"And do you think I want to know that? It's not even on our exam syllabus. I *never* had to know that. So now it's your turn to pick up a few pairs of shoes and make *ooh* and *aah* sounds for me because Jo ate prawns and she's allergic to prawns and she got sick and couldn't come and I'm not sitting on a bus on my own for five hours. OK?"

Nat takes a deep breath and I look at my hands in shame. I am a selfish, selfish person. I am also a very sparkly person: my hands are covered in gold glitter.

"OK," I say in a small voice. "I'm sorry, Nat."

"You're forgiven." The coach doors finally slide open. "Now get on this bus and pretend for one little day that you have the teeniest, tiniest smidgen of interest in fashion."

"All right," I say, my voice getting even smaller.

Because – in case you haven't worked this out by now – here's the key thing that really divides Nat and me:

I don't.

4

So, before we get on the bus, you might want to know a little more about me.

You might not, obviously. You might be thinking, *Just get on with it, Harriet, because I haven't got all day*, which is what Annabel says all the time. Adults rarely have all day, from what I can tell. However, if – like me – you read cereal boxes at the breakfast table and shampoo bottles in the bath and bus timetables when you already know what bus you're getting, here's a little more information:

1. My mother is dead. That's usually the bit where people look awkward and start talking about how rainy the sky looks, but she died when I was three days old so missing her is a bit like loving a character from a book. The only stories I have of her belong to other people.

2. I have a stepmother, Annabel. She married Dad when I was seven, she's alive and she works as a lawyer. (You would not believe the amount of arguments my parents have over those two facts. "I am living," Annabel will scream. "You're a lawyer," Dad will shout back. "Who are you kidding?")

3. Dad's In Advertising. ("Not in adverts," Annabel always points out when they have dinner parties. "I write them," Dad replies in frustration. "I'm as In Advertising as you can get."

   "Apart from actors," Annabel says under her breath, at which point Dad stomps off to the kitchen to get another bottle of beer.)

4. I'm an only child. Thanks to my parents, I am destined to a life of never having anyone to squabble with in the back seat of the car.

5. Nat isn't just my Best Friend. She gave herself this title, even though I told her it was a bit unnecessary: she's also my Only Friend. This might be because I have a tendency to correct

people's grammar and tell them facts they're not interested in.

6. And put things in lists. Like this one.

7. Nat and I met ten years ago when we were five, which makes us fifteen. I know you could have worked that out by yourself, but I can't assume people like doing equations in their heads just because I do.

8. Nat is beautiful. When we were young, adults would put a hand under her chin and say, "She's going to break hearts, this one," as if she couldn't hear them and wasn't deciding when would be the best time to start.

9. I am not. My impact on hearts is like an earthquake happening on the other side of the world: if I'm lucky, I can hope for a teacup tinkling in its saucer. And even then it's a bit of a surprise and everybody talks about it for days afterwards.

Other things will probably filter through in stages

– like the fact that I only eat toast in triangles because it means there are no soggy edges, and my favourite book is the first half of *Great Expectations* and the last half of *Wuthering Heights* – but you don't need to know them right now. In fact, arguably, you never need to know them. The last book Dad bought me had a gun on the front cover.

Anyway, the final defining fact that I may already have mentioned in passing is:

10. I don't like fashion.

I never really have, and I can't imagine I ever will.

I got away with it until I was about ten. Under that age, non-uniform didn't really exist: we were either in our school uniform, or our pyjamas, or our swimming costumes, or dressed like angels or sheep for the school nativity. We had to go and get an outfit especially for non-uniform days.

Then teenagehood hit like a big pink glittery sledgehammer. Suddenly there were rules and breaking them *mattered*. Skirt lengths and trouser shapes and eye-shadow shades and heel heights and knowing how long you could go without wearing mascara before people accused you of being a lesbian.

Suddenly the world was divided into the right and the horribly, horribly wrong. And the people stuck between, who for the life of them couldn't tell the difference. People who wore white socks and black shoes; who liked having hair on their legs because it was fluffy at night-time. People who really missed the sheep outfit, and secretly wanted to wear it to school even when it wasn't Christmas.

People like me.

If there had been *consistent* rules, I'd have done my best to keep up. Made some sort of pie chart or line graph and then resentfully applied the basics. But fashion's not like that: it's a slippery old fish. You try to grab it round the neck and it slides out of your grip and shoots off in another direction, and every desperate grab towards it makes you look even more stupid. Until you're sliding around on the floor, everybody is laughing at you and the fish has shot under the table.

So – to put it simply – I gave up. Brains have only got so much they can absorb, so I decided I didn't have space. I'd rather know that hummingbirds can't walk, or that one teaspoon of a neutron star weighs billions of tonnes, or that bluebirds can't see the colour blue.

Nat, however, went the other way. And suddenly the sheep and the angel – who hung out quite happily in the fields of Bethlehem together – didn't have as much in common any more.

We're still Best Friends. She's still the girl who lost her first baby tooth in my apple, and I'm still the girl who stuck one of her sunflower seeds up my nose in primary school and couldn't get it out again. But sometimes, every now and then, the gap between us gets so big it feels like one of us is going to slip through.

Something tells me that today that person is going to be me.

5

Anyway.

What all this means is: I'm not thrilled to be here. I've stopped whining, but let's just say I'm not spinning round and round in circles, farting at intervals, like my dog Hugo does when he's excited. In fact, I did two years of doing woodwork *specifically* so I didn't have to come on this textiles trip. Two years of accidentally sanding down my thumbs and cringing to the sound of metal on metal, purely to get out of today. And then Jo eats prawns and does a little vomiting and *BAM*: here I am.

The first step on to the coach is uneventful, just one step, directly behind Nat's. The second step is slightly less successful. The coach starts before we've sat down and I'm thrown sideways, in the process kicking a nice fluffy green bag the way I've never, ever managed to kick a football in my entire life.

"Moron," Chloe hisses as she retrieves it.

"I'm n-n-not," I stutter, cheeks lighting up. "A

moron only has an IQ of between 50 and 69. I think mine's a little higher than that."

And then it all goes wrong. On the third step, the driver sees a family of ducks on the road, hits the brakes and sends me flying towards the end of the bus. I instinctively grab whatever will protect me from slamming my face on the floor. A headrest, a shoulder, an armrest, a seat.

Somebody's knee.

"Ugh," a voice shouts in total disgust, "she's *touching me*."

And there – staring at me as if she just sicked me up – is Alexa.

6

<u>People Who Hate Harriet Manners</u>

1. Alexa Roberts

Alexa. My nemesis, my adversary, my opponent, my arch-enemy. Whatever you want to call somebody who hates your guts.

I've known her three days longer than I've known Nat and I've yet to work out what her problem is. I can only conclude that her feelings towards me are very similar to what I've read about love: passionate, random, inexplicable and totally uncontrollable. She can't help hating me any more than Heathcliff could help loving Cathy. It's simply written in the stars. Which would be quite sweet if she wasn't such a cow all of the time.

And I wasn't totally terrified of her.

I stare at Alexa in total shock. I'm still clinging to her tight-covered leg like a frightened baby monkey clinging on to a tree. "Let *go*," she snaps. "Oh my *God*."

I scrabble away, trying desperately to stand up. There are approximately 13,914,291,404 legs in the world – over half of them in trousers – and I had to grab *this* one?

"Ugh," she says loudly to anybody who will listen. "Do you think I might have caught something? Oh, God, I can already feel it starting…" She cowers in her seat. "No…The *light*… It *hurts…* I can feel myself changing… Suddenly I want to do my homework… It's too late!" She puts her hands over her face and then pulls them away, crosses her eyes, protrudes her teeth and pulls the ugliest expression I've ever seen on public transport. "Nooooooo! I've caught it! I'm… I'm… I'm a geeeeeeeeeeeeek!"

People start sniggering and from somewhere on the left I can hear a little ripple of applause. Alexa bows a couple of times, pulls a face at me and then goes back to reading her magazine.

My cheeks are flushed, my hands are shaking. My eyes are starting to prickle. All the normal responses to ritual humiliation. The thing I want to make really clear right now is that I don't mind *being* a geek. *Being* a geek is fine. It's unimpressive, sure, but it's pretty unobtrusive. I could be a geek all day long, as long as people left me alone.

The thing is: they don't.

"*Seriously*," Nat snaps in a loud voice from a few metres in front of me. "Did you sniff wet paint as a child or something, Alexa?"

Alexa rolls her eyes. "Barbie *talks.* Run away and play with your shoes, Natalie. This has nothing to do with you."

I'm trying desperately to think of something clever to say. Something biting, poignant, incisive, deeply wounding. Something that will give Alexa just an ounce of the hurt she gives me on an almost daily basis.

"You suck," I say in the tiniest voice I've ever heard.

Yeah, I think. *That should do it.* And then I hold my chin up as high as I can get it, walk the rest of the way down the aisle and sink into the seat next to Nat before my knees give way.

I'm in my seat for about three seconds when the morning promptly decides to get worse. I barely have time to open my crossword book first.

"Harriet!" a delighted voice says, and a little pale face pops over the back of the seat in front of me. "You're here! You're really, actually, actually *here*!" As if I'm Father Christmas and he's a six-year-old whose chimney I've just climbed down.

"Yes, Toby," I say reluctantly. "I'm here." And then I turn to scowl at Nat.

It's Toby Pilgrim.

Toby "my knees buckle when I run" Pilgrim. Toby "I bring my own Bunsen burner to school" Pilgrim. Toby "I wear bicycle clips on my trousers *and I don't even have a bike*" Pilgrim. Nat should have told me he'd be here.

I'm now following my own stalker to Birmingham.

7

Imagine you're a polar bear and you find yourself in the middle of a rainforest. There are flying squirrels, and monkeys, and bright green frogs, and you have no idea how you got there or what you're supposed to do next. You're lonely, you're lost, you're frightened and all you know – for absolute certain – is that you shouldn't be there.

Now imagine you find *another* polar bear. You're so happy to see another polar bear – *any* polar bear – that it doesn't matter what kind it is. You follow that polar bear around, just because it's not a monkey. Or a flying squirrel. Because it's the only thing that makes it OK to be a polar bear in the middle of a rainforest.

Well, that's how it is with Toby. One geek, incoherently happy to find another geek in the middle of a world full of normal people. Thrilled to discover that there is someone else like him. It's not me he wants. It's my social standing. Or lack thereof.

And let me get something straight: I'm not going

to have a romance with someone just because they're made out of the same stuff as me. *No.* I'd rather be on my own. Or – you know – in unrequited love with a parrot. Or one of those little lemurs with the stripy tails.

"Harriet!" Toby says again and a little bit of bogey starts dripping from his nose. He promptly wipes it on his jumper sleeve and beams at me. "I can't believe you came!"

I glare at Nat and she grins, winks and goes back to reading her magazine. I am not feeling very *harmonised* with her at the moment, if I'm being totally honest. In fact, I sort of feel like hitting her over the head with my crossword puzzle.

"Yes," I say, trying to edge away. "Apparently I had to."

"But isn't this just wonderful?" he gasps, clambering up on to his knees in his unbridled enthusiasm. I notice that his T-shirt says **THERE'S NO PLACE LIKE 127.0.0.1.** "Of all the buses in all the towns in all the world, you walk on to mine. Can you see what I did there? It's a quote from *Casablanca*, except that I replaced the words *gin joints* with *bus* and the word *into* with *on to.*"

"You did, yes."

Nat makes a snuffle of amusement and I subtly pinch her leg.

"Do you know what I learnt this morning, Harriet? I learnt that the phrase *rule of thumb* came from a time when a man was only legally allowed to beat his wife with something the width of his own thumb. I can lend you the book, although there's a pizza stain on page 143 which you might have to read round."

"Erm. Right. Thanks." I nod knowingly and then lift my book so that Toby realises the conversation is over.

He doesn't.

"*And*," he continues, holding it down so he can see me properly. "You know the most *unbelievable* thing?"

It's funny, when Toby behaves like this, I can suddenly see why I'm so annoying.

"Well, did you know that..." The coach swerves slightly into the middle lane. Toby swallows. "That..." he continues and licks his lips. The coach swerves back into the slow lane. "That—" Toby's face goes abruptly green and he clears his throat. "I don't want you to think I'm easily distracted, Harriet," he finally continues in a little voice, "but I'm suddenly not feeling so well. I don't take too kindly to vehicles, particularly the ones that move. Do you remember the ride-on lawnmower in Year One?"

I look at him in horror and Nat immediately stops smirking. "Oh, no," she says in a dark voice. "No, *no*." Nat obviously remembers it too.

"Harriet," Toby continues, licking his lips again and going an even stranger colour. "I think we might need to stop the bus."

"*Toby*," Nat snaps in a low, warning voice. "Breathe in through your nose and out through your—"

But it's too late. The coach makes one more sudden movement and – as if in slow motion – Toby gives me one look of pure apology.

And vomits all over my lap.

8

In case you were wondering, that's what Toby did on the ride-on lawnmower in Year One too. Except this time he manages to broaden his horizons in the most literal sense and hit Nat too.

She's not happy about it. I mean, I'm not happy about it either. I don't relish being hit by the contents of other people's digestive tracts. But Nat's *really* not happy about it.

She's so unhappy about it that when the coach finally pulls up to The Clothes Show at the NEC, Birmingham – two and a half hours later – she's *still* shouting at him. And Toby's telling both of us how much better he feels now because, "Isn't it funny how it feels OK when all the vomit's gone?"

"I don't *believe* this," Nat is still snapping, stomping across the carpark. We're both now wearing PE kit: luckily two of the boys had football practice straight after the trip, so – after a lot of whining – Miss Fletcher managed to convince them to lend us their kit. We're wearing orange football shirts, green football shorts and white knee socks.

I quite like it. It's making me feel quite sporty. Nat, on the other hand, isn't so keen. We were forced to keep our shoes on, and – while my trainers look quite normal – Nat's red high heels... don't.

"Do you *know* how long it took me to choose my outfit this morning?" she's yelling at Toby as we approach the front doors.

Toby contemplates this like it's not a rhetorical question. "Twenty minutes?" he offers. Nat's face goes slightly puce. "Thirty?" Nat's jawline starts flexing. "An hour and a half?"

"A really long time!" she shouts. "A really, *really* long time!" Nat looks down at herself. "I had a brand-new dress and *leggings from American Apparel,* Toby. Do you know how much they cost? I was wearing *Prada perfume*." She picks up a piece of green nylon between her fingers. *"And now I'm wearing a boy's football kit and I smell of sick!"*

I pat her arm as comfortingly as I can.

"At least my vomit was sort of chocolatey," Toby says cheerfully. "I had Coco Pops for breakfast."

Nat grits her teeth.

"Anyway," Toby continues blithely, "I think you look awesome. You both match. It's super trendy."

Nat scrunches her mouth up, clenches her fists and furrows her brow right in the centre. It's like watching somebody shake a bottle of fizzy drink without taking the lid off. "Toby," she says in a low hiss. "Go. *Now*."

"OK," Toby agrees. "Anywhere in particular?"

"*Anywhere*. Just *go. NOW.*"

"Toby," I say in a low voice, taking him by the arm. I'm really, genuinely scared for his safety. "I think maybe you should go inside." I look at Nat. "As quickly as possible," I add.

"Ah." Toby contemplates this for a few seconds and then nods. "Ah. I see. Then I shall see you both anon."

And – giving me what looks disturbingly like an attempt at a wink over his shoulder – he skips off through the swing doors.

When he's gone and I know that Nat can't rip his head off and feed it to a large flock of pigeons, I turn to her.

"Nat," I say, chewing on a fingernail anxiously. "It's not that bad. Honestly. We smell fine. And if you put my coat on over the top, nobody will see what you're wearing. It's longer than yours."

"You don't get it," Nat says and suddenly the anger

pops: she just sounds miserable. "You just don't *get* it."

I think Nat underestimates my powers of empathy. Which is a shame because I am a very empathetic person. *Em*pathetic. Not *pathetic.*

"Sure I do," I say in a reassuring voice. "You don't like football. I get that."

"It's not that. Today was *really important,* Harriet. I *really* needed to look good."

I stare at her blankly. After a few seconds, Nat rolls her eyes and hits herself on the forehead in frustration. "*They're* in there."

I stare at the revolving doors. "*Who's* in there?" I whisper in terror. I think about it for a few seconds. "Vampires?"

"*Vampires.*" Nat looks at me in consternation. "You have got to start reading proper books."

I don't know what she's talking about. Just because I own a lot of books about things that don't actually exist in real life in no way indicates that I'm not connected to the real world. I totally am.

Nat takes a deep breath. "I put the prawns in Jo's dinner," she says, avoiding my eyes.

I stare at her. "Nat! Why would you do that?"

"Because I need you today," she says in a tiny voice.

"I need you for support. *They're* in there." And she looks again at the doors and swallows.

"*Who?*"

"Model agents, Harriet," Nat says as if I'm an idiot. "Lots and lots of model agents."

"Oh," I say stupidly, and then think about it. "*Ohhhhhhh*."

And I finally understand what I'm doing here.

9

We were seven when Nat decided that she wanted to be a model.

"Gosh," somebody's mum said at a school disco. "Natalie. You're getting gorgeous. Maybe you could be a model when you grow up."

I paused from filling my party dress pockets with chocolate cake and jelly sweets. "A model of what?" I asked curiously. And then my greedy little hand went out to grab a mini jam roll. "I have a model airplane," I added proudly.

The mum gave me the look that I was already used to by then.

"A model," she explained, looking at Nat, "is a girl or a boy who gets paid ridiculous quantities of money to wear clothes they don't own and have their photo taken." I looked at Nat and already I could see her eyes starting to glow: the seed of the dream being planted. "Just hope you grow tall and thin," the mum added bitterly, "because if you ask me, they all look like aliens."

At which point Nat put her chocolate cake down and spent the rest of the night sitting on the floor, with me pulling on her feet to make her legs longer.

And I spent the rest of the night talking about space travel.

It's finally here.

Eight years of buying *Vogue* and not eating pudding (Nat, not me: I eat hers) and we've finally made it to the very edge of Nat's destiny. I feel a bit like Sam in *The Lord of the Rings*, just before Frodo throws the ring into the fires of Mount Doom. Except in a more positive, magical way. With slightly less hairy feet.

Nat doesn't look as excited as I thought she would. She looks terrified and as stiff as a board standing, totally still, in the middle of the NEC entrance. She's staring at the crowd as if it's a pond full of fish and she's a really hungry cat, and – honestly – I'm not even sure she's breathing. I'm tempted to put my head on her chest just to check.

The thing is: she's doing it all wrong.

I know a lot about stories and magic – thanks to reading loads of books and also belonging to a forum on the internet – and the most basic rule is that *it has to come as a surprise*. Nobody hopped into a wardrobe to find Narnia; they hopped in, thinking it was just a wardrobe. They didn't climb up the Faraway Tree, knowing it was a Faraway Tree; they thought it was just a really big tree. Harry Potter thought he was a normal boy; Mary Poppins was supposed to be a regular nanny.

It's the first and only rule. *Magic comes when you're not looking for it.*

But Nat's looking for it, and the harder she looks, the less likely it is to turn up. She's scaring the fashion magic off with her knowing, waiting vibes.

"Come on," I say, trying to distract her by pulling at her (or technically *my*) coat sleeve. I need to get her to think about something else so that the magic can do its thing. "Let's just go and shop, OK?"

"Mmm."

I don't think she can even hear me any more. "Look!" I say enthusiastically, pulling her to the nearest stall. "Nat, look! Handbags! Shoes! Hair bobbles!"

Nat gives me a distracted glance. "You're dragging my coat on the floor."

"Oh." I bundle it back under my arm and start tugging Nat towards the next stall.

"What do you think?" I say, picking up a small blue sequined hat and plopping it on my head. When we were little, we'd spend hours and hours in department stores, trying on different hats and pretending we were going to a royal wedding.

"Uh-huh." Nat gets a little bit more tense and looks over her shoulder.

"Come on, what about this one?" I pick up a large floppy hat covered in big pink flowers and put it on. "Look." I wiggle my bottom at her.

Nat abruptly whips round. "Oh my God," she whispers and it takes me a few seconds to realise that it has nothing at all to do with my bottom.

"Have you seen one?"

"I think so!" She looks again. "Yes, I think I can definitely see an agent!"

I peer into the crowd, but I can't see anything. They must be like fairies: you can only see them when they want you to.

"Stay right here, Harriet," Nat whispers urgently. She starts moving into the crowds. "Don't move a muscle. I'll be back in a second."

Now I'm confused. "But..." This makes no sense. "Don't you need me with you?" I call after her. "Isn't that why I'm here? For support?"

"*In spirit will do just fine, Harriet,*" Nat shouts back. "Love you!"

And then she disappears completely.

10

Is she kidding me? *In spirit?*

I could have done *in spirit* quite happily from my bedroom, thank you very much. I could have texted Nat support from my own fake deathbed. I pick up another hat crossly. Next time Nat wants me to go shopping, I am *so* throwing myself down the stairs.

"Excuse me?" a voice interrupts, and when I turn around, there's a lady staring at me with a deep crease between her eyebrows. "Can you read?"

"Umm," I reply in surprise. "Yes. Very well, actually. My reading age is over twenty. But thank you for asking."

"Really? Can you read that sign there? Read it out loud."

Poor lady. Maybe she didn't go to all of her English lessons at school. "Of course," I say in a friendly and – I hope – not patronising tone. Not everyone benefits equally from a full education system. "It says, *Don't Touch The Hats*."

There's a pause and then I realise that she probably doesn't have a literacy problem after all. "Oh," I add as her meaning sinks in.

"That's a hat," she says pointing to the one in my hand. "And that's a hat." She points to the one on my head. "And you're touching them *all over*."

I quickly put the one in my hand back on the stall and grab the one on my head. "Sorry. It's, erm, very..." What? How would you describe a hat? "*Hatty*," I improvise, and then I pat it and put it back on the stall. At which point my chewed nail snags on a flower.

We both watch as the flower separates itself from the hat and throws itself on the floor, like a little child having a hissy fit. And then – as if in slow motion – what was clearly just one piece of thread breaks and, one by one, every other flower on the ribbon follows it.

Oh, sugar cookies.

"That's a very interesting design concept," I say after clearing my throat awkwardly a couple of times and starting to back away. "Self-detaching flowers? It's very modern."

"*They're not self-detaching*," Hat Lady says in a low, angry voice, staring at the pile on the floor. "*You detached them*." And then she points at a felt-tip sign that says *You Break It You Buy It,* followed by the most inappropriately placed smiley face I have ever seen in my entire life. "And now you're going to have to pay for it."

God. She sounds a little bit like someone from the Italian Mafia. Maybe the Italian Mafia has a hat section.

"You know," I say, backing away a little bit faster. "You are very lucky that hat didn't kill me. I could have choked on one of those flowers and died. The playwright Tennessee Williams died from choking on a bottle cap. *Then* how would you have felt?"

"I'll take a cheque or debit card details."

I take a few more steps backwards and she follows. "Tell you what," I say in the most lawyer-y, Annabel-like voice I can find. "How about *I* forget that you tried to kill me if *you* forget that I broke your hat? How does that sound?"

"Pay for the hat," she says, taking another step towards me.

"No."

"Pay for the hat."

"I can't."

"Pay for the h—"

At which point fate or karma or the universe or a God who doesn't like me very much steps in. And sends me flying bottom-first into the rest of her stall.

11

<u>*People Who Hate Harriet Manners*</u>

Alexa Roberts

Hat Lady

Owners of stalls 24D 24E 24F 24G 24H

I try to blame Nat's coat dangling on the floor, but Hat Lady is having none of it. There is a lot of squeaking: mine, mostly, followed by hers. And then the crowd gets suddenly bigger.

Apparently I haven't just knocked over the hat table. Her stall has dominoed into the stall next to it, which has dominoed into the stall next to *that*, and before I know what's happening there are six stalls, strewn creatively over the floor, with me lying in a heap in the middle. It's the fault of those silly fake partitions, in my opinion. They just aren't stable enough.

Clearly, neither am I.

"This is why I didn't want you to touch the hats," Hat Lady is screaming at me as I struggle to get up.

Every time I put my hand down, something crunches. And not in a good-crunch kind of way. In a hand-through-hat kind of way. "You've ruined *everything*!"

From my position on the floor I can see that the tables have crushed at least seven hats, and another three have been hit by the jug of water on one of the now tipped-over chairs. Along with the sign. Another four hats have shoe-shaped dents in them and footprints on the brim. I'm sitting on at least three.

OK, she has a point.

"I'm sorry," I'm saying over and over again (*crunch, crunch, crunch*). Everywhere I look are the faces of people who don't seem to like me very much. "I'm *really* sorry. I'll pay for it. I'll pay for *all* of it."

I have no idea how, but I suspect it's going to involve a lot of car washing and about six hundred years' worth of groundings.

"*It's not enough,*" the woman yells. "*This is my biggest sale day of the year! I need to attract a client base!*"

I look around briefly. From the size of the crowd, she's definitely attracted something.

"I'm sorry," I say again, with my face flaming – because I really, truly, honestly am – and I'm just about to burst into guilty tears when a man wearing a fluorescent yellow jacket and a jaunty black hat leans forward and grabs hold of my hand.

"I'm afraid you're going to have to come with me," he says firmly. Then he looks at Hat Lady. "Don't worry, Sugar," he adds. "She's going to pay for the hats. I'll make sure of it personally." And he starts leading me away from the carnage.

I gape at him, totally speechless.

So far today, I have nearly died of my own fake illness, fallen over – three times – been shouted at, humiliated, vomited on, abandoned and I've managed to trash an entire section of an indoor market. And now, just at the point where I thought it was impossible for things to get worse…

I've just been arrested.

12

This is what happens when I'm forced to go out in public.

"I didn't do it!" I gasp as the man pulls me through the crowds. He's holding my hand and – I have to be honest with you – I'm not sure he's allowed. I think it might be against the law or something. "I mean," I clarify, "I *did* do it. But I didn't mean to. I'm just..." How can I put it? "Socially disadvantaged."

And – just so you know – that's what I'm going to plead in court as well.

"Cherub-cheeks, that sounds so *fun*," the man says over his shoulder in a high voice that doesn't seem to fit him properly. "Society is *tedious*, don't you think? *Sooo* much better to be pushed out of it."

What did he just call me?

"I haven't been pushed out of it," I tell him indignantly. "I just don't seem to be able to get in it in the first place. Anyway," I add as firmly as I can, "you should know I'm only fifteen." *Too young to go to jail,*

I want to add, but I don't want to give him any ideas.

"Fifteen? *Perfectomondo*, my little Sugar-kitten. So much potential for free publicity."

The blood drains from my cheeks. *Free publicity?* Oh, God, he's going to use me as a warning to other underage wannabe hat vandals.

"Before you take me anywhere," I say quickly, "I need to find my best friend. She's not going to know where I've gone."

He stops walking and swivels round with his spare hand on his hip.

"Mini-treetop, once I have a photo of you, you can go wherever the tiddlywinks you like." And then he tinkles with laughter.

I freeze. "A photo?"

"Well, *yes*, my little Peach-melba. I could draw a picture, but Head Office thought that was *ever* so unfunny last time." He giggles and pushes me away with a limp wrist. "Oh," he adds casually. "I'm Wilbur, by the way. That's *bur* not *iam.* From Infinity Models."

My knees abruptly buckle, but Wilbur-not-iam keeps tugging as if I'm on wheels. Suddenly I know how Toby feels when he tries to do the high jump.

Infinity Models?

No.

No, no, no, *no*.

No no no no no no NONONONONO.

"Oh, it has just been a *mare* this morning," Wilbur continues as if he's not dragging me bodily across the floor.

"But *w-w-why*?" I finally managed to stutter.

"Oh, you know, total chaos. The Birmingham Clothes Show: highlight of the fashion year etcetera etcetera. Well, apart from London Fashion Week, obviously. And Milan. And New York. And Paris. Actually, it's quite far down the list, but hey, it's still a *blast*."

I can't really feel my mouth. "N-n-not why is it busy. Why would you want *my* photo?"

"Oh, Baby-baby Panda," he says over his shoulder. "You're, like, so *tomorrow* you're next Wednesday. No, you're the Thursday after. Do you know what I mean?"

I stare at him with my mouth slightly open. I think it's safe to say that the answer to that question is no. "But—"

"And I am *loving* this look," he interrupts, pointing at the football kit. "So new. So fresh. So unusual. *Inspired.*"

"My jeans had sick on them," I blurt out in disbelief.

"My Jeans Had Sick On Them. *I love it.* Such an imagination! *Darling*-foot—" and here Wilbur pauses so that he can pull me through a particularly dense crowd of really angry-looking girls – "I think you might be about to make my career, my little Pot of Tigers."

One of the girls behind me mutters in confusion: "Hey, she's *ginger*."

(She's wrong, by the way: I'm not. I am *strawberry blonde*.)

"I don't underst—"

"All will become clear shortly," Wilbur reassures me. "Maybe. Maybe not, actually, but hey, clarity is *so* overrated." He pushes me against the wall. "Now stand there and look gorgeous."

What? I don't even know how to *start* attempting that.

"But—" I say again.

Wilbur takes a Polaroid picture, shakes it and puts it on the table. "Now turn to the side?"

I stare at him, still frozen in shock. None of this is making sense. He tuts and gently pushes my shoulders round so I'm facing the other wall, and then takes another photo.

"*Wilbur*—" I turn to frantically search the crowd for Nat's dark head, but I can't see anything.

"Baby-pudding," Wilbur interrupts, "you know you look *just* like a treefrog? Darling, you could climb up a tree with no help at all and I wouldn't be shocked in the slightest."

I pause and stare at him with my mouth open. Did he just say I look like something with suckers on its feet? Then my mind clears. *Focus*, Harriet. For God's sake, *focus.*

"I have to go," I explain urgently as Wilbur twists me round and takes a final photo. "I have to get out of here. I have to—"

But I can see Nat heading straight towards us. And I know two things for certain:

1. The magic has gone horribly wrong.
2. Nat is going to kill me.

13

Hiding under the table probably isn't the best impromptu decision I've ever made, but it's the only one I can think of. Which is a problem.

First of all, because Wilbur knows I'm here. He just saw me drop to my knees and crawl away. Second, because the table cloth doesn't quite reach the floor. And third, because there's already somebody else under here.

"Hi," the person under the table says, and then he offers me a piece of chewing gum.

There are times in my life when the synapses in my brain move quite fast. For example, during English exams I've normally completed the essay with plenty of time to doodle little relevant pictures in the margin in the hope that it gets me extra points. However, there are other times when those synapses don't do anything at all. They just sit there in confused silence, shrugging at me.

This is one of them.

I stare at the chewing gum in shock and then blink at the boy who's holding it. He's so good-looking, it feels like my brain has collapsed and my skull is about to fold in on itself. Which is actually not as unpleasant a sensation as you might think.

"Well?" the boy says, leaning back against the wall and looking at me with his eyelids lowered. "Do you want the gum or not?"

He's about my age and he looks like a dark lion. He has large black curls that point in every direction and slanted eyes and a wide mouth that curves up at the edges. He's so beautiful that all I can hear in my head is a high-pitched white noise like a recently switched-off television.

It takes an interaction of seventy-two different muscles to produce human speech, and right now not a single one of them is working. I open and shut my mouth a few times, like a goldfish.

"I can see," he continues in a lazy accent that doesn't seem to be English, "that it's an extremely important decision and you need to think about it carefully. So I'll give you a few more seconds to weigh up the pros and cons."

He has really sharp canine teeth, and when he says *F*s, they catch on his bottom lip. There's a mole under his left eye and he smells sort of green, like… grass. Or vegetables. Or maybe lime sweets.

One of his curls is sticking up at the back, like a little duck tail. And I've just realised that I'm still staring at him, and he's still looking at me, and he's still waiting for me to answer him. I quickly trawl my mind for an appropriate response.

"Chewing gum is banned in Singapore," I whisper. "Completely banned." And then I blink twice. It's probably not the best introductory statement I've ever opened with.

His eyes shoot wide open. "Are we in Singapore? How long have I been asleep? How fast does this table move?"

Nice one, Harriet.

"No," I whisper back, my cheeks already hot, "we're still in Birmingham. I'm just making the point that if we *were* in Singapore, we could be arrested for even having chewing gum in our possession."

Stop talking, Harriet.

"Is that so?"

"Yes," I gulp. "Luckily we're not in Singapore, so you're safe."

"Well, thank God for UK legislation," he says, leaning his head against the wall again. His mouth twitches. And then there's a long silence while he closes his eyes and I go red all over and try to work out whether it's possible to make a worse first impression.

It's not.

"I'm Harriet Manners,"I admit finally and then I put my hand out to shake his, realise it's sweaty with nerves, swoop it back in and pretend I'm scratching my knee instead.

"Hello, Harriet Manners," Lion Boy says and all I can think is: *I know there's something outside the table that I'm supposed to be running away from, but I can't quite remember what it is.*

"Erm..."*Think, Harriet. Think of something normal to say*. "Have you been here long?"

"About half an hour."

"Why?"

"I'm hiding from Wilbur. He's using me as bait. He keeps chucking me into the crowd to see how many pretty girls I can come back with."

"Like a maggot?"

He laughs. "Yes. Pretty much exactly like a maggot."

"And have you... caught anything?"

"I'm not sure yet," he says, opening one eye and looking straight at me. "It's too early to say."

"Oh." I glance briefly at my watch. "It's not that

early," I inform him. "Actually, it's nearly lunchtime."

The boy looks at my watch – which has a knife, fork and spoon instead of hands – raises an eyebrow and stares at me hard for a few seconds. His nose wiggles a little bit. And then – clearly fascinated by the mesmerising first impression I've made – he closes his eyes again.

With Lion Boy apparently unconscious, I suddenly feel a great need to ask him all sorts of questions. I want to know *everything*. For instance, what is his accent and where is he from? If I get a world map out of my bag, can he point to it for me? Does it have strange animals and really big insects? Is he an only child too? Were the holes in his jeans there when he bought them, like Dad's, and if not, how did he get them?

But nothing is coming out. Which is lucky, because people don't tend to like it very much when I interrogate them relentlessly while they're trying to sleep.

"Do you often hide under furniture?" I manage eventually. He grins at me and his smile is so wide that it breaks his face into little pieces and my stomach immediately feels like a washing machine on spin-dry mode.

"I don't make a habit of it. You?"

"All of the time," I admit reluctantly. "*All* of the time."

Whenever I panic, actually. Which means, because I panic a lot, that I've been under many types of things. Dining tables, desks, side tables, kitchen counters... Any kind of furniture that allows me to disappear. Which is, actually, how I met Nat.

And I've just remembered what I'm doing here.

14

In case you're wondering, I met Nat under a piano.

It was the second day of school and I'd had enough. Alexa had already taken a shine to me – or whatever the opposite of that is – and I had become the butt of all of her most intricate five-year-old jokes. Who smells the most? Harriet. Who has hair like a carrot? Harriet. Who spilt their milk on their lap, but *actually, it's pee*? Harriet.

So I'd waited until everyone else had gone outside and then I'd crawled under the piano. Where I'd found a heartbroken Nat, crying because her dad had just run off with the check-out girl at Waitrose. We bonded straight away, probably because we both only had half of a parenting team left: a bit like discovering the missing bit of a friendship necklace. I'd offered her a part-time share in my dad, she'd offered me a bit of her mum and – just like that –we'd become Best Friends. And we have been ever since.

At least, from that moment until… *this* one.

*

"Harriet," a voice says from somewhere outside the table cloth. Two red shoes can be seen underneath it. "I don't know whether you're under some kind of impression that you've become invisible in the last thirteen minutes, but you're not. I can still see you."

My stomach swoops again and this time it has nothing to do with the boy sitting next to me. "Oh."

"Yes, *oh,*" Nat agrees. "So you may as well come out now."

I look back at the Lion Boy, who still has his eyes shut, whisper, "Thanks for sharing the table," and struggle back out of my terrible, terrible hiding place.

Nat looks furious. Even more so than when I accidentally knocked her new bottle of Gucci perfume out of the window as a result of an impromptu dance routine that she didn't want to see in the first place.

"What," she whispers to me, glancing in confusion at Wilbur, "are you *doing,* Harriet?"

"I..." I start, already panicking. "It's not what it—"

"I can't believe this," Nat interrupts. Her cheeks are getting redder and redder and her eyes keep flicking to Wilbur. "I *know* you don't like shopping, Harriet, and I *know* you didn't want to come today, but hiding under *this* table... I mean, of all the tables..." She looks at

Wilbur again in total embarrassment.

I frown. What is she talking about? Then I realise, in a horrible rush. Nat doesn't know I've just been spotted. She didn't see me having my photo taken. She just saw me here and assumed I'd followed her and then crawled under a table because being a total plonker is the only thing I really excel at. And – at exactly the same moment – I glance at Wilbur and a jolt of shock hits my stomach. His expression is totally blank. He's not interested in Nat. *She hasn't been spotted.* Which means – and my stomach suddenly feels like it's been electrocuted – that I haven't just accidentally hitched a ride on the back of Nat's lifelong dream.

I've *stolen* it.

I look at Nat in alarm. "Well?" she says and her voice starts to wobble. "What's going on, Harriet?"

I can save this, I think in a rush, *it's not too late*.

I don't have to break Nat's heart and crush her dream, and I don't have to do it in the most humiliating way possible: in the very place she thought it would come true, in front of the very person who could have given her what she wanted.

"I was looking for unusual table joints," I say as quickly as I can. "For woodwork homework."

A beat and then, "Huh?"

"Woodwork homework," I repeat, trying hard to look into Nat's eyes. "They said local craft can be very interesting and we had to look in other parts of the country. Like… Birmingham."

Nat opens her mouth and then closes it again. "*What?*"

"So," I say, my voice getting fainter, "I thought from a distance that this particular table looked very… solid. In terms of construction. And I thought I'd have a closer look. You know. From… underneath."

"And?"

"And?" I repeat blankly. "And what?"

"What were they?" Nat asks, her eyes narrowing even more. "What kind of table joints? I mean, you were under there quite a long time. You must have been able to tell."

She's testing me. She's checking to see if I'm telling the truth and I can't really blame her. After all, I started the day by covering my face in talcum powder and red lipstick.

"I think that…" I start, but I have absolutely no idea. And there's a really good chance that Nat's about to kneel on the floor and check. "They're…" I say again and the sentence trails to an end.

"They're dovetail," a voice says and Lion Boy climbs

out from under the table.

"Nick!" Wilbur cries, looking delighted. "There you are!" And then he looks at the table in astonishment, as if it's some kind of door to an alternative universe. "How many more of you are there under there?"

Nat stares at Lion Boy and then at me. And then at him again. The creases in her forehead are getting deeper. "*Dovetail?*"

"Yep, dovetail," Nick confirms, flashing her a lopsided smile.

Nat looks at me and blinks three or four times. I can see her trying to process the situation, which is obviously totally unprocessable.

"Mmm," I say in a faint voice. "That's what I thought too."

There's a silence. A long silence. The kind of silence you could take a bite from, should you be interested in eating silences. And then – just as I think I might have got away with it and everything is going to be OK – Nat glances at Wilbur's hand. There, in his grip, are the three damning Polaroids of me. Developed purely to show Nat the truth of my evil lies, like three miniature pictures of Dorian Gray.

The silence breaks. Nat makes a sort of sobbing noise at the base of her throat, and I automatically step forward to try and stop it. "Oh, *no*, Nat, I didn't..."

Nat steps away from me with her face crumpled. She knows, and she found out in the worst way possible. In public, smack bang in the middle of me lying to her.

I should have stayed in bed this morning.

Or at least under the table.

"*No*," Nat whispers.

And with that final word – the one neither of us can take back – she jumps off the stage and runs away.

15

People Who Hate Harriet Manners

Alexa Roberts

Hat Lady

Owners of stalls 24D 24E 24F 24G 24H

Nat

Back-stabber. Betrayer. Fink. Apostate. Miscreant. Quisling. Snake. It's a good thing I brought my thesaurus with me because Nat refuses to speak to me for the rest of the day so I have an awful lot of time to ponder my wrong doings.

Quisling. I quite like that word. It sounds like a baby quail.

What's even worse is that by the time I've pulled myself together enough to move from the dirty little corner I'm scrunched up in, a *real* security guard has found me and dragged me into an office full of yet more people who look angry with me. Apparently I – or my legal guardians – owe The Clothes Show stallholders £3,000.

This is what happens when you set tables covered in ink pots next to tables covered in dresses next to tables covered in hats next to tables covered in hot wax candles and every single one of them has a ***YOU BREAK IT YOU BUY IT*** sign and insufficient insurance.

I'm not one to moan unnecessarily. In fact, I like to think of myself as a positive, life-affirming person, albeit one who also has a full grasp of the darkness and tragedy inherent in modern living.

But it has to be said: today is turning out to be just *full* of sugar cookies.

The rest of my Thursday can be summarised thus:

- *Nat tells me to bite her.*
- *I don't.*
- *I am forced to sit next to Toby for the entire two-and-a-half-hour return coach journey.*
- *He tells me that water is not blue because it reflects the sky, but actually because the molecular structure of the water itself reflects the colour blue and therefore our art teacher is wrong and the authorities should be alerted.*

- *I pull my jumper over my head.*
- *I stay under my jumper for the next two hours*

By the time we get back to school I'm so high on my own carbon dioxide and deodorant fumes that my powers of apology have been severely stunted. Before I can even focus my eyes properly Nat has raced off the bus and disappeared, and I'm left to walk home on my own.

And no, in case you're wondering. None of this makes sense to me either. I've turned the facts over and over in my head like Chinese marbles for eight hours, but there is still no feasible explanation for anything that has happened today. Unless I have somehow landed in an alternative universe where everything is inside out and all the trees are upside down and people talk backwards and we walk in the sky with the earth as a ceiling and flowers growing downwards. And that seems unlikely.

I've even worked out an equation for the situation.

$$M = (1/W/H \times P + NSM)\,C + S + X$$

Here, M stands for *Model*, W is *Weight*, H is *Height*, P

is *Prettiness*, NSN is *Nice-shaped Nose*, C is *Confidence*, S is *Style* and X is *Indefinable Coolness.* Each element (apart from Weight and Height, obviously measured by the metric system) is given an objective mark out of ten, and the higher the overall result, the better you would be as a model.

By my calculations, Nat comes out at 92.

I'm 27.2. And I was being quite kind about my nose.

Anyway, I've given up thinking about it. There has clearly been some kind of mistake, and at this precise moment somebody is smacking Wilbur round the head and putting him in a nice jacket that ties his arms behind his back.

And – just so you know – I'm not thinking about Nick either. He hasn't popped into my head once, with his big liony curls and his lime-green smell and his duck-tail tuft at the back. In fact, I can barely remember him. I meet head-smashingly beautiful foreign boys all the time. I can't hide under a table without finding one there. There is no reason whatsoever that this one would stick in my memory or make my stomach twirl at intervals.

And I definitely *didn't* walk past the Infinity Models stall six or seven times during the rest of the day in case he was there. Which he wasn't.

Unfortunately, there isn't a *whole* lot else to think about. My head feels like it's fallen off the top of a great wall and I'm waiting for all the king's soldiers to come and put it back together again. There's only one thing left to occupy myself with. And it isn't that much fun to dwell on. Can you guess what it is yet?

Uh-huh.

Now I have to go home and tell my parents.

16

Debt = £3,000

Pocket money = £5 per week

Total time to pay off debt = 600 weeks = 11.1 years

Age when debts cleared = 26.11

Conversation Starter Option One

Dad? Annabel? I've been spotted by a modelling agency and I owe £3,000. Oh, and can you wash my jeans? They smell of sick.

Conversation Starter Option Two

Dad? Annabel? I owe £3,000 and I've been spotted by a modelling agency. Oh, and can you wash my jeans? They smell of Coco Pops.

Conversation Starter Option Three

Dad? Annabel? I'm moving to Mexico and yes, this is a fake moustache.

The problem with making meticulous and well-constructed plans is that people tend to ignore them. Other people. Not me; I stick to them religiously.

As I open the front door, I'm already clearing my throat. I've decided to lead with the modelling because hopefully my parents will be so paralysed with confusion and shock that I can slip the vast quantity of money they now owe various stallholders in there without them noticing: like doing a root canal after local anaesthetic.

"Dad?" I say nervously, shutting the door behind me. "Annabel?"

Hugo immediately barrels into my legs and starts pawing at my stomach. He has obviously just been to the hairdresser's because I can now see where his eyes are instead of just guessing by their proximity to his nose.

"Hey, Hugo," I add, bending down. "You're looking very elegant." He licks my face, which I think means, "Thanks very much," or possibly, "You smell of hotdog." Then I look back up. "Dad? Annabel?"

Silence.

You know what? The welcoming atmosphere in this house needs to be worked on. I've been away all day and it's dark. Why aren't they standing in the hallway, waiting anxiously for me to arrive home safe and in one unharmed piece? What kind of parents *are* they?

"Dad?" I repeat again, getting a bit snarly. "Annab—"

"Harriet?" Annabel interrupts from the living room. "Come in here, please."

I sigh loudly, put my satchel down on the floor and then do as I've been told. Annabel is sitting on the sofa in her office suit, inexplicably eating sardines out of a tin, and Dad is in the armchair opposite her.

You know what I was saying about young children, and how non-uniform doesn't really exist? It's the same for lawyers. Annabel's either in her suit, or her dressing gown, or she puts her dressing gown on top of her suit. When she goes out for dinner, she has to buy an outfit especially.

"What are you *eating*?" I ask immediately, sitting down on a chair and looking at Annabel's tin.

"Sardines," Annabel says – as if I didn't mean *why are you eating that?* – and she pops another one in her mouth. "Now, Harriet," Annabel says as soon as she's swallowed it. "Your dad's in trouble at work."

"Annabel!" Dad exclaims. "For the love of… Don't just throw that at her! Lead up to it, for God's sake!"

"Fine." My stepmother rolls her eyes. "Hello,

Harriet. How are you? Your dad's in trouble at work." Then she looks at Dad. "Better?"

"Not even slightly." Dad scowls. "It's nothing, Harriet. Just a small difference in opinion."

"You told your most important client to go and French Connection UK himself, Richard. In the middle of reception."

Dad picks a bit of fluff off the sofa. "Well, he wasn't supposed to *hear* it, was he?" he says in his most defensive voice. "It just came out loudly because of the acoustics. That place is all stone walls."

"And we're keen that you have a sterling example of adult behaviour to follow, Harriet."

"*It was the walls*," Dad shouts in exasperation.

I look at Annabel. Under a cosy layer of flippancy she looks really worried. "How bad is it?"

Annabel puts another sardine in her mouth. "Bad. They've called him into a disciplinary tomorrow."

"It's just a formality," Dad mutters. "I'm creative: I'm supposed to be unpredictable. I'm the sort of guy who wears brown suede shoes when it's raining; they just don't know what to do with me. I'll probably get a pay rise for being such a maverick."

Annabel lifts one eyebrow and then rubs her eyes. "Let's hope so because we really can't afford to just live on one salary at the moment. Anyway. What about you, Harriet? Did you have a nice day? I hope you had a fragrant day at least because when I went into the bathroom, it was knee-deep in your grandmother's vanilla talcum powder."

"Oh." I look at the floor. "Sorry. I meant to clean that up."

"Of course you did. If only your actual cleaning was as good as your intended cleaning, we would have a very tidy house indeed. Did you manage to get out of whatever it is you were trying to avoid this time?"

"Actually," I say, ignoring this extremely slanderous insinuation, and then I take a deep breath and stand up. "I have something to tell you both."

On second thoughts, maybe I won't tell them about the money *right* now. Honesty is very important within families. But so is timing. Especially when it comes to amounts like £3,000 while your father is in the process of throwing his job out of the window.

"Well?" Annabel prompts after a pause. "Spit it out, sweetheart."

"I, uh," I start. "Well, it's..." I take a deep breath and prepare myself for the...well, whatever reaction you get from parents to news like this. "*I've been spotted*," I finally manage to blurt out. There's a silence. "Today,"

I clarify. "I've been spotted today."

There's another silence and then Annabel frowns. "*What?*" she snaps. "Let me see." She puts the sardine can down and drags me up from the chair and pulls me under the light. She looks carefully at my face, and then she looks at my hand and turns it over. She stares at my wrist and the inside of my upper arm. Then she gets Dad to stand up and look at my wrist and the inside of my upper arm. What the hell are they doing?

"No, Harriet," she finally says firmly. "There're a couple on your forehead, but I think that's just teenage acne."

"Since *when* is spotted a human adjective?" I snap impatiently. "I'm not a leopard or a stingray. *Spotted*. Verb, not adjective. Scouted. Picked up. Discovered. Found." They still look blank, so I continue even more crossly. "By a *model* agent. By Infinity Models, to be more specific."

Annabel looks even more confused. "To do what?"

"To pack potatoes."

"Really?"

"No! *To be a model*," I yell in distress. It's one thing thinking you're not pretty, but it's quite another having that confirmed by the only people in the world who are supposed to think otherwise.

Annabel frowns again. When I look at Dad, however, he appears to be shining with the light of a million smug fairies. "They're my genes, you know," he says, pointing to me. "Standing right there. That's my genetics."

"Yes, dear, they're your genes," Annabel repeats as if she's talking to a child. And then she sits down again and picks up her newspaper.

I look from Annabel to Dad. Is that *it*? I mean, *seriously*?

OK, I didn't expect them to start dancing round the coffee table, waving their Sudoku books in the air like exotic bird feathers, but a *bit* more enthusiasm would be nice. *Fantastic, Harriet,* they could say. *Maybe you're not as totally disgusting to look at as we all thought you were. How wonderful for the whole family.*

Or something that acknowledges that this would be the most exciting thing that had ever happened to anyone, if I was someone else and this was a totally different family.

Annabel looks up to where I'm still standing, mouth open. "What?" she says. "You can't do it, Harriet. You're too young and you've got exams coming up."

"She can't do it?" Dad repeats in an incredulous tone. "What do you mean she can't do it?"

Annabel looks at him calmly. "She's fifteen, Richard. It's totally inappropriate."

"It's Infinity Models, Annabel. Even *I've* heard of them."

"Hundreds of beautiful women in one place? I bet you have, darling. But the answer's still no."

"Oh my *God,*" Dad yells at the top of his voice. "*This is so unfair.*"

You see the problem? It's really hard being a child in my family when that space seems to already be taken.

"I don't actually want to do it," I interrupt. "I'm just telling you. But you could say well done or something."

"*You don't want to do it?*" Dad yells at me.

Oh, for God's sake.

Annabel looks at me. "It's modelling. Fashion." She pulls a face. "What's there to be excited about? Why is everyone getting so worked up?"

I look from her to Dad and then at Hugo. Hugo gets off the chair, tail wagging, and promptly licks me. I think he knows I need it.

"Right," I say in a slightly deflated voice. "Fine."

The only remotely exciting thing that has ever happened to me and it's over already. It lasted about as long as I thought it would. I feel a little bit like sulking. Dad still looks totally shell-shocked.

"Now," Annabel says, shaking the remote control to get the batteries working and turning the television on. "Who wants to watch a documentary about locusts?"

17

I sulk for about twenty-five minutes and then get bored and spend the rest of Thursday night a) *not* thinking about Nick and b) getting ready to woo Nat into Best Friendship again. Flowers, cards, poetry: I even bake special, personalised, sugar-free muffins with photos of me and her on top (not edible photos – I didn't have time – real photos). And then I put them all in my satchel and prepare to take them to school, where I will ambush Nat and convince her of my guilt and/or innocence.

Whatever it takes to make her anger with me disappear.

It's all a total waste of time and effort and flour. Apparently I don't need to woo Nat at all. On Friday morning, at precisely 8am, the doorbell rings.

"Nat! You're here!" I gurgle in surprise, halfway through a jam sandwich. It comes out a sticky, strawberry-flavoured, "*Nnnnnaaatcchh uuuhhh hhiiii!*"

"For *breakfast*?" she says, looking pointedly at the

other half, which is perched in my left hand.

I stick my nose in the air in my most dignified way. "Jam sandwiches have all the necessary nutrients needed to survive. Sugar, vitamins, carbohydrates. I could live entirely on jam sandwiches and lead a totally normal life."

"No, you couldn't," Nat says, pulling me out of the door. It's lucky I already have my shoes on or I'd be walking to school in my socks. "You'd be The Girl Who Only Eats Strawberry Jam Sandwiches and that's not normal." She looks at me and then coughs. "Can I have the other half, though? I'm totally starving."

I give her the other half in surprise and then look at her while she eats it. Firstly, Nat never eats food with high sugar content. *Ever*. Not since that fateful disco, eight years ago. And secondly, is this *it* then? The big dramatic scene I've been dreading all night? I made muffins without sugar especially and now *nobody* is going to eat them.

"Nat," I start and at exactly the same moment she says "Harriet?" and then she clears her throat.

"I'm sorry. For getting mad at you and stomping off."

"Oh." I blink in shock. "That's OK. I'm sorry too. For… getting spotted and stuff."

"The lying was the main problem, Harriet." Nat twists her mouth up in an awkward half-smile and licks her fingers. "Can we just forget about yesterday?"

"Of course we can," I beam at her.

A huge wave of relief washes over me: it's all OK. I was being neurotic and oversensitive as normal.

And then – just like waves – the relief abruptly disappears. Nat clears her throat and I look at her again, but a little more carefully this time. Suddenly I can see what I didn't notice before: that her neck is tense and her shoulders are all bunched up. Her collarbones have gone red and splotchy. The rims of her eyes are pink. She keeps biting her bottom lip.

"Cool," Nat says after an infinitely long pause, and then an anxious flush climbs up her cheeks and sits there, staring at me. "So..."And she clears her throat. "Did they..."She swallows. "You know... ring you?" She clears her throat for the third time. "Infinity? Did they ring you?"

She hasn't forgotten about yesterday at all. Not even a little bit.

"No." *I didn't give them my number*, I add in my head, but somehow I'm not sure saying that out loud is going to help.

"Oh." Nat's cheeks get darker. "That's a shame. I'm

sorry. So let's just put it behind us, right?"

I frown. *I thought we'd already done that.* "OK."

"And pretend it never happened," Nat adds in a tense voice.

"...OK."

Every time she tells us to put it behind us, it's becoming more and more clear that Nat hasn't done that.

"We'll just carry on as normal," Nat adds.

"...OK."

Then there's a long silence and it's not comfortable. In ten years, it might be the first uncomfortable silence there has ever been between us. Apart from the time she peed herself on the ballet-room floor and it hit my foot. That was a little bit awkward too.

"Anyway," Nat says after a couple of minutes, as she pats her hair and straightens her coat and pulls up her school tights with one hand. "So, Harriet." She looks at the bite of sandwich left in her hand. "Where's the protein in this thing, huh? I'm sorry, but I don't think you've done your research properly."

Finally, the topic has moved back to territory I can handle.

"I *have* done my research properly!" I shout back, pretending to be totally outraged. "The protein's in the..." What can I say to move the conversation as far from modelling as it is possible to move it? "Chicken," I finish and then grin at her. "There's chicken in it too. Did I forget to mention that? Strawberry and high-protein chicken sandwiches. Mmmm. My favourite."

"Strawberry and *chicken*?" Nat laughs and my shoulders relax a little bit.

"You can totally live on strawberry and chicken sandwiches," I clarify, trying not to meet her eyes. Is there any way we can just avoid the subject of yesterday until it goes away completely? Is that how Best Friendship works? Maybe. Maybe not.

But we both spend the rest of the journey to school trying to find out.

18

The really great thing about Toby Pilgrim is that you can always rely on him to treat a delicate situation with sensitivity and consideration.

"Wooooaaah," he says as Nat and I walk into the classroom. We've got to school in one piece – just. I've talked about the Greek origin of the delphinium flower (*delphis*, because it looks like a dolphin), just how many wives Henry VIII *actually* had (between two and four, depending on whether you're Catholic or not) and the fact that the Egyptian pyramids were originally shiny and white with crystals on the top. Nat has stared into the distance, nodded and grown progressively quieter, stiffer and pinker around the collarbone.

But the important thing is we've managed to avoid talking about modelling or dream stealing or the bone-crushing disappointment of thwarted lifelong ambitions. Or the fact that there's palpable tension between us.

Anyway. "Woooooaaaah," says Toby. "Look at the

palpable tension between you! It's like the Cold War, circa 1962. Harriet, I think you're probably America. You're sort of trying to make lots of noise in the hope it goes away. Nat, you're more like Russia. All kind of cold and frosty and covered in snow." Then he pauses. "Not literally covered in snow," he clarifies. "Although it's terribly wintry today, isn't it? Do you like my new gloves?"

And then he holds out a pair of black knitted gloves with a cotton-white skeleton hand attached to the back. There's an embarrassed silence while Nat and I put a lot of energy into getting our books out of our bags. All our morning's hard work has just been totally undone.

Thank you, Toby.

"You know," Toby continues obliviously, turning his gloves over and over with an affectionate expression, "I had to sew these bones on myself. I was inspired by an old Halloween costume, but it just wasn't warm enough for December." He holds a glove up to my face. "Plus, I thought it would be an excellent way of developing my medical knowledge."

I can now see that on quite a few of the 27 white bones in the hand he's written in grey pen the Latin name for them: *carpals, metacarpals, proximal phalanges, intermediate phalanges, distal phalanges.*

"Very nice, Toby," I say in a distracted voice because Nat's already getting out of her seat.

"I've just got to go hand in my biology homework," she says in an awkward voice. "See you at breaktime, OK?"

For the record, Nat and I don't have any lessons together. Despite trying very hard to get put in the same sets last year (Nat studied more and I did my best to answer things wrong), I'm still in the top sets and Nat is in set two or three for everything.

"OK," I say. She's still not really looking at me. "Meet you in the school canteen?"

"Sure," she says, and then she flicks me a smile and shoots out of the classroom faster than I've ever seen Nat shoot out of anything.

The rest of the day can be summarised thus:

- *Every time I see Nat, she smiles and ducks behind her hair.*
- *At morning breaktime, she has a detention to go to.*
- *At lunchtime, she has another detention to go to.*
- *At afternoon breaktime, she has a third detention to go to.*

· *I spend the entire day on my own.*

By the time the final class comes around and she tells me she's going to be kept behind after school as well, I'm fairly convinced that Nat is specifically getting detentions just to avoid me. I'm torn between being devastated and simultaneously impressed by her extremely cunning strategic bad behaviour.

Toby has been making the most of Nat's absence to follow me around like a small kitten follows a ball of wool; he even pats me now and then to check that I'm still there.

"*Harriet*," he whispers during sixth period English literature. "Isn't it lovely to spend so much time together?"

I make a noncommittal grunt and doodle another eye on my textbook.

"I really feel that I know you better now," Toby continues enthusiastically. "For instance, I know that at ten o'clock exactly you tend to go straight to the toilet, and when you come back out, your hair is much neater so I can only assume that you redo your ponytail in front of the bathroom mirror."

I continue doodling.

"And," he whispers in excitement, "at five past

twelve you go back to the bathroom and when you come out at twelve fifteen, your eyes are sort of pink and gummy around the edges. Which I can only conclude means that you go in there to cry in private."

I glare at him. "I don't do that every lunchtime, Toby."

"No?" He gets out a little notepad and opens it to a page that appears to have a list on it. He draws a line through the corresponding entry.

I can sense that I'm about to lose my temper. I've hurt Nat, it's been a rubbish day and I suspect that Toby is about to bear the brunt of it.

"And," he continues, "at approximately three pm you go to the bathroom again, but this time you're in there for the entire break so I believe you might be avoiding me. Either that or you're… you know. Engaged in intricate bowel activities."

I can feel my cheeks suddenly flame. He was right the first time, but I'm not happy with that second insinuation. I don't like talking about bowel activities, regardless of intricacy.

"Could you just leave me alone perhaps?" I whisper and I can feel my voice getting louder with every word. "I mean, is there any chance that you could – I don't know – *find someone else to stalk*?"

Toby looks astonished. "Who?" he says, looking around. "There's nobody else worth stalking, Harriet. You're the only one."

I grit my teeth. "Then don't stalk anyone." My voice is getting more abrasive. "How about you just don't stalk anyone, Toby? Otherwise known as LEAVE ME THE HELL ALONE."

And then there's a silence. Toby looks at me in astonishment. A low snigger ripples round the classroom.

When I look up, Mr Bott has paused writing on the board and is staring at me with an expression that a geek like me doesn't see very often. One of anger, frustration and a fervent desire to punish.

It looks like I might be seeing Nat after school today after all.

19

I look at Mr Bott with round eyes.

"Miss Manners," he says icily from the front of the classroom, and I suddenly remember that we're supposed to be reading act four, scene five of *Hamlet*. "Do you have a thought you would like to share with us?"

"No," I say immediately and stare at my desk.

"I find that very hard to believe," Mr Bott says in an even sharper voice. "You always have a thought to share with us. In fact, it's usually difficult to stop you from sharing it with us."

"I've no thoughts," I tell him in a meek voice.

"Good to know. That's what I like to see: a student approaching her exams with nothing at all in her head."

Alexa looks up from where she's been texting somebody under the desk and snorts with laughter.

Oh, yes, Alexa's in the top sets too. Unfortunately, she's both mean and smart. I have at least another three years left of her to look forward to, and then she'll probably follow me to university. Although, given the amount of time she spends on her phone in our classes, I can only assume she's really, really good at last-minute cramming.

"Alexa?" Mr Bott snaps, whipping round to face her. "Is something funny?"

Alexa looks over to me and raises an eyebrow. "No," she says in a meaningful voice. "Quite the opposite. Mostly sad, I'd say."

Nice. She's managed to insult me in front of the teacher and he hasn't even noticed.

"Well," Mr Bott says, but he doesn't look happy either. In fairness, he rarely looks happy. I don't think he teaches because it fills him with a deep inner light. "How about Little Miss Shouter and Little Miss Giggles both come up to the front here and give us your perspectives on a little question I have."

Alexa's face goes suddenly pale, and as we walk to the front, she's throwing metaphorical daggers in my direction.

"Now," Mr Bott says, "turn and face the whole class, please."

My cheeks are getting hotter and hotter. I turn so that my body is in the right direction, but try to focus on the floor.

"So, Alexa Roberts and Harriet Manners." Mr Bott sits down and gestures gracefully to the board. "As you are both clearly fascinated by this text, would you like to explain the significance of Laertes in *Hamlet*?" He looks at Alexa. "Please go first, Miss Roberts."

"Well..." Alexa says hesitantly. "He's Ophelia's brother, right?"

"I didn't ask for his family tree, Alexa. I want to know his literary significance as a fictional character."

Alexa looks uncomfortable. "Well then, his literary significance is in being Ophelia's brother, isn't it? So she has someone to hang out with."

"How very kind of Shakespeare to give fictional Ophelia a fictional playmate so that she doesn't get fictionally bored. Your analytical skills astound me, Alexa. Perhaps I should send you to Set Seven with Mrs White and you can spend the rest of the lesson studying Thomas the Tank Engine. I believe he has lots of buddies too."

Alexa's face suddenly goes bright red and she looks utterly humiliated. I feel really sorry for her, actually.

Mr Bott then turns to me. "It's your go, Miss Manners. Anything to add?"

I stare at the floor for a few seconds. Answering interesting intellectual questions correctly in public is possibly my single greatest weakness. Every time I do it,

I make myself even less popular. But I can't help myself.

"Well," I say slowly, and even though I know I should say in my most stupid voice, *No idea, sorry*, I say: "Laertes is a literary mirror for Hamlet. The play is *ostensibly* about Hamlet avenging the murder of his father, but actually, it's about Hamlet procrastinating instead. Laertes is a sort of alternative universe Hamlet, because when Hamlet murders *his* father, Laertes takes immediate revenge and pushes the play to its conclusion straight away. So as a *literary construct*, I think he's there to show what would have happened if Hamlet had been somebody else instead. It's sort of Shakespeare's way of saying that our stories are driven by who *we* are and what *we* do, and not by the events that happen to us."

I take a deep breath. Toby starts clapping, but I shoot a look that stops him.

"Very good, Harriet," Mr Bott says, nodding. "Excellent in fact. Possibly even a degree-level answer, although a distinctly second-class one." He looks at Alexa coldly. "Alexa, English literature doesn't have any right answers. But it has a hell of a lot of wrong ones. And your cracker was one of them."

"Sir!" Alexa exclaims indignantly. "This isn't fair! We haven't got to the end of the play yet! Harriet cheated!"

"It's not called cheating," Mr Bott says tiredly, putting his hand over his eyes. "It's called having a vague interest in the storyline." Then he puts his fingers briefly on the bridge of his nose and breathes out.

"But—" Alexa says, cheeks even redder.

"I can see my time here is well spent," Mr Bott interrupts. "And on that encouraging note, I am going to go and collect some more textbooks from the staffroom. At least three members of this class appear to be reading *Romeo and Juliet*, hoping I won't notice the difference." He sweeps a look of total disdain round the classroom. "Entertain yourselves for five minutes. If you can."

And then he leaves. Like a circus master who has just bashed an angry tiger on the nose and then locked it in a cage with his assistant.

I turn slowly to face Alexa, and somewhere in the distance – outside of the terrified buzzing that has just started in my head – I can hear the sound of thirty fifteen-year-olds sucking in their breath at the same time.

"Well," Alexa says eventually, turning to look at me, and I swear she sort of growls. "I guess now it's just you and me, Harriet."

20

You know in romantic films, there's always that moment where the love interest just can't hold back how they feel any more and has a sudden need to declare themselves in public?

It's always totally predictable, and always totally expected, yet the heroine is always shocked and surprised, as if it's out of the blue. I've never understood that. I mean, how dense is she? Couldn't she see it coming a mile off? Couldn't she feel the gradual build-up of tension, like everyone else?

Now it all makes a little bit more sense. You don't see things happening *to you*. Only when they're happening to somebody else. Alexa's passionate, inexplicable hatred for me has nowhere else to go. It has come to a big pulsing head and now it's going to come bursting out.

I look at the door desperately. Should I try to escape? Or keep my head down and try to get through it? We're at school. Just how bad could it be? And you know the scary bit? There's still a part of me that's about to correct her grammar. "You and I," I'm tempted to reply. "Not you and me. Now it's just you and *I*, Alexa."

"Well," Alexa says again and I can tell the whole class is still holding its breath. "Harriet Manners."

I swallow and take one step towards my seat.

"Oh, no. No, no. You're not going anywhere." She grabs the back of my school jumper and pulls me to the front of the class. It's not a violent tug; it's gentle, almost like a mother trying to stop her child from walking across the road when a car is coming. I stop and stare at the floor, making myself as small as possible.

"Could you have made me look any more stupid?" Alexa asks, almost conversationally. "I mean, *ostensibly*? Did you actually use the word *ostensibly*?"

"It means 'apparently'," I explain in a whisper. "Or 'supposedly'."

Why didn't I use 'supposedly'?

This seems to make her even angrier. "I know what it means!" she shouts. "God, you really do think I'm thick, don't you!"

"No," I whisper.

"Yes, you do. You and your smart little comments and your crap little facts and your geeky little face." She pulls that expression again: the one with the crossed eyes and protruding teeth. Which is really unfair: she knows I had my braces taken off years ago, and my left eye is only lazy when I'm tired. "You really think you're better than everyone else, don't you, Harriet Manners?"

"No," I mumble again. The humiliated burn has spread to my neck and my ears and is creeping up my scalp. I can feel the entire class staring at me the way they stared at the monkey at the zoo with the red bottom. "I don't."

"I can't hear you," Alexa says more loudly. She walks closer – way past my personal space boundaries – and for a brief second I think she's going to slap me. "I'll rephrase. *Do you think you're better than everyone else, Harriet Manners?"*

"No," I say as loudly as I can.

"Yes, you do," she hisses, getting even closer, and even in my shock I can't believe the expression on her face: pure, almost shining, hatred. As if it's burning on the inside of her and lighting her up like one of those little round candles with pictures of penguins on the outside. "You have no idea how much of a loser you really are."

"That's not true," I whisper.

Because I totally do. I know *exactly* who I am. I'm Harriet Manners: A++ student, collector of semi-precious stones, builder of small and perfectly proportioned train sets, writer of lists, alphabetiser and genre-iser of books, user of made-up nouns, guardian of twenty-three woodlice under the rock at the bottom of her garden.

I'm Harriet Manners:

GEEK.

Alexa ignores me. "So I think it's time we put it to the test," she continues and then she looks around the room. I can feel my eyes filling up with water, but I'm totally frozen. Even my tongue feels numb. *"Who in this room,"* Alexa says slowly and loudly, *"hates Harriet Manners?* Put your hand up."

I can't really see anything because the whole room is wobbling.

"Toby," Alexa adds. "Put your hand up or you're going down the toilet every lunchtime for the next week."

I close my eyes and two tears roll down my face. I think it's really important that I don't see this.

"Now open your eyes, geek," Alexa says.

"No," I say as firmly as I can.

"Open your eyes, geek."

"*No.*"

"Open your *eyes*, geek. Or I will make this worse for you today, and tomorrow, and the day after that. And I will keep making it worse for you until you realise what you are and what you are not."

So even though I know precisely what I am – and even though I'm not sure it's even possible to make it worse – I open my eyes.

Every single hand in the classroom is up.

I wish she had just punched me.

And, with that final thought, I burst into tears, grab my satchel with GEEK written all over it and run out of the classroom.

21

<u>People Who Hate Harriet Manners</u>

Alexa Roberts

Hat Lady

Owners of stalls 24D 24E 24F 24G 24H

Nat?

Class 11A English literature

By the time I get home, I'm crying so hard it sounds like somebody sawing wood.

I'm not really a crier, though, and there's a good chance my parents won't understand what I'm doing, so I scoot into the bush outside my house until I can be absolutely certain – without a shadow of a doubt – that I can breathe without either hiccuping or a bubble of snot coming out of my nose. Then I sit in the bush in the hole that Toby's made for himself in four years of stalking and sob quietly into the sleeve of my school jumper.

I'm not sure how long I cry for: it's like a never-ending circle of tears because every time I calm down and look up, I catch sight of the red letters on my satchel and it sets me off again. It even feels like they're getting bigger and bigger, although rationally I know they must be staying the same size.

GEEK

GEEK

GEEK

GEEK

GEEK

And I can't pretend it doesn't matter any more because it does. Because they just won't leave me alone.

I'm so tired of it all. I'm tired of not fitting in; of being left out; of being hated. I'm tired of having everything I am ripped up and strewn around the room the way a puppy wrecks an abandoned toilet roll. I'm tired of never doing anything right; of constantly being humiliated; of feeling like I'm just not good enough, no matter what I do.

I'm tired of feeling like this. And most of all, I'm tired of being a polar bear, wandering around the rainforest on my own.

When the letters are two metres high and flashing, I finally lose it completely. I give a little scream of frustration and attack the word with my belt buckle until the material's so ripped you can't read anything. And then – finally calmer – I curl out of a ball, climb out of the bush, wipe the mud off my uniform and try to pretend that I'm behaving in a totally rational way for 4pm on a Friday afternoon.

I sniff my way to the front door.

"Dad?" I say quietly as I open it, wiping my nose on my sleeve. "Annabel?" Then I stop, startled. Because Annabel, Dad and Hugo are all standing in the hallway.

And they all appear to be waiting for me.

22

OK, are you *kidding* me?

Now that I just want to go straight to bed without being hassled my parents have finally started working on the house's welcoming atmosphere?

"What's going on?" I ask, embarrassed and quickly rubbing my eyes with my hand. Hugo jumps up at my trousers and starts experimentally licking at the mud. "Is everything all right? Dad, did you have your meeting?"

Annabel frowns and peers at me. "What's wrong, Harriet? Have you been..." And then she stops, confused. I can see her searching her mind for a word that matches my face. "*Crying?*" she finishes uncertainly.

"I have a cold," I explain firmly, sniffing. "It started this morning." And then I look at Dad, who has his mouth clamped shut. "Dad? Your important meeting? Did it go OK?"

"Huh?" Dad makes a face. "Yeah, no problem. They

said I was a maverick like I predicted they would, but I asked for a pay rise and they said no." Then he looks at Annabel and bounces up and down on his toes a couple of times. "Tell her, Annabel." Dad nudges her with his elbow. "Tell her."

"Tell me what?" I look at Annabel and she stares back in silence. "*What?*"

Annabel sighs. "They rang, Harriet," she finally says in a reluctant voice. "The modelling agency. They rang. While you were at school."

My mouth opens slightly in shock. "They rang? But..." I stop for a few seconds in total confusion. "I didn't give them my number. How could they ring?"

"Well, they found it anyway and they rang!" Dad shouts, exploding and punching the air. Hugo responds by taking a few steps backwards and barking. "*Infinity Models*, Harriet! This is *massive*! This is more massive than massive! This is *massiver*! They rang and they said they love the photos and they want to see us all! Tomorrow, first thing! In the agency! With them! And us! And them again!"

"*Massiver* is not a word, Richard," Annabel sighs. "Anyway, what they want is irrelevant. As we discussed, Harriet's not doing it. She doesn't even want to do it." Then she looks at me. "Right?"

There's a long silence.

"*Right?*" Annabel repeats in confusion.

I look at my parents – Annabel with her hands on her hips and Dad bobbing around like a happy little duck – and suddenly I can't really see them. I can't really see anything at all. It's as if the whole world has just gone strangely dark and quiet and I'm standing in the middle, waiting for everything to start making light and noise again.

And then it hits me, like a metaphorical train or a hammer or a fist or something fast and heavy and absolutely inescapable. And it's so clear I don't know how I didn't see it before, except that maybe I couldn't because I didn't need it like I need it now, at this exact moment.

This is it.

This is what I can do to change things.

This could be my metamorphosis story, like Ovid's or Kafka's, or Hans Christian Andersen's *The Ugly Duckling* or even *Cinderella* (originally called *Rhodopis* and written in Greece in 1BC). I could go from proverbial caterpillar to butterfly; from tadpole to frog. From larva to dragonfly (which is actually only a half metamorphosis, but still – I think – worth mentioning).

MODELLING COULD TRANSFORM ME. And I'd no

longer be Harriet Manners – hated, ignored, humiliated. I'd be… someone else. Someone different. Someone cool. Because if I don't do something now, I'm going to be me forever. I'm going to be a *geek* forever. And people are just going to keep hating me and laughing at me and putting their hands up. Forever. And things will never, ever change.

Unless I do.

"I…I…" I start stammering, and then I stop and swallow because I can hardly believe what I'm about to say.

"Well?" Annabel and Dad say, except with totally different tones.

"I… think maybe I want to see them."

There's a stunned pause. "*What?*" Annabel finally gasps. "*You want to what?*"

"I want to see them," I repeat, but this time my voice is clearer. For a few seconds, Nat's face flicks into the back of my mind. My Best Friend's tense, flushed, miserable, heartbroken face. And then Alexa's flicks up next to it like a double slide show and I switch them both off. "I want to go and see the modelling agency," I confirm.

Dad jumps up in the air. "You *said*, Annabel!" he

crows. "Do you remember? We fought and I won and you said if she wanted to do it, we'd go and see them!"

"I didn't think she'd actually want to," Annabel huffs. "You tricked me, Richard. I can't believe you tricked me."

"Please?" I say, looking at her with my widest eyes. When I look to the side, Dad's doing the same thing. "Just to see? Please, Annabel?"

Annabel opens her mouth and then shuts it again. She's looking at my face as if it's a maths sum and the answer is harder than she was expecting it to be. "You actually want this?" she asks in a totally shocked and slightly disgusted voice, as if I've just said I'd like to pick fleas from stray cats for the rest of my life, and possibly eat them. "*Clothes*, Harriet? Photographs? Fashion? *Modelling?*"

"Yes," I say and I look her straight in the eye. "Maybe," I clarify.

Annabel looks straight back for a few seconds and then sighs and puts her head in her hands. "Has the world gone topsy-turvy?"

"Definitely," I confirm.

"Then…" And Annabel breathes out crossly. "Well, I'm sort of trapped by my own integrity, aren't I?"

"*Yesssss*," Dad shouts as if he's just scored a goal,

and – when Annabel gives him a short, sharp look – he clears his throat. "I meant, good decision, darling. Excellent. Very sensible."

"Don't get carried away, Richard," Annabel snaps. "I said we'd *see* them. That is all. I've made no other promises. I'm not agreeing to anything right now."

"But of course," Dad says in an apparently insulted voice. "That's also very sensible, darling."

But as Dad winks at me and runs off into the kitchen to do a celebration dance, I realise I'm not really listening. Because all I know is – after ten years – I'm finally doing something to make things better.

And – frankly – it's about time.

23

The first thing any good metamorphosis needs is a plan. A nice, well thought out, structured, considered and firm *plan*.

And if that plan happens to be in a bullet-pointed list, typed out and then printed from the computer in Dad's 'office' (the spare room) then so much the better.

It goes like this:

<u>Plan for Today</u>

- Wake up at 7am, and press the snooze button precisely three times.
- Don't think about Nat.
- Find an outfit from my wardrobe suitable for a visit to a modelling agency.
- Go downstairs wearing said outfit. My calm and supportive parents say things like ooh and aah and tell me they didn't realise I had so much inherent style.

- Blush prettily and agree because I probably do have inherent style.
- Don't think about Nat.
- Leave the house at 8.34am on the dot, to catch the 9.02am train to London.
- Arrive just in time to eat a pain au chocolat and drink a cappuccino in the local café because this is what models do every morning.
- Get transformed into something amazing.

Admittedly, the last point on the list is a bit vague – because I'm not quite sure what they're going to do, or how they're going to do it – but it's fine. As long as I have control over the rest of my plan, everything should go exactly as it's supposed to.

Unfortunately, nobody else appears to have read it.

"*Richard Manners,*" Annabel is shouting as I come down the stairs. It's already not going well: I pressed snooze fifteen times, and finally got out of bed to the calming, dulcet sounds of my parents trying to scratch each other's eyes out. "I cannot *believe* you ate the last of the strawberry jam!"

"I didn't!" Dad is shouting back. "Look! There's some here!"

"What use is that much strawberry jam to anyone?

Do I look like a fairy to you? With little tiny fairy pieces of toast? I'm five foot ten!"

"How do I answer that without accidentally calling you fat?"

"Be *very careful* what you say next, Richard Manners. Your life depends on the next sentence."

"Well... I... *Harriet*?" and Dad turns to me. I'm not sure how the argument's turned to me when I'm barely in the room, but apparently it has. "What the hell are you wearing?"

I look down indignantly. "It's a black all-in-one," I say with my nose as high as I can get it. "I don't expect you to understand because you're old. It's called fashion. *Fash-ion*."

Now it's Annabel's turn to look confused. "Is that last year's Halloween outfit, Harriet?" she says, scraping some of the jam off Dad's toast and putting it on her own. "Are you dressed as a spider?"

I cough. "No."

"Then why do you have a leg hanging off your shoulder?"

"It's a special kind of bow."

"And why are there seven remaining circles of Velcro down your back?"

"Style statement."

"And the cobweb stuck to your bottom?"

Oh, for God's sake.

"Fine," I snap. It's not that I'm unnecessarily emotional or worked up, but *why won't anyone just stick to the plan*? "It's my Halloween Spider outfit, OK? Happy now?"

"I'm not sure that's the best choice for today," Dad says dubiously as he starts stealing his jam back, and I can tell he's trying not to laugh. "I mean, there are other trendier insects. Bees, I hear, are very big this season."

"Well, tough," I bark again. *"Because it's all I have, OK?"*

"What about a wasp?" Dad offers, voice breaking.

"Everything else I own has a cartoon on the front."

"Or a grasshopper?" Annabel suggests, winking at Dad. "I like grasshoppers."

At which point I lose it completely. They're not being calm or supportive at all. *"Why are you such terrible parents?"* I yell.

"I don't know," Dad yells back. *"Why are you such a naughty little spider?"* And then Annabel bursts out laughing.

"Aaaargh!" I scream in frustration. "I hate you I hate you I hate youihateyouihateyouihateyou."

Then I run out of the room with as much dignity as I can muster.

Which – as my spare leg gets caught in the door frame until Annabel unhooks me in peals of laughter – isn't much.

24

My door doesn't slam nearly as loudly as it used to. I think my parents must have sanded it down. Which is very underhanded of them, and also suppresses my legal freedom to express myself creatively. I shut it three times to make up for it.

Once I'm lying flat on my bed, though, I start to feel ever so slightly ashamed of myself. The thing is I broke the plans myself before I'd even got down the stairs. I've been thinking about Nat all morning. It was the first thing I thought about when I woke up, and that's what I was doing for fifteen snoozes. Picturing Nat's face when I tell her where I've been today. Imagining Nat's expression when she realises I've stolen her dream, for all the wrong reasons. Not because I love fashion, but because it's my short cut out of *this*.

And I can't get it out of my head.

So, yes, I'm pretty irritated with my parents for going on about insects, and I'm also a bit frustrated that the inherent style I was hoping I might have is either not there or is so inherent that it's never going to come out. Like the last bit of toothpaste.

But mostly I'm just angry at myself.

"Harriet?" Annabel says as I'm huffing and puffing and helping myself to one of the chocolate bars I keep stashed in my bedside table. "Can I come in?"

She never normally asks, so this must mean she's feeling quite sheepish.

"Whatever," I say in a sulky voice.

"Now you know 'whatever' isn't a grammatically correct response to the question, Harriet." Annabel puts her head round the door. "Try again."

"If you must," I correct.

"Thank you. I will." Annabel comes into the room and sits down on the bed next to me. Her arms are full of plastic bags and despite myself I'm curious. Annabel likes shopping about as much as I do. "Sorry we wound you up," she says, brushing a strand of hair out of my eyes. "We didn't realise you'd be so nervous about today."

I make a noise that is intentionally ambiguous.

"Is something wrong?" she sighs. "You're all over the place at the moment. You're normally so sensible."

Maybe that's the problem. "I'm fine."

"And there's nothing you want to talk about?"

For a few seconds all I can see in my head are thirty hands in the air. "…No."

"Then…" and Annabel clears her throat, "I've bought you a present. I thought it might cheer you up."

I look at Annabel in surprise. She rarely buys me presents, and when she does, they absolutely *never* cheer me up.

Annabel unfolds a large bag and hands it to me. "Actually, I bought this for you a while ago. I was waiting for the right moment and I think this might be it. You can wear it today." And she unzips the bag.

I stare at the contents in shock. It's a jacket. It's grey and it's tailored. It has a matching white shirt and a pencil skirt. It has very faint white pinstripe running through the material and a crease down each of the arms. It is, without any question of a doubt, a suit. Annabel's gone and bought me a mini lawyer's outfit. She wants me to turn up looking exactly like her, but twenty years younger.

"I guess you're an adult now," she says in a strange voice. "And this is what adults wear. What do you think?"

I think the modelling agency are going to assume we're trying to sue them.

But as I open my mouth to tell Annabel I'd rather go as a spider *with all eight legs attached*, I look at her face. It's so bright, and so eager, and so happy – this is so clearly some kind of Coming of Age moment for her – I can't do it.

"I love it," I say, crossing my fingers behind my back.

"You do? And you'll wear it today?"

I swallow hard. I don't know much about fashion, but I didn't see many fifteen-year-olds last week in pinstripe suits.

"Yes," I manage as enthusiastically as I can.

"Excellent," Annabel beams at me, shoving some more bags in my direction. "Because I bought you a Filofax and briefcase to match."

25

The entire plan was a total waste of time. And Dad's paper and printer ink.

By the time I'm dressed up like some kind of legal assistant and my parents have stopped fighting about Dad's T-shirt ("It hasn't even been washed, Richard,"; "I won't bow down to the rules of fashion, Annabel,"; "But you'll bow down to the rules of basic hygiene, right?"), we've missed our train and we've also missed the train after that.

When we eventually get to London, there isn't time for a *pain au chocolat* or a cappuccino, and apparently, even if there was, I wouldn't be allowed to have one.

"You're not having coffee, Harriet," Annabel says as I start whining outside the window.

"But *Annabel*..."

"*No*. You are fifteen and permanently anxious enough as it is."

To make matters worse, when we finally locate the

right street in Kensington, we can't find the building: mainly because we're not looking for a blob of cement tucked behind a local supermarket.

"It doesn't look very…" Dad says doubtfully as we stand and stare at it suspiciously.

"I know," Annabel agrees. "Do you think it's…"

"No, it's not dodgy. I saw it in the *Guardian*."

"Maybe it's nicer on the inside?" Annabel suggests.

"Ironic, for a modelling agency," Dad says, then they both laugh and Annabel leans over and gives Dad a kiss, which means they've forgiven each other. Honestly, they're like a pair of married goldfish: squabbling and then forgetting about it three minutes later.

"Well," Annabel says slowly and she squeezes Dad's hand a few times when she thinks I won't notice. She takes a deep breath and looks at me. "I guess this is it then. Are you ready, Harriet?"

"Are you *kidding* me?" Dad says, ruffling my hair. "Fame, fortune, glory? She's a Manners: she was born ready." And – before I can even respond to such a shockingly incorrect statement – he adds, "Last one in is a total loser," and runs to the door, dragging Annabel behind him.

Leaving me – shaking like the proverbial leaf in a

very enthusiastic proverbial breeze – to sit down on the kerb, put my head between my knees and have a very non-proverbial panic attack.

26

After a few minutes of heavy breathing, I'm still not particularly calm.

This might surprise you, but here's a fact: people who plan things thoroughly aren't particularly connected with reality. It seems like they are, but they're not: they're focusing on making things bite-size, instead of having to look at the whole picture. It's procrastination in its purest form because it convinces everyone – including the person who's doing it – that they are very sensible and in touch with reality when they're not. They're obsessed with cutting it up into little pieces so they can pretend that it's not there at all.

The way that Nat nibbles at a burger so that she can pretend she's not eating it, when actually she's eating just as much of it as I would.

Despite my rigorous planning, I can't break this down into any smaller pieces. Walking into a modelling agency and asking strangers to tell me objectively whether I'm pretty or not is one big scary mouthful, and the truth is I'm terrified.

So, just as I think things can't get any worse, I abruptly start hyperventilating.

Hyperventilation is defined as a breathing state faster than five to eight litres a minute, and the best thing you can do when you're hyperventilating is find a paper bag and breathe into it. This is because the accumulation of carbon dioxide from your exhaled breath will calm your heart rate down, and your breathing will therefore slow.

I haven't got a paper bag, so I try a crisp packet, but the salt and vinegar smell makes me feel sick. I think about trying the plastic bag that came with the crisp packet, but realise that if I inhale too hard, I'm going to end up dragging it into my windpipe, and that would cause problems even for people who weren't struggling to breathe in the first place. So, as a last resort, I close my eyes, cup my hands together and puff in and out of them instead.

I've been puffing into my hands for about thirty-five seconds when I hear a human kind of noise next to me.

"Go away," I say weakly, continuing to blow in and out as hard as I can. I'm not interested in what Dad thinks. He plays games of Snap with himself when he's stressed.

"This isn't Singapore, you know," a voice says. "You can't just fling yourself around on the pavement. You'll get chewing gum all over your suit."

I abruptly stop puffing, but I keep my eyes closed because now I'm too embarrassed to open them again. My suit is grey and the pavement is also grey; perhaps if I stay very still and very quiet, I'll disappear into the background and the owner of the voice will stop being able to see me.

It doesn't work.

"So, Table Girl," the voice continues, and for the second time today somebody I'm talking to is trying not to laugh. "What are you doing *this* time?"

It can't be.

But it is.

I open one eye and peek through my fingers, and there – sitting on the kerb next to me – is Lion Boy.

27

Of all the people in the whole world I didn't want to see me crouched on the floor in a pinstripe suit, hyperventilating into my hands, this one is at the top of the list.

Him and whoever hands out the Nobel Prizes. Just – you know. In case.

"Umm," I say into my palms, thinking as quickly as I can. *Hyperventilating* doesn't sound very good, so I finish with: "Sniffing my hands."

Which, in hindsight, sounds even worse. "Not because I have smelly hands," I add urgently. "Because I don't."

I take a quick peek through my fingers again and see that Lion Boy is lazily flexing his feet up and down and staring at the sky. Somehow – and I don't know how he has done this – he has managed to get even better looking than he was on Thursday.

"And how are they?"

"A bit salty," I answer honestly. Then I nervously

blurt out: "Do you want to smell them?"

I trawl through fifteen years of knowledge, passions and experience and the best I can come up with is: *Do you want to smell my hands?*

"I'm trying to cut back," he says, lifting an eyebrow. "But thanks anyway."

"You're welcome," I reply automatically and then there's a short silence while I wonder if – in an alternative universe somewhere – another Harriet Manners is having a conversation with a ridiculously handsome boy called Nick without making herself sound like a total idiot.

"So," Nick says eventually. "Are you ready to go upstairs yet? Because your parents are waiting in reception, and judging by the look on your mum's face five minutes ago, everybody up there may already be dead."

Oh, sugar cookies. I knew Annabel was going to start channelling *Tomb Raider*: she's been in a scratchy mood all morning. "How do you know they're my parents?" I ask coolly, hoping to pretend that I've never seen them before in my life.

"Your mum is wearing exactly the same thing as you, for starters. And you have the same hair colour as your dad."

"Oh."

"And they keep saying, '*Where the hell is Harriet?*' and looking out of the window."

"Oh," I say and then I stop talking. My hands are shaking and I'm not sure I can handle any more shades of embarrassment. I'm already purple as it is. "You know," I say, after giving it a little thought, "I think I might just stay here."

"Hyperventilating on the kerb?"

I look up and see that Nick is grinning at me. "Yes," I tell him curtly. He has no business laughing at breathing problems. They can be very dangerous. "I am going to stay here and I am going to hyperventilate on the kerb for the rest of the day," I confirm. "I've made an executive decision and that is how I shall entertain myself until nightfall."

Nick laughs again, even though I'm being totally serious. "Don't be daft, Harriet Manners." He stands up and a little flicker of electricity shoots through my stomach because I've just realised he has remembered my name. "And don't be nervous either. Modelling's not scary. It can actually be sort of fun sometimes. As long as you don't take it personally."

"Mmm," I say because frankly I take *everything* personally. And then I watch as he starts wandering lazily back towards the building. Everything Nick does is slow, as if he lives in a little private bubble that's half the speed of everything around it. It's mesmerising. Even if it does make me feel like everything I do and say is too fast and frantic and sort of unravelling like the cotton on my grandma's sewing machine.

"And you want the *really* good news about modelling?" Nick says, abruptly turning round.

I glare at him suspiciously and try and ignore the flip-flop feeling as my stomach turns over and starts gasping for air, like a stranded fish. "What?"

"It's an industry *full* of tables to hide under. If you decide you don't like it, you can literally take your pick."

Then Nick laughs again and disappears through the agency doors.

Forty-eight hours ago, the most exciting thing that had ever happened to me was having my hand accidentally touched by the least spotty boy in the local bookshop, and that was just because he was handing me a book. Now I'm expected to get off the pavement and follow the best-looking boy I have ever seen into an internationally famous modelling agency as if it's the most natural, normal thing in the world.

So let me clarify something, in case you don't know me well enough by now.

It's not.

28

I wait as long as I can because it's important to maintain a high level of personal dignity at all times and also to show that you're not madly in love with someone by chasing them up the stairs. And then I get off the kerb and walk as fast as I can.

It's no use: Nick stays just ahead of me, as if he's the carrot and I'm the eternally optimistic donkey. By the time I reach the reception of Infinity Models (three floors up) he has disappeared completely, and all that's left is a slightly swinging door to convince me I didn't just invent him in the first place.

One quick glance, however, shows me that he was right and Annabel is totally fuming. While Dad bounds around the room, annoying the hell out of the receptionist, Annabel is sitting in total silence, bolt upright, with her back nowhere near the chair. The tendons in her neck are standing out like the bubbles in our living-room wallpaper.

Then I realise why. Somewhere in the direction

Annabel keeps looking, I can hear the distant sound of a girl crying.

"Where have you *been*?" she demands as soon as I walk in, but I'm saved by Wilbur, who bursts through the reception door in an explosion of orange silk trousers and a shirt with paint splashes all over it, except they're clearly not a result of anyone painting.

"Gooooood mooooorrrnniiiinnng," he squeals, clasping his hands together. "And if it isn't Mr and Mrs Baby-baby Panda! Just right there in front of me, like two little matching pots of strawberry fromage frais! Ooh, I could just eat you both up. But I won't because that would be terribly antisocial."

Annabel's eyes have gone very round and her mouth has dropped open. Even Dad has stopped bounding and he takes a slightly frightened seat next to her.

"What?" she whispers to him. "*What* did that man just call us?"

"This is fashion," Dad murmurs reassuringly, taking her hand gently as if she's Dorothy and he's the White Witch. "*This is how they speak here.*"

"And it's Mini-panda herself!" Wilbur continues obliviously, waving at me. "In a suit this time, no less! What's the inspiration this time, Monkey-chunk?"

I glance quickly at Annabel and see that she's

mouthing *Monkey-chunk?* at Dad, who shrugs and mouths *Mr Baby-baby Panda?* back. "My stepmother's a lawyer," I explain.

"My Stepmother's a Lawyer," Wilbur repeats slowly, a look of growing amazement on his face. "Genius! I'm Wilbur, that's with a *bur* and not an *iam*," he continues happily, semi-skipping over and grabbing Annabel and Dad's hands, "and I am so thoroughly, *thoroughly* giddy to meet you both."

"It's an – erm," Annabel manages, and Wilbur holds his fingers up to her mouth to stop her speaking.

"Ssssshhh. I know it is, my little Pumpkin-trophy. And I have to tell you I'm totally *incandescent* right now about your beautiful daughter's *visage*. It's special. New. Interesting. And we don't get much of that round here. It's all legs up to *here,*" (he points to his neck) "and eyelashes out *here,*" (he moves his hand a few centimetres in front of his face) "and lips out here," (he keeps his hand in the same place). "Dull, dull, dull." He turns to me, beaming. "You don't have any of those things, do you, my little Box of Peaches?"

I open my mouth to answer, and then realise he's telling me I don't have any of those things. Otherwise known as *beauty*. Fantastic.

In the meantime, Dad is still staring at the hand

Wilbur is holding. "Um," he says, trying to tug it away as politely as he can.

"I know," Wilbur agrees, holding on tighter. "Doesn't it feel like a whirlwind of adventure?"

And before either of them can say anything else he pulls both Annabel and Dad to their feet and starts dragging them across the reception floor.

29

"Now I'd love to stand on ceremony," Wilbur says as he physically pushes my parents into a little office at the back of the room. "But we don't have a minute to lose. I have another engagement in six minutes. So let's get this done speedio and make the magic happen, right?" He holds his hand up to Dad.

"Right!" Dad says and high-fives him.

"For crying out loud," Annabel sighs as Wilbur shows us to little plastic seats. "Will somebody other than me please take this seriously? And you should know that I'm making notes," she adds sternly, getting out her notepad.

"How funalicious!" Wilbur cries. Annabel writes one word down, but I can't see what it is. "Now," he continues, "are we definitely set on the name Harriet?"

We all look at him in shock because… well, it's my *name*. I've been sort of set on it for the last fifteen years.

"My name," I tell Wilbur in the most dignified voice

I can find, "was inspired by Harriet Quimby, the first female American pilot and the first woman ever to cross the Channel in an aeroplane. My mother chose it to represent freedom and bravery and independence, and she gave it to me just before she died."

There's a short pause while Wilbur looks appropriately moved. Then Dad says, "Who told you that?"

"Annabel did."

"Well, it's not true at all. You were named after Harriet the tortoise, the second longest living tortoise in the world."

There's a silence while I stare at Dad, and Annabel puts her head in her hands so abruptly that the pen starts to leak into her collar. "*Richard*," she moans quietly.

"A *tortoise*?" I repeat in dismay. "I'm named after a *tortoise*? What the hell is a tortoise supposed to represent?"

"Longevity?"

I stare at Dad with my mouth open. I don't believe this. Fifteen years of the worst name ever and I can't even blame my dead mother for it?

"We could try Frankie?" Wilbur suggests helpfully. "I don't believe there were any famous reptiles, but I'm sure there must have been a cat or two."

"She stays Harriet," Annabel says in a strained voice.

"You have to admit it was worth a punt," Wilbur whispers to me, but I'm too busy giving my father the evil eye to say anything back.

"Now," Annabel continues. I can see that she has a list in front of her. "Wil*bur.* You're aware that Harriet's still at school?"

"Of course she is, Fluff-pot; the others are decidedly too old."

Annabel glowers at him. "I see I need to rephrase that. *What happens with Harriet's school work?*"

"We work around it. Education is so *very* important, isn't it? Especially when you stop being beautiful and perhaps get a little fat."

Annabel's eyes narrow a bit more. "How much is this going to cost?"

"Gosh, she's to the point, isn't she?" Wilbur says approvingly, winking at Dad. "If it's a testshot, everyone works for free and it costs nothing. If it's a job, Harriet gets paid and the agency gets a cut of that. That's sort of the point, isn't it? I'm not here just for the free dinners." Wilbur pauses thoughtfully. "I'm a little bit here for the free dinners," he corrects. "But not entirely."

"And who looks after her? She's only fifteen."

"You do, poppet. Or Panda Senior over there. At fifteen she has to have a chaperone at all times, and I'm going to suggest that it's one of you two because the total strangers we drag off the streets just don't seem to care as much."

I glance quickly at Dad and note that his excitement levels are getting dangerously high. Annabel scowls at him. "And who was that crying earlier?" she hisses. "*Why* were they crying?"

Wilbur sighs. "We had to turn a girl away, Darling-cherub. If we made everyone who wanted to be a model a model, we'd just be an agency for human beings, wouldn't we? Fashion's exclusive, my little Butternut-squash. That means *excluding* people."

"That was a child," Annabel says in an angry voice.

"Maybe, maybe not," Wilbur shrugs. "It's hard to tell: sometimes they just don't eat very much. Confuses the growth hormones, you know? Either way, we sent them packing." And then he beams at us all. "I won't be sending *you* packing, though, because you're here by special invitation of *moi*." And he throws the Polaroids from The Clothes Show on the table. "Your daughter is adorable. I've never seen such an alien duck in my entire life."

"A *what*?"

"Frankie here looks just like the ginger child of an alien and duck union, and that is so *fresh* right now."

"*Her name is not Frankie*," Annabel hisses in barely contained frustration. "It's *Harriet*."

"Could you not at least have smiled, Frankie?" Dad sighs as he studies the photos. "Why do you always sulk?" He looks apologetically at Wilbur. "She ruined eighty per cent of our photos when we were in France last summer."

"*Her name is Harriet!*" Annabel almost shrieks at Dad.

"Oh, no," Wilbur says earnestly. "That works for me. People like their high-fashion models to look as deeply unhappy as physically possible. You can't have beauty *and* contentment: it would just be unfair." He looks at the photos again with a satisfied expression. "Harriet looks thoroughly miserable: she's perfect. Once we've straightened out that lazy eye, obviously."

"*What are you talking about?*" Annabel shouts and her voice is getting higher with every sentence, as if she's singing it. "*Harriet does not have a lazy eye.*"

"Sorry, sorry," Wilbur says, waving his hands around in an attempt to calm her down. "What's a more politically acceptable way of putting it? Directionally challenged?"

Annabel looks like she's about to bite him.

"Are you sure," I finally manage to interrupt before Annabel rips the entire room to shreds, "that I'm what you're looking for? That there isn't some kind of mistake?"

Because with all of the nerves and the tension and the shouting, I haven't been able to get a word – or a thought – in edgeways, but some of the things I've heard have kind of stuck. Words like: *ginger, tortoise, alien, duck, lazy* and *eye.* This isn't quite the magical metamorphosis moment I was looking for. I don't feel very beautiful at all. In fact, I think I feel worse than I did before I came in here.

"My little Tortoise," Wilbur says, reaching out to grab my hand as my squinty, directionally challenged, short-lashed alien eyes start welling up. "Cross-eyed or not, there's no mistake. You're perfect just the way you are. And it's not just me that thinks so."

"No, your daddy does too," Dad says, leaning over and ruffling my hair in an attempt to make peace with me. I growl and bat his hand away crossly.

Wilbur smiles. "*Actually*, I'm rather enigmatically referring to an *enormously* important fashion designer who saw the Polaroids and wants to meet Harriet asap." He pauses and looks at his watch. "Asap is an abbreviation of as soon as possible," he adds.

There's a long silence while Annabel, Dad and I stare at Wilbur with blank expressions. After twenty seconds of nothing, Annabel finally snaps. "What the hell are you talking about, you strange little man? *When?*"

Wilbur's watch starts beeping. "Now," he says, grinning and standing up. "It's the other engagement I was talking about."

"*Now?*"

"Yes." And then Wilbur looks directly at me. "She's sitting next door."

30

Now I know many things.

I know that the word 'mummy' comes from the Egyptian word for 'black gooey stuff'. I know that every year the moon steals some of the Earth's energy and moves 3.8cm further away from us. I know that when you sneeze, all bodily functions stop, including the heart.

And I know nothing about modelling.

However, I'm pretty sure that this is not how the story is supposed to go. The agency are supposed to assess me and then think about it, we're supposed to assess them and think about it, and then we're all supposed to make lots of careful decisions and go through lots of boring waiting time before anything interesting happens. *If* anything interesting happens.

They're not just supposed to lob a fashion designer at me the way Alexa lobs a netball at my head before the game has even started. What's more, I haven't been transformed at all yet. I'm not ready. *I'm still a caterpillar.*

"*What?*" Annabel finally stammers in total disbelief. "She's *what*?"

In the meantime, Wilbur has manually picked me out of my chair and is pushing me towards the door on wobbly Bambi legs. "She's next door," he repeats. "You know, they sell the most fabulous little ear syringes in chemists that will clear these hearing problems right up for you."

"I don't think so," Annabel hisses, starting to get out of her chair too.

"Oh, they do," Wilbur insists. "It's like *pop*, and suddenly you can hear again."

Annabel clicks her tongue in frustration. "I mean, Harriet's going nowhere."

Wilbur looks at Annabel in confusion. "But it's a *super important designer*, my little Door-frame. I don't think you quite understand. Frankie's a very lucky little girl to even get a chance to meet them."

"I don't give a flying duck if they're Queen of the World," Annabel snaps. "Harriet's not just being thrown into it like that."

Wilbur sighs. "Let's be rational about this, *non*? You haven't signed anything and you haven't decided anything. You can still say no. But isn't it best to know what you're saying no to? That's just basic maths."

"It's not maths," Annabel sighs. And then her head furrows in the middle. I can see the logic has started worming its way in.

"Plus, Annabel," Dad says anxiously. *"What if it's the Queen of the World?"*

"Oh, for the love of *Pete,*" Annabel says after staring at Dad for a few seconds, and then she turns to me. ("Are you Pete?" I hear Wilbur whisper to Dad.) "Do *you* want to meet this person?"

"Uh," I say because everything has suddenly gone very far away and quiet, and my whole body is shaking – even my thumbs.

This cannot be happening. This is not on the plan. This is not on *any of the plans.*

They want me to go in without a plan?

Yes. Apparently that's exactly what they want me to do.

"*Perfectomondo!*" Wilbur cries and – before I can work out what my next thought is going to be – he pushes me out of the door and closes it behind us.

31

"Now," Wilbur says as we stand alone in the hallway and I start hyperventilating again. I knew I should have bought the crisp packet with me. "There's nothing to worry about, Plum-cake. This woman can't hurt you." He thinks about this statement for a few seconds. "Actually, that's not totally true. She can and she might. But try and forget about that because if she smells fear on you, it'll make her worse. She's like a vicious Rottweiler, except with less muscle mass and much better table manners."

"B-b-but who is it?" I stammer.

"If I tell you, you'll panic," he says, frowning at me.

I'm already panicking. I'm not sure he can say anything that's going to make it worse. "I won't," I lie.

"You will. You'll panic, and then I'll panic, and then you'll panic again, and she'll be able to tell we're weak and she'll eat both of us."

"Wilbur, I *promise* I won't panic. Just tell me who it is."

Wilbur takes a deep breath and grabs my arms. "Darling Strawberry-mush," he says in a reverential voice. "It's *Yuka Ito*."

And then he waits for my reaction. Which is obviously extremely disappointing for him because, after a short silence, he shakes me gently and taps my head. "Are you still in there? Has the shock killed you?"

"Who?"

"*Yuka Ito.*" Wilbur waits a little longer for the penny to drop and then sighs because the penny is clearly going nowhere at all. "Legendary designer, personally discovered at least five supermodels? Best friends with eight *Vogue* editors around the world? Has her *own personalised seat* at New York Fashion Week? Current Creative Director of Baylee?" Wilbur pauses and then sighs again. "Bunny-button, this woman doesn't work in fashion, she *is* fashion. She is the beginning of it and she is the end of it. A bit *more* panic might be appropriate."

According to scientists, the slowest that information travels between neurons in the brain is 260mph. I don't believe them because my brain is working nowhere near that fast.

My mouth has gone suddenly dry. I haven't heard of Yuka Ito, but I have heard of Baylee. People at school buy the fake version handbags at the local market. And they're just going to send me in like *this?* In a *suit*? Without any preparation at all? Where the hell is my metamorphosis?

"B-b-but w-w-what do I d-d-do?"I start stuttering because my ears have done what they always do when I'm extremely frightened: they've gone totally numb. "W-w-w-what do I s-s-say?"

Wilbur sighs in relief. "That's better. Total breakdown. A much more respectable reaction." He pats me and pushes me towards the second glass cubicle. "*You* don't do anything, Doughnut-face. Yuka Ito *does.* Trust me, she'll know straight away if you're what she's looking for. And if you're not... Well. She'll probably just bite you."

"B-b-b-but..."

"It's OK, she's totally sterile. This is the moment when the rest of your life takes shape, Harriet," Wilbur says, putting his hand reassuringly on my shoulder. And then he considers this statement. "Or fails completely," he amends. He opens the door. "No pressure," he adds.

And pushes me forward.

32

Ok.

Deep breaths. In, out. In, out. But keep them subtle: I don't want Yuka Ito to think I'm going into labour.

Everything is dark, except I don't know whether it's just my brain closing down in shock or my eyes adjusting to the light. The whole room is pitch-black, and there's just a small lamp in the corner. And right in the middle, sitting in a chair, is a very small woman.

She's very still, and very silent, and she's wearing black from head to toe. *Everything* is black: her long hair is black, her minuscule hat is black and the lace hanging over one eye is black. Her dress is black and her shoes are black and her tights are black. The only thing on her that isn't black is her lips, and they're bright purple. Her hands are folded very neatly in her lap, and the only other way I can think of to describe her is that she's everything that Wilbur isn't: quiet, controlled and absolutely rigid. She looks exactly like a fashionable spider.

I *knew* I should have stuck to my first outfit choice.

As if on cue, Wilbur cries, '*Sweetheart!*' and flounces across the room to greet her. 'It's been tooooo long!'

She looks at Wilbur without a flicker of expression on her perfect, pale face. "I saw you eight minutes ago. Which I believe is two minutes longer than we agreed."

"Precisely! Tooooooo long!" Wilbur runs back to me, totally unfazed, and pushes me forward. "I had difficulty retrieving this one," he explains happily, as if he's Hugo and I'm some kind of really nice stick. "But retrieve her I finally did."

He gives me another nudge with his fingertips until I'm standing awkwardly in front of Yuka. There is something so queenly about her that I find myself suddenly dropping into a curtsy, the way I was taught to in ballet class before the teacher asked Annabel not to bring me back because it was "impossible to teach me grace".

Yuka Ito looks at me with a stony face and then – almost without moving – touches a little button on a remote control on her lap. A bright spotlight fades in dramatically, almost directly above me, and I jump a little bit. Seriously. What kind of room *is* this?

"Harriet," she says as I squint upwards. There's no

inflection to her voice, so I'm not sure whether it's a question or a statement or whether she's just practising saying my name.

"Harriet Manners," I correct automatically.

"Harriet Manners." She looks me up and down slowly. "How old are you, Harriet Manners?"

"I'm fifteen years, three months and eight days old."

"Is that your natural hair?"

I pause briefly. Why would anyone dye their hair this colour? "...Yes."

Yuka raises an eyebrow. "And you've never modelled before?"

"No."

"Do you know anything about clothes?"

I look down at my grey pinstripe suit. It must be a trick question. "No."

"And do you know who I am?"

"You're Yuka Ito, Creative Director of Baylee."

"Did you know who I was before Wilbur told you thirty seconds ago?"

I glance at Wilbur. "No."

"But she's *very* bright," Wilbur bursts enthusiastically, clearly no longer able to contain himself. "She picks things up ever so quickly, don't you, my little

Bumblebee? Once I told her who you were she didn't forget straight away at all."

Yuka slowly slides her gaze over to him. "At what point exactly," she says in an icy voice, "did it seem as if I was attempting to engage you in conversation, Wilbur?"

"None at all," Wilbur agrees and takes a few steps back. He starts gesturing at me to get behind him.

"And," she continues, looking at me, "how do you feel about fashion?"

I think really hard for a few seconds. "It's just clothes," I say eventually. Then I close my mouth as tightly as possible and mentally flick myself with my thumb and middle finger. *It's just clothes?* What's wrong with me? Telling the fashion industry's most powerful woman that *It's Just Clothes* is like telling Michelangelo, *It's Just A Drawing*. Or Mozart, *It's Just A Bit Of Music.* Why is there no kind of net between my brain and my mouth to catch sentences like that, like the one we have in the kitchen sink to catch vegetable peel?

"Would you mind explaining why you want to be a model in that case?"

"I guess..." I swallow uncertainly. "I want things to change."

"And by *things* she means," Wilbur interrupts, stepping forward, "famine. Poverty. Global warming."

"Actually, I mean *me* mainly," I clarify uncomfortably. "I'm not sure fashion is going to help with anything else."

Yuka stares at me for what feels like twenty years, but is actually about ten seconds with a totally blank expression on her face. "Turn around," she says eventually in a dry voice.

So I turn around. And then – because I'm not sure what else to do – I keep turning. And turning. Until I start to worry that I'm going to be sick on the floor.

"You can stop turning now," she snaps eventually, and her voice sounds high and strained. She flicks her finger again and the light above me abruptly switches off and plunges me back into the dark. "I've seen enough. Leave now."

I stop, but the room continues spinning, so Wilbur grabs me before I fall over.

I can't believe it. That was my chance and I blew it. That was the escape hatch from my life and I managed to shut it on myself within forty-five seconds. Which means I'm stuck being me forever.

Forever.

Oh, God. Maybe I am actually a moron after all. I

might have to recheck my IQ levels when I get home.

"Go, go, go," Wilbur whispers urgently because I'm still standing in the middle of the room, staring at Yuka, totally paralysed with shock. "Out, out, out."

And then he bows to Yuka, shuffles backwards out of the room with me behind him and shoves me back into the real world.

33

The real world, as it turns out, is even icier than the fashion one.

I stomp back miserably into the little office where my parents are waiting: Annabel, with her head in her hands, and Dad, pointedly ignoring her and staring out of the window in huffy silence.

"Tell your stepmother you don't mind being named after a tortoise," Dad immediately demands, still staring out of the window. "Tell her, Harriet. She won't talk to me."

I sigh. Today is really going downhill. And given the start, I wasn't sure that was possible. "I suppose I should just be grateful you weren't browsing the FBI's Most Wanted lists as well as scanning the *Guinness Book of Records*, Dad."

"Tortoises are incredible creatures," Dad says earnestly. "What they lack in elegance and beauty they more than make up for in the ability to curl up and defend themselves from predators."

"What, like me?"

"That's not what I was saying, Harriet."

"Then what are you saying?"

"No," Annabel snaps suddenly, lifting her head.

Dad remains nonplussed. "They do, Annabel. I saw a documentary about it on telly."

Annabel whips round and her face is suddenly the colour of the paper she's still gripping in her hands. "Why you felt the need to tell her about that bloody *tortoise* I have no idea. What's wrong with you?" Dad looks at me for help, but I'm not going to drag him out of this one. "And," she continues, turning to look at me, "I mean *no*; you're not modelling. Not now, not next year, not ever. Full stop, the end, *finis*, whatever you want to put at the end of the sentence that makes it *finite*."

"Now hang on a second," Dad says. "I get a say in this too."

"No, you don't. Not if it's a stupid say. It's not happening, Richard. Harriet has a brilliant future in front of her and I'm not going to have it ruined by this *nonsense*."

"Who says it's brilliant?" I ask, but they both ignore me.

"Have you been listening to a single word that crazy

man has been saying, Richard?"

"You just want her to be a lawyer, don't you, Annabel!" Dad shouts.

"And what if I did? What's wrong with being a lawyer?"

"*Don't get me started on what's wrong with lawyers!*"

They're both standing a metre away from each other, ready for battle.

"Do I get a say in this?" I ask, standing up.

"No," they both snap without taking their eyes off each other.

"Right," I say, sitting down again. "Good to know."

Annabel puts her handbag over her shoulder, quivering all over. "I said I would think about it and I have. I've even made notes and I have seen nothing that convinces me that this is right for Harriet. In fact, I've only seen things that convince me of exactly the opposite: that this is a stupid, sick, damaging environment for a young girl, it was a terrible idea and it needs to stop now before it goes any further."

"But—"

"This conversation is over. Do you understand? *Over.* Harriet is going to go to school like a normal fifteen-year-old and she is going to do her exams like a normal fifteen-year-old and have a normal, fifteen-year-old life so that she can have a brilliant, successful, *stable* adult one. Do I make myself clear?"

I could point out that it's irrelevant – seeing as I've just blown any chance I have – but Annabel looks so scary and we can both see so far up her nostrils that Dad and I both duck our heads and mutter, "OK."

"Now, when you're ready, I'll be outside," Annabel continues from between her teeth. "Away from all this *rubbish.*"

And Dad and I continue to stare at the table until we hear the front door close, with Annabel safely on the other side of it.

34

We continue to stare at the table for quite some time: me absorbed in thought and Dad possibly just really interested in the table.

You know, the human brain never stops surprising me. It's always evolving: not just through the centuries, but from day to day, and minute to minute. Always in a constant state of flux. Forty-eight hours ago, I would have laughed if somebody had told me I couldn't be a model or perhaps stared at them as if they were strange alien beings with feet coming out of their heads. I've always wanted to be a palaeontologist, or maybe a physicist. But… I don't want to go back to my life the way it was.

Not now I've imagined an alternative.

I look at Dad and realise he's studying my face. "What do *you* want, Harriet?" he says gently. "Never mind Annabel, I think it must be her time of the month. You know, when she turns into a werewolf. What is it you want to do?"

I think about Nat and how devastated she would be if this went any further. I think about Annabel and her fury, and then I think about Yuka Ito and her open contempt.

"It doesn't matter," I say in a small voice. "It's not going to happen anyway."

At which point Wilbur bursts back into the room and flings himself dramatically into the chair that Annabel just vacated. He doesn't seem to realise that anyone's missing.

"You got the job," he says abruptly, flinging his arms out in a wide motion. "She loves you."

I stare at him in silence. "B-b-but – no, she doesn't, she *hates* me," I finally manage to stammer. "She turned the light off on me and everything."

"*Hates* you?" Wilbur tinkles with laughter. "Golly-knickers. Did you *see* what she did to the other girls? Well, no, obviously not. We'd have all sorts of tribunals on our hands if anyone did. She does not hate you, my little Goldfish. She didn't even turn the light *on* for most of the other candidates."

"What's going on?" Dad is still saying. At least, I think he is. My brain is making that high-pitched TV noise again. "*What job?*"

"The job of the century, my little Crumpet of Loveliness; the position of the millennium. The employment opportunity to end all employment opportunities."

"Which *is*?" Dad snaps crossly. "Drop the jazz, Wilbur, and just tell us."

Wilbur grins. "Gotcha. Yuka Ito wants Harriet to be the new face of Baylee. We're on a deadline, so we start shooting tomorrow. In Moscow. For a twenty-four-hour whirlwind of fashion."

I feel like I'm in an elevator, dropping thirty storeys in three seconds. My stomach doesn't even feel remotely attached to my abdomen.

Dad opens and shuts his mouth a few times.

"For real?" he says eventually, and even in my catatonic state I cringe. I wish Dad would stop trying to be 'street'.

"So real it could have its own TV show," Wilbur confirms seriously. "We've been looking for the right person for ages. The advertising spaces are already booked and the crew is on standby. Now we've found her, it's *lift-off*."

"Gosh," Dad says and he suddenly looks strangely calm. I thought he'd be up and dancing around the room, but he looks very composed and very – you know

– *fatherly*. "Right," he says in a faraway voice. "Wow." He looks at me again. "So it's actually happening then. Who'd have thought it?"

The white noise in my head is getting louder and louder. "Dad?" I manage to squeak. "What do I do?"

Dad clears his throat, leans toward me and puts his hand on my head. "Harriet," he says gravely, in his most un-my-dad-like voice. "Think about it carefully. If you don't want this, we walk now. No questions. If you do want it, I'm behind you."

"But Annabel..."

Dad sighs. "I'll deal with Annabel. She doesn't frighten me." He thinks about this. "OK, she frightens me. But I'll just frighten her back."

I try to swallow, but I can't. The door has just been thrown wide open when I thought it was locked. This is the forked road that the poem talks about. I can take my old life back. I can be Harriet Manners: Best Friend to Nat, Prey to Alexa, Stepdaughter to Annabel, Stalkeree to Toby. Stranger and total Hand-sniffing Weirdo to Nick. *Geek*.

Or I can try to become something else entirely.

Something inside me breaks. "I want to do it," I hear myself saying. "I want to try and be a model."

"Well, *duh*," Wilbur says happily.

"But what happens now?" Dad asks, taking hold of my hand and squeezing it. I squeeze it back. My whole body is trembling.

"Now?" Wilbur says, laughing and leaning back in his chair. "Well. Let's just say that Harriet Manners is about to become very fashionable." And he laughs again. "Very fashionable indeed."

35

So Dad and I have worked out a cunning plan. It's not particularly complicated and it consists of one simple step: *lie.* And that's it.

We debate the telling-the-truth option for about thirty seconds, and then decide that it's probably much better all round if we just... don't. Because we're scared mainly. As Dad says, "Annabel is absolutely *bonkers* at the moment, Harriet. Do you really want to awaken the Kraken?"

So we're going to lie to Annabel. And – I add this silently in my head – Nat. We're obviously not going to lie to them forever. That would be ridiculous. We're just going to keep the truth from them until the timing is right. And it feels like a suitable moment.

And we have absolutely no other alternative. Which makes me feel no better about anything at all, so as soon as we're home from the agency, I make my excuses and go straight to the only place in the world I go when I need to run away.

The local launderette.

It's about 300 metres away from my house, and I've been coming here since I was allowed to leave the house on my own. For some reason it always makes me feel better. I love the soft whirring sounds, I love the soapy smells, I love the bright lights, I love the warmth coming out of the machines. But most of all I love the feeling that nothing could ever be bad or wrong in a place where everything is being cleaned.

I dig fifty pence out of my pocket and put it in one of the tumble dryers. Then – when it's switched on and hot and vibrating – I lean my head on the concave glass window and shut my eyes.

I don't know how long I sit with my head on the dryer, but I must nod off because I suddenly jerk awake to the sound of: "Did you know that the average American family does eight to ten loads of laundry each week, and a single load of laundry takes an average of one hour and twenty-seven minutes to complete from wash to dry? That means that the average American family spends approximately 617 hours a year doing laundry. What do you think it is for England? Less, I think. We just seem to be a bit dirtier."

And there – sitting on top of a washing machine – is Toby.

I stare at him in silence.

"Hey, you're awake!" he observes. "Look!" And then he points to his T-shirt. It has a picture of drums on it. "It's interactive! When I press the drums, they make the sound of drums." *Thud, thud.*

"Toby. What are you doing here?"

"Did you hear that?" He's wearing a yellow bobble hat and it's bobbling in excitement. *Thud, thud, thud.* "They're realistic, aren't they? Do you think if you got one with a guitar on it, we could start a band?"

"No. What are you doing here?"

"Obviously I'm doing laundry, Harriet."

I raise my eyebrow. He looks completely at ease with this terrible excuse, which – considering the fact that he has no laundry with him – is a little worrying. "Did you just follow me here?"

"Yes."

"Why?"

"You looked sad. And also because it's dark and it could be dangerous if you wander around on your own."

I scowl. "Yes, Toby. I might be at risk from *stalkers*."

Toby looks around us. "I think it's just me, Harriet.

I've not run into any others while on the job. Are you excited about the modelling assignment?"

I stare at him for a few seconds. *"How the hell do you know about that?"*

How am I supposed to keep it a secret from Nat and Annabel if I can't even keep it secret from Toby?

"Well, I wouldn't be a very good stalker if I didn't, would I?" Toby laughs. "I'd have to hang up my stalker gear in shame." He thinks about it. "Which would be unfortunate because all I've really got is this flask and I'm quite attached to it." He pulls out a red flask and shows it to me. "Soup," he explains. "In case I get hungry."

"Toby, nobody is *supposed to know.*"

"So that makes this a secret between the two of us, right?" I glare at him. "Which makes us kindred spirits? And – correct me if I'm wrong – *soulmates*?"

"We're not soulmates, Toby. You can't just go round stealing secrets and then forcing people into being your soulmate."

"OK." He seems unabashed by the rejection. "But you're glad I gave that model man your number."

For a few seconds all I can do is stutter without any noises coming out. "*You* gave the modelling agency my number?"

"You ran off at The Clothes Show so quickly I think you forgot. Good, huh?" Toby grins at me and the yellow bobble bounces up and down cheerfully. "Now the whole world is going to see you the way I already see you. I've always been a little bit ahead of the trends."

I point to the scraped-up word on my satchel. "And what if they see me the way everyone at school sees me, Toby?"

Toby considers this for a few moments. "Then I think you're going to need a bigger bag." And he hits the drum on his T-shirt. *Thud, thud.*

Suddenly I'm not so sure the launderette was a good idea after all. "I'm going home."

"OK. Would you like me to follow a few metres behind?" I frown at him, but he doesn't seem to notice. "By the way," he adds, "did Nat tell you what she did yesterday? She was amazing, Harriet. Like Boadicea, except without the chariot. Or the horses, or the swords, but still: it was *awesome*."

I stop near the door. "Nat?" I say, totally confused. "What are you talking about?"

"She heard what happened to you in Mr Bott's English class and she went *crazy*. She stormed into the changing rooms while Alexa was getting ready for hockey and did a whole world of yelling." Toby pauses. "I didn't see this because they wouldn't let me in. Apparently that room is only for girls and I am not one of those, Harriet. I assure you. Whatever Alexa might say. I am all man."

My blood is running cold, and not just because Toby just said the phrase *all man*.

"And you want to know the best bit?" Toby adds, apparently totally unaware that every single muscle in my face is now twitching with guilt and horror. "You want to know what else she did?"

"What?"

"Honestly, you won't believe it when I tell you."

I almost snarl at him, I'm so tense. "*Tell me*," I pretty much shout across the launderette. "*Tell me what she did.*"

"She chopped Alexa's ponytail off. Right off. At the base. With some scissors. And then she said, '*Now let's see how you like everyone laughing at you*,' and stormed off." Toby laughs. "Apparently Alexa looks a bit like she's all man too now."

Oh my God. I groan and put my hand over my eyes. This is the school equivalent of the assassination of Archduke Franz Ferdinand in Sarajevo in June 1914, which led to Austria-Hungary declaring war on

Serbia, which led to Russian mobilisation, which led to Germany declaring war on Russia. *Which led to World War One.*

Nat just started a war for me. In defence of me. Because of me.

And I am not worth it.

This is about as horrible as it's possible to feel. I've reached new heights of self-shame (or lows, depending on which way up the scale is). "I...I..." I say faintly, holding on to the door handle. "I really have to go home, Toby."

And I run out of the door as fast as my legs will carry me.

36

I run all the way home.

OK, that's not true. I don't run *all* the way. I just wanted you to think I could if I needed to. Because I probably could. I run most of the way and then I Brownie Walk for the rest of it (walk twenty paces, run twenty paces). But I can't run fast enough to get me away from what it is I'm running from. Which is me, mainly.

What am I doing? I'm about to screw over my Best Friend while she defends me, my stepmother while she protects me and possibly – depending on exactly how bad I am at this modelling thing – Wilbur and the entire fashion industry.

My head feels like it's starting to rattle with words bouncing around inside it like balls. Every time *Moscow, Nick, Baylee* or *Metamorphosis* hit the side, my entire body jolts with excitement. Every time *Nat* and *Annabel* make contact, I feel like I'm about to implode with guilt and anxiety. And every time the *Alexa* ball bounces, I feel like vomiting.

But it's too late. I've made my choice. So I spend the rest of the evening making an imaginary box in my head. And into this box I put all of the balls. I close the lid. And then I lock it up and temporarily misplace the key.

I'm going to Russia, I'm going to be transformed and there is nothing anybody can do to stop me.

First thing on Monday morning, the lies begin.

<u>Lie No.1</u>

Nat, I have a bad cold. Really do this time. Not coming to school today or tomorrow probably. Hope you're OK. See you Wednesday XX

<u>Lies No.s 2 and 3</u>

Annabel: "Why are you wearing your Winnie the Pooh jumper, Harriet?"

Me: "...It's non-uniform day."

Annabel (*long silence*): "And why haven't you gone to work already, Richard?"

Dad: "It's non-uniform... Hang on. No. Late start today. Going in later. Look: I bought some strawberry jam."

Annabel: "Why? I *hate* strawberry jam."

Lie No.4

Me: "Annabel, do you know where my passport is?"

Annabel: "Why on earth would you want your passport at 8am on a Monday morning?"

Me: "...International school project?"

Annabel: "Why does that sound like a question? Are you asking me or telling me?"

Lie No.5

Toby, have gone to Amsterdam for a shoot. H

By the time Annabel's frowned at both of us, checked me for a temperature and gone to work, Dad and I are running late for the airport so packing consists of throwing everything I own into a little suitcase, bouncing on top of it to get it to shut and contemplating just trimming round the edges as if it's some kind of pie.

I've decided if I'm doing this, I have to do it properly, so I've made a bubble chart plan on the computer and given a copy to Dad. My lies are pink bubbles, Dad's lies are blue bubbles and the lies we have to share are – obviously – purple.

In synopsis: Nat thinks I'm at home, sick, Annabel thinks I'm at Nat's tonight for a sleepover, followed by school, and Annabel also thinks that Dad's flown to Edinburgh for a late emergency client meeting that will run over until tomorrow evening.

"I can't believe you made a *bubble chart*," Dad keeps saying in disbelief as we finally climb into our plane seats.

"It's the most suitable kind of chart for this kind of plan," I tell him indignantly. "I made a flow chart and a pie chart, but they didn't work nearly as well. This one is a lot more sensible."

Dad looks at me in silence. "That's not what I meant," he says eventually.

"I made a timeline graph too," I tell him as we buckle our seatbelts. "The lies are spread across it on an hourly basis. But if I show it to you, you might get confused. I think it's best if I simply alert you when you're supposed to be saying something that isn't true."

Dad stares at the bubble chart again. "Harriet, are you sure you're my kid? I mean, you're sure that Annabel didn't bring you with her and swap you in?"

I scowl at him and then wince in pain because the universe has apparently decided to wreak vengeance upon me by making my metaphorical devil horns literal. By the time the air hostesses start pointing to the exits, my entire forehead is hot and throbbing; by the time they bring round the free peanuts, I can't really frown without it hurting, and by the time we start the descent into Moscow, Dad's calling my brand-new and massive zit "Bob" and talking to it like a separate entity.

"Would Bob like a drink of orange juice?" he asks every time a flight attendant walks past. "Perhaps a piece of cracker?"

It takes every single bit of patience I have not to ask the pilot if we can just turn round and drop my father back in England because he is *not behaving*. None of this, however, is enough to crush my excitement.

I'm going to Russia.

Land of revolutions and preserved leaders with lightbulbs stuck in the back of their heads. Land of the Kremlin and the Catherine Palace and the lost Amber Room, which was covered in gold and somehow 'went missing' during World War Two. Land of big fur hats and little dolls that fit inside each other.

And if I have to model while I'm there, so be it.

"This is it," Dad says as the plane comes down. He nudges me with his elbow and grins. "Do you know how many teenagers would kill for this, sweetheart?"

I look out of the window. There's a flurry of soft white snow and everything is covered in white powder, like a postcard. Russia looks exactly as I imagined it would. And trust me, I've imagined it a lot. It's on my Top Ten List of Countries to Visit. Number Three, actually. After Japan and Myanmar.

I swallow hard. Things are starting to change already. From this point on, everything is going to be different.

"You're living the dream," Dad smiles at me, looking back out of the window.

"Yes," I say, smiling back at him. "I think I just might be."

37

The really great thing about Moscow airport is that it's so *Russian*.

The signs are in Russian. The books are in Russian. The brochures are in Russian. The shops are in Russian. All the things in the shops are Russian. All the people are Russian. OK, maybe all the people aren't *Russian* – most of them are getting off planes from the UK and America, and if I'm totally honest, everything is also in English – but everyone looks sort of… different. Exotic. Historical. Revolutionary.

Even Dad looks more sophisticated, and he's still wearing that nasty T-shirt with the robot on the front of it. None of which seems to have made any impression on Wilbur.

"Oh, my Billy Ray Cyrus," he sighs when we finally find him. He's sitting on top of a pink suitcase, wearing a silk shirt covered in little pictures of ponies, and the second he gets close to me he puts his hands over his eyes as if I'm about to poke them out with my zit. "Where did *that* come from? What have you been *eating*?"

"Chocolate-chip cereal bars," Dad informs him helpfully. "She had three for breakfast."

"You look like a baby unicorn, Twinkletoes. Could you not have held off for another twenty-four hours before you started sprouting horns?"

I scowl in humiliation, wince, and try to push the spot back in again. "It's only one," I mumble in embarrassment. "Horn, *singular.*"

"Stop trying to *climb* the mountain with your fingers, Cookie-crumble," Wilbur sighs, gently smacking my hand away. "Unless you're planning on sticking a flag on top for posterity."

Dad laughs so I thump his arm. Adults really need to learn to be more sensitive about teenage skin problems. They can be devastating to mental health, and to confidence, and also – I'd imagine – to modelling careers. "It'll cover up with make-up, though, right?" I ask nervously.

"Treacle-nose, putting make-up on *that* is like sprinkling sugar on the top of Mount Fuji. Thank God for computers, that's all I'm saying." Then Wilbur takes a step back and surveys my outfit. "*Luckily*," he exclaims, "we've saved the day with another moment of sheer fashion brilliance. Turn around, my little Rhino."

I squint at him and then look down. "My Winnie the Pooh jumper?" I say in disbelief. "And my school skirt?"

It was all I had that still fitted and wasn't a) in the wash, covered in sick, b) a football kit c) a suit or d) designed with an insect as a template.

"Winnie the Pooh Jumper and School Skirt," Wilbur says, looking at the sky in wonder and slapping himself on the forehead. "You are truly an original, my little Jellyfish. *Anyhoo*, while I could stand here all day and talk about dermatological disasters and your sense of style, sadly I'm being paid to make sure I don't."

And he starts wobbling across the airport with his suitcase in one hand and the other held inexplicably high in the air.

"But where are we going first?" I say as Dad and I trot along behind him. I'm so excited now that little insects feel like they're rocketing around my stomach, the way they rocketed around the jam-jar trap we made at primary school. "The Gulag History Museum? The Tretyakov Gallery? The Novodevichy Convent? The Worker and Kolkhoz Woman is in Moscow, you know. It moved from Paris."

Not that I've spent the entire journey reading a guidebook about Moscow or anything. Or – you know – three. And studying a map.

"Oh, good Lord. They sell lots of vodka here, right?" Dad asks. "I think I might need one."

"My little Ginger-cakes," Wilbur says, turning to look at us with his hand on his hip. "We're not sightseeing *or* drinking vodka. This isn't a romantic weekend for three, although – " and he looks at Dad – "Mr Panda Senior over here is definitely a cutey."

Dad looks momentarily stunned, and then grins and winks at me. "I keep telling Annabel I am, but she never believes me."

"So where are we going?" I repeat impatiently. I'm going to throttle Dad before this trip is over.

"We're going straight to set, Sponge-finger," Wilbur says in a businesslike voice, "and we don't even have time to drop your bags off at the hotel first. However, we *do* have to find the other model before we go anywhere."

I stare at Wilbur in shock. He's started walking towards the taxi rank and is waving his hands around as if his feet are on fire. "Wooohooo?" he adds at the top of his voice. "*Avez-vous* a spare taxi, anyone? Silver plate?"

I continue looking at his back, slightly distracted by

the fact that he seems to think we're in France. "Other model? What other model?"

Another model is *not* on the bubble chart.

"It's a paired shoot, Puppy-toe," Wilbur explains, looking at his watch. "I'm certain I explained it all to you, although that could have been a dream. And not one of my most interesting ones either." He looks at his watch again and sighs. "But he's predictably late, *as usual*."

My stomach falls into my knees. "*He?*" I finally stammer.

"That's the personal pronoun we use when the subject is male, Petal. And, if I remember correctly, you've met this one before. You were talking about doves, or was it pigeons? Some sort of bird anyway."

My stomach drops all the way to the floor. And then my heart and my lungs and my kidneys and my liver all follow it until they're lying in a smashed-up pile at my feet.

There is *no way* this is happening.

"*Finally*," Wilbur says, turning round and waving. Because there – leaning against a lamp-post in the snow, wearing a big army jacket and looking impossibly beautiful – is Nick.

Again.

38

What were the chances?

I'll tell you what the chances were. Approximately 673 to one. And that's if Yuka Ito was only casting male models who were based in London. If you count the rest of the globe – which is equally full of beautiful people – then the statistics get even more improbable. Thousands to one. Thousands and thousands to one little tiny one.

And how have I worked this out so quickly? That's not important. But if, say, I *happened* to stumble upon all the main modelling agency websites while I was bored last night, and I *happened* to count up all the male models, and I *happened* to calculate the chances of seeing Nick again soon, then that would be my prognosis. If I *had.*

As I said, it's not important.

Approximately 673 to 1 and yet here he is, climbing into a taxi next to me. And my dad. Which is mind-boggling because I sort of assumed that if my planet and Nick's planet weren't supposed to collide then his planet and my *dad's* planet were probably on different orbits, in different solar systems, in totally different universes.

Dad takes one look at Nick, sitting on the backseat next to me with his hair covered in snowflakes, and coughs. "I think I'm starting to understand why you were so keen to be a model, Harriet," he says in the most unsubtle voice I've ever heard. I kick him on the ankle.

"What?!" Dad pretends to look innocent and offended. "I'm just saying, from a fifteen-year-old girl's perspective, things are making a lot more sense all of a sudden." And then he grins at me.

It's not possible to be this embarrassed. If I open the taxi door while it's moving and physically *push* my dad out, will I get arrested for murder? It might be worth it.

"*Dad*," I whimper and stare out of the window as hard as I can. Moscow is zooming past – all snow and big buildings – but I can barely focus on it. Not only is Nick here when he's not supposed to be, he's even *more* handsome than last time I saw him. He gets better looking every day, as if he's taking some kind of magic beautifying potion made from the tongue of a unicorn and the hair of a dragon or something.

Perhaps I should ask if he has any spare.

"You met under the table at The Clothes Show, do you remember?" Wilbur says innocently, waving his hand between us.

Dad's all-knowing expression has deepened. "Is that *so*?"

Nick half smiles at me and puts his feet up on the seat in front of us. "Harriet Manners," he says in his slow, lazy voice. "Dedicated to law enforcement."

"She gets that from her stepmother," Dad explains and I quickly try to calculate how much injury I'll cause if I wait until there's a red light and then just casually kick Dad's car door open.

"I didn't know you'd be here," I say as nonchalantly as I can.

Nick shrugs. "I got the Baylee gig a while ago," he says as if he's just landed a Saturday job at the local supermarket. "They were just waiting to find the right girl."

Oh my God. *I'm* the Right Girl? I'm usually the Girl That Will Have To Do I Suppose Because That Other One Got Chicken Pox (Year Five play *Cinderella*).

Wilbur leans forward. "Plum-pudding," he says in an awe-filled voice. "He's done it all. Gucci, Hilfiger,

Klein, Armani. Barely sixteen years old and one of the most successful young male models in London. You're very lucky to work with him, my little Pot of Bean Paste. He can hold your hand. Walk you through it."

I look briefly at Nick's hand. *I wish*, I think wistfully. And then my cheeks go pink.

"It's nothing to be worried about, honestly," Nick says in a calm voice, staring out of the window. "We rock up, we do our job, we get snowed on, we go home again. It's no biggy."

I nod quickly, my whole head now zinging with nerves. *No biggy.* The closer we get, the more real it's starting to feel, and the more I can feel the panic rising. The last few days have been less like a funfair rollercoaster and more like one of those round balls they strap astronauts into in preparation for space. I'm never quite sure which way is up any more.

But it's fine: this is *no biggy*. It's just me, Dad and Wilbur, hanging out in Moscow for twenty-four hours, taking photos. Casual, breezy photos, with a really expensive camera. And one of London's top male models and a famous photographer. And maybe fashion legend Yuka Ito drinking coffee 100 metres away and switching lights on and off with a disgusted look on her face. Just six people and one of them is Lion Boy.

No biggy. Sure.

My heart is starting to hammer like one of the little toy soldiers in a Christmas cartoon, and my mouth has gone suddenly fuzzy. I lick my lips and try to focus. This is what I wanted. This was my choice. This is what I'm lying for. And what's the point if I'm so scared I can't enjoy my own transformation?

I look out of the window while I try to calm my breathing down. It *is* really beautiful. The buildings are massive and majestic, everyone is wrapped up in furry hats and scarves and there are Christmas lights twinkling between the snowflakes. And every so often, if you look really hard, it's possible to see a man in uniform, standing on a corner with a massive gun in his hands.

Which distracts a little bit from the Christmas *ambience*, but still.

And then there's the river: huge and shining with the lights stretching out in reflections across the water. Exactly like the books I have at home and much, *much* better than *La Seine* in Paris.

Which is not being racist towards rivers. I'm just saying.

"We're nearly here, my little Chocolate-drops,"

Wilbur says as the taxi turns a corner. "Baby-baby Unicorn, how are you feeling? Calm? Cool? Deeply and irretrievably fashionable?"

I give the least convincing nod of my life. "I feel fine," I lie as the taxi stops. My hands suddenly feel like live fish in my lap: all slippery and incapable of staying still. "I feel great," I continue, looking out of the window. "I feel—"

Then I stop. Because in front of us is a huge square, filled with snow. On one side is an elaborate red wall and on the other side is a large white palace, delicately carved. I know that if I was to turn round, there would be a red castle behind us, but directly in front of us is the most beautiful building I have ever seen. Red, and blue, and green, and yellow, and striped and starred and carved like the most expensive cake you could possibly imagine.

And in front of that are about thirty-five people, sixty lights, trailers, chairs, hangers full of clothes, clusters of passers-by and – inexplicably – a small white kitten on a pillow, wearing a lead.

And it looks like every single one of them is waiting for us.

39

Lion Boy lied.

There's no other way of putting it: he totally and utterly lied. This *is* a biggy, in every possible sense of the word. As soon as we get out of the taxi in Red Square – which is where I've already worked out we are – we're surrounded. It's like being in some kind of zombie movie, except that instead of the undead wearing ripped clothes and trying to eat us, it's fashionable people wearing black and fur and trying to talk to us about our journey.

"At last!" somebody shouts at the back. "They're finally here!"

"Sweetums," Wilbur announces as he gets majestically out of the car. The snow has slowed down, but Wilbur still opens a huge umbrella in case his hair gets "damp". "I'd like to say it was the traffic, but it really wasn't. It's just so much easier making an *entrance* when everybody's waiting already, isn't it?"

I'm glaring at Nick so hard that my eyebrows are starting to hurt. "No biggy?" I hiss as we're helped out into the snow. "*No biggy?*"

Nick grins at me and shrugs. "Oh, come on," he says in a low voice. "If I'd told you the truth, you'd have just tried to climb out of the taxi window."

He's right. "I would *not*," I snap back because climbing out of windows isn't a very elegant image for him to have of me, and then – to regain a little bit of dignity – I toss my head as angrily as I can. Although it's pretty hard staying mad when you're standing in the middle of a fairytale in front of a castle with somebody who looks just like a prince.

Not that I think of Nick like that. We're just colleagues.

Dad, in the meantime, is sucking the attention up as fast as physically possible. "*My* daughter," he's saying to anyone who will listen. "The strawberry-blonde one. Can you see?" He keeps pointing to his own hair. "Genetically mine. It's actually a recessive gene so she was very lucky because her mother was a brunette."

"*Dad*," I whisper again and roughly four more ways to kill him race through my head. "*Please.*"

"Harriet, this is all *so... so...*" Dad sighs happily while he looks for the right word, dusting off his nineties vocab. "*Rad*," he finishes and I have to put my hand over my face to hide my embarrassment.

It's not enough to ruin this moment, though. I'm in *Red Square*. To my left is the Kremlin, which houses Lenin's Mausoleum, and in front of me is St Basil's Cathedral, one of the most amazing and famous pieces of architecture in the entire world. There's the GUM department store, and the State Historical Museum, and the Kazan Cathedral. There's even a bronze statue of Kuzma Minin and Dmitry Pozharsky, although it's so covered in snow I can't see who is who.

It's stunning, which shouldn't really be a surprise. It's not called Red Square because it's red. It's because the Russian word for red – *красная* – also means *beautiful*. This is their *beautiful square*.

There are so many people making so much noise – so many objects I don't really recognise – that it takes me quite a few moments to realise that Nick has disappeared completely again and the crowd is starting to part in the middle, like the Red Sea except Black.

It slowly gets quieter and the parting widens until there's a distinct snowy pathway up the middle. Even Wilbur stops talking and the only sound left is the kitten, who now and then makes a small squeaking sound like a door shutting.

"Here she comes," somebody whispers in what sounds a lot like terror, and all heads turn in one direction.

Stalking up the pathway on the highest black heels I've ever seen is Yuka Ito. And she's staring directly at me.

40

Now I could be wrong, but Yuka Ito appears to be wearing exactly the same outfit, except with bright orange lipstick instead of purple. For somebody so high up in the fashion industry, she seems to have even fewer wardrobe options than I do.

Yuka stops two metres away from where we're all standing, totally mesmerised. She doesn't look happy. Although obviously I'm not sure what happiness looks like for Yuka Ito. Let's just say the snow on her shoulders doesn't appear to be melting in the slightest.

"Wilbur," she says in a voice so appropriately icy it's like it's coming from the sky. "What, precisely, do you think your job is?"

"Other than being generally fabulous?"

"Debatable," Yuka snaps. "Would you say that your job entails getting my models to me at the time I've asked you to get them to me?"

Wilbur thinks about this for a few seconds. "I would say it's definitely on the list, yes."

"Then could you explain why they're both forty-five minutes late?"

"Darling," Wilbur sighs, rolling his eyes. "Turning up on time is so *keen*. Not *cool.* Plus –" and he makes a little gesture and lowers his voice, as if telling us a secret –"it's *snowing*."

"Yes, I was vaguely aware of that. Although everybody else managed to get here on time because in Russia snow is not, shall we say, *unexpected*." Yuka's lips press together in a straight line and then she looks at me. "Could you also explain why the female face of my new collection is sporting some kind of head accessory?"

Head accessory? What is she... *Oh*. My whole being goes bright red. She's talking about the spot. If there was a light above my head, I suspect it would be turned off about now.

"If you cast a *teenager*," Wilbur says patiently, "that's a risk that comes with the territory. They're skinny, yes, but just *full* of hormones and pus. It's like employing a tiger and then complaining because it has whiskers."

Yuka looks at me impassively. I've definitely felt prettier. She makes a clicking noise with her tongue. "Fine," she says in a snipped voice. "We'll digitally enhance her beyond recognition anyway. Take her to the hotel to get ready while we set up and do Nick's solo shots. You've got an hour and a half." And then she clicks her fingers at a handful of people standing directly to her right. "There's a list. Follow it *exactly*. Let me make this clear: this is *not* your time to shine creatively." She scowls at the crowd in general. "*Now*," she adds. "Why are you all still standing there? I'm finished."

And then she walks back through the black sea, which closes neatly around her.

I look at Wilbur in bewilderment.

"List?" I say finally. "What list?"

"I believe, Munchkin-face, that'll be the list of what we're going to do about *this*." And then he waves his hand in my direction.

Apparently by *this* he means *me*.

"But," I finally manage to blurt, "I thought you said I was perfect just the way I was?" At which point Wilbur throws his head back and roars with laughter.

And that, apparently, is my answer.

41

So I have a confession to make: I haven't come here totally unprepared. I mean, I can't expect them to do everything, can I? If I want to be cool, I have to put a little effort in. Participate in my own metamorphosis.

So I spent a few hours last night doing some research on the internet. I know a whole lot more about the fashion industry than I did before. And I'm kind of excited because now I get a chance to prove it and, maybe, start making a little progress in the right direction.

"Sit down, sweetheart," one of the women wearing black says. I've been taken out of the snow and put into a little hotel room just behind Red Square. I've never seen so many beauty products, make-up items and hairbrushes. There's even one of those headlamps set up, like the one my grandma uses when she gets a perm.

I sit down. Another woman gets a piece of paper out and looks at it. "Are you kidding me?" she says in disbelief. "*No cat eyes?* Doesn't Yuka know it's all about cat eyes this season?"

The other woman shrugs. "Prada have just done it so it's officially over already."

I blink. This isn't quite the conversation I was gearing up for, but I shall do my best to keep up.

"You know," I say, clearing my throat and trying to look as casual as possible, "cats' eyes have a mirror-like membrane on the back to maximise light exposure. That's why they shine in the dark."

The two ladies look at me. "That's... nice."

"And on the subject of fashion," I add quickly, mentally trawling through the research I did last night, "did you know that in the eighteenth century it was very hip to stick on eyebrows made out of mice skin?"

They gaze at me in silence.

"Also," I add, determined to keep going until they're impressed, "did you know that there are buttons on coat sleeves because Napoleon ordered them to stop his soldiers wiping their noses on their jackets?"

"That's gross," one of them points out.

"But weirdly interesting," the other one adds.

See? I told you my research would pay off. I've already won over a little bit of the fashion industry with my hip knowledge.

"Now," she continues, looking at the list again, "we've got just enough time to do your make-up after. And get you into the clothes."

I stare at her and then I stare at Dad who's wandering around the room picking things up and putting them down again. ("Look, Harriet! A Russian Bible! It's all in Russian!") Dad shrugs nonchalantly as I raise my eyebrows at him. "No idea what anyone's talking about, sweetheart. Don't look at me."

"After what?" I ask tentatively, looking at Wilbur.

We've got an hour and a half. How much time does it take to put on a bit of lipstick and a dress? How much time does it take to make me into a model? How ugly do they think I am?

Wilbur claps his hands together. "Ah, my little Pineapple-chunk, this is the best bit," he explains. "I've been excited about it ever since I saw The List."

I look around the room and already I can feel a sense of impending doom. "What's going on?"

"Oh, come on," Wilbur shouts in excitement, starting to jump up and down. "What happens to the Ugly Duckling to turn her into a swan?"

The blood drains from my face. "You're making me go swimming?"

"*Yes!*" Wilbur shouts excitedly. "We're making you

go—" and then he stops. "What? No, honey. We're *giving you a haircut.*" At which point the door opens.

"And *that,*" Wilbur adds, pointing to the incredibly short man who has just walked in, "is the wizard who is going to transform you."

Right, I'm not sure what fairytales Wilbur has been reading, but at no stage in any of Hans Christian Andersen's stories does the Ugly Duckling get a haircut.

The Ugly Duckling gradually becomes the beautiful bird on the outside that he always was on the inside. It's a story about inner beauty and embracing who you truly are and fulfilling your destiny (and also ignoring mean ducks who have a go at you in the process).

He doesn't just *get a haircut*. I've tried explaining this to Wilbur, but he's having none of it. "What are you talking about, Treacle-bottom?" he says distractedly, still dancing round my chair like some kind of excited leprechaun. "So how does he go from all ratty and grey to beautiful and smooth and white then? Are you telling me a hairdresser wasn't involved?"

I'm not quite sure what to say to that, so instead I shut up and stare at the hairdresser – a French man called Julien – who is walking solemnly round in the opposite direction.

"Now," Julien says, "*ma petite puce*. Wot iz your name again?"

"Harriet Manners," I say, sticking my hand out awkwardly. Did he just call me a *flea*?

Julien stares at my hand in shock. "*Mon Dieu*," he says, appalled. "I am *French*. We do not *touch 'ands.* It is un'igienic."

"Sorry," I say, pulling it back as quickly as possible and wiping it on my trousers.

"*Non*, instead we do a little kissin'. Like zis." And he leans forward and kisses Wilbur three times on the cheeks and then once lingeringly on the lips.

Wilbur giggles. "Best bit of my trip," he whispers to me behind his hand. "I do *love* Frenchmen."

"Ze lip bit was just for Wilbur," Julien explains. "We don't do zat in France. *Alors.*" He grabs my face and stands behind me, looking into the mirror. Then Wilbur's face pokes up to the right, and Dad's face pokes up to the left until all three are staring at me like a bad eighties album cover.

"Zis 'air," Julien continues. "It iz big."

"Yes," I agree.

"It iz *too* big. It iz… 'ow you say… *flooding you*."

"Drowning?" Dad offers helpfully.

"*Mais oui*. You are nuthin' but a little wave in an

ocean of 'air. We cannot see your features. It iz all lost." Julien looks at Wilbur and then looks back at me. "Yuka iz right," he says finally, and Wilbur gives a little squeal as if somebody just trod on his toe and he's happy about it. I'm not feeling as comfortable with this conversation as I should be.

"Your 'air," Julien explains in a nonchalant voice, "iz too big for your 'ead."

"It's *supposed* to be," I explain. "More room to hide."

"*Non*." Julien pushes me back down again. "A little 'ead needs little 'air."

"And a little ego needs *lots*," I argue, but it's too late. Julien has put a thick lock of my hair between his scissors and he's moving them closer and closer to my head. "Dad!" I yell. "Do something!"

"Touch a hair on my daughter's head," Dad says firmly, standing up, "and my wife will sue you all."

"OK," Julien shrugs.

And then he lops the whole lot off.

42

My dad is having a breakdown.

He keeps looking at my head and then murmuring, *Oh God, Oh God, Oh God*, and putting his hands over his eyes. "I think Annabel is going to notice this one," he says eventually.

I touch the hair clutched between my fingers. An hour ago it was waist-length and now it's bobbed to just below my ears. I also have a short spiky fringe which is going to be standing vertically for the rest of my teens.

Julien is calling this look "*La Jeanne d'Arc* for the New Decade". I think it means that I'm going to be sent to the wrong toilet in restaurants until it grows back again.

"Darling," the stylist says, patting me on the shoulder, "I know you must be gutted: the loss of your femininity and so on. But we don't really have time for this. We need to get you ready."

I nod, and then pull myself together and get off

the bed. I can't complain just because my idea of a *transformation* apparently isn't the same as anyone else's, i.e. to make me look better.

"OK," I say bravely, getting into the make-up chair. I'm going to just let them do whatever it is these people want to do.

Which is, apparently, bore me to death.

Being transformed is incredibly dull. It's like watching somebody you don't know paint by numbers. They inexplicably paint my face with something the same colour as my face, then put pink stuff where I was blushing before they covered it up, and then give me lots of black mascara that goes into my eyes, and then bright pink lips.

Then they put shimmery stuff on my shoulders, and shimmery stuff in my hair, and then they hand me my 'outfit'. I've used quotation marks, for the record, because it's not an outfit. It's a short fake fur coat and a pair of the highest red heels I have ever seen. And that's it.

No, sorry. I've also got a pair of big black knickers you *just* can't see under the coat and a sheer pair of tights that are totally transparent and do nothing apart from make my legs look weird and shiny, like the legs of a Barbie.

I stare at it all for a few seconds in disbelief and then take it into the bathroom to maintain my modesty, which for some unknown reason everybody seems to think is really funny. Then I sit on the seat of the toilet to put 'the outfit' on.

Ten minutes later, I'm still sitting there.

"Harriet?" a concerned voice eventually says, accompanied by a knocking on the door. "It's Dad. Are you all right, sweetheart?"

"She's probably so mesmerised by her own beauty she can't move away from the mirror," I hear Wilbur stage-whisper. "It's why I'm always late." Then he knocks on the door as well. *"Look away from the reflection, baby,"* he shouts through the wood. *"Just look away and the spell will be broken."*

"Dad? Can you come in here? I'm on the toilet."

There's a pause. "Darling, I love you very much. You're my only child and the apple of my eye and whatnot. But I'm not coming in there if you're on the toilet."

I sigh in frustration. "With the seat *down*, Dad. I'm sitting on the toilet. As a chair."

"Oh. OK." Dad pokes his head round the door. "What are you doing?"

"I can't stand up."

"You're *paralysed*? How did that happen?"

"No, I literally can't stand up. The heels are too big, Dad. I can't walk in them." I try to stand up and my ankles buckle and I collapse back on to the toilet.

"Oh." Dad frowns. "Why hasn't Annabel been teaching you how to walk in heels? I thought we had an agreement: I teach you how to be cool and she trains you how to be a girl."

I stare at him in silence. This explains so much. "I've never worn heels before. So what am I going to do?"

Dad thinks about it and then starts singing 'Lean on Me' by Al Green. He bends down and I take one wobbly step and hang on to his shoulder like a tipsy baby koala hanging on to a eucalyptus tree. Then Dad spins me round so I'm facing away from the door.

"What are you doing?" I snap crossly. I'm currently failing to be a *girl*, let alone a model. "The exit's that way."

"Before we go anywhere, I want you to see this," Dad says and he points in the mirror.

Next to a reflection that looks exactly like my dad is a girl. She's got white skin and sharp cheekbones and a pointed chin and green eyes. She has thin long legs and a long neck and she's sort of graceful yet clumsy-looking, like a baby deer. It's only when I lean forward a bit and see that her nose turns up at the end just like mine does that I fully register that it's me.

That's *me*? Wow. The beauty industry actually works. I look… I look… I look kind of *OK*.

"You can say what you like," Dad says after a moment. "But I think me and your mum must have done something right."

I make an embarrassed but pleased peeping sound.

"Don't get me wrong, I'm taking full credit for the hair. But she had all the beauty. She'd be so stoked right now." Then Dad spins me round again so that my toes are on top of his feet and starts half-carrying, half-dancing me out of the bathroom. "Roar for me?" he demands.

"*Rooooaaaar.*"

"That's the one. Now let's go get 'em, Tiger."

"I think this is leopard, actually," I point out, looking at the coat. "Tigers have stripes."

Dad gives me his widest grin. "Then let's go get 'em, Leopard."

It takes another four minutes to get out of the bathroom, and by the time I'm back in the hotel room, Dad has corrected the leopard analogy to "baby giraffe learning how to ice-skate".

Which is extremely unkind. I'd like to see *him* try and walk with eight-inch spikes attached to his feet. Plus, giraffes never lie down and there are at least three points where I'm sort of horizontal.

"Well, *this* isn't going to work, is it?" Wilbur points out eventually. "At this rate you'll be *way* too old to model by the time we get down to the shoot, Angel-moo. You'll probably be in your early twenties and what good is that to anyone?"

"I could put my trainers back on?" I suggest, getting them out of my bag.

Wilbur visibly flinches. "A next season, perfectly cut, limited edition Baylee coat worn with… are they supermarket own-brand trainers?" He swallows. "I think I just sicked up in my mouth. Fashion sacrilege. I can't allow it. Not while there's a breath left in this beautiful body of mine." He frowns and looks around the room. "Luckily I'm brilliant as well as stunning," he adds happily. "And I have an idea."

Ten minutes later, I enter Red Square with my entourage behind me. It's not *exactly* the entrance I was hoping for. In fact, I believe I've got my head in my hands for all of it.

Nick takes one look at the wheelchair, accurately

guesses why I'm in it and gives a very uncool shout of laughter so loud that pigeons fly off the top of a nearby statue. Yuka isn't quite as impressed.

"Would somebody like to tell me," she hisses as she stalks towards where I'm sitting, glaring at the seven people standing behind me, "*who broke my model?*"

43

Elegant. Dignified. Graceful.

Three words that don't describe me in the slightest. Five people have to pick me out of the wheelchair and carry me to where Nick is waiting in the snow, in front of St Basil's Cathedral, and when they plop me down, it takes another few minutes to get me balanced enough to remain vertical on my own. Which I can just about manage. As long as I focus really hard, don't move a muscle and scrunch my toes up into claws inside the shoes for leverage. And keep my hands out at the sides like a tightrope walker. None of which is aided by Dad's continuous laughing.

Or – for that matter – Nick's.

I'm briefly introduced to the photographer, Paul, who is a thin blond man without – as far as I can see – one single flamboyant tendency. He looks totally focused on the job, which is actually even more worrying. At least with Wilbur, it's possible to forget that there's a great deal riding on me.

It's not a little metamorphosis experiment any more. It's a job. It's very expensive. It's very important. And it matters to a lot of people.

"Look at me doing wheelies in the snow!" Wilbur screams in the background, spinning around in the wheelchair.

The photographer takes one look at him, grinds his teeth and looks back at Nick and me. "I just need to set up lighting," he says in a tense voice, looking up at the sky. It's starting to snow harder and the sky is a little darker than it was before. "Can somebody get my light reflector?"

A young boy races off and then runs back with a big gold circle.

"Just make yourself comfortable for a few minutes," he says, fiddling with a little black box as the boy starts flicking the gold circle around. "I'll take a few test shots when everything's perfect." He fiddles with the box again and then looks up. "Somebody might as well get Gary."

Gary? *Gary?* Who the hell is *Gary*?

I look at Nick, who I've managed to avoid making eye contact with since I came back from the hotel. I feel extremely self-conscious now that my hair's all gone.

Like the Wizard of Oz after the curtain's come down. Nick has his hands in the pockets of a large army-style coat and his hair gelled into a Mohican. He scrunches up his nose at me and my internal organs turn inside out again.

Shouldn't I be immune to him by now? Or is he like the human version of the common cold?

"You want to watch out," he says in his slow drawl. "Gary's vicious."

I look around in alarm. "Is Gary another model?" I whisper in terror. "A stylist? A hairdresser? Yuka's assistant?"

"Nope," Nick says and the corner of his mouth is twitching. "Worse. He's a monster. Raises hell wherever he goes." And then he looks past me and nods. "Here he comes. Watch yourself." And out of the crowd comes a woman holding the teeny-tiny white kitten.

OK, first impressions are deceiving. As soon as the lady hands him over to me, Gary nips my finger and starts clawing his way up my shoulder, hissing like an angry kettle. It's just not natural for something so cute and fluffy to be so nasty.

I look at Nick in distress. "Why is he spitting at me?"

"Maybe he thinks he's a llama."

I grab the kitten, who has changed his mind and is now scrabbling back down and trying to use my arm as a springboard. I don't think that's a good idea. He's small and white: if he lands in the snow, there's a really good chance we'll never find him again.

"OK, guys," Paul finally says. "We're ready to do some test shots." He pauses and looks at me. "Harriet. What are you doing to that animal?"

I look down to where I'm sort of hanging on to Gary by his back legs while he scrabbles away with his front ones. "Bonding?" I offer weakly.

"Could you bond in a way that looks a bit less like animal cruelty?" Paul clears his throat. "Right, I'm going to take a dozen or so frames. It's not *too* important what you do now, but this might be a good time to practise."

I nod nervously, grimly hold on to the cat and try to pretend that there isn't a large group of people in a semicircle, all watching every single thing we do.

Right, this is it. I'd expected a little more training – perhaps a little step-by-step instruction sheet on modelling – but... this is fine. I'll just go with it. Let the inner model out. Wilbur and Yuka obviously saw something deep within me, which has just been waiting to burst forth and impress everyone. Like a...

dragon. Or a really big dog.

I stare at the camera with my most modelly face. There's a pause and then Paul looks up. "What are you doing, Harriet? What's that face?"

I gulp. "It's my modelling face."

"Your…" Paul says in confusion and then he rolls his eyes. "You *have* a modelling face, Harriet. You don't need to strain it as if you've got a bad case of constipation. *Relax.*" There's another silence. "*Now* what are you doing?"

"Smiling?"

Paul sighs. "Have you ever seen a fashion magazine in your life? Take a look at Nick, Harriet. What is he doing?"

I look at Nick. "He's, erm… Just standing there."

"Precisely. He's being natural, in the best-looking way possible. Just pretend the camera's not here, sweetheart, and focus on being as beautiful as you can be."

The cat's clearly not convinced that I'm capable of this either; he makes a mewling sound and scratches in terror at my other shoulder. Which makes me wobble dangerously on the heels, so I have to reach out and grab Nick's shoulder.

"Sorry," I mumble in embarrassment and stare

hard at the snow.

Why didn't anyone explain that there was actually some kind of *skill* involved in being a model? Why didn't somebody tell me I'd have to actually *do* something? Why didn't they know I'd be rubbish?

I can feel my eyes starting to well up, and somewhere in the background I hear the make-up artist starting to panic loudly about my mascara. I look at Nick in open desperation and he gives me a crooked smile.

"Right," he says under his breath. "Give me the cat," and he takes it off me. Gary immediately makes a small meowing sound, curls up happily in Nick's arm and goes to sleep. Even *Gary* is in love with him.

"Now blow a raspberry."

I look at him for a few seconds in silence. "You want me to blow a raspberry?"

"Yup. Loud as you can. Make it a nice wet one."

I can feel my cheeks getting pink under the foundation. "I'm not blowing a raspberry," I tell him in a dignified voice. "I'm nearly an adult."

"Blow a raspberry."

"No."

"Blow it."

"No."

"Blow."

"*Fine*," I snap in exasperation and I blow a half-hearted raspberry.

Nick frowns at me. "That wasn't even a strawberry."

"Oh, for the love of..." I sigh and then I blow a much louder raspberry. I'm not even going to look at Yuka. I don't think this is why she employed me. "Happy now?"

"Much better. Now wiggle your shoulders. And your neck."

I wiggle my shoulders and my neck.

"Knock your knees together."

I knock my knees.

"And do the funky chicken."

I giggle and obediently do the funky chicken.

"Can you handle cold feet? Because if you can, I reckon you should take those stupid shoes off and hold them."

I glance at Paul, who is concentrating on adjusting one of the lamps to his right. And then I glance to the left where Yuka Ito is sitting in a black chair, glaring at us both with the face Annabel pulls when she eats oysters.

"OK," I say, shrugging, and take my shoes off. I'm so nervous I can't feel my feet anyway. Plus, I'm not sure I can get much worse at this. The only way is up.

Apparently Nick's thinking the same thing. Literally. "Now," he says, grinning. "I'm going to hold your hand. And when I say jump, *jump*, as high as you can. Look straight at the camera, keep your face calm and *jump*. OK?"

I nod, with my head now numb.

"Relax?"

I nod.

"Funky chicken?"

I nod and waggle my arms a bit.

"*OK, jump*," Nick whispers.

And I jump.

44

I'm holding Nick's hand.

I'm actually holding Nick's hand. And nobody made him do it. He did it for free.

Or, you know. For a modelling fee. *But he didn't have to.*

It was his idea.

Not that this is the only thing going through my head for the rest of the shoot, obviously. I'm a professional. I think about lots of… modelling related things. Like clothes, and make-up, and hair, and sticky eyebrows made out of mice.

And… and… no.

That's all I think about. The fact that Nick is holding my hand and I've never had my hand held by a boy before in my entire life unless you count when I was eight and forced into being Prince Charming's mother in the school play, and I don't.

And this time it's Lion Boy.

This time it's Nick.

*

It turns out that when Nick said *jump*, his idea was that he *also* jumped, and so we both leapt into the air at the same time as high as we could. Nick held on to the kitten, I held on to the red shoes and we both jumped together.

And *everyone* loved it. Paul loved it. Wilbur loved it. Dad loved it. The crowd loved it. Even Yuka stopped threatening to sack everyone in a ten-mile radius. Gary wasn't quite as keen, but you can't please everyone.

When we've finished jumping in the air from a standing position, we throw caution to the wind and try running along from left to right, jumping. And then from right to left, jumping. Eventually I'm so relaxed and having so much fun they actually manage to get me to *not* jump for a few shots, just for variety. They even get close to my face and I don't flinch or start twitching because I'm too busy thinking about… erm. Make-up. And clothes. And hair. And mice. And so on and so forth.

Before I know it, we're done.

I'm a *model.*

"My little Pea-pod!" Wilbur squeals as soon as Paul shuts down the camera. Nick immediately lets go of my hand, and by the time I turn around he's gone again. *Poof*. Like the proverbial genie. "Look at you, just bouncing around like a little kangaroo in the snow!"

Dad pushes past him. "All right, kiddo?" he says, and it looks like his face is going to snap in half, he's smiling so hard. "Chip off the old block, that was. I used to do high jump for the under-sixteens. Won trophies and everything."

"Dad, you won a bronze medallion on Sports Day once when you were thirteen. It's still on top of the fireplace."

"Trophy, medallion, who's counting? Anyway, I'm very proud." He gives me a hug. "I thought for a horrible minute there we were going to have to pay for our own flight home. Now did someone say free vodka?" And he scampers off happily in the direction of the hotel.

I look at my empty hand again. I can't believe Nick's gone already. I've never seen anyone capable of becoming invisible quite so quickly or unexpectedly. And I can't help wishing he wouldn't.

"London, Poppet," Wilbur says kindly, patting my shoulder.

"Hmm?" I'm still gazing in the direction I think Nick went.

"He's gone back to London. He has another shoot for a different designer in the morning."

I swallow in embarrassment and quickly look away. "Who? I don't know what you're talking about."

"Oh, please, Petal-pants. You're all lit up like Lenin, and you don't have the excuse of a lightbulb in the back of your head."

I clear my throat crossly. "Nick and I are just colleagues," I say with as much indifference as I can muster and an improvised shrug. "We work together."

"Not any more you don't," Wilbur says matter-of-factly, patting me on the head. "His bit's over. Yuka's not as bothered about the male fashion end of the spectrum. Not bad money for a four-hour gig, hey?"

A swoop of disappointment hits my stomach and I bite my bottom lip in case it reaches my face. I should have realised. I'll probably never see Nick again, unless it's on the pages of a magazine in a doctor's surgery and half his face will probably be missing from where somebody's ripped out a coupon from the other side.

I can feel my cheeks tingling. And he didn't even say goodbye.

"So," I say as calmly as I can, "is my bit over too then?"

I've done a shoot, I've got a new haircut, I'm wearing make-up and I've held a boy's hand, but…

I still feel like me. Something's not working the way it's supposed to.

Wilbur starts pealing with laughter. "*Is my bit over? Is my bit…* Oh, my little Bookworm," he sighs eventually, bending over and putting his hand in the crease of his waist. "You *do* crack me right down the middle."

Honestly, I wish people would just answer questions properly when I ask them.

"It's not over then?" I reiterate.

"Nope." Wilbur wipes the tears of laughter out of his eyes. "Now is the *really* fun bit. We're going to another part of Moscow."

For some reason, I'm not feeling as excited as I should be. Nick's gone and I'm on my own this time.

"For dinner?"

Wilbur starts squealing again. "*Dinner?* You're a model, Sugar-plum: you no longer *do* dinner. Or lunch. Or breakfast, actually, unless you plan on regurgitating like a little snake. No, we have a Baylee fashion show to attend."

"A fashion show? And I'm going too?"

"Well, I hope so, my little Chicken-wing," Wilbur says, straightening out my fringe affectionately. "Because you're starring in it."

45

OK, how the hell am I supposed to concentrate on turning into a butterfly when I don't have a clue what's going on from one minute to the next?

Although – to be fair – I'm not sure what I'd have done if they'd told me. I am not a big fan of fashion shows. That's not a gloomy, defeatist attitude either. It's hard-won knowledge that comes from plenty of experience. I spent a large portion of my ninth summer walking up and down a 'catwalk' (the patio at the bottom of Nat's garden), holding on to a skipping rope pulled in a straight line down the middle.

It was part of a deal Nat and I made: I practised 'The Walk' with her, she rehearsed lines from *The Song of Hiawatha* with me and we both pretended to enjoy it. But no matter how hard I tried, or how carefully Nat shaped our 'couture' plastic bin-bag dresses or arranged daisies on our heads as accessories, something always went wrong. A stumble. A rip.

A trip over a piece of pavement that resulted in a

trip to A&E and seven stitches.

Until Nat decided it was probably less dangerous if I handled half-time refreshments and 'directed' the show from the safety of a deckchair on the lawn. And she got on with the modelling.

Nat.

Ugh. The metaphorical box in my head feels like it's going to open and the contents are about to burst all over the floor, so I mentally stick an extra nail in each corner.

"Fashion shows are fantabulous," Wilbur reassures me as he forces me into yet another taxi. "Obviously we're going to need to work on your walking skills, Chuckle-bean, because I don't think the wheelchair is going to fit on the catwalk, but we've got at least twenty minutes to train you up."

I feel a bit like vomiting.

I get the Bubble Chart of Lies out of my bag and switch my phone on. "Dad," I say, turning to him, "You need to send something to Annabel to make her believe you're in a really boring business meeting that's running over."

"Like *what*?" Dad asks in confusion.

"I don't know," I snap back irritably. "I can't do *everything*. Just send whatever you'd normally send."

Dad frowns. "First of all, if I'm in a meeting, I don't normally text people under the desk. It's not school. Second of all, Annabel and I have been married for eight years: we don't send texts updating each other on our emotions about everything. And third of all, I'm a man. I *never* send texts updating people on my emotions about everything. *Anything* in fact."

"Oh, for God's sake," I grouch because my head feels like it's about to explode. "Send a text message, Dad. Just *follow the Bubble Chart*, OK? I don't have the energy for your maverickness today."

Dad looks at me, shrugs and gets his phone out. "All right. Don't blame me if she gets suspicious. This is your adventure: I'm just the sidekick."

"You're not the sidekick, Dad."

"I am. I'm like Robin. Or maybe Dr Watson."

I scowl at him. "Try Chewbacca," I mutter under my breath. My phone has been going crazy on my lap. I'm trying to pretend I haven't heard it because I'm not sure I'm ready to deal with the rocket of guilt and shame I'm about to have launched at me.

"Is this a teenage thing?" Wilbur eventually asks in excitement when it beeps yet again. "It's been a couple of years since I was a teenager, so maybe I'm out of the loop. Do you have a special ringtone you can't hear or something?"

Dad coughs. "A couple?" he says, gazing out of the window. "A couple of years?"

Wilbur sticks his nose in the air. "I just have a very carved face," he says haughtily. "Like Wolverine. It's always been carved."

Dad and I both look at him for a few seconds. If Wilbur's under forty, I'll eat that gold light reflector.

"No," I sigh eventually, picking up my phone. "I can hear it. Unfortunately." And then – extremely reluctantly – I click on the text messages.

H, how are you? Wish you were here. Shall I bring round soup after school? I can pick up some of that green Thai chicken stuff you like Nat x

H, no green stuff. Is red OK? Nat x

Dear Harriet, Toby Pilgrim here. Things are erupting at school. To wit: Alexa's torturing Nat. Shall I come to Amsterdam and bring you home to avenge her like a flaming angel? Yours truly, Toby Pilgrim

Harriet, don't forget to floss Annabel

H, is red too spicy? There's a picture of three chillis. Is that bad? Nat

Nausea rises up my trachea and I stare at my phone, totally frozen.

I'm the devil. I'm actually the devil. Any minute now the horn that matches Bob is going to sprout and my hair is going to catch fire. I've been prancing around in the snow like a shoeless idiot, while Nat runs around fighting for me and buying me soup, and Annabel worries about my dental hygiene. And all I can think about is holding a boy's hand.

I touch the painful spot on my forehead and tap my feet on the floor of the car. They're starting to sound a little bit like – oh, I don't know – *cloven hooves.*

I quickly type out a reply.

Nat, no soup thanks – am going straight to sleep. Am also contagious so don't come round. See you soon. H x

I stare at it for a few seconds then press send.

That's another lie. Two in fact. The balls inside the box in my head are going crazy, so I mentally sit on the lid so they don't all come bursting out at the same time.

When I glance to the side, Dad looks pretty uncomfortable too. "Hell's a pretty cosy place, right?" he says, closing his phone. "I mean, it's probably not as bad as they say, I reckon."

"Let's hope not," I sigh as we draw up outside an astonishing, white, beautiful, huge carved building with a red carpet spread out in front of it.

Because I have quite a strong feeling we're about to find out.

46

The Baylee fashion show is being held in a proper red-velvet-seated Russian theatre. A runway has been built down the middle of the room, in the bit where I'd imagine they normally sell ice cream, and there are chandeliers hanging low over the centre of it. Russian architecture isn't exactly known for minimalism: true to form, the entire room is gold and gilt and carved and embroidered and mirrored.

"Oh, my heavenly mango juice," Wilbur says when we walk in, putting his hand over his eyes and making a loud retching sound. "It's like the Sugar Plum Fairy exploded in here."

"If you don't like it, William," Yuka says, stalking past in her heels, "I can send you somewhere a lot less fancy." She walks up to the front of the stage.

Wilbur looks at me in shock. "Where did *she* come from?" he whispers, placing a hand over his heart. "Am I right in thinking that was a physical threat?" He looks resentfully at Yuka, who's now checking the runway. "And it's *bur* not *iam*," he points out loudly.

"I can't begin to tell you how little I care," Yuka snaps and beckons me over to where she's standing. "Harriet Manners," she continues seamlessly. "Everyone's getting ready backstage. Please go and join them. Important people are going to start arriving imminently and I can't have the face of my new campaign standing here in a hamster and horse jumper."

I look down, momentarily stunned. "He's not a *hamster*. He's Winnie the Pooh. A *bear*." And then I turn round and point to my back. "Eeyore's a *donkey*."

Yuka studies me for a few seconds. "I don't like donkeys," she decides eventually. "Or bears. Please go away and get into the outfit I've chosen for you, which features neither. Your name is on the tag."

I nod meekly. I'm not sure what to say to a woman who doesn't recognise Winnie the Pooh.

"And Harriet?"

I turn round on the stage, where I'm trying to find my way behind the curtains. My foot is caught in one of them. "Yes?" I say, trying to extricate it as subtly as possible.

Yuka's eyes slide down until she's staring at it. "If somebody offers to shave your legs," she snaps, "let them."

*

Well, I've found all of the Russian people.

All of the really good-looking female ones anyway. They're tucked into a little room behind the stage, crammed together like beautiful, thin, blonde sardines. I've never been so uncomfortable. There is skin *everywhere*. It's not flashes of puppy fat and training bras either. Really tall, toned girls are wandering around, laughing and almost naked, as if it's the most natural state in the world.

And I don't care what documentaries on television say: it's *not*.

I've climbed down the backstage stairs, beyond a screen, and now I'm standing by the doorway. Nobody has noticed I'm here; they're just walking past me as if I'm on work experience. At school, Alexa is the Cool girl, Nat is the Beautiful girl and a girl called Jessica is the girl who insists upon stripping down to her underwear at any possible opportunity. I'm the hairy-legged geek in the corner with the white ankle socks. I think the scale has just shifted and I should be in a hole under the floor somewhere.

I start backing out of the door I just came through.

"My daughter *needs me*," a voice yells from behind me. When I look round, Dad's standing on his tiptoes by the door, trying to see over the screen. "She *needs me*, I tell you."

"I don't need you," I call back.

"You see?" Dad says again, doing little jumps so that the top of his head bobs up and down. "I demand you let me into the room full of tall Russian models *this minute*."

Oh, for the love of sugar cookies.

"Dad," I hiss through the screen, "if you embarrass me any more, I'm sending you home. I mean it."

There's a pause and then Dad sighs dramatically. "*Fine*," he snaps in a sulky voice. "I'll just go and eat pickled cabbage at the back of the hall, shall I?"

"Yes, please."

"Being a sidekick *sucks*," he mutters and strops back into the theatre.

I look at the room again, which is getting more overwhelming by the minute. There's commotion and chaos everywhere: mountains of clothes, dozens of people, the shine of bright lights, the smell of hairspray, the roar of hairdryers and girls. People taking off clothes and putting them back on again. Confidence oozing out of every pore in the room. I am totally and utterly out of my depth.

I reckon if I just tucked myself into a ball in one

of the prop cupboards, nobody would notice I was missing. I mean, how important can I be?

"There she is!" somebody shouts, running forward and dragging me into the room by my arm. "The most important model of all!"

Oh.

I guess that's my answer.

47

This is a new start, I keep reminding myself as I'm pulled through the crowd of girls. What's the saying? *You've got to fake it to make it*. It's time I start pretending to belong and then maybe I will.

This isn't school after all. I can be someone else here. Someone cool. Someone different. I don't have to be a geek any more. I look down at my satchel. The red words are still vaguely visible and I hastily put my hand over it. I have *got* to get a new bag.

"Hello," I say confidently to the models who have all stopped what they're doing and are now watching me with their eyes narrowed. "I'm Harriet Manners. It's nice to meet you."

It's totally working. They've all stopped talking, and I can tell from the expressions on their faces that any minute now they're going to stand up, envelop me in a warm group hug and start arguing over who will get to be my Russian penpal. I grin in relief and hold out my hand to an astonishingly beautiful brunette.

"Bite me," she says in a strong accent, and then she turns round and continues putting on black stockings.

"Black with no sugar. Don't forget the lemon," another giggles and she high-fives her friend, who starts muttering darkly in Russian.

"I lost the Baylee campaign to *her*? Seriously? Has Yuka gone totally insane?"

"She looks like a little boy," another one says in a perfectly audible whisper.

"Maybe she is. Let's see what happens when she takes off her skirt."

"I reckon she doesn't have *anything* going on down there. Like Action Man."

"Have you ever seen freckles *like* it?"

"Yeah. Definitely. On a, like, *egg*."

"Or, like, a *Dalmatian*."

I can literally feel my face collapsing. This is exactly like school. Except that they've all got a fewer clothes on, which somehow makes it even worse.

I've said nine words so far. How can it have gone so badly wrong already? *How do they know all the same insults?*

"Actually," I say in the most reprimanding voice I can find, "there are no animals that have no reproductive organs at all. Even hermaphrodites have both sets, for instance the great majority of pulmonate snails, opisthobranch snails and slugs. So that is a physical impossibility."

There's a surprised silence and then the room erupts into nasty giggles. It's probably not going to go down in history as one of my most incisive comebacks.

"And," I add, looking at the girl with the stockings, "I'd rather not bite you. I don't know where you've been."

The giggling stops.

That's better, Harriet. That's the sort of thing Nat would have said.

The girl blinks at me a few times in shocked silence. "*What* did she just say to me?" she eventually snaps to the girl next to her and her forehead starts to get all scrunched up in the middle. "I'm the face of *Gucci*. I'm *Shola*. People don't talk to me like that. I *won't be talked to like that.*"

"Don't get worked up, honey," a blonde with huge blue eyes whispers back. "It'll just make you ugly and we're about to go on. *Vogue*'s out there. Stay pretty for *Vogue*."

Shola swallows and concentrates. "Thanks, Rose. I am *so* not getting wrinkles for *her.*" She looks back at me and narrows her eyes. "You're *how* old?"

"Fifteen and three-twelfths."

"My God, you still measure your age in fractions. I'm not getting worked up over a *child*. I'm just *not*. I am a *woman.* I am the face of *Gucci Woman.* It's right there in the title."

"It is," Rose agrees, patting her on the shoulder. "It's right there on the advert under your face, Shola. *Woman.*"

"Harriet?" a friendly lady in red says, tapping me on the shoulder just in the nick of time. Models are clearly bonkers. "This is your outfit." And she unzips a clothes bag.

A general hiss goes round the room as I stare at the contents. It's a long, silky gold dress with thousands of tiny little gold feathers layered around the bottom. It has thin straps made of sort of gold fish scales and it shimmers when you touch it, like a magic cloak. It's really, really beautiful: even I can see that. Although it *is* going to make me look a bit like the toffee finger in a box of Quality Street.

"That's mine? For me?"

"It is, darling. You're the Closer."

Another slightly louder hiss goes round the room. "I'm the what?"

"The Closer. You're the last girl on the catwalk. All

eyes are going to be on you, honey."

I quickly look into the mirror, and behind me I can feel every single eye in the room glaring at my back.

"You're the new face of the line," she continues. "Yuka wants you to be as prominent as possible."

I can see Shola's face getting paler under her make-up. She glances quickly at Rose and a look passes between them, but I've no idea what it means.

"OK," I say, trying to ignore the new clenching sensation in my stomach. "But..."And then I take a deep breath. "The... Ummm." I stop. How can I put this subtly? "The... er." And then I take in as much oxygen as I can. "What shoes am I wearing?" I finally blurt out.

The lady smiles at me kindly. "These," she says. And then she holds out a pair of little gold-scaled shoes with one-inch kitten heels. I almost collapse with relief.

"Yuka says she would prefer it if you could stay upright," she says with a wink. "Now, Miss Manners, let's get your hair and make-up sorted so we can have a little practice, shall we?"

48

People Who Hate Harriet Manners

Alexa Roberts

Hat Lady

Owners of stalls 24D 24E 24F 24G 24H

Nat?

Class 11A English literature

Models in general, but particularly Shola and Rose

I can do it.

I can actually do it. I can walk up and down a room with a pretty dress and heels on and not rip anything, ruin anything, break anything or fall over.

It seemed like an impossibility an hour ago. But… I've practised and practised backstage for about an hour until I'm pretty sure I can get through this evening without a disaster. I mean, it's *one walk*. A toddler could do it, with a bit of encouragement and maybe one of those push-along toys. How hard can it be?

"Thank you *so* much," I say to Betty, the stylist who

has been helping me. She's even managed to find time to quickly de-fluff both my legs without causing any damage.

Betty winks at me. "My pleasure, chicken. Quick revision: what are you walking in time to?"

"The music," I say eagerly. She gave me her iPod to practise with. I have no idea what the music is, but it's actually quite nice. At least I know when to put each foot forward.

"And what do you do when you get to the bottom of the runway?"

I'm back in my comfort zone: studying and revision. "I pause with one hand on my hip, and then I face towards the left, and then the right, and then I pause again, and then I turn round slowly and walk back."

"Facial expression?"

"Totally blank and slightly bored."

"Excellent. And what side are you walking on?"

"Centre, and when you see a girl coming, keep to the left."

"I think you're set." She smiles at me and points at the door. I was taken out of the area where everyone was getting ready so that I could concentrate, and also so that I could fall over without anyone laughing at me. "Knock 'em dead," Betty adds.

Which – given the probability of that happening – is not the *best* thing she could have said to me.

And she gently nudges me back into the world of fashion.

It is now manic.

The earlier commotion was obviously just the buzz before the mania: the whole room has exploded into a mess of lights and noise and panic. I can hear the music pumping from the stage and I don't think the girls have time to be nasty any more: they're whizzing in and out of clothes and being shouted at by people wearing headsets as if they're working in call centres.

"Next!" an angry man shouts. "Come on! We don't have time for a lipgloss touch-up! Get on the stage!"

There's a small queue of models forming this side of the curtains and I'm totally mesmerised. They're all twice my height, and willowy, and curvy in the right places, with the most amazing faces. Every single one of them looks like a different example of beauty, from a different imagination. And now they look like a collection of amazing birds, or butterflies, covered in greens and blues and reds and sparkles and feathers. It's less fashion, I think, and more… plumage.

It's like that butterfly farm I go to every summer with

Annabel: the room is covered in colours. I feel a sudden pang of envy. I'm the little brown moth, going round and round the light bulb. Then I look at the mirror next to the stage. My eyes have been painted dark black, and my hair's been fluffed up and pinned at the back. My cheeks are pink and flushed and the light is reflecting off the top of my head, and off my shoes, and off the straps over my back. The gold dress sort of shoots straight down because there's nothing to stop it – but… it still looks pretty. Sparkly.

I'm not a moth, I realise with a lurch. I'm not one of them exactly, but maybe I'm still a butterfly. One of those little white ones that doesn't live very long, but is happy just to get the chance to be there for a little while.

"Harriet?" the man with the headset on shouts. "Where's Harriet?"

"I'm here," I say as clearly as I can and realise my hands are damp. Dad's somewhere out in the audience: Yuka reluctantly gave him a seat near the back. I have to make him proud. I *have* to. I have to make Annabel proud too, even though she isn't here and doesn't know about it.

"Get ready," the man says. "You're nearly up."

I stand against the curtains and notice that there

are three girls in front of me. Rose, Shola and a girl I haven't spoken to – or been shouted at – before with a set of earphones in. A very, very beautiful girl with pale brown hair in curls.

"I'm Harriet Manners," I say automatically, holding out my hand and trying to stop it shaking.

She takes her headphones out. "Hmm?" she says. "Sorry. I listen to music to help calm my nerves before a show."

"I'm Harriet Manners," I say again. "Nice to meet you."

"I know who you are," she says, nodding and giving me a wry smile. "I'm Fleur. I'm not the face of anything." And she gives me an almost imperceptible wink.

"This is the Closer," Shola says, nodding at me. Fleur shrugs and puts her headphones back in again, and Shola smiles sweetly. "So they told you about the change of plans, right?"

"What change of plans?"

"*They didn't tell you?* Oh, that's just so *like* them. They told us while you were out the back, doing your little walking practice." She looks at Rose. "*So cute*," she adds, smirking.

"What's changed?" I can feel myself starting to

tense up again. I've learnt everything by heart; I'm not sure I can just alter details at this late stage. This *never* happens in exams at school. It's why we have revision guides.

"Well, this is *Moscow*," she explains as if I'm not aware of this already. "And we drive on the *right* here. So although Yuka's not Russian, she's decided last minute that models have to go *right* on the runway. Not left as they normally would. To make things more… *realistic.*"

"Huh?" I frown.

"I can't believe they didn't tell you. That was a close call." Shola makes a face of massive relief. "Could have screwed *everything* up."

I take a deep, confused breath. Honestly, I don't know whether to believe her or not. Is she telling me that so I make a mistake, or is she genuinely telling me so that I *don't* make a mistake?

Shola looks at me with massive, heavily made-up almond eyes. "We're on the same side," she says innocently. "Us models. We have to stick together. The better you look, the better I look, right?"

I look at her for a few quiet seconds, my mind twirling like a ballerina in a music box. "OK," I finally whisper. "Thank you." Rose has gone on stage now and it's nearly my time. My legs are starting to wobble and I can feel my feet shaking.

"My pleasure." And then Shola frowns. "What are you doing?"

"Blowing a raspberry," I explain, doing a funky chicken so subtle I'm not sure she can see it. "Sorry. I'm just trying to relax."

"Oh. Whatever," Shola says, turning her back on me and rolling her eyes when she thinks I can't see, and then she walks up the stage steps.

This is it.

I'm so terrified that when I try to lick my lips, my tongue doesn't come out. Somewhere on the other side of the curtains is a huge audience, and in that audience is Dad, waiting for me to be amazing. It's time to prove to him that I can be.

And maybe prove it to myself while I'm at it.

"You're up," the man with the headset says. "Good luck, Harriet."

And I climb up the stairs into the bright lights.

49

For a few seconds, I can't move.

The theatre looks nothing like it did when I walked in. The lights are so bright I can hardly see anything, but there's just enough visibility to ascertain that every single chair in the building is filled. Even the carved golden boxes near the ceiling have people in them, and if there were still tsars in Russia, I'd imagine that's where they'd be sitting.

I glance in terror to the right, where I can vaguely see Yuka sitting in the centre of the front row, her face like a mask. And, somewhere at the back, I think I can see Dad holding both thumbs up in the air.

I stand there, paralysed, for a few seconds. Then I take a deep breath and I start walking.

Apparently I've been walking since I was nine months old and hanging on to the bottom of Dad's jumper, but it has never felt like this before. It's never felt so difficult, or so surreal. It feels less like *I'm* moving forward and more like it's the floor moving backward and I'm just trying to keep up. Like… ice skating. Or walking down the aisle of a moving coach.

And as we know, I'm not so good at that.

I keep my face totally blank and try to focus on the music. All I have to think about is just one foot in front of the other. Looking as bored as I possibly can.

Somewhere near the bottom of the stage, I see Fleur, pausing and looking to the right and the left, just as I've been told to. Now that she's at a distance I can appreciate what she's wearing: emerald green, covered in little bits of floaty green material like a mermaid. And the biggest silver heels I've ever seen in my life. Bigger even than the red ones I had to wear in Red Square. She hasn't even been given a wheelchair.

Now *that's* what I call a model.

Fleur gives a little dignified toss of her head and starts walking back up the centre of the stage towards me, at which point something in my chest abruptly lurches in a panic.

If I believe Shola, I go right. If I don't believe Shola, I go left. So right or left?

Left or right?

I can trust Shola. I *have* to believe that human beings are essentially good. That girls don't destroy each other just because they can. I start veering towards the right. Then Alexa's face pops into my head. Alexa would send me in the wrong direction. She would want a collision. What if Shola is another Alexa?

So I start moving towards the left. But if I start to believe that everyone is like Alexa, doesn't it mean she's won? If I start to lose faith in humanity, isn't that worse than a million hands in the air? I can't let that happen.

I start veering towards the right again.

We're getting closer and closer and I can see a look of sheer panic starting to appear on Fleur's face.

I don't know what I'm doing.

Oh, God. Left or right? Right or left?

I'm changing my mind by the millisecond, and as I walk, I'm making almost unnoticeable movements towards each direction. They're so small, I don't think the audience can tell. But Fleur can, and the look of panic on her face is getting more and more pronounced. It's like we're in a game of chess, trying to second-guess the other's movements.

We're almost in the middle now and I still don't know which way to go. I can feel myself starting to wobble. I'm going to lose my balance and topple, even on these low heels. And then it hits me: that's what Shola wants. She doesn't want a *collision*. She wants me to fall over.

Which means I *have* to keep going. At which point everything starts happening in slow motion. Fleur starts to wobble too. She sways from side to side like a tree, except that her heels are much, much bigger than mine. And they can't take it.

Time almost stops.

One of her ankles buckles completely.

And – with the smallest of gasps – Fleur plummets like a stone on to the runway.

50

I'm paralysed with horror. The whole audience has taken one loud, audible breath.

I have just ruined an entire fashion show.

And it's *all my fault.*

I stare numbly at Fleur, who is now desperately trying to stand up. Her heels keep slipping, and I can see her eyes filling with tears and her cheeks starting to flame, even under the thick make-up. And with a sick lurch of my stomach, I recognise the humiliation and shame, the disbelief and horror. It's like looking in a mirror. I've just done to Fleur what I promised I would never, ever do to anyone.

I've turned her into me.

The entire audience is staring, but the only thing I know now is I have to do something to help her. *Anything*. Just so Fleur knows she isn't on her own. So I take a deep breath and sit down on the stage next to her.

There's a stunned silence. And then, from somewhere

at the back, comes the sound of one person clapping as hard as they possibly can.

"Woooooooooo!" Dad shouts at the top of his voice. "That's my girl! Woooooo!"

The whole audience turns to look at him and Fleur grabs my hand. Slowly, we stand up.

And together we walk off the runway, back behind the curtains.

51

As soon as I'm backstage, I find the nearest table I can and crawl straight under it.

I don't know much about fashion shows, but I don't think that's how they're supposed to go. And I have a suspicion I'm about to get into really, *really* big trouble.

"Harriet?" a voice says after about forty minutes, and a pair of black trainers appears under the tablecloth.

"Monkey-moo?" another voice says and a pair of shiny orange shoes with blue toes appears next to them. There's a bit of whispering and then I hear Wilbur say: "Is it, like, some kind of fetish? Is it just tables, or all types of furniture?"

"She's frightened," Dad explains. "She's done it ever since she was a baby." And before I know it he's crawling under the table next to me. "Harriet, sweetheart," he says gently. "What you did was very noble. Nobody's going to shout at you."

Wilbur sticks his head under the tablecloth. "That's not *necessarily* true," he amends. "Yuka's on her way backstage now and I've never seen her lips so thin. The bottom part of her face looks like an envelope."

"I'm sorry," I say, with my knees pulled right up to my chest. "I didn't know what else to do."

"*Sorry?*" Wilbur gasps and he puts his hand over his chest. "Baby-baby Panda, Baylee couldn't have *bought* that much publicity if they'd hung Yuka Ito upside down from the chandelier with her trousers down around her ankles."

"Which they're not going to do," a cold voice says from somewhere beyond the tablecloth. Another pair of shoes appears: black and shiny and spiky. "I'm a fashion goddess. Goddesses don't wear trousers."

"Yuka, darling!" Wilbur says, retracting his head. "I didn't see you there! Mainly because I don't have eyes in my bottom."

"Fascinating, William," Yuka snaps. "Harriet? I am going to speak to you immediately. I would therefore prefer it if this conversation was not held with a piece of laminate wood."

I look at Dad, take the biggest breath I can find and crawl out from under the table. "I'm sorry, Yuka."

"I don't recall asking you to do anything other than wear a dress and walk in a straight line. It really shouldn't have been that difficult."

"I know," I mumble. "Am I fired?"

Yuka looks at Wilbur. "William? How did the front row react?"

"It's *bur* not *iam*," Wilbur points out, sighing. "The editor of *Elle* said Harriet was fresh. *Harper's* said she was delicious. *Vogue* thought she had unexpected warmth."

"My daughter's not a loaf of bread," Dad points out in surprise.

Yuka raises an eyebrow at him and then looks at me. "In that case, Harriet, you're not fired and neither is Fleur. But in future, if I want you to sit down, I shall ask you to sit down. I shall give you a step-by-step plan, an X on the requisite spot and a detailed description of how I want you to do it."

"OK," I say, feeling my spirits starting to lift. The more I get to know Yuka, the more I like her. She reminds me of Annabel.

Yuka looks at her watch. "There is an after-party being held in the penthouse suite of our hotel. The other models have gone there, and every important editor and celebrity in Europe is currently drinking my profits."

My stomach twists uneasily and Dad's face starts to beam.

"Yuka," I start anxiously, "I'm not sure that—"

"Obviously," Yuka continues as if I haven't opened my mouth, "you will be going straight to bed and you will go nowhere near it. If I so much as catch you out of your room for the rest of the evening, there will be a world of pain."

I sort of want to hug her. I'm so tired. This has probably been the longest day of my entire life.

"Oh, *what*?" Dad moans under his breath. "This is so unfair."

"The same applies to you," Yuka says to him sternly, narrowing her eyes. "A world of pain. Understood?"

"Understood," Dad says in a shamed voice, staring at the floor. Which makes me feel even more at home.

Because that's exactly what Annabel would have said as well.

52

Somehow, I manage to get a full ten hours of sleep. Despite Dad doing everything he possibly can to sabotage this. I've been given the queen-size bed and he has the sofa on the other side of the room "as befits a sidekick".

"You know," he says as I'm brushing my teeth, "if I were to wake up in the middle of the night, say, and find you putting your make-up back on, I would assume it was a mirage and go back to sleep."

I nod sleepily.

Ten minutes later, as I'm crawling under the duvet in my penguin pyjamas and yawning, Dad coughs. "And if I were to wake up in the middle of the night and see that your bed was empty, I would presume I was dreaming and put it down to an overactive imagination."

"OK, Dad." I close my eyes and snuggle into the pillows.

"And if you were to come back in, smelling of – say

– *celebrity party*, I would say nothing of it the next day. To *anyone*."

"OK," I murmur, starting to drift off. Suddenly the bedroom lights snap on.

"Are you seriously telling me you're not going to this celebrity party?" Dad says in loud disbelief. "You're not going to sneak out for even a little bit?"

"You can go if you want," I mumble with my eyes shut. "I'm going to be asleep."

"Oh, *great*, just guilt trip away, why don't you, Harriet? No, it's fine. I don't need to meet Liz Hurley. I'll just sit here on the sofa and eat pickled cabbage."

I yawn again. What is this obsession with pickled cabbage? "OK, Dad. You do that."

"I will," Dad says, turning off the light again. "Who needs a celebrity fashion party? I mean, who needs to meet Liz Hurley and drink Martinis and eat little olives and bits of cheese on sticks when you can just sit, wide awake, on a spare... sofa... and... eat... pickled... "And the word *cabbage* is replaced by the sound of Dad snoring so loudly it sounds like somebody is drilling through the wall next to my head.

I open my eyes and look at the ceiling. Somewhere, floors and floors above us, a party is going on. A party full of beautiful people and important people and famous people: laughing, drinking, kissing the air, sparkling, having their photos taken. Wearing beautiful clothes and eating beautiful food – or pretending to. And I really couldn't care less.

I listen to Dad snoring his head off for a few minutes and then I close my eyes and join him.

We have the entire following morning to look around Moscow. Yuka has told us that we're "free to do whatever it is ordinary people do during daylight hours".

So we go to the Kremlin and look around the Cathedral of the Archangel where the Romanov tsars are buried, and the Ivan the Great Bell Tower which is covered in beautiful gold leaf and is thought to be the very centre point of Moscow. Then we go to the Peter the Great Monument and the Bolshoi, and a huge park where the lake is covered in ice and peeved-looking ducks. The amazing morning is only ruined by the fact that I keep having to lie to Nat by text and Annabel keeps ringing Dad up and crying.

Which is disconcerting because Annabel never cries. *Ever*. This is the woman who watches gazelles get mauled by tigers on television and gives them marks out of ten for tidiness.

"Sweetheart," Dad says into the handset as we pay

for some authentic Russian merchandise (I've got some hand-painted Russian dolls and a teddy bear that says **I RUSHED THROUGH RUSSIA**, and Dad has a T-shirt that says **RUSSIA HOUR**). "You're wrong. I *do* understand."

There's some squeaking on the other end of the phone. From a distance it sounds a bit like Dad is talking to a mouse.

"But darling, it's just milk. You can clean it up." There's more squeaking. "And we can buy you some more cornflakes." More squeaking. "And a new bowl." *Squeak, squeak*. "Yes, exactly the same shade of white, sweetheart. Now stop crying."

The Russian merchandise seller loudly asks Dad in broken English if he wants his **ONLY FOOLS RUSSIA IN** baseball cap gift-wrapped. There are a few more squeaks on the phone. "Hmm? Wrapped?" Dad says anxiously. "No, Annabel. That's just the... coffee lady. She wants to know if I want my coffee... flapped." *Squeak, squeak*. "It's street talk for... cooled down."

Eventually, Dad puts the phone down, wipes his hand over his face and looks at me.

"Phew. That was close," he says after a long, strained pause. "Luckily I'm an excellent liar. Annabel's gone all Sylvia Plath on us. What are we going to do?"

I swallow guiltily and tug at my shorn hair. "Not show her this?" I suggest.

Dad nods. "We need to wait out werewolf season." And then he thinks about it. "But Harriet... What if she's just... *crazy*?"

We both look at Dad's phone, which has started ringing again. And then Dad looks at the stall in front of us, covered in huge furry Russian hats. "Let's get you one of these," he sighs eventually. "I'll turn off the central heating and we'll tell Annabel you have a cold head."

"Do you think she'll buy that?"

"No." Dad looks at his phone again. "Take a good long look at my face, Harriet, because by tomorrow it'll be chewed right off." He opens his phone. "Darling?" *Squeak, squeak*. "Then throw the burnt bits away, sweetheart. And get some more bread." *Squeak*. "I know it's not the same." And then he looks at me, puts his finger up to his forehead and twirls it. *Bonkers,* he mouths to me.

And I swallow nervously and buy as many Russian hats as I can fit into my bag.

By the time we get back to England, though, everything

is starting to feel a lot more promising. My hair is covered with a nice big Russian hat – it's very cosy and goes well with my orange snowflake jumper – and the world is looking brighter already.

In fact, as we get off the train from London and start walking home – and I say goodbye to Dad and veer off to the shops to buy myself a Welcome Home Harriet chocolate bar – it feels like things are starting to go the right way finally.

I've been to Moscow, I've had an adventure and I appear to have got away with it. OK, I haven't really changed at all, except I'm now considerably less hairy and the owner of a Russian teddy bear. But it *feels* like life might be getting ready to improve. I mean, even caterpillars spend between four and nine days inside a cocoon before anything happens. And I *do* know some things I didn't know a few days ago. Like, for instance, if you put primer on your eyelids, it helps eyeshadow last longer. And pink lipstick has a tendency to get on *everything*.

Maybe it's just a matter of thinking positively. Believing that we can all change, if we try hard enough. Which is when it hits me. Because just as I'm reaching a point where the world is starting to make sense and happy thoughts are making me feel all sort of glowy on the inside, a yellow banana sweet comes flying through the air.

And whacks me straight on the head.

53

It takes a few moments to work out where the bananas are coming from. Within seconds, I've got sweets in my hat, in the collar of my jumper and a half-chewed one stuck to the sleeve of my coat.

Inexplicably, I look upwards.

"Hey, *geek*," a voice yells. It's only as I turn round that I realise the sky isn't raining sweets after all. Alexa is standing on the other side of the road just outside the local shops with her hand in a paper bag. "*GEEK*," she shouts again and then she laughs.

I freeze. Alexa has the single ugliest haircut I've ever seen on a girl in my life. Somehow I don't think this is going to be a friendly encounter. A confused buzzing has started in the back of my head. *Aren't things supposed to be different now?*

"Leave me alone," I say more firmly than I feel and start walking away as fast as I can.

She follows me. "As if that's going to happen." Another banana smacks me hard on the back of the head. "I saw a documentary about monkeys last night and I think you look just like one, Harriet. And you move like one too. A little ginger orang-utan. All orange and hairy." She looks at the bananas in the bag she's holding. "You know," she adds, "it's lucky these taste like perfume or I'd probably just eat them."

"Umm," I say. Does she want me to thank her?

Alexa looks back at me and her lips pull back so I can see her teeth, except it's definitely not a smile. "What do you think, Harriet? Do you like my hair?" And she points to her head.

Don't engage in conversation. It's going to make it worse. "It's, umm," I say because yet again the connection between brain and mouth has snapped. "Very... snazzy."

"Yeah?" Alexa says. "Personally I'm not so keen." She runs her hands through it. "In fact, I'm pretty hacked off about it."

I burst out laughing at the pun and then bite my lip in horror.

"You think this is *funny*?" Alexa yells, suddenly losing her cool. Her face changes colour. "You think I'm *laughing*?"

"No." I put my suddenly sweaty hands around my satchel straps so that when I have to run, it doesn't slow me down.

"The hairdresser can't fit me in until tomorrow. I've had to go to school like this for *two entire days*. Two days, geek. Do you *know* how many boys have stopped fancying me now?"

"Two?"

"It was a rhetorical question!" Alexa looks furious. "Nat said she did it for you. So *I'm going to make you pay for it.*"

I take a few jittery steps backwards because she's going to hit me. Finally – after years of vaguely promising it – she's going to get down to bullying basics and smack me right in the face.

I quickly run through the options.

- *Run.*
- *Wait until she hits me then run.*
- *Wait until she hits me, hit her back and then run.*
- *Hit first then run.*

I'm so surprised that I nearly forget about the fifth choice:

- *Stand still and stare at her like a total idiot.*

"Are you going to punch me?" I ask, feeling numb and strangely relieved. I wish she had done this years ago. Maybe then she'll be finished with me.

Alexa frowns and then laughs. "Punch you? Why would I *punch* you? What on earth would I get out of that, apart from a load of trouble?" Then she pulls something out of her bag. It looks a lot like a newspaper. "You forget, Harriet, that I've known you for ten years. I don't *need* to punch you."

I'm so confused my whole head feels like it has been stuffed with cotton wool. And yet somehow I know that whatever it is Alexa's about to do, I'm going to wish she'd just used her fist.

I look at the paper. "W-w-what's that?"

"This?" Alexa looks at it. "It's an article, Harriet. About some fifteen-year-old schoolgirl apparently. Took the fashion world by storm yesterday in… where was it? Moscow."

My entire body goes cold and I feel like I'm going to throw up.

"That's in Russia," she adds. "In case you were wondering if I knew."

No. *No.* There's no way this could have happened. It would have to have gone to print… Last night.

Sugar cookies.

Alexa smirks and moves close enough for me to see. There – in full glory – is a large photo of me yesterday. Sitting on the catwalk, with Fleur next to me. The headline says English Schoolgirl Knocks Fashion World Off Its Feet.

"I…" I start mumbling, but my insides are ice and my ears are completely numb. "I… I…"

"I, I, I," Alexa echoes and then she looks at it again. "I know. It's beyond me why anybody would want a photo of *you.*"

At the back of my brain, I finally feel the horror of comprehension. "You haven't… *shown* anyone, have you?" I whisper and my voice sounds like I'm being strangled. "You haven't shown anyone else this article?"

Alexa looks shocked. "Like who? Like our headmistress? Who'll be interested to know why you haven't been at school for two days? I went all the way back to school to hand her a copy especially. Punishment for taking time off school without permission is normally suspension, right? Or possibly," and she looks at the paper again, "expulsion."

My head is starting to spin. I'm going to get suspended? I don't get suspended. And I definitely don't get *expelled.* I shake my head. There's something more important. "Have you shown it to… anyone else?"

Alexa crows. "What, Nat? The girl who has made every single class speech about wanting to model since we were seven? The girl who wouldn't talk to anyone after The Clothes Show and has been crying in the loos ever since? The girl who told everyone you were sick with a cold for the last two days *and seemed to believe it*?" Alexa raises her eyebrows. "Why?" she says in a faux-innocent voice. "Was I not supposed to?"

Oh, no. Oh, no, no, no.

Nonononononono.

"*Did you tell Nat?*" I shout at the top of my voice. "*Did you tell her?*"

"No," Alexa says. "I just dropped an extra copy of this page through her letterbox." And she turns round and touches her hair. "It's known as *retribution*, Harriet. Or *requital. Vengeance. Comeuppance.* Pick any noun you like."

And – just as quickly as it started fitting back together – my whole world falls apart again.

54

I run as fast as I can, but it's no good. As soon as I turn my phone on, I know my life is in meltdown. I have fifteen voicemails from Wilbur and nobody else is picking up their phone.

"*Hello. This is Richard Manners. I'm probably with Liz Hurley right now, but leave a message and I'll ring you back when she's gone home. BEEP.*"

"Dad," I gasp into his answering machine, still running. "We've been caught. Don't let Annabel buy—" and I screech to an abrupt halt on the pavement. I have no idea what paper this article is in. "Don't let her buy *anything*. Just stop her leaving the house. She can't find out this way."

Then I recommence running. I need to get to Nat. Before the newspaper does.

Apparently I'm the only person in the entire world with any sense of urgency. By the time Nat's mum finally opens the front door, I'm screaming *Fire* through the letterbox and scratching at the paintwork.

"Harriet?" she says and even in my panic I stop, confused for a few seconds.

Nat's mum is blue. Not a bit blue: totally blue. Like Annabel, she only really ever wears a dressing gown; unlike Annabel, she doesn't just have one and it doesn't have baked beans down the front. This one is a pale blue silk kimono. She also has a white towel wrapped round her hair and her face is painted in a pale blue face mask. When Nat's mum doesn't look like a giant Smurf, she looks a lot like Nat. Except twenty years older and modified by huge amounts of plastic surgery.

"What's going on? Are we all dying?"

"Yes. I mean no. Not immediately. Is Nat here, please?"

"No idea. Four Botox injections and I can't move a muscle. Look at this!" She makes a pained expression with her eyes.

"I need to see her."

"Is everything all right?"

"Not really." I start removing my shoes so I don't track mud into her white carpet. "Has anything been delivered to your house today?"

Nat's mum strains around the eyes again. "Not as far as I know."

I pause in the middle of a shoelace. The wave of relief is so powerful that for a second I think I'm going to fall over. Maybe Alexa got the wrong address. "Really?"

"I don't think so."

I take a deep breath and feel the panic starting to seep back out. I'm still going to tell Nat, but now I can do it gently, sensitively, apologetically, delicatel—

"Unless you mean the envelope that came through the door half an hour ago."

My breath stops.

"I took it up to her a few minutes ago. I'm not sure I'd call it a *delivery* exactly, but it seemed important. Handwritten and everything."

Oh, no, no, *no.*

And before Nat's mum can say anything else, I rip my shoes off and race upstairs.

55

I'm too late.

That's the only thing I know for certain when I open Nat's bedroom door. She's sitting on her bed in her pyjamas with the newspaper next to her. And on her face is the most hurt expression I've ever seen on anyone. Ever.

"Nat—" I start and then grind to a halt. "Nat, it's not what it looks like." Then I pause because actually, it's *exactly* what it looks like.

"What's this?" she asks in a bewildered voice. She holds the newspaper up. "Harriet? What's going on?"

I'm not sure I've ever heard her sound so young. It's like we're five years old again. "It's… It's…" I say and then I swallow and look at the floor. "It's exactly what it looks like."

"You haven't been sick?"

"No."

"You were in Russia?"

"Yes."

"You're a model?"

"Yes."

"I defended you…"

"I know."

"And you left me to Alexa and didn't even tell me why?"

Oh God. "Yes."

"You've been lying about…" Nat pauses for a few seconds. "About *everything*?"

"I was going to tell you, but I was looking for the right way to do it."

"Via national newspaper?"

I stare at her in confusion and then the penny drops. I look at the envelope. On the front is printed in familiar red capital letters: **NAT, IT WAS THE EASIEST WAY TO TELL YOU.**

Alexa really is a piece of work.

"*No*," I gasp. "You weren't supposed to know for *months*." Then I flinch. I'm not sure that's the best thing I could have said.

Nat's eyes widen. "You were going to keep lying for *months*?"

"Well, *no*… you know… just… a few more days," but I'm not even sure what the truth is any more. Was I ever going to be honest, unless I was caught? Have I been lying to myself as well as everyone else?

Nat's cheeks are getting pinker and pinker. "*Why?*"

"Because... Because..." It all made so much sense at the time, but it suddenly doesn't any more. "You were so angry at The Clothes Show..."

"*Because you lied*, not because you were *spotted.* I told you that."

"It would have hurt you."

"More than this?"

I lick my lips. "I thought you would ruin it for me."

"*You thought I would ruin it for you?*" she repeats, amazed. "I'm your *best friend*, Harriet. *Why would I ruin anything for you?*"

"You wouldn't understand and... and... you wouldn't want to be my friend any more."

The excuses are coming thick and fast. But the truth that I can't even admit to my best friend is that I lied because it was easier.

Because I'm a coward.

Because I clearly don't think very much of the people I love.

Because all I was thinking about was me.

Nat stands up and the hurt five-year-old suddenly disappears. "No," she says abruptly. "Now I don't want to be your friend any more. *Get out of my bedroom.*"

"But..." I start. I open my mouth and promptly shut it again. All I've done is think about myself and lie compulsively. I don't have a leg to stand on.

"*Now*," she yells, totally furious, and she starts rummaging in a plastic bag at the foot of her bed.

"Nat, I'm sorry."

"*Out*," she screams and I've never seen her so angry. "What are you waiting for, Manners? *Soup?* You still want *soup*?" And she pulls something out of her bag and throws it. A carton of green Thai soup hits the wall behind me and explodes. *"There's your bloody soup."* She rummages in her bag again, and before I know it for the second time this afternoon food is hitting my head. *"And there's the bread. I hope you feel better soon. NOW GET THE HELL OUT!"*

And – just as I think things can't get any worse – Nat puts her hand in the air and looks at it. My chin starts to wobble: of all the hands in the air this week, I think this might finally be the hand I actually deserve.

Then, because I'm frozen to the spot, Nat pushes me across the room and into the hallway.

And slams the door behind me.

56

All I want to do is crawl into bed and cry, but I can't. The minute I open the front door I know things are about to get even worse.

Hugo's lying in his basket with his chin on the edge. His eyebrows twitch unhappily and he immediately looks at the wall as if he's blanking me. According to scientists, dogs can make approximately 100 facial expressions and it's quite clear which one Hugo is using right now.

"Annabel?" I whisper. "Dad?"

There's a long silence, so I put my bag down and tiptoe into the living room. Then I tiptoe into the kitchen, and the bathroom, and the garage, and the laundry room, and Annabel and Dad's bedroom. It's only when there's nowhere else to tiptoe that I go into my own bedroom and find Dad sitting on the floor with his back against my chest of drawers.

He looks at me desolately. "You know," he says, "for somebody so organised, you're incredibly untidy."

There are clothes everywhere: books strewn all over the floor, sweet wrappers across the bottom of the bed, teddybears stuck halfway behind the wardrobe, clothes scattered. He has a point. I'm just not sure it's the most important one right now.

"Dad, where's Annabel?"

"She's gone."

"What do you mean gone?"

"She's gone, is what I mean. She'd gone by the time I got your message and managed to get back to the house. She took her bags with her and the cat."

"But why?"

Dad shrugs. "It was her cat."

"No, why did she leave?"

Dad reaches into his pocket. "She wrote this." And he hands me a yellow Post-it.

SICK OF BEING LIED TO. HAVE GONE.

A

Then he pulls out the article from the newspaper. "This was next to it."

I stare at it, my heart making little sputtering sounds. "This is all my fault."

"Not really."

"Of course it is, Dad. What else would she be talking about?"

"A couple of things maybe." He reaches in his pocket and pulls out another piece of paper. "This was on the kitchen table too."

It's a letter from The Clothes Show lawyers, addressed to my parents.

"Dad, I..." And my voice breaks. "I'm sorry."

The amount I'm saying that at the moment, maybe I should just get a little MP3 track with it on loop so that I can simply press a button and offer out earphones.

Dad shakes his head. "That's not everything." Then he looks at the carpet and rummages around in his pocket again. What he pulls out appears to be a tax form. More specifically a P45. "This was also on the table."

I look at it in confusion.

"I've been lying too, Harriet. I didn't get permission from work to come with you to Moscow."

"But..." And when I look at him, I realise he's been wearing the same clothes now for five days, he smells of vodka and he looks exhausted. In fact, he's looked exhausted all week. I've just been too wrapped up in myself to notice.

"I don't understand, Dad. Why not?"

"Because I didn't need to, sweetheart. The agency lost their biggest client because of me and they fired me on Friday. On the spot."

"But you said..."

"I know. I lied. I thought Annabel would be angry."

"Oh."

"It turns out she's much, *much* angrier now."

It feels like the whole world has tilted up on itself and everything is falling off the top of it. "Oh," I say again.

"Yeah. *Oh* pretty much sums it up for me too," Dad agrees and then he lies down on the carpet. "We're not very good at this, are we, Harriet?" he says.

And he closes his eyes.

It's only once I've helped him up and put him in front of the TV that I turn the yellow Post-it over.

PS HARRIET, YOUR FATHER NEVER TURNS NOTES OVER. DON'T TELL HIM I'M PREGNANT.

57

<u>People Who Hate Harriet Manners</u>

Alexa Roberts

Hat Lady

Owners of stalls 24D 24E 24F 24G 24H

Nat

Class 11A English literature

Models in general, but particularly Shola and Rose

Mrs Miller, our headmistress

Annabel

Harriet Manners

My name is Harriet Manners and I am an idiot.

I know I'm an idiot because I'm lying in my bed, looking up other words to call myself. Ninny. Dunce. Blockhead. Twit. Ignoramus. *Fool*. Which is the origin of the word 'geek' so I think we've just come full circle.

I've made a mess of everything.

Alexa has won. Nat's not talking to me. Annabel has gone. Dad's unemployed. I owe £3,000. The entire population of England is laughing at me. My hair looks like a ball of orange fuzz.

I don't know if I've been suspended or not, but only because I'm refusing to go to school to find out. For the first time in my life, I've decided I don't care about my education. It hasn't made me any smarter at all. I've actually managed to transform in the *opposite* direction. I'm like a caterpillar that's gone back to being an egg, or an unemployed Cinderella without even a hearth to scrub.

One simple metamorphosis story and I couldn't even get *that* right.

Dad and I spend the entire night trying to fix things. I haven't told him about the back of the note, though. I *think* about telling him, but Annabel asked me not to. I've betrayed her quite enough already without adding that to the list as well.

"We've got to do something *dramatic*," Dad tells me sternly after staring at the wall for half an hour. "We have to *prove* to Nat and Annabel how sorry we are."

So we make 'sorry' cakes, we make cards, we film ourselves singing an apologetic song. I take Nat a mix CD, a little silver necklace that splits in half and a box of chocolates. Then a barely used bottle of perfume, then flowers with a cunningly amended poem on the card. She trashes everything apart from the chocolates, which she eats without offering me any.

Dad goes to Annabel's law firm and stands outside with a bunch of flowers and a sandwich board that says *I am so very sorry, Annabel* (and on the back says *Seriously. Very, very sorry*). He stands there until the security guard comes down with a note saying:

GO AWAY, RICHARD, OR I'LL BACK CHARGE YOU FOR WASTING MY TIME.

MY RATES ARE £300 AN HOUR AND YOU OWE ME TEN YEARS.

ANNABEL

Dad says he's not good at maths, but that's not a number he wants to calculate.

Finally, totally defeated and unsuccessful, we give up and sit on the sofa for the rest of the evening. Then we get up the next morning and sit on the sofa for the rest of the next day. I have no idea what we watch on television because I'm not really watching it.

All I'm thinking, over and over and over again, is: *How? How do I make everything go back to exactly the way it was?* Because I'll go through everything again – the bullying, the ugliness, the unpopularity – just to have my old life back. I've traded the only things that mattered to me for a whole load of stuff that doesn't matter to me in the slightest. And I did it on purpose. Out of choice.

My IQ is clearly nowhere *near* as high as I thought it was.

"My little Tadpole," Wilbur gasps when I eventually pick up my phone. "Where have you been?"

"On the sofa."

"Jelly-bean, we have things to do. Everyone wants a piece of you, my little Ginger-cake. Journalists, television shows, designers, big brands. My phone hasn't stopped, Sugar-plum, apart from when I turned it off so I could drink a coffee. The genius that is Yuka Ito has turned your little sit-down-athon into a PR coup. She's telling everyone you've inspired her. You're her new muse."

"Uh-huh," I say without really listening.

"You know what that *means*, my little Frog?"

I continue staring impassively at the television. "No."

"It means you're *hot*, darling. You're at *boiling point.* Your saucepan simmereth over."

There's a silence. Modelling is how I got into this mess in the first place. OK, technically *lying* is how I got into it. But I wouldn't have had to lie if the modelling had never happened. Nothing's going to get better if I keep going down this path.

"I don't care," I say. "Sorry, Wilbur."

Wilbur laughs. "That almost sounded like *I don't care*," he says, giggling. "But obviously I misheard you. This is… this is… the stuff of dreams."

"Not of mine."

And I put down the phone.

I'm not sure what my next plan should be. But it's going to start with Annabel.

58

The best way to make amends for lying is probably not by lying, but I can't really see an alternative. Not after the way Annabel responded to Dad.

Luckily the receptionist is new, which makes the process significantly easier. As long as there isn't a little warning photo of me taped behind the desk: you know, like the photos they have of terrorists and people who steal penny sweets from newsagents.

"May I speak to Annabel Manners, please?" I ask sweetly, taking the fur hat off and making myself look as small and vulnerable as physically possible.

The receptionist reluctantly puts down her magazine. "Do you have an appointment?"

"Yes." I widen my eyes to make my face a vision of innocence. "Gosh, that's a nice ponytail you have. Did you do it yourself?" And when she turns round to try and look at it, I lean over the desk and quickly scan the schedule. "My name is Roberta Adams," I say as she turns back.

She frowns at the list. "Bit young to have your own lawyer, aren't you?"

"I'm suing my parents," I say calmly.

Her expression immediately clears. "Oooh, I thought about doing that too. Let me know how much money you get. Go straight up."

And she buzzes me through before I get a chance to change my mind.

This building has always scared me. When I was young, I refused to come in alone when Annabel was working late because I thought it was haunted.

"It's not haunted," Dad said when I told him. "Haunted buildings are full of souls with no bodies, Harriet. A lawyer's office is full of bodies with no souls. There's a big difference."

And then he'd laughed until Annabel put salt in his wine glass.

Even the lift feels like some sort of creepy horror-movie glass coffin. When I finally get to Annabel's office, I can see through the window that she has her head down and is writing some kind of report.

"Ahem," I say softly.

"Roberta," she says without looking up. "Take a seat. I've been going through the file and I think getting custody of the guinea pig isn't going to be a problem."

I take a seat despite not being Roberta and squirm. I've just realised that Roberta is a real person and not just a name on a sheet, and she might actually turn up too. Annabel writes a few more things down and then glances up. She fixes me with a long stare, while I try desperately to activate the dimples in my cheeks.

"Well, Roberta," she says eventually. "Can I just say that you have grown a lot younger in the three weeks since I saw you last. Being away from your husband is clearly doing wonders for your complexion."

"Annabel—"

"And," she says, looking at my head, "that's a great improvement on your last hairstyle. Although as your last hairstyle was a purple rinse, that's not necessarily saying much."

"Annabel, I—"

She looks at the hat in my hand. "I thought for a moment perhaps you had brought the guinea pig with you, but I'm relieved to see that's not the case. I *would* suggest, however, making sure that whatever that *is*, is definitely dead. It looks like it might bite."

"Annabel—"

Annabel leans forward and presses a button on her phone. "Audrey? When the *other* Roberta Adams turns up, please keep her in reception until I alert you otherwise. And for future reference, none of my clients are schoolgirls. Thank you."

And then she leans back in her chair and looks at me in silence.

59

After what feels like forever, I finally manage to say, "Hello, Annabel."

"Hello, Harriet."

"How are you?" This seems like a good conversation opener. Actually, I think this is the only conversation opener. I don't know how she is at all.

"Sleeping on the floor of my office, which is never ideal, but apart from that I'm just dandy, thank you."

I stare at her stomach. It doesn't look any different, but I can't stop staring. It's amazing really. A few days ago it was a stomach containing strawberry jam and now it contains a person. I'm actually really excited, even though it does mean that every minute I've spent in the last five years researching *famous only children* on the internet was a total waste of my time. "So it's true?" I ask. "What you wrote?"

"That I am gravid, parous, fecund, *enceinte*, teeming with child?"

"Umm." I think Annabel's thesaurus is bigger than

mine. "Yes?"

"Absolutely. I'm gestating like nobody's business."

"Wow." I'm so overwhelmed with this information. I don't know anything about babies: it's a massive hole in my general knowledge base. I'm going to have to go home and do some research.

"Does your father know?"

"No, you told me not to tell him."

"Quite right. The man should learn to turn a Post-it over now and then."

It feels like something tight in my chest is finally starting to unravel; as if everything from the last week is starting to melt. Why didn't I just come to Annabel in the beginning? Why did I tell her I was OK when I wasn't?

"Annabel," I say, folding my arms round my knees. "Can I ask you a question?"

"As long as it's not about bodily functions. I'm not going to start discussing disgusting things just because I'm pregnant."

"It's not about bodily functions." Then I close my eyes and say in a rush: "Do you hate me?"

Annabel raises an eyebrow. "No," she says after the longest pause that has ever existed in the history of the world. "I don't hate you, Harriet."

I take a deep breath, and without warning everything in my chest comes pouring out. "I didn't want to lie to you, Annabel, I really didn't. I mean, I *did* want to lie to you because that's why I lied to you, but I didn't do it to hurt you or because I don't respect you or I don't think that you're usually right all the time, because you are. It's just... haven't you ever wanted to be somebody else?"

Annabel looks at me as if I'm mad. "Not really," she says finally. "Who in particular?"

"*Anybody*. Just to see what it's like? Just to see if it's better? To see if things can be different?"

Annabel thinks about it. "No," she admits. "Never."

"Well, that's what I wanted. I was so tired of being me. And I thought maybe if I became a model instead of a geek, I would be somebody else and my life would change, or maybe everyone else would change, or maybe the way they saw me would change."

Annabel crosses her ankles under the desk. "Hmm," she says.

"But nothing's changed and all I've done in the last week is make a big mess of everything, and I don't know what to do to take any of it back."

Annabel folds her hands together. "Huh," she says.

"And my list keeps getting longer," I continue in

a slightly smaller voice. "Longer and longer. I'm in trouble with just about everyone I've ever met and I don't know what to do now, Annabel. I'm out of my depth and I don't know how to fix it. Just... Just... *Please.* Tell me what to do. Tell me how to make it all better again."

I'm not going to cry. I'm *not*. But now I can feel a lump in my throat I can't quite swallow. Like when I'm taking those huge vitamins Dad makes me eat in the winter.

Annabel nods calmly. "And what list is this?"

Oh. I forgot she didn't know about my list. I reach in my pocket, get it out and hand it over the desk. You thought that was just a mental list, for your benefit? No, it's a real one. I carry it around in my pocket and update it regularly.

"Well, it's very neat and well spaced," Annabel says approvingly. "Underlined with a ruler?"

"Of course." I feel a little burst of pride. "Two lines, actually, if you look carefully."

"Nice," Annabel agrees. "Now give me the pen and the ruler. May I mark the list?"

I nod because it's a bit rude to tell her I don't really like other people editing my lists.

"Right. So first of all, we're taking this one off."

And she draws a neat line through her own name. "And I'd appreciate it if you'd stop putting people who love you very much on to lists like this." She looks at the list again with the pen lid in her mouth and crosses another one off. "And you can take off Mrs Miller too."

I shake my head. "She's going to suspend me for missing school."

"No, she's not." Annabel looks straight at me. "Harriet, when are you going to realise that you are just as bad at lying as your father is? I saw your faces when you came out of the agency and therefore kept in daily – sometimes minutely – touch with Wilbur. I gave my permission for you to have your hair cut and I also rang Mrs Miller and explained that you would be taking three days off school and I would supervise the catch-up: two for the trip to Russia and one to recover."

There's a stunned silence while my mouth makes an O shape. "But—"

"However clever you think I am, Harriet, I'm much, *much* cleverer." Annabel looks at the list. "And you can take Hat Lady and the stall owners off too: I paid them. Or, I should say, I recalculated the damages and paid them what they were actually worth, and then I threatened to sue them for extortion."

I stare at her with my mouth still open.

"You can pay me back if you want to, but trust me: the amount you earned this week – and Wilbur promised me he wouldn't tell you how much that is – you won't even notice." Annabel looks at the piece of paper again. "As for the models, we can obviously put that down to the fact that they're models and also women."

She crosses them off as if that explains itself.

"But everyone at school… everyone in my class, they—"

"Put their hand up? Nat rang and told me. Has world history taught you nothing, Harriet? Countries will always side with those who have the biggest weapons. Your classmates were scared of Alexa and not scared of you. You should take that as a good thing, unless you have dictator ambitions."

And she crosses them off the list as well.

I blink a few times. I suppose I hadn't thought of it that way, but countries with lots of nuclear weapons tend to have an awful lot of allies.

"And as for Alexa…" Annabel pauses. "I don't know what's wrong with the girl. The point is: who cares?"

"I care."

"I know you do," Annabel says and her voice is gentler now. "That's the problem. You need to stop caring what people who don't matter think of you. Be who you are and let everybody else be who they are. Differences are a good thing. It would be a terribly boring world if we were all the same."

"But, Annabel, I'm a... I'm a..." I can't get the word out, so instead I lift my satchel and point at what's left of the red word.

"A..." Annabel squints slightly. "CE-H? What's a Ceh?"

"A geek. It says GEEK. Or, at least, it used to."

"Oh." Annabel shrugs. "So? Some of the best people are. And – for the record – I didn't want you to model precisely because I didn't *want* you to become someone else." She picks up the newspaper and points at the article of me. "But I was wrong. You've stayed you and I'm so proud. What you did was kind. It was courageous. It was strangely inspired. It was everything I love best about you. It came from a good place."

"Russia?"

Annabel gives me a long look. "No, Harriet. Not Russia. *You*." She lifts an eyebrow and then looks back at the paper. "Take yourself off the list and you'll find that the rest start to disappear as well."

And she draws the final line.

I can feel my head starting to go swirly again.

Annabel looks at me in silence and then she hands me the paper.

People Who Hate Harriet Manners

~~Alexa Roberts~~

~~Hat Lady~~

~~Owners of stalls 24D 24E 24F 24G 24H~~

Nat

~~Class 11A English literature~~

~~Models in general, but particularly Shola and Rose~~

~~Mrs Miller, our headmistress~~

~~Annabel~~

~~Harriet Manners~~

"There's still one on there," I point out sadly.

"What did I tell you about putting people who love you very much on this list, Harriet?"

"Nat doesn't—"

"Don't be daft – she's just hurt and angry. Nobody likes being lied to by somebody they trust. When you've worked out what it is Nat needs from you, you'll be able to cross her off too."

"Is it…"

"No, it's not personalised flapjacks, Harriet."

I nod and tuck the list in my back pocket. I don't

know why I didn't come here first of all: Annabel always knows how to organise the world for me so it makes sense again. Just as she does when she tidies my room. "Are you coming home, Annabel? Ever?"

Annabel sighs and looks back at her report. "I don't know. Your dad has his own list to think about. And unlike you, he's old enough to do it on his own."

Her phone beeps.

"Annabel? Roberta Adams says if she doesn't get back soon, Fred is going to start getting anxious."

"God forbid I should make a guinea pig feel unloved. Send her up, Audrey." Annabel looks at me. "Now go home and study that list," she adds in her normal sharp voice. "You know where I am if you need me. My bed is in the cupboard."

And as I turn round and walk back out of the office with the paper in my hand, I realise how happy I am that Annabel knew about everything the whole time. It reminds me of that famous fridge magnet: the one about footprints in the sand.

I wasn't as on my own as I thought I was.

60

So I no longer have a plan.

The universe has shown me, repeatedly, that it has no respect at all for bullet points or pointers or lists or charts. Plans don't work and even when they *might* work and *should* work, people ignore them. So I'm going to try a brand-new strategy: not having a plan.

For the first time in my life, I'm just going to attempt to bumble through from one moment to the next and see where I end up. Just like a normal human being.

Or, you know. A bee.

"Are you *kidding* me?" I say as I open the front door. Dad's still in his dressing gown from yesterday, and the only difference is that he now has a family-size packet of gummy sweets nestled in the crook of his arm. I read somewhere that in an average lifetime we each use 272 cans of deodorant, 276 tubes of toothpaste and 656 bars of soap, and it is quite clear that since

Annabel left, Dad hasn't touched one of them.

"Look how depressed I am," he says as soon as I walk into the room. He holds up a sweet, looks at it sadly and then puts it in his mouth. "I'm even eating the green ones. I have nothing to get up for any more. *Nothing*. I think I'm just going to stay here until I grow into the sofa and they have to winch me out of the window every time I need the toilet."

"Dad," I say, sitting next to him. The situation is clearly critical. Dad is starting to sound like he thinks he's in some kind of made-for-TV film. I have to do something. "Dad, does Annabel like strawberry jam?"

Dad frowns and puts another sweet in his mouth even though he hasn't swallowed the one he's chewing yet. "What are you talking about?"

"Does she like strawberry jam?"

"No. She's always hated it."

"So *why is she eating strawberry jam*, Dad?" Then I look at him with the most obvious meaningful expression I can get on my face. I promised Annabel I wouldn't tell him, but I never told her he wouldn't work it out for himself.

Although frankly, at the rate my dad's brain works, there's a really good chance the baby will be in school by the time that happens.

"Do werewolves eat jam?" Dad asks in surprise.

I roll my eyes. "No. They eat people."

"So does Annabel. Do you think maybe she's trying to scramble my brain up and trick me into divorcing her by accident?"

"No." God, this is like pulling teeth. "Is Annabel any plumper than normal?"

Dad nods knowingly. "It's all the strawberry jam. Or people."

I look at him so hard it feels like my eyes are going to pop out. "Yes," I say meaningfully. "*Or people*."

Dad stares at me blankly.

"So," I continue slowly, "she's *getting fat*. She's *eating things she hates*. She keeps *changing her mind* about things. She's *crying* about inconsequential things and *shouting a lot* and *peeing all the time*."

I'm ticking the points off on my fingers and holding them pretty much under his nose. There is no way he won't get this now. No *way.*

Dad nods slowly, a look of realisation starting to dawn on his face (he has a red and yellow stain on the corner of his mouth and I'm trying really hard not to look at it). "My God," he says in a stunned voice. "She's... she's..."

"Yes?"

"She's... *having an affair with a strawberry jam manufacturer?*"

"Oh, for the love of *sugar cookies*," I shout, standing up. How have I managed to grow into such a balanced, reasonable person with him as a role model? "She's *pregnant. Annabel is pregnant.*" Then there's a long silence while Dad's entire face goes white.

Oops. I didn't mean to just throw it at him like that. He's quite old. Over forty. He'd better not have a heart attack.

"Sh-she *can't* be," Dad finally stammers. "It's utterly impossible."

"Is this the part where I have to tell you about the birds and the bees and the fact that it has nothing to do with either?"

"No, I mean the doctors have always said she can't have children. Almost totally impossible. We've been trying for years."

OK: ugh. That's disgusting.

"Too much information," I interrupt. "Well, she is. The proverbial bun is cooking in the proverbial oven."

"She's *pregnant*?" Dad says again. He looks like he'd fall over if he wasn't already sitting down.

"I just saw her. Trust me, she's pregnant."

Dad inexplicably looks even more astonished. "You

just *saw her*?"

"She's not the Loch Ness monster, Dad. She's in her office, doing paperwork."

"She's pregnant. With a baby?" For some reason Dad looks at me questioningly.

"Yes, with a *baby*. What else is she going to be pregnant with?"

"A mini werewolf perhaps," he mumbles. Then there's a long silence while he puts his head in his hands. "I'm an idiot, aren't I?" he mumbles through his fingers. "A total idiot."

There's no beating around the bush here. "Yes. I think it must be in our gene pool."

"I need her. I need to tell her I need her *immediately*."

"No, you don't." I shake my head crossly. "You need to show her that you're there for her when she needs you."

And then I shut my mouth in surprise. Oh. *Oh*.

Is that why Nat is so angry with me?

Dad looks at me in shock. "When did you get so smart, missy?"

I put my nose in the air, totally offended. "I've always been smart, actually."

"Not that kind of smart, you haven't." Dad thinks about it and then stands up and dramatically takes off his dressing gown like some kind of superhero transforming. Underneath, he's wearing jeans, a T-shirt and a cardigan.

"Hey!" I say crossly. "That's my trick!"

"Like I said, I'm a maverick. And you're a chip off the old block." Dad stretches the muscles in his neck. "Now grab your coat, Harriet. We're going to get your not-so-evil stepmother back."

61

I have absolutely no idea where we're going.

"Annabel's office isn't in this direction," I point out as Dad pounds down the street in the steadily increasing drizzle, with me jogging along behind him. I've never seen him looking so purposeful (apart from when he's on the Easter egg hunt, and that has chocolate at the other end of it).

"She's not in her office."

"But she *is*, Dad. I was just there."

Dad looks at his watch. "The cleaners come in at seven and Annabel hates the sound of a vacuum cleaner. She'll have gone. I know my wife. Werewife or not."

He takes another turning and I can feel myself getting steadily more anxious (which is not helped by the fact that my phone keeps vibrating in my pocket). "We're going shopping?" I say as Dad takes an abrupt right turn into a clothes shop.

"Trust me, Harriet." Dad picks up a shopping

basket and throws a green floral dress into it. "This is part of the master plan." I look with concern at the yellow ruffled shirt he's chucking on top of it, followed by a pink catsuit and a sequined boobtube.

"Have you ever met Annabel before?" I ask in concern as he shovels more hideous clothes into the basket. "They're not suits or dressing gowns."

"They're not for Annabel."

I look with alarm at the purple hotpants he's just picked up. "Tell me they're not for you, Dad."

Dad laughs.

"Or *me*," I say sternly. I'm still looking at the hotpants.

"They're not for you, Harriet." Dad marches abruptly into the baby section.

"They're not going to fit the baby either."

Dad picks up a pair of baby socks and strides over to the cashier. If he screws this up, I'm going to have to move into Annabel's office with her. And – frankly – I'm a little concerned about just how many beds she can get in her cupboard.

"Right," Dad says when it's all paid for. "Let's go to the park."

"Annabel's in the park?" I huff as we charge to the bit of grass about fifty metres away. It's not really a park because there are no flowers or trees, but now is probably not the best time to split that particular hair.

"Have you met Annabel before?" Dad says as he hands me the hotpants, puts the baby socks in his pocket, throws the rest of the brand-new clothes in the mud and starts jumping up and down on them. After a couple of minutes, he looks up. "That doesn't look very much like helping me, Harriet," he says.

"But—"

"Pipe down and stamp on the shorts, kid. As hard as you can."

So even though I am quite distinctly not a baby goat, I pipe down, throw the recently purchased hotpants on the floor and start jumping up and down on them like Rumpelstiltskin when he finds out that he's been tricked out of the Princess. Three minutes later, we're both exhausted, dripping wet and covered in mud. We stop and look at each other. "That should do it," Dad says, nodding, and then he grabs the clothes and puts them back in the bag.

"But where are we—"

"All will become abundantly clear imminently," Dad explains in a mysterious voice. "Learn some patience, sweetheart."

Which – frankly – is a bit rich coming from him.

And then he starts charging back towards our house again, trailing mud behind him.

It's only when Dad takes an unexpected turn that I finally realise where we're going. I stop, very still, on the pavement and stare at him.

"We're going to the *launderette*?" I finally manage to say. This makes no sense at all. This is where I come. This is my hiding place.

"It's where Annabel always comes when she's upset, Harriet. She used to take you with her when you were tiny."

Suddenly a memory comes bursting forward. Annabel and I, sitting in the launderette, listening to the washing machines. Me curled on her lap, sleepy and sniffing the soap bubbles and feeling totally content. And then it hits me. I don't come here by chance, or by magic, or by coincidence. I come here when I'm sad or scared or anxious because – without even knowing it – it reminds me of Annabel and makes me feel safe again.

"There she is," Dad says. And my heart figuratively skips a beat, and possibly literally skips a beat too,

I'm so surprised. Because Annabel is asleep in the same chair I fell asleep in a few days ago. Her head on the same tumble dryer.

62

Dad looks at the sleeping Annabel with a silly expression on his face and then opens the door as quietly as he can.

"Annabel—" I begin, inexplicably wanting to climb back into her lap, but Dad motions for quiet. She hasn't opened her eyes yet and I'm guessing from this gesture that he doesn't want her to.

Dad opens the bag of wet, muddy clothes and dumps the contents on the table. Then he opens a washing machine and starts putting each item in, very slowly. My pocket has started vibrating again, but I studiously ignore it.

"The thing is, Harriet," Dad says loudly, "I've made a real mess of things." I look at Annabel; her eyes are still shut. "You see this shirt, Harriet? I really mucked it up. It was lovely, and now it's not, and it's my fault."

I glance at Annabel again. She hasn't moved, but one eye has opened a little bit.

"And do you see this jumper?" Dad continues,

holding up a green one. A big dollop of mud falls off the sleeve on to the floor. "It was beautiful and now it's ruined."

"Mmm," I say and peek at Annabel again.

"I can't help it," Dad continues, picking up a skirt and putting it in the washing machine. "I'm an idiot and sometimes I don't even know I'm mucking things up until they look like this." He holds up a pair of dripping brown trousers. "And I'm so angry with myself because they were such an awesome *pair*." He pauses for a few seconds and then adds, "Of trousers."

Annabel has both eyes open now and is quietly watching Dad fill the washing machine. Dad is pretending he can't see her. "And it's so sad," he says, picking up some gloves, "because they made such an amazing *couple*." He pauses again. "Of gloves. What do you think, Harriet?"

I clear my throat. "I think I messed things up too," I say, pulling out the hotpants and holding them up. "And I'm so sorry because I really love them."

I don't, just to make that clear. I don't love the hotpants. But I love Annabel and that's what the hotpants stand for. At least, I think that's what the hotpants stand for.

"Exactly." Dad continues to fill the washing

machine. "And you should always look after what you love properly and keep it safe." He pauses. "And not jump up and down on it in the mud." Then he makes a large sweeping gesture with his hand and moves into the centre of the room.

"You've gone too far," I whisper to him under my breath. "Rein it in, Dad."

"Sorry," he whispers back. "But maybe," he says more loudly, holding his hands together, "it's not too late. Maybe we can make everything lovely again."

"Maybe," I say, glancing at Annabel again and moving into the middle of the room to support him.

"I hope so. I'll do anything it takes because I really don't want to screw these up too." Dad promptly pulls the clean baby socks out of his pocket and dangles them in the air.

And then – I'm going to assume this is the final scene of the final act – he closes the lid of the washing machine and stands there like a wally, holding the baby socks and staring at Annabel with the expression Hugo makes when he pees on the carpet.

There's a long, long silence, broken only by the comforting sound of a tumble dryer going round and round.

Finally Annabel sits up and rubs her eyes. "You

know what gets things clean?" she says, yawning.

"What?" Dad says eagerly. He takes a few excited, dripping steps towards her.

"Turning the washing machine on." Annabel looks at it pointedly.

"Oh."

"And you know what else gets things clean?"

"Saying sorry again?"

"Washing powder."

Dad and I both stare at the washing machine. We've piled all the clothes into it and then just left them there. Presumably to clean themselves.

"Now just wait a minute," Dad says in a horrified voice. "I actually have to wash the clothes? I mean, *actually* wash them?"

Annabel glances at the ceiling. "Yes, Richard. You have to actually wash them. They're covered in mud and dripping wet."

"But they're a *metaphor*," Dad explains. "They're supposed to symbolise our relationship, Annabel. Are you telling me I have to wash the metaphor?"

"Yes, you have to wash the metaphor. You can't just leave them in the washing machine like that. It's a public washing machine."

"Can I take them out and throw them away?"

"No. We'll wash them and take them to a charity shop."

Dad looks shell-shocked and then visibly rallies himself. "Am I forgiven, though? Will you take me back, with all of my adorable foibles and charming idiosyncrasies?" He thinks about it. "And handsome quirks?" he adds with round eyes.

Annabel's mouth twitches, but I don't think Dad sees it. He looks really anxious, although this might be partly because he really doesn't like doing laundry. "We'll discuss it while you're doing the washing. And the drying. That should take a good couple of hours at least."

Dad sighs and looks at the washing machine. "I guess this is fitting punishment," he says in a humble voice.

"Oh, no," Annabel says, winking at me so that Dad can't see it. "This isn't the punishment, Richard. This is the metaphor for the punishment."

Dad looks terrified, and then sighs and takes her hands. "No matter what you do to me," he says, slipping effortlessly back into B-movie mode, "no matter how hard you try, I'll always be glad I knew where to find you."

"Me too," Annabel says and then she flicks his nose

hard with her thumb and middle finger. There's a pause while they both look at each other and something unspoken passes between them, something I don't really understand. Which is good because I don't think I'm supposed to.

"High five for Medical Miracle Baby?" Dad finally says, holding up his hand and grinning at her. Annabel bites her bottom lip, and then laughs and hits it twice.

"High ten," she corrects. "Although we're going to have to work on a better name than that."

Which must mean Annabel's coming home again.

63

Now I don't want to be smug or anything, but not having a plan seems to be working miraculously well. In fact, you could say that the plan of not having a plan – because that's how I'm now thinking of it – is working a treat. I've fixed Dad and Annabel pretty much single-handedly and left them in the launderette. And next on my not-plan plan is Nat.

My phone rings again.

"*Pamplemousse*?" Wilbur says as soon as I pick it up. It's been vibrating in my pocket at three-minute intervals for the last four hours and I can't ignore it any more. There's a really fine line between playing it cool and just being rude, and I think any more than four hours is pushing it. "Is that you, my little *Pamplemousse*?"

"It's still me, Wilbur."

"Oh, thank holy chicken monkeys. Where have you been?"

"The launderette."

"I can't help but feel your priorities are a little out of whack, my Chestnut-bean. But if clean clothes are what you need to be a star, who am I to argue?"

I sigh. I couldn't feel less like a star now if I tried. I'm covered in splashes of mud and I smell vaguely of washing powder and socks. "Did you want something, Wilbur?"

"Banana-muffin, I need to talk to you about an opportunity that's come up, but they need to see you tomorrow mor—"

"I can't do it." I look at my watch and immediately pick up speed: I need to get where I'm going faster. I frown, and then bend down in a moment of pure inspiration and click the little button on the side of my trainers so that the little inbuilt secret wheels pop out. And *no*, I am not of an age group too old to be wearing these. No matter what Nat says. Just in case you were wondering. They wouldn't make them in this size if I was.

Anyway.

"You *can* do it," Wilbur protests.

"No," I say again as I start wheeling down the pavement. "Whatever it is, I can't do it, Wilbur."

"But you don't underst—"

"I'm sure it's great, I'm sure it's amazing, I'm sure that every girl in the world wishes she had the same opportunity." I wheel-hop over a double drain. "But I don't, OK? This isn't me, Wilbur. None of this is me. I'm not the swan. I'm the duckling. No, I'm the *duck*. I just want things to go back to how they were before I met you."

Wilbur laughs. "You really *do* make me giggle, my little Darling-pudding," he titters. "As if that makes any difference!"

I'm so busy calculating if I'll get where I'm going faster if I start running rather than wheeling, but have to stop again in a few minutes – average speed versus immediate speed – that I'm hardly listening to him.

"Difference?" I say distractedly, skipping over a crack in the pavement.

"Kitten-ears, you're under contract."

I slam the stopper on the toes down and abruptly stop in the middle of the road, with the sound of the wheels still whizzing behind me. "I'm under *what*?"

"Contract, Sweet-bean. You know the pieces of paper you signed? That's what they call them in the legal industry apparently. Visa-vee: Yuka owns you.

Plumptious, she wants you to do this so you *have* to do it. Or she'll just go right ahead and sue you."

My stomach abruptly folds in half. *Why do people keep trying to sue me?*

"A contract?" I finally repeat in disbelief. Was I so blinded by the excitement of my own metamorphosis that I signed a contract without actually reading it first? Without making notes? Without looking at every single word of the small writing and then looking it up in a legal dictionary? I mean, of course *Dad* did. Dad would sell his soul for a pink marshmallow. But me?

Who have I *been* this week?

"I know! Isn't a 'contract' just the least fun name for anything in the world ever? Annabel was *furious* that you did it, but it still stands: just one parental signature needed, my little Squeaky-kettle. So I'll ring you with details about tomorrow later, OK? Toodle-pip, *bella*."

I make a few confused mumbling sounds, say goodbye and hang up. I can't believe I'm in trouble with the law again. For the second time this week. Doesn't nine years living with a lawyer rub off at all?

I can't think about this now. I'll think about it

later. There's somewhere I need to be and it's far more important.

And I abruptly click the button on my shoes so that the wheels disappear and start running.

64

I was only here a couple of days ago, yet everything feels so different.

It even looks different. Everything is lit by a bright green light and there's a little red flask on the ground. Somewhere in the background, I can hear the faint, tinny sound of *Swan Lake* by Tchaikovsky coming out of a wind-up, hand-held radio. Which was actually performed first at the Bolshoi Theatre in Russia, so everything seems to be fitting into place like a magical puzzle.

Or, you know. A normal one packed simply full of coincidences.

"Toby?" I say, crawling back into the bush outside my house.

He's sitting inside it, just as I suspected he would be, reading a battered copy of *Don Juan*. He looks up, sniffs and then lifts the green torch he's holding so that it shines directly in my face like a sort of Halloween-themed Gestapo. "Harriet!" he says in astonishment. "What an unexpected surprise! I didn't expect you for – " and he clicks the red light on his watch – "another twenty-eight minutes. Did you not get any laundry done? Or did I miscalculate the dryer times?"

OK, Toby is much, *much* better at this stalking malarkey than I thought he was.

"Aren't you cold?" I ask, clambering in next to him.

"Not at all. This flask prevents the energy loss of the vibrating molecules of my soup and thus is still nice and toasty." Toby sniffs again. "Sadly, I think I may need a flask for my nose, as it is suspiciously icy and may be about to fall off, if that is a physical possibility."

I laugh. "Not at this temperature."

"Well, that's a relief." Toby looks around the inside of the bush with an embarrassed expression. "If I'd known you were coming, I'd have tidied up. Honestly, it's not always like this."

"It's OK. Isn't it my bush anyway?"

"Which makes me your tenant, I suppose." Toby fiddles with the volume button on the radio, which is now playing Vivaldi. "I shall try and keep it down so as not to disturb the neighbours."

"*I'm* your neighbour, Toby." I laugh again and make myself a little bit more comfortable on the blanket.

The entire time I was running/wheeling here, I knew I had to ask him something – something important – but I didn't know quite what it was.

Suddenly I do.

I look at Toby's skeleton gloves, and the hat with the little bear ears built into it, and the trainers with the laces that look like piano keys, and the battered copy of a book he'll never *have* to read, not even for university. I look at his flask and his blanket and his face, with the slightly shiny, drippy, wet-looking nose. I look at his simple, transparent happiness that I'm here. And then I take a deep breath.

"Toby," I say, "can I ask you a question?"

"Sure." Toby thinks about it. "Was that it? Did I just answer it?"

"No."

"Then sure, go right ahead."

"OK." I close my eyes, swirl the question around my mouth a few times, take a deep breath and spit it out. "Toby, do you ever feel like a polar bear, lost in a rainforest?"

Toby narrows his eyes thoughtfully. "What kind of rainforest?"

"Does it matter?"

"Absolutely, Harriet. Different rainforests have totally

different vegetation. It will dramatically affect how easy it is to be found again. Some have significantly more ground foliage and then it will be mainly cutting at plants with the paws." Toby waves his hands in front of his face to illustrate this.

There's silence again as I stare at him. "It's a metaphor, Toby. I'm speaking *metaphorically.*"

"Right. Gotcha." Toby thinks about it for a few minutes. "In that case, sure I do, Harriet."

My stomach flips over. He knows? "And then do you ever feel as if…" I pause, trying to think of how to put it. "As if no matter what we do, we're made of the wrong stuff and everyone can see it?"

Toby nods knowingly. "And we just want to get back again…"

"…to somewhere snowy, where the other polar bears must be…"

"…but we don't know how to…"

"…so we just wander around on our own."

Toby and I stare at each other for a few seconds and I can feel my entire body vibrating.

Not with romance. Just to make that clear. It's not a *romantic vibrating*. To make the point separately, Toby's nose chooses that moment to drip on to his scarf. But still: *he understands.*

"So what do we do?" I finally manage to blurt. "How do we get out, Toby?"

Perhaps there's a map I don't know about. Or – at the very least – a signpost.

Toby pulls a face, shrugs and wipes his nose with his finger. "Polar bears are awesome." He wipes his finger on his coat. "They're the largest land carnivores in the world, and did you know their skin is actually black and their hair is translucent, but looks white because it reflects light?"

I stare at him and my stomach is sinking already. So close and yet so far. "*Metaphorically*, Toby," I sigh. "We're still talking about metaphorical polar bears."

"I know. That's what I'm trying to say. We're awesome, Harriet." Toby picks up his flask and unscrews the lid. "We've got big paws so we can catch tropical fish out of rivers. And as we're genetically related to European brown bears, I think with a bit of practice we could climb trees too. Even the really tall ones."

"But..." And I pause. "We still don't *fit in*, Toby. Doesn't that bother you?"

"Nope." Toby takes a swig of soup.

I can feel myself starting to stammer. Toby knows, but he doesn't care? "B-b-but what about the others?" I start mumbling in confusion, almost to myself now.

"The frogs, the parrots, the... the tigers, the flying squirrels... What about them? They *know*, they see it, they don't want anything to do with us, they laugh at us..."

"In fairness, most of them end up getting eaten, Harriet. We've all got our bad points. The rainforest is an extremely harsh environment and shrinking in size. Just as the ice caps are. That's a much bigger issue."

"But—"

Toby puts the cap back on his flask and straightens out the blanket. "Just enjoy being a polar bear. Appreciate the size of our paws." He makes his hands into paws and waves them in front of his face again. "Plus," he adds, "we're deceptively fluffy and cute."

I stare at him, too surprised to say anything. Suddenly, cross-legged and bathed in the green light of his pocket torch, Toby looks otherworldly. Mysterious. Knowing. Almost... Yoda-like.

And then he sticks his finger up his nose and goes back to being Toby again.

We sit in silence: Toby fiddling with the channel on the radio and me picking distractedly at a leaf on the bush. There are so many things to think about and yet – somehow – I don't need to think about them. They're presenting themselves to me now, fully formed.

I clear my throat and start crawling out from under the bush. I finally know what it is I have to do. "Right," I tell Toby over my shoulder in my bossiest voice. "You're coming with me."

Toby looks at me with wide and delighted eyes. "I am? With you? When?"

"Now. Bring your green torch, Toby."

I'm going to need all the additional wisdom I can get.

65

I'd like to say that our ensuing journey is a profound one: filled with adventure and inspiration and self-discovery. That would be nice, wouldn't it? A little bit like *Pilgrim's Progress*, without the overwhelming religious analogy.

It's not.

"Are you sure you wouldn't like me to walk ten paces behind you?" Toby asks in consternation as we hurry down the pavement. "Would it make you more comfortable?"

"Toby, when does walking ten paces behind ever make someone more comfortable?"

"It depends on whether they see you or not. Although, I have to say it gets a bit tricky *measuring* the ten paces. It usually requires running up to them and then pacing away again. Which isn't as subtle as you might think."

I decide to ignore this. "Just walk next to me, Toby. Like a non-stalker."

"Golly." Toby seems overwhelmed. "This is a break with tradition, I have to say. If you change your mind, Harriet, just say the word and I'll duck behind a tree and pretend to be reading a newspaper or checking for woodworm, OK?"

"OK." I smile at him. Why have I always been so mean to Toby? He just wanted another polar bear to play with.

"Would you mind terribly if I attempted to hold your hand?" he adds, skipping next to me. "For just a short time? On this beautiful winter day?"

All right, I'm not feeling that sorry for him.

"Yes," I snap, stuffing mine in my pocket. "I would mind terribly, Toby."

Toby starts rummaging in his backpack. "I shall make a note of that," he tells me earnestly. He scribbles something in his notebook. "Perhaps in six months?"

I think of Nick's hand, the hand I'll never hold again. My stomach gives a sad little flip and I shake my head.

"Not a problem," Toby says cheerfully, making another note and putting his book away. "Seven months it is."

Nat's house seems even bigger now, although I'm pretty sure it's the same size. It's just my guilt making it loom like something out of a Tim Burton film.

"Stand back," I tell Toby quietly as we approach her front door. "Nat isn't happy with me. And, much like an angry *Camponotus saundersi…"*

"Commonly known as the Malaysian ant," Toby interjects.

"There's a good chance that when we get close, her head is going to literally explode."

Toby obediently stands a few metres back and the door opens. Nat's mum blinks at us a few times. She's now entirely pink: pink dressing gown, pink towel round her head, pink face mask. She even has a pink eye mask strapped to her head, like inflatable glasses.

"Harriet!" she says, delighted. "Are you here with gifts again? I finished the chocolates and arranged what I could salvage of the pink roses strewn around the driveway. Although the bits with the teeth marks obviously had to go in the bin."

Sugar cookies. I knew Nat preferred lilies.

"Is Nat here, please?"

"Still sulking somewhere, I believe, yes." Nat's mum glances behind me and waves. "And this must be your little stalker, Toby. I remember you from the school fête a few years ago. You were shuffling around the raffle on your belly with binoculars."

Toby steps forward, beaming. "That's me," he says, puffing out his chest proudly. "Although my Harriet-following skills have improved *immeasurably* since then. It's very nice to meet you properly, Mrs Nat's mum."

"It is indeed." She smiles at him, and then smiles at me, and then smiles at Toby again. And then – and I can't actually believe this – she winks at me. She'd better not be winking for the reason I think she's winking.

Ugh.

"Ahem." Nat's mum clears her throat and then gets a small hand-held microphone out of her pocket. "Excuse me," she explains to us, "but shouting up the stairs is causing unnecessary wrinkling in my forehead. So I've invested in an alternative." And then she clicks the little red button on the side. "Natalie?" she says into the microphone, and somewhere in the distance her voice starts bouncing around the stairs. "You have a couple of visitors."

Silence.

Nat's mum rolls her eyes and fiddles with the volume control. A loud screeching fills the house and she puts her hand over the top. "It's linked up to a speaker outside her bedroom," she whispers conspiratorially. "I put one under her bed too, although she hasn't found that one yet. Natalie? *Natalie?*" She listens for a few seconds, sighs and holds the microphone up again. "Don't make me turn it up to ten, young lady."

"All right, all right," I hear Nat shout, storming down the stairs.

Nat's mum turns the microphone off, winks at Toby and me, retreats into the living room and shuts the door. Leaving us to face Nat.

And – from the look on her face – I believe she's about to give the head-exploding Malaysian ants a run for their money.

66

"Well?" Nat says after a few seconds. "I'm surprised you're here again, Harriet. I thought you'd be busy auditioning for *A Midsummer Night's Dream*."

I blink a few times in surprise. "No. I'm not."

"You should be. I heard they're looking for an *ass*."

Oh.

Now why can't I think of quips like that when I need them? Does she sit and make them up beforehand or do they just pop out like that, fully formed? If she ever talks to me in a non-violent way again, I must remember to ask her.

Toby holds his head up very high and looks Nat dead in the eye. "Natalie Grey," he says in a stern voice. "Harriet has come here in great and glorious dignity – and, if I may say so, quite mesmerising beauty – to apologise to you. The very least you can do is stand there and listen politely. Otherwise you're nothing but a... a... a..." I can see him looking around desperately. His eyes fall on the ground next to the front door. "A flowerpot head," he finishes triumphantly. "Full of lavender."

Toby clearly has the same problem I do. Nat lifts an unimpressed eyebrow.

"I don't want to apologise again," I say in a rush.

"Then what are you doing here? Are you going to give me more pointless gifts that I can enjoy breaking?"

"No. I just want you to come with me somewhere."

Nat's shocked into silence for a few seconds. "And why the hell would I do that?"

"Because neither of us is happy like this."

Nat makes a *hmph* sound. "Actually, being without you is extremely liberating, Harriet. I never knew how much time there would be in life when it's not being filled with documentaries about humpback whales migrating."

That's a low blow. She *liked* the humpback whale documentary. She said they were very "splashy".

"Please, Nat? Twenty minutes and if you still hate me then you can spend the rest of the night cutting my face out of all our photos."

"How do you know I haven't already done that?"

We glare at each other obstinately for a few seconds, neither of us willing to budge.

Toby clears his throat. "If you need somewhere to

put all the cut-out Harriet heads," he interjects, "I'd be happy to take them off your hands."

We both turn slowly to stare at him, but luckily my response is interrupted by the sound of the invisible Nat's mum tapping the top of the microphone. "Ahem," she says, like the disembodied voice of some kind of ancient goddess. "Go with them, Natalie."

"What?" Nat says to thin air.

"I'm not having you marching around the house with a face like a smacked bottom for the rest of the week. Go with them."

"*No.*"

"All right." The voice of the goddess clears her throat. "It's on six, Natalie." A screech starts filling the house.

"*Mum.*"

"Seven." The screech gets louder. Nat starts chewing on her bottom lip.

"At eight, Natalie, your ears are going to start hurting."

Nat puts her hand over her face. "Please, Mum—"

"Nine. Ringing in your ears for the rest of the day. Don't make me go to ten. I will."

"Fine!" Nat shouts, glaring behind her and grabbing her handbag. She violently forces her feet into a pair of shoes next to the door. "Fine, all of you. Happy now? I'm coming." She stalks out of the door and slams it behind her.

But not before we hear the faint sound of disembodied laughter.

I lead the rest of the way.

I have to: nobody else knows where we're going. And even if they did know where we were going, they wouldn't know how to get there. I'm the only one with that magical knowledge, thanks to a party eight years ago that Nat missed because she was having her tonsils out. The first and last party I ever went to without her. Although I haven't exactly been *wading* through solo invitations.

"Right," I say nervously as we get to a large front gate and I click the latch. "Just let me do all the talking."

"Harriet," Nat says crossly as we walk up the garden path. "Where the hell are we? And when do you ever *not* do all the talking?"

I know I'm supposed to be making peace with her, but with comments like that she is making it very difficult.

"You think I don't know what friendship is, Nat," I say, lifting up the knocker and letting it fall noisily. "But you're wrong. And I know how to be honest too." I lift it again and let it fall. "I just forgot for a little while, that's all. And now I'm going to prove it to you."

Slowly, with an ominous creak and a struggle – and some mild swearing – the front door opens.

And there, with a very surprised look on her face, is Alexa.

67

If you guessed this is where I was coming then your mind clearly works just like mine does. In a linear and sensible and yet simultaneously creative and poetic fashion.

Nat and Toby's minds, however, obviously don't. Their mouths have fallen open in perfect coordination with Alexa's.

"This," Nat says clearly behind me, "tops the list of most stupid things you've ever done, Harriet. That's a pretty huge achievement."

"*Harriet*," Toby stage-whispers, "*did you know Alexa Roberts lives here? What were the chances?*"

I clear my throat. Alexa's face is going through emotions the way Annabel flicks through channels on advert breaks: shock, followed by incredulity, and then a long moment spent on anger and a brief glimpse of embarrassment. And for a few fragments of time I almost see… respect. Respect for my audacity. On second thoughts, no. It's not respect.

It's a reaction to the smell of Toby's powerful aftershave: the wind's blowing it straight into the house.

"Alexa," I say and I take a deep breath. I'm not absolutely certain what I'm going to say, even though I've been thinking about it all the way here. I just know that – whatever it is – it has to be perfect and it has to fix everything.

No pressure then.

"Harriet," Alexa says, beaming at us. "Natalie. Toby. What a pleasant surprise. Would you like to come in for a cup of Darjeeling tea? My mum's just bought a new box of Bakewell tarts and there's plenty to go round."

My deep breath rushes out of me all in one go. "Huh?" I say in confusion. "What? Seriously?"

Nat puts her head in her hands.

"Sure," Alexa says, folding her arms in front of her. "We can all sit in the living room and discuss the likelihood of a white Christmas."

"Really?"

The beam disappears. "*No*, not *really,* you moron. I have no idea what you're doing here and I don't care. Get off my doorstep before I set the dogs on you."

Toby takes a few steps backwards. Admittedly, I can't hear any dogs, but that doesn't mean there aren't any; they might just be really quiet ones.

I bite my bottom lip hard. "Not until I've said what I need to say."

Alexa's frown deepens and she starts making a whistling sound. "Rex? Fang? Come here, boys. It's geeks for tea."

Nat breathes out loudly and tugs at my arm. "OK, Harriet. You've made your point, you're risking your own safety to defend me, you're very brave, I love you again, now let's drop it and go home, all right?"

"No." I fold my arms, partly to look determined and partly because my hands are shaking with nerves. "I'm not going anywhere. Not until I've told her."

"Told me what?" Alexa stops whistling and her eyes narrow. "You're standing there like the three little pigs on my doorstep so that you can tell me *what*?"

There's a long silence while I look at her, my brain making whirring sounds. *The Three Little Pigs.* And their three little houses. One made out of straw, one made out of wood and one made out of brick. That's it.

I'm going to tell Alexa that if we're the three little pigs, then it's OK because there are three of us, and we're not in a house of straw, we're in a house of brick. So she can huff and puff as much as she likes, but she can't blow us down.

And if she has a problem with this analogy – I do, actually, because in Tudor times houses were made out of straw and *they* didn't seem to have a problem with the elements – then I'll switch to *The Three Bears* and tell her it doesn't matter how much of our porridge she eats and how many of our beds she sleeps in: we've finally found the strength to run her back into the woods.

And then I'll turn to *The Three Brothers*, and I'll just keep going with the fairytale triumvirate analogies until she understands that we're not frightened of her any more. And she can't hurt us again, however hard she tries. Because we won't let her.

I prepare myself to launch an attack verbally way below my range, but abruptly stop. I don't need to say any of it. I know. Nat knows. And Toby knows. We're here and that's enough. But there is something I do need to say.

"We're sorry about your hair." I point to Alexa's head. "That's what we came to say. What we did was horrible, malicious and wrong, and we are sorry."

Alexa lifts her eyebrows. "You came all the way over here to tell me you're sorry about my hair?"

"Yes." I turn to Nat, who looks totally speechless. "Aren't we, Nat?"

"I'm sorry too," Toby interjects. "Despite having nothing to do with it in a *literal* sense, as leader of this gang I feel I should take responsibility for its actions."

Nat and I look at each other. We'll just let Toby have that one.

Nat scowls and her cheeks go pink. I know she's been feeling bad about it too. She's just not mean enough to think it was acceptable behaviour. "Yeah," Nat says finally, her shoulders relaxing. "I lost my temper, Alexa, and I shouldn't have. I'm sorry." She pauses. "But if you do anything like that to Harriet again," she mutters so that only I can hear her, "I'll give you a buzz cut."

Alexa touches her hair. "Luckily my face shape can pull off just about anything. Are we done now?"

"Yes," I say slowly, looking at her hard. "We are done now."

And I really, really mean it.

"Then please feel free to go to hell. All of you." Alexa looks at the three of us. "Geeks," she adds, almost as an afterthought.

And closes the door on us.

68

We dance all the way home. Although we wait until we're out of Alexa's driveway first obviously. We're not on a suicide mission.

"*Did you see that?*" Toby keeps shouting, wiggling his hips. He's opened his jacket up and is accompanying our triumphant movements with the electric keyboard on his T-shirt. "Take *that*, Alexa! *WHAM!* We came all the way to your house and *everything*!"

I twirl round in a happy little circle with my hands over my head. It's all over. If the big bad wolf wants to get us, she's going to have to climb down the chimney. Where we're going to keep a big cauldron of hot water, just in case.

It feels *amazing.* Even Nat does a little triumphant shoulder wriggle when she thinks nobody's looking.

"You know," she says breathlessly when we've all finally stopped glorying in the moment, "that felt really good. Alexa's never going to say sorry for anything, which makes us the good guys, right?"

"Well, we know we're not the bad guys," Toby says earnestly. "If we were, we'd be wearing black with little skulls and we'd probably have moustaches."

"I still can't believe you cut her hair off."

"I *know*. What was I thinking?"

"Where did you even get the scissors?"

"The art room. Everything went a bit blurry for a few minutes and the next thing I knew I had a ponytail in my hand. I've felt horrible about it for days."

"Nat," I say seriously, slowing my skipping down a little. "I am sorry. For everything. For lying to you. For stealing your dream. And I know that you'll probably hate me forever, but..."

Nat rolls her eyes. "I was never going to hate you *forever*, Harriet. Just a couple of days."

"But you said..."

"We were *fighting*. What did you want me to say? *I'll hate you for about thirty-six hours until I've calmed down a bit?*"

Oh.

"Yeah, that would have been nice, actually," I tell her, slightly huffily. "Just a heads-up could have been really handy. I was in the depths of despair."

Nat laughs. "Drama queen as always. Although if you had a temper like mine, I probably would have kept the modelling secret too. I am *terrifying*." She looks proudly at her nails and blows on them. "Unpredictable and absolutely *terrifying*."

"So we're…" I venture.

"Yeah." Nat shrugs and grins at me. "Whatever."

I'm just about to throw myself into her not-even-slightly open arms when my phone rings and Toby holds his hands up.

"It's not me," he points out. "Just in case anyone's wondering. I'm not ringing you, Harriet. Although I could because I've totally learnt your number off by heart."

"Wilbur?" I say, grabbing it out of my pocket.

"Hello, my little Crunchie-nut," Wilbur says happily. "I'd love to sit and chat about all sorts of girly fun, but I want to go home, so here's the details for this thing Yuka wants you to do. It's tomorrow morning, Petal-moo; an interview for a fashion special on *WakeUp UK*. They need you there nice and early so you'll still get to school on time." He pauses. "If your school starts at 10am obviously."

I look at Nat, who's pretending she can't hear the entire conversation. Wilbur's voice carries like a Sports Day whistle.

"I can't do it, Wilbur." Nat's eyes go very round,

but we've only just resurrected our friendship: I can't risk it. "You're just going to have to tell Yuka to sue me. Remind her that I'm underage, please, and my stepmother's a really, really great lawyer."

I can feel it already. Nat and I will be like the dolphins at Sea World again, jumping in perfect harmony. Living in synergy; one stream of consciousness, with never a cross word between us. Two minds in one bod—

The phone gets snatched out of my hand.

"Wilbur? Hello. This is Nat. I'm the girl who cried in your reception on Saturday morning. Harriet says it's a fantastic and exciting opportunity and she'll be there. Text her the time and address. Thanks." And she hangs up.

I stare at her for a few seconds. *Nat's* the girl who was crying in the agency?

"Nat? What the hell are you doing?" I finally blurt.

"What I would have done at the beginning, if you'd let me."

69

Statistics aren't important, they're just numbers. Irrelevant, arbitrary numbers. So obviously I don't spend the evening on the internet, researching how many people watch *WakeUp UK* every morning.

(3,400,000.)

And I don't find out the demographic of the viewers.

(Extremely widespread: students getting ready for school, families having breakfast, workers as they get ready to leave the house.)

And I *definitely* don't find out roughly how many people watch the internet videos of the interviews.

(300,000 for a guy talking about trimming the edges of your lawn neatly.)

Most importantly, the thing I most absolutely don't do is skip breakfast because I'm locked in the toilet, breathing in and out of a paper bag, and then spend the entire taxi journey to the studio tearing the bag to shreds and scattering it all over my lap.

Why would I do that? I'm not the old, anxious

Harriet any more. I'm cool. I'm calm. I'm taking all of this in my stride.

Obviously.

"Harriet?" Dad says finally. *Everyone* has decided to come with me this time: the taxi is so full that the driver has started making grumpy sounds about what his insurance covers. Annabel's taken the front seat and Dad, Nat, Toby and I are all crammed in the back, trying to put our feet in places that don't already have feet in them. "Are you under the impression that you're some kind of hamster or possibly bird?"

I look at the papery mess on my trousers. It's true: if I was suddenly rendered much, much smaller, it would make excellent bedding.

"I'm making an ancient style of puzzle," I tell him loftily. "When I have time, I will consider putting it all back together again."

"Would you like me to make a start on it?" Toby asks eagerly. I tried to evade him, but after he explained how many buses he was going to have to catch to follow me, I relented. It's easier if he just stalks me in the same taxi.

"No. But thanks."

"I'm going to need to get out again I'm afraid," Annabel says from the front. "I need to pee."

"*Again?*" Dad sighs. "Honey, do you need a catheter?"

"No, it's fine, Richard. I'll just urinate all over this nice man's seats and then we'll just walk the rest of the way. Hang on, isn't this your favourite jumper, darling? Maybe I can use it to mop up the mess."

Dad's face goes pale. "*Stop the taxi.*" He looks at all of us. "Never lend a pregnant woman cashmere."

"I was going to anyway," the taxi driver tells us, pressing the little green light so that we can hear him through the speakers. "We're here."

The taxi turns a corner and we all fall silent. Partly because it's a little overwhelming arriving at an international television studio at 6.30am. And partly because Wilbur's waiting for us. Wearing a bright pink top hat and silver jumpsuit.

"Is it me?" Annabel says as the taxi pulls to a stop and Wilbur takes his hat off and bows. "Or does that man just get weirder and weirder?"

Once we've disembarked, Wilbur adjusts the pink hat slightly and then sends everyone to sit in another part of the studio while I go with him to "get beautiful". He looks at the frizz-ball masquerading as my hair. "Although, Baby-baby Panda," he adds sadly, "it looks like we're going to have to start from scratch again, doesn't it?"

Just in case I was under some illusion that I may have transformed even *slightly* in the last week, it's nice to be set straight.

"I can't control it," I explain in a small voice as he shepherds me down some skinny corridors towards a closed door.

"I can see that, Apple-blossom," he sighs, narrowing his eyes at the top of my head. "Any chance that it's controlling *you*?" He looks at my outfit. "Glad to see you're styling it out, though. Are these your pyjamas, Bunny?"

I ignore him. I'm getting quite used to doing that now. They're not my pyjamas, for the record. It's a snowman-themed T-shirt and baggy patterned trousers from the Moroccan shop in town. These are the only clean clothes I have left.

"So what do we do first?" I ask nervously. "Do I have any lines to learn?"

"Even better than that, my special Sugar-peanut. I've got *this*." And he holds out a small piece of plastic.

"A hearing aid?"

"I'm wiring you up, darling. With five million viewers, we reckon you might need some help."

Five million? The internet lied to me?

I look at the little plastic thing with a mixture of relief and horror. "You're going to tell me what to say?"

Wilbur throws back his head and laughs. "*I'm* not, Monkey-tiger. Can you *imagine*? I just don't think my vocabulary would fit in your little mouth, darling. No, Yuka Ito is. Word for word."

Oh, God. She's here? "And all I have to do is repeat it?"

"And all you have to do is repeat it," Wilbur confirms. He giggles again. "You see? I should *so* have been a model."

I look at the earpiece apprehensively. OK, I can do this. Say whatever it is Yuka wants me to say and then get back to my normal life. School. Trigonometry. History club. Walking to school, instead of getting a taxi via Shepherd's Bush and five million people.

"Now," Wilbur says, "let's get you ready and then we can get you both on to the sofa."

My brain twangs. *Both?*

"But if Yuka's sitting next to me," I point out, "how can she…"

"Oh, Yuka's not sitting next to you, Sweet-pudding," Wilbur laughs, throwing open the closed door. "Nick is."

My brain is now pinging in frantic little elasticated

movements around the inside of my head.

Nick looks up, grins at me and then goes back to doodling on a notepad.

Would people please stop doing this to me?

"Did I forget to mention he was being interviewed too?" Wilbur adds, looking carefully at my face and then winking. "Oops."

70

Does anybody – *anybody* – have any idea how hard it is to concentrate on getting ready to talk in front of five million people with an unexpected *Nick* sitting a few metres away?

Well, let me tell you: it's like trying to tune a digital radio while Mount Vesuvius erupts in the background.

"Why is he *here*?" I whisper under my breath as a nice lady called Jessica does my hair and make-up. I've already been put into a blue dress that I would never, ever have picked for myself. Mainly because it doesn't have cartoon characters on it.

"He's the male face of Baylee, Plumptious," Wilbur whispers back as if I didn't already know this. "Maximum brand exposure." He looks to the ceiling as if he's just seen an angel. "Yuka's a total publicity *legend*."

"Hmm." Nick's lazing around on the sofa – flicking his pen in the air and catching it again – as if national television is something he does all the time. Which, actually, it might be. Today he is wearing a warm grey jumper and a pair of dark blue jeans. His hair is all sort of quiffed up at the front and now and then he puts his finger in his mouth and bites the—

"Hey, Manners," he says, looking up.

I look away quickly. *Sugar cookies*. "Y-yes?" I stammer, trying to look as nonchalant as possible.

He gestures towards the coffee table. "It's low, but if you really squidge, you might be able to do it."

Is that all he's going to say? After we held hands and everything? "I have grown out of my table-hiding days as it happens," I tell him in a cold voice. "It was a childhood phase, that is all."

"That's a shame. If we lived somewhere with lots of earthquakes, you'd be a really good person to know."

I glare at him. For somebody so gorgeous, he really knows how to be annoying. "Actually, there have been nineteen earthquakes in the UK in the last ten years," I snap. "Which makes me a good person to know right now."

"It does," he agrees, grinning at me and going back to his doodle.

I grind my teeth and feel my cheeks get hot. What's that supposed to mean? That I'm a good person to know, but only nineteen times in ten years? That's not a very good ratio.

"Now then, my little Squabbling-beans," Wilbur interrupts. He pushes a little bit of plastic in my ear, pulls the wire under my collar and pops another bit of plastic in a pocket at the back of my dress. "We don't have time for all this adorable Darcy and Lizzie tension, Kitten-cheeks. Let's get you on air so that your stepmother can stop texting me at three-minute intervals, Harriet. She's extremely anxious that we get you to school on time today."

I nod. I am too, actually. I don't want something to go horribly wrong later in life because I'm supposed to know about metaphysical poets and don't.

I notice that the little green light on my hearing aid has been switched on. I look at Nick. "Do you have one too?"

Nick and Wilbur both laugh.

"Harriet," a cold voice in my ear says. "This is Yuka Ito."

I look around, trying to locate her. "Don't look around trying to locate me," she snaps. "I'm in the production-control room."

"Can you see me?"

"No. I just know that's what you're doing. Are you ready?"

"I'm ready," I say as clearly as I can. Nick is standing just behind me, yawning and rubbing his face with the sleeve of his grey jumper. How come Yuka Ito isn't shouting in his ear like the little caterpillar in *Alice in Wonderland?*

"Just say what I tell you to," Yuka says, "and everything will go as planned. And please, Harriet..."

"Yes?"

"*Try* and behave yourself this time."

71

I'd always assumed that on TV, when it looks like the presenters are in a living room, they're actually, you know, *in a living room*. With a nice painting, a fireplace and maybe a few bookshelves for perusing while the cameras weren't rolling.

But it's just a stage with a few sofas, and a big open black space full of wires and intense-looking people. Frankly, I can't help but feel a little cheated.

"Good morning, sweetie," the chirpy blonde presenter says as I perch nervously on the edge of one of the sofas. "I'm Jane. I bet this is early for you, isn't it?"

I nod, even though I'm not quite sure what Jane's talking about. It's 7.30am – precisely the time I'm normally shouting at Dad to get out of the shower.

"And I'm Patrick," a slightly older man says, leaning forward to shake my hand, and then leaning a little further to do the same to Nick. "Don't be nervous, guys. This is just a bit of fun, right?"

"You know," Nick says in his slow drawl, "I just can't remember when I've had more." Patrick nods enthusiastically.

Yuka clears her throat in my ear. "Tell Nick that if he doesn't stop being facetious, he's doing his next show in a dress."

I lean forward and pass the message on.

"Awesome," Nick says, laughing. "Tell her to make sure it has sequins on it this time."

I keep looking anxiously into the dark space, but I can't see Nat, or Dad, or Annabel, Wilbur or even Toby. What was the point in stuffing themselves into that taxi if nobody's here now? Where's my stalker when I need him?

I look at Nick with my eyes wide. "Remember," he whispers under his breath. "No biggy."

I breathe out and can feel the panic starting to leave again. It's only six minutes. Just six minutes of saying whatever Yuka wants me to say, and then I can go to school and be normal again.

"Getting ready to go live," one of the cameramen shouts. "In ten, nine, eight..."

I look around the dark again.

"Seven, six, five..."

Where are they?

"Four, three, two..."

And suddenly – with the softest of shuffles – the five of them scoot into the room at the back. My entire body relaxes as if somebody's just cut all of the cords holding me upright. Nat holds her thumbs up and Dad points dramatically to Annabel's lower stomach, mimes going to the toilet and shrugs. Wilbur gives a little dancing move and then shoots me with the imaginary gun of his fingers. Toby simply stands there and grins at me.

"One," Jane says. And I'm live on air.

72

I jump a little bit and then – to cover it up – cunningly pretend I'm checking out the bounciness of the sofa.

"As part of our fashion special," Jane continues as if she hasn't noticed that I'm bouncing up and down on national television, "we have with us this morning Harriet Manners, the fifteen-year-old schoolgirl who made headlines across the world as the newest face of fashion powerhouse Baylee. How are you, Harriet?"

"I'm fantastic, thanks, Jane," Yuka says in my ear.

"I'm fantastic, thanks, Jane," I repeat like a robot.

"And we also have Nick Hidaka, the sixteen-year-old male face of the brand. How are you, Nick?"

"I'm barely awake, thanks, Jane." And then he grins at her so that his dimples pop in and out. "But I'll do my very best."

Are you *kidding* me? And *I'm* the one being spoon-fed lines?

Jane blinks a few times. "Amazing. Now, Nick, am I right in thinking that this wouldn't be your first big campaign? You've done Armani, Gucci, Hilfiger..."

"Apparently so."

"...And now Baylee. I remember there was a bit of controversy when you were first cast. Tell me, what's it like to work with your Aunty Yuka? Extra pressure or is it nice keeping it in the family?"

Nick laughs. "Well, let's just say if I screw it up, it's going to make for an uncomfortable Christmas dinner."

What?

My whole head has gone numb. Yuka is Nick's *aunt*? Nick is Yuka's *nephew*? They're *related*? They're *family*? The same blood runs through their... well, you get the picture.

And nobody told me?

"...you've caused a bit of a commotion yourself already, Harriet." Patrick's leaning forward and I suddenly realise that while I'm silently freaking out, he's trying to engage me in conversation.

"*Listen*, Harriet," Yuka hisses in my ear. "Or at least pretend to."

"Ahmmm," I mumble, smiling at as many people as possible.

"Fifteen years old, plucked from obscurity less than a week ago." Jane looks at her notes. "You caught legendary designer Yuka Ito's eye straight away, I hear. Gosh. That doesn't happen that often, does it? Isn't that just a fairytale?"

I look at her blankly.

"Yes, Jane," Yuka whispers. "It's a fairytale come true for any girl."

"Yes, Jane," I say obediently. "It's a fairytale come true for any girl."

"And Yuka's even designing a special outfit for you in her next show."

This is news to me. I stare at Jane.

"She is," Yuka says and I repeat. "I'm extremely lucky."

"Truly amazing." Jane shakes her head as if she wants to jump across the sofa and slap me jealously across the face. "Who wouldn't want that at fifteen?" She laughs gaily. "Who am I kidding: who wouldn't want that at any age? And it says here you're her new muse. Wow. Tell me, Harriet, have you always wanted to model?"

"Ever since I was a child," Yuka says clearly in my ear. "I used to dress up in my mother's clothes and twirl around my bedroom in front of the mirror. I have always been captivated by fashion."

"Ever since I was a child," I say dutifully. "I used to

dress up… in… my… m-m-m—" I swallow. Dad gave all my mum's clothes to the charity shop when she died. There was nothing to dress up in. And when Annabel came along, the only thing available would have been a suit.

I briefly imagine a skinny little red-headed girl twirling around in a huge pinstripe suit complete with tie and clunky office shoes and have to stifle a giggle.

"Harriet," Yuka snaps. "Say it."

"…in my mother's clothes and twirl around the bedroom in front of the mirror," I continue, trying to straighten my face out and not cry at the same time. "I have always been captivated by fashion."

"And how have you managed to balance it with your schoolwork so far?" Jane asks. "It must be hard, combining the two?"

"Baylee always puts my schoolwork first," I chime after Yuka has spoken. "It's of key importance to them."

Apart from – you know – the bit where they made me take two days off to go to Russia. And this morning.

"And your favourite school subjects?" Patrick winks at the camera. "I think we can guess what they'd be!"

Maths. Physics. Chemistry.

"Textiles and art, of course," I say diligently after waiting a nanosecond for my cue.

"And what about your school friends? You must be a very popular girl now."

I think of Alexa's scowling face and the shouts of *Geek*. I think of thirty hands in the air. "Uh-huh," I say.

"*Uh-huh* was not what I just said," Yuka snaps.

"As the new muse of one of fashion's biggest players," Jane says in excitement, "is the fashion life everything you thought it would be?"

Yuka clears her throat and I wince slightly: it's really unpleasant having that sound shot straight into your head.

"Modelling is everything I dreamed it would be..." I repeat. "And I love fashion because it's really about individuality, and creativity... and... and self-belief... and self-exp..." I trail off into silence.

Jane leans forward. "Self-exp?" she prompts.

"Self-expression," I say in a small voice. Then I stare into the black space where my family are sitting. There's a commotion behind the camera and somewhere in my ear I can hear Yuka starting to panic.

What the hell am I doing?

I'm sitting here, in front of five million people, repeating someone else's lines about self-expression. I'm harping on about individuality in a dress somebody else put me in, with a haircut somebody else gave me, wearing make-up somebody else did. I'm talking about self-belief when I became a model because I didn't have any.

Have I learnt *nothing*?

I take the microphone out of my ear and abruptly sit on it. Underneath my bottom, I can hear the tinny sound of Yuka yelling.

"It's not true," I say, taking a deep breath.

Jane flinches and I can see Patrick furiously reading the autocue.

"I didn't dream about being a model," I say firmly, refusing to look at Nick. "I dreamed of being a palaeontologist. I didn't do any twirling when I was a child, my favourite subjects are maths and physics, nobody at school has ever liked me and I don't think this is going to help much."

"Well," Jane says, laughing nervously, "isn't that just..."

"And I don't love fashion," I say because I can't stop now; this suddenly feels like the most important thing I'll ever say. "It's just clothes."

There's a gasp from around the studio and even the microphone under my bottom has stopped vibrating.

"And self-belief and self-expression and individuality are really important," I continue, looking into the dark and talking too fast, "but if you're wearing what everyone tells you to wear and saying what everyone tells you to say and thinking the way everyone tells you to think then – well... you don't have any of those things, do you?"

Patrick is starting to look frightened and there's a pink patch forming on Jane's cheeks. "You don't like it?" she says, her forehead creasing in the middle. "You don't like modelling?"

I think about going to Russia, and jumping around in the snow, and walking down that catwalk, and the butterfly girls. I think about how much fun it can be and how I feel when I'm doing it. I think about Dad's excitement, Annabel's pride and Nat's selflessness. "Actually, I *do* like modelling," I say in surprise. "But I don't want to be somebody else to do it. I still want to be me, and if that means wearing a suit and doing my trigonometry homework ten days before it's due then that should be OK."

"But if you hate fashion—"

I shake my head because I've suddenly realised that's not true either. "You know, Jane, cavemen used to wear different skins and bones to differentiate themselves from each other and from other tribes."

"Erm…"

"So if fashion's a creative way of showing the world who you are and where you belong, that's a good thing, isn't it? But if who I am is a Winnie the Pooh jumper then I should be allowed to wear it." I pause and look into the dark where Toby is standing. "Or a T-shirt with electronic drums." I look at Dad and Annabel. "Or a robot T-shirt or a pinstripe suit." And then I look at Wilbur. "Or a pink top hat for no reason at all."

"But—"

"But they're still *just clothes.* They can't make you something you're not. They can only help to say who you are."

Stop talking, Harriet. Stop talking *right now.*

I think I've sort of forgotten I'm on television. I'm having my little epiphany on air, in front of five million people. But at least I'm not lying any more.

Patrick is sweating and one of the cameramen is making a winding motion with his finger. Nick leans forward. "I disagree," he says and I flinch. *Of course he does*. He's Yuka's nephew.

Jane smiles at him. "You do?"

"Piglet is far superior. Harriet's made quite an error of judgement."

I gape at him. What is he talking about?

"*Piglet?*" I snap. "What has Piglet ever done of any importance?"

"Helped to pull Winnie out of Rabbit's door, for one thing."

Nick and I look at each other for a few seconds and something passes between us. Except – yet again – I'm not quite sure what that thing is.

"Well," Jane says finally, breaking the silence. "That was a very interesting insight into..." she thinks about it, "something, wasn't it?" She glances at Patrick and puts her finger to her ear. Does she have a microphone as well? Is anybody round here just saying what's in their own heads? "Sadly, that's all we have time for. Coming up after the break, how to compost the hair from your pet brush." Jane grins at the camera and picks up her script again.

"And *cut*," the cameraman shouts.

And I'm done. Finished. Actually, considering what I just said on live television, I think that's probably true in more than one sense.

"Sorry for ruining your interview," I say in a small voice to nobody in particular. Or, you know. Everybody.

And I pull the microphone out from under my bottom, whisper, "Sorry, Yuka," into it and run to the back of the room.

73

It's not hard to see where my family is, even in dim lighting.

Dad's doing his dance again. Toby's bobbing up and down on the balls of his feet and Nat's standing on a chair and clapping. Even Annabel's nodding her head to what looks suspiciously like an internal beat. Wilbur is sitting on the edge of a box with his head in his hands and his hat off.

"Whoop!" Nat shouts across the room.

"Whoop," agrees Toby gravely. "And again, what Nat said: whoop."

"My daughter!" Dad cries as soon as I get close. He punches the air, scruffs my hair up and then folds me into a bear hug in one seamless movement. "Feminist, pioneer, trailblazer, general bottom kicker."

Annabel nods. "Harriet Quimby would be proud," she says approvingly, leaning forward and touching my face.

"As would Harriet the tortoise," Dad adds, nodding

up and down. Annabel rolls her eyes. "What, Annabel? She *would*."

"I'm glad you guys liked it," I say, my face going pink with pleasure. "I think that might be it for my modelling career, though. I'm so sorry, Wilbur. I let you down."

Wilbur looks up with a pale face. "No, you didn't," he says in a quiet voice. "That was really brave, Harriet. Don't worry about Yuka. I'll deal with her."

"Nobody *deals* with Yuka," a sharp voice says from behind us and we all spin round. Yuka Ito is standing in the middle of yet another spotlight, totally in black lace, but this time with bright red lips.

OK, does she just carry the spotlight around with her or does she just stop when she gets to one?

Yuka looks straight at me. "I do not appreciate being sat on, Harriet. Don't do it again."

"I'm sorry," I mumble. "This time I'm definitely fired, right?"

"Why would you be fired? If I had known you would say that, I wouldn't have given you an earpiece in the first place."

My mouth falls open. "But wasn't it just a PR..."

"Of course not. If I believed that fashion was about being the same as everyone else, would I dress like a negative of Miss Havisham every single day for thirty years?"

"I guess not."

"Then this conversation is over. You'll sign your next contract with me tomorrow morning."

Yuka turns around and starts walking back towards the door.

"On one condition," I hear myself say in a clear voice. She stops and turns slowly back around to face me. "I'm not missing any more school. If you want me, you'll have to do evenings, mornings and weekends. Like a..." I think about it briefly. "A paper round."

Yuka narrows her eyes. "Did you just compare working for me to doing a *paper round*?"

I nod. "Yes."

She shuts her eyes for a few seconds and then opens them again. The corner of her mouth twitches. "Condition accepted. I'm hiring you for another season so you keep me on my toes. After that, I'll probably ditch you for somebody younger." She glances in the air. "Nick?"

Nick steps out of the dark where he's been standing, unseen. My whole stomach squeezes shut. "Yes, Aunty Yuka?" he says with a cheeky grin.

"Call me *that* again and you can collect your P45."

"Yes, Aunty Yuka?"

Yuka sighs. "Get your own taxi home, Nicholas. Like your father, you're far too irritating to sit with." And she turns around again and abruptly stalks out of the room.

I giggle slightly, feeling about six years old, and then turn back round to introduce Nick to the people I love most in the world. Except I can't.

Because they've all sugar cookied off.

74

"Well," I say after an embarrassed silence. There's still a door swinging, and if I listen *very* hard, I can hear the distant sound of my loved ones betraying me. "Everyone was here a minute ago." I cough a couple of times.

"*I'm* still here," Wilbur points out, standing up slowly and putting his top hat back on. "And wouldn't you know it, my little Chuckle-bum, Nick is here too. What a *coincidence*."

My cheeks are bright pink and when I glance at Nick, I notice with a spark of surprise that his cheeks are starting to… It must be a trick of the light. It's very dark in here.

"Well," I say, squeezing out the most unnatural laugh I've ever heard. "I guess we do work for the same person."

"And why is that, do you think?" Wilbur shifts his pose so that his chin's on his hand, like Rodin's *The Thinker* statue. "Nick? Any idea?"

Nick coughs too. "Nope. No idea at all."

Wilbur gives him a stern look. "So what was the point in doing all that Jane Austen stuff if she doesn't know about it, Poodle-bottom?"

The blush drains out of my body so quickly my head feels like it might float away. "W-what?" I manage to stammer.

"Nothing." Nick glares at Wilbur. "Have you been sniffing glitter again?"

"Harriet, my Baby-baby Panda," Wilbur says, rolling his eyes and sticking his tongue out at Nick. "*I* didn't discover you, honey, Nick did. Yuka recruited him to find the female face for the collection and then you fell into that hat stall... And the rest, as they say, is geography."

"History," I correct automatically.

"Yes," Wilbur agrees gravely. "His story indeed. *Nick* pointed you out to me, *Nick* gave your photos to Yuka and *Nick* said you'd be perfect for the campaign in Russia. With – as it just so happened – *him*."

I can't really breathe any more. Nick is the reason I'm here?

"But the table..." I say in confusion. "The pavement..."

"The table was a coincidence," Nick sighs, visibly

giving up. "You just happened to crawl under there. How was I to know you'd dive under it? Normal people don't do that and wannabe models definitely don't." He laughs. "And the pavement… I came to get you. I knew you'd freak out."

"But…" My head still feels like a helium balloon. "*Why?*"

Nick looks blank. "Because you always freak out."

I shake my head. My voice feels like I've swallowed it. "I mean, why do you care if I freak out?"

There's a long silence.

"Well," Wilbur finally bursts, "I can take a shot in the dark, if you want."

"*Seriously*," Nick snaps, making his fingers into a gun shape. "I'm going to take a shot in the dark in a minute and it *will make contact*."

Wilbur looks charmed. "Isn't he adorable?" he says fondly. "My duty as Fairy Godmother is complete, anyhoo, and I believe it's time to spread my magic dust elsewhere. So many pumpkins after all; so little time." And Wilbur makes a few skipping steps backwards, takes a little bow and disappears with a dramatic flourish behind the door.

I'm going to pretend – simply for the sake of this moment – that I can't hear whispering on the other side of it.

There's a long silence. "I like you," Nick says finally. He's still speaking slowly, but the laziness that is always there seems to have disappeared. My whole body feels like it has a light bulb in it.

He likes me?

Lion Boy likes me?

"But… *Why?*" I manage to stutter.

Nick shrugs. "You're different."

I frown at him. "Good different or bad different?"

He grins. "Good," he says. "And bad. But even the bad bits are good different and they always make me laugh."

"That makes no rational sense at all," I tell him, crossing my arms. "There are 6,840,507,003 different people in the world. You clearly just haven't met that many."

"I've met enough," he says, twinkling at me and taking a step forward. His cheeks have gone pink now as well. I didn't know it could happen to boys.

A human heart is supposed to beat between sixty and ninety times a minute, while resting. A hedgehog's heart beats up to 300 times a minute when standing still. Honestly, I think I might be turning into a hedgehog.

Oh, God. Is he going to kiss me? It's my first kiss. My

first... *anything*.

I haven't brushed my teeth for hours and hours.

"Are you sure you don't want to meet a few more before—" I start and then I hear the door behind me open.

"Harriet? It's Toby." I turn round and only his fluffy head is visible. "I just want to reassure you that I am fine with this development. Fifty-three per cent of all marriages in the UK end in divorce and so statistics are actually on my side."

"Shut up, Toby," Nat says and I see a hand reach round and yank Toby back behind the door. Then the hand reappears, gives me a thumbs up and disappears again.

I look at Nick and clear my throat. I'm not a hedgehog any more. I'm a rabbit: 325 beats per minute.

Nick takes another step.

Now I'm a mouse: 500 beats a minute.

Another step.

A hummingbird: 1,260 beats.

And as he leans forward, all I can think is the following realisation: *nobody really metamorphoses*. Cinderella is always Cinderella, just in a nicer dress. The Ugly Duckling was always a swan, just a smaller version. And I bet the tadpole and the caterpillar still feel the same, even when they're jumping and flying, swimming and floating.

Just like I am now.

And in the fraction of time before Nick kisses me and every other thought in my head explodes, I realise: I didn't need to transform after all.

My name is Harriet Manners and I am a geek.

And maybe that's not so bad after all.

Acknowledgements

Thanks to Dad – a constant source of inspiration, encouragement and laughter – and Mum, for "doing the voices" at bedtime. Thanks to my little sister, Tara, for a lifetime of believing I'm better than I am; to Grandma and Grandad, for their never-ending wisdom and support and supplies of Jaffa Cakes; to Aunty Judith, who read the first few chapters and gave me the confidence to keep going. Thanks also to Hel, for reminding me to "write what I know". It shortened the process significantly.

Thanks to my agent, Kate Shaw, who rescued Harriet and has fought patiently and valiantly for both of us ever since; to Pippa Le Quesne, a wise guiding hand not unlike a literary Gandalf; to Lizzie Clifford, the most brilliant and sensitive editor a writer could ask for. Thanks also to the entire team at HarperCollins, for embracing geeks so warmly and wholeheartedly.

Finally, there is one person without whom this book would not exist: my very own "Alexa". You gave me a reason to write *Geek Girl*, and I will always be grateful.

Thank you. x

Read on for a sneak peek of . . .

1

My name is Harriet Manners, and I am a model.

I know I'm a model because:

1. It's Monday morning, and I'm wearing a gold tutu, a gold jacket, gold ballet pumps and gold earrings. My face is painted gold, and a long piece of gold wire has been wrapped around my head. This is not how I normally dress on Mondays.

2. I have a bodyguard. The earrings cost so much I'm not allowed to go to the toilet without a large man checking my earlobes afterwards to make sure I haven't accidentally flushed them.

3. I haven't been allowed to smile for two hours.

4. Every time I take a bite of doughnut to keep my strength up everybody breathes in sharply

as if I've just bent down and given the floor a quick lick.

5. There's a large camera pointing at my face, and the man behind it keeps saying, "Oi, model," and clicking his fingers at me.

There are other clues – I'm pouting slightly, and making tiny movements every couple of seconds like a robot – but they're not necessarily conclusive. That's exactly how my father dances when a car advert comes on TV.

Anyway, the final reason I know I'm a model is:

6. I have become a creature of grace, elegance and style.

In fact, you could say I've really grown up since you last saw me.

Some glittering reviews for the GEEK GIRL books:

"Loved *Geek Girl*. Wise, funny and true, with a proper nerd heroine you're laughing with as much as at. Almost"
James Henry, writer of Smack the Pony and Green Wing

"I would highly recommend *Geek Girl* to anyone who likes a good laugh and enjoys a one-of-a-kind story"
Mia, Guardian Children's Books website

"Smart, sassy and very funny"
Bookseller

"Brilliantly funny and fresh . . . A feel-good satisfying gem"
Books for Keeps

"There's laughter and tears in this hilarious roller-coaster story"
Julia Eccleshare, Sun

"Touching, true, and always very funny... beneath the shiny surface is a heart of solid gold"
Andrea Reece, Lovereading4kids

"I love the zany and warm-hearted way that Holly Smale writes"
Eloise Percy-Davis, age 12, Lovereading4kids

GEEK GIRL

MODEL MISFIT

HOLLY SMALE

HarperCollins *Children's Books*

For my sister, Tara.
In calm or stormy weather.

GEEK GIRL

MODEL MISFIT

Photograph © Georgina Bolton King

Holly Smale is the author of *Geek Girl* and *Model Misfit*. Clumsy, a bit geeky and somewhat shy, she spent the majority of her teenage years hiding in the changing-room toilets. She was unexpectedly spotted by a top London modelling agency at the age of fifteen and spent the following two years falling over on catwalks, going bright red and breaking things she couldn't afford to replace. By the time Holly had graduated from Bristol University with a BA in English Literature and an MA in Shakespeare she had given up modelling and set herself on the path to becoming a writer. Between then and now she also spent two years living in Japan. Holly is currently writing the third book in the *Geek Girl* series.

Photograph © Georgina Bolton King

Holly Smale is the author of *Geek Girl*, *Model Misfit* and *Picture Perfect*. She was unexpectedly spotted by a top London modelling agency at the age of fifteen and spent the following two years falling over on catwalks, going bright red and breaking things she couldn't afford to replace. By the time Holly had graduated from Bristol University with a BA in English Literature and an MA in Shakespeare she had given up modelling and set herself on the path to becoming a writer.

Geek Girl was the no.1 bestselling young-adult fiction title in the UK in 2013. It was shortlisted for several major awards including the Roald Dahl Funny Prize and the Branford Boase Award, nominated for the Queen of Teen Award and won the Teen and Young Adult category of the Waterstones Children's Book Prize. Holly is currently writing the fifth book in the *Geek Girl* series – *Head Over Heels*.

www.facebook.com/geekgirlseries

For Mum. Who has given me so many stories.

GEEK GIRL

ALL THAT GLITTERS

HOLLY SMALE

HarperCollins *Children's Books*

First published in Great Britain by HarperCollins *Children's Books* 2015
This paperback edition first published in Great Britain by
HarperCollins *Children's Books* in 2015
HarperCollins *Children's Books* is a division of HarperCollins*Publishers* Ltd,
HarperCollins Publishers
1 London Bridge Street
London SE1 9GF

The HarperCollins *Children's Books* website address is: www.harpercollins.co.uk

5

ISBN 978-0-00-757461-2

Printed and bound in England by Clays Ltd, St Ives plc

glitter [glit-er] verb, noun

1 To sparkle with reflected light

2 To make a brilliant show

3 To be decorated or enhanced by glamour

4 Tiny pieces of shiny ornamentation.

ORIGIN from the Old English *glitenian:* 'To shine; to be distinguished'

1

My name is Harriet Manners, and I am a genius.

I know I'm a genius because I've just looked up the symptoms on the internet and I appear to have almost all of them.

Sociological studies have shown that the hallmarks of extraordinary intelligence include enjoying pointless pursuits, an unusual memory for things nobody else finds interesting and total social ineptitude.

I don't want to sound big-headed, but last night I alphabetised every soup can in the kitchen, taught myself to pick up pencils with my toes and learnt that chickens can see daylight forty-five minutes before humans can.

And people don't tend to like me very much.

So I think I've pretty much nailed this.

Other symptoms of genius I recognise include:

1. *Difficulty sleeping*
2. *Random temper tantrums for no reason at all*

3. Messiness

4. General strangeness.

"I'm confused," my father said when I triumphantly showed him my ticked-off list. "Aren't they also the symptoms of being a sixteen-year-old girl?"

"Or a baby," my stepmother added, peering over at the list. "Your sister also appears to fit the list."

Which just goes to show why so many of the intellectual elite are misunderstood. Even our own *parents* don't recognise our brilliance.

Anyway, as the biggest sign of a high IQ is asking lots of questions and I got to the page by googling…

Am I a genius?

…I'm feeling pretty optimistic.

Which is good, because this morning is my first day back at school so I'm going to need all the extra brain-power I can get.

That's right, I am now an official sixth former.

By my calculations I have spent exactly eleven years of my life at school so far: 2,145 taught days, or approximately 17,160 hours (not including homework or the free tests I downloaded to take on holiday).

In short, I have invested *over a million minutes in education* in preparation for this precise moment. The day when all my carefully collected knowledge will be valued and appreciated, instead of just irritating people.

Finally, school is getting serious.

Gone are the homework-haters and eye-rollers, and – thanks to an influx of new students from other schools – in their place are people who really *want* to learn. People desperate to know that gerbils can smell adrenaline and a caterpillar has twelve eyes, or that there's enough carbon in your body to make 900 pencils.

People just like me.

And I couldn't be more excited.

As of today, I have five A levels to study, two universities to introduce myself to early and a bright career in palaeontology to begin pursuing in earnest. I have statistics to analyse and frogs to dissect and thigh exercises to start so I don't get cramp when I'm brushing soil away from dinosaur fossils in the not-so-distant future.

I have brand-new, like-minded friends to make.

It might be the same school with a lot of the same people, but things are about to change. After eleven years of scraping insults off my belongings and retrieving my shoes from the cisterns of toilets, this is my chance to

start all over again. A new beginning.

A chance to shine.

This time, everything will be different.

Luckily, one of the really *great* things about being a genius is that it's easy to multitask.

So this morning I decide to make the most of it.

I learn that there are forty different muscles in a bird wing while I'm getting out of bed.

I discover that a sea urchin can walk on its teeth while I'm combing my hair, and that parasites make up 0.01 per cent of our body weight while I'm brushing my teeth.

Clothes, socks and shoes are all picked out and donned as I fully absorb the fact that a snake smells with its tongue and hears with its jaw. I study the names of British kings and queens as I run down the stairs, and by the time I reach the kitchen I'm on to Secret Service code names (Prince Charles is "Unicorn", which is a shame because I was hoping one day they'd use that one for me).

"Did you know," I say as I lean down to kiss Tabitha on her little round cheek, "that the average person will eat 500 chickens and 13,000 eggs in a lifetime?"

My baby sister clearly didn't, because she gurgles happily at this new and unprecedented information. Then

I reach over her fluffy head to grab a hard-boiled version of the latter listed from the table.

"Harriet," my stepmother says.

"And we'll each eat thirty-six pigs," I continue as I start peeling the egg with one hand. "And thirty-six sheep."

"Harriet."

"And eight cows."

"Harriet."

"And 10,000 chocolate bars." I pause with the egg halfway to my mouth. "I think I may have eaten my rations for that already, though. Maybe I should become a vegetarian to balance it back out."

A hand lands on my arm.

"Good morning, Annabel. How did you sleep? I'm fine, thank you. Isn't it a beautiful day today? Thanks for making me breakfast, even though I am now leaving bits of shell all over the kitchen floor for you to clean up."

I blink at my stepmother a few times, then at Dad. I've lived with Annabel since I was five, yet sometimes she is still a total mystery to me.

"Why is Annabel talking to herself?"

"She's an alien unsuccessfully trying to fit in with the rest of the human race," Dad says knowingly, dipping a bit of toast in egg yolk and then dripping it on the table. "Is there anything in your book to help us figure out what

she wants with us poor earthlings before she sucks our brains out with her tentacles?"

I start flicking eagerly through the chunky tome in my hand. There are 729 pages and I'm only 13/20ths of the way through, so there's almost definitely some kind of precedent.

Or at the very least something interesting about spaceships.

"Sadly, all signs suggest that your brain is already gone, Richard," Annabel says grimly. "So I'm probably going to starve."

Then she pulls a chair out and gestures at it.

"Put your fact book down, Harriet, and have some breakfast. I start back at work tomorrow morning and none of us have heard a sensible word out of you for the last twenty-four hours."

I don't know what my stepmother is talking about. Every single sentence I've said has been scientifically and historically accurate. There's a bibliography proving it in the back.

I shove a piece of toast into my mouth.

"Can't," I say through a spray of buttered carbohydrates. "No time. Things to learn, places to go, kindred spirits to meet."

Quickly, I stomp into the hallway and grab my satchel

from the corner whilst simultaneously discovering that in 1830, King Louis XIX ruled France for just twenty minutes.

"Look how awesome she is," Dad says proudly as I open the front door. "That's my daughter, Annabel. My genetics, right there. Harriet Manners: model and style icon. Fashion legend. Sartorial maverick extraordinaire."

I stick one ear of my headphones in.

"Harriet," Annabel says. "Hang on a second. Where are you going?"

I'm not entirely sure how I'll use the Louis XIX information, by the way. Not everything I read is potentially useful or relevant, even to me.

"School!" I put the other ear in. Tchaikovsky's *Swan Lake* starts blaring out at full volume. "See you this evening!"

And my first day as a proper sixth former begins.

2

So, I've done a little studying on the art of making new friends and I'm happy to report that there appear to be a few basic rules for us all to follow.

I have boiled it down to: find things in common, smile and laugh lots (this indicates a sunny and welcoming personality), ask questions, remember details and never wear the same outfit as them without asking first.

Which sounds deceptively easy.

Over the last sixteen years I've successfully made just four friends: my stalker classmate, Toby Pilgrim; my dog, Hugo; a Japanese model called Rin (who would happily befriend a sausage); and my Best Friend Nat, who I met when I was five and literally couldn't have less in common with if I tried.

So I think it's fair to say I need all the advice I can get.

The way I see it, the fact book in my hand isn't just fascinating trivia, relevant to the trials and tribulations of daily living (which it also is). It's a *bridge* between me and

other people. With these scientifically proven nuggets of information, I'll be able to find things in common with *everyone*.

Oh, you like tennis? Well, did you know that the longest ever match lasted eleven hours? You're a big fan of keeping fit? The most push-ups ever performed in one day was 46,001!

Have a cat? Cats kill more than 275 million creatures a year in the UK alone!

It doesn't matter whether it's film or sport or songs or animals or a fondness for fizzy drinks (they dissolve teeth!): somehow, I'll be able to find a connection. A link between me and them. Something to pull us together.

All friendship requires is focus and dedication.

And a little bit of knowledge.

I learn all about crocodiles as I wander down the road to school and past the bench where Nat usually meets me (except now she's at fashion college on the other side of town).

Caterpillars get a brief look-over as I quickly glance around for Toby – there's no sign of him – and pull my phone out of my pocket to check for texts from my modelling agent, Stephanie (as per usual, absolutely zero – my fashion career appears to have fallen into

some kind of coma).

US presidents fill in the gap as I clumsily open and walk through the school gates.

The world's largest lakes occupy my opening of the stiff front door and stroll down the silent corridor into my empty classroom.

Then I take a seat, turn to a page about the London Underground, and wait.

I've specifically chosen to get to school early today so I have plenty of time to adjust before my new form arrives. Thanks to Dad's job at the time, I was living in America for the first few weeks of term – being tortured by a tutor who turned out to be a fake, and fainting on fairground fashion shoots – so I really need the extra time. This way I can acclimatise to my new environment, cram some last-minute knowledge in and maybe stop my stomach from rolling over and over like a sick guppy while I'm at it.

Nervously, I clutch my book as tightly as I can.

Focus, Harriet.

The London Underground is the world's first underground transport system. It has a network of 402 kilometres, carries 1,265 billion people a year and is actually more overground than it is undergr—

"Harriet Manners?"

I swallow. This is it. This is where my new beginning

starts. *Be cool, Harriet. Be casual. Be as full of relevant yet breezy information as physically possible.*

With a deep breath, I plaster on my biggest and friendliest smile and put my book down.

"Good morning," I say in my brightest voice. "It's super nice to meet y—"

Then I stop.

Because standing in front of me is a group of what appear to be fully grown adults, holding clipboards and pens.

And every single one of them is staring at me.

3

For the first few seconds, I assume my classmates have just aged quite a lot over the summer holidays.

That's how weird teachers look in casual clothes.

Then – like the Magic Eye picture of a galloping horse Dad has stuck in the garage – strange colours and shapes slowly start to make sense.

Mr Collins from biology in high-waisted jeans and a green polo-neck jumper. Drama teacher Miss Hammond in a beige jumper, tie-dye pink skirt and woolly lilac socks. Receptionist Mrs O'Connor – devoured by an enormous yellow jumper that says DEFINE 'NORMAL'!!! – and my English teacher Mr Bott in his standard black suit, white shirt and thin black tie, like a magician on his way to a funeral.

I blink as the entire school staff gradually crowds in from the corridor so they can stare at me curiously, the way little children gather around a pink-bottomed rhesus monkey at the zoo.

Any minute now, somebody's going to throw me a banana and ask me to dance.

You know what?

I'm so confused right now, I might just go ahead and do it.

Finally Mr Bott takes his pen out of his mouth. "Would you like to explain what you're doing here, Miss Manners?"

"Umm." I look back at my book in bewilderment. "I'm studying, sir."

"That's as maybe. But the school is closed for teacher training today. You're not supposed to be here."

And – just like that – I suddenly see my morning all over again. The empty roads. The blank phone. The closed school gates. The wedged-shut front door, silent corridors and empty seats.

The fact that Toby wasn't following three steps behind me for the first time in known history.

Annabel's confusion as I left the house.

Oh my God.

There's a special kind of reef fish called the *Enneapterygius pusillus* that glows with a bright red light in order to communicate with the fish around it. From the heat in my cheeks right now, it feels like I'm attempting it too.

Every other student on the planet is trying to get out of school. I'm the only one who accidentally breaks *in*.

I stand up quickly. *Think, Harriet.*

"I was just, umm..." *What?* "Bringing a gift for you all. For the... errr... teachers. To wish you luck. With... the training."

Then I hold out the stupid *Big Book of Trivia for the Loo* that got me into this mess in the first place. In fairness to the authors, the warning was in the title. I probably should have left it there.

Miss Hammond beams and takes it off me. "That's so sweet of you, Harriet! How thoughtful! And *what* a spectacular outfit you've chosen for today," she adds brightly. "You've really harnessed your inner rainbow."

I look down and my cheeks promptly go supernova.

Thanks to getting dressed while reading, I'm apparently wearing a yellow T-shirt, a red jumper featuring a Christmas pudding – in October – a pair of pink pyjama bottoms with blue sheep all over them and the bright purple knee socks Nat bought me "as a joke", slouched down around my ankles.

On one foot is a green trainer.

On the other is a blue one.

My daughter. Model and style icon. Fashion legend. Sartorial maverick extraordinaire.

Maybe I'm not such a genius after all.

4

Anyway.

While I'm stuffing my mismatched shoes in my satchel and shuffling home in my not-a-whole-lot-better socks, I may as well update you on what's been happening since I returned from New York, right?

That's what you want to know.

Exactly what I've been doing with myself since I split up with Nick Hidaka – Lion Boy, ex-supermodel and love of my life – on Brooklyn Bridge just over three weeks ago, and flew home without him.

So here it is:

Nothing.

Not literally, obviously, or I'd be dead.

Over the last three weeks I have breathed approximately 466,662 times and processed 4,200 litres of blood with my kidneys. I have produced thirty-seven litres of saliva

and 9,450 litres of carbon dioxide.

I've had eighteen showers, four baths, brushed my teeth forty-two times, eaten sixty-seven meals and consumed more chocolate bars than I can be bothered to count (and that's really saying something).

But that's about it.

Other than basic survival – and packing up the house in Greenway while we waited two weeks for our flight back to England – almost the only thing I've done voluntarily is read. With my curtains shut and my bedroom door closed, I've devoured words like never before: buried myself in books and submerged myself in stories.

I've read during breakfast and lunch and dinner; until the sun's come up and gone down and come up again.

And not just fact books.

I've fought dragons, attended balls and chased a whale. I've won wars, lost court cases, travelled India, ridden broomsticks and stranded myself on numerous islands.

I've died a dozen times.

Because here's the thing about a book: when you pick up a story, you put down your own.

For a few precious moments, you become somebody else. Their memories become your memories; your thoughts turn into theirs. Until, page by page, line by line,

you disappear completely.

So until today – until my new beginning – that's exactly what I've done.

Because I thought maybe if I could just bury myself deep enough, for long enough, I could shut the world out and myself out with it.

And then I wouldn't have to think about how the last time I saw Nick is the last time I'll see him, and the last time I kissed him is the last time I'll kiss him. About how life keeps going on as it always has.

Or how my heart can beat 100,000 times a day.

Even when it's broken.

5

Unfortunately, vanishing has its side effects.

And – as I quietly turn on to the path leading back up to my house – I can see two of them: standing on my front door step.

Without a sound, I quickly dive into a nearby bush.

Maybe there are advantages to walking around in your bare socks after all.

"Are you *sure*?" Nat is saying, shifting from one foot to the other. Her dark hair is curly, and hanging down her back like well-behaved snakes. "You're *certain* Harriet's not here?"

"I'm definite," Annabel confirms gently. "Unless she's scaled the outside wall and re-entered through her bedroom window, but given Harriet's inherent fear of PE it seems unlikely."

That's putting it mildly. Frankly, there's more chance of me growing wings and flying back in.

"It's actually easier than it looks," Toby says cheerfully.

Even from a few metres behind I can read the orange letters on the back of his T-shirt: VOTED MOST LIKELY TO TRAVEL BACK IN TIME, CLASS OF 2057.

"If you take the first flowerpot on the left there's a little toe-hole in the wall just above it, and then you can use the ivy trellis as leverage the rest of the way." He pauses. "You should probably reassess your exterior plant framework, Mrs Manners. It's not very security-conscious."

The corner of Annabel's mouth twitches. "Oh, I'd imagine we will now."

"If you want, next time I'm up there I'll stick a little warning note on the outside of the window telling all other stalkers to go away."

My stepmother laughs because she obviously assumes that Toby is joking.

I, however, know better.

I am literally never opening my bedroom curtains again.

"*Focus*, Pilgrim," Nat says crossly, leaning to the side and poking his arm. "What kind of rubbish stalker are you, anyway? You don't even know where Harriet *is*."

"In fairness, my concentration has been a little distracted with an exorbitant level of homework, and also the TARDIS I've been building in my garden."

Toby holds out bright blue fingers as evidence.

Nat stares at him for a few seconds in disgust. "What *is* your problem?"

"I'm glad you asked," Toby says happily. "I'm struggling to make it look as if it has truly travelled through time and space. Any suggestions?"

There's a silence, then my best friend sighs and turns back to Annabel. "I haven't seen or heard from Harriet *all weekend*. She's not picking up calls, she's not answering texts and she didn't remind me seven times about the parrot documentary on telly. I really need to talk to her."

"She's just jet-lagged, sweetheart. It takes a little while to settle back into a new time zone, that's all."

"And you don't know where I can find her?"

There's a tiny pause. "I don't, I'm sorry."

"Right." Nat's shoulders slump slightly. "Well." She looks sharply up at my bedroom window, and then kicks the front doorstep a couple of times. We've been home six days and my best friend is not an idiot: we're five hours ahead of New York, not in a different solar system. "I have to go to college. Will you tell her I called again?"

"Of course." Annabel nods and looks at Toby. "And I'll tell her you popped by too."

"You don't need to," he says proudly. "She'll know. I've left one of my new calling cards." He points to the

wall and there's a little round, bright green dot stuck there. "It says TPWH™, which stands for Toby Pilgrim Was Here, Trademarked."

"I'm impressed," Annabel smiles. "Very organised and efficient."

Literally nothing fazes her. She's like Gandalf but less beardy.

Nat glances at my bedroom window again.

She kicks the doorstep a few more times.

Then, with an audible exhalation, my best friend swirls round and stomps back down the garden path in bright silver shoes.

With my stalker trailing after her.

6

I watch Nat leave with a guilty twist of my stomach.

Then I wait as long as I can.

I am invisible. I am undetectable. I am a ninja of imperceptibility, as hidden as a leafy sea dragon, elaborately constructed to blend into my surroundings, and—

"You can come out now, Harriet."

Oh. So – maybe not.

Slowly, I creep out from inside the bush and brush dried mud and dead leaves off my pyjama bottoms.

"You know," Annabel says, gently removing a small spider from my eyebrow. Apparently I'm even more camouflaged than I intended to be. "I'm not enjoying all this subterfuge very much, Harriet. It's much more your father's style."

"I know," I say awkwardly. "Thanks for lying again."

In Greek and Roman mythology there's a three-headed dog called Cerberus who guards the entrance of the

underworld to prevent the dead from escaping and the living from entering.

For the last few days, that's exactly what my stepmother has been doing for me.

On cue, my phone beeps three times in quick succession:

When one door of happiness closes, another one opens! :) xx

A break-up is like a broken mirror. It is better to leave it broken than to hurt yourself trying to fix it! :) xx

If you walk away and they don't follow, keep walking. :) xx

And this is exactly why I'm avoiding Nat.

Ever since I returned from America, it's been like having my own personal therapist crossed with a woodpecker. What exactly happened? *Peck.* What did Nick say? *Peck.* Do I miss him? *Peck.* Was it definitely the right decision? *Peck peck.* Can't we make it work? Has he been in contact? How do I *feel*?

Peck peck peck peck until the tree falls over.

And it doesn't matter how many times I tell her I

don't want to talk about it, Nat has decided that we are heartbroken and she's committed to working through it.

Together.

Incessantly, over and over and over again.

Without a single moment's peace, and with the help of quite a lot of fridge magnets, motivational T-shirts and quotes off the internet.

Never mind picking the lock: my best friend is trying to smash me open with a sledgehammer.

I take a deep breath and type:

Very wise! Speak soon! :) x

Then I put my phone back in my pocket and glance desperately over Annabel's shoulder at the house. I've got the works of Terry Pratchett waiting on my bedside table. If I take two stairs at a time, I can be balanced on the back of four elephants and a giant turtle within thirty-five seconds.

I love Nat.

She's my best friend: the person who knows me inside and out, who can finish my sentences when I don't even know what it is I want to say yet. But – as a magnet might tell me – I can't start the next chapter of my life if I keep re-reading the old ones.

I just want a new story, that's all.

"Harriet?" Annabel says as I start racing desperately towards my next escape.

I turn round blankly. "Hmm?"

"You don't need to shut us all out, sweetheart. Me, your dad. Natalie. You can talk to us about it."

"Sure," I say, and then start heading back to my bedroom.

Because for the first time ever, that's exactly the problem.

Maybe I don't want to.

7

So, my plan for the next morning is as follows:

1. Try not to notice Toby crouched behind a nearby pot plant outside my house.

2. Or standing behind a tree.

3. Or lying on the grass, pretending to be part of the foliage.

4. Tell Toby that he may be my self-confessed stalker turned-comrade, but now we're sixth formers he really needs to find another hobby because his obsession with me is getting a bit embarrassing.

5. Walk to school, paying close attention to any sign that may say SCHOOL CLOSED FOR TRAINING on the way.

6. Make brand-new friends.

7. Have a brilliant and thoroughly educational day.

Admittedly, the last point on the list is a bit vague, but I'm leaving it up to the teachers.

That is what they're paid for, after all.

The way I see it, yesterday was just a dress rehearsal: one that went spectacularly badly. Statistically, a first impression is usually cemented in seven seconds (although obviously I've disappointed people far more quickly than that).

This time, I'm not taking any chances.

At 8am, I stand on the doorstep and double-check my carefully selected outfit. A quick study of the psychology of colours has established that white clothes make strangers think you're honest, yellow clothes make them think you're friendly and orange implies that you're a whole lot of spontaneous fun.

So I'm wearing a white jumper, orange leggings and yellow pumps. Hopefully this will silently represent an excellent personality before I've said a word.

It may even be powerful enough to make me appealing *after* I've said some too.

Then I roll my eyes at the enormous rustling purple

hydrangea to my right. "Come on, Tobes. We're friends now. Why don't you just walk to school *with* me instead of hiding in bushes?"

There's another rustle and a small squeak. Then Annabel's cat, Victor, struts out from behind the pot with a piercing expression that says: *I'm not going anywhere with you, weirdo.*

Flushing slightly as a neighbour gives me the kind of glance you give to people who talk to plants, I decide to go ahead and just start walking to school on my own.

"Tobes," I say with a small smile when I reach the tree at the bottom of my road, "you're not being very subtle. I can totally see you..."

A squirrel runs out.

"Toby..." I say as a jogger runs past.

"Tob—" I start again, but it's just a leaf skittering along the ground.

With growing confusion, I continue walking: past the bench Toby isn't crouching behind, in front of the lamp-post Toby isn't pretending to fix with a small screwdriver, past the old man with a big newspaper held up to his face.

"Sorry," I say after I've pulled it down and shouted "Ha! Gotcha!"

"Girls these days," the man snorts angrily, burying

himself in it again. Which is really unfair: I'm pretty sure I'd have done that if I was a boy too.

By the time I approach the road to school and – somewhat reassuringly – spot a group of students in school uniform, I'm starting to feel a little off-centre. I hadn't realised quite how much of my day is constructed around various degrees of pretending to be irritated with Toby.

Finally, I spot him: crouched on the floor next to the front school gates in a pale brown T-shirt with little flecks all over it. He's obviously pretending to be a boulder. Or a huge tortoise. Or something else that would never, ever be found outside a British school in a million years.

"Toby," I say with a huge wave of relief. "There you are. I really don't think you need to—"

"Hello, Harriet!" he says, redoing a shoe and standing up. His pale sideburns are fluffy and sticking out, and I realise he must have grown another four centimetres over the summer: he's starting to look like a lightning bolt. "Did you know that Velcro was inspired by the tiny hooks on a burr that stuck to the inventor's dog? I prefer it to laces, even if evidence of string *does* date back 28,000 years."

I beam at him.

That is *exactly* what I needed to make me feel

grounded and secure this morning. A fascinating, shoe-based historical fact, guest-featuring dogs.

"That's interesting, becau—" I start enthusiastically, but I don't get any further because Toby sticks two thumbs up and starts powering towards the school gates, slightly-too-short trousers flapping around his ankles.

"See you later, Harriet!" he calls over his shoulder.

"But," I stutter in amazement, "w-wait, Toby. Don't we have class together? Shouldn't we... go in at the same time?"

Or – you know – with him ten paces behind me.

It's kind of a tradition.

"We're in different forms now, Harriet!" Toby says cheerfully. "Plus I have a super important project to get on with before class starts. Have a great day!"

And my stalker disappears into school.

Leaving me following ten paces behind him.

8

It's amazing what a difference a day can make.

Or – you know.

An open and functioning school you don't have to break into.

As I push through the glass sixth-form doors, I can feel a terrified, nervous hopping sensation starting at the bottom of my stomach. It takes fifty hours for a snake to fully digest a frog, and for part of that time the frog is still alive. Given the feeling in my stomach, I'm starting to wonder if I've accidentally swallowed one too.

Everything has changed.

There is now noise and chaos everywhere. Classrooms and corridors are filled with people: giggling, laughing, shouting, singing. Chair legs are being scraped on the floor, various items are flying through the air – rubbers, crumpled-up notes, packets of crisps – and there's a faint smell of board-marker and furniture polish that's halfway between a cleaning cupboard and a sofa shop.

People I don't recognise are stomping up and down the stairs proprietorially, and students I do know have transformed completely. Braces are off, long hair has been chopped, short hair grown and extended. Acne has erupted or disappeared. A few tentative moustaches have sprouted like shadowy upper lip infections. Everything that was banned last term is scattered defiantly: heels, short skirts, piercings, lipsticks, shaved heads. All worn with pride and triumphant chins.

It's the same school, yet – somehow – not at all.

Sixth form has been open just four weeks and it already feels like everyone has made this world their own. Now it's my turn.

With another froggy stomach hop, I reach the door of my new classroom and stand outside on one foot for a few seconds, peeking through the window.

Then I anxiously pull out my phone.

Really wish you were here. Hx

I press SEND and wait a few seconds.

There's a beep.

Me too. Raid the vending machine for me. ;) Nat x

I smile – I was obviously going to do that anyway – and take a deep breath.

You can do this, Harriet. You are a goddess of insight and possibilities; a warrior of chance and fate. A goldfish of optimism and opportunity.

Oh God. My brain is shutting down already.

Then, with all the courage I can muster, I hold my breath, square my shoulders and lift my chin high.

And push into my brand-new world.

9

The really great thing about having the head of drama as my new form teacher this year is – thanks to my role in last year's production of *Hamlet* – I already know her.

The not so great thing?

She already knows me.

"Harriet Manners!" Miss Hammond looks up from her desk so enthusiastically that the beaded fringe on her tie-dye scarf gets caught on a pencil pot. "You've returned to us for the second time! How utterly wonderful!"

Oh, *sugar cookies.* I really hope she's not going to bring out the book I gave her. I don't want my first introduction to the class to involve the word *loo.*

"*You guys,*" she continues chirpily, waving a hand around. There are so many bracelets, she sounds like an enormous Slinky. "For those who haven't had the pleasure of meeting her before, Harriet Manners has veritably *boomeranged* back after a glamorous adventure in Nooooo Yaawwwk!"

I flush a little bit harder.

"Apparently Americans eat more bananas than any other fruit," I blurt anxiously. "And twenty-five per cent of them think the sun orbits the earth."

Oh my God. What is wrong *with me?*

"Which isn't why I came back," I add quickly, the back of my neck starting to prickle. "I like bananas."

I like bananas.

Yup. There are over a million words in the English language, and I chose those three in that particular order to impress a group of strangers.

I am never reading a fact book again.

The students in the class murmur "Hey, Harriet" while they try to make sense of me too.

"Why don't you plop yourself down there?" Miss Hammond says, pointing to a free seat. "We're doing a team-building exercise first thing, so it's perfect timing! You're going to fit back in like a kitten in a straw basket full of other kittens. I can tell already."

Still blushing, I walk cautiously to the corner of the class and place my satchel on the floor. Then – trying not to notice the thirty-two eyes still following me – I take out my new folders: three colours with dividers for easier organisation.

Followed by my new school diary and a set of biros.

Five pencils, an eraser, three highlighters, glue, a hole punch, ruler and Post-its. A tape-dispenser and compass. A calculator and protractor.

A full, rainbow-hued box of felt-tip pens. A traditional fountain-pen.

With little ink-pot.

Finally, I add a couple of shiny blank notepads with pictures of dinosaurs all over the front.

What? I just really like being prepared, that's all.

When it's all laid out neatly and at perfect right angles on my desk I feel much calmer again, so I fold my hands tightly on my lap and survey the slowly expanding class with a growing sense of excitement.

I vaguely know some of them already.

The two leads from the play last year are on opposite sides of the classroom: Christopher (Hamlet), sullen and still wearing a black polo-neck, and pretty Raya (Ophelia, obviously) with a glossy black ponytail, camel-like eyelashes and permanently pouted lips. I also recognise Eric, the school football captain, now slightly pirate-like with a shaved head and a gold hoop earring, and my old classmate Robert, who has apparently developed an interest in hair gel – the front of his hair looks like if he ran fast with his head down he could probably kill somebody with it.

Two of Alexa's key minions – Liv and Ananya – are seated together at the back: one with pale skin and a bleached white top-knot, the other with dark skin and a large, black high-bun. They're wearing the same floral onesies in contrasting colours and are united by identical, intensely bored expressions.

But much *more* excitingly, there are also at least a handful of faces I don't recognise at all.

Which one of these is going to be my new kindred spirit?

The girl with pink glasses? She looks like she's on first-name terms with her optometrist too. The girl with neon purple hair and a rainbow-coloured nose ring? I'm a big fan of bright colours too. How about the boy with freckles and a red bag? I, too, have freckles and a—

OK, I think I might just be clutching at similarity straws now.

Finally, almost every chair but the one next to me is taken.

"Oh, *shoot a hamster*," Miss Hammond says, slapping her head lightly with her wrist. "What a twit I am! I left the register in the staffroom." She stands up and jingles a few times. "Back in two ticks, peeps."

And – in a whirlwind of orange and pink – our form teacher disappears into the corridor.

The room immediately starts bubbling with noise again, and I cautiously start staring hard at individuals and then giving them my brightest, friendliest smile. The kind that says *I can't wait to ask you questions and then remember the details!*

A few of them actually smile back.

You know what? I like sixth form already. People are glancing at me, but it doesn't feel hostile.

It feels curious; quizzical and interested.

I can feel my entire body starting to relax.

I was so right: this was *exactly* what I needed. A fresh start. A new beginning. The closure of an old page, and the opening of a new one. The unfolding of a different story.

Except it isn't.

Because, just as I'm congratulating myself on making such an excellent – albeit fruit-enthused – first impression, the classroom door opens again. And in walks the Captain Hook to my Peter Pan; the Voldemort to my Potter.

The Cruella De Vil to my hundred spotted puppies.

Alexa.

10

No.

11

No no no *no no no*.

12

NO NO NO NO NO NO NO NO NO NONONONONONONO NONONONONONONONONONONONONONONONO NONO.

13

If you yelled for one year, seven months and twenty-six days, you would produce enough sound energy to heat one cup of tea. Hook up my brain right now and I should be able to boil ten in three seconds flat.

This can't be happening. It *can't* be.

Alexa isn't doing any of the same subjects as me. She has a totally different schedule: English, History, Geography. I was *sure* she had a different form room. I rang and checked with Mrs O'Connor to confirm that I'd been moved to another class, just in case.

And emailed. Five times. With a supporting text.

I thought I was finally *free.*

With a flick of the grown-out blonde hair which Nat chopped off for being horrible to me nearly a year ago now, Alexa strolls into the room and looks at us through heavily lined eyes.

"*Hi,*" she says with a small cat-smile.

"How *are* you all today?"

She's the only person I know who can make a general greeting sound like a specific death threat.

"Lexi! Over here!" Ananya sits up straighter and sticks a hand in the air. "Thank God you're here: this class is *so boring.*"

"Ohwowowow," Liv squeaks, bopping up and down in her seat, "areyoukiddingLexiyoulook*amazing*todayIlove yourskirtI'vetotallygotonejustlikeitexceptit'sredanda differentlengthandshapebutit'sprettymuch*identical*."

When an elephant lies down it only needs to breathe four times a minute. Every time Liv gets excited, I can't help wondering if she has a similar lung capacity.

Alexa ignores them and swivels to look in my direction.

I'm not kidding: her entire face has just lit up. As if she's six, it's Christmas morning and I'm a solid gold bike somebody's left under the tree.

The frog in my stomach has suddenly gone very still.

"Do you mind if I take this seat?" she says, sashaying towards me in sharp-heeled black boots: the kind you can skewer somebody's soul with.

"Yes," I say as clearly as I can. "Immensely."

But apparently it's a rhetorical question, because Alexa kicks back and puts her feet on our desk, knocking my compass on to the floor.

I'm going to leave it there. I don't think drawing my bully's attention to a sharp metal object with a stabby point is the smartest possible decision at this precise moment.

"I'm *so* delighted you're finally back," she says flatly, picking one of my notepads up and staring at the T-Rex on the front with a wrinkled nose. "Overjoyed, in fact."

"Are you?" I say tightly.

"Totally." She's now fiddling with my ink pot. "School's so *dull* without somebody fun to play with."

Which would be quite sweet if we were five and she didn't mean the way a tiger plays with a three-legged goat or a cat plays with a mouse just before she rips it apart.

Skeletal muscle consists of 650 striated layers connected to bones, and I'm so cold and rigid now every one of my fibres feels like it's made out of stainless steel.

This is a disaster.

Actually, no: it's a catastrophe; a cataclysm; utter ruination. A meteorite could be about to obliterate England, and it would still be second on the Worst Things That Could Possibly Happen Today list.

There's no *way* I can make new friends and start again with Alexa snapping at my heels. She's going to make

everybody hate me before I even get a chance.

Again.

"And I just love the look you're going for today," she adds in a voice so loud it could blister paint. "Ducks are so hot right now."

Ducks? I look down in confusion at my white jumper, orange leggings and yellow shoes and then flush bright red. She's right: I look exactly like a member of the Anatidae family.

That is *not* the sophisticated first impression I wanted to give at all.

"Hey, you guys," Alexa continues at the top of her voice, gesticulating with one of my pencils. Everybody in the class is now staring at us in silence. "For those of you who haven't met Harriet Manners, we've known each other a really long time, haven't we?" The frog in my stomach is now totally frozen. *No. No no no no.* "A really, really long time. Eleven years, in fact."

"Alexa—"

"Oh, they're just going to *love* our childhood memories, Harriet. They're *adorable.* Do you remember when we were five and you peed yourself on the story-time carpet and they had to buy a whole library of new books?"

"OMG!" Ananya laughs from behind me. "I remember

that, Lexi! That was *hilaire*."

"*So gross*," Liv squeaks. "Like, *ewwww*."

I feel sick. "It was *milk* and I squeezed my carton too hard."

"What about the time you took your skirt off during Year Four Cinderella and ran around the stage in your knickers?"

Oh God. Oh God oh God oh God –

"*The button fell off and I didn't notice*."

"And goodness, everybody," Alexa says, taking a nice big breath while she unsheathes her claws and gets ready to rip my metaphorical intestines out. "Just *wait* until you hear about the time that Harriet Manners—"

The door smacks open.

14

"Guys!" Miss Hammond breezes into the room, carrying roughly twenty-five toilet rolls. "I just found these and had the *best* idea for our team-building game. This is going to be so much fun and—"

She abruptly stops and peers over the top of them. As if she's protected by the world's softest, strongest, most absorbable wall.

"Alexa Roberts?"

"Hey, miss! Wow, is your tummy feeling OK? Are they all for you?"

Miss Hammond is slowly changing colour.

Six months ago, Alexa single-handedly attempted to destroy *Hamlet* before getting detention every day for a month. From the energy crackling between them now, it looks like neither of them has forgotten about it.

"What are you doing in here?" Miss Hammond says sharply, dumping all the rolls on the desk so hard that three bounce straight on to the floor. "This is Form A.

You're in Form C, with Mr White."

"*Am* I?" Alexa stands up and flicks her hair. "Oh no. I must have got lost on my way there, somehow. Or maybe I was just *drawn* here by some invisible and irrepressible force."

She smiles and I can't help thinking that if Alexa put this much obsessive compulsive behaviour into her schoolwork she'd have graduated school by now. And university. And possibly obtained some kind of PhD.

"Out," Miss Hammond snaps, pointing at the corridor. "Now."

"But miss..."

"*Now.*"

"I just think..."

"*Immediately*."

"*Fine*." My nemesis stalks towards the corridor, and then turns round. "But I think it's really important that you all know about the time that Harriet once—"

"Nobody cares, Alexandra," Miss Hammond snaps, slapping her hands on her desk. "And if you come near this room again, you're suspended, effective immediately. Do I make myself clear?"

"But—"

"No buts. *Scoot*."

Miss Hammond crosses the classroom quickly, slams

the door on Alexa and pulls down the blind so we can't see her. Then she turns back to a stunned, silent class and smooths down her skirt.

Like a warrior in 100% organic cotton.

"Right," she says softly, and her voice is all sunshine and kittens in baskets again. "Grab a toilet roll each, guys, and let's get out on the playing field, build teams and really *connect.*"

I've never brought an apple in for a teacher before, but – as almost the entire class smile at me sympathetically and start grabbing their bags – I think I might just do that.

I'm getting my fresh start after all.

15

So, here are some facts about toilet roll:

1. It was invented by the Chinese in 600 AD.
2. Britons use 110 rolls each a year, which is the equivalent of six miles of tissue.
3. 72% of people hang toilet paper with the first sheet going *over* the roll.
4. The US military used toilet paper to camouflage their tanks in Saudi Arabia during the Desert Storm war.
5. Novelty paper includes: glow-in-the-dark, money, Word of the Day and Sudoku.

How do I know this?

Let's just say a few months ago I had a bad cold combined with a long car journey with Toby that I've never fully recovered from. I've sworn not to blow my nose anywhere near him again.

Miss Hammond appears to be even more excited than Toby about its possibilities.

She giddily ushers all of us outside: past the enormous tug-of-war being conducted by Mrs Baker, beyond a taciturn Mr Bott and small groups constructing tables out of newspaper, far away from Mr White and rings of students passing balloons between their knees and laughing.

(Every couple of minutes there's a loud BANG that I suspect is not unrelated to Alexa.)

"Right," Miss Hammond says cheerfully, planting a stick in the ground with a stripy pink sock taped to the end. "We had a *very* enlightening teacher training session yesterday, didn't we, Harriet?"

The whole class turns to look at me.

Excellent. Now I look like an undercover teacher trainer.

"And we were reminded of how we are all part of the *same beautiful puzzle*. Held together by the invisible *threads of harmony and happiness.*" She pauses. "Please stop hitting Robert with the roll of tissue, Eric."

"But we're just bonding, miss," Eric objects, doing it

again. "Our thread of happiness depends on it."

"Lovely! That's the spirit!" She beams at us all and then gestures at a blonde girl to take her roll off the top of her head. "So we're going to play a little game to help us form lifelong *connections.* After all, there's no *me* in team!"

"Yes, there is," Christopher objects. "It is literally right there."

"And meat."

"Mate." "Meta." " Atem."

"That's not how you spell atom, idiot."

"See how you're already working together?" Miss Hammonds claps. "So in a *burst* of inspiration, I am calling this game *The Riddle of the Mummy.*"

Liv's hand goes up.

"Mine is in Vegas right now, miss. She goes there after every summer holiday to recover."

"Er, excellent, Olivia! And your eventual arrival, Mr King, is always a pleasure, however unpredictable."

A boy in a yellow T-shirt shrugs and takes a place at the back of the group.

"So," Miss Hammond continues brightly, "I'm going to ask you all riddles, and in teams of three you'll try to answer them as quickly as possible. The team that gets it right first gets to take three steps towards *The Sock of Survival.*"

I can feel an excited, fizzy feeling starting to run down the back of my neck.

I *love* riddles.

They're like facts, except backwards and you can solve them and that's even better. Plus, competition really helps to sharpen my mind and bring out the best in me. Miss Hammond couldn't have picked a better way for me to make new friends if I'd sent in a handwritten request form.

Which I didn't, just to clarify.

"To make things a bit more jolly," she continues, beginning to wind the end of a loo roll round her ankle, "I'm going to turn myself into an Egyptian mummy and chase you, to help motivate you to keep moving forward! If I tap you on the shoulder, you become a mummy too and you're out of the race. And so on and so forth."

Oh my God.

This is getting better and better. I love ancient history *too* (although mummies technically originated in South America but maybe that's not super relevant to the game right now).

Miss Hammond keeps winding the tissue until it's binding her legs together like a penguin after knee surgery.

"The team that reaches The Sock of Survival first –

without all turning into mummies – wins!"

A flurry of hands immediately go up.

"What do we win, miss?"

"The satisfaction of knowing you did it together!" There's a pause while all the hands come down again, and Miss Hammond adds slightly reluctantly: "And a ten-pound voucher for the school tuck shop."

A murmur of approval goes round the class.

I'm now buzzing so hard it's as if I'm filled with bees or electric toothbrushes, and not just because the prize is sugar.

This is it. This is going to change *everything.*

From this point onwards, I will no longer be Harriet Manners, pee-er on books, skirt-dropper and irrational lover-of-bananas. I'll be the Riddle Master. Sweet Winner. Saviour of Socks. Avoider of Mummies and Destroyer of Toilet Rolls.

This is going to be *amazing.*

Miss Hammond starts grouping people together, and then hops over to me. "Harriet Manners? I've put you with India Perez and Olivia Webb."

I smile shyly as the girl with neon purple hair and Liv walk towards me. India smiles back and my insides do another excited little frog hop: *and so my new close and irreplaceable lifelong friendships start.*

Honestly, I'm kind of fascinated by her already.

Apparently Queen Elizabeth the First used to pretend that there was a piece of glass between her and the rest of the world to make her feel more royal, and it kind of seems like India has one too. Beneath My Little Pony hair and scowling eyebrows, she has dark eyes and an air of dignity and nobility. She reminds me of a powerful Egyptian princess.

We are *definitely* going to win now.

"Anya!" Liv calls as we stand behind a line made out of skipping rope. "Ans! A! Ani! Over here! We'll totally share answers, right?"

India frowns as Ananya pretends to have temporarily lost her hearing facilities.

"You will totally not," she says steadily. Then she turns to me. "Does this sort of exercise happen a lot at this school? Because it would have been extremely useful to have that in the brochure."

"Umm, I think it says *We are a school dedicated to the creative exploration of the individuality of our students*," I admit. "Page eight. Halfway down, under the photo of people making forts out of boxes."

India lifts a black eyebrow so it looks like a tick at the end of an essay. "Did you memorise the sixth form brochure?"

"N-no," I lie. "I just... umm..." *Sound more hip, Harriet.* "I used that page as kindling to build a really cool fire... for no reason, because I... err, burn stuff I don't care about, etcetera."

India puts her eyebrow back down.

"OK," she says, and I relax again.

I think I just passed my first social test.

"All right, my little intrepid puzzlers!" Miss Hammond calls, now covered head to toe in white, like an overexcited golden Labrador puppy. "Are you ready to journey back 5,000 years to a time of mystery and intrigue?"

There's a chorus of "yeah," "suppose so," "whatever," "I guess," are we going to be recycling all this tissue because this is kind of environmentally unfriendly?"

(That last one was me.)

"And..." She shakes a tiny tambourine that seems to have appeared out of nowhere. "*Go!*"

16

It starts off perfectly.

"How far," Miss Hammond says, looking up and down the line, "can a person run into the woods?"

There's a short silence while people whisper.

"We don't know how big the woods are," India murmurs as our group crowds its heads together. "There must be information missing. That can't be the whole question."

I grin at the other two while my brain clicks away happily. This is *so much fun* already. It's so intimate. So *bonding*. I really feel like part of a *team*.

"I've got this one," I whisper back conspiratorially, and then stick my hand up. "Halfway, miss. Because if you run any further, you're running back out of them again."

"Excellent, Harriet Manners! Take three steps forward!"

I high-five Liv and India like BFFs and we move towards our goal. Miss Hammond closes her eyes, shuffles

forward with a small embalmed-dead-person groaning sound and taps Robert on the shoulder.

"Ah, *man*," he says as he starts wrapping himself up in toilet tissue. "This is utter b—"

"Language, Robert." Miss Hammond claps her hands. "I am the beginning of the end, and the end of time and space. I am essential to creation, and I surround every place. What am I?"

"God!" Christopher's group yells.

"Santa Claus!"

"Taylor Swift!"

"Nope!" Miss Hammond says to all three groups. "Sorry! Take a step backwards, guys."

I wink at my group jubilantly as two more people are reluctantly ingratiated into ancient Egypt.

"You are the letter E, miss," I say loudly.

"I am indeed, Harriet!" We step forward again. "What loses its head in the morning but gets it back at night?"

My hand goes straight up, with the speed of a question-answering ninja. "A pillow!"

And – riddle by riddle, answer by answer – my group starts racing towards the goal. I know what is so fragile that saying the word breaks it (silence). I know what has many keys but can't open a door (a piano) and what gets wetter and wetter the more it dries (a towel).

Between us, we even know how many months have twenty-eight days in them. India lowers her head to whisper, although we're so far ahead by now that there's no real point.

"All of th—"

"Four!" I shout in excitement. "Twenty-eight days hath September, April, June and November!"

"I'm afraid it's all of them," Miss Hammond says gently. "All months have *at least* twenty-eight days. One step back, team."

Oops.

But luckily it doesn't matter if we make a mistake now and then, because nobody can catch up. We're too far ahead for even the mummies to grab us.

Finally, we get within touching distance of the sock.

Studies have shown that during competitive games, cortisol, prolactin, testosterone and adrenocorticotropic hormone levels increase dramatically. I'm now so rabid with excitement I'm basically floating on a fluffy cloud of my own chemical cocktail.

It's just my team, Christopher and Raya left.

"What kind of room has no doors or windows?"

My mind starts racing, jittering, turning itself inside out and back again. A prison? No, because how would you get in or out? Maybe a cellar, if a trapdoor in the floor

didn't count as either…

Is it a play on words? A groom, a broom, a…

"A cupboard?" Raya suggests, but I suddenly know. *Wham*. As if my brain was in the dark and a light's just been switched on: once you see the answer, you can't *unsee* it.

I punch the air.

"I've got it!" I yell, and beam triumphantly at Liv and India. "It's a *mush-room,* miss!"

Then, with three quick hops, I reach the sock and start automatically doing my happy dance: hands punching the air, knees bent, bottom wiggling.

"We win!" I squeak jubilantly. "We win we win we win! Woooooooo!!!"

17

My cheeks are flushed. My knees are shaking.

All the standard responses to success, adrenaline and unexpected physical activity.

I *knew* it. Best. Day. *Ever.*

This is *exactly* like Rebecca's birthday party eleven years ago when I won all the games. We played Pass the Parcel and I explained the rules to anyone who held on to the package for too long, and Musical Chairs where I encouraged anyone who was walking too slowly to hurry up, and Musical Statues when I helpfully pointed out people who were moving and… and…

And nobody wanted to play with me ever again.

Cucumbers consist of ninety-five per cent water. Without warning, it suddenly feels as if I may have become one. Every cell in my body is rapidly turning into liquid.

No. No no no *no*.

I abruptly stop wiggling my bottom and – with infinite slowness – turn around.

And there it is.

Every single one of my peers is standing in silence: arms folded, faces sullen. Glaring at me with narrowed eyes and raised eyebrows. Unimpressed. Outraged. Bored stiff by a game they haven't participated in.

Precisely the same as when we were five, except they're considerably bigger now and even angrier because this time they're covered in broken up bits of toilet roll and they're not quite sure why.

Oh my God: I've done it again.

I was so desperate for my team to win, I didn't think about anything else. I was trying my hardest, but in doing so I've made the entire game about…

Well. *Me,* I guess.

With a sick lurch, I'm suddenly not so sure I need Alexa to make me unpopular after all.

Oh, who am I even kidding?

Maybe I never actually did.

Swallowing, I turn slowly to Liv and India. Their arms are folded as well. I hold up my hand to awkwardly high-five them. "We won, guys. Yay?"

They both stare at it, suspended in the air. The loneliest hand that has ever existed in the 65 million years since our primate ancestors first evolved them.

"Not really," India says finally. "*You* won, Harriet. All by yourself."

And – as she turns in silence and starts walking back to the sixth-form building, followed by every member of my class – I can't help but marvel at the irony.

Because, despite my best efforts, *all by myself* is exactly how I've ended up.

18

The poet John Donne once wrote that no man is an island. I'd like to seriously question the accuracy of that statement.

In the middle of the South Atlantic Ocean, 1,700 miles from Antarctica, lies Bouvet Island. It has an area of forty-nine kilometres squared, is covered in glaciers and ice, and nobody lives there or ever has. According to Wikipedia, it is the remotest island in the world.

Thanks to today's misadventures, it is *still* a more popular destination than me.

The rest of the morning can be summarised thus:

1. I apologise to India and Liv and give them my share of the tuck-shop voucher.
2. They tell me it's fine, honestly, and then avoid me.
3. I overhear a girl in maths say I'm "still an arrogant, weird know-it-all".

4. I briefly consider telling her that *weird* originally meant "has the power to control fate" and if that was true I wouldn't be in this mess in the first place.
5. I realise it'll prove all three points and think better of it.

News of my unsporting smugness and apparent *In Your Face* dance spreads around sixth form with the speed of a forest fire. By the time I get out of double physics with Mr Harper, it's everywhere.

I try to outrace it – attempting to start friendly conversations with strangers as fast as I can – but it's impossible. The flame hops from student to student via whispers and raised eyebrows until all I'm doing is circling the common room like a desperate squirrel with its tail combusting.

I'm smiling, trying to find things in common, asking questions and remembering details as hard as I can.

But it's too late.

My seven seconds are up. The first impression has been made, and with every attempt to undo it I just look even more pathetic. It doesn't matter what I do or what I say any more.

I am the school weirdo.

Again.

By the time I'm ejected from my sixth failed conversation attempt ("Did you know that pirates used to wear gold hoop earrings because they thought it improved their eyesight?") I've officially given up.

I haven't seen Toby all morning. I should probably focus the remainder of my efforts on the one person in the year that still wants to talk to me.

But he's not in the common room, he isn't in the dining hall and when I take my lunch to his normal spot in the bush behind the gym hall, he's not there either.

Seriously. For a stalker, Toby is becoming ridiculously difficult to track down.

By the time I eventually find him, tucked into the corner of the art studio, I've basically resigned myself to playing noughts and crosses on the floor of the playground. I've already got two chalks ready, just in case I can persuade a year seven to play with me.

Although, given how quickly my leper status is whizzing around the school, even that's looking optimistic.

"Hey, Toby!" I say, pushing through the art room door. He looks up with slightly mad eyes, like a miniature Albert Einstein except without the moustache or Nobel prize.

"Harriet Manners!" he says, pulling his earphones out and quickly flipping over a piece of paper in front of him. "What an unprecedented surprise!"

I am so, *so* happy to see him.

"Are you having lunch in here today?" I say, bouncing forward and slamming my satchel enthusiastically on the table. "Did you know that in the average lunchtime you eat 150,000 kilometres of DNA? Although I'm afraid this cheese sandwich may have a few less, judging by the state of the lettuce." I plop it on the desk in front of him.

"Want to share?"

Toby gently pushes the sandwich off his piece of paper and brushes a few crumbs away.

"That's very kind of you, Harriet. But Mum made me sushi." He prods a little Thomas the Tank Engine lunchbox on the chair next to him. "Except we didn't have any fish so it's beef and I'm not keen on wasabi so it's mustard." He opens it and peers in. "With bread instead of rice."

"So," I say slowly, "it's a beef sandwich, then?"

"Absolutely," Toby agrees, holding one up. "Except Mum cut the crusts off and rolled it up into little balls so I'd feel like I was getting an interesting cultural experience."

I grin and glance briefly around the room.

Thanks to a total lack of artistic interest and even less ability, I've spent as little time as possible in this part of the school. There are paints and brushes everywhere, bright canvases leaning against walls and a general atmosphere of creativity.

I don't like it.

Entirely subjective grades make me uncomfortable.

Toby looks, if possible, even more out of place. The front of his brown T-shirt says COME TO THE NERD SIDE – WE HAVE PI and he's wearing trousers with an electronic computer keyboard across the lap, though he isn't actually plugged into a computer. At the moment anyway.

"So what are you doing?" I say, sitting down on the edge of his desk and reaching curiously for the piece of paper.

Toby moves it away. "It's my project for the Science Fair."

"Oooh." The Fair isn't for another three months, but maybe I need to get started on mine too. "What's yours on? Can I see?"

"I'm afraid not," Toby says, shifting the paper into his satchel. "Showing you would jeopardise its top-secret status by definition of it no longer being a secret of any kind."

"That's very true." I frown. "So if it's science why are you in the art room?"

There's a tiny pause while Toby stuffs a sushi-sandwich in his mouth, and then says:

"It's quiet and private and away from… people."

"Cool." I look at the sunshine streaming through the windows. "I might do my project on the effect of music on animal behaviour using Hugo and Victor as voluntary subjects, or maybe study the Oort cloud because the edge of it is 4.6 trillion miles from the sun so I can investigate the composition of the—"

"I have a question for you," a voice interrupts from behind me. "Maybe you can add this to your investigation while you're at it."

I spin round in surprise.

Somebody is sitting in the corner near the door, almost totally hidden behind an enormous sculpture of an angel made out of plaster, clay and wire. I had no idea there was anyone else in here: that's how quiet they are and how big the sculpture is.

And how little my genuine interest in the art room has been, obviously.

"Umm," I say, blinking a few times. I *do* love a good question, after all. "Sure. Hit me with it."

"Do you ever," the voice says, "and I mean *ever*,

think about anyone other than yourself?"

And I don't even know who they are yet.

But I asked them to hit me with it, and it feels like they just did.

19

Apparently, there are over 6,000 languages in the world and by the turn of this century half of these are expected to die out. Judging by my speechlessness at this precise moment, my brain thinks English is one of them.

"S-sorry?" I finally manage.

Then I take a few steps forward until I can see a boy behind the sculpture.

He's pale and tall, with mousey hair, thick dark eyebrows and a round face, and – for some reason I can't fathom – he looks slightly magical. It's only as I get a few metres away that I realise he has two slightly different coloured irises: one pale blue, the other light brown.

Otherwise known as *heterochromia iridis* and entirely a result of melanin levels in the eyes rather than enchantment or a Harry Potter spell.

Sadly. I checked.

"Seriously," the boy growls, grabbing some clay and sticking it into the angel's leg, "I've never known anyone

so obnoxiously wrapped up in themselves. It's quite amazing."

His magical quality takes another enormous step down.

"Sorry? We haven't even met, have we? I don't think I've ever even seen you before in my entire life."

The boy looks at me steadily for a few seconds.

"I'm in your form. I was in the team next to you this morning. For a full hour."

I get a little closer, and – now I'm not distracted by the thought that he might be a wizard – I can see that, yup: he's the new boy in the yellow T-shirt who was late this morning, except now he's disguised by blue overalls.

In fact, I think when we went back to the form room at the end of team-building to do the register he was sitting at the desk directly in front of me as well.

OK. The defence isn't looking good right now. Annabel would tell me to start plea-bargaining immediately.

Instead, I automatically go on the counterattack.

"Well," I say, desperately sticking my nose in the air and crossing my arms, "you didn't say hello to me either."

"Yes, I did," he retorts bluntly. "Twice. You were too busy telling India about the essay you wrote for your English exam. Four months ago."

I flush. It was all about masculinity and gender in

Othello and I thought it might be a good way of making peace with her. I don't think it worked.

"But—"

"And now this poor guy just wants peace and quiet to work on his project, and you follow him in here, ignore his pretty obvious hints and gab away about yourself again."

Follow *him*? *Excuse* me?

"Actually Toby's *my* stalker," I snap indignantly. "*Not* the other way round." I pause slightly while I consider how that sounds. "OK, that's not exactly what I..."

The guy with the heterochromia snorts.

"Yeah, my mistake," he says, grabbing a piece of wire and bending it into a C shape. "You're lovely. I can see why you fit into glamorous New York with all the bananas."

My mouth flaps in silence a few times – he wasn't even there when I said that; I *knew* people were talking about me and my bananas – and then I turn desperately to Toby. Why isn't he protecting my honour?

Because he hasn't heard a single word, that's why.

His head is bent over the piece of paper again, his earphones are back in, and he's lost in Toby-land: scribbling away frantically, humming the theme tune from *Star Wars* under his breath.

I rush over and pull out an earphone.

"Hello again, Harriet!" he says, quickly folding his arms across the desk. "Maybe I could encourage you to wear a bell round your neck so people know you're coming? Our cat's got one. It's very handy."

"Toby." My cheeks are getting hotter and hotter. "Tell this... this *boy*..."

"Jasper. For the third time today, my name is Jasper."

I'm not sure how, but this is getting steadily worse. "Please tell Jasper I'm actually quite nice if you get to know me!"

Toby turns to Jasper with reproach in his eyes.

"Harriet Manners," he says with total sincerity, "is the sweetest girl in the entire universe. She is a sterling example of what great niceness the human race is capable of. Should we ever need an ambassador for outer space, I will be voting for her to represent us."

A little grateful knot of embarrassment forms in the base of my throat, and I turn to Jasper triumphantly.

"S—" I start, but before I can get to the "ee" Toby continues:

"Sometimes she is so kind she even lets me sit on her doorstep when it's raining and she's too busy to let me in."

Oh my God. That just made it a billion times worse.

But if I let him in *every* time I'd never be on my own again.

"Right," Jasper says flatly, picking up another piece of wire. "Sorry. She sounds utterly charming and not at all like a stuck-up princess."

I can feel myself starting to get angry.

"Toby," I say, turning back to him. "You don't really mind me being here, do you? I'm not in the way, am I?"

Then I look triumphantly at Jasper with my *ha* face at the ready.

"Actually," Toby says, "you are a bit in the way, Harriet. It would be useful if you could go away today. I really need to focus on my project. And maybe tomorrow too, actually."

"But—"

"And Thursday."

"I—"

"In fact, while we're discussing it, could you maybe leave me alone for the rest of the week? Next week would also be extremely handy as well."

It feels like something is starting to tighten inside my chest. Toby doesn't want to hang out with me either?

Then I turn back to Jasper and the corner of his mouth is turned upwards slightly in a little smirk.

That does it.

A lightning bolt is 54,000 degrees Fahrenheit, and it feels like one has just shot through me: white-hot anger

is scorching and fizzling from the top of my head down to my fingertips and back again.

Swallowing, I stick my chin in the air and start heading towards the door in dignified silence.

Somehow I don't quite make it.

"You don't know me," I say, spinning round. "You don't know who I am, or how I think, or why I do the things I do. You know *nothing about me at all*."

"You're totally right," Jasper says as the bell for the end of lunchtime rings. He stands up and pulls off his blue overalls so that the yellow T-shirt is fully visible again. "And you know what?"

"What?"

"That's just fine by me."

And without another backwards glance, Jasper walks straight past me and out of the door. Leaving both the angel and me speechless, white and rigid behind him.

20

By oneself. Excluded. On your tod.

It's a good thing I brought my thesaurus with me, because I have plenty of quality *me time* to expand my vocabulary over the rest of the day.

For the next four hours, I am completely *unescorted*.

I am *solo* as I eat my sandwich in the corner of the common room and drop it down my top, *companionless* as I mess up a rat dissection in biology because nobody wants to pair with me and *lonesome* when an experiment in chemistry goes wrong because I can't hold both the test tubes at the same time.

I even try to make myself feel better by replacing these words with positive synonyms: I *independently* stare out of the window, I chew my nails *unaided* and *unassisted.*

But it doesn't matter how many different words I use, they all boil down to the same thing.

It's my first day back at school.

And I am completely alone.

*

"Anyway…" I say as I wait for the final school bell to ring. I'm now sitting on the little wall next to the playing field, kicking my duck pumps on and off at the heels.

The caretaker picks sheets of tissue off the ground and throws them in a black plastic bag.

"He doesn't even *know* me," I say quietly. "He's just so *rude*."

"*Can I borrow some toilet rolls*, she says," the caretaker mutters, picking up another few bits. "*Just a few*, she says. And next thing I know every roll in the school is all over the grass and nobody's got anything to wipe their bottoms with for the rest of the week."

"Exactly!" I say triumphantly. "Or almost exactly, anyway. That's nearly the same thing."

I kick my feet against the wall despondently.

At least I've found somebody who will talk to me. I hadn't expected my first kindred spirit in sixth form to be a fifty-seven-year-old man in dungarees and a tool belt, but beggars can't be choosers.

Plus he spends a lot of his time under tables and in cupboards, so we actually have a surprising amount in common.

Steve bends down again. "I'm supposed to be practising my spinning tonight, not cleaning up after

hours. That hippy can bring in her own supplies next time."

I shake my head in empathy. Then I hop off the wall so I can pick up a few bits of tissue and pop them in the bag. I like to spin round too: maybe he has a special office twirly chair like Dad?

We work industriously together in companionable silence for a few minutes, and then I clear my throat and say: "I've got a miniature game of Scrabble in my satchel – would you like to play it with me tomorrow?"

There's a thoughtful pause while Steve considers this.

"Hang on... Chicken wire? Did you say the statue is made out of chicken wire? I *knew* I was missing a roll. That little blighter."

"Isn't he just the most horrible, unpleasant—"

"Quack quack," a familiar voice says and I immediately stop moving with my hand still clutching a bit of tissue: bent double, with my bottom firmly poking in the air.

I can't help feeling as if I'm not as well protected as I could be.

Slowly, I straighten up and turn to look at Alexa.

She's standing a few metres away with her hands on her hips. Ananya and Liv are at either side, and India is standing just behind them.

Huh. That was fast.

I guess she's picked her team already.

I look at the wad of crumpled tissue in my hand, then at the black bin bag. Then at the middle-aged man I'm chatting to. On my own. Voluntarily, when I could just go home.

There's a piece of loo roll stuck to my knee, and another attached to the toe of my shoe. Tuna is still coating my front, and I smell of a day's worth of embarrassed dry sweat.

In the meantime, Alexa is noticing exactly the same things.

"You're hanging out with the *staff* now? Like, people who are actually *paid* to be here all day?"

"Actually, Steve's..." *only part-time,* I'm about to say, and then change my mind.

"So where are your little sidekicks now, Harriet? Where's Team Geek?" Alexa elaborately looks around her. "I can't see them. Are they hiding?" She picks up a bit of loo roll and pretends to look under it. "Helloooo? Geeks? Come out, come out, wherever you are."

"Nat's gone to fashion college," I say as firmly as I can, even though Alexa already knows this. "And Toby's really, really busy with something super important."

"Oh *yes,*" she says, narrowing her eyes and putting the paper back down again. "That's *right*. You're totally

on your own now, aren't you?"

Alexa has always known how to find the rusty nail and smack it straight on the head.

My eyes start prickling.

"No," I say with as much dignity as I can muster. "I'm not alone. I have..." *Steve,* I'm about to say, and then change my mind for the second time.

"This is pathetic, even for you." Alexa sounds genuinely cross. "Where's the *fun*, Harriet Manners? Where's the challenge? You've ruined everything." She clicks her fingers and turns away. "She's not worth it, guys. We've got better things to do."

As if I'm one of the fabric mice we give Victor and he's chewed all the catnip out of it, rendering it useless and of no interest any more.

The bell rings and Alexa starts marching towards the front gates with her Underlings behind her. India looks at me with disdain for a few seconds, then turns and follows them.

My eyes are smarting, my vision is starting to wobble and my throat feels like there's a sofa cushion stuck in it.

Then my phone beeps.

How was your first day?? Tell me tell me! Nat xxx

How am I supposed to answer that with any self-respect?

A-maz-ing!! SO MUCH FUN!! Couldn't have gone better!!! Can't wait for two more whole years of this!!!! Hxx

With a lie, that's how.

I put my phone away, hiding my face behind my hair so Steve can't see my chin starting to crumple.

"It's all right, love," he says, giving me an awkward pat on the back as I head towards the school gates. "Those nasty little minxes will get what's coming to them."

"Sure they will," I say over my shoulder, even though I know they obviously won't.

Because Alexa's right.

There's a big difference between not-popular and *un*popular, and I hadn't even noticed that until I was on the other side. I may have spent years struggling to make friends at school, but this is the first time since I was five that I've had *none.*

And of the two options, I can't decide which is worse:

a) being brought down a peg or two every school day of your life for eleven years

or

b) finally being so far at the bottom that there's nowhere left to go.

21

They say that every cloud has a silver lining.

Which is obviously untrue.

Most clouds don't: just the rain clouds with the sun directly behind them. Given the size of the sky, that makes it statistically uncommon.

However, I'd like to think that I'm the kind of person who at least *looks* for the sunshine. A positive, optimistic girl, who hopes for the best even when the signs aren't looking good.

And – let's be honest – they're really not right now.

At all.

The first schools were established in 425 AD. I'd be quite surprised if anyone has had a less successful first day in the history of formal education.

On the upside, at least I'll be able to focus on my schoolwork properly now. Without any distractions or discussions or interesting debates. All day, every day,

for the next two years.

Most of the evenings too.

And possibly quite a few weekends, if Nat gets really busy with college.

Oh my God.

Of all the planets in our solar system, we would weigh the most on Jupiter. I'm starting to wonder if I've somehow accidentally ended up there instead.

Bits of the day are beginning to rattle around inside my head like coloured balls inside a lottery machine, and every time they collide with each other, another little piece of me gets heavier.

I like bananas! My lungs. *I've got this one!* My tongue. *It's a mushroom!* My kidneys and liver. *Do you ever think about anyone but yourself? Maybe you could leave me alone?* Eyeballs, spleen, pancreas, veins, muscles.

She's not worth it: every single one of my bones.

Until, organ by organ, I weigh so much I'm surprised I don't have to drag myself down the road by my fingernails.

Finally, I manage to reach the bench on the corner of the road where Nat and I have met every morning for the last ten years, even when our parents had to come with us.

I stand and look at how empty it is.

Then I turn around again and start walking towards the only place in the world that could possibly make me feel lighter again.

The local launderette.

22

No, in case you're wondering.

I haven't been back here since Annabel and Dad broke up and then had their big romantic laundry reunion nearly a year ago. Initially, I thought it was because it had become *their* place, not mine any more. Then I thought it was because I'd just worked out how to clean my clothes for free at home, like a normal human being.

But now I'm wondering if it's simply because I haven't needed it the way I need it now.

When I don't know where else to go.

I still love this place.

I love the bright lights, the soapy smells, the soft purring of the machines. I love the heat and the shininess of the glass in the tumble driers. But most of all I love the way that nothing could ever feel alone in a place where so many things are jumbled together.

I rub my eyes and pull a chair over to my favourite machine. The glass is still warm, and there are baskets filled with piles of abandoned clothes everywhere. Somebody's even left a shoe behind: it's peeking out from behind a particularly large heap of jumpers and underwear.

I pull a blue sock out of my bag and a memory suddenly flashes: snow, warm cheeks, a cold hand squeezing mine.

So I swallow and put it in the drier as quickly as I can.

Then I start fumbling through my satchel for the fifty pence I need to put it on a quick spin. Followed by another fifty pence.

Then another pound in shrapnel.

And a two pound-coin.

After the day I've had I may be here some time. I am about to own the driest sock in existence.

I'm just chipping a bit of melted chocolate off a pound so that the machine recognises it as something other than a snack when something small and shiny flies through the air and lands in my lap.

I blink at the newly arrived coin, then at the empty room.

Maybe there's some kind of strange gravitational pull levitating the money out of the machines and throwing

it at my head. I suppose I could do my science project on that instead.

Reaching into my bag, I pull out another ten pence and there it is again: money, soaring through the air.

Except this time it's a pound, which is even better.

I look around the empty room – still nothing – and am just quickly calculating how long I'll have to stay here before I am rich enough to buy a castle when somebody laughs.

"You actually think it's magic flying money, don't you?"

Then I see the shoe in the pile moving. A pointy, silver shoe that stormed down my driveway yesterday morning, attached to my best friend.

"Nat?"

A dark, curly head pokes out from behind an enormous pile of clean jumpers and trousers. She's obviously been lying in them, like some kind of enormous cat.

"Obviously. God, you took *ages*. I was starting to think I might actually have to do some washing." She stands up, puts *Vogue* down and picks off a pair of huge beige knickers attached by static to her jumper.

"Gross," she adds, flinging them into the corner

so they hit the wall with a *fffpp*. Then she turns to where I'm still sitting, frozen in surprise. "How's it going, Manners?"

23

Seriously.

I have *got* to start checking rooms before I walk into them. Apparently chameleons and dragonflies have 360-degree vision, and I am clearly neither. If I were a small animal, I'd definitely have been eaten by now.

"Nat, what are you doing here?"

She hops on top of one of the machines. "Finding you, obviously. I've got a selfie with Vivienne Westwood – she was nowhere *near* as difficult to pin down."

I jump with considerably less nimbleness on to the machine next to her. "I'm sorry."

"What's going on? I'm so worried, I've just spent an hour sitting in a laundry basket, covered in old-lady clothes. I may never fully recover."

I take a deep breath and decide to confront the metaphorical elephant in the room head-on. "I'm fine, Nat. Honestly. Nick quit modelling and went back to Australia, and we both decided together that a long-distance

relationship was too painful. I know we made the right decision, I just don't want to talk about it, that's all."

"Really?"

"Really really."

"Really really really?"

"All of the reallies."

"So you're OK?"

"Yes," I say as confidently as I can.

Nat studies my face carefully, then her shoulders relax very slightly. "Thank God, because I need to tell you something and if I don't I'm going to explode all over my second-best dress and then we really *will* need a launderette."

Suddenly I notice again how perfectly curly her hair is.

In fact – now I'm not hiding in a bush fifteen metres away, being attacked by spiders – I can see a general shininess about Nat, as if her insides have just been dipped in something twinkly. Her eyes are sparkling and her cheeks are pink; there are little dimples in the corners of her mouth and her skin looks like it could glow in the dark.

I look down: the varnish has been chewed off every single one of her nails.

Then I remember her on my doorstep yesterday.

I really need to talk to her.

Oh my God, why did I automatically assume it was about me? Ugh. Maybe Jasper has a point after all.

"Is it François? Are you back with him?"

"*Who*?" Nat frowns. "Oh, the French dude. Ugh: no. He won't stop sending me postcards with rabbits cuddling in front of the Eiffel Tower. This one is called Theo. He's studying photography at college, and we kissed on Friday night for the first time. He's all right, I guess. For a boy."

My best friend is playing it cool, but her entire face is luminous as if something has been set on fire behind it.

I stare at Nat in confusion. She has left literally fifty-six messages on my phone over the last few days, and not a single one of them mentioned this.

"But... why didn't you just tell me?"

"Because you're my best friend and you've just had your heart broken and this is terrible timing and I didn't want to make you sadder."

I suddenly love my Best Friend so much it's hard to swallow.

"Nat," I say finally, "do you know what happens to metal when it touches another piece of metal in outer space?"

"It makes a really loud screeching sound and the universe goes *aaaaaargggh stop it*?"

I grin at her. "There's no sound in space, so no. What

happens is that those two bits of metal weld together permanently. Nothing that makes you happy could possibly make me sad, Nat. We're *welded*."

She considers this briefly and then pulls a face. "Remind me never to go into space with Toby, in that case."

We both laugh, then sit in comfortable silence for a few seconds with one shoulder touching.

"So how did you know I'd be here, anyway?"

Nat stretches and yawns. "I tagged you with an electronic chipping device while you were sleeping. Like a cat."

My hand automatically goes up to my neck.

"Plonker. As soon as I got that last text I knew where you'd be, Harriet. You never use exclamation marks in a text unless you're lying. So I figured your first day back had blown, and you'd be heading straight here."

I blink at her in amazement.

See what I mean? Nat had known I was coming to the launderette before I even knew it myself.

Now, *that's* a best friend.

"Well," I start, ready to tell her everything: about Toby and Alexa and Jasper, and how nobody likes me. About how lonely I am without her already, and how I want her to come back to school so it can be just us again, the way it always has been.

Then I stop.

If we're welded, it works both ways, right? My sadness will make her sad too, and I don't want that. It's her turn to be happy now. I've had my big, amazing romance. My best friend deserves to have the world light up for her too.

"*Au contraire*, Natalie," I say as airily as I can, with a quick hand flourish. "In fact, I'll have you know I won the class quiz in my very first hour."

This doesn't have the impact I'm hoping for.

"Oh my God," Nat sighs, putting her hand over her eyes. "How bad? Post-it on the back of T-shirt bad or head-down-the-toilet bad?"

Just *once* I'd like Nat not to see straight through me.

"The former," I admit. There was a Post-it saying *I AM A KNOW-IT-ALL* on my satchel at breaktime. "But don't worry: it's just a brief hiccup. I'm sure they'll forget about it eventually."

"Of *course* they will." Nat puts her arm round me and leans her head against mine. "Lots of people make a slightly bumpy first impression and nobody ever remembers."

We're both lying, by the way: scientists have found that first impressions are very difficult to undo and can often be permanent.

"Exactly!" I drop off the machine with as much enthusiasm as I can muster. "And a school year is only 190 days, right? 1,330 hours will be over before I know it."

There's a short silence.

"That's a really long time, Harriet."

"Actually, it's only three days on Mercury. Plus I've got you and Toby – as soon as his project is over, anyway – so what else does a sensible girl really need?"

"But Harriet, I'm not—"

"So do you want to come to mine tonight? I've designed a game of fashion Monopoly for us to play and it has a doll's house sewing machine you can use as your little placer."

Let's just say that last free period was *really* boring.

There's another short, uncomfortable silence.

Then Nat frowns and hops off the machine, landing on a half-open detergent box with a little puff of white powder like a dragon.

She stares at the floor for a few seconds.

"I... can't tonight. I mean, it sounds great. But if you... If we... Some other time?"

"Oh." I feel slightly popped. "I guess you're busy with Theo tonight, right?"

"Huh? Oh. Mm-hmm."

I nod as another memory flashes: a seagull, a swing, a fur hat.

A kiss.

Then I swallow and push it away as fast as I can.

"Excellent!" I try and grin. "Can't wait to meet him! Have fun!"

Nat gets to the door then bites her lip, runs back and abruptly throws her arms around me so hard she almost knocks me over.

"Don't give up, Harriet. They'll love you as much as I do, I promise. Just give them a bit of time, OK?"

She kisses my cheek, hard.

Then my best friend bursts back out of the laundry doors into the dark, leaving a white fog of soap behind her.

24

I wait until Nat has definitely gone.

Then I sit back down in the chair, lean my cheek against the warm tumble dryer and watch the sock going round and round and round in never-ending circles.

Just like my stupid little life.

My phone beeps.

My little chunky-chip! Is this the face that launched a thousand lips?! Sparkle monkey everywhere! Fairy wins again! Gravy

I stare at it for a few seconds, then turn my phone upside down in case it reads better the other way up.

It does not.

It's midday on a Tuesday in New York right now. My bonkers ex-agent has clearly had *way* too many cups of coffee.

Although at least Wilbur's still in contact: we may not

be working together any more, but he still talks to me more than my current modelling agent.

The last three times I rang Infinity Models I never even got past the receptionist.

Still bemused, I type:

Wilbur, have you been eating sequins again? xxx

I wait a few minutes – he's obviously peaked and passed out – pop my phone back in my bag and make a mental note to ring him tomorrow when he's slept through the caffeine spike.

Then I close my eyes and try not to notice how, despite coming to my happy place, there's an organ in the middle of my chest that still belongs on Jupiter.

25

According to scientists, it takes sixty-six days to form a new habit.

I'm obviously going to need every single one of them.

As I walk slowly home, every bush is stared at, every flowerpot glanced behind, every tree trunk checked. At one point I find myself making a little detour around a rubbish bin, just in case there's somebody lurking there. Honestly, I haven't behaved this weirdly since I went on a rampaging Flower Fairy hunt, aged six.

Or had so little success.

Because it doesn't matter how hard I look, or how slowly I walk, or how many times I whisper *I believe in you*: it's no good.

There's nobody following.

Nobody listening, nobody watching.

For the first time in five years, Toby isn't there.

"Dad?" I say as I push open the front door. "Tabitha? Did

you have a nice d—"

I freeze.

Newspapers are strewn around the hallway. The sofa has been dismantled; blankets and clothes are scattered down the stairs. One living-room curtain is closed, every drawer is out, every cupboard is open. The rubbish bin is lying on its side: contents splurged all over the floor.

There are approximately 35,000 robberies reported every month in the UK, and it looks like we've just become one of them.

"Dad!" I shout in a panic, dropping my satchel. "Tabitha! Are you OK?"

What if they've taken my laptop?

Nobody will ever see the presentation I was making about pandas doing handstands.

"Dad!" I yell as I race into the bathroom. The medicine cupboard has been pulled apart. "Dad!" I yell in the kitchen where the fridge door is still open. "Dad!" I shout in the totally ransacked cupboard under the stairs. "Da—"

Dad walks in through the back door with Tabitha, snuggled up in his arms. "Daughter Number One! The conquering heroine returns!"

I fling myself at them so hard I may have crushed my little sister irreversibly. "Oh my goodness, you poor

things. Did they hurt you? Did they threaten you? You could have been *kidnapped*!"

Actually, they *may* have been kidnapped and then returned. If I was a robber, I'd have brought my dad back pretty quickly too.

"Did the who which what now?"

"The burglars!"

"We've been *burgled*?" Dad says in alarm. "When did that happen? I was only in the garden for thirty seconds. Blimey, they move fast, don't they?"

I look at him, and then at the chaos around us.

Now I come to think of it, nothing seems to be *missing*. It just appears to be... heavily rearranged. There isn't a single cup left in the cupboard: they're all sitting next to the sink, half full of cold tea. The plates aren't gone: they're just randomly distributed around the living room, covered in ketchup.

"*You* made all this mess?"

"What mess?" Dad glances around. "Looks fine to me. I tell you what, I don't know what Annabel was going on about. This stay-at-home-parent malarkey is a *doddle.* I even wrote a poem after lunch. Do you want to hear it?"

"You wrote a *poem*?"

"I did indeed. I rhymed artisan with marzipan. And Tarzan." Dad looks at my sister smugly. "We're just trying

to work out how to get *partisan* in there too, aren't we, Tabs. *I am partisan to a little marzipan while watching Tarzan.*" He thinks about it. "If only it was *Tarzipan*. Such a shame."

Oh my God. The only thing missing in this house is the thing between my father's ears.

"But—"

"I feel a bit cooped up now, though," he continues cheerfully. "I might take Hugo for a walk, stretch the legs, get the air moving around the brain again. You can take care of Tabitha, right?"

He plonks her in my arms before I can tell him there's clearly enough air moving around his brain already.

"But Dad—"

"Oooh, *medicine-man*!" he says as he grabs his jacket, whistles at my dog and marches out of the door I left hanging open in panic behind me. Hugo bounds after him, giddy with excitement. "That rhymes too! God, I'm a creative genius. See you in a bit, kiddos!"

And the door swings shut behind them.

My sister and I look at each other in disbelief for a few seconds. Not for the first time, we are entirely on the same page. *You think that's bad*? her round blue eyes are saying. *I've had eleven hours of this and I'm only four*

months old. I can't even physically crawl away yet.

I glance at the clock on the kitchen wall.

It's five-thirty and Annabel will be home from her first day back at work in an hour. Exhausted, drained and desperate to spend time with her tiny baby. I could be wrong, but I don't think washing up, re-folding towels in a cupboard and reading Dad's inaccurate attempts to rhyme *marzipan* are on that list.

Which gives me no other choice.

With a quick sigh, I give my sister a kiss on the cheek and put her back in her little bouncy chair so that she can keep me company.

Then, like all the King's soldiers and all the King's men, I roll my sleeves up.

And start putting the house back together again.

26

Here are my top three days in history:

1. *The day in 1877 when S. W. Williston discovered the first diplodocus fossil.*

2. *March 12th, 1610, which marked the publication of The Starry Messenger by Galileo, thus proving that the solar system didn't revolve round the earth.*

3. *My birthday. Obviously.*

Suffice to say, today is not on this list.

Frankly, it wouldn't even make it into the top 5,000.

I had so many brilliant plans for my first day back at school. Facts and stats and equations and carefully controlled explosions; laughter and soul-searching and conversations about life and death and what our favourite

trees are (mine – the Socotra dragon blood, followed closely by the rainbow eucalyptus).

I was prepared for everything and anything on my first day as a sixth former.

I just never thought I'd spend quite so much of it *cleaning.*

By the time I've finished vacuuming the hallway, all I want to do is crawl to my bedroom, bury myself under a pile of books like a hedgehog and never come out again. I can be one of those people who says *reading is to the mind what exercise is to the body* while never moving another muscle.

"Harriet!" Annabel says in surprise, coming in through the front door as I'm halfway up the stairs with Tabby in my arms: she's earlier than I thought she'd be. "How was school? I thought you might still be at some kind of extra-curriculum or social activity."

Then she pauses, rubs her eyes and looks round the spotless house. "Crikey," she adds with a grimace. "Now I feel terrible. I'd assumed your father would spend the day trashing the place and writing terrible poetry. I clearly don't know my husband at all."

I really don't have the heart to break it to her.

"School was great," I say brightly, clipping a smile on

like Lego. "How was work?"

"Amazing. Frankly, I'd forgotten how much I enjoy telling people I'm going to sue them."

Annabel grins at me – attired once more in her fitted suit and black heels and obviously feeling completely herself again – and I smile back.

Then I pull my phone out of my pocket and stare at the empty screen. "Oooh, six missed phone calls and seven text messages from like-minded people with similar interests who want to spend quality time with me. Better go reply to them all."

Annabel takes Tabitha off me with a gentle, "I missed you, squirrel." Then she looks up with dark eyes. "I'm so glad your first day back went well, sweetheart. I was worried it would be tricky to fit back in so late into term."

I nod. For once, I'm glad my stepmother is too exhausted for her mind-reading superpowers to kick in properly.

"Not at all! It was ace!!!!" *Fake quadruple exclamation marks.* "I just have a little extra reading to do before tomorrow!! So I shall say goodnight!!!"

There go five more.

Then I do a weird little royal wave all the way up the stairs until I'm locked safely inside my bedroom.

Where I fling myself face down on my bed.

And promptly start to hyperventilate.

Apparently if you hyperventilate before you go underwater, you can hold your breath for much longer because CO^2 levels in your bloodstream are lower.

Frankly, I'm breathing so fast now I'm basically a mermaid.

What's the expression? *Be careful what you wish for.*

I wished for everything to be different; I thought that way it would change for me too. I'm not sure it was such a smart ambition after all.

Everybody else has moved on already.

Nat has college and Theo. Toby has a brand-new, top-secret project that doesn't involve me. Annabel has work, Dad has "poetry" and Tabby has the imminent hurdle of solid foods to attend to. My grandmother Bunty is painting murals in a beach hut in Rio, Wilbur's still creating fashion havoc in New York, Rin's moved to South Japan.

My modelling agency has forgotten who I am.

Nick's still gone.

Even Alexa and her minions have found something better to do.

And in the meantime, I'm just the same old me, doing the same old things, over and over again. Carrying the past around with me, exactly as I always have.

There's a humpback whale in the ocean that sings at fifty-two hertz: too low for any other whale to hear. Scientists aren't sure if it's a genetic anomaly, or a sole survivor of an extinct species, or just a whale who accidentally learnt the wrong song. They just know that it's probably the loneliest mammal on earth.

I know exactly how it feels.

As if I'm swimming desperately round and round in repeating circles, singing as hard as I can, but nobody can hear me.

For the first time since I left America, I put my pillow over my head.

And burst straight into tears.

27

According to a recent study, the average teenager cries for two hours and thirteen minutes a week. Thanks to saving it all up, I'm very close to hitting that target in just one session.

I cry until my face hurts and my pillow's wet.

I cry until my chest aches and there are no tears any more: just an exhausted *ng ng ng* sound.

Never mind Jupiter: my heart is now on the sun. It's on a white dwarf. It's somewhere on a neutron star, weighing millions of tonnes and about to rip a channel to the bottom of my toes.

Because there's the massive lie I told Nat: one with a gaping, obvious hole in it.

I am not *OK* at all.

Finally, I stop crying.

I wipe my nose on my duvet and sit up. I grab a piece of paper and a pen from my bedside table.

And I start writing.

Dear Nick,

Here are some things I know about you.

From the moment you were born, there have been 276 major earthquakes and 87 volcano eruptions; 39 solar eclipses and 85 super-moons. The seas have risen by 5 centimetres, and the average temperature of the earth has increased by 0.2 degrees centigrade.

Over the last seventeen years, the planet you are on has travelled 138,253,139,000 kilometres around the Milky Way, 22,673,602,167 kilometres away from the Voyager Probe and 16,590,377,250 kilometres around the sun, taking you with it.

You have had 70 birthdays on Mercury, 27 on Venus, 9 on Mars, 1 on Jupiter (and you will be 29 years old before you have your first birthday on Saturn).

Your heart has beaten 654 million times.

But none of these things are going to stay the same. With every day, you're going to travel a little further, get a little older: the sea will rise, volcanoes

will erupt. And all these things I Know about you won't be true any more.

Just one thing will.

I miss you, and that's never going to change.

Harriet xxx

28

Quickly, I cram the letter into an envelope.

I scribble an address on the front and stick three rare stamps on it that will carry the letter far, far away: to a strange, foreign place I've never been before. Then I shove my trainers on and run down the stairs before pride or shame or hope can stop me.

"Harriet?" Annabel says as I run through the hallway and fling open the front door. "I thought I could hear crying. Is everything OK?"

"Yes," I say as I close the door softly behind me. "At least, I think it will be now."

I run all the way to the postbox. Which isn't saying much: it's only at the bottom of the road.

But still.

And as I run, Nick runs with me.

*

Home, Hertfordshire – January (10 months ago)

"Did you know that snow isn't actually white? It's translucent. It just reflects light uniformly, which makes it *look* white."

"Jump," he instructed, hopping over a large slushy ice puddle and squeezing my hand with his warm, dry fingers. I'd taken my left glove off, claiming it was because I had one randomly hot hand.

This was a small white lie.

Or possibly a translucent one, reflecting light.

My stomach flipped over, and I jumped too late to avoid a totally wet and icy sock.

"Like polar bears, right?" Nick continued as we kept running towards the train station. "They're not actually white either, are they?"

I was impressed: I told him that *months* ago. His ability to retain useless but fascinating information was getting nearly as good as mine.

"Exactly," I said, slipping slightly so that his arm went temporarily round my waist. "We – I mean *they* – aren't what they look like at all."

Then I cleared my throat in embarrassment.

Oops. It was one thing comparing myself to a misfit polar bear in a rainforest in my head occasionally: quite

another to do it out loud to my boyfriend.

"I was twelve the first time I saw snow," Nick grinned as we started running down the stairs to the train platform. "I was so excited I got out of bed at 3am and tried to make a snow angel in shorts and a T-shirt."

I rolled my eyes.

"Half of the world's population has never seen snow, Nicholas. Considerably fewer would be that stupid."

He shouted with laughter and my heart squeezed shut for a few seconds, just as it had the first time he did it in Moscow.

"Luckily, I've now got the world's biggest smarty-pants to balance me back out again."

With a quick spin, Nick stopped, wrapped his arms round me and pulled me so close I could feel his breath warming the end of my cold nose. I had just a second to notice that everything was white and still and calm, like a snowglobe just before it gets shaken.

Then he kissed me and it all disappeared: the snow, my wet sock and both my feet with it.

When we finally stopped kissing, we'd missed the train.

"I think I need to balance you faster, in that case," I laughed, cheeks ridiculously warm. "It's an hour to the next train and now you're going to miss your Hilfiger casting."

"Totally worth it. Tell me something else about snow."

"Umm." I rummaged through my brain for a few seconds while Nick opened his big grey coat and pulled me inside it so I wouldn't get cold. "Anything?"

"Tell me anything, Polar Bear Girl," he said, wrapping his arms round me. "Anything at all."

"OK." I found my best snow fact and smoothed it out for a few seconds until it was all neat and clean. "If you had a million snow crystals and compared two of them every second, you'd be there for nearly a hundred thousand years before you found two that matched."

Nick wiped a snowflake off my cheek and pulled me a bit closer. "Funny," he said as it started snowing again. "I must be smarter than we thought. It only took me seventeen years."

And he kissed me again.

I run until I reach the bright red postbox.

For a disorientating second, I can almost believe Nick's here and not on the other side of the world. That it's snowing again and I have one cold sock and two hot cheeks. That he's still with me.

That I'm not on my own.

"I miss you," I whisper, kissing the envelope and posting it through the hole.

And it's like magic: I immediately feel lighter.

As if I've pulled out all the heavy words and sent them far, far away, where they can't weigh me down any more. *I miss you* is gone and – just like that – my heart lifts to a white dwarf, then to the sun, then to Jupiter. Then Neptune and Saturn.

Until, finally, I'm on earth again.

Back where I belong.

29

You know what?

People can say what they like about my hippy grandmother – and judging by my parents they often do – but Bunty told me once that sometimes all you need is a good cry and an even better pen.

I think she might have been right.

By 7am the next morning, I'm feeling infinitely brighter and more positive. In fact, I've even found the massive flaw in my First Day Back plan.

I didn't have one.

After years of careful strategising, I can't believe I tried to fit back into a new life with nothing but a toilet book and an apparently pathological interest in bananas to win people over.

I will never be winging anything again.

Luckily my new plan – aka Harriet's Win People Over And Make Them Like Me Again Plan (HWPOAMTLMAP, for short) – is *so* well designed it starts working before I'm

even through the school gates.

That's how powerful it is.

"Hey," a girl in a yellow dress says, tapping me on the arm. "Do I know you from somewhere? We played volleyball last year, right? Or were you at Meg's party in February, dancing on a table?"

Volleyball. Party. Dancing on a table.

"That doesn't sound like me," I say doubtfully. "If I'd been there I'd have definitely been under it."

She laughs, even though I wasn't actually joking.

"No worries – I'll work it out. Catch you around!"

The girl wanders off and I stare in amazement at the enormous bag I'm carrying with the plan inside it.

Goodness. It's not even *open* yet.

Another two students smile as I wander through the corridors, a girl I vanquished in debate club two years ago nods at me and a group of three boys abruptly stop talking as I walk past.

And no: I'm not dressed as a bumblebee or a duck, my trainers are matching and my clothes are seasonally appropriate.

For the first time ever, I've actually checked.

"Yo, Harriet," Robert says as I reach the classroom. I open my bag and pull a pink plastic Tupperware box out. "It *is* Harriet, isn't it? You look really… nice today."

I blink at him. "Sorry?"

"Yeah. You look really… Err. Cute."

Robert has been in my form for five years, and he once sat on my foot: that's how utterly invisible I usually am to him. I stare at him in shock, then at the box I'm holding, and it all promptly makes sense again.

Oh my goodness: the poor, poor boy.

His parents clearly aren't feeding him properly. His blood sugar levels must be dangerously low.

"Thanks, Robert," I say gently. "You look nice too."

"Do I?" He grins and leans forward until I'm at risk of being stabbed in the eye by one of his gel-points. "Maybe we could look nice together at lunch sometime?"

"Sure," I say sympathetically, awkwardly patting his arm. "I'll save some sugar for you."

"That's what *I'm* talking about," he says, wiggling his eyebrows. "I reckon there's a bit of sugar with my name all over it."

Huh? How does he know that?

"There is, actually," I say in surprise, pushing the classroom door open. "And chocolate chips too, and quite a lot of peanut butt—"

But before I can get any further, every person in the room swivels round.

And the room explodes around me.

30

All I can hear now is a chorus of my name.

"Good morning, Harriet!" "Hey, Harriet!" "How was your evening, Harriet?" "What did you get up to, Harriet?" "Over here, Harriet!"

As if my class has been replaced by a flock of twittering, excited birds.

"Harriet!" Ananya says as I take a bewildered seat. "Or can I call you Ret?"

Ret? That makes me sound like a man with a big moustache and a Panama hat.

"Umm, of course," I mumble in surprise, putting the box on the desk in front of me and getting an even bigger one out. "Ret. Retty. Or… you know. Harriet is also fine."

"I'm so sorry we didn't get a chance to catch up properly yesterday. Sixth-form homework is *mad*, right? I mean, where do they think we get the time from? Does it grow on *trees*?"

"Actually, thyme is a flowering herb," I say distractedly,

still blinking at the rest of the class. "It grows best in pots."

Ananya stares at me blankly, and then explodes in a fit of giggles. "Oh my God, that's so funny! How do you think that quickly?"

I don't know what she's talking about. One neuron in the brain fires 200 times a second, but none of mine have done a single thing since I walked into the room.

I knew my plan was good, but this is ridiculous.

"Oh wow-wow-wow," Liv breathes, pointing at me. "IsthatChanelI*love*itit'sso*retro*IreallywishIhadonetoo wheredidyougetitfrom?!"

I glance down in confusion at my bright jumper. I don't know much about designers, but I don't think Coco Chanel was a big fan of badgers wearing top hats and bow ties.

"My grandmother embroidered it for me."

I mean Granny Manners: not Bunty, obviously. The latter would rather poke her own eyes out with a biro than get caught appliquéing knitwear.

"OMGthatis*so*unfair. My nan died *years* before badgers became cool. That is literally so *typical.*"

I'm not quite sure how to respond to that.

Then I glance cautiously around the room. Everyone's still staring: Robert keeps winking at me, five girls are whispering and even India gives me a brief nod.

This lot must be *starving.*

I can't help but notice that Jasper is still facing the front, utterly unmoved.

We'll just see about that.

With a sense of triumph, I open my Tupperware box and the comforting smell of freshly baked butter and sugar rises into the air. Inspiration hit me last night, at some point around the fiftieth mumbled *sugar cookie.*

All I needed was something simple and traditional. Something that would show the class that I care about them and want to be their friend: that I'm not as stuck-up as I made them think.

So – in a flash of positivity – I rushed down to a late-night supermarket.

Then I spent the entire night making, icing and decorating three hundred dinosaur-shaped sugar cookies. Pink *Isisauruses* and green *Tangvayosauruses*; purple *Argentinosauruses* and orange *Camarasauruses*. Each one personalised so that everyone in my class had their very own biscuit: name written in silver balls and jelly sweets perched on top.

With enough to win over the rest of the year too.

Maybe a few extra for the teachers.

Three for Steve, obviously: he looks like he has a sweet tooth.

And I might be exhausted, and I may still have flour in my eyebrows, but I don't care. The word *mate* comes from the Middle Low German word *gemate,* which literally means *to eat together.* So maybe this is my best shot at making friends.

Because as people start smiling, chattering to me and munching their way through the biscuits, I think I've actually done it.

I am finally part of a team again.

31

News of my awesome dinosaur biscuits spreads far and wide.

In fact, I don't want to sound smug but I may need to rethink my career objectives. Had I known my baking talents were this prodigious, I'd have taken home economics instead of woodwork.

Unless you intend to be an undertaker, there are only so many wooden boxes a girl needs to make.

During double maths, Raya sits next to me and asks "how I did it" because "it's the sort of thing she's *always* wanted to do but never had the confidence."

"Well," I say. "It's actually surprisingly easy."

Then I explain all about the importance of making sure the room is cool and how it's essential to really focus on the dough. "Although you don't want to work it too hard," I add helpfully. "It'll make it tough."

Raya shakes her head in amazement. "I've *heard* that it can be tough," she says with wide eyes. "Is there… you

know. A *lot* of dough involved?"

"It depends," I say, thinking about it honestly. "On this particular occasion, huge amounts. Like, ridiculous quantities. Masses."

I mean, it was 300 cookies, after all.

During breaktime, the girls from the netball team tell me how "lucky" I am because they're "so amazing".

"Thank you, but it's not really luck," I say as modestly as I can. "There's an awful lot of hard work involved and a lot of horrible ones get thrown out in the process. I have to stop my dog eating them."

"Your *dog*? How does that work?"

"I lock him in the laundry room for an hour or so."

"Huh."

By lunchtime, I've been asked to go ice-skating, offered an "ironic" pen with a plastic, fluff-coated unicorn coming out of the top, and gifted a bracelet made out of pink and yellow rubber bands.

I obviously make the best biscuits in the world.

Seriously.

Recent studies have shown that a combination of fat and refined sugar can reduce levels of neurofactors produced by the hippocampus, thus slowing brain capabilities. I'm slightly concerned I may have chemically damaged my classmates permanently.

Let's put it this way: I may postpone trying any until I've at least finished my AS levels and maybe graduated university.

Plus I offered Toby one and he didn't take it.

I think enough said.

By the final period, I've basically set up my own market stall in the corner of the common room. There's a flurry of people lounging around it: chatting and eating and laughing merrily, covered in a fine layer of icing sugar like plastic snowmen.

"Harriet! Want to go shopping this evening?"

"Or down to the local park?"

"Hey, Harriet! How about we go to the cinema and watch something with..." Robert looks me up and down. "Talking cartoon penguins in it?"

I beam at him. I do *love* a good cartoon penguin.

"That's hilarious," Ananya says flatly, taking his sixth biscuit off him. "Are you actually kidding? I think Ret's got slightly higher standards than a sixteen-year-old schoolboy with a face she could buy in Pizza Hut, thanks very much."

Liv appears from behind her.

"I mean, as *if* you could ever compete. Make a wish, fall asleep and dream on." She starts giggling. "OMG, that's brilliant. I'm so funny."

India looks up from the sofa and stares at Robert levelly in silence for a few seconds. "Don't be so creepy," she says coolly. "Also, consider holding back on the hair gel. It's not a dangerous weapon."

Robert glances at all three girls, and then shrugs.

"Oooh, I'm so *intimidated,*" he says, taking another biscuit. "Hubble bubble. Laters, witches."

He wanders out of the door, winking at me and still munching away, and I blink at the girls now flanking me: one in front, and one to either side.

Quietly, the rest of the group around the table is dispersing: four girls make an impromptu trip to the vending machine, Christopher decides he has a monologue to learn somewhere far away and Raya apparently needs to redo her make-up in a different room.

Why does it suddenly feel like I've got another three-headed Cerberus? And – much more importantly – what on earth are they talking about and what is going on?

"Umm..." I say awkwardly. "I'm not sure you had to be that..."

Unkind, I'm about to say when I spot two different-coloured eyes in the corner of the room, fixed firmly on mine. There's a plant called the *Mimosa Pudica* that curls up abruptly when touched: folding in on itself to protect itself. It suddenly feels like that's what my

stomach is doing too.

Jasper and I stare at each other for a few seconds as my insides retract sharply.

Then he looks away with a scowl, picks up his bag and starts pounding with a rigid back towards the door of the common room. At which point it flings open and Alexa storms in, staring at her phone.

"Hey," he says, dodging to the side. "Be careful where you're—"

But it's too late.

Alexa keeps walking and – with an enormous crash – the two people who like me least in the world collide.

Straight into each other.

32

There's a very good reason why anacondas and crocodiles aren't kept in the same zoo enclosure.

The same logic should probably extend to these two.

Jasper's art bag has fallen open and paints have gone everywhere: smashing into little pieces all over the floor. Reds and blues and greens and yellows are spread in a powdery, wet rainbow across the carpet. A couple of sheets of white paper have fallen out, and they're soaking it all up like soggy rectangular butterflies.

"Brilliant," he sighs, bending down. "Just... brilliant."

He holds the paper up, and for a few seconds I catch an incredibly beautiful pencil sketch of a large orange leaf with an autumn forest drawn inside it: browns and oranges and reds, now ruined by a thick splodge of black and purple.

In the meantime, Alexa is still finishing her text.

"Watch where you're going," she says without looking up. "Freakazoid."

"Oh, I'm so sorry." Jasper throws his paints back in his bag. "I hadn't realised I was the invisible man. Huge apologies for your inability to walk straight through me. I'll look into a way of rectifying that as soon as possible."

Then he flings his bag back over his shoulder, crumples up the ruined pages, throws them into a nearby bin and thunders out of the door. Honestly, there's some comfort to be taken from seeing that Jasper seems to dislike Alexa nearly as much as he dislikes me.

Some comfort. Not lots.

He's still not calling her names or refusing to eat any of her home-made peanut butter biscuits. Despite my best efforts, he hasn't touched a single one.

"Whatever," Alexa snaps absently, still staring at the screen of her phone. "Bye bye, mutant eyes."

Then she presses a final button and looks up.

Slowly, she scans the common room with a bored expression until her eyes finally alight on my corner.

"Oooh," she says, stalking over to me and wrinkling her nose. "Are you selling upside-down ferret biscuits, geek? How adorable."

Excuse me? Upside-down ferret biscuits?

I indignantly draw myself up to my biggest possible

size and make my voice as confident as possible.

"They're Sauropods, actually, Alexa. It means *lizard-footed*, and they were dinosaurs originating in the Triassic period with long tails and long necks. *Diplodocus* and *Brontosaurus* are the most famous versions, although technically the latter was a mistaken *Apatosaurus* and so has never actually existed. It is a dinosaur *myth.*"

"Still looks like an upside-down ferret," she says, putting one in her mouth. "Tastes a bit like one too."

Actually, now I'm looking at them again I suppose they kind of do. *Bat poop.* I might need to invest in some proper cookie cutters.

Alexa turns to her minions.

"What are you all doing in here? I told you to meet me on the tennis courts. There's a year ten and she's totally losing it with her boyfriend. It's hilarious. I want to go heckle."

She spins and starts sauntering out of the room again.

"And I thought I told you not to bother with *her* any more," she calls over her shoulder as Ananya and Liv stand up to follow her. "Let's go. As in, *now.*"

Except – as she pushes open the sixth-form door – for the second time in two days my nemesis doesn't get quite the exit she was hoping for.

"No," a sharp voice says from behind me. "Actually, Alexa, we're not going anywhere."

33

Crayfish warn each other by emptying their bladders at the first sign of danger. As the scariest person I've ever met slowly turns to face us, I'm a bit concerned I'm about to do the same thing.

I've known Alexa Roberts for eleven years, and I've never seen this expression before. Her face is very still and calm, but I'm pretty sure something is about to burst through the surface.

Like, maybe an alien or a great white shark.

"Excuse me? Would you like to repeat that, new girl?"

"Which of those seven words are you struggling with?" India says coolly, picking a little silver ball off a biscuit and sticking it in her mouth. "I'd imagine it's *no*, so I'll give you a few more pointers. We are going to stay here with Harriet today. All three of us. Is that any clearer, or would you like me to draw you a picture?"

Ananya and Liv are now frozen in the space between us mid-step, like enchanted forest fawns turned to stone.

They glance at Alexa, then India, then Alexa again.

Then at me.

Until it looks like they're watching a really confusing and awkward game of ping-pong.

Finally Ananya clears her throat.

"Actually," she says slowly, unfreezing and taking a small step back, "Indy's right, Lexi. It's a bit cold outside today. Maybe we should stay here. What do you think, Olivia?"

"Like, *totally.*" Liv folds her arms and takes a step towards me as well. "Also, I think you might be a bit over right now, Lexi. Sorry."

For the first time in history, my nemesis and I now have exactly the same facial expression. A mirrored series of Os: two for eyes, one for a mouth and two tiny ones for shocked, flared nostrils.

She turns slowly towards me, and I'm just about to leave a terrified, Harriet-Manners-shaped hole in the wall when her face abruptly changes.

Muscle by muscle, Alexa relaxes.

Her shoulders lower, her eyes normalise, her nose wiggles, her mouth twitches and a small bubble of sound pops out of her mouth. My entire stomach twists into the shape of a fresh pretzel.

Worse than anger, more dangerous than vengeance.

Is Alexa actually… *laughing*?

"*Oh*," she says, putting a hand over her eyes. "Oh, of *course*. I *get* it now. This is brilliant. How stupid *are* you? You actually think a bus stop is going to *change* things? That everything will be *different* now?"

"A bus stop?" I echo in confusion. "I'm not a bus stop."

At least, I don't *think* I am. I'm so discombobulated right now, though, I wouldn't put any money on it.

But Alexa's not even looking at me any more: she's focused intently on Ananya and Liv. "She's still *Harriet Manners*. The geek who once brought a woodlouse to school and tried to make us hold it."

OK: I was six, his name was Malcolm and I thought he was cute.

"That was a really long time ago," Ananya says, taking another step towards me. "People change."

"*Yeah*," Liv adds. "Maybe we actually *like* her."

"Nobody actually *likes* Harriet," Alexa laughs. "Even her creepy little stalker is nowhere to be seen any more. She's on her own for a *reason*."

My stomach pretzels a little bit further.

"That's your opinion," India says firmly. "We don't agree."

"Exactly." Ananya takes another few steps until she's

right next to me. "And this is getting a bit boring, Lexi. It's the same old thing, over and over again."

"*Yeah,*" Liv says, standing on my other side. "Also, hanging out on the tennis courts is *so* Year Eleven. Move on, babe. Let it go."

I'm staring at this exchange in bewildered silence.

I'd always seen the Underlings as faceless, voiceless henchmen: existing purely to provide background and visual support, but without identities of their own.

I was obviously very, very wrong.

I'm kind of expecting Alexa to break now the way I would – going red, possibly crying and hiding under a table – but she still looks intensely amused. I can't help being slightly impressed, in spite of myself.

That is pretty majestic self-confidence.

"You're right," she says finally, shrugging. "Things *were* getting a bit boring, weren't they? This way is *so* much more fun. Let's shake it up a bit."

I blink at her. What? What are we shaking?

Oh, God. I bet it's me, isn't it.

"See you around, Harriet Manners," she continues as I stare at her in amazement. "*Enjoy.*"

And the girl who likes me least in the world blows a kiss in my direction and exits the room.

Leaving her three closest friends with me.

34

Here are some things I know:

1. *The average human eye can distinguish between 500 shades of grey.*

2. *Greenland is the coldest country on earth.*

3. *We all have muscles in our ears that could once be used to move them.*

4. *A comet's tail always points away from the sun.*

Unfortunately, *what the hell is going on* is not on that list.

Call me deeply intuitive – although nobody ever does – but something is starting to tell me that this isn't all about biscuits.

I wait until the bell for the end of school rings and the girls leave in a wave of enthusiastic kisses and hugs. Then

I reach forward and break the tail off a *Camarasaurus*. Or it could be a *Giraffatitan:* honestly, they all just look like upside-down ferrets now.

It's not great.

In fact, I'm going to be honest with you: on a scale of biscuits I've ever eaten (which is a lot) it's pretty near the bottom. Plans to bolster my future palaeontology earnings with a bakery probably won't be materialising.

Frowning, I pull my phone out of my satchel and my ears suddenly go numb with shock. There are ten missed calls from Nat and eight from Stephanie at Infinity Models.

RING ME NOW THIS IS INSANELY URGENT. Nat x

Hands starting to sweat, I hit 1 on Speed Dial. Nat picks up on the first ring, and that's when I know it's serious.

"Meet me in town," she says. "Now."

"But—"

"Seriously, Harriet. You need to see this."

35

I don't even make it to the fountain.

Next to where a large proportion of my year hangs out after school, eating crisps, throwing the packets into the water and then being forced by passers-by to pick them back out again, is a bus stop.

It's where most of the buses pass through on their way to school, on their way home from school, on their way to the shops, to the hospital, to rollerskating, to… anywhere, actually.

In other words: it's right in the middle of everything.

As I slowly approach it, I see a girl I recognise.

Her face is very white and freckled, her eyes are wide and bright green, her nose and chin are slightly too pointy for comfort and her hair is pale red and unbrushed: hanging in a fluffy, knotted mass around her shoulders.

She's sitting in a lake, surrounded by glitter.

Her white dress is sparkling with a thousand tiny flashes of light, the water is glowing and shimmering

around her, and a purple sky is starred above. Behind her is an enormous, pointed mountain with a white tip and a few glowing clouds spiked on top of it. Her eyes are shining, and she's enormous: at least fifteen foot tall, if she stood up.

And next to the sparkling girl is another, much smaller one I also recognise. This one is leaning against the bus stop, against the poster. Her brown eyes are narrowed and her eyebrows are drawn together in consternation.

I reach them both in silence.

"That's not even everything," Nat says after a few seconds, grabbing my hand. "Just wait 'til you see the rest of it."

I am literally *everywhere.*

There's a huge poster of me in the designer section of the local department store: this time floating in Lake Motosu, hair and lights swirling round me as if I'm the Lady of Shalott, except set on fire.

In the make-up department is another photo: me, locked in a glass box in Akihabara, with pale pink hair, gigantic green manga-eyes and bright pink, glossy lips.

The bus-stop photo where I'm crouched in front of Mount Fuji has been turned into shiny flyers and is now being distributed outside the shopping centre to anyone who walks past.

In the window of the local chemist's is an extreme close-up of my face: eyes bright and burning and fixed slightly to the left, as if I'm staring at somebody important that the camera can't see.

Which – obviously – I was.

Nick was standing slightly behind the photographer, and he had just kissed me in the middle of a lake at sunset: I was finding it quite hard to concentrate properly.

With a shake of her head, Nat clicks on Facebook and holds her phone up in silence. I'm running in long adverts down the side of the page, wearing a gold tutu with gold paint all over my face (and tiny physics revision stickers – which I had all over my arms at the time – presumably Photoshopped out).

This doesn't make any sense. At all.

The majority of these are shots I did for designer Yuka Ito's new fashion line – clothes, accessories, make-up, the lot – in Tokyo last summer. Except that was cancelled: the whole campaign was shut down after fashion-house Baylee found out Yuka had broken her contract with them to set up her own label.

So what am I now doing all over everything?

With a sudden brain-click, yesterday's text abruptly makes sense: as if I've just plugged it into Wilbur-Translate on Google.

Wilbur	**Every other human in the world**
My little chunky-chip!	Hello!
Is this the face that launched a thousand lips?!	Your face is now selling lip gloss on a lot of posters.
Sparkle monkey everywhere!	Seriously, a lot of posters.
Fairy wins again!	Look how great I did!
Gravy	OXO = hug, kiss, hug

The *Alvinella Pompejana*, commonly known as the Pompeii worm, grows a layer of bacteria around it that protects it from high temperatures, allowing it to survive at 80°c. It is the most heat-tolerant animal on earth. Judging from the state of my cheeks right now, I may need to turn into one before I burst into flames completely.

Today's conversations are starting to replay in my head, except now they suddenly sound slightly different.

Or – you know. A lot.

Oh, there are huge amounts of dough involved. Ridiculous quantities. Masses. You really need to focus on making the dough. That's the important part.

You just need to stay as cool as possible.

I am sometimes very hot, yes. Baking, in fact. [I snort with laughter.]

Oh my God. We weren't talking about biscuits *at all.*

I stare at Nat in silence with my cheeks flaming. Why isn't there some kind of magic potion I can drink to stop me being such an idiot? Or at least make me very tiny so I can climb under a toadstool where nobody will hear me say things.

"Hey!" a girl exclaims as she walks past and double-glances at the enormous poster directly behind me. "Oh wow! Is that you?"

She points at the girl in the lake: Photoshopped and glossed and de-flawed, but – thanks to the bright orange hair, pointy nose and lack of make-up – still recognisably me.

That and the blank expression, obviously.

"Umm," I say, swallowing anxiously. "I guess so. Yes?"

"That is so cool! You're, like, famous!"

And before I can stop her, the girl snaps a photo of me with her phone and walks off.

Panic is starting to rise up like an icy tidal wave.

What is she going to do with that? American Indians used to believe that every photograph stole a part of your soul, and it suddenly feels like I've just given an irreplaceable bit of mine to a total stranger with a crystal

heart stuck on the front of her bag.

Oh God. Oh God oh God oh God oh—

"Harriet?" Nat says, grabbing my arm. "Are you OK?"

"Uh-uh," I say blankly as the panic keeps rising: to my ankles, to my knees, to my stomach and my shoulders. "Mmmm. Brilliant. Superbo."

"Totally not a word," Nat says gently, patting me as if I'm a small puppy on firework night. "This is *freaking awesome*, H. I'm *so* proud of you." She strokes my arm a few more times – eyes shiny and far away – and then adds in a burst of triumph: "I *knew* you'd be a megastar eventually."

And that does it.

Panic washes up from my shoulders, into my throat and over my head until I can't breathe. Leaving me with no other option but to abruptly crouch down on the floor outside the chemist's, put my head between my knees.

And have a very un-awesome panic attack.

36

Experts say that the best way to stop a panic attack is to find something else to think about.

Unfortunately, there's a massive flaw in this logic.

I'm now so anxious about finding something else to think about I can't inhale at all.

In desperation, I close my eyes and begin reciting the periodic table loudly: starting at the alkali metals and working to the right until I can feel myself beginning to calm down again. *Lithium. Sodium. Potassium. Rubidium.* Then Alkaline earth metals. *Beryllium, Magnesium, Calcium, Strontium.* Then Transition metals*: Scandium, Yttrium, Titanium.*

I'm all the way into the noble gases before I'm stable enough to look up again.

The irony of which does not escape me.

"You know..." Nat says, sitting on her coat next to me. She hands me half a chocolate-chip biscuit she must have found at the bottom of my satchel. "You may be

the only supermodel in the world who repeats the entire periodic table when stressed."

"It wasn't the entire thing," I admit sheepishly. "I still had lanthanoids and actinoids to go. And ununoctium." Then I stuff the entire cookie in my mouth and anxiously spray: "And I'm not a supermodel, Nat."

Except it comes out *nmnaspamdlnatttt.*

"Maybe not quite," Nat agrees, grinning with excitement. "But you're *definitely* about a million steps closer."

A few more waves of terror ripple through me.

You know what's utterly ridiculous?

I've been modelling for nearly a year now – since I was unintentionally spotted at a fashion event that Nat dragged me to. Ten full months of getting paid to stand in front of a camera and wear beautiful clothes in foreign countries – first Russia, then Japan, then New York – and this is the first time it's actually felt *real*. All this time, I've used modelling to run away, to run towards – to escape, find myself, lose myself, transform – but never as an end in and of itself. I've been so focused on the verb – *modelling* – that it never once occurred to me that I'm also the noun.

Harriet Manners: *model*.

Or that my face might actually one day be used in

public to, you know: sell things.

Because apparently I'm an intelligent girl with no grasp of cause and effect, who thought she could have all these great fashion adventures and then the evidence would just up and vanish as soon as she was done.

Poof! Like the magical fairytales they were.

Seriously. I'm supposed to be getting smarter as I get older. Nobody told me it would be the other way round.

"What is this dress even made of?" Nat continues, staring at the leaflet. "How does it light up like that?"

"It's thin woven optical fibres," I say distantly. "They're hollow, which allows photons of light to bounce down the centre of them and—"

A sudden memory flashes.

Nick, looking like the world's most beautiful banana in yellow wellies and a yellow waterproof coat. I can remember the exact coldness of the water, the precise warmth of my stomach and fingers and toes. The position of the stars and the lights; the shape of the mountain and the lake. The happy glow in his eyes.

The happy glow in mine.

Now immortalised and stuck all over town to remind me of exactly what I don't have any more every time I need to buy deodorant.

Without equal.

Oh my God: of all the shoots I've ever done, why did they have to stick *this* one in the window of the chemist? I'm going to smell for the rest of the year.

Wobbling slightly, I get to my feet.

Abruptly, I need to get as far away from both the shopping precinct and this particular photo as fast as physically possible.

"Harriet," Nat says, jumping up too, "I know you're freaking out right now, but I honestly think you just need a little time to process how amazing this is. This is *huge*, H. It's *epic*. You've really made it."

I stare at my best friend blankly.

"Here," she adds, thrusting a leaflet into my hand. "I'm so sorry, but I need to run back to college for a late class on evening gowns. I only popped out to pick up some extra material."

Nat pulls a bit of black satin out of her bag to show me, gives me a tight hug, then starts trotting towards the bus stop. "Call me when it's sunk in, OK?" she yells over her shoulder.

I nod, but honestly: she may be waiting some time.

According to the Oxford English Dictionary, the word *epic* can mean *impressive or remarkable*.

It can also mean *heroic or grand in scale.*

Since I was five years old, I've thought about all the

ways I might eventually make my mark on the world. Dragons I could fight and winged horses I could fly and elements I could magic into being with my bare hands. Then – when I got a little older – I dreamed about diseases I could cure, dinosaur fossils I could unearth and stars I could discover and then name.

I've spent eleven *years* of my life studying as hard as I can in the hope that one day – with enough knowledge, enough commitment and enough dedication – I might eventually achieve something worthwhile.

Something heroic. Something grand.

Something *epic*.

I just never thought for a single second that my most tangible achievement would come at sixteen years old for sitting in a lake, wearing somebody else's clothes and staring at a camera.

Doing absolutely *nothing*.

37

On the upside, somebody else knows what I look like too now. As soon as Nat's gone, I somehow stumble to the bench near my house, plonk myself down and make the obligatory call-back.

My hands are shaking, my head is spinning.

My fingers are so sweaty it takes four attempts before I can get my phone to stop taking accidental selfies up my nostrils.

"Lovely *girl*! How *are* you, darling? We haven't *spoken* for simply *ages*!"

I pull my phone away from my face and stare at Stephanie's voice for a few seconds. We haven't spoken for simply ages because last time I rang Infinity Models I heard her say:

"Who? Tell her I'm out."

"But I can hear her," I observed, and the receptionist passed the message on.

"Then tell her I'm dead. Freak polo accident."

"I can still hear her," I said sadly. "But thanks for trying."

I've rung Infinity Models thirteen times over the four months since my return from Tokyo, and this is the first time Wilbur's replacement has ever picked up. It's quite difficult to really get to know someone properly when they're pretending to fall off horses.

"I'm fine, thank you." I'm slightly tempted to point out she sounds pretty buoyant for a recently deceased person.

"That's 'triffic!" she trills. "And *how's* your..." There's a pause while she tries to remember anything about me. "*Anyway*, I was just calling to say that my phone has been on *fire* this morning with *love* for my best model. Those photos are *just scrummy.* What a *seuw-per* time you must have *had* in China!"

"Japan."

"Exactly! I just *adore* Mount Kilimanjaro!"

"Fuji."

"Yah! I have some *very* big designers who want to see you, ey ess ey pee. Gucci, Prada, Versace, you name it. Pop in on Monday and I'll set up some meetings."

I blink. "I'm sorry, Stephanie, but I'm at school."

"*Are* you, darling? How *delightful*! What *for*?"

"Umm." I've never had to explain the concept of education before. "Knowledge. Learning. Books and my future and so on."

"Ri-iiiiight. And that can't be cancelled?"

I haven't actually met Stephanie before, but I suddenly remember that Wilbur isn't exactly a fan, to say the least.

"Not really, because… you know. It's *school*."

"That's terribly inconvenient. Perhaps we should consider phasing it out. You know, gradually doing less of it." There are a few loud taps on a keyboard. "Yah, no, yah. I'll work something out. In the meantime, how does first thing tomorrow sound?"

"Sorry, sound for what?"

"Three days in Marrakech. Lovely job for Levaire, just come through today."

We each blink an average of 6.25 million times a year, but if I'm not careful this phone call is going to use up the rest of my year's rations and I'll have to walk round until Christmas with my eyes shut.

"Levaire? As in Jacques Levaire, the jeweller?" Even *I've* heard of him. Nat's unsuccessfully had a Levaire necklace on her Christmas list ever since she realised Santa was actually her mother. "Marrakech as in… *Marrakech*?"

"Yah, darling. Spain, Europe. Vah hot. Sand and so forth."

"Morocco," I say automatically. "North Africa." I'm starting to wonder if Stephanie needs me to send her a world map.

"Exactly, darling. That's what I said."

I stare at my phone.

An hour ago, I assumed my fashion career was completely done. Now my face is all over town and I'm being invited to *Africa* to shoot for *Jacques Levaire.*

With an abrupt lurch, my heart does a familiar, excited humpback whale leap: into the sky, twisting around.

I'd *love* to go to Morocco.

I know quite a lot about it already: it's the westernmost country in the Arab world, and some say Hercules himself forced apart Europe and Africa with his bare hands, thus forming the Straits of Gibraltar. It's also considered by many as one of the most dramatic, exotic and compelling destinations there is, and I've studied all the guidebooks already.

Just – you know – in case.

It would mean modelling again, and I've actually kind of missed it.

It would be an adventure.

Plus, most importantly, it'll give me something to do other than sitting on my doorstep, staring at the sky and *waiting.*

"I'll—" I start, then stop.

The whale crashes back into the water again with an enormous splash.

I can't *keep* using modelling to run away, can I? I have polynomials and factor/remainder theorem to learn at school tomorrow.

My parents will go *mad.*

Not to mention the fact that I've just discovered I don't really like seeing my face on posters very much. It gives me anxiety attacks on the floors of shopping malls.

But… *Morocco.*

"Stephanie, may I have a couple of minutes to think about it?"

"Absolutely. And Hannah, dahling?"

"It's Harriet."

"Yah. This one is fifteen."

I blink a few more times. Fifteen years? Fifteen carrots? Fifteen bottles, hanging on the wall?

"Pounds?" That's not a *huge* amount of money, but I'm really not super experienced, I haven't worked in a month, the flights must cost quite a lot and then there's hotels to think about and…

"Fifteen grand, darling. Think about it."

And the phone goes dead.

Stephanie may be gone – although probably not to the Other Side just yet – but I'm still staring at the phone.

Fifteen *thousand* pounds? Somebody wants to give

me fifteen *thousand* pounds for something I'd happily do for free?

That is an *awful* lot of money.

Not just for a sixteen-year-old, either. It's three years' income for a single man in possession of a good fortune, according to *Pride and Prejudice.* It's 911 times what Jo March sold her hair for in *Little Women* and nearly two months of James Bond's salary. It's – perhaps slightly more relevantly – one and a half whole years at Cambridge University.

My head is starting to spin; my hands are shaking.

So I take an enormous breath and decide to ring the only person left in the world who might actually have some answers.

And that is really saying something.

Wilbur.

38

It takes eighteen attempts to finally reach him, but I just keep staunchly going until I do.

Frankly, I have never played it cool in my entire life.

I don't think now is the time to start.

"Squirrel-hips!" he squeaks finally. "Hold your Shetland ponies, this boy has written the wrong name on my pumpkin-spiced latte." Wilbur's voice gets a little more distant. "It's with a *bur*, not an *iam*. Yes, like the pig in *Charlotte's Web*.... *Excuse* me?"

"My little sugar-lump," he says, coming back to the phone. "I don't care how adorable this American barista is, if he oinks at me again I *will* report him to the RSPCA."

It suddenly feels like there's a piece of apple lodged in my throat. I hadn't realised when Wilbur left England for a new fashion job in New York quite how big the hole he'd left in my life would be.

"Wilbur, what outfit are you wearing?" I really need to visualise him. "At this precise moment, what have

you got on?"

He takes this very creepy question completely in his stride. "A fake fur panda poncho with sticky-up ears and fluoro pink trousers that just *scream* I'm All That And A Bag of Kale Chips, darling. I look fabulous. Everybody wants to be me, or date me, or dehydrate me and keep me *forever*. Like a fig or maybe a raisin."

I smile in satisfaction. I could be in New York right now, trying hard not to cuddle him like a massive rainbow kitten.

"So what's cookin', my little pookin'? Did you get my text?"

"Umm. Yes." I swallow and to my horror, there's a slight wobble in my voice. "That's actually why I'm ringing. Wilbur, I don't understand. What's happening? Why is my face everywhere? I thought Yuka's campaign wasn't going ahead any more."

Wilbur snorts loudly with laughter.

"Oh, *dilly*-dandelion," he giggles. "That was *never* going to happen. Yuka obviously took Baylee to court immediately, like the rabid Rottweiler of fashion she is. After she won she decided to go *hugeungous* with her new label to make a point. *Shoe-fungous, moo-gungous, boo-gungous*."

One day – when we've got less to discuss – I'm going

to ask Wilbur why he doesn't just say *big*.

"But why with me?"

"I thought that was obvious, monster-munch. You've always been her favourite ginger-frog. So much love in the room."

Over the course of my modelling career, Yuka Ito has shouted at me, turned lights off and on over my head, locked me in glass boxes, thrown me into cold water, surrounded me with dead things and fired me. She must put models she's *not* fond of in the oven and then eat them.

"But what about the gold-painted photo?" I ask in confusion. "That was for Baylee, wasn't it?"

"Indeed it was," Wilbur laughs. "Yuka poached you off them too: I think this is their way of fighting witch with fire. Oooh, that reminds me. She had a message for you and I'll remember it just as soon as this caffeine hits my bloodstream. It's a triple shot so it won't take long."

I can hear him blowing on his coffee 3,459 miles away: bright blue sky above him, yellow and orange leafy Central Park behind him, Empire State Building looming over. Brooklyn Bridge is suddenly so close I can almost see it.

I feel a homesick pang in my chest. Which is weird because I'm sitting right next to the house I actually live in.

"Boom," Wilbur continues jubilantly. "She says: *done*."

"*Done?* What does that mean?"

"Sugar-munch, if I understood what Yuka Ito was talking about I'd be the only person in the world and would have an entirely different and very lucrative career as a Yuka-whisperer."

I frown. She probably means *done*, as in *cooked*: marinated and ready for frying, quite possibly.

And then it hits me.

Last December, I stood in Infinity Models with a spotlight over my head and told Yuka I wanted to model so that *things would change.*

More specifically: me.

That's what she's done: she's given me exactly what I asked for. It just didn't happen according to the schedule I originally laid out for it, that's all.

I'm starting to realise maybe nothing ever does.

"So…" I'm ripping at the skin around my fingernails with my teeth. "What happens next, Wilbur? What do I do?"

"Chipmunk," he laughs. "I'm your fairy godmother, not your fortune cookie. Tell me, is Stephanie still wearing scrunchies without any kind of irony? She should *not* be allowed in fashion. The woman is single-handedly

preventing velvet from coming back in again."

It's only now starting to hit me that I've never done this before without him and I'm not sure I know how to.

"Wilbur, if I take the job in Morocco, will you come with me? Please?"

"I'd love to, munchkin," he sighs. "I am so over New York I could hurdle it in eight-inch heels. But fairy godmothers don't go to the ball, as much as we might want to. We simply get you ready and send you on your way."

I stare at the pavement, because maybe that's the problem. "But what if I'm *not* ready?"

"Then don't go," Wilbur says more gently. "Fame, fortune, success: you can take them or leave them, baby-baby-panda. We've given you the fairytale. What you do with it now is up to you."

39

Head still spinning, I say goodbye to Wilbur.

Then, slowly, I open the sweaty, crumpled photo I have scrunched in my hands.

I stare at the glittering girl in the lake.

Underneath **YUKA ITO** in small, gold letters is a picture of a glass perfume bottle that looks like a flame: frosted white glass that starts dark gold at the bottom and gets clearer and lighter towards a tip that curves upwards. There's a tiny light built into the base, so the entire bottle looks like it's glowing from the inside.

Beneath that is one large, silver word:

SHINE

And I suddenly feel like I'm splitting down the middle: torn into two pieces.

On one side is Harriet Manners, *geek*.

Shy, clumsy, anxious and unpopular. Awkward and constantly apologetic. Collector of stick insects, inventor of personalised Monopoly games, dryer of socks. Dressed like a duck, hyperventilating on floors and hiding under tables.

Embracer of other people's stories instead of her own.

Heartbroken, lonely and left behind.

On the other side is Harriet Manners, *model.*

Traveller through exotic foreign countries, grabber of opportunities, chaser of adventures. Successful and interesting. Wearer of designer clothes, desired employee of the fashion industry, explorer of strange cities and adored girlfriend of Nicholas Hidaka.

Loved, wanted and remembered.

Today at school suddenly flashes in front of me.

That's what has changed, isn't it?

Thanks to these impossibly beautiful and glossy photos, everybody has seen another side to me. The geek they've known for years has evaporated overnight, and in her place is the seemingly confident, successful version of me. Fearless and mysterious; intrepid and brave.

They've seen this glittering girl and they like her.

And you know what?

I think I do too.

I stare at the photo for a few more seconds, and – with an abrupt *crack* – I suddenly know which one of these two girls I want to be. And clue: it's not the one who hides under her duvet, crying and wishing life was different.

"Stephanie?" I say when she picks up on the second ring. "I'm taking the job. In fact, from this point onwards I'll be taking all of them."

"*Seuwper*," she says, tapping on a few keys. "I've just put the phone down on Gucci, Wang and McQueen so we'll sort something out for when you're back. This is just the start, darling. You're going to be *huge*. Deets on the way."

As I hang up, a tidal wave rushes over me again, except this time it's not cold or panicky.

It's warm and hopeful, and it leaves me glowing.

Everything in my life has already changed, and this is my only chance to change with it. To pick up my own story and turn the pages.

To start moving forward again.

Because whether I wanted to or not, nearly a year

ago I split in half. There are now two Harriets, two lives, two people I can be.

Wilbur was right: it's up to me which one I want.

And I choose the one that shines.

40

So, here are some interesting facts about lying:

- *By the age of four, ninety per cent of children understand the concept of telling falsehoods.*
- *Sixty per cent of adults can't make it through a ten-minute conversation without saying something that isn't true.*
- *Compulsive lying makes you scientifically smarter.*
- *We're much likelier to lie to the people we love than to strangers.*
- *I do it a lot.*

Like, a *lot* a lot.

I don't *mean* to, obviously. It's just that I've worked out over a period of sixteen years that the chances of upsetting people, not getting what you want and finding yourself in trouble tend to be *considerably* higher if you tell the truth.

However, I have *also* learnt that building an intricate web of deceit almost always results in me getting caught in the middle of it, like a really stupid spider.

So I sit on the bench for a few minutes and think really hard. I do a little internet research. I make a couple of important decisions.

Then I decide to try something brand new.

Something unprecedented; something nobody would ever expect me to do in a million, billion years.

For the first time in known history, I resolve not to wear a thematically brilliant costume or make a fiercely relevant PowerPoint presentation. I won't be typing out any clever arguments about insects or writing pie charts or flow charts or area graphs and then forcing them on my parents.

I'm not going to run away, or cry, or cover myself in dots of lipstick and coat myself in a fine layer of talcum powder to feign sickness, and I won't pretend to fall down the stairs or break an arm or fake my own death with a very noisy vacuum cleaner.

Nope.

This time really matters, so I need to bring out the big guns. I need to concentrate all my persuasive powers and give it everything I've got.

So I do something I've never, ever done before.

I walk calmly home. I walk calmly into the living room. I sit down calmly with my parents.

And I tell them everything.

Or nearly everything, anyway.

I give them the leaflet and explain in detail about the impact of this campaign on my fashion career, and how Jacques Levaire now wants me to go to Morocco for a shoot.

But I keep my new mission to myself.

The truth can be a powerful thing; it's not sensible to overdo it.

"I'm confused," Annabel says when I've finally finished, still staring at the glittering girl clutched in her hand. "Where's the PowerPoint presentation? What's happening?"

"It's a trick," Dad says, narrowing his eyes at the corners of the room. "Mark my words, there's a camcorder here somewhere, humiliating us on telly as we speak."

He winks and blows the DVD player a kiss.

"It's not a trick," I say even more calmly. "Parents are statistically the most lied-to section of society, and I think I speak for all of us when I say I am normally at the very forefront of this movement. I just thought I'd experiment with a different approach this time, that's all."

There's a silence while Dad checks under the coffee table.

Then he explodes into the air.

"OH MY GOD my daughter is a SUPERMODEL and I'm going TO *MOROCCO*!" he shouts, running into the hallway and tugging his suitcase out from under the stairs. "Finally! Casinos, Formula One and Grace Kelly! This is the life to which I've intended to become accustomed for *ages.*"

"That's Monaco, Richard," Annabel says, still looking at the flyer. "You're thinking of Monaco."

"Oh." He pauses. "Does Morocco have private jets? Because if so I think I could be equally happy there."

Finally my stepmother looks up and stares steadily at me, as if I'm a foreign film she's trying to translate and it's much, much harder than she expected.

My hands are starting to sweat again. I've had an entire lifetime of trying to fool my parents. This was an *extremely* risky moment to stop doing it.

I grip my hands together a little more tightly.

Frankly, I know exactly who I have to convince, and it is not my father. I could have won him over with half a packet of crisps and a chocolate digestive.

"Please, Annabel. I miss modelling, it's an amazing opportunity, a *lot* of money and I will make up the two

days I miss from school. I'm even prepared to take Dad with me."

Prepared. Which is not the same as *willing*.

"WOOOOOOOO!" my father yells from the corridor. "Yachts! Helicopters! A tax haven full of parties and glitz and—"

"Still Monaco, Richard." Annabel hands the leaflet back to me. "That's a lovely photo, Harriet. You look absolutely beautiful. The answer's yes."

I nod slowly.

"I understand. Thank you for your time and considera— Sorry, what?"

"You can go. Absolutely. Yes."

"But..." My calmness has now evaporated. "*What* would you – *why* would you... *Why*?"

"Why not? You've just proved to me that you're not a little girl any more. You've explained things logically, you've been honest and it makes total sense. It's entirely our fault that you missed the first four weeks of term, so I don't think two more days are going to make a vast amount of difference. In fact, I think a bit of an adventure in Morocco is just what you need right now given... everything. I'm wholeheartedly behind it."

I stare at Annabel in amazement.

What? She has got to be kidding me. I can't believe

I've spent so many years slamming doors: I could have saved *so* many hinges if I'd just tried this approach earlier.

I close my eyes tightly for a few seconds – relief rushing through me – then impulsively throw myself on the sofa and bury my nose in my stepmother's pinstripe shoulder-pad.

"*Thank you,*" I whisper, lobbing my arms round her. "I'm going to be *so good,* Annabel. I'll do everything I'm told, I won't break anything, I won't get into any trouble, and I'll..."

Somehow lose Dad.

Maybe exchange him for a camel, or a really useful leather footrest.

"Oh, I know," Annabel says calmly, folding up her crossword and kissing the top of my head. "Because this time, I'm coming with you."

41

Dad sulks for the rest of the evening.

"You went to Russia with Harriet," Annabel explains as she retrieves our summer clothes from under her bed. "It's my turn, isn't it?"

"Well, if I'd known it was a *choice*, I'd have picked this trip," Dad complains. "It was *really* cold out there, and there was nothing but cabbage to eat. Plus none of the Russian supermodels would talk to me. This is *so unfair.*"

This is so unfair is then repeated for the rest of the evening.

It's so unfair as we pack our suitcases, and so unfair as we fold up our maps and get out our guidebooks. It's unfair as we pull the suncream out of the cupboard, and *really really really* unfair when we look at the temperatures and discover it's twenty-six degrees in Morocco and climbing. It's unfair as we put our suitcases in the car the next morning, and unfair as Dad drives us to the airport.

But by the time my father leaves us at the security gates, he appears to have finally made peace with the decision.

"On the bright side," he says cheerfully, kissing us both goodbye, "when Harriet goes to the Maldives, I'm first in line, right?"

"Absolutely," Annabel says, kissing him back and snuggling the top of Tabitha's head. I give my sister a little kiss as well and she squeaks so adorably I'm temporarily tempted to put her in my bag and take her with us.

"Take care of my baby, OK?"

Although – frankly – by this point it's not really clear which one of the two she's referring to.

In the meantime, my excitement levels are rising rapidly and exponentially. With the help of my guidebooks, my fact books, my translation books and my detailed maps of Marrakech, I've spent pretty much the entire last fifteen hours studying.

I know about the prehistoric rock engravings of the Figuig region. I know about the 50,000-year-old remains of a sixteen-year-old Neanderthal boy discovered in a cave near Rabat, and the magical city of Chefchaouen: painted entirely blue to symbolise the skies and the heavens.

I also know that nobody else wants to know these things: the old man next to me pretends to fall asleep

halfway through me reading him the Moroccan Political History Chart on page four of my chunkiest guidebook.

But as the plane climbs through the grey clouds over London and pops into a bright blue, shiny sky, it feels like the excited bubbles inside me are multiplying by the second: not unlike the experiment we did in biology last year with micro-organisms in a Petri dish.

Except hopefully slightly more glamorously.

And with slightly less fuzzy green mould.

"Ssalamu lekum," I say experimentally to the air hostess as she brings us round peanuts. (This means *hello* in Arabic.) "Sbah el kheyr," I say cheerfully as she gives me a wet towel. (*Good morning.*) "Me ssalami," I chirp as she offers us breakfast.

"We don't have salami," she frowns. "It's a cheese or beef sandwich."

"I was trying to say *goodbye* in Arabic," I explain.

"Then that's m'a ssalama."

I quickly scan my translation book for *thank you.* "*Shukrun bezzef,*" I attempt.

"Beef it is," she says, plonking it in front of me.

By the time large, dusty expanses of land outside the plane window start to speckle with exotic peach and orange buildings, I'm so high on adrenaline I'm tempted to run up and down the aisles of the plane, clapping my

hands together and screaming.

Except there's already a four-year-old doing that, and it's not making her very popular.

So I probably won't.

Finally, the plane makes a smooth landing and the two of us – both child and I – break into uproarious applause. Then Annabel and I tug our suitcases through a white, delicately carved airport that looks exactly like an ornate wedding cake, towards a man holding a sign that says **HANNAH MANNERS**.

I'm way too thrilled to correct him.

According to my research, there are three Harriet Manners in the world, and for the next half-hour I am more than happy to no longer be one of them.

The driver leads us in silence out of enormous, glass airport doors into hot, dense, fragrant air. Then I hesitate for a few seconds and fiddle anxiously with a piece of paper in my pocket.

Annabel looks at me steadily.

She's let me chatter in excitement the entire way here: for six solid hours. In fact, when the lady sitting in front of us turned round and glared at me with a loud, pointed sigh, Annabel took her glasses off and stared until the lady went pink and disappeared again.

Now it feels like my stepmother's reading me as

carefully as I've been reading any of my guidebooks. I just don't know quite what she's looking for, that's all.

"Umm." I clear my throat. "Annabel, will you give me a few seconds? There's just something quick I have to do before we get there."

My stepmother studies my face a little longer.

Then she puts her sunglasses on.

"Absolutely. Take your time. I'll be in the car, making sure your father hasn't already exchanged our youngest for a PlayStation."

She winks at me and I wink back.

Then I walk across a bright, sunlit pavement into the shade of an enormous palm tree, feeling more full of hope than I have in weeks.

Maybe this time I don't need Wilbur after all.

42

Cautiously, I move around the side of the tree until Annabel can't see me. Then I open the scrumpled piece of paper that has been clutched tightly in my hand ever since I printed it out this morning: the online research I did while sitting on the bench last night.

The bit of truth I kept from my parents.

<u>How To Find Your Inner Star!!!</u>

1. ***Be Confident!*** **You are a creature unlike any other!**
2. ***Take Risks, Be Brave!*** **There is no limit to what you can do!**
3. ***Be Stylish!*** **Shake it up and try something new!**
4. ***Inspire!*** **Lead, never follow!**
5. ***Don't try too hard!*** **It just looks desperate!!!!**
6. ***Believe in yourself!*** **Soon everyone else will to!**

I've been surreptitiously reading and memorising it since I found it.

I didn't write it, obviously.

If I *had*, I'd have corrected *to* to *too* and held back on quite a few of the exclamation marks. That much punctuation is basically the grammatical equivalent of grabbing somebody by the collar and shaking them while screaming right into their face.

Which is exactly why I screenshot the list directly off the internet and left them all there. This is incredibly important, and I don't want to get anything wrong because I've gone and corrected some grammar.

Also, maybe this kind of aggressive positive energy is *exactly* what I need in my life right now. Something to get me moving in the right direction, when I'm not sure quite how to do it by myself. It's like having my very own perky, bouncy life coach in my pocket, or maybe some kind of tiny sergeant major.

Jubilantly, I kiss the list that's going to alter my life.

I put the paper in my pocket, walk to the car and climb into the back with the most confident swish of my head I can possibly manage.

Then – just for added impact – I put my sunglasses on.

They're bright red and they've got glitter all over them. I got them in the airport and they remind me of Dorothy's magic slippers.

Except I didn't have to kill anyone to get them.

Obviously.

"Ready?" Annabel says as the car pulls away from the airport and begins its dusty, winding journey into the centre of Marrakech.

"I am." I smile brightly at her. "I'm ready."

Because if you do the same thing over and over again, you can't expect different results.

If I really want *things to change*...

They have to start with me.

43

When I was ten years old, I had my tonsils out.

And I *still* managed to tell the entire hospital ward that for thirty minutes after they've been removed, human tonsils can bounce higher than a rubber ball if dropped on the floor.

What I'm trying to say is: it takes an awful lot to shut me up. Within three minutes, Morocco has somehow achieved it.

As we drive slowly into the ancient medina, the world outside the car windows begins to unravel into a carnival of colour and noise. Narrow, dusty streets are crammed with people in long turquoise robes, pink scarves, blue and red and green hats, embroidery in white and grey and purple. Cars are everywhere – beeping at each other and parked willy-nilly in streets while drivers talk to each other, yell, laugh and shout – and scooters weave nonchalantly in and out of the traffic.

Dotted here and there are animals: horses, trotting

along the road drawing little green carriages; wild-eyed ginger cats, streaking down alleyways; brown donkeys laden with brightly woven bags and camels chewing patiently in little huddles.

And as we get out of the car and start wheeling our bags through narrow, cobbled streets, it intensifies yet further.

From uneven peach and yellow walls hang fabrics in every colour of the rainbow; red and yellow bags, silver jewellery, rows of sparkling slippers in greens and oranges, glass lanterns, carved wood and painted ceramics.

Sunshine stripes the walls and floors with lines of yellow, and the smell changes every few seconds: from fruit to incense to flowers to a faint scent of urine mixed with leather.

Sounds are blended – French, Arabic, English, American, laughter, music, shouts – and piles of food lie glistening on tables: pointed mounds of musky spices, trays of figs, mountains of oranges in carefully constructed pyramids.

Every time I turn my head, there's something else to see, something else to smell.

Finally, the driver stops outside a small, heavy wooden blue door and knocks on it.

With a loud squeak, it swings open.

And the world transforms yet again.

The chaos has abruptly disappeared.

A long turquoise pool stretches across the floor, lit from below. Lanterns line pale, marble floors with arched doorways, tinkling flute music plays, columns and ornate iron balconies stretch upwards in a mass of stone carvings.

Enormous stained-glass lights hang from the ceiling, and flowers, mirrors, incense sticks, elaborately painted furniture and silk cushions are scattered everywhere like a carnage of tired butterflies.

It feels as if we've climbed inside the lamp of a particularly house-proud genie.

"Right," Annabel says after a few minutes of totally awestruck silence. She sinks into one of the velvet sofas with a little sigh. "This is my new house, Harriet. If your father wants me, tell him I will be in this exact position for the next three years."

"That's what I like to hear." A gentleman walks towards us in white trousers and a white tunic. He has two tiny glasses of steaming honey-coloured liquid, which he places calmly in front of us. "I'm so glad you like it. Alan wa Salan. Mint tea?"

"Make that five years," Annabel says, gratefully taking her glass. "Six if there's a ginger biscuit."

"Hello, Alan," I say, sticking my hand out *confidently* and plonking my suitcase down. "It's nice to meet you,

and also super cool that your first name rhymes with your last name. You must have very poetic parents."

Alan laughs.

"*Alhan wa salhan* means *welcome* in Arabic. My name is Ali, and I'm the manager of this riad. There is a Berber proverb that says you have to calm the surface of the lake to see to the bottom." He waves a hand gracefully around. "That is what I try to achieve here. Anything you wish, it is my pleasure to grant."

I beam at him. Looks like we found the genie.

"Eight years," Annabel whispers, standing up and looking at the carved stone ceiling. "Nine if there's a garden."

"I'm afraid you only have a couple of minutes to freshen up," Ali continues, gently pivoting both our suitcases and leading us quietly through a little marble hallway into a powder-blue room, full of flowers and lilac silks and bright paintings. "The crew is setting up in Jemaa el-Fnaa at the moment."

There's a four-poster bed, which I immediately sit on and start happily bouncing up and down.

"Ali, did you know that Morocco contains one of the most ancient civilisations in the entire world? The oldest ever child's skull was found here. It dates back a hundred and eight *thousand* years, which means it's all the way

from the early Pleistocene period. Isn't that cool?"

"Very cool," Ali says with a small smile. "The director and stylist are in the lounge now. When you're ready, I'll take you down."

"Thank you so much." I bounce a few more times. "Also, did you know that in Morocco you have *forty* different ecosystems of animals, which used to include lions and bears and—"

I abruptly stop. Hang on a minute.

"Sorry, *director*? Do you mean… photographer?"

"Apologies," Ali says, bowing slightly. "I'm not totally up to speed with fashion terminology. What do you call a man who directs a television commercial?"

A man named Ashrita Furman holds the current world record for the most forward rolls ever done in one hour (1,330). He also holds the record for the fastest somersaults, longest top spinning, quickest leapfrogging and most star jumps, and is arguably a very twisty and flippy kind of man.

I think my stomach just beat him at all of them.

Oh my God.

I'm here to shoot a television commercial?

"I think th-there's been some kind of mistake," I eventually stutter, jumping up and grabbing Ali's hand.

"I'm not an actress, I'm a model and I'm here to shoot a campaign for Jacques Levaire and—"

"I'm afraid there's no time," Ali says brightly, handing me three sheets of A4 paper covered in very small writing. "See you in a few minutes, Hannah Manners."

44

Here are just a few occasions when I have failed to move as expected in public:

- *The time I sat down on a catwalk in Moscow in front of three hundred of the fashion elite*
- *The moment I smashed my way out of a glass arcade game in Akihabara*
- *The destruction of a couture dress as a result of irritating an octopus until it squirted me with ink*
- *Every single time I try to put a straw in my mouth without concentrating properly*
- *Approximately a billion other occasions.*

Frankly, my clumsiness has already been pretty well documented.

I'm not entirely sure we need any more evidence.

Especially not on film.

With my brain making small, desperate clicking sounds,

I stare in confusion at the paper I've just been given. It appears to be some kind of brief, with JACQUES LEVAIRE INTERNATIONAL TIMEPIECE ADVERTISING CAMPAIGN typed at the top. With a CV and photo stapled to the front.

It's definitely me – I recognise the freckles, the too-far-apart eyes, the pointy nose and vacant expression – but underneath it in neatly italicised letters is written:

HANNAH MANNERS
model-artist-performer-dancer-actress

I've been hyphenated *five* times?

Even in my panic I can't help feeling quite impressed: pushy American model Kenderall would be so jealous of me right now.

"Trained at RADA?" Annabel frowns over my shoulder. "Graduated from a dance programme with the Royal Academy of Arts? A summer with the Royal Shakespeare Company? Harriet, do you have a Nobel peace prize knocking around somewhere that I don't know about?"

The entire document is packed with achievements.

Short films I've starred in, awards I've won, songs I'm capable of singing entirely *a cappella*. There's a brief

summary of the time I triumphed in *The Phantom of The Opera*, and a paragraph all about just how wide my splits are and how fast I can backflip. My emotional *range*, apparently, is quite outstanding.

Except none of it was me, obviously.

Having known me for a year now, I'd imagine you've already worked that out for yourself.

"Stephanie's sent them the wrong details," I say in a blank voice. "She actually, literally thinks I'm Hannah Manners."

Yah, Hannah, darling. That's what I said.

I look at Annabel with wide eyes.

I can't do this. I can't film an *international television commercial* as if I'm somebody who knows exactly what they're doing. I struggle to behave like a normal human being in private, let alone when it's being recorded for posterity and shown to millions.

I glance at the brief again.

Like, literally millions. This is being shown in England. France. Italy. America. South America. Spain. Portugal. Russia. Australi—

Oh my God. Ohmygodohmygodohmygodohmy—

Hydrogen. Lithium. Sodium. Potassium...

"Harriet, sweetheart." Annabel sits down next to me on the bed and gently pulls my hands away from

my face. "This is exactly why I'm here: to sort out misunderstandings like this. Just give me a few minutes, and I'll go and explain everything."

She stands up and grabs her briefcase: always ready to fight some kind of legal battle, even on holiday.

Except… then what?

Annabel tells them I have the *emotional range* of a peanut, and then what happens? It's too late to get sent home now. I'll have to model anyway: they'll just know I'm not good enough before I've even started.

Plus… isn't this what I wanted? The opportunity to be someone better? Someone… starrier? Even if it means – temporarily – being someone *else*? Maybe Hannah can teach me a few things on my list while I'm at it.

And that does it.

"Don't tell them," I say firmly, standing up and forcing my breathing to slow back down again. "Annabel, if this is the girl they want, then *this* is the girl they're going to get."

I wave the paper in the air.

I can be risky. I can be confident. I can be *brave.*

Annabel frowns and looks at me steadily for a few seconds. "Are you sure? Because, sweetheart, you really don't have to do this."

"I know," I say, putting the paper on the table. "This time I want to."

45

In the forests of central Africa grows a plant called the *Pollia condensata*. It produces tiny iridescent fruit that reflect pinpricks of light, and biologists claim that it is officially the shiniest living organism in the world.

It used to be, anyway.

Ali politely takes Annabel to the riad *hammam* for a complimentary massage while I 'get ready'. ("Fifteen years," she says, grinning at me. "Tell your father to drag me out by my toenails.") Then he leads me into the atrium and introduces me to a small, blonde, spiky-looking stylist called Helena.

Over the following hour, I am transformed from a human being into something that could be attached to the side of a car and used as a wing-view mirror.

With little dobs of glue, Helena gradually covers me head to toe in sequins and tiny bits of glass, beads, silver and gold, necklaces and bangles and hair clips and fake purple lashes. My dress is sparkly: red and pink and gold

and silver. Even my face and hands have been sprayed so heavily with twinkle that every time I look down my vision glints, as if I've got a temporary case of glaucoma.

Seriously: *National Geographic* may want to send someone over. I am definitely breaking some kind of light-reflective record.

Finally, Helena daubs me with sticky red lip gloss, blue eyeshadow and three inches of very pale foundation, and then secures an enormous, heavy gold watch round my wrist. It looks like something that could be used to locate a submarine underwater.

"Try not to lose it," she whispers to me under her breath. "If that's even possible. It looks like it has a tracking device inbuilt."

"It doesn't," a voice says from the doorway. "Sadly, because that would be *super* useful. Oh, you're just a veritable *phantasmagoria,* Hannah! *Exactly* as I dreamt it. Well done, lady whose name I can't remember."

"I just followed your directions," Helena says, holding up a stick-figure picture she's been glancing at the entire time. I'd assumed it was a nostalgic keepsake from her five-year-old daughter. "The credit is *all* yours, Kevin. Please. Take all of it."

"It just *came* to me, you know? I wanted Bollywood crossed with Strictly Come Dancing and I think we've achieved

it. Or *I've* achieved it, really. You just did the sticking."

A young, thin, slightly goat-like man hops into the room and holds his hand out to me. He's wearing little brown furry boots, a white T-shirt, brown skinny jeans, a tartan scarf and a small curly beard, and for a few seconds he reminds me so much of Mr Tumnus, I'm tempted to check him for horns and warn him about the perils of fraternising with humans.

"I'm Kevin Holland, the director. But of course, you already know that."

I shake his hand carefully.

How would I already know that? Is he wearing a name badge I haven't spotted?

Be *confident,* err... Hannah.

"Oh yes. Kevin Holland. Of *course.*"

"Constantly being recognised everywhere I go is *such* a nuisance," he continues, rubbing a hand over his beard. "I wasn't prepared for this level of fame, you know. All the awards. All the attention. Just this time last year, I had thirty Twitter followers. *Thirty.* Can you believe that?"

He looks at me with shock and indignation.

Studies have shown that we like people more when they mirror our own actions back at us, so I rub my chin too: inadvertently scratching myself with a sequin in the process.

"No, Kevin, because that is unbelievable."

"Now I have a blue tick and thirty-five thousand followers, and who are they all? Who knows? Who cares?"

I'm tempted to say: thirty-five thousand people probably know and care, but I bite my tongue.

"Then I meet Jacques Levaire at a big Hollywood party in Hackney and he's all, '*Hey, Kev, Kevin, Kevin Holland. I know you normally do profound art films that really mean something, but I would like to pay you an OBSCENE wad of money to bring that astonishing creative vision to my new line of expensive watches.*'"

I stare at Kev-Kevin-KevinHolland in surprise.

Huh. Maybe that's just how people talk in Hackney.

"I totes see what normal people miss, you know?" he continues cheerfully. "Like a superhero with x-ray vision, except I can view straight into the *human heart,* which is even more useful."

It really isn't.

Unless you're a surgeon, and judging by the state of his nails, this seems unlikely. But that sounds like a *very* geeky and Harriet Manners response, so instead of sharing this thought I toss my head back with a little laugh.

You can do this, Harriet. You are star-like.

"Absolutely!" I laugh loudly. "And what is your...

modus operandi for this particular direction? I'd really like to *channel* the right *creative vision.* Are we thinking *Marlowian*? *Millerian*? A touch of *Stoppardian* with an air of *Wildean*?"

Kevin blinks a few times, as well he might.

I have literally no idea what I just said: I'm just naming playwrights I know and making long words out of them.

"*Modus operandi?*" he says faintly. "Creative vision? Stoppardian? Millerian?"

I flush. "Umm, by which I meant…"

"Oh, I know what you *meant*," he says, grabbing my hands and kissing both of them. "*Finally*, they send me a professional I can actually *work* with."

He drags me over to the door of the riad, bangs it open with a flourish and spreads his arms out wide in the sunshine.

"Now, Hannah, let's *make some art*, shall we?"

46

Jemaa el-Fnaa is an ancient marketplace in the centre of the walled city of Marrakech. It's an enormous open square used by both locals and tourists, and the origin of its name is unclear.

It means either 'courtyard in front of a mosque', 'the mosque of death' or 'assembly at the end of the world'.

I'm going to vote for the latter.

It's dusk by the time we get to the square and it feels exactly like walking into an exotic fairyland, or maybe Christina Rossetti's enchanted goblin market.

During the day the square is filled with orange-juice stalls, ladies painting hands with intricate patterns of henna, medicine men selling cures and potions, tooth-pullers with teeth laid out in front of them and people selling little glasses with MOROCCO painted on them just in case anyone has forgotten what country they're in.

But at night, everything changes.

The sun sets and the city shifts: music starts and spaces

are filled with acrobats, dancers and musicians. Storytellers sit on the ground, fortune-tellers under umbrellas, snakes fight, monkeys dance and drums thump.

Lights are everywhere: scattered on the floor on tablecloths covered with candles and night-lights, and every now and then a whizzing blue light launches into the air: thrown by an enthusiastic child.

Marrakech during the day is wonderful, but Marrakech at night-time?

Totally magic.

"Gosh," Annabel says as Ali leads us quietly between stalls. She's now glowing and relaxed, and also sneaking quite a lot of little confused glances at my make-up and costume. "Harriet, you look very…"

Then she pauses for at least thirty seconds while she considers her internal thesaurus.

"Dazzling," she finally settles for.

I pull a face, because I know exactly what she means. Held at the right angle, I could be used to create a small fire.

Ali smiles slightly and walks us past a vulture perched on the floor with a chain round its neck, beyond a group of backflipping dancers, to a corner that's been sectioned off.

In the middle of it are enormous bright white lights

and a team of people, holding cameras and looking in little screens.

And around *them* is an even larger circle of tourists.

Chatting, laughing, taking photos. Waiting patiently for the performance to begin.

I abruptly feel a bit nauseous.

There are a lot of fascinating attractions in Jemaa El-Fnaa, and it looks like I just became one of them.

"*Sooooo* sorry," Kevin says, barging forward and dragging me through the crowd. "They must have heard I was here. There's just no *privacy* for the famous, is there? No respect for the integrity of artists."

"Is that Steven Spielberg?" somebody whispers. "Is this the new Indiana Jones film?"

"Is that the blonde girl from *Twilight?* She's not as pretty in real life, is she?"

"OK," Kevin continues as he pushes me quite aggressively into an open space and leaves me there while he runs next to the camera and picks up a blackboard. "I really want this to be *fresh* and *unstilted.* Feel *the moment*, you know? So I'm going to start rolling immediately, see how the two of you *interact*. See what the chemistry is like."

I blink and stare in concern at the growing crowd.

The two of us? Oh my God. Not *again.*

Over the last ten months, I have modelled with a beautiful Australian boy, a white kitten called Barry, a strident New Yorker, a cockroach, a sad girl called Fleur and an octopus with very little patience for my shenanigans.

I fell in love with one, knocked the other over and made the rest of them hate me. As far as *chemistry* goes, it's not a brilliant start.

"*Bring out Richard,*" Kevin shouts, clicking his blackboard together. "*ACTION.*"

I turn in astonishment – half expecting to see my father – and out of the crowd walks a little brown furry creature on all fours: round brown eyes, tail straight upwards.

They have got to be kidding me.

Because I've said this before, obviously, but I've never meant it literally.

Richard is a monkey.

47

Now, I *love* monkeys.

Monkeys share ninety-three per cent of their DNA with humans. They communicate with accents, play games, recognise photos of their friends and express affection by cuddling each other. They have even been known to lie to each other: yelling *tiger* so that the others retreat to the trees and they can keep a special food treat for themselves.

Monkeys are one of the sweetest, most curious and most fascinating species on the planet, and they're third on my list of all-time favourites (under 1. elephant and 2. panda).

But I *don't* love seeing them with a chain round their neck. I *don't* love seeing them dragged across the ground of a paved market square.

And I definitely do *not* love having one shoved into my arms while the chain is secured tightly round my wrist and a little man with a beard is yelling: *"Go on then,*

Manners! DO something!"

Richard wraps his little furry arms round my neck and stares into my face with huge, sad eyes and a little leathery nose.

And I suddenly want to cry.

"This is a macaque," I say, disentangling his tiny hands gently. "A Barbary macaque."

"Stop shooting!" Kevin shouts as Richard starts curiously picking at a bit of shiny plastic on my dress. "No, it's not. It's a monkey."

"You don't understand." My throat is starting to tighten. "A Barbary macaque *is* a monkey. It's the only macaque not found in Asia, and it's an endangered species. There are fewer than six thousand of these left in the wild."

Kevin frowns. "Well it's not in the wild now so what are you complaining about? *Action.*"

I make the chain looser, and Richard – monkey, not father – clambers up on to my shoulder, then sits firmly on top of my head.

"You're upsetting him," I say fiercely as I feel his little furry tail curl down the back of my neck. "He shouldn't be here. He should be out in the mountains with his mum and dad. Or his girlfriend."

"CUT," Kevin yells. "I thought you were used to

working with animals? What about all that time at the circus?" He clacks his board again. "I'm not paying you to whine. *Action*."

The crowd is starting to murmur unhappily.

"I don't think he's famous *at all*," somebody whispers.

"And I'm not sure she is either. She's *definitely* not pretty enough to be in *Twilight*. Or Indiana Jones, for that matter."

Richard clambers back down into my arms and stares at me again, hand carefully placed on my chin, and I look up in a panic to where Annabel is standing at the front of the crowd in a sharp white shirt and grey trousers, arms folded.

She looks exactly as furious as I feel and is clearly just waiting for some kind of sign from me to leap into action.

Help, I communicate silently, and with a quick motion my stepmother stands directly in front of the camera so that it's totally blocked.

"Stop filming," she says coldly. "I'm a lawyer, and if this shot isn't cut immediately, animal rights organisations will be contacted. Your client does not need that kind of publicity. Do I make myself perfectly clear?"

Kevin glares at her like an irritated seven-year-old.

Any second now, he's going to stamp his feet, tell her he hates her and wishes he'd never been born before

stomping to his bedroom. I can't believe I ever thought Yuka Ito was insensitive. By comparison, she was an angora rabbit.

"*Fine*," Kevin finally sighs angrily, flinging his scarf on to the ground. "Take the flaming monkey away. He was rubbish on camera anyway."

A man comes and grabs Richard from me. He clings for a few seconds, little chocolate-coloured eyes still fixed on mine, then lets go.

I watch him leave with a lump in my throat.

Then I give myself a little shake and try to snap back into a slightly less antagonistic, fierce kind of mood. I'm here to do a job, after all. "I'm really sorry if I ruined your advert, Kevin. Would you like me to… umm." What can I offer him instead? "Handstand? Cartwheel? Make a long string of origami cranes?"

I can only do one of those things, so I may have to learn the others pretty quickly.

"No, thank you. I've got a *much* better idea."

Kevin looks around at the still mesmerised crowd and gives the first broad smile I've seen since I met him.

"Ladies and gentlemen, bring out the snakes."

48

I'm not a *lot* happier, draped in four poor snakes.

But I'm supposed to be a professional, so I try my absolute hardest to look like I might be.

With the cameras rolling, I start swaying as gracefully as I can – waving my arms assertively – so that the film crew can capture me "at one with nature". Despite the fact that nature doesn't look like it really wants to be at one with me.

The large green one keeps trying to tie itself round my neck, and I'm not entirely sure I blame it.

"Kiss it," Kevin hisses as the smaller brown one slides over my shoulder and peers with a tickling tongue into my ear.

"Excuse me?"

"Kiss the snake. Just a quick peck. And make sure the watch is on show the whole time."

I glance at the gold still weighing down my wrist. I don't think there's an alternative, frankly: you could see

this thing through a dark pair of curtains.

Then I look at the snake doubtfully.

There are 3,000 species of snake in the world, and 600 of them are venomous. If I had any poison, a random redhead trying to kiss me would be my very first target.

I swallow, take a deep breath and give it a quick peck.

"Yes!" Kevin shouts. "Again!"

I peck it again.

"Again!"

I kiss the snake again. I think in some countries we are now married.

"AND CUT!" Kevin claps his board so sharply somebody in the audience gives a little squeak. "Now, let's see what else we can do that won't get us *sued*, shall we?"

I spend the rest of the evening wandering aimlessly through the winding, narrow souks of Marrakech with a film crew trailing four metres behind me.

And every few steps, somebody yells at me.

Occasionally, it's a stall owner who thinks I have an eye for a bargain. "Hey, lady!" one shouts, trying to grab my hand. "Hey, Rihanna! You want to buy a scarf? Lovely scarf for you and your family! I give you super good price!"

"Hey, Beckham! You like nice carpet?? I have so many nice carpets!"

"You are a pretty lady! Come and have a butcher and a wag of the chin!"

But mostly, I'm just yelled at by Kevin.

Every time I reply to the stall owners, or laugh, or walk the wrong way, or say thank you very much but I already have a carpet at home, my director explodes at me.

"I said *no*, Hannah! No talking! Laughing is not fashion! Do it again! Take a left! A right! No, a *right*! Look at the watch! Faster! Slow down! And make sure you look at the *watch*! This isn't an advert for orienteering!"

Until I'm starting to feel very confused, very lost and very late for something important: I'm just not entirely sure what, exactly. Like a particularly rubbish version of the rabbit from *Alice in Wonderland.*

I'm so disorientated that during an especially enthusiastic head-toss one of my enormous dangly earrings gets caught in a long yellow scarf hanging from a pole and renders me abruptly immobile.

"What are you *doing*?" Kevin yells at me as I lurch backwards with a wince and cover my ear with my hand. "What is *this*?"

"I'm..." I pretend to rub the scarf on my face while I try to surreptitiously unhook myself. "I'm just... Really

getting *into* it, you know? Into the *vibe.* Of this… uh, summer accessorising."

Into it, on to it, attached to it: pretty much the same thing.

Kevin scowls at me as I start pretending to sniff the scarf instead. "Well can you *stop*? It does not look sophisticated and expensive *at all.*"

The cameras keep filming as an outraged stall owner charges forward and unhooks my earring while muttering loudly. In the meantime, all the other stallholders are now filming me on their mobile phones.

"Americans!" one says cheerfully, shaking his head. "Always making my day."

You know what?

If I can find a hole through to another universe, it might be best for everyone if I just jump straight down it.

Once released I wander a bit more – stumbling into a gutter full of dirty water – and then I accidentally venture into a one-way street at which point I have to confidently put my hand on my hip and pretend it was entirely intentional.

Finally, Kevin decides he's probably got enough footage for the day.

That or he's given up on me entirely.

It's hard to tell.

"Done!" he shouts as his phone starts ringing, grabbing it out of his pocket. "I can just pay somebody to edit all the rubbish out. Get an early night, peeps. It's a long way to Erg Chebbi, so we'll precede at four."

Then he disappears down a dark little path that presumably leads back to the riad, still yelling into his phone.

There's a short silence.

"It's *midnight,*" Helena finally sighs. "How exactly are we going to get an early night? Time travel?"

"He means four *am*?" Joe the cameraman moans. "In *four hours*?"

"No *wonder* the money for this was so good."

Annabel and I wait until the entire crew has stumbled off to bed – still grumbling and rubbing their eyes – then we look at each other.

"Are you sure you still want to do this?" she says calmly. "Because this is a man that doesn't know the difference between *proceed* and *precede,* and our life is in his hands."

I nod sleepily and grin.

Despite being shouted at so much – and despite getting so much wrong – I'm actually having a surprising amount of fun, living life so far on the edge I'm basically tipping over.

Maybe I'm more like my dad than I hoped I was.

"All right, then," Annabel says with a swift nod. She gets a guidebook out. "In that case, the good news is that Erg Chebbi consists of fifty-kilometre dunes of sands blown by the wind, and it's part of the Sahara desert."

I open my eyes, suddenly very alert.

I've had a Sahara desert poster in my bedroom since I was seven, and I may or may not have cut a photo of myself out and stuck it on top to look like I'd already been there.

"And the bad news?"

Annabel puts the guidebook back in her bag and rubs a hand over her eyes. "It's an eleven-hour drive away and we're taking a bus."

49

Eleven hours on a bus is a long time.

Eleven hours on a bus with Kevin sitting behind you is an infinity.

Before sunrise the next morning, we're piled in the back of a tiny white van, driven out of the city... and into the Atlas Mountains.

As the sky slowly begins to lighten, we see the outline of dark peaks speckled with snow. Sweeping valleys and gorges are dotted with trees and rivers and here and there small turreted, castle-like *kasbahs* are perched randomly on the hillside.

We drive past goats and sheep, market stalls and little villages, including the incredible Ouarzazate: a red-walled Berber city made of mud, and the setting for *Lawrence of Arabia* and *Gladiator.*

And Kevin doesn't see any of it.

"I just came from *nowhere,*" he says as we all watch

a man walking a donkey with a little bell along the road. "BOOM. Nobody knows how I did it.

"I suppose I've always been creative," he ponders as we stop for some traditional Moroccan *tagine* for lunch: stewed chicken with vegetables and currants in a clay pot. "Some of us are just born to really *see* the world, you know?

"Oooh!" he says as we pull over to take photos of a pretty village with peach walls and yellow flowers. "Seventeen retweets! Eighteen! Twenty!"

By the time the land starts to get dustier and the mountains flatten into brown plains, scattered with little piles of sand, the only thing stopping everyone on the bus from literally killing Kevin is the knowledge that we must be nearly there now. That, and the fact that Morocco still officially has the death penalty for murder.

Finally we pull into a small, crunchy car park and stop.

Helena and I wobble quickly off the bus into the sweltering heat, then dive into a small cement building so I can get changed again before the sun sets: this time into a long yellow, blue and orange silk dress covered in gold sequins, as dictated by an even more elaborate stick figure.

She covers my face in yet another thick layer of gunk

and secures the watch with the same horrified face as yesterday.

Then she leads me to a long line of camels, grunting and chewing with the laconic, disinterested expressions of old men with grudges. Every now and then one opens its mouth and makes a loud, grumbling sound: halfway between an angry dinosaur roar and a really acidic belch.

Annabel is standing cautiously next to them.

"Apparently the Arabic language has 160 words for *camel,*" she says, grimacing slightly. "I can probably think of a couple more. However, if this is what's next on the list then..."

"Oh, there isn't a camel for you," Kevin says brightly, ambling past on an enormous brown one, with a blue scarf tied elaborately round his head. "You weren't on the crew list, lady. Frankly, you're lucky there was even room in the bus. I was all for leaving you in Marrakech."

Annabel's jaw clenches. "You're so kind."

"My charity work is well documented," he agrees. "Hannah? I'm not paying you to stand and stare gormlessly at the transport. Get on Zahara immediately, please."

He points at an enormous, white fluffy, curly camel, who turns and gives me a slow, long-lashed blink, like

a flirty film star from the 1920s.

Take risks, Harriet.

I clamber nervously on and squeak slightly as Zahara slowly stands up with her back legs first – tipping me terrifyingly forward – then with her front legs, so I'm flung backwards again like a rag doll.

Annabel writes something in the little notepad she's started carrying around with her. I'm not sure what it is, exactly, but from her expression I'm guessing it's not a love poem.

"Are you sure you don't need me, Harriet?" she says, holding a flat hand up and squinting against the sunshine. "Because if you do, I'll steal one of these furry old man animals. But if you don't... I suppose I could stay here and make a few phone calls."

Her fingers twitch unconsciously towards her briefcase.

It's only *just* occurring to me now that this must be the longest Annabel's ever been away from Tabitha. Plus she's just started back at work after maternity leave, and it's a Friday afternoon: she must have work coming out of her ears. This isn't a fun sunny holiday for Annabel at all.

The *only* reason she's here is to look after me.

"I'll be absolutely fine," I say as confidently as I can

while Zahara experimentally licks my left ankle. "Give Dad and Tabby my love. See you when I get back, OK?"

I blow her an affectionate kiss.

Then I ride off alone into the orange sands.

50

I should probably have said: *if* I get back.

Camels aren't known as 'ships of the desert' for nothing, and it turns out I'm not a very good sailor. As we start walking across little heaps of sand towards the dunes, Zahara begins to sway dramatically from side to side, up and down, round and round: staggering, belching, shuffling, clambering up the first of the dunes, twitching her tail and sliding back down again.

Which is a bit of a problem.

The film crew has been set up fifteen metres away so they can film me, wobbling precariously past with my head jiggling loosely like one of those little plastic dogs that go on the dashboard of a car.

I lurch one way, then the other.

I swerve and dip and squeak, and at one point slip so violently I'm hanging off the side of the camel and one of the Moroccan camel-men has to grab me as I close my eyes and hang on to the poor animal's neck for dear life.

"*Stop. Strangling. The. Camel,*" Kevin hisses from his position to my right. "You are so *not* good with animals."

Finally, I find a kind of awkward rhythm.

Together, Zahara and I climb slowly up a particularly enormous and powdery dune to the very top. At which point every bit of remaining breath leaves my body in one big *whoosh*.

Annabel has disappeared. The bus has disappeared. The gravel car park has disappeared.

All that's left is sand.

Approximately eight octillion grains of sand, to be precise: spread across three and a half million square miles in tiny, sea-like ripples and enormous soft, cascading mountains, all in golds and oranges.

To my left, the shadows of the camels are stretched to the horizon, perfectly outlined in black with long, thin legs like the elephants in the famous Dali painting.

The sky is bright pink, and little yellow and tangerine clouds are scattered above us; below us the ground keeps shifting like magic from rust to orange to crimson. Little stars are beginning to pop out and the air is utterly silent. Not a bird, not a plane.

Just perfect stillness.

Modelling has opened the world up for me.

I've seen the bright lights of New York and the

candy-like turrets of Moscow in the snow. I've watched Mount Fuji as the sun goes down, and the neon colours of Tokyo as it comes back up again. I've walked the streets of Marrakech and navigated empty warehouses in London.

But of all the places I've ever been, this is by far my favourite.

It's just a shame I have to share it with Kevin.

"*Remember*," he yells from several metres away, cupping his hands round his mouth. "You are *a queen*! You are *an empress*! You are the monarch of everything you survey! Now *look at the flaming watch*!"

But as we pause on top of the dune and the crew films me for a few minutes, staring at the horizon with my dress floating in the wind, I suddenly feel every single muscle in my body start to relax. Kevin can shout at me as much as he likes: I am the luckiest girl in the entire world.

And for a brief fragment of time, I don't need to act.

As I sit on the camel and stare at the calm, empty, limitless sands spreading millions of miles around me, that's exactly how I feel: like a queen.

Brave, confident and capable of anything.

Because after a childhood of dreaming and imagining, I am finally here.

I am in the Sahara desert.

51

Things that live in the Sahara desert include:

- *500 species of plant*
- *70 species of mammal*
- *90 species of bird*
- *100 species of reptile*
- *200 million people.*

Kevin appears to think he's the only one.

"Does anybody have reception?" he yells as we roll carefully back down the dune again and are brought to a juddering halt. "I need to upload this selfie, and I've got *jack.*"

Carefully, I'm helped off the camel.

I give Zahara a little pat and a thank-you.

Then I'm led to a flat piece of sand between two dunes while the crew starts setting up lights in a semicircle. I glance around expectantly: so far I've been buddied up with a camel, a monkey and four snakes.

My next task will no doubt involve subduing a fire-breathing dragon with my bare hands while simultaneously attempting some kind of whimsical recorder playing.

"Right," Kevin says, leaning nonchalantly against his camel. "This is my final shot, Hannah, and will be my *Pièce de Résistance*. Do you know what that means?"

I nod in relief: finally, something I can answer properly. "Yes. It's French for *piece of resistance*, and it traditionally refers to the most substantial dish in a meal."

"Wrong. It means this is the bit that will make me famous. *More* famous. So I need you to really dig deep and bring out your best stuff. You know. Do your thing."

I stare at Kevin for a few seconds in bewilderment.

"Sorry, my thing?"

Does he want me to do complex algebra for the cameras? Analyse a bit of metaphysical poetry? Experiment with the migration of manganite ions?

Kevin bends down and pulls two little yellow boxes out of his bag.

Then he wedges them in the sand.

"I'm thinking *nomadic.* I'm thinking *free spirit.* I'm thinking *my classic timepiece by Jacques Levaire is so glorious I can't control my happiness.* Pretend there's a campfire and sparklers if you need them. We can always CGI that in later. ACTION."

Then he waves his hand at the cameras and clicks a button on his iPod.

Oh my God. What is happening?

Except as huge white lights switch on with a bang and the cameras start whirring, I think I already know. Sure enough: a loud, tinny beat begins to thump across the sand. *Thud. Thud. Thud thud thud thud.* Then a little voice starts screeching *oooooooooh babyyyyyy hiiiighhhh iin theeee skkyyyyyyy yeahhh baby.* An electronic keyboard joins in, followed by what appears to be a random fake owl sound.

The kangaroo rat has wide toes that turn its feet into sand shoes, allowing it to run across sand really fast in the opposite direction to danger without sinking in.

I may need to quickly grow some too.

"Now," my director confirms as he leans back on the camel again and throws his hands out widely. "*Dance.*"

*

So I dance.

Or – more specifically – Hannah does.

With the skills she learnt during a short stint with the Bolshoi Ballet Academy, she swirls and spins, pirouettes and squats, jumps and curtsies. She rolls around a bit on the floor, getting sand in her eyes and mouth and hair and trying to surreptitiously spit it back out again in the most glamorous way possible.

She fake-drowns and jives, shuffles and wiggles.

She even attempts a little break-dancing. And you know what? Harriet Manners can't do any of this. But Hannah Manners?

Apparently she's not that bad at it.

I must have harnessed her powers more accurately than I ever dared dream could be possible, because for the first time Kevin hasn't got a single word of criticism.

"*Superb!*" he yells as I attempt to moonwalk across the sand. "*Marvellous!*" he shouts as I huff and puff through three extremely low star jumps. "*Genius!*" he exclaims as – in a panic – I steal a few of Dad's key moves and start doing 'wobbly-knees' and making big boxes with little boxes inside them with my hands. "This is *precisely* what I wanted! It's fresh, it's unorthodox! It's visionary! Could you, perchance, try a little *krumping*?"

Which I assume is dancing like a crumpet.

So I obediently roll myself on to the sand and try to look as bread-like as possible.

Finally, the music stops and I crash in exhaustion to the ground and end with tired jazz hands. I'm sweating all over and breathing so hard I sound like a tree being cut down.

"AND THAT…" Kevin yells, clacking his little board for the final time, "…IS. A. WRAP! Could you take a photo of me jumping?" He hands his phone to Helena. "I need one for my Facebook profile."

I sit for a few seconds in the sand, trying to get my breath back.

Then I look upwards at the sky.

The light is fading, pink has deepened to a purple-blue and stars are popping out and multiplying by the second like freckles in the sun. I give a little sigh and try to quickly take as many mental photos as I can. I'm only sixteen, after all. I can always come back and enjoy my first ever night in the desert without somebody yelling I CAN JUMP HIGHER! DO IT AGAIN! another time, right?

Right?

"You know," Joe the cameraman says, helping me up. "After careful consideration, I think I might need a couple of extra shots of the dunes. A long, long way over there."

He points far away in the distance.

"I'll come with you," Kevin says, reappearing as if by magic. "I know *exactly* the shot you're thinking of and you can't do it without me because I'm the *director.*" He holds his fingers up in a square. "Oh yes, I *see* it already. I see it *all.*"

Joe winks at me as Kevin begins sliding through the sand in the direction Joe indicated and – as if by some strange, wonderful enchantment – the air gets quieter and quieter until it's completely silent.

I can almost hear the desert heaving a sigh of relief.

Then I quickly whip my shoes off while mouthing a grateful *thank you.*

"You've got fifteen minutes," Joe says with a small grin as I start heading towards the biggest dune I can find. "Get as far away as you possibly can."

And it looks like the desert is finally mine.

52

Scientists estimate that there are 70,000 million million million million stars in the known universe and at least 170 billion galaxies stretching 13.8 billion light years away from us in all directions.

Our galaxy alone contains 400 billion stars.

With all the energy I have left, I scramble on all fours up the dune. It takes a surprisingly long time: for every two scrabbles forward I slide back one, as if I'm trying to climb a mound of warm, soft sugar.

Finally, I reach the top and lie down. I spread my arms out wide with my fingers buried in the sand.

And I look upwards, at a sky now coated in glitter.

Hertfordshire/Sydney – February (9 months ago)

"I know you miss me but try and be cool, Manners. There's no need to lick the computer."

I laughed and pulled Hugo off the webcam.

He got a bit overexcited every time he saw my boyfriend, but I couldn't exactly blame him.

In fairness, so did I.

"Saliva is antibacterial," I told Nick airily. "We just like keeping things clean." Then I poked my face round my dog's little white fluffy head. Hugo immediately started licking my ear instead. "Is it nice being home?"

Nick was making the most of shooting a huge campaign in Australia by spending the weekend with his parents.

"It's great, but I keep getting this niggling feeling I've left something behind."

"You did," I said, holding up a blue sock. "I found this under my bed yesterday. It doesn't smell great. In fact, I have considerable doubts about your laundry skills."

Nick threw his head back and laughed, and every one of my two billion heart-muscle cells stood up silently and did a little invisible dance of triumph. "I gave that to you when you jumped in the snow puddle, plonker. So technically you were the last one to wear it."

"Oh." I flushed with happiness. "Of course. In that case, it smells of sunshine and roses and I've never inhaled anything so delightful in my life and shall sleep with it forever under my pillow."

We both laughed, and then the screen flickered.

"Hello?" I clicked a few buttons. "Are you still there? Nick?"

It flickered a few more times: his face appearing and disappearing again. "Harri—"

"Nick?"

"*Shoot,*" a disembodied voice said. "Why is this connection so bad?"

"It's OK, we'll just..."

Then the sound cut out too.

Over the two and a half months we'd been dating, I had grown to hate video calls with a passion. They gave me a pixelated picture of Nick – like he had been drawn or painted – but I couldn't curl up with my head on his shoulder or smell his lime-green smell or kiss him.

And there were these little unexpected awkward bits: the moments where we talked over each other, or the sound lagged, or the screen froze and we were suddenly disjointed and pulled apart.

The screen went bright again and I could see his beautiful face: fuzzy and frozen in the middle of expressing a *U* shape.

"Are you..." we both said at the same time.

"...Here."

"...There. What?"

"Huh?"

There was an awkward silence again while I flushed. My face was now frozen in the corner of the screen, like a constipated goblin. I felt strangely shy, as if we were back at the beginning.

My boyfriend was 10,552 miles away, and I could suddenly feel every single one of them.

"What were you—"

"I was just—"

"You go—"

"No, I was just saying—"

Another long silence while we both fiddled with our laptops and I tried my hardest not to throw it on the floor and stamp on it.

"Take me to the window," Nick said finally.

"Oh God, it's not *that* bad, is it? I mean, you're not going to virtually jump, are you?"

"Maybe," he laughed. "Let's see how I feel when I get there."

I clambered off my bed and took my laptop to the windowsill. Our neighbour was trimming his lawn with a dark blue fleece on. Not even vaguely romantically: I could hear him swearing and kicking the machine through the glass.

"Now turn me round so I can see the sky."

"But you can't see anything, Nick. It's just grey."

"Obviously. You're in England so that goes without saying. Now I'll do it." Nick held his computer up and I peered forward. "What can you see?"

"Black."

"Because I'm currently in the southern hemisphere, and you're in the northern hemisphere. We have two almost totally different skies, so it's dark here while it's light there."

I turned the camera round so I could blink at him incredulously. Maybe this was what happened when you became a model: people tried to explain the notion of a spinning earth to you.

"Thanks for that, Nick. That is fascinating geological knowledge that I didn't learn when I was six years old at all. Please, tell me more about the basic concept of night and day."

"I wasn't finished," he laughed. "May I continue?"

"Yes. Unless you're about to tell me that rain comes out of clouds and gravity makes things, like, fall down. In which case, no."

He growled at me so I stuck my tongue out.

"I said we have *almost* two totally different skies, smarty-pants. But there's still a crossover point and it's always there. Three—"

Nick's face suddenly went very quiet and stationary.

Oh my God, I thought, *you have to be kidding me*.

"Nick?" I shook my laptop desperately. "Three what? Three squirrels? Three blind mice?"

But there was nothing: just emptiness and silence.

"Nick?" I said in a smaller voice, shaking it again. "Come back."

And the screen went black.

Thanks to almost no light pollution, I can now see more stars than I've ever been able to before: thousands and thousands of lights slowly scattering themselves across the sky like the blue sparkle Nat used to throw all over everything when she was seven.

But I'm only looking at three of them.

After five minutes of cursing my laptop, I'd finally worked it out: Orion's Belt, also known as The Three Kings.

Alnitak, Alnilam and Mintaka.

Three of the brightest stars in the sky, and – because of their position near the equator – visible in both the northern and southern hemisphere: Morocco and Australia.

Last week I read that the heart has its own electrical pulse, which means it can function even when it has been separated from its body.

Which I thought was pretty handy.

Given that mine has been on the other side of the world now for quite some time.

But as I dig myself into the warm sand and look upwards, it suddenly feels a tiny bit closer again: beating and hopeful, as if I'm not quite as empty any more. And as I think about my letter, I feel a little closer to being whole again: more than I have in a long time. Since I walked off Brooklyn Bridge and left the boy I love still standing there without me.

Because tonight, these stars are mine.

But in a few hours, they'll belong to Nick again.

No matter where we are, no matter how dark it gets, no matter which of us can't see them, this is one connection that is never going to break.

The part of the sky we share.

53

Luckily, the return journey is a lot easier.

This is mainly because I borrow earplugs, curl up with my head on Annabel's lap and sleep the entire way back to Marrakech.

By the time the crew staggers off the bus at 7am and figuratively crawls back into the riad, Kevin and I are the only upbeat people in the party. I'd like to pretend it has nothing to do with my fifteen minutes with the stars, but that would be lying.

I honestly feel happier than I have in weeks.

My brighter mood is enhanced yet further when my director calls me a "triumph of casting" and air-kisses my hand – albeit from a considerable distance.

"I am about to have a very happy client," he chirps, grabbing his enormous suitcase and heading straight back towards the riad door. "*Kev,* Jacques Levaire is going to say, *Kev, Kevin, Kevin Holland. If only they gave Oscars for adverts, you would win them all.*"

I beam at him: I think that means it went well.

"Now I'm off to the South of France to restock my fragile, butterfly-like creative juices on a yacht," he continues. "Catch you on the fame train, Hannah."

"Kevin?" I say as he pulls on a little black felt hat and pushes the door open. I clear my throat anxiously. "I'm not actually Hannah Manners. My name is Harriet."

He's given me two of the most amazing days and an entire desert: the least I owe him is the truth.

"Whatevs," he says, shrugging.

And he closes the door behind him.

"We have a Berber proverb in Morocco," Ali says thoughtfully, appearing as if out of thin air with two more steaming glasses of mint tea. "*Every dog thinks of its own fleas as gazelles.* I think Kevin assumes his are unicorns."

Annabel opens her eyes from where she's been propped up with a straight back against the reception desk.

"Unicorns?" she says sleepily, glancing around the room. "Where? I like bees."

I smile and gently remove the phone still gripped tightly in her hand. My stepmother was sending emails when I fell asleep on the bus and still sending emails when I woke up: there's a small but real chance she may have been suing people in her sleep.

I kiss her cheek as she puts her sunglasses on over her

glasses. "I think it's time to go home now, Annabel."

"Sadly, you would be right," Ali says, forcing a tea into her hand. "But you have one hour left in Morocco before I must take you to the airport. Is there anything special you'd like to do?"

He really is our magic genie.

There's just one wish I haven't had granted yet.

"Actually, Ali," I say, glancing at sleeping-again Annabel. I don't need to check it with her: I know we're on the same page. Or we will be when she wakes up, anyway. "We have a little favour we'd like to ask before we go, if you don't mind?"

"Harriet Manners," he says, grinning and bowing slightly. "Nothing would delight me more."

By the time we get home, everything on my list has been ticked off neatly.

Everything that matters, anyway.

"You're back!" a voice shouts as we at last push through the front door. "Finally! You were gone for *years and years*."

Annabel and I stand in the hallway and stare in amazement at the living room. I'm pretty sure we were gone three days, but for a few seconds I'm convinced Dad might actually be right.

There's fabric everywhere. My spare bedding has been spread over a couple of bits of string, Annabel's best embroidered white cotton throw is forming a vast canopy in the middle, and inside the world's worst home-made tent is every pillow in the house.

My sister is lying in a furry cocoon of fleece jumpers in the entrance, patiently tugging on one of Hugo's ears.

"I built a fort!" Dad cries, still hidden. "We have everything you could possibly need. Biscuits, and movies, and milk, and a wooden donkey I found in the loft and—"

He pokes his head out of the sheets and then stops in amazement.

We both turn slowly to look at Annabel.

Her face is bright scarlet and peeling, the normally perfect blonde fringe is fuzzy and sticking upwards, there's orange juice down her front and ink on her face from where she fell asleep on her crossword on the flight home.

Yup.

My stepmother is one of the country's top barristers.

She has gone through twenty years of education, two postgraduate degrees, one teenage stepdaughter, one baby, nine years of marriage to my father, hundreds of court cases and thirteen hours of labour without ruffling a single eyelash.

Three days of fashion have broken her.

"Harriet Manners," Dad says sternly, looking at me, "what did you do to my wife?"

Annabel gives me a long, sleepy look and then nods in satisfaction. "It was exactly what we needed," she yawns, crawling into the tent. "But it's nice to be home."

With a happy little sigh, she picks Tabs up, kisses her face and tummy enthusiastically then lays her gently on her own stomach. My sister immediately makes a delighted squeaking sound and attempts to stick a whole hand up Annabel's nose.

Then Dad gives my stepmother the kind of kiss that makes me look awkwardly at the ceiling for a few seconds.

I crawl in next to them and for a while the four of us lie quietly under the white canopy.

"You know what I'm thinking?" Annabel says eventually.

"Yes," Dad nods with his eyes shut. "You're thinking: why isn't there mouse-flavoured cat food?"

"Nope."

"You're thinking why doesn't Tarzan have a beard when there are no razors in the jungle?"

"Well, I'm thinking that now, yes. But no."

Dad sighs sadly. "I have to take the awesome fort down, don't I?"

"Nope," Annabel says, closing her eyes. "Right now, it's perfect. I'm thinking Bahamas, Maldives, Hawaii, wherever Harriet goes next, Richard. They're all yours."

54

We have a little family nap for half an hour.

Then Tabitha and Hugo start clamouring simultaneously for something to eat, so I leave them to my disorientated parents and climb out of the fort as fast as I possibly can.

I carefully inspect the post next to the front door for a few minutes to see if anything has arrived for me over the last few days. Then I check under the indoor mat, because something important might have slipped into the wrong place.

And under the outdoor mat.

Tentatively, I wave my hand around inside the letter box a few times, in case a bulky, romantic gift was simply too huge to get all the way through.

But there's nothing there.

Not today anyway.

Still standing in the open doorway, I send Nat a quick text to check if she wants to hang out this weekend,

now I'm back from Marrakech earlier than I thought.

A few seconds later my phone beeps:

Wish I could, but I already have plans. ☹ Can't wait to hear about your trip! Nat xxx

I send a quick reply – **OK! Have fun! X** – put my phone back in my pocket, tug my suitcase up to my bedroom and sit on the floor with my back against the wall.

Then I pull my crumpled Inner Star list out of my pocket, retrieve a pen from my desk and hover over it in deep concentration for a few minutes.

Over the last three days, I have: been on two aeroplanes, skipped school, bussed through winding mountain roads, break-danced, ridden a camel in the desert, been vigorously draped in snakes and monkeys and held quite a few conversations with a man called Kevin.

I don't want to sound smug, but I think the anonymous author on the internet would be incredibly proud of me right now. I've never taken so many potentially lethal risks in my entire life.

With a smile, I draw a neat little tick next to the two entries I've been primarily concentrating on.

1. ***Be Confident!*** **You are a creature unlike any other!**
2. ***Take Risks, Be Brave!*** **There is no limit to what you can do!**

Then I focus my attention on my next targets.

3. ***Be Stylish!*** **Shake it up and try something new!**
4. ***Inspire!*** **Lead, never follow!**

With a deep breath, I fling my suitcase open wide and energetically start pulling out the contents like some kind of magician.

Bright yellow scarves and white sequin wraps. Turquoise and purple shawls with tassels; embroidered green waistcoats; orange and blue trousers, red leather shoes and enormous silver spangly earrings. Sparkles and sequins and things with beads all over them.

Until it's all in a rainbow heap around me.

As of Monday morning, things are going to change.

The geek is gone, and in her place is a much better version of Harriet Manners. Somebody strong and brave, cool and confident. A girl who can inspire others; who believes in herself so that everybody else will too.

Or – you know. *To*.

Because if there's a star inside everybody, it's only logical that there must be one inside me as well.

Now I just need to find a way to coax the rest of her out, that's all.

55

Unfortunately, the Inner Star list's author hasn't given any more details on exactly how to do that.

Which is a shame.

Because, as of 8:30am on Monday morning, I could really do with a little more guidance.

By the time I reach the end of my road, there are four first years following me with huge eyes, like barn owls in too-big dark green blazers and little white ankle socks.

Every time I speed up, they speed up.

Every time I stop, they stop.

Until my only options appear to be: a) run b) crawl inside a bush or c) curl up on the floor in a ball like a hedgehog until they either lose interest or accidentally stand on one of my fingers.

Except that's exactly what the old Harriet Manners would do, so instead I take a deep breath and spin round.

"Yes?" I say as brightly as I can. "Is there something I

can help you with, ladies?"

Brilliant.

Now I sound like a Gap assistant after somebody has just tangled up my jumpers.

"Umm." The little redhead has started hopping from one foot to the other, glancing at her friends. "Is your name *Harriet Manners*? Are you really a *supermodel*? Because my sister's in your year and she says you're famous but Fee thinks you're not pretty enough so we're not sure."

She points at a blonde girl, who immediately goes red.

"I didn't say that! Oh my God, Lydia, you're *so embarrassing*!" Fee looks at the floor. "I just said you're quite normal-looking for a model, that's all."

Normal-looking. Honestly, that's probably the nicest thing anybody at school has ever said about me.

"Yes, my name is Harriet," I say as we start walking again. "The rest, I'm afraid, is massively inflated."

"*Massively inflated*," they breathe to each other. "*Coooooool.*"

Then they start skipping down the road next to me.

"Do you live in a *castle*?" "Does it have turrets?" "Have you ever been to Jamaica?" "My aunty's been to Jamaica and it rained." "I'd rather go to Barbados. It *never* rains there." "Don't be stupid, Lydia, it rains *everywhere*."

"Not in Antarctica it doesn't," I interrupt automatically. "The Dry Valleys are the driest spot in the world as winds of speeds up to 200 miles per hour blow there and evaporate all surface water, snow and ice."

They stop skipping and stare at me with round eyes until I can feel myself flushing bright red.

Then they explode again.

"Oooooh." "200 miles per hour is *so fast.*" "That's faster than a *car.*" "That's faster than a *speedboat.*" "What else do you know, Harriet Manners? Do you know *everything*?"

To my surprise, I can feel my chest puffing out like a little pigeon. I'm not used to strangers enjoying my facts quite so enthusiastically. "Not at all. But I have a lot of books like this one which really help."

I reach into my satchel and pull out *Wise Up In The Bathroom*. I really wish publishing companies would stop assuming the only place to learn trivia is on the toilet.

"*Ooooooh.*" They crowd around it. "This is *so awesome.*" "This is, like, the *awesomest thing* I've ever seen." "My mum says fact books are only for nerds but she's so *wrong.*"

I study their faces carefully, but there isn't a trace of sarcasm or facetiousness. They're not mocking me or

being ironic. They honestly think my fact book is super cool.

Even weirder, they appear to think *I* am too.

We're outside the lower building now, and for a few crazy seconds I'm tempted to go in with them so we can discuss interesting facts about bridges. They might actually be my kindred spirits.

Or – at the very least – my spirit animals.

Instead I say: "Would you like to borrow my book for the day? There's a *really* interesting section about sharks on page 143."

They take it as if it's some kind of holy grail.

"When I'm grown up, I want to be *just like you*," Lydia says, staring at it reverently.

There's suddenly a little lump in my throat. I've never been considered a goal before.

Or – who are we kidding – a grown-up.

"If you like it there's *plenty* more where that came from," I beam at them. "And if you want to meet me before school tomorrow at the bottom of the road I can give you some more."

They're going to *adore* my humorous potted history about the Tudors.

"Yay!" they squeak, jumping up and down. "We love you, Harriet Manners!" "You're the best, Harriet

Manners!" "See you tomorrow, Harriet Manners!"

And – waving shyly – the four girls run through the lower school doors.

Leaving me lit up with pleasure behind them.

56

I wait a few minutes until they've gone.

Mainly so I can wipe the stupid grin off my face and compose myself into a more sophisticated sixth form kind of mentality.

Then I glance down at my outfit.

Bright purple linen trousers, turquoise kaftan, a yellow shawl, enormous silver earrings with orange stones, three scarves – pink, green and blue – and little red leather slippers. There are sequins on at least four of those items, and tinkling bells on three.

Yup: *nailed it*.

With a satisfied sigh, I get my list out of my pocket and draw little ticks beside the next two items.

Be Stylish! **Shake it up and try something new!**
Inspire! **Lead, never follow!**

Then I anxiously contemplate the next goal:

***Don't try too hard!* It just looks desperate!!!!**

Hmm.

Of everything on this list I've attempted over the last few days, this is going to be my biggest challenge yet. In Year Seven, I leapfrogged so hard I flung myself into a wall and dislocated my shoulder; in Year Eight I debated colonialism in history so enthusiastically I started crying; in Year Two I played Mary with such conviction I stole baby Jesus and…

Well. You get the picture.

Whichever part of the brain allows you to participate in anything half-heartedly, I just don't have it.

I try too hard at *everything.*

But there are four exclamation marks, which means this must be pretty important. So I stick my nose in the air as high and nonchalantly as I can physically get it.

Be confident, Harriet! You are a creature unlike any other! Unique! As special as a snowflake! As exceptional and rare as a…

A…

Northern Hairy-nosed Wombat, of which there are only 115 left in the wild.

Yup: that should do it.

And I push boldly and carelessly back into my classroom.

57

Or try to, anyway.

I'm so careless one of my three scarves gets caught on the classroom door handle and Miss Hammond has to untangle me patiently before I accidentally strangle myself.

So far not trying hard has nearly killed me.

"Harriet!" my form teacher says cheerfully, releasing me from the furniture. "You've returned yet again! It's very exciting, wondering if you'll be at school or not. A veritable Russian roulette of attendance."

In the meantime, the entire class has stopped talking and spun round to face me.

"Harriet! There you are!" "How was your weekend?" "Your earrings are *lush*!" "*Loving* this look, Harriet! It's so *quirky*!"

"Retty, you're back!" Liv squeaks as I blink at them all. She elbows Ananya sharply. "Yay! We were so worried you'd moved back to New York!"

"Where *were* you?" Ananya says, politely moving her feet so I don't have to step over them. "Did you do something exciting, Ret?"

I make my way shakily to my seat.

The urge to tell them every single thing I have ever learnt about camels and snakes and how the mortality rate if bitten by a black mamba is over ninety-five per cent is *immense*.

But I can't.

Don't be desperate, Harriet.

"Um." I sit down as airily as I can. "I was actually in Morocco for a few days, filming a television advertisement for Jacques Levaire."

Television advertisement?

Why couldn't I say *TV ad*? I sound like somebody who has never seen a telly before.

A few of my classmates start dragging their seats closer to me. "Morocco?" "You're really going to be on telly? No way!" "When does it come out?" "Did you get paid loads?" "What was it like?" "I bet you hung out with *loads* of stars, right?"

They're all talking at once, which makes it really hard to focus. It's normally me interrogating people relentlessly, not the other way round.

I'm not really trained for this.

"*Loads* of stars," I agree anxiously. "I've actually never seen so many stars in my entire life. Some of them were *huge*. It was pretty cool."

A few more people gravitate towards my desk.

"Which ones were they?" "Would we know them?" "I bet Harry was there, wasn't he?" "Do you have *lots* of celeb mates?" "Do you know any really hot models?"

As fast as I can, I count them up on my fingers.

Rin, obviously. Poppy from my flatshare in Tokyo. Fleur and Kenderall from New York. Shola and Rose in Moscow. The two girls who locked me in a cupboard last year just before my audition for *Hamlet*. An entire room full of models backstage at a fashion show who said I looked like an egg.

"Maybe eight or nine?" I say, still staring at my hand. "Plus twenty or so Russian supermodels in their underwear."

"Oh *sweet mother of all that is good and holy*," Eric whimpers, staring at the sky and putting his hands together. "*Thank you,* Universe."

"Everybody!" Miss Hammond calls sweetly, clapping her hands. "Everybody! We're in the middle of taking the register, remember! Let's do this thing *together*!"

Everybody ignores her and inches a little closer to me instead. I stare at them in amazement.

Is this… Is this *still* working?

"What was Tokyo like?" "Did you really live in a penthouse in *Manhattan*?" "Is it true you were spotted on a school trip?" "Are there *loads* of glam parties?"

I gawp at the chaos.

"There are parties pretty much every night, I reckon," I tell them. "Poppy went to all of them."

"*Poppy?* As in Poppy Page? Oh my God – she's *huge.*" "You are so *lucky*." "Is there champagne?" "Is it true that Yuka Ito has named a handbag after you?"

"If she has I don't want to know what it's called," I admit doubtfully. "The last word Yuka had for me was *pus-filled.*"

To my total astonishment, there's a loud burst of laughter.

Real, genuine laughter.

And – with a *whoosh* – a warm rush of happiness spreads over me: from my cheeks down into my chest and straight into my arms until I feel like light is about to shoot out of my fingertips, like Beast just after his enchantment was broken.

I sit for a few blissful seconds, basking in the warm glow of friendly faces. It feels as if I'm bathed in sunshine, steeped in rainbows, cuddled by a billion furry teddies, covered all over in sparkle and—

A copy of *Vogue* is pulled out of a bag and opened on the desk in front of me.

"Do you know *him*? Because if you do, I officially want to climb into your skin so I can be you *forever.*"

And my happiness rushes straight back out again.

58

The glittering girl in the photo is back again.

Except this time, she's not sitting in a lake. She's standing in the middle of a huge sumo stage with a sea of bright lights behind her.

Tiny white lights are flashing from the cameras in the audience, yellow lights are hanging in spots above her head and little cream orbs are reflected from the wooden floor under her bare feet.

Her head is tilted back, her eyes are painted dark and her bright red hair has been pulled into a tight bun. Her dress is long and dark blue, with slits up the sides and little holes cut in the bottom so that the lights shine through like stars.

It's a different kind of sparkling this time – harder, brighter, angrier – but it's still there: shot through the photo like fine gold thread woven through dense fabric.

At the bottom of the page is a glass bottle shaped

like a light bulb, lit internally from the bottom, and the large silver word:

LUMINATE

And below it are the words

BY YUKA ITO

It's a beautiful photo, a beautiful dress and it's a two-page spread in *Vogue*. But, frankly, I couldn't care less.

Because next to the girl is a boy.

He's tall and dark: all angles and points. Hips, cheekbones, eyes are slanted in parallel directions like identical flicks of the same God-like pen. His hand is resting gently on her waist, his head is lowered, and his nose is centimetres from the nape of her neck. As if nobody else is watching and it's just the two of them.

As if he's trying to tell her something.

According to my science books, the atoms that make up human bodies consist of almost entirely empty space. If you took it all out you could compress each of us into a cube 1/500th of a centimetre across.

Staring at the boy in the photo, it suddenly feels like

that's what somebody's trying to do to me too.

I wasn't prepared to see him again.

At least, not like this.

Nick.

59

Tokyo – June (4 months ago)

"Exactly how long do we have?"

"An hour, darling," Bunty said, inexplicably looking at the sun even though she had a watch on. "Or sixty-five minutes max, if I pack the lining of my clothes with coins and try to break the airport metal detector. Let's just say it won't be my first attempt."

I looked at Nick doubtfully as my maverick grandmother started rummaging through her multicoloured woven handbag.

His skin was darker than normal – deepened by the sun – and his hair was still all ruffled from where we'd kissed each other for twenty straight minutes, sitting on the pavement by an enormous zebra crossing in Shibuya.

"Make that seventy," Bunty added triumphantly, pulling out a large bottle of shampoo. "Seventy-five minutes if I can sneak in the bottle opener."

"That still isn't much time," I said anxiously, peering into my satchel. "We don't have a proper map. Or a guide. I've lost my guidebook and—"

"It's long enough," Lion Boy laughed, putting his arm round me so I was tucked into the ridge of his collarbone. "And you don't need one any more. You've got me."

A shock of electricity ran all the way from the back of my shoulders up my neck and into my head, as if I'd accidentally covered myself in warm water and stuck my finger in a socket.

Except in a beautiful kind of way.

I did. *I had him.*

"So what do you want to do?" he continued, kissing the top of my head. "For the next seventy-five minutes I am utterly at your disposal."

"Umm."

I pulled out my To Do list and stared at it blankly, brain now pleasantly fried. What did one do with just seventy- five minutes left in Tokyo?

We could go to the robot restaurant, and watch giant mechazoid robots fight dinosaurs to the bitter death. We could try to find a (very short) tea ceremony, or wander through a Zen garden hand in hand, or visit the Bunny Cafe (like a Cat Cafe but better, because – obviously – no cats).

We could attempt an hour of karaoke, or eat an hour's worth of sushi, or visit the Shitamachi Museum to look at miniature reconstructions of buildings from the late Meiji period.

There were still so many things left in Tokyo I had always wanted to do. So many things I still wanted to cross off my list.

But – for the first time ever – none of them seemed to matter much any more.

Because it wasn't just about me.

"You used to live here, right?" I said, looking up at him. "In Tokyo?"

"I did," Nick grinned. "When I was eleven my parents split up and I came here with my mum and spent three somewhat confusing years not understanding anyone."

"Then I want to see your favourite bit." I put my list back in my bag and flicked a switch that magically turned my watch into a stopwatch. "Show me the bit of Tokyo you love the most."

"Are you sure?" he frowned. "That list isn't going to tick off itself."

I loved that Lion Boy knew how much I needed to tick things off, and how important my lists were to me.

But I loved him more than any of them.

"I'm sure," I said, clicking on the timer button. "You

have 4,500 seconds, Nicholas Hidaka. Think you can manage it?"

He wiggled his eyebrows.

"Oh," he said. "I think I probably can."

"Ready?"

"Never readier."

"Steady?"

He laughed. "In my entire life, Harriet Manners, I have literally never been steadier. Especially by comparison."

"Show-off." I stuck my tongue out at him: I hadn't fallen over in *hours*. "Now... GO."

"Gone," Nick said, and he grabbed my hand.

60

"Harriet?"

"Hmm?" The entire class is still staring at me. "Sorry, what was the question again?" I suddenly miss Nick so much it's like an enormous hand is squeezing me shut.

Raya taps the photo again and I flinch and focus on a bit of desk slightly to the left.

"Oh," I say slowly. "Yes, I know him."

"Is he single?" "Is he as hot as he looks in pictures?" "I can't believe he's *touching* you. You actually got to *touch* him."

Quick, Harriet. Change the subject.

"Umm," I say faintly, clearing my throat. "Did you know that when you speak your throat's vocal folds vibrate inside your own skull, which means the voice you hear sounds nothing like you actually do to everyone else?"

There's a brief pause.

"Did she answer the question?" somebody whispers.

"Was that it?"

"I don't think that was it," somebody whispers back.

"Oh my *goodness*," Ananya says, suddenly pushing her way to the front of the group with her hands. "Don't you guys know *anything*? That is Nicholas Kou Hidaka. Ret's long-term *boyfriend* and love of her *life*."

"*Yeah*," Liv echoes, shoving forward too, except a little less successfully. "You obviously don't know our Retty at *all*."

I stare at them both in astonishment.

OK: they have done some *serious* research. Nick managed to convince me that the middle K in his name stood for Koala for nearly six months, and Kookaburra for another two.

"How did you—"

"We can't *wait* to meet him," Liv breathes, gripping her hands together. "I ship you two so hard I can't even."

She *ships* us? Like, in a boat? Or a spaceship?

A spaceship sounds a lot more fun.

"Uh." I blink a few times. "I'm afraid we're not… I mean, Nick's not… I'm not…"

Apparently girls speak an average of 20,000 words every single day – I don't know where all mine have suddenly gone.

I just can't say it.

I can't say *Nick and I have broken up* out loud: it's lodged somewhere in the middle of my oesophagus.

"You are the *luckiest* girl in the entire universe, Harriet!" "Does he live in London?" "Does he ever pick you up from school?" "Does he have any *friends* you could introduce me to?"

"I..." I swallow painfully. "Nick's in Australia right now."

"On a shoot?" "I saw him on a bus a few weeks ago." "On a bus? Like, a passenger?" "Obviously not, idiot. As a poster. Boys like him don't take *buses.*"

"Uh." I swallow and try to find my voice again. Nick takes buses all the time. He's just a boy: not the Queen. "Actually, it's..." I swallow *again*. "I mean, there are times in our life when paths go in different directions and – uh. There's a fork in the road that..."

"Is she answering the question again?"

"I'm *so* confused."

There's a sharp voice at the back of the room.

"Right." A purple head appears from the crowd, and India walks forward, closes the magazine with a snap and hands it back to its owner with an icy expression. "This school dynamic is deeply disturbing and I think that's quite enough. Does nobody have any respect for privacy?"

Bizarrely, everyone immediately shuts up and I sigh with relief. I'm obviously not the only one who thinks

India might be royalty.

"*Yeah,*" Ananya sighs. "You guys are *vultures.* Ret comes to school to get *away* from all this stuff."

Liv folds her arms. "Such *hyenas*."

Actually vultures provide an invaluable service to the ecosystem by eating dead carcasses that are otherwise rendered inedible due to their bacterial content, whereas hyenas follow vulnerable animals and rip them apart while still alive.

It's really not fair to lump them together like that.

I'm just about to explain this in detail when the door swings open.

"Jasper!" Miss Hammond calls cheerfully from the front. I'm going to assume for the last ten minutes she's been gallantly taking the register and then answering it herself. "Better late than never! Join the crowd!"

He glances in surprise around the empty classroom, and then at the spot where every student is clustered in a mob around me.

My phone beeps and I pull it quickly out of my pocket.

Hannah darling! Kev THRILLED with Levaire shoot! Gucci director asked to see your book – call me!! Stephie xx

I'm too surprised at "Stephie" to hide my phone.

"No way!" somebody loudly squeaks over my shoulder. "*Gucci!* You're going to model for *Gucci!*" "Oh my God, that's amazing!" "Oh wow!" "Have you written a *book*, Harriet? What's it about?"

I flush in embarrassment, quickly shove my phone back into my satchel and look up again.

Jasper and I lock eyes for a few seconds and my stomach clenches slightly.

"You know what?" he says finally, still staring straight at me. "I think this particular crowd is quite big enough already, don't you?"

And he disappears again with a loud BANG.

"Jasper..." Miss Hammond says tiredly this time, scanning her register with a small sigh and then drawing a little tick. "Yes, Miss Hammond. Here, Miss Hammond. Have a lovely day, Miss Hammond."

The bell rings and everyone suddenly disperses to collect their bags, attention now focused on whatever their next class is going to be.

But I'm still staring at the door.

What is Jasper's problem? Why does he always have to be so horrible? I made him a dinosaur biscuit, didn't I? What more does he want from me?

More importantly, why do I even *care?*

61

The rest of the week can be summarised thus:

1. Under considerable duress, I surreptitiously teach a group of girls how to "catwalk" in double chemistry
2. Mr Harper tells me if I don't stop "stomping like an elephant" around the classroom he's going to give me a detention
3. I politely explain that I am, in fact, walking like a cat
4. Everyone laughs
5. I get a detention
6. Almost every girl in the year inexplicably wants to sit next to me for the next three lunchtimes.

Basically, I don't have a second to myself for the next five days.

In chemistry, I explain my "best beauty trick" to a big group of girls (toothpaste on my spots) and how to perfectly balance your dietary nutrition (chicken and

strawberry jam sandwiches). In maths we all have a long and apparently very interesting conversation about castings, and then everyone wants to see my 'book'.

So – flushed with pleasure – I get *Bleak House* out and show it to them all under the desk. For some reason they seem a bit bemused.

In physics, I start using Kirchhoff's Law to find the internal resistance of a cell. "Want to work this out together?" two of the new girls ask, pulling their graph paper over to mine. When I help them out, "You see?" one says triumphantly to the other measuring voltage, "Harriet knows everything!"

Eric wants to discuss Russians for a whole breaktime, Raya is adamant for three hours in double biology that Nick *must* have an identical twin brother and the sixth form netball captain thinks I'm *just the cutest* after I regale the team with a story about the world's most expensive coffee while waiting in line for the vending machine.

"But it's made from the droppings of an Asian palm civet," I clarify again, because I'm not entirely sure she's heard me. "That's poop. Basically mongoose poop."

"*Poop coffee!*" she exclaims, putting a delighted arm round me. "You are just so *adorable*."

On Tuesday I bring in all my extra Moroccan purchases and enthusiastically distribute them, and by Wednesday

morning bright colours are scattered everywhere: silver earrings and bangles and scarves attached to people like bird feathers. Even the boys are participating: they're using spare bangles as tiny hoops to throw around cans and high-fiving me every time they succeed in their target.

Every morning and afternoon after school I meet the first years to hand over more of my books, like a private librarian service.

I have to explain – six times – to Stephanie that I can't take any more time off school to meet designers and she'll have to arrange interviews at weekends instead. Eventually she gets the idea and schedules something for the weekend after next.

By Friday, there are so many ticks on my Inner Star list it looks like one of the essays I used to write and then mark myself when I was seven. I have been confident, over and over and over again. I have been risky, repeatedly. I've been brave and limitless seven times, stylish three and inspirational at least twice.

And it has totally and utterly worked.

Whatever the opposite of lonely is, I've never been so *that* in my entire life.

I just haven't done any homework. At all.

No *wonder* I've got excellent grades for the last eleven years.

I had literally nothing else to do.

"Ret!" Ananya calls as I finally stagger out of the sixth form doors on Friday afternoon and blink sleepily in the sunshine. One of my pink scarves has been wound round her neck and a pair of my enormous silver earrings are glinting in her dark hair. "Retty! Where are you going?"

"We haven't seen you all *day*," Liv squeaks, wrapping her arms tightly round me. "Where *were* you? We *missed* you." I'm still finding her huge enthusiasm for me a little overwhelming, but it's nice that she's so affectionate.

"We're having a sleepover tonight at Indy's. It's going to be *ace*. You're coming, right?"

I freeze in surprise – have I just been voluntarily invited to my first ever non-Nat social outing? – then try to stifle a massive yawn.

Honestly, I had no idea trying so hard not to try hard could be so physically and mentally *exhausting*.

Fresh connections are made in the brain every time you form a new memory. Mine is now so stuffed full of new names and facts and conversations about body parts of celebrities I've never heard of before that I think I may have just run out of space.

"Of course I would *really* love to," I say politely, rubbing my eyes. "But do you mind if I come another time

instead? I've got such a huge amount on this weekend."

Sleeping. Reading. Catching up on homework. Eating biscuits in my penguin pyjamas, hopefully with Nat, and watching documentaries about insects in case anything has changed in the last five days.

"See you on Monday?" I add with a little wave, and start wandering sleepily towards home.

Ananya's voice cuts through the air like a sword.

"Oh. Right. So it's like *that*, is it?"

I stop in confusion, and turn round slowly. "Huh?"

"We get it. It's *fine*, Harriet," she says with her arms crossed. "You've obviously got more *important* things to do than hang out with us now. We *totally* understand."

"*Yeah*," Liv agrees, folding hers too. "I mean, I thought we were a *gang*, but if you're too *busy*, Harriet, then just let us know. We wouldn't want to be *in the way*."

The words are nice, but something about the way they're saying them doesn't quite match. An unpleasant memory from last year is beginning to niggle at the back of my brain: one I killed and buried quite a long time ago.

At least, I thought I had.

"It's not that at all," I stammer, face starting to get hot. "I just haven't done any work this week and I'm really tired and there's a lot to—"

"No no," Ananya interrupts, holding up her hand.

"No need to explain, Harriet. You've got *so* much on, now you're a *celebrity*. I'm sure you have much *better* things to do than spend quality time with *us*."

And there it is.

With that word – *better* – the memory comes tumbling forward: out of my frontal lobes, through my hippocampus and straight into the middle of my forehead where it sits, flicking me hard with its fingers.

You really think you're better than everyone else, don't you? Who here hates Harriet Manners?

Put your hands up.

My entire body has suddenly gone cold, as if I've plunged myself headfirst into the freezer.

No.

No no *no*. Not again.

I can't do this again. Not again not again not again not again not again not again not again…

It suddenly feels like all my hard work over the last ten days is unravelling and I don't know why, or how to stop it. I must have deviated from the list, somehow. And now they seem to think I don't want to spend time with them…

And it's really *not* that.

I'm having *fun*. I'm just *tired*, that's all.

But as I stare at Ananya and Liv's tense faces, it suddenly

hits me that there is no time off from this plan. If I'm not extremely careful, the old Harriet Manners will return, and one by one all the hands that have come down are going to start going straight back up again.

Until finally I'm right back where I was last year, except worse.

Because this time it'll be all my fault.

And I'll know it.

"Umm…" I say, desperately trying to think. My brain is jittering around: picking up ideas and putting them down again. "Could we maybe do something awesome together next week? A… museum visit? An… art exhibition?" They're still staring at me. "A… little gathering or something?"

They glance at each other.

"OhmyGodohmyGodohmyGod," Liv squeaks, lobbing herself at me again. "*Really?* Doyou*mean*itIcan'tbelieveit you'rethebestwillyoureallythrowusa*party*?"

Huh? Where did a *party* come from? I meant tea and biscuits. Maybe a slice of chocolate cake.

"Well, I—"

"OhmyGodohmyGodHarriethowareyousoamazing howdoyou*live*tellmesoIcanbreatheyourairandabsorb yourpowersandliveinyourmagickingdom*forever*."

"Wait," Liv blinks a few times. "Was that me?"

We all turn round simultaneously to see a pretty blonde girl, perched comfortably on a bollard behind us in silence. Like a hawk: the powerful kind with a pointy beak and muscular legs and a habit of tearing unsuspecting rabbits into pieces.

I haven't seen Alexa once all week. I'd almost forgotten she was in my year: that's how utterly invisible she's been.

She's not invisible any more.

And as she unsheathes her talons and looks at us steadily, I have a horrible feeling she's about to destroy everything.

62

In the 1970s, a man called Michael Lotito ate an entire aeroplane. Bit by bit, he chewed through every part of a Cessna 150: glass, metal, engine, leather and tyres. It took him two years but he finally swallowed all of it.

My hands are starting to sweat, but I'm somehow managing to keep my face composed.

After all, I've had more than eleven years of Alexa now. As Lotito proved, you can get through anything with enough practice and a decent set of teeth.

Be brave, Harriet.

"So," Alexa says smoothly, smiling as I push my shoulders back as far as I can get them and lift my chin, "how goes Project Reinvent Harriet Manners? Is she everything you hoped she'd be and more?"

Ananya and Liv take a step forward until they're standing on either side of me, like identical bookends. "Of course she is. We just totally *love* her."

"Harriet's the *best*."

"*Isn't* she just?" Alexa says, her cat-smile curving a little more. "Hasn't this last week been *so much fun*? I've *loved* watching Harriet transform into an icon right in front of my very eyes. It's like a Disney film or something."

My stomach suddenly feels like it's full of aeroplane too. What does *that* mean? Has Alexa been watching me the whole time?

Ugh. It feels a bit like pulling off a shoe and then discovering an enormous cockroach has been sitting inside it for the last six hours.

"Yeah, well, whatever," Liv says stiffly, putting her hands on her hips. "Harriet's having a *party.* A *big* party. An *amazing* party."

"Yup," Ananya says coolly, staring at her fingernails. "And guess what, Lexi? *You can't come.*"

OK: tea and biscuits is rapidly spiralling out of control.

"A big *party*?" Alexa says, hopping off the bollard. "Really? That sounds like such a *brilliant* idea. I bet you really blow everyone away. You've always had such an incredible imagination."

I stare at her in amazement.

I know it seems crazy, but it sounds like she really, genuinely means it. *Could* she mean it? Maybe an entire week of being ostracised has made Alexa realise how I've felt for the last six years. Maybe this is her way

of making amends.

I'd have preferred a traditional apology – maybe a handwritten card with a dolphin on the front – but I'll take what I can get.

In a flush of hope, I step forward.

"Alexa. It's more of a… gathering, really. But if you want to come, then… you can. You're invited. I'd really like you there."

That last bit isn't true at all, but baby steps.

"Harriet," she says, breaking into a wide smile. "I would *love* to come. Thank you *so* much for inviting me. Let's try and put the past behind us, shall we? It's time we moved on, don't you think?"

Alexa kisses my stunned cheek.

"This is *so exciting*," she whispers into my ear. "I am *beside myself* with anticipation." Then she gives us all a little wave and saunters down the road, swinging her bag jauntily behind her.

I watch her walk away in bewilderment.

OK… Did my lifelong nemesis and arch-enemy just *kiss* me?

"Well," Ananya says grumpily when Alexa is finally out of earshot. "I don't see why you had to invite *her*. But I guess it's your party, so you can do what you want."

"Lexi won't come," Liv says confidently. "She always

says she will and then she never does."

An old, bright-purple car stops outside the school and India's head pokes out of the driver's seat. "Are you getting in or what, BANANA? I draw the line at being your private chauffeur service."

Wow. India must already be seventeen and she can drive: no *wonder* she has such an air of distinction and gravitas.

Also, she matched her car to her hair.

That is *so freaking cool.*

"Coming, Indy!" Ananya calls, waving. Then she turns to me. "This is *so* brilliant, Retty. You're too good to us, you know that?"

"Eeeeeep!" Liv squeaks, chewing on the end of her ponytail.

"Iwon'tbeabletosleepIcanalreadyfeelitohmygoshwhat amIgoingto—"

"*GET IN THE CAR, MUPPET!* Liv too if she wants," India shouts, slamming hard on the horn four times. "Are you coming as well, Harriet?"

I shake my head apologetically, and India nods and turns back to fiddle with the radio. Ananya and Liv give me a hug that threatens to permanently change the shape of my windpipe, then climb into the back of the car still chattering excitedly and drive away.

At which point the sixth form door opens and a familiar fluffy head appears, pauses for a few seconds and starts charging in the opposite direction.

So I take a deep breath, tug my satchel on to both my shoulders and begin racing after the only person in the year who *hasn't* spoken to me in the last five days.

Toby Pilgrim.

63

A mouse's tail is precisely as long as its body.

Toby is literally the only person I know who would find this fact interesting, and possibly try to hunt one down so he can measure it with a ruler.

Apart from me, obviously.

And – as I start shuffling after him in my little leather slippers – that's suddenly all I want to talk about. How every human has between two to four million sweat glands, and how on just one square centimetre of our skin live eight million microscopic animals.

All I want to do this weekend is play scrabble and debate in great detail which of the twelve Dr Whos is the best. Toby asked me to stay away from him until the end of this week, so I've obediently done exactly that. But his secret project should be finished now. It's time to spend some proper time together.

I had absolutely no idea how much I would miss him.

Unfortunately, I also hadn't realised how fast Toby was

capable of walking. By the time I've finally caught up with him, every one of my three million sweat glands has done its job and I'm covered in a fine film of water.

I suspect our PE class would be similarly surprised at his speed.

Had Tobes shown this kind of athletic capacity over the last five years, he could have spared himself a lot of wedgies.

"Toby?" I say for the fifteenth time. "Toby? Tobes? Toby Pilgrim?" He keeps walking, so I try to run in front of him. "Toby?"

Then I grab his arm. "Hello, *Toby*?"

"Oh, hello, Harriet," he says finally, taking enormous white headphones off and clipping them backwards round his neck so he looks a bit like a vicar. "I was busy listening to vocal and instrumental sounds combined in such a way as to produce beauty of form, harmony and expression of emotion."

I beam at him. Only Toby would say all that instead of *music*.

"How are you, Tobes? I haven't seen you at all this week. Did you finish your project? Did it go well? Because if you have, I was thinking maybe we could spend this evening—"

"I've got a new jacket, Harriet," he interrupts. "It's a

Secret Agent jacket, and it has thirty-five pockets. Here's one to warm my hands. One for a torch. One for ID. One for glasses. One for sunglasses. One for spare glasses…"

We may be here some time.

"Brilliant! Why don't you come to my house and have a cup of tea, and we can look at all of them together! We can find other things to put in them and…"

"Here's one for a laser."

"Yes…"

"And one for an iPod."

"OK."

"But I'm afraid I need no pocket in which to put the time I have for you right now, Harriet," Toby says, putting his headphones back on. "Because I sadly have none at all at this precise moment."

I stop walking and stare at his back blankly. "What?"

"I'm spending this evening with Jasper," he explains over his shoulder, while fiddling with his iPod. "We're going to fight."

For a few seconds, I'm not sure which of those two statements is more astonishing. "*Fight?* Jasper? You're going to fight *Jasper*?"

A wave of relief rushes through me.

I *knew* Toby would come to my aid eventually. I just

hadn't realised it would be with such uncharacteristic violence.

"Tobes," I say, running after him again. "That's so sweet of you, but just because Jasper and I don't get on it doesn't mean *you* have to dislike him too."

"I don't," he says in surprise, fiddling with his iPod again. "Why would I dislike him? He's a thoroughly nice chap with many interesting and valid points. We've become excellent friends."

I blink. "...Oh."

"Did you know that he's a purple belt in Jiu-Jitsu, Harriet? As I have just discovered Bartitsu, a classic gentleman's martial art from the 1800s, we're going to see which one we like best. It should be rather fun."

I blink again in response.

"Although," he adds slightly sadly, "my fighting involves umbrellas, snuffboxes and top hats and was used by Sherlock Holmes, so I will probably vanquish him effortlessly. Hopefully he won't hold it against me."

Then he clicks a button.

Giraffes have no vocal chords, and it seems neither do I right now. *Jasper?* Despite my noble statement thirty seconds ago, *obviously* I wanted Toby to dislike Jasper on my behalf. Of all the people he could have befriended, Toby's picked the one who hates my guts?

In a sudden rush of suspicion, I lean over and look at Toby's iPod. There's no light: just a dark battery picture, lodged in the middle of the screen.

Which means he could hear me.

Which means he carried on walking anyway; which means he was *ignoring* me.

I suddenly feel a bit dizzy. I'm now trying desperately to remember what was drawn on the paper he hid from me in the art room last week. All I actually *saw* was a rabbit and a badly executed outline of Darth Vader.

Oh my God. Is there even a science project?

Has there *ever* been one?

"What about tomorrow?" I blurt, racing after him again. I'm wrong: I have to be. This is *Toby*. "Saturday evening? Sunday?"

"I'll be very busy," he says, avoiding my eyes. "Super busy with many interesting and exciting things that don't involve you."

I stare at him for a few seconds, eyes beginning to prickle. "Toby, that's incredibly hurtful."

"Oh." He looks confused. "I'm so sorry, Harriet. I didn't mean it to be. What's a more sensitive way of saying I'm not allowed to spend time with you right now?"

Giraffes have nothing on me. An oyster is more capable of putting together a coherent sentence.

"Uh."

"Well, this has been a very interesting catch-up," Toby says finally as I stare at him in silence. "It was nice to see you, Harriet Manners. I hope you are enjoying all your brand-new friends."

Then, without another word, Toby makes an abrupt left and dives straight through a hole in a hedge.

And crawls out the other side, away from me.

64

I stand for a few minutes and watch Toby army-crawl across the grass as if I can't see him.

Enjoying all my brand-new friends?

Not *allowed* to spend time with me?

What the *sugar cookies* have Jasper and Toby been talking about for the last two weeks in the art room? How many *excellent and valid points* has Jasper made, exactly, and what about?

Or – more specifically – about *whom*?

I blink back the hurt as my ex-stalker attempts an enthusiastic somersault and disappears round a wall. He *asked* me to stay away last week, so I did. Why is he being so weird now? What have I done wrong? Is he angry with me for something?

Then I swallow and tighten my hands into little balls.

If Toby wants to take sides against me, *fine*.

He wasn't really part of my gang anyway: he was a late insertion, an involuntary addition who forced his

way in via totally socially unacceptable methods, such as stalking. If he's going to be like this, it can just return to normal again: Nat and I together, like fish and chips, or ketchup and mustard or banana and Marmite, which I quite like even though nobody else I know does.

Except…

I haven't really heard from my best friend all week either. We've exchanged a few messages – having a great time, super busy, etc. – but other than that she's been pretty quiet. I've been giving her some space to enjoy the first few heady days with her new boyfriend.

But I think I've finished doing that now.

So I get my phone out.

Hey – want to hang out this weekend? Hxxx

My phone beeps almost immediately.

You OK? ☺ N xxx

Brilliant! I just thought we could watch that model show you like. I think somebody gets punched this week. ☺ Hxx

Love to! But super busy again. ☹ Another time? ☹ Nx

Monday or Tuesday? Wednesday? H

Something in my throat is starting to hurt.

I may not understand relationships, but I understand punctuation.

This is rapidly growing tension composed entirely of kisses and passive aggressive emoticons. Three kisses to two to one to none: we're both getting irritated. Strategically placed smiley and sad faces: she's feeling guilty, I'm getting needy.

And there's really no way Nat's *that* sad.

She lives three minutes' walk away: not in the outer Hebrides.

I wait an inordinately long time – given that we are *in the middle of a conversation* – then my phone beeps.

Out every night this week too. ☹ I'll ring soon? ☹ Love you. Nat xxxx

I stick my tongue out at my phone – two sad faces and four kisses is really pushing it – then type:

No worries! Let me know when you're free! ☺ Hxx

Insincere winky face.

A part of me totally understands: of course it does.

I know exactly what happens when you meet someone you really, really like. I know how it feels as if the world is shutting down and opening up at the same time: as if it's somehow getting bigger, but only for the two of you. How every sentence of a book, every line of a song, every scene of a film, has a little fragment inside it just for you.

How anything that doesn't starts to melt away.

But no matter how much time I wanted to spend with Nick, I always tried to find a way to put Nat first. To include her. To make sure she didn't feel shut out. Always. Because falling in love doesn't have to mean dropping your best friend in the process.

Except – as I put my phone back in my pocket and start wandering slowly home again – I'm starting to realise I might be wrong.

Maybe sometimes it does.

65

Every hour in Britain we throw away enough rubbish to fill the Albert Hall. It looks like they've just found a new place to put it.

The house has exploded, yet again.

As I push the front door open slowly, I spot about eighteen different receptacles scattered at random all over every possible surface: cups, mugs, glasses, vases, the yellow bucket we normally keep in the garden. Tiny bits of debris are scattered all over the hallway, as if a particularly stupid Hansel and Gretel got lost somewhere near the entrance.

So far this week I've tidied the house every single night before Annabel got home.

And – frankly – I've had enough.

"*Dad*," I say, slamming my satchel on the floor. "Do you think we have *pixies* or something?"

"Don't be ridiculous." My father pokes his head round the corner of the living-room door. "I don't believe in

pixies, Harriet, or fairies either for that matter. I'm a fully grown man in his forties. Do I look like an idiot?"

I stare at him for a few seconds. I can't believe that appears to be a genuine question.

"You have a tea towel on your head."

"Yes, well." He sticks his nose in the air in a gesture I may have to stop doing sharpish. "Your sister and I have spent the day adventuring, and I was keen to give her as realistic an experience as possible."

"With a tea towel on your head?"

"I couldn't find my Indiana Jones hat, and Tabitha thought it was hilarious." He holds Tabby out from behind the doorframe. She has a tiny towel on her head and is grinning widely. "So, don't you want to know what we found?"

At any other time, I absolutely would: yes. I admit I'd be donning a tea towel and marching around the house with my compass.

But right now, I'm not really in the mood.

"No," I say a little too sharply, putting one foot on the stairs. "Feel free to discover-stroke-destroy the house without me, Father."

"First we found a half a hamster wheel in the shed, which is *very* mysterious given that this family has never had a hamster."

Another step and a sigh.

"We did, Dad. It ran away on day two."

"Ah. Smart little man. We *also* found a quarter of a person, which your sister thought was hysterical."

He pulls out the Hug Pillow Rin sent me from Japan a few weeks ago, straight after I got back from New York. It consists of half a torso, one arm and a pink T-shirt that says *I am made for the loving of us.*

"A gift from a friend," I say, taking another grumpy step. Then I turn back slightly. "Actually, give me that."

Dad throws it and I catch and hug it to my chest.

It might just be time to start using it.

"Don't you want to know what else we found, Harriet? They appear to be addressed to you."

"If they're flyers from the Chinese takeaway then it's because I told the man in the shop that fortune cookies were actually invented in San Francisco and…"

I stop.

Dad's grinning and wiggling his eyebrows.

With a sudden lurch, I glance back at all the glasses, mugs, vases and buckets. They're not randomly distributed at all: they've been placed carefully. And the debris looks like… petals and leaves.

Oh my God.

I *knew* it. I *knew* I'd hear from Nick again.

In a single day, one human heart produces enough energy to drive a truck twenty miles. As I leap back down the stairs and start following the trail, mine suddenly feels like it could propel me around the country.

The petals are scattered in the kitchen, out on to the back step and down the garden. I run after them, with Dad jogging carefully after me with Tabby in his arms.

Then I open the shed and my little sister gives a shout of happiness that's only very slightly louder than mine.

There are flowers everywhere.

Hundreds of yellow roses, pink alstromemeria, purple and white sweetpea, pink gypsophila, cream freesias and red carnations. They're arranged in bunches on every available surface: on top of the lawnmower, hanging off a large rusting fork and lined along the window ledge.

It smells like Granny Manners' house, except it doesn't come from a spray or a potpourri inside a particularly creepy teddy bear.

I open my mouth and shut it again.

"I spent all day arranging them for you," Dad grins from behind me. "They came with that."

He points at the old hamster ball, balanced haphazardly on a chair in the middle.

In it is a little yellow envelope that says:

HARRIET MANNERS

And my heart abruptly shoots like a truck to the moon.

66

I've never been sent flowers before.

Or I have – obviously – because I'm sixteen and what kind of self-respecting teenage girl has never received flowers?

I'm just not entirely sure they count if they're from your family, you're ten and you've just had your tonsils out. Gifts don't seem to mean quite as much if you have to chop a bit of your body off first to get them.

But as I run back into the house with my hug pillow over one shoulder, my arms full and my hand clenched tightly round the envelope, it hits me: these aren't just proper flowers, romantic flowers.

They're *fairytale* flowers.

The kind you send someone when they win an Oscar, or have their first opening night in a theatre, or break a world record.

Or if you love them unstoppably.

Hands shaking, I reach my bedroom, close the door

gently behind me and sit on the floor. I carefully place some cornflowers so I can stare at them, chest still zooming upwards.

Then I turn over the little yellow card.

With infinite slowness – the kind that really, really irritates Nat every Christmas – I peel it open. Carefully, delicately. As if I'm performing some kind of open-heart surgery.

Which, in a way, I kind of am.

Then I stare at the paper inside it.

My little Cinder-doll! I am sage and onioned with pride right now. Best hat I've ever found.

All my turtle dove.

Your F-G, Wilbur

And my nose abruptly starts to prickle.

Wilbur.

I feel like I'm splitting in half again: divided between being incredibly touched by this gesture, missing Wilbur so hard it hurts, and hating myself for…

For wishing it was from someone else.

No wonder I never get sent flowers. I'm a horrible, ungrateful hat and I deserve to have things cut out of my body without receiving any floral arrangements at all.

Blinking, I stare at the letter a little longer.

Then I give it a gentle hug, put it on the floor and fiddle with a blue cornflower petal while I wait for the annoying prickle in my nose to go away.

But it doesn't.

Slowly, it spreads across the bridge of my nose, along my cheeks, into my forehead and creeps between my eyebrows. Like ivy, it tendrils outwards: stinging and bristling and spiking all the way across my face until finally it wraps itself round my throat and crawls into my eyes.

I try to take a deep, calm breath: *It's OK, Harriet, it's OK, Harriet, it's OK it's OK it's OK it's OK...*

But it's no good.

The vines wrap tighter and tighter until I can feel the panic rising: my eyes wobbling, my chin crumpling.

I can't do this any more.

I need Nick here, right now. I need to put my head on his chest and have his feet on top of mine; I need the smile that goes all the way round; I need his calmness and his kindness. I need his fresh green smell, and the scar he got from a seagull, and the way he brings things down from high shelves in supermarkets for strangers without being asked to.

I need him to tell me things are going to be OK.

That he hasn't gone for good; that I can do this without

him. Because he's coming back.

But I just don't know if I believe any of it any more.

So I do the only thing I can to bring him closer. I sit up; I wipe my face and grab a piece of paper and a pen.

And I start writing again.

Dear Nick,

I know we made this decision together.

I know we both thought it would be less painful to break up before the distance did it for us. I really believed it was the right thing to do: that it wouldn't hurt as much this way. But I can't imagine anything could be harder than this.

And I don't think I'm OK.

I came back from New York and I was so devastated I shut myself away from my best friends, and now they've shut themselves away from me too.

I've done everything I can to feel happy again. I've been to Morocco and ridden on camels and danced in the desert: I've chased my inner star. I've thrown myself into modelling and done whatever it takes to make new friends at school so I'm not alone, even though I don't really understand them most of the time and I don't think they understand me either. I'm trying so hard to

move on without you.

But I'm not, Nick. I'm not moving anywhere.

All the things I wrote in the last letter... they weren't true. Or they were, but it wasn't what I really meant. I was hiding behind facts and figures because I didn't know how to say this:

Every day you're changing, you're growing, you're living, you're out there being you, and the only thing staying the same is me.

I'm still here, holding on to you.

Stuck in the past. Trapped in it. Burying myself in it. Drowning in it. And I don't know what to do to make it better.

I miss you, Nick. I've missed you every day, every hour and every second since you've been gone.

And I miss the bit of me you took with you.

Harriet xxx

67

I have never run so fast in my entire life.

With my envelope in my hand, I fly down the stairs, out into the street and towards the postbox as if my feet are on fire.

As if there are tiny wings on my heels and six rocket engines on my back. As if I have a magical cape; as if I'm a paper aeroplane.

As if I'm a comet, or a falling star.

And as I run, I chase Nick.

Tokyo – June (4 months ago)

"3,358 seconds."

We passed through tiny side streets, past dark wooden houses with white fabric hanging from the doorways like half-open gifts, under little archways and curved roofs, popping out into bustling, noisy roads and then back into

the quietness again.

"3,247 seconds."

We raced past a little train station.

"2,320," I told him as we ran over a beautiful wooden bridge stretching across a canal, painted red and stuck with long, red flags. "Nick, where on earth are you taking me?"

He laughed and turned round.

"Harriet..."

As he turns, Nick's face flickers slightly: like a broken projection of an old movie scene. Then it melts, as if I'm passing through it like smoke.

Maybe I'm just not running quickly enough.

So I run faster.

I run until my thighs burn and my eyes blur and the world judders from side to side. Until my breath is coming in high-pitched squeaky noises and all I can hear is thumping under my feet.

Focus, Harriet.

"1,986 seconds." We jogged breathlessly through grey cement streets as skyscrapers started closing in around us.

"1,653."

Up some steep stairs. "1,454."

"Harriet..."

But Nick's starting to evaporate again.

Now I can't see the exact shape of his nose, or the precise shade of his eyes, or exactly the position of the mole on his cheek. I can't remember the angle his mouth turns down in just before he smiles, or the exact tone of his voice when he's tired.

So I frown and keep running.

Through the park with the roundabout where we spun in circles last summer.

Across the path where we kissed in the rain; down the road where my foot got wet and he gave me his sock.

Past the first postbox, where he posted my first ever letter.

"1,223 seconds," I said. "I don't understand where we're—"

"Harriet..."

Now his chin is gone, the shape of his ears, the colour of his back in the summer, the curl of his lips.

"Harriet."

I can't remember what his hand felt like.

"Harriet."

I can't remember the expression on his face.

"Harriet."

And I'm running as fast as I can: as if my legs are the wind-up handle on the old movie projector, and maybe all I have to do is get them moving quickly enough for long enough, and – with a little click – I'll be able to see him again.

Smiling and waiting for me to catch up.

But it doesn't work.

Every time Nick turns round, his face flickers and fades a little more.

And as I come to a juddering stop by the second postbox, it finally hits me just how pointless this is. My letters aren't being read. They're not being answered. What's left of Nick is all in my head, and when that goes dark, so will he.

Whether I'm ready or not.

Over the past year, Nick has disappeared so many times.

But this is the first time he's actually gone.

68

I post the letter anyway.

I've run so far and so hard it seems silly not to.

Then I slide breathlessly down the postbox until I'm sitting on the floor with my head in my hands. Nat and Toby don't want to see me. Rin, Bunty and Wilbur are thousands of miles away.

Nick isn't here.

And now I have two whole days stretching ahead of me that seem impossibly empty.

Forty-eight hours of homework and documentaries and hiding in stories that aren't mine again. Two days of rearranging the cans in the kitchen into reverse alphabetical order and trying to wiggle my earlobes when I'm pretty sure I don't have the necessary muscles.

A full weekend of being the old Harriet Manners.

And something inside me snaps.

I wait until I've got my breath back, which – I'll be honest – takes longer than the NHS says it probably

should for a girl of my age and size.

Then I grab my phone out of my pocket.

As fast as I can, I click on every number I've carefully collected over the last week at school: Ananya, India, Liv, Chloe, Mia, Raya, Eric, Robert and a plethora of other people whose names I couldn't quite remember. (They're A, B, C, D etc. in my phonebook, because it seemed rude to tell them that.)

I grit my teeth together.

Then I write the following text message:

I'm having a big party next Friday and would love you to come! Details on their way. ☺ Harriet Manners xx

There are 250 different types of bees in the UK. Over the following two minutes it sounds like they're all trapped inside my phone.

Buzz.

Yes! I'm in! You're THE BEST! X

Buzz, buzz, buzz.

No way! You rock! Xx

You legend! Bringing the whole footie team!

Epic! Can I invite the boys' school? x

Buzz buzz buzz buzz buzz buzz buzz.

And as replies start rolling in by their dozens – even from people I haven't sent the message to – I put my still vibrating phone back in my pocket and stand up.

I know what it is I have to do.

I'm going to throw the partiest party the world has ever seen. It'll be huge. Enormous. Prodigious, humongous, jumbo, bumper, almighty. A monstrous, princely, towering and stupendous party to end all parties.

And when it's over, the old Harriet Manners will be gone forever and she won't be coming back.

Because this isn't a game any more or a fun chance to tick things off a list. It isn't a way to distract me, or keep me busy, or help me forget the people I miss.

The glittering version isn't just the life I've chosen any more.

It's the only one I have left.

69

I spend the rest of the weekend planning.

With Tabby perched on my lap, I spend three hours in Dad's home-office: typing, formatting and printing out two hundred individual invitations on different-coloured paper.

Then I hand my sister back for health and safety reasons and spend another four hours carefully cutting all my invitations into cool shapes and drawing really relevant images all over them.

I make a dozen phone calls, compile six different planning lists and do a little shopping.

I even borrow some of the money I made on my Moroccan job from Annabel, on the strict understanding that I pay it all back just as soon as it comes through.

My stepmother is surprisingly on board, actually.

"A *party*?" she says, lurking in the door of the office as I start enthusiastically laminating all my various bits of paper. Everybody knows that a party isn't official until all

the invites are rendered completely waterproof. You just never know what's going to get spilt on them, further down the line.

"Yes," I say firmly, taking a warm piece of plastic out of the machine. "I need one, Annabel."

Then I add one of the little gold stickers I normally save for myself when I get an A+ on an essay.

There's a short silence.

"Would you like some help?"

I glance up at Annabel in surprise, and then at the bullet-pointed argument I carefully prepared for the moment I had to fight her on it. I'm starting to wonder if having a baby has relaxed my stepmother a little too much: she seems to have become alarmingly easy-going.

The moment she starts doing yoga, I'm calling the authorities and asking for some kind of brain scan.

"I think I need to do this on my own," I say gratefully. "But thank you."

Plus there's always a risk she'll make everyone sign some kind of legally binding contract before they get through the door, and that's just not the look I'm going for.

In the meantime, Dad is bouncing around the house as if all two floors have become a trampoline overnight.

"I *love* parties. What's the theme? Can we make it

food-related so I can dress as an Italian chef and turn Tabby into a lobster and carry her around in a really big pot?"

I look at Annabel in alarm.

If my father so much as shows his face, my hard-earned new image is going to go up in flames. Especially if he's wearing a fake moustache and pretending to boil my sister.

"No, Richard," Annabel says firmly. "If Harriet needs us we'll be on hand, but otherwise we're staying very much out of it."

Seriously: any minute now she's going to tell me quinoa is pronounced *keen-wa* and start extolling the virtues of meditation.

"*So unfair*," Dad says for the six billionth time. "Well if you change your mind, I've got the costume anyway. Harriet wore it fifteen years ago and made a very charming crustacean. She used to cry when we made her take it off."

Which – now I'm thinking about it – explains more about my life than I'd like it to.

By the time I get to school on Monday morning, I'm pretty much ready. I don't want to sound smug, but this is going to be the most awesome party anybody has ever seen in

the history of social gatherings.

I'm even getting pretty excited about it myself.

And I'm not the only one.

"No *waaaay*," Lydia and her little friends squeak as I hand them invitations, tucked into my latest *Giant Bathroom Reader*. "For *us*? We can come? *Really*? You're the *best*, Harriet Manners!"

"*Amazing*!" Chloe beams at me, studying it carefully. "You're so *adorable*!"

"*Ace*," Eric and co grin as I hand them all shiny slips of plastic. "This is *so cool* of you, Retzer."

(That's my name now, by the way. Retzer. I sound like something you take when you've got a funny tummy.)

Liv takes one look at the invitation and immediately starts hyperventilating.

"Look! LooklooklookIcan'tbelieveitwhatamIgoingto wearthisisamazingI'mjusttotallygoingto—"

"*Olivia*," India snaps, rolling her eyes. "Calm *down* or you're going to pop something."

"It's just the best idea *ever*, Ret," Ananya says, giving me a huge hug. "Is *everyone* coming? Will I know them all?"

I beam at her. "Hopefully! They all texted back straight away so it looks like it!"

Ananya and Liv both squeak.

"I'm going to take *loads* of photos," Liv says, kissing my invite. "This is *so exciting*!"

Six hours of burning my fingertips on melting plastic were *totally* worth it.

Everyone loves them. So much so, even I am a little surprised. The last time I saw my peers this excited about anything, we were six and Father Christmas took an impromptu assembly with three real-life reindeer.

I'm handing out invitations in form time and biology, maths and physics and chemistry. I stand outside French and English and history, even though I don't take those classes. I do the rounds in the dining room at lunch, and construct a little booth in the common room at breaktimes.

The most important thing is I don't leave anybody out.

Even if that means giving one to Alexa.

Then – slightly less courageously, because she's still staring at me in silence – running away again.

Finally, when almost all my bits of laminated plastic are gone, I head to Toby's form room. Despite still being cross with him, I'm kind of hoping he'll get over it eventually. Hopefully by Friday evening: I spent extra time drawing on his invitation, and used all of my very best stickers.

"Thank you for this, Harriet Manners," Toby says rigidly as I jump out from behind the door and thrust it

in his face before he can spot me and run away again. Except he's still not meeting my eyes and it's impossible not to notice. "I'll need to check first. I'm afraid I don't think I'll be allowed."

I nod sadly.

Then I glare daggers at Jasper from across the hallway until he blinks and looks away again.

By Wednesday morning, I can't move a single step down a school corridor without being high-fived, hugged, kissed and affectionately pretend-punched on the top of my arms.

"Hey, Ret!" "Yo, Retty!" "Retzer! How's it going?" "Looking *coooool* today, Retty-girl!"

And as the lower school starts to slowly fill up with sequins and bright scarves and red leather satchels, I realise in bewilderment that maybe I was right.

Maybe it really is this easy.

Because as I smile confidently and wave bravely – as I laugh riskily and high-five people carelessly back – it occurs to me that maybe I've finally found my Inner Star.

And it wasn't as far away as I thought.

10

By Thursday afternoon, *Harriet's party* is the only thing anyone can talk about.

My entire biology class has been moved outside to the netball courts while we wait for the two other classes to join us, and it's raining hard. We're all standing in the cold: huddled and shivering under little umbrellas.

But nobody seems to have even noticed.

Everyone is using the extra time to animatedly discuss their favourite parties over the years. Apparently there have been a plethora of imaginative themes, ranging from 80s Lycra to toga to Halloween, and they've all had varying degrees of success.

Which I wouldn't know, obviously, because I wasn't invited to any of them. I'm getting as involved as I can, but apparently Tudor regalia isn't as cool as I thought it was, and neither is 'Victorian Orphan'. 'General home appliances' isn't cutting it either.

"But honestly, Ret," Chloe says as we stand in a little

group of girls. "I think your one on Friday is going to be better than *all* of them."

"It's *such* a cool idea. What made you think of it?"

I consider this carefully. "It's just nice to share the things you love with other people, you know?"

"*Totally.* Oh my God, that is *so true*."

"It's *so* kind of you to share them with us."

"*Girls*," Mr Collins says as the second sixth form biology class walks out of the building to join us in the rain, "I've asked you to stand in silence, please."

"So what should we wear? Something shiny, right?"

"The last party I went to I had this awesome bee costume with adorable antennas that wobbled when I danced."

Huh. I didn't know Attractive Animals was a socially acceptable dress theme.

In fact, I thought it was kind of illegal.

"Oooh," I interject excitedly. "Research shows that bees use their right antenna to determine whether another bee is friend or foe. Did you use that to flirt with boys?"

They all stare at me for a few seconds, and then burst into loud laughter.

I wasn't joking at all – I thought it would make an excellent icebreaker – but I can now feel myself puffing

up so hard I may need to hold on to the school fence to stop me floating away.

I *love* being so unexpectedly funny.

"*Girls*," Mr Collins says again, frowning, "what did I just say? Am I talking to myself? Can anyone actually hear me?"

"*Or*," I continue, thinking hard, "a honey bee uses its dance to communicate information about the location of food. You could have choreographed one around the snack table!"

They laugh even harder. "Hilarious!"

"Or you could have worn a tiara and acted like a Queen Bee and—"

"Girls," Mr Collins sighs, trundling over to us. He has a large, round chest, a rolling gait and has always reminded me slightly of a disconcerted badger. "*What* is this commotion?"

I look at the sniggering group and suddenly feel slightly light-headed. "Sorry, sir," I say, winking at them, "we didn't see you *bee*-hind us."

They giggle harder and I beam.

"Did you not?" Mr Collins frowns. "I'm sure you were facing this way."

"*Bee* serious, sir," I say, wiggling my eyebrows. "That's just un-*bee*-lievable."

The girls are now howling in hysterics.

Mr Collins is starting to look annoyed, but I'm far too giddy to stop now. I want *more. More* laughter. *More* approval. I *knew* my fondness for clever puns would come in handy one day.

"In fact, have you heard the Beatles song, *Let It Bee*, sir? It's really *bee*-eautiful. It really helps us *bee*-have."

Something in Mr Collins' face suddenly twitches.

"*Right*," he snaps, pointing to the middle of the playground. "I've had enough. Get over there, Harriet. *Now.*"

I blink. "But—"

"This is because I have honey sandwiches every day, isn't it? They're simple to make and easy to pack and I will *not* be mocked for my eating habits by a sixteen-year-old. Frankly, I don't know what's come over you this year, young lady. Mr Harper and Miss Lloyd say you've been causing trouble in their classes too."

And – just like that – geeky Harriet Manners reappears again with a *pop*.

I feel a bit sick.

Now the *teachers* don't like me? Why is it so impossible to keep everybody happy?

"Oh no, sir," I say desperately, cheeks flushing, "we weren't laughing at you. We were just talking about this

party I'm going to be—"

That does it.

"I SAID GET IN THE MIDDLE, HARRIET," he yells flatly. "RIGHT THIS SECOND."

I glance to the side, but the girls now have totally straight faces: my hilariousness has evaporated.

Swallowing, I put my head down.

Then I start shuffling awkwardly through the rain towards the yellow circle drawn in the middle of the netball court. Somewhat ironically, centre is a position nobody would ever give me voluntarily in a million years.

Then I stand in silence and wait.

It's really pouring now, and I'm getting soggier by the second. Within a minute, my hair's plastered to my head, water is running down my cheeks and dripping off the end of my nose, and my leather pumps are making little squelchy sounds every time I move.

Of all the days I picked to be accidentally naughty, I could have at least chosen one with slightly better weather.

Slowly, Mrs Harris and the final biology class join the crowd at the edge of the court: a total of thirty-three freezing students.

Every single one of whom is staring directly at me.

In tropical and subtropical oceans all over the world,

you can find a frogfish of the family *Antennariidae*. It is bright red and silent, and notable because of its penchant for creeping slowly along the sea floor on its pectoral fins.

We're now basically indistinguishable.

I'm so embarrassed, I am literally centimetres away from dropping to the floor and shuffling off on my belly too.

India's standing under a bright yellow umbrella, and she gives me a little *What's going on?* frown.

I respond with an *I did a bad thing* wince back and shrink a little smaller.

"Right," Mr Collins says angrily, blowing a whistle. "We are all grouped here together today to practise sampling and classification for your Biology AS-level coursework."

"Yes, sir," everyone says, still staring at me.

"But *some* people seem to think they have more important, exciting things to talk about right now. Apparently this is an inconvenient distraction from their social calendar."

My biology teacher points at me unnecessarily: the entire department is already focused on the middle of my forehead.

I stare at the floor, suddenly grateful it's raining.

I'm so humiliated, it's the only thing that's going to stop me bursting into spontaneous flames.

"If you can't show this class and your teachers the respect and focus they deserve," Mr Collins continues clearly, "then you can stand in the rain with Harriet Manners. Am I crystal?"

"Yes, sir," say thirty-three students.

Water drips off the end of my nose and my cheeks feel like they're on fire.

I'm just trying to work out if there's a way of harnessing the rain and dissolving completely like the Wicked Witch of the West when a throat clears.

And a hand goes up.

71

"I just have a quick question, sir."

There's a short pause as Mr Collins frowns and peers at the speaker through his glasses. "Yes, Miss… Sorry, I don't know your name."

"India," she says smoothly. "India Perez. I moved here from Leeds at the start of term."

"Ah." Mr Collins nods. "Yes. I've heard your name in the staffroom. What would you like to know?"

"Sir, are your atoms, molecules or ions arranged in a highly ordered, microscopic structure?"

He blinks. "Excuse me?"

"Have you ever known yourself to form a lattice shape, and under a microscope are you largely geometrical?"

"Sorry?"

"Are any members of your family a) a snowflake –" India's now ticking off on her fingers – "b) a diamond or c) table salt?"

"*India*," Mrs Harris whispers nervously.

"I'm sorry, but this *teacher* wanted to know if he was crystal. I'm simply trying to find out by means of classification. We *are* in a biology class, aren't we?"

All three classes have started sniggering, and Mr Collins is slowly turning the same colour as India's hair.

"Oh, *another* funny one," he snaps. "We're a veritable stand-up comedy show round here, aren't we. Get in the middle too, Miss Perez. Go on. In."

India slowly closes her umbrella and walks towards me through the rain.

I watch her approach in bewilderment.

Honestly, I kind of thought India didn't like me very much. I've caught her looking at me with disdain *way* too many times for it to be a coincidence.

"I don't think he's crystal at all," she says as she stands next to me. "It's extremely disappointing."

I smile soggily at her. "You didn't have to do that."

Her hair is getting steadily darker and a raindrop is collecting on her nose ring.

"Yeah," she says flatly. "I kind of did. He shouldn't have picked on you like that."

In the meantime, Mr Collins' temper seems to be slowly winding down again. "Right," he says sharply, picking up his clipboard once more. "Anybody else fancy getting wet today? Or can I get on with my class now?"

There's a moment of silence.

The kind of silence you could slide down, should you be interested in sliding down silences.

Then two of the boys put their umbrellas down. "Yeah, go on then. It's getting a bit dry here anyway."

"Yup." Another umbrella disappears. "I fancy a bit of rain action."

"Me too. Mutiny!"

"Well, if everyone else is then…"

One by one – slowly at first, and then with increasing speed – all three classes close their umbrellas and start walking towards me through the rain. My heart is now expanding so quickly it feels like it's going to squeeze out between my ribs in ribbons, like the red plasticine in a Mr Potato Head.

Because it doesn't seem possible. It *can't* be possible.

But it is.

Slowly but surely, the entire playground moves from one side to the other until every biology student in the year is in the middle of the playground, soaking wet.

Standing behind… me.

72

All but one.

I didn't even know Jasper *did* biology until this moment. That's how quiet he is, and how far at the back he's been standing.

"Oh for the love of..." he sighs from his solo position by the fence. "Seriously, what is it with this girl? Is she made of chocolate or something?"

And without warning, a hot, red firework of anger starts fizzing inside me like a spinning Catherine wheel.

I *hate* this boy.

This is one of the most triumphant, glorious moments of my entire life and Jasper's *ruining* it. *Again.* He's already taken Toby away from me. Why does he have to try and take the rest of the year too?

Why can't he just leave me *alone*?

"*Actually,*" I snap, folding my arms furiously. "There is a *direct* correlation between the amount of chocolate a country consumes and the number of Nobel laureates

they produce. So *there*."

Yeah, I know.

Everyone is looking at me: I panicked.

"That doesn't even make *sense*," Jasper exhales. "You literally just took one word out of what I said and attached an unrelated fact to it."

Sugar cookies. That's exactly what I did.

"So?" I manage, the firework fizzing again. "What do *you* know about chocolate?"

"An average of eight insect parts are found in each bar," he says flatly. "Which makes it a lot less nice than everyone thinks it is. Hey – maybe you're made out of chocolate after all."

My cheeks flame. That is *very* hurtful.

And scientifically accurate, which makes it even worse.

"Well the compound *theobromine* is found in chocolate and it can be lethal in large quantities. So maybe you have something in common with it too."

Yup: I panicked again.

"I am so confused right now," somebody whispers. "What are they talking about?"

"Now..." Mrs Harris says, stepping forward and gripping her hands together anxiously. "Let's be nice, you two. We're here to... to... study ecological diversity,

so why don't we all grab a clipboard, a white tub and a bit of rope and..."

There's a cough.

"Just hang on a second," Mr Collins says, stepping between us and rubbing his chin with his hand. "Am I right in thinking that you, Jasper King, do not like Harriet Manners?"

"No," he agrees, glowering until something inside me does an angry little flip backwards. "I think it's fair to say I do not."

"And would I be correct in assuming that you, Harriet Manners, are not terribly fond of Jasper King?"

"Correct," I say, narrowing my eyes at him until my eyebrows hurt.

Mr Collins breaks into an enormous grin: as if all his Christmases have come at once, along with half his birthdays and a couple of Hanukkahs too.

"Excellent," he says, zipping up his jacket triumphantly. "That saves me giving the entire class a detention. Harriet Manners, maybe you need to spend a little time with somebody who understands what kind of behaviour this sixth form expects from its students."

Jasper and I glance at each other in confusion, and then my stomach goes rigid.

No. No no no. *No no no no NO.*

"Harriet and Jasper will be working together for the rest of the day," Mr Collins confirms cheerfully. "Have fun. Class dismissed."

73

Here are some classic enemies in popular culture:

1. Captain Hook and Peter Pan
2. Shere Khan and Mowgli
3. Maleficent and Aurora
4. Ursula and Ariel
5. Scar and Mufasa

And yes, they're also all Disney characters but I still think cartoons perfectly reflect the modern world and all its conundrums and aren't just intended for young children at all.

Whatever Nat might say.

Or the British Board of Film Classification.

But as Jasper and I silently grab our roll of string and clipboards and start heading into the long, wet grass at the bottom of the field, I can't stop wondering which one I am: the villain or the hero.

After all, *I'm* the one in trouble and *he's* the one I'm supposed to be trying to emulate.

But I'd *know* if I was the bad guy, wouldn't I?

"Would Your Highness like me to take my coat off and throw it across a puddle for you to tread on?" Jasper growls as I pick my way precariously through the muddy grass. "Or should I carry you on my shoulders while playing some kind of celebratory trumpet?"

This is so typical.

I've spent the majority of my life stomping across mud in supermarket trainers, looking for flowers to press/dandelions to wish on, and now I actually have to do it for grades: *now* is when I'm wearing soggy cotton and little leather slippers with no grip at all.

By comparison, Jasper is dry, warm and comfortable in waterproof boots, jeans and a light blue anorak.

I really, really despise this boy.

We reach a particularly thick section of grass next to a big oak tree and stop. The rain has finally slowed down, and everything is starting to sparkle slightly.

"First of all," I snap, unrolling a piece of blue string

and pinning it to the floor with a metal spike. "I am not Queen Elizabeth the First, despite similar colouring. Second of all, you *wish* you were the famous explorer Sir Walter Raleigh. And third of all, the cloak across the puddle story is fiction made up by clergyman Thomas Fuller so..."

So what?

"Stick that in your face and stuff it," I finish lamely.

"That's the worst comeback I've ever heard. And why would I want to be Raleigh, anyway? He had his head embalmed and given away in a bag."

"Well, I don't know about everyone else," I retort, forcing another stake in the ground, "but my fingers are firmly crossed for a repeat performance."

"Ouch. Historical burn." Jasper glares at me as I start stalking off with the roll of string. "Where are you going, princess? That's not a right angle. You know we need to section off a perfect square to get an accurate area."

"This *is* a right angle."

"It's seventy five degrees, at best," he says, taking the string off me. "Do you even understand what a right angle is?"

Oooooh.

"How *dare* you," I snap, taking the string back off him. "I knew what a right angle was before you were *born*."

"When were you born?"

"...August."

"Right. So you must have been one of those genius unfertilised eggs everyone talks about." Jasper pulls the string into the final fourth side of the square. "Why don't you just sit on a log and contemplate how amazing you are while I start measuring the diversity of species in our area?"

Another little flash of fury pulses through me.

Made significantly worse by the fact that my feet are now so cold and wet that sitting down for a bit actually sounds quite appealing.

"I've found an insect," Jasper adds sharply, crouching on the floor. "Wings."

I look at the key we've been given. "One pair or two?"

"Two."

"Membranous or hard and leathery?"

"Membranous."

"Covered in a kind of white powder?"

"Think so. The wings are held over the body, not lying flat to the sides."

"Then it's a lacewing. A *Neuroptera*, actually." Then – before I can stop myself – I blurt: "Did you know that lacewings can detect bats using hearing apparatus in their wings?"

"I did, yes," Jasper says, unrolling the string to its final corner. "Because I, too, am a sixth form biology student. But thanks for the patronising information."

Another little dagger of anger flashes through me.

"Why are you even *doing* biology?" I bend down and peer into the grass. "I thought you were an *art* student. Write down frog."

"What kind of frog?"

"Smooth moist skin, green, stripes on back legs, hops. *Frog.*"

"Are you sure?"

"It's a *Rana temporaria*," I snap. "I know a common frog when I see one."

"Maybe you should try kissing it then, Your Highness. See if another prince pops up."

My cheeks go bright red. I have no intention of kissing anything, frog or otherwise.

But I resent the implication that I might.

"And I like biology," Jasper adds, kneeling into the grass. "Write down earthworm."

"Maybe you should kiss *that*," I say fiercely, scribbling it on my clipboard. "See if yet another slimy creature without a proper functioning heart pops up."

Jasper makes a weird snorting sound, and I glance up. It sounded like a laugh, but his face is completely

composed again.

"Work on that one," he says sharply, standing up. "One day it could develop into an actual joke."

Oooh.

We're only a metre away from each other now, and I'm so angry I'm trembling slightly. For the first time, I'm close enough to see that there are six freckles scattered across the bridge of his nose and his eyes aren't two different colours at all. They're both bright blue, but one has a large splodge of brown in it. As if somebody dropped a little splash of the wrong paint on wet paper.

It's really pretty, actually, which makes me even angrier. Jasper doesn't *deserve* interesting, genetically rare eyes. This horrible boy should have boring matching ones, just like everybody else.

We stare at each other for a few seconds.

A line of blue string is running round us in a perfect square, and we're in the middle: tense and pulsing with anger.

Exactly like a boxing ring.

Any minute now a man in a tuxedo with a microphone is going to jump out from behind a tree.

3. 2. 1. FIGHT!

At that precise moment the whistle blows – calling us back for our first round of results – and Jasper turns

abruptly, rolls the string back up and hands it to me.

"Torture's over," he says sharply, before pounding across the grass towards school. "I hope that lesson was as illuminating for you as it was for me."

And I've had just about enough.

"Why do you hate me so much?" I say angrily, running after him. "Is there a particular reason, or is being nasty just a fun extracurricular hobby?"

Jasper keeps walking.

"I don't hate you, Harriet. I just don't like you very much."

I know that should be a relief, but for some reason I don't quite understand, it feels kind of worse.

"But *why*?" I say breathlessly, still running to catch up. "I know we didn't get off to the best start but—"

"Everyone in the entire world doesn't have to worship you, Harriet," he sighs. "Gliding through life surrounded by fans, with your *I'm-so-cute-and-quirky* dinosaur biscuits and random facts. I just find you a bit full of it, that's all. I'm only one person and very much in the minority. Why does it matter?"

I stop running and flap my mouth a few times.

Full of *what,* exactly?

And I can't believe I've spent my entire life being ostracised and now I finally have lots of friends it's being

used against me. Plus – I'm not trying to be cute. I just really, really like dinosaurs.

This is *so unfair.*

"Well I may not be *your* cup of tea," I say, trying to run past him, "but I've *always* been Toby's. So why have you told one of my best friends not to play with me any more?"

Then I flush.

Great: I just made myself sound about six years old. As if somebody took my favourite teddy bear off me and I'm getting a bit hysterical about it.

Probably because that's exactly how it feels.

"If somebody doesn't want to be part of your fan club," Jasper says tiredly, "it has absolutely nothing to do with *me*."

He pointedly lifts an eyebrow.

And that does it.

The little angry firework stops twisting in my stomach, and – with an abrupt *whoosh* – bursts up through my chest, into my head and out of my ears in a shower of sparks.

"I *hate* you," I hiss, spinning round and whipping the blue string through the air at him. "You mean, horrible, unkind—"

But I don't get a chance to find the right noun.

Jupiter has the fastest spinning rate of any planet in

our solar system at 28,273 miles an hour. Not for the first time this term, I may have ended up there.

Because as I watch the string sail through the air – two metres to Jasper's left – I just keep right on rotating.

Round and round and round.

And as my hand clutches at nothing and my silly slippers try to find some traction, I give a little squeak and slip forward, still spinning slightly.

Straight into the mud.

74

There have been a lot of embarrassing moments in my life.

The time I walked around the supermarket with my skirt tucked into my knickers until a sales assistant had to point it out to me. The time I had cinnamon powder on my top lip and everyone thought I'd grown a "little ginger moustache".

Peeing myself during storytime when I was five because I got too excited about *The Faraway Tree*.

(I lied: it wasn't milk.)

Lying flat on my face in mud in front of a field full of thirty students, my new nemesis and three teachers is an event now very much on that list.

"Crap, are you OK?" Jasper jumps forward. "You're not hurt, are you? Nothing's broken, is it?"

I stare coldly at the hand he's holding out.

My palms are stinging, my knees are stinging, my eyes are stinging and my cheeks are stinging: all the familiar symptoms of humiliation and falling over.

In my peripheral vision, I can see groups around the field, starting to head in this direction.

Am I hurt? No. Am I angrier than I have literally ever been in my entire existence?

Absolutely.

"Oh you know me," I snap, shakily trying to get to my feet. "I'm so *full of it* I can't even stay upright. *Don't* touch me."

Jasper grabs my arm anyway. "At least let me help you up, Harriet. We don't have to be friends, but I'm not a monster. Let me get you off the floor."

"I said *do not touch me*." I shake him off furiously. "*Ever*. The next thing you hold out gets bitten off."

He laughs, and it takes everything in my willpower not to lean forward and scrabble at his face with my little dinosaur claws.

"Fair enough," he says, shrugging. "Sorry. Maybe I should have put down that cloak after all. Could have provided a bit of padding."

"*Ooh*," I say, getting on to my knee. "I'll get a bit of padding and stuff it right in your—"

But I don't get any further.

My foot hits another slippery spot, and this time I slide backwards.

Into the mud again.

75

You know what? I think I'm just going to stay here.

The universe seems to be strongly suggesting that lying on the floor, covered in 360 degrees of wet dirt, is exactly where I'm supposed to be.

The bell for breaktime rings.

With a clatter, people burst out of the sixth form doors, pause and then a large number start running towards me.

I automatically close my eyes and wait for the inevitable laughter. *Geek. Loser. Idiot. Why do you always make a mess of everything, Harriet?*

"Oh my God, are you all right, Ret? What happened?"

"You poor thing, you're totally *dripping*."

"The biology department should be ashamed of themselves, sending us out in this weather. My parents are going to write in and complain."

Cautiously, I open one eye.

Dozens of faces are now hovering over me, creased with concern. There isn't a glimmer of laughter: not a

single sign of a snort, an eye roll or a chuckle. Nobody's whispering or taking photos and videos and then uploading them straight on to the internet.

Seriously?

I slipped over into wet mud *twice*. I'm one banana skin away from being a Charlie Chaplin film.

India silently helps me up.

"I... umm." I wipe a strand of hair out of my eye, almost definitely making the mess worse. "I thought it was important to get a close-up view of our biology project. From... you know. Ground level."

Everybody laughs.

A clomp of wet mud and grass falls off my knee with a *plop* on to the floor and there's a sympathetic *awwwww*. Somebody hands me a useless but well-intentioned tissue.

"In fact," I say, my cheeks gradually starting to return to their normal colour, "baby elephants have been known to throw themselves into mud on purpose when they're having a temper tantrum. That's pretty much what I was doing too."

It's not that far from the truth, in fairness.

There's another laugh. I head towards the sixth form block to try and dry off, and the crowd begins to disperse. But just as I'm walking off, Liv arrives.

"What *happened*, Retty?" she says breathlessly, running to my side.

"She got pushed," Ananya says, barging through. "I *saw* it. That *freak of nature* lost his temper and shoved her over, then he *laughed*."

She points at Jasper, and some of the remaining students abruptly turn back towards him.

"Oh my God, what a *weirdo*." "What is *wrong* with you?" "Douchebag!"

"Such a *mutant*," Ananya says fiercely, crossing her arms. "Where did you come from, anyway? Is one of your eyes made out of glass or something?"

"*Yeah*," Liv hisses. "Freakazoid. No wonder you hide in the art room on your own like a total loser."

The sudden vitriol is so thick, so intense, it feels like you could open your mouth, take a chunk out of the air and swallow it.

African wild dogs are one of the most efficient pack hunters in the world. When working together, they have a successful kill rate of eighty per cent.

Some of my classmates' ratio may be even higher.

I look in surprise at Jasper.

Is this what they're always like to him? Is this why he's in the art room all the time? Is this why he's so angry and hostile constantly? How hadn't I noticed?

Jasper lifts his chin, clenches his jaw and glares at me defiantly. *Go on then*, he seems to be silently saying.

Do it.

This is my chance, and we both know it.

All I have to do is say four little words – yes, he pushed me – and I'll have the ultimate revenge. This horrible boy has insulted me, called me names, judged me and twisted my friend against me. Now it's my turn.

After all, he *started* this, didn't he?

Except…

Except as I stare silently at Jasper's round face, with a lurch I suddenly recognise it all. The tenseness of his jaw. The too-brightness of his eyes. The twitch in the muscle next to his mouth. A group of people facing one way, and only one facing the other.

He's pretending he doesn't care, but he does.

I know, because eight days ago – and for eleven years before that – it was me.

"Jasper didn't push me," I say quietly, still looking at him. "I slipped twice because I'm an idiot, and he was just trying to help me. And he's not a freakazoid, so please don't call him that. The chances of having *heterochromia iridium* are six in a thousand, so – to quote Professor Xavier – it's actually a very groovy mutation."

Jasper blinks.

"Also," I say, reaching firmly into my trouser pocket, "here's your invitation to my party, Jasper. I'm sorry I didn't give it to you earlier."

I pull out a piece of muddy plastic and wipe it clean on my scarf. *Ha. Told* you laminating everything was a good idea. When you fall over as much as I do, you learn to take precautions.

Still dripping, I hold the invitation out and Jasper takes it in silence. His face is slowly turning from pale to a strange, mottled pink.

"*Well,*" Ananya says, uncrossing her arms. "We were only *defending* you, Retty. As long as you're OK, that's all that matters."

"Definitely." "We didn't *mean* it. We were only *teasing*." "He should *totally* come to the party."

Jasper's face still hasn't moved.

We look at each other for a few seconds.

Then I resume limping soggily back to school.

The last thing on my list is *believe in yourself,* and this is exactly what it means, isn't it?

It means knowing who you are, even when it's incredibly tempting to be someone else instead.

I'm not Hook, or Khan, or Ursula, or Scar.

Maybe in another life, I might have been.

In an alternative universe – one where everybody

always laughed at my jokes and invited me to parties and never hid my pencil case at the back of a toilet cistern – maybe it would have been harder not to hurt somebody who's hurt me.

But for the first time in eleven years, I'm glad I've spent a lifetime with *GEEK* written all over my satchel. I'm glad I know exactly how it feels to always be on the outside, looking in.

I might finally be on the inside now.

But I am not – and never will be – the villain.

76

Which means there's one more thing I have to do.

"Harriet!" A blue front door swings open and a face coated in thick brown gunk pokes out. "Darling! Just look at the two of us! Snap!"

Nat's mum holds her hand in the air, so I high-five it.

It seems churlish to point out that only one of us is covered in mud intentionally.

"Hello, Miss Grey," I smile, picking a bit of wet grass from my hair and flicking it into a bush. "How are you?"

"I'm just *dandy*, sweetheart. No botox in six months and I've got so many expressions I'm terrifying the postman." She wiggles her face and grins. "I don't think I've seen you since you got back from Nooo Yowwwk, darling. Are you *terribly* glamorous and sophisticated now?"

I look down.

Nearly a year ago, Toby vomited on me and I was

forced to walk around Birmingham wearing little blue nylon shorts, a yellow T-shirt with the number 9 on the back and knee-high green socks.

I am now in a boy's football kit again, complete with little studded boots. You can say what you like about the universe, but it obviously has a very symmetrical and ironic sense of humour.

I just wish it wasn't always aimed at me, that's all.

"Absolutely," I grin. "Or as good as I'm ever going to get, anyway."

Then I clear my throat.

After I'd raided the PE lost property box, I took a deep breath and raced to Nat's house as fast as I could. I still haven't given her an invitation to my party, and it doesn't matter how hurt I am by her, she's my best friend, I love her, and I need to make sure she has one.

Two, actually: one for Theo as well.

He'd seriously better be worth all this trouble. I'm going to be very annoyed if he's as drippy as François.

"Umm." I step into the hallway and hand Nat's mum two pieces of laminated plastic. "I just brought these round for Nat. Can you give them to her? Also, is it OK if I run upstairs and get something from her cupboard?"

Every fun thing I own in the world is currently in a cardboard box that has NAT AND HARRIET'S WORLD OF

FUN written on the side in purple Sharpie.

My party doesn't need it – obviously – but it's always nice to have a fall-back plan.

"Of course, darling," Nat's mum says as I tug off a football boot. I might look into getting some for myself: they're remarkably grippy. "But why don't you just give them to her yourself? She's in her bedroom, watching a film."

I pause, still holding on to a red lace. "What?"

"*Roman Holiday*, I think. She said it's for her course but I'm not entirely convinced it isn't just an excuse to watch Gregory Peck drive a scooter."

"But…" I blink a few times. "Nat said she was out every night this week."

Nat's mum laughs. "In that case, she's been climbing up the chimney like Santa Claus. To the best of my knowledge, Natalie has barely left the house for anything but college in a fortnight."

My stomach flip-flops.

"Then I must have misunderstood," I say slowly as I take the other shoe off and start climbing the stairs.

"You definitely have some kind of wires crossed," Nat's mum says brightly.

"Huh," I say, frowning. "Weird."

But as I climb the stairs, I check my phone again: just to make sure.

I'm out every night this week. ☺ I'll ring soon. ☺ Love you. Nat xxxx

Two sad faces, four kisses.

And she never rang me.

So you can analyse and pull it apart as much as you like, but there isn't a lot of ambiguity in that sentence.

I don't think I've misunderstood at all.

77

The Birch and Swinnerton-Dyer conjecture is one of six unsolved Millennium Prize Problems. It's regarded as one of the most challenging mathematical problems in the world, and it's so hard there's a $1,000,000 prize for the first one to solve it.

By the time I reach my best friend's room, three floors up, I've decided I'd rather be giving that a shot right now than trying to work out what's going on here.

None of this makes any sense.

Nat has repeatedly told me she hasn't got any time to see me, but she's been in *every night*? What the *sugar cookies* is going on?

Has Jasper got to her now too?

Maybe he's written a list of my failures as a human being in the sky with plane smoke and trailed it all over Hertfordshire.

Frowning, I lurk anxiously outside Nat's bedroom for a few seconds.

Then I knock politely on the door. We normally have a strict no-knocking policy, but I no longer feel totally comfortable just walking straight in.

"I said *in a minute*!" Nat yells through the wood. "I'm still drying, Mum! You know I can't eat pizza with wet nails! Enamel is not a topping!"

"It's not Mum," I say in a slightly bewildered voice. "It's Harriet."

There's a short silence and a little clatter.

Then the door swings slowly open.

Nat's wearing a bright green dressing gown with cotton wool balls stuck between each of her toes, fingers spread wide in the air in a large Y shape and a white blackhead strip plastered across her nose.

"Harriet! What are you doing here?"

"I could ask the same of you," I say, folding my arms tightly. My throat is starting to hurt again. "You said you were out all week, and yet… *here you are*."

A familiar, guilty red pattern has started making its way across Nat's collarbone and I watch it travel suspiciously up her neck and on to her jawline.

"I'm just… getting ready to go out again."

I fold my arms a bit tighter. "Funny, because your mum just told me you haven't left the house much in weeks."

"Right." The pink rash climbs a little higher on to her

cheeks. "Well, I've been sneaking Theo in. You know… without Mum knowing."

My shoulders relax a little bit, but not entirely.

That might be true, but Theo's certainly not here right now: I've known my best friend skip a maths exam because she had an unsightly blocked pore. She's not going to be sneaking in a boy while dressed like Kermit.

"OK," I say slightly stiffly. "Well…" There's an uncomfortable pause. "If he's not here now can I come in, then?"

"Oh." Nat nods and opens the door properly. "Yes, please do come in."

"I will," I say awkwardly, walking forward and taking an uncomfortable seat on the edge of her bed like an old matron aunt. "I'll come in. Thank you very much."

Then I twiddle my thumbs.

"Nice weather we're having," I say experimentally, even though it's been raining all day. "Unseasonally warm."

"It… umm. Is," she says. "They say there's a storm coming."

I've never, ever felt like this around Nat before.

Together, we've made it through eleven years, three countries, three break-ups, six million fights and three hundred chicken and jam sandwiches, but there's never

been this kind of distance between us before.

I just don't understand where it's come from.

"Well." I stand up and clear my throat. "I thought you should know that I'm having a party tomorrow, Natalie. You are most welcome to come."

Natalie. I just called my best friend *Natalie.*

"A *party*?" Nat stares at me for a few seconds. "You're having a *party*?"

"Yes."

"Like, a proper party? With proper people? *Real* people?"

"Yes." I'd be offended if ninety-five per cent of our guests in the past hadn't consisted entirely of teddy bears, Mickey Mouse and a shaved-headed Barbie doll. "Real people."

Nat's eyes are so round she looks like an ocelot. "A physical, real-life party, with people and music and food and lights and—"

"I understand the basic concept of a party, Nat." I'm getting a bit irritated now. "Yes, a *party*."

She frowns and stares into space.

My stomach suddenly flips, and every single bit of stiffness abruptly melts away in a wave of guilt.

"Oh please don't be angry with me, Nat," I say, jumping off the bed and grabbing her hands. "I know I

didn't tell you, and I know it's normally just us, and I know we normally arrange it all together and it's a tradition, but you weren't around and I didn't know what else to do and… *Please* don't hate me, Nat."

Nat blinks a few more times. Then her face clears.

"What on *earth* are you talking about? I couldn't be more delighted. A *party*. Harriet Manners is throwing a *party*!"

Like a soldier she drops to the floor and starts rummaging under her bed until she's dragged out a huge, familiar cardboard box.

Then she hops up and claps her hands.

"So," she says brightly, rushing across the room and flinging open her cupboard with a flourish, "we'll need to sort you something to wear, obviously. It's important to get it *exactly right,* because otherwise… tragedy. Chaos. And we can't have that."

She pulls out a yellow dress, holds it up critically, then shakes her head and lobs it on the floor.

I can feel every single cell in my body starting to uncurl. It's all going to be OK again. The Super Team are back.

"You really don't mind? Really?"

"Of *course* I don't mind, you silly billy. A *party*." She laughs. "An actual *party*. Who'd have thought it?!"

"Not me," I say fervently, starting to laugh too. "I'm

throwing a party. *Me.* Can you believe it!"

We're both snorting with laughter now.

"Hey, what's that big party you've heard of?" Nat chuckles. "Oh it's *only* Harriet Manners'! Biggest party of the year, dontcha know."

"What's that?" I giggle, holding my hand up to my ear. "Want a ticket to the bestest party of the year? Well, you only need to speak to *Harriet Manners.*"

"Hahahahahaha!" Nat shakes her head as she drags an orange dress out of her wardrobe and then lobs it on the floor too. "Unbelievable! So who's coming? How big is it? What's the plan? How did this come about? I need to know *everything.*"

"*Well,*" I say excitedly as Nat pulls a green dress out and holds it against me with narrowed eyes, "it's going to be pretty amazing, Nat. I've thought of *everything*, and almost everyone in my form has RSVPd, I think. Quite a lot of the boys' football team, the girls' netball team..."

"Maybe with blue shoes," Nat murmurs, now lost on Planet Fashion. "Silver? Black?"

"Most of my biology class," I continue happily, ticking them off on my fingers. "Physics and maths. Lydia and her friends."

"*Gold,*" Nat says triumphantly. "Gold shoes, green dress, earrings in... silver?"

"And then my new gang, obviously." I hold my hands up thoughtfully. "So that's India – she's new and she's got this really cool bright-purple hair I think you'd love – Liv and Anan—"

Both Nat and the green dress suddenly go very still.

Oh my God.

What is *wrong* with me? Why isn't there a draft box in my head to save statements like that before I say them? We were doing *so well.*

"What?" Nat says sharply, all signs of giggling now gone. "What did you just say?"

"Uh." I stare past my best friend's left ear for a few seconds, brain now scrabbling desperately. "Liver and onion, that's what India and I call ourselves. We're all like, *Hey, Liver and Onion! How you doing, Liver and Onion?*" I cough. "It's an… umm… Leeds thing."

Sorry, Leeds.

In April 2005, a pond in Hamburg made international news when toads started exploding for no apparent reason. Judging by the colour my best friend's face is now turning, exactly the same thing is about to start happening here.

I bend down quickly and pick up the cardboard box of fun.

"Liv and Ananya? Did you just say your new *gang* is

Olivia and Ananya?"

"Well..." I'm sidestepping out of the room now like a nervous morris dancer. "It's not a *gang* exactly, Nat. That was a bit of an overstatement. It's more like an... informal group. A good thesaurus might say it was a squad, or a troop or even a—"

And Nat promptly goes BANG.

78

Fact: the toads didn't explode for no reason at all.

Everyone just *thought* they did.

Eventually a top amphibian expert, Franz Mutschmann, realised crows had pecked out and eaten their livers, leaving the toads to explode from their own protective swelling.

Which is a bit disgusting, so I'm sorry about that.

Although it's worth noting that maybe the collective noun is a *murder of crows* for a reason.

What I'm trying to say is: Nat's not exploding inexplicably. It might look to the untrained eye like she is, but I am an expert on Natalie Grey and I understand it perfectly.

It's only ten steps to the bedroom door.

If I can use this cardboard box as a protective shield there's a remote chance of getting out of here without being blown to shreds first.

"ANANYA AND LIV?" Nat yells as I quickly trundle

towards the exit. "YOUR NEW BEST FRIENDS ARE ANANYA PEREZ AND OLIVIA WEBB?"

"Girls?" her mum calls up the stairs. "Keep it down or take it into the attic."

"Alexa's *henchmen*?" Nat hisses in a lower voice.

"They're not her henchmen any more," I try to explain, shuffling another step. "Actually, they're on my side now."

"Why would you *want* them on your side? They're *horrible*. And I don't know who this 'India' girl is, but if she's hanging about with them I guarantee she's just as bad, if not worse. She probably *wants* something from you. Are you doing her homework for her, or something?"

My cheeks are getting hot and my stomach feels like I've been eating aeroplane again. "That's a terrible thing to say, Nat. You don't know them."

"I totally *do*, Harriet. They've been cheerleading behind Alexa for the last eleven years. Sneaking around, yes sir, no sir, three muppets full, sir. Next you'll be telling me *she's* coming to your party too."

There's a short silence.

"Alexa really wanted to come," I say defensively, taking another step towards the door. "She told me she did, she said we could have a clean start and—"

"*No*," Nat says, eyes widening. "Oh my God, you have

got to be kidding me. This isn't what I… It wasn't in the… Have you forgotten *everything they did*?"

"Of course not." My cheeks are getting hotter and hotter. "But they're all sorry, Nat. I'm sure they are. We were only children – everyone should get a second chance and people *change*, don't they? I mean, *I* have so—"

"No, they *don't.*" Nat grabs the edge of the cardboard box closest to her and tugs it, hard. "When are you going to learn this lesson, Harriet? *People don't change.* You're not having a party with them. No. Nu-uh. I *forbid* it."

I try not to think about Ananya turning on Jasper earlier – she was just worried about me, she didn't mean it – as something in my chest starts to burn.

I can hear Alexa's voice again: *You think things are going to change? You think things are going to be different now?*

Has everything I've done been for *nothing*?

"You *forbid* it?" I tug the box back. "I'm sorry, are you the entirety of the British legal system?"

"Don't be so incredibly naive, Harriet." Nat tugs on the box again. "They're *using* you. A total *idiot* could see that."

My chest burns a little bit more.

"Using me for *what*? And I'm naive for thinking people might actually just *like* me? I'm an idiot for believing I'm

worth spending time with?"

"That is not what I..."

"So you're allowed new friends and a new boyfriend and a new life, and I just have to sit on my own for the next two years, is that it?"

"Why are you being like this?" Nat frowns. "Is this really about Nick? Because if it is..."

And – with an enormous eruption – the burn in my chest comes roaring out of me like a volcano.

"*This is not about Nick!*" I yell at the top of my voice. "Everything in the world is not about Nick! HE IS GONE AND HE IS NOT COMING BACK. This is about *me*, Nat. *Me!* My story is not over just because *he's not here*."

Nat blinks, but it's all still bursting out like lava in one steady, bubbling stream. "And I'm trying as hard as I possibly can to move forward, and now you're taking it all away from me! You're *ruining* it!"

"Harriet! How can you even *think* I..."

But I've been holding on to this for too long now and there's nowhere left inside me to keep it all.

"You *left*, Nat." My chin is starting to wobble and I tug on the box more sharply. "Don't you understand that? You *left me on my own.* You chose college, then you chose Theo, and now you're always busy and you're never around and *what was I supposed to do*?"

I tug the box again.

"But Harriet I only said I was busy because—"

"And you know what?" The flames are rising up: into my cheeks and flicking between my eyebrows. "Maybe I'm *glad* you're gone. Maybe I'm *glad* you're not around. Maybe this is what we both needed, because maybe *you're* the one who's been holding me back in the first place."

Nat goes very still. "*What?*"

I want to stop. I need to stop.

But the lava is hurtling down the mountain. It's burning everything and everyone who gets in its way, and there isn't a single thing inside me that can halt it.

"My life is better without you in it, Nat. I'm more confident. I have friends. People *like* me. I've moved on. Maybe this is what's supposed to happen. I mean, it's not as if we have anything in common any more anyway."

The colour suddenly drains from Nat's face, as if somebody's pulled some kind of plug inside her. She stares at me in silence for a few seconds, then her eyes get very bright and very hard.

"Right," she hisses, tugging hard at the box. "I've heard enough. This isn't yours – let go."

"No." I tug back. "It's not yours either. *You* let go."

"Let GO."

"*You* let go."

"YOU."

"*You.*"

"HARRIET. LET. GO. OF. THE. BLOODY. BOX."

And – with one almighty rip – we both tug on NAT AND HARRIET'S WORLD OF FUN at exactly the same time and it splits right down the middle.

Exploding on to the floor between us.

79

We stare at the mess for a few seconds in silence.

Scrabble tiles and Monopoly hotels have gone everywhere. Face paints have smashed into pieces. Deflated balloons with little eyes and mouths have rolled under the bed and a tail from an old donkey is lying on top of my foot.

Organs have been spilt: there's a kidney and pancreas from an old game of Operation still rocking back and forward slightly on the floorboards.

Old blue glitter is spread across the rug.

Then – with astonishing speed – Nat bends down and sweeps it all up into her arms. The Maglev train in Shanghai is the fastest train in the world, but at this moment I feel like Nat could probably beat it.

She runs towards the door.

"Don't!" I shout after her, because I know exactly what she's going to do and if she does I don't know how we're going to fix it. "DO. NOT. DO. THIS!"

But Nat does it anyway.

Without a word, she runs to the bathroom and lobs every house, every chess piece, every card, every paint, straight into the toilet.

Then she pulls the chain.

Slowly at first, and then with increasing speed, eleven years start to disappear in front of us.

Every late-night giggle. Every shared nose snort.

Hours and hours of *Cinderella* and *Shrek*. Hundreds of soda floats and pizzas and muffins.

Years and years of hiding under a duvet together, with a torch, so we could stay up a little later. Doing whatever we could to make the night last longer. To spend a bit more time together: just the two of us.

All spinning and turning until they've totally vanished.

Gone.

"There," Nat snaps, facing me coldly. "*Now* we don't have anything in common any more."

We stare at each other, shoulders heaving up and down.

"Maybe you shouldn't come to my party after all," I say finally. "I think maybe we need some space."

"I agree," Nat hisses, face completely white. "After all, I wouldn't want to *hold you back* any more than I have already."

And with a firm kick of the radiator Nat storms out of the bathroom, slamming the door behind her.

Now, I know a lot about space.

I know it's big, and dark, and lonely, and we don't really understand it. I know that all stars are moving away from each other, and that the galaxies at the outer reaches of the universe are racing away from us at ninety per cent of the speed of light.

But as I let myself out of the bathroom and start charging angrily home, I can't help wondering if maybe that's what is happening to Nat and me too.

Because it feels like my universe and everything in it is slowly pulling apart.

And there's nothing I can do to stop it.

80

There's an altitude point that occurs between 18,900 to 19,350 metres above sea level, called Armstrong's Line. It's the exact level where atmospheric pressure becomes so low that water boils at 37°C.

In other words: precisely the temperature of the human body.

My blood is now bubbling so fast I suspect I may have crossed it.

In a fury, I rip home and charge straight up the stairs.

I fling open my cupboard and get my Arts and Crafts kit out. I pull out my baking kit and my notepad. And I start party-preparing like I have never prepared for anything before in my life.

And as I prepare, I chatter angrily.

"Oh I'm *sooooo* fashionable and cool," I snap as I start blowing up balloons and squeakily drawing on them with pens. "Oh I know *sooooo* much about eyeshadow," I mutter as I cut little shapes out of shiny paper. "Oh I

am just *sooooo* pretty with my swishy black hair and my glowing brown skin and I never ever get zits because I eat *allll* my vegetables and drink two whole litres of water a day."

Then I realise I'm essentially just being really nice about Nat under my breath, which isn't making me feel any better at all.

So I focus my anger and give it another shot.

"Fickle and disloyal," I hiss as I mix flour in with eggs. "Volatile," I complain as I shape ham and cheese sandwiches. "Nowhere *near* as good at Jenga as she thinks she is."

That's more like it.

In an angry whirlwind – not unlike the Tasmanian devil, the world's largest carnivorous marsupial and generally deemed to have one of the worst tempers on the planet – I whizz round the house: cutting and sticking, baking and mixing. I paint and blow up, pop accidentally and blow up again. I attach strings and ribbons and twinkle and put things in cardboard boxes.

But it's still not enough.

By the end of Thursday night, I'm nowhere near ready, and I'm definitely not calm. In fact, I'm more charged up than ever. Instead of defusing, the anger is just hardening and stiffening like cement between each of my cells until I

lie awake all night, staring at the ceiling because I'm now too rigid to roll over.

This isn't just a party any more. It's a *battle.*

A battle made of streamers and balloons and music and carefully arranged snacks, and I have to win.

I'm going to show Nat.

She's going to *rue the day* she ever doubted me. I'll throw such a successful party, such an *amazing* party, that she will be forever known as The Girl Who Had Nothing To Do With It, Actually. For the rest of time, Natalie Grey will be asked where *she* was the night Harriet Manners triumphed socially, like the first time humans walked on the moon.

And any ideas I had for Friday night – which were quite a few anyway – are now accelerated, heightened, turbo-charged.

There is *nothing* I will not do to make my party victorious.

With a bolt of defiant adrenaline, I bounce out of bed on Friday morning and carefully pack everything away neatly in the car so that Dad and Tabby can help me drive it to The Venue.

I remind my father, for the billionth time, that he's not invited.

I listen to *It's so unfair* another 1,298 times.

Then I use every breaktime, lunchtime and all of my free periods at school to run out and start setting things up. I specifically hired a venue as close to school as possible so it would be convenient for everyone to get there.

Not least me.

"Can't we *help*?" Ananya says as I trot out of the front gates for the third time, holding a pair of scissors (upside down, obviously – I don't have a death wish). "Are you sure there isn't anything we can do? Can't we at least be at the gates to greet people?"

"We *so* want to be involved," Liv explains, chewing on a nail. "It's the best theme *ever, I can'twaittoseewho comesandwhatthey'rewearingand—*"

"*Olivia*," India sighs, putting a hand over her eyes. "Stop. Only killer whales can hear you now, and as far as I know, none of us are members of the orca family."

"Sorry, Indy. ButI'mgoingtofangirlsohardandohmyGod I'mbringingmyphoneandcameraand..."

India slowly lifts her bag and puts it in front of Olivia's face until she stops talking.

"That's so nice of you all," I say, shaking my head. "But I really want this to be a big surprise for everyone, so I'd like to do it myself, if that's OK?"

"Absolutely," Ananya says, nodding sweetly. "Just

know we're here if you need us. For *anything.* Anything *at all."*

By my fourth visit, I can feel the cement running through me starting to soften again.

The Venue has finally started taking shape.

As each table goes up, as food gets carefully laid out in strategically planned and organised patterns, as decorations get pinned to the walls and the ceiling, lights are unplugged and re-plugged, and a corner is set aside for a dance floor, I start to fill with a warm, confident glow of satisfaction.

And by the time I've quickly run home, jumped into the shower and tugged on my brand-new outfit, there's no question in my mind that I've done the absolute best I can possibly do.

Now there's nothing left to do but wait.

81

You already know what the theme is, by the way.

Of course you do.

If you've been paying attention, and if your mind works like mine does – in a logical, strategic, slightly obsessive-compulsive kind of way – there was really only one possible choice: one area I knew I could shine in.

But – just in case you've missed it – here's the invitation:

Night of Stars
8pm 'til late
132 Earl Street
Dress code: All That Glitters

Let's be honest: it was the only option that wasn't dinosaurs or group-solved crossword puzzles.

And yes, I know the Shakespeare quote is from *The*

Merchant of Venice and is technically "all that *glisters*" but glisters sounds a bit too much like *blisters* and I don't want people at my party getting accidentally confused and coming as one of those instead.

At 7:59pm exactly, I count down the last ten seconds of the hour as calmly as I can.

Ten, nine, eight, seven, six, five, four, three, two –

Then I fling the doors open wide.

I'm wearing a gold T-shirt customised all over with black star stickers, black leggings individualised carefully with tiny gold stars and a black headband with a large cardboard gold star stuck to the front. And I've used every single make-up trick I learnt in Morocco to help make me look suitably celestial.

Gold eyeshadow and eyeliner, highlighter, a bit of twinkle spray that's supposed to be used on trees at Christmas.

Behind me are reams and reams of hand-dyed black sheets, hanging from ceiling beams, with white fairy lights also borrowed from our family Christmas box wound carefully round them. The floor is covered in little hole-punched silver circles, and precisely three hundred and fifty hand-cut gold and silver paper stars are stuck to the ceiling in accurate constellations: *Chamaeleon, Octans, Reticulum, Indus, Pavo, Norma, Carina, Volans.*

Balloons are bunched in the corners with stars drawn on the front in Sharpie, and from the rafters hang two round red rubber balloons, two yellow, two blue, a teeny tiny brown one and a green-and-blue-mottled one I coloured in myself.

On the tables – on top of black sheets covered in little dobs of white Tipp-Ex – is an array of appropriately themed foods: sandwiches cut into stars, jellies shaped into stars, cupcakes with icing stars stuck on top, pizzas cut into stars, biscuits cut into stars, melon pieces cut into...

Well. You get the drift.

Let's just say I really made the most of my new star-shaped cookie cutters.

Bowls of Mars bars and Milky Ways have been distributed at random for the peckish and non-diabetic, the lights have been turned down low and in the corner is Tabitha's little fluffy turtle night-light, borrowed for a few hours: shining bright white and moving stars on all the walls.

(I obviously have a glow-in-the-dark constellation in my bedroom too, but the stars are stuck on the ceiling with superglue and Annabel wouldn't let me "dismantle the house" despite my desperate pleading.)

And – in the middle, at the back – is my *pièce de*

résistance. The main meal: the showpiece, the highlight, the pinnacle of all my achievements.

My own, personal DJ.

Hovering over a table with huge earphones on, looking as cool as can be and ready to hit the music just as soon as the first people arrive. Because that's the great thing about having so many friends: you can call in little favours.

Believe it or not, I haven't had to pay for a single thing: it's all been offered for free, out of the kindness of people's hearts.

Which includes the perfect venue.

Precisely seven years, three hundred and three visits, seven orienteering holidays and a camping trip where I was chased by a very large cow across a field have finally come to full fruition. One quick phone call and the head of the Girl Guides Association was more than happy to lend me their local wooden hut for the evening.

"Harriet," she said when I asked how much it would cost, "according to my memory, you got a hundred and two badges as a Brownie and Guide, not including whatever you achieved as a Rainbow."

"Seven," I said immediately. "I got my I've Had An Adventure Badge, my I've Been On A Sleepover Badge, my Aim High Badge, my Happiness Badge, my Loyalty

Badge and—"

"Stop stop stop," she laughed. "The hut is on us. I think you've earned it."

And as the first sounds of footsteps and giggles can be heard in the dark outside, I turn round quickly and stick my thumbs nervously in the air.

"All set?" my DJ calls from the back of the room, finger poised over the GO button, or – you know. Whatever the trendy disc jockey equivalent of that is.

Timing is paramount, so I wait a few seconds until the voices are so close I can hear them whispering *"You* go first," "No you," "No *you*".

Then I take my deepest breath and nod. *"Go!"*

With a flourish, Steve the caretaker hits a button.

As the air fills with the buoyant, triumphant perfection that is *The Planets* by Gustav Holst, I can feel my smile getting broader and broader until my whole face feels like it's glowing from the inside out.

As if it has its very own source of solar energy.

And as the music swells and I swell with it, it's all I can do not to lift into the air too.

That's how brightly I'm burning.

"Hello," I say at the first small and polite knock on the door, "and welcome to the stars."

82

The first head round the door is Lydia's.

"Oh *wow*," she squeaks, jumping out with her bright orange hair flying and running into the middle of the room. "This is what I think *heaven* should look like. Because a) it's awesome, b) there are stars everywhere and c) cake!" She spins round a few times and runs over to the table. "AND *MARS BARS*!" she shouts. "THERE ARE MINI MARS BARS!"

Then she opens two and crams them both into her mouth simultaneously.

Yup. She's my spirit animal.

"*Lydia*," Fee hisses, poking her blonde head round too. "You're *so* embarrassing. *Try* and remember we left primary school four whole *months* ago."

Two more familiar little heads appear. "We're *so* sorry, Harriet Manners. Please don't send us home again, Harriet Manners."

I smile affectionately and beckon them in. They shuffle

forward shyly, self-consciously tidying up little spangly skirts and straightening their T-shirts with sequins that say LOVE, PARIS and MEOW.

Lydia's wearing a jumper with a sun on it and is now rocketing round the room with a mouth full of chocolate, prodding things at random.

"Oh, look! Balloons painted to look like planets! That's so clever!" She spins the little brown one round. "Except planets aren't stars, are they, Harriet? I thought they were celestial bodies in orbit? Did you cheat on the theme?"

I think I've just found the missing link between me and Tabitha. I may have to ask my parents if they've misplaced a child at any stage in the last decade.

"Planets are in between us and the stars," I explain, resisting an urge to high-five her. "So they represent the journey we take to them."

And also because let's be honest: there aren't that many snacks called *Fomalhaut* or *Kornephoros.* Mars Bars were much easier to source.

"*Ooooooooohhh,*" all four say, clasping their hands together and gazing at the ceiling with round eyes. "*Coooolioko.*"

Then they start skipping around the room, examining every detail – the tiny star candles, the big star cake, Tabby's fluffy night-light – and waving at the DJ booth.

"Hey, Mr Barker," they say cheerfully, stuffing sandwiches in their mouths. "You look *so* cool out of your overalls."

"Darn right I do!" Steve grins, taking his orange trilby hat off and doing a little bow. "Now let's party, shall we?" And he starts smashing his head to a particularly rambunctious cello solo.

In the meantime, I'm lurking anxiously by the entrance, staring at my watch.

The invitation said 8pm, and it is now 8:03pm.

Where *is* everyone?

Maybe they're not coming. Maybe this was a huge mistake. Maybe this is going to be like when I had a big order of books delivered and they said they would be there on Saturday afternoon and I waited all day on the sofa and they didn't show up at all.

Except, you know: a billion times worse.

Because that wasn't utterly humiliating or emotionally devastating or a waste of cupcakes and it's not like I was actually intending to leave the house all day anyway.

I check my watch again as the first years start dragging Twister from the Games Corner and laying it out on the floor, then again as they begin giggling and shouting colours and directions at random.

Then again.

And again.

Brain-imaging studies have shown that our perception of time stretches backwards when our eyes shift from one point to the other, meaning that the second hand on a clock feels like it's taking longer than a second to tick if we stare directly at it.

My second hand doesn't seem to be moving at all.

Like: at all.

It's apparently been 8:05pm for the last three hundred years.

Cheeks starting to flush, I sit on a little chair by the entrance and try to breathe as calmly as I can. The stomach of a hippopotamus is three metres long, and mine is now dropping so fast it feels like it may have stretched to similar proportions.

Then I hear it.

Another wave of noise outside the door: faint at first – a few giggles, a few faraway shouts – and then louder. Louder and louder and louder until the gravel in front of the Guide Hut starts crunching noisily.

I look up.

"Is that *them*?" the first years whisper with round eyes, frozen in terror with their feet and hands in the air. "Is that *the sixth formers*?"

Eyes widening too, I nod.

There are three tables in this room right now and for a brief second it takes all my willpower not to crawl under one of them.

Instead, I straighten my shoulders.

Be confident, Harriet. Be brave.

Harness your Inner Star.

And with a loud burst, my entire year comes pouring in.

83

Within moments, my classmates have flooded the room and settled all over everything, like one of the plagues of Biblical Egypt.

Except instead of locusts or frogs or lice or flies, it's sixteen-year-olds.

And instead of boils they've erupted into sequins.

Seriously, there is sparkle *everywhere.*

Never mind embracing the theme: this lot have wrestled it to the floor and got it in an aggressive headlock.

Almost all of the girls are wearing dresses, and some of them are in full evening gowns, covered in beads and twinkle and glitz. There are a few big net skirts, a number of tiaras and huge earrings and quite a few wobbling knees thanks to enormous heels: the entire female population has grown five inches in the last four hours.

Most of the boys are in shirts and black trousers; a few are in ties, and a couple have donned black tuxedoes with little sequin bow ties like magicians.

Lips are red, enormous eyelashes are stuck on, hair is carefully curled or straightened, messed up or cleanly shaven. (Apart from two little cautious moustaches: Robert and Adam.)

My gang have really gone for it: India's in a knee-length purple dress – like a very beautiful Barney the dinosaur – and Ananya and Liv are resplendent in floor-length satin red and pink gowns.

Honestly, I've never seen them all look so lovely.

So glamorous. So *glitzy*. It's like they've come to a prom, or a ball, or maybe the party Cinderella threw after she became a princess.

And they've made all this effort for *me*.

I mean, it's a little more glam than I was expecting for the Guide Hut, but the support is seriously appreciated.

I can feel a lump starting in my throat as the year spreads through the now relatively tiny room as if by osmosis, staring at the decorations in astonishment. They've gone very, very quiet. They must be *so* impressed.

I have obviously blown their minds.

"This is..." "Wow." "...Unexpected." "*Retro.*"

"Crikey." Raya picks up a little cup of jelly and blinks at it. "Is this *jelly*? Like actual jelly? With *glitter*?"

"Yes, but don't worry," I say quickly as her eyes widen. "It's totally safe to eat. I checked."

"Cu-ute," she says slowly, putting it down again.

"So where are the drinks?" Chloe asks, rubbing her hands together. "We're *parched.*"

"Over there." I beam and wave my hands with a flourish at the table on the left. "We have everything you could possibly want. Lemonade, cola floats, ginger beer, fizzy orange and my very own personal invention, Milkywayshake."

Then I snigger slightly.

"See?" I explain as she continues staring at me. "It's a space-themed play on words. Milkshake? Milkywayshake?"

"Oh," she says, not taking any of them. "Yeah."

The rest of the group is still staring in silence around the room, amazed at how creative I've been. The music is getting louder, and a few people are cocking their heads to the side curiously.

"What *is* this? Is it some kind of hymn?"

I turn to Steve and quickly make the international *next track* circle-finger gesture. The entire crowd follows my eyes.

"Is that your *dad*?" "Your *dad* is the DJ?"

"Don't be ridiculous," I laugh, shaking my head. "Please! As if I'd invite my *dad* to my own party! That's Steve."

"Steve… Steve the school *caretaker*?"

"All right there, spring-chickens!" he yells, bopping up and down to what is now *Waiting For a Star to Fall.* "DJ Earthling rocking the microphone for the free-range stylers!"

There are a few giggles.

Steve's *spinning* skills may be top-notch but I might quietly ask him to hold back on the comedy.

"Isn't it *brilliant*?" Lydia says, picking up the night-light and holding it in the air. "Isn't this just the best party *ever*? When I'm in sixth form I'm going to have one *exactly* like it except with even *more* chocolate and also *Galaxy* bars because Harriet forgot about them."

There's a short silence while everyone in the room stares at her. "Hang on – is she..." "Are they *first* years?" "Are there *eleven*-year-olds at this party?"

"She's twelve, actually," Fee says, pointing at Keira, the quietest of the four. "She was twelve last week."

"*Lydia?*" Chloe says in alarm, stepping out of the crowd in a glitzy blue strapless number. "What the hell are *you* doing here?"

Lydia folds her arms. "Mum said I could come as long as she could collect me at half nine and you're not allowed to say *hell*, Clobo, so *there.*"

"*Mum*'s turning up at half nine?" Chloe's cheeks are going purple and she turns round to a now-giggling-again

group in a fury. "*Shut* it. I'd like to see *your* kid sisters turning up to ruin everything."

I can feel my stomach starting to get tense and cement-y again. It hadn't occurred to me that my peers might not actually want the first years here. Isn't the expression *the more the merrier*? I mean, we were all first years once, weren't we? Exactly how much can change in five years, anyway?

Quite a lot, judging by my classmates' expressions.

"I invited them," I start protectively as the four begin to look in a panic at the exit. "It's my fault, they're here because I asked them, and they're actually really sweet and—"

"And they're welcome." India walks firmly to my side. "This is a great party, it was kind of you to invite everyone and we're all really happy to be here, *aren't we*."

This isn't a question, by the way. She's telling everyone they're happy to be here.

It seems to work. Some of the netball team start to mill by the drinks table, Robert picks up a sandwich.

"But of *course* we are," someone says. "We didn't mean it like *that,* Retzer! Don't be silly!" "We were just surprised, that's all." "It's a really *nice* gesture, Retty." "This is the *sweetest* party ever!"

"It's so *awesome,*" Ananya says loudly, pushing

through to my other side and linking arms with me. "We're *so* impressed, Ret. With your... er... outfit too. And I love what you've done with the theme! Such a clever pun!"

"*Hilarious!*" Liv agrees, standing slightly behind me. "You're *so* smart, Retty. And *so* generous."

A flush of intense gratitude rushes through me.

Nat was wrong. I'm not sure what she thought these girls were using me for, exactly, but these are my comrades. My posse. My gang.

My *friends.*

Although – I have to be honest – not for the first time I'm not entirely sure what Ananya's talking about. *What* clever pun?

This party is the most literal thing I've ever done.

"Ah *shoot,*" Steve says, looking around him in confusion. "I've left my box of CDs at home. Back in twenty mins, party people. I've put Now Eighteen on to keep you all going in the meantime."

There are a few more little sniggers as he tries to high-five three or four students on the way out.

"*So,*" Ananya says as Steve disappears out of the wooden door. "*Tell* us all about the stars, Retty. Everyone is just *dying* to know."

Really?

I beam at the now silent, awestruck crowd in front of me. I've been preparing for this question for ages.

All my life, some might say.

"OK," I say happily, taking a deep breath. "The closest star to earth is obviously the sun, which is four point six billion years old and a yellow dwarf measuring one million, three hundred and ninety-two—"

"You're so *hysterical*, but I mean the *other* ones."

I stare at Ananya. "What other ones?"

"The *other* stars."

"Umm." She's very impatient: I was just getting round to them. "Uh, OK. There's Alpha Centauri, which is the second closest star… to earth but… actually consists of three…"

I gradually slow to a halt.

Everybody's looking really confused now. What on *earth* is going on?

Why does everyone keep glancing at the door?

"*Harriet*," Ananya says finally, putting a hand on my shoulder. "Just tell us when all the celebrities are getting here."

84

In 1961, the Museum of Modern Art in New York hung Matisse's painting *Le Bateau* upside down for forty-seven days before a stockbroker finally noticed.

That's exactly how I feel now.

As if I've been looking at everything the wrong way up this whole time and I didn't have a clue.

Night of Stars.

My second hand is never going to tick again: that's how slowly everything is now moving.

"C-c-celebrities?" I stutter faintly.

"Yes," Liv squeaks, hopping up and down. "All the hot models and the actorsandthepopstarsandpeople offtellyohmyGodthisis*so*excitingIdon'tknowifIcaneven containmyselfanylongerand—"

"*Olivia.*" Ananya glares at her. "For God's sake. Will you *ever* be cool?" She looks back at me and smiles, except now I'm noticing for the first time it doesn't quite reach her eyes. In fact, I'm not totally sure it ever actually

has. "They're all coming late, of *course*. They're *famous. Obviously* they're not going to get here on time. But who do you think will make it?"

Is everyone coming? Will I know them all?

I stare at Ananya blankly, then at the crowd still looking at me. All the excitement. All the sparkle. All the pretty dresses. All the lipstick and heels and eyelashes. All the *bow ties*. They're not for me at all. They think this is a party of *stars*. *OF.* STARS.

Oh my God.

I've done it again, haven't I.

This is *just* like the dinosaur biscuits, except I've somehow managed to turn a horrible misunderstanding into an entire evening's entertainment.

With a sickening jolt, my brain is starting to replay conversations from school all week.

Oh yes, lots of the stars are single! Most of them in fact!

Actually most stars are pretty much the same, believe it or not: some are just much bigger than others.

Of course I know the really massive ones!

I think I might vomit. I *knew* my love of astronomy would get me into trouble one day.

Quick, Harriet. Be bold.

"I've got a quiz for us," I say desperately, rushing

over to the microphone and grabbing it in my sweaty hand. "There's a handmade cake for the winning team! Umm." My knees are literally starting to tremble. "First question – what are stars primarily made of?" I clear my throat. "Anyone? Anyone at all?"

Nobody answers.

"It's hydrogen and helium!" I squeak. My voice is so high now I think I may have eaten one. "Second question – which of the following is *not* a star: a) a red giant, b) a white dwarf…"

"Oh my God," somebody says flatly. "She means stars. Actual stars. It's not a pun."

"This is *it*. This *is* the party. It's just us."

"With *jelly*." "With a *caretaker*." "And hymns." "And *first* years." "And a baby's *night-light*."

"*Such* a geek."

"It's a green dwarf!" I say loudly, except the microphone is starting to make little *thd thd thd* noises from where my hand is shaking. "Next question – what category does our sun fall int—"

"Hang on." Ananya walks forward and takes the microphone off me. "Harriet, are you saying that *none* of your celebrity friends are coming this evening? Like at *all*? Why the hell *not*?"

OK: firstly, it looks like I'm back to being *Harriet* again.

Secondly, I can't believe I've got myself into a situation where this is even a question I'm actually being asked.

"Because I don't *have* any."

There's a short silence, then several people pipe up. "What do you mean you..." "But you *said*..." "We *asked* and you told us..." "You *lied* to us."

"I didn't lie," I say in bewilderment. "You asked if I knew any models and I said yes because I do. I've met *lots*. But they're not my *friends*."

"But what about Poppy Page?"

"She hates me," I admit. The last time I saw Princess Poppy she literally asked me to leave the country. "Passionately. Like, I'm her least favourite person in the world."

"Yuka Ito?"

"The last time I was in the same place as her she fired me. So probably not." I glance around at my bits of black crepe paper. "Honestly, I'm not sure she'd have come to this even if she hadn't."

"*What about the Russian supermodels, where are the Russian supermodels, I want to meet the Russian supermodels.*"

That's Eric. Obviously.

"They're not coming." My cheeks are now bright red. "I'm so sorry. I didn't realise you thought... I didn't

know… They don't like me either."

There's a long silence.

Then the students clustered closest to Ananya and Liv erupt into disappointed cries. "But she said she went to all the *parties*." "Oh my God, I broke up with my boyfriend for *this*?" "Isn't she supposed to be loaded?" "Why are we eating home-made biscuits *again*?"

"But at least *Nick's* coming, right?" Liv says, frowning. "I mean your famous supermodel *boyfriend* will be here, won't he? With his face and his hair and his hip bones and all his beautiful supermodel single friends?"

And this is exactly what happens when you don't tell the truth, even to yourself.

Everything starts to fall apart.

That's what they're all here for, isn't it.

Ananya, Liv, India, the others… They're here for Nick and beautiful Russian supermodels. For Nick's non-existent identical twin brother and famous designers and celebrities and clothes and all the glamour and glitz they think go with being a successful model.

I've been such an idiot.

They didn't look at the Tokyo photos and see a confident, inspiring girl they wanted to get to know better. They didn't see another, less geeky side to me: a brave, starry version I so badly wanted to live up to

in real life.

They just saw the glittery lifestyle they thought the girl in the lake had, and they wanted a piece of it.

Which means Nat was right.

And so was Alexa.

I can see my entire new life at school teetering precariously on the edge, about to fall over with an almighty crash. For just a brief second I almost lie to keep it hanging there for a few more precious moments. *Oh, how funny! My supermodel boyfriend is just busy right now! He'll totally come to the next one!*

But I still want to believe in myself: even if nobody else does too.

Or, you know. *To.*

"No," I say as firmly as I can, lifting my chin and meeting their eyes without a flicker. "Nick is not coming to this party. He won't be coming to any of them. We've broken up."

My insides are shutting down, piece by piece.

I can feel the room slowly changing. All the warmth is gradually seeping out, along with all the laughter. They think I lied to impress them. I'm not funny any more. I'm not adorable, or cute, or interesting. I'm just back to being what I always was.

A geek who got really, really lucky.

"Well, *I don't care*," a little voice says from the back. "Harriet's still *amazing* and you're all *horrible*." Lydia comes charging through the crowd with her elbows out, cheeks pink. "And *look*. I just found the new Jacques Levaire watch advert on YouTube so you can *bite* me, sixth formers. Harriet Manners is more successful than you will *ever* be."

And she holds her phone high in the air.

85

I am graceful. I am elegant.

I am fluid and flowing and supple: moving with the grace of a ballet dancer, the poise of a gazelle, the lightness of a gentle *Diplulmaris antarctica* jellyfish gliding through the icy water.

Effortlessly, I move through the orange sands of the Sahara with total composure and confidence. As piano music plays, the wind catches my red hair and clothes and flings them gently around me: the light glows warm on my cheeks and my eyes are full of emotion, of hope, of joy.

Frankly, I have never been more beautiful in my life.

Or glittered so hard.

"That's not Harriet," somebody says, grabbing the phone and peering at it. "That's not Harriet *at all.*"

The screen gets handed to me.

The perfect red-haired girl spins again towards the camera and grins. Her make-up is almost completely

imperceptible. Her bright green eyes are framed with pale lashes and she's flushed and natural, her freckles visible even on this tiny screen. Her dress is simple white cotton and knee length: as she laughs her hand comes up to cover her mouth and you see a bright, momentary flash of a gold watch.

It's fresh. It's modern. It's captivating.

There's no dancing. No monkeys or snakes; no camels or running or chasing. No krumping.

And it's not me at all. Not even vaguely.

No wonder it's so good.

JACQUES LEVAIRE CLASSIC TIMEPIECES flashes up at the end, and then a make-up blogger's pretty face pops up as she starts talking about how she does her hair when she's in a hurry.

"You lied *again*?" somebody says as Lydia's phone gets passed around the room and the advert plays repeatedly. "Why on *earth* would you pretend you got a modelling job you didn't get?"

"I didn't pretend," I say, blinking at them all. "I went to Morocco. I got the Levaire campaign. I *promise* I did."

Except now I'm even starting to question that myself. *Did* I? Where *was* I last week? What was the shoot *for*?

"That's kind of lame, Harriet." "Seriously, who *does* that? Are you *that* desperate for attention?" "Oh my

God, where did you get those Moroccan clothes from? I am *so* confused right now."

"I..." My mouth is opening and shutting. "I don't know what to..."

"And I just googled Nick Hidaka and found a recent interview," somebody says, holding their phone in the air too. "I *bet* she lied about going out with him as well."

A human body has enough iron in it to make a metal nail three inches long.

It feels like mine has just done exactly that.

"Please," I say quickly, leaping forward. "Don't. Don't play it. Please don't play the—"

"Funny you should say that," a familiar, twangy voice jokes and I freeze where I am: every cell in my brain suddenly turning to ice. "Dozens of dolphins follow me everywhere I go, actually. It's a bit of a problem. They're such creepers."

A faceless girl gives a little besotted laugh.

I have no idea what the question was – I'm guessing *Have You Ever Swum With Dolphins* – but at the sound of Nick's voice it suddenly feels like I'm holding the nail at arm's length and an incredibly strong magnet is starting to draw it back towards me again, point first.

"And what's Australia's favourite male model doing now he's taking a break from the cameras? We've heard

you've voluntarily gone back to full-time education. We have just one question for you: *why*?"

"Because over the last year I've been reminded repeatedly just how much of a thicky I am," Nick says with a small laugh. "Seriously, though, a very special English girl inspired me. I realised how much of the world there is I still want to know about. How much I still want to do."

A huge lump suddenly rises up my throat.

"You're a mad person. Who gives up a successful career as a supermodel to go back to *school*?"

"I do," Nick says calmly. "And I am honestly loving it."

"So how's the *romantic* situation?" I can literally hear the optimism in the girl's voice. "Is this *very special* English girl still on the scene? Or should we all start sending you our CVs?"

Oh my God. No. No no no. *No no no no nonononononononono...* For just a fraction of a second the iron nail quivers, then it starts speeding towards me.

Turn it off. Turn it off turn it off turn it off turn it off turn it off turn it—

"Please," I whisper, holding my hand out towards the sound. "I don't want to hear this..."

"I don't really want to talk about it," Nick says after a short pause. "But no, we broke up. I'm just focusing on

the future now."

"Awwwww," the interviewer says insincerely. "Well I'm sure there are lots of girls out there who would happily take her place."

"I don't want them to," he says simply. "She kind of broke my heart."

With a final shudder the nail I made completely out of myself glints slightly in the light.

And plunges straight into my chest.

86

There's a long silence.

The video's finally been turned off, but it doesn't really matter: I'll be hearing it for the rest of my life anyway.

She kind of broke my heart.

My brain is starting to switch off, but on the edges of my vision I can see everybody in the room now whispering at each other uncomfortably. "English girl..." "It *was* her", "Harriet dumped *him*? I did *not* see *that* coming."

Then they turn self-consciously to face me.

Another deep silence.

"Well," a voice finally says from the back of the room. "This is a bit *awkward*, isn't it?"

With one blink I refocus my eyes just enough to see Alexa, sitting at the back in one of the little plastic seats I carefully put out, wearing black jeans, a plain grey T-shirt and enormous black heels. She's the only thing in this room that isn't bouncing rays of light in every direction.

I don't know when she arrived or how long she's been sitting there.

Frankly, I no longer care.

"I think that's enough *drama* for me," Alexa says, standing up. "Girls, my parents are away for the weekend, the home cinema is set up and I've got an unlimited supply of pizza. Coming?"

There's a short pause while Ananya assesses Alexa.

Something unspoken is passing between them.

It's not *friendship*, exactly – or not my definition of the word – but it's similar. Understanding. Respect. Eleven years of shared history and experiences that aren't going anywhere.

"Yes," Ananya says finally, looking me up and down. "What a total waste of time. You were right, Lexi: Harriet's not who we thought she was. What a *geek*. Let's go."

Ananya's not a minion, I realise dully as she gives me one more icy assessment: she's Alexa's equal and always has been.

"OhmyGodthisissucharelief I'mso*hungry*whatfilmare wegoingtowatchanddoyouthinkwecangetpepperoni because..."

Olivia, maybe not so much.

I look at Alexa emptily for a few seconds. There's a snake found in Mexico and Central America called the

Cantil. It has deadly venom, but instead of chasing prey it simply stays where it is and wiggles the yellow end of its tail. Birds, frogs, little mammals and lizards assume it's a worm and approach enthusiastically.

They never even see it coming.

Alexa didn't need to destroy me this time. She just had to sit back quietly and watch me destroy myself.

My nemesis gives me a little *told you so* shrug.

Then – without another word – she and the two girls I thought were my friends walk out of the room without so much as a glance over their shoulders, taking five or six other girls with them.

I look vaguely at the only one of my 'gang' left.

India's face is twisted in disgust, her top lip is curled and disdain is pretty much dripping from the tips of her fingers. "*So* disappointing," she agrees coldly, narrowing her eyes at the room.

Then she grabs a sandwich off the table, pulls the door open, shouts "*ANANYA, WAIT!*" at the top of her voice and slams it behind her.

I turn slowly towards the rest of the party.

They're now shifting awkwardly from foot to foot, trying to work out where to look. Frankly, I'm not surprised they're so uncomfortable. In 44 BC Roman conspirators threw a big gathering for Julius Caesar and

then stabbed him to death.

This party is even worse than that one.

"I think maybe you should all go too," I say blankly. "Please."

I just want them out of here now.

They're not my friends, and I'm not theirs. Honestly, I don't even blame them. It's starting to hit me that I was using them just as much as they were using me. I still can't remember most of their names: I was so busy trying to fill my life with as many people as possible, I didn't really care who they all were.

And it looks like they didn't care who I was either.

There are a few guilty nods, even sympathetic glances.

But then one by one the rest of my classmates filter out of the room and into the dark.

"*We're* not going," Lydia says, staunchly folding her arms in the doorway. "*We* love you, Harriet. You've still got *us.*"

"*Yeah,*" Fee adds. "We still think you're *awesome.*"

But it's too late.

"Thank you," I say, gently spinning them towards the exit. "But the party's over now."

I usher them out of the door.

Then I walk back into the darkness I made, covered in stars, and sit in the middle of the empty dance floor.

You actually think that everything will be different now?

She's still Harriet Manners.

There are many survival strategies in nature.

The tortoise draws its head and limbs up inside a hard outer shell, rendering it completely protected from predators. The hedgehog has damaging prickles; the skunk ejects sulphuric compounds from its bottom. When threatened, the mother-of-pearl caterpillar launches itself backwards at thirty-nine times its walking speed, somersaulting the entire way.

But all I'm thinking about now is a sea snail.

When I was three years old, scientists discovered a *Crysomallon Squamiferum* at the bottom of the ocean: the only creature in the known world to literally build metal into its coat of armour. They found that its thick shell is made from layers of metallic sulphides, including iron pyrite.

Otherwise known as *fool's gold.*

I tried so hard.

I wanted so badly to be the glittering girl: confident, stylish, brave, inspiring. I so wanted to protect myself from my normal life. But all I was doing was covering myself in a layer of fake gold and I couldn't deceive anyone for

long: just one little hole, and the world could see the real me again.

And I was pulled out and torn to pieces.

I look down at my shiny outfit, and then up at the cut-out stars. Then at the sparkle I threw all over the floor.

It was right there in the theme: I wrote it myself.

All that glitters... is not gold.

I don't have an Inner Star at all. I was the glitter and the fool, and now I'm right back to the beginning again.

Except worse, because Nat and Toby have gone too.

This time I've lost everything.

87

Tokyo – June (4 months ago)

"3,358 seconds."

We passed through tiny side streets of Tokyo, past dark wooden houses with white fabric hanging from the doorways like half-open gifts, under little archways and blue curved roofs, popping out into bustling, noisy roads and then back into the quietness again.

"3,247 seconds."

We raced past a little train station.

"2,320," I told him, as we ran over a beautiful wooden bridge stretching across a canal, painted red and stuck with long, red flags. "Nick, where on earth are you taking me?"

He laughed and turned round.

"Harriet, do you have some kind of exploding watch you haven't told me about? Because if you have, I think it's only fair I know about it. It is *seriously* going to

affect my schedule."

I grinned. "Say that again."

"Schedule."

"Again."

"Harriet Manners, don't you *dare* affect my schedule."

I pulled Nick to a stop and stood on my tiptoes so I could kiss him. "I love it when you talk itineraries to me, Lion Boy."

Nick kissed me back. Then he leant forward until I could feel his breath in my ear and whispered:

"*Timetable*."

There are 7,000,000,000,000,000,000,000,000,000 atoms in my body, and at that precise moment every single one of them was his.

"2,228 seconds," I whispered back.

And he took my hand again and started running as I kept counting down: through the quieter streets, into the large, silver buildings of Roppongi. We ran over grey pavements, under an enormous, thirty foot bronze spider with an egg sac containing marble eggs and towards a huge, glass skyscraper.

Then we caught our breath in a lift that shot us fifty-seven floors into the air.

"At what point in our relationship," I said, leaning against the wall and panting slightly, "did we decide

there would be so much running? I mean, you've met me before, right? I'm not exactly renowned for my athletic abilities."

"Well, my little geek," Nick said as the lift doors opened, "did you know that when you run you spend more time in the air than you do touching the ground? So if it helps at all, that means it's the closest we can get to flying."

Then he wiggled his eyebrows at me.

I glared at him crossly. That did help, yes. Nick was officially the only person in the world who could make me voluntarily do physical activity.

"Whatever," I said faux-grumpily. "If I really wanted to fly that badly I could just get on a trampoline and..."

I stopped talking.

While I was muttering we'd walked up tiny stairs on to a wooden deck surrounded by barriers of glass. People were scattered around us, taking photos, and in every direction was Tokyo. Stretched out and sparkling in the sunshine, leant against a backdrop of clear, bright blue.

And – far away – on the horizon, was a little cone shape.

Mount Fuji.

Nick reached out, tugged me into his side and kissed my head as I stared at it in amazement. I wanted to see

Tokyo, and he had given me all of it in one go.

"Without equal," he grinned, holding his arms out with a flourish and bowing. "Told you I could do it in the allocated time."

"Oh my God, that's so romantic. Say that again."

"Allocated," he said into my hair, "time."

"*Thank you*," I whispered, kissing the edge of his chin. Then I looked at my watch. "Although, you've still got fifty-two seconds left, according to my calculations."

"Don't need them," Nick laughed. "Actually, I didn't need any of them in the first place. I was just making you run for the sake of it."

I blink at him. "What are you talking about? This isn't your favourite bit of Tokyo?"

"Nope." He touched the end of my nose with his finger. "I was there already. My favourite bit of anywhere is you."

And then he kissed me.

88

Slowly, I pull my satchel out from under a table.

Gently, I touch the little coloured beads hanging in a circle round my neck: Mercury, Venus, Earth, Mars, Jupiter, Saturn, Uranus, Neptune and Pluto.

My very last gift from Nick.

Then I open my bag, tug a box from inside it and start pulling everything out carefully, as if I'm playing a very volatile game of Operation.

A Clothes Show ticket from the first time I ever met Nick under a table.

An advert torn from a magazine, depicting a boy, a white kitten and a girl, jumping in the Russian snow: the first time he ever held my hand.

The tiny toy lion he brought me when I was sick with flu, and the (unused) tissue and (unopened) packet of Lemsip that were supposed to make me better, but I kept instead.

A little postcard with a T-rex on the front that arrived a

few days after I said I had an inner dinosaur in Tokyo, and the letter that followed our race from the roundabout: *Told you I was faster. xx*

The folded, crumpled 1,000-yen note he gave me on the edge of Lake Motosu.

A very, very dry blue sock.

Finally – when the box has been excavated until it's all lying in front of me, like a strange archaeological dig – I get a pristine envelope out. I pull a clean, smooth piece of paper from it and unfold it gently.

And I start reading.

Dear Harriet,

You're going to be OK.

I know this, because you're Harriet Manners. You walk through this world seeing every tiny detail, but you don't see yourself. You don't see how beautiful you are, or how graceful: even in your clumsiness. You don't see how kind you are, even in your tempers. Or how brave and strong you are, even when you're scared. You never notice just how

much you touch the people around you, just by being you.

So I know you're going to be OK, but I don't know *if* I will be. I have to go back now to a world without polar bear hairs and matching snowflakes: without knowing that otters fall asleep holding hands to stop themselves drifting apart. Without being told, at random, that duels are legal in Paraguay, or how many senses a shark has (eight) or what shape an octopus's pupil is (rectangular). I have to go back to a world that just doesn't spin the way you always spin it.

And I don't want to.

I think we've made a mistake, Harriet. I want to make this work, and I'll do whatever it takes. I'll come back to England, I'll take up modelling again, I'll travel back and forth. Whatever I have to do, I'll do it.

Just send one word and I'll come back. But if I don't hear from you again, I'll understand. And I'll do my best to move on.

Three words, three stars: AlnItak, ALnilam and Mintaka.

LionBoy xxxx

89

I stare at the box in my lap.

Oh, you thought I meant I carry the past around with me *metaphorically*?

No, I meant literally.

At the bottom of my satchel, under all my schoolbooks and fact books and dictionaries and thesauruses, so I know it's there.

I don't always tell you everything, you know.

I'm an unreliable narrator. We all are.

We don't unfold ourselves like pieces of paper for everyone to see: that's not how humans work. There are always parts of us we shut away or hide. Bits of ourselves we can't touch because they're too precious and buried too deep.

Fragments of truth we barely admit to ourselves.

Because sometimes editing our own story is the only way to get through it.

So here are the three facts you didn't know.

Fact 1

My letters were going abroad, but they weren't going to Australia. They were going to a little village in Brazil, so that Bunty could look after them.

"Darling," she said when I rang her in tears from my bedroom in Greenway, New York, five weeks ago. "Sometimes all you need is a good cry and an even better pen. Write it all down and send it to me, and I'll keep it safe for you."

So that's what I did.

When I couldn't hold it in any more, I pulled my heartbreak out like a splinter and sent it to my grandmother to look after. Because it helped, somehow: knowing she would protect the parts of me I couldn't hang on to any longer.

It made me lighter.

Fact 2

What happened on Brooklyn Bridge didn't stop being true, just because it hurt.

Nick and I had three choices.

a) He could carry on living a life he didn't enjoy just

to see me: doing a job he hated, putting his future on hold, flying to and fro across the world for a few grabbed moments together. I could watch him grow increasingly lost, unanchored and unhappy: divided between a real life and a girl he loved.

b) We could stay together, seven thousand miles apart, and watch as our connection slowly shattered every day: until the awkward silences lengthened, the frozen moments expanded, the distances pulled at us, until finally all we had left were memories and stars.

Or c) I could force Nick to move on.

Instead of tearing him to pieces so I could keep a few bits for myself, I could make him take all of it with him. To live wholeheartedly without me in a way that would, eventually, make him happier.

Which is – I think, from his voice on that video – what he's started doing.

Because....

<u>Fact 3</u>

I got Nick's letter six days before I left New York.

I've had it all along.

So he didn't reply to my letters because he didn't get

them. He doesn't know how much I miss him because I haven't told him. And he doesn't know why I broke his heart because I couldn't let him know mine was broken too.

Over the last year, Nick has made so many sacrifices for me. He has been there when I needed him, gone when I didn't: appeared and reappeared and disappeared, entirely for my sake. He has adored every bit of me, without question and without judgement.

He has given me the kind of romance some people never get in an entire lifetime.

And I'll be honest: if he'd tried one more time – one more letter, one text, one single flower – I'd have crumbled and changed my mind: it would have been impossible not to. So I guess the lonelier I got, the more I waited and hoped for it as hard as I could.

But he didn't. Instead, he grabbed happiness and started moving forward again.

Which means I finally know I made the right decision.

I may not be the girl Nick thinks I am.

Over the last month, I've been lost, scared, weak, unhappy and – at points – quite shockingly stupid. I've lost my best friends, clung to the wrong people for the wrong reasons and done a whole lot of things I'm not proud of.

But this is not one of them.

The Oxford English Dictionary says that *love* is both a noun and a verb. And – because of Nick – I know now what I didn't know a year ago.

It's not enough to say it; it's not even enough to feel it.

Love is a *doing* word: an action you have to complete continuously, every day, however much it hurts. Whatever it ends up costing you. And this time loving Nick properly means letting him go.

After all, he has saved me, over and over again.

It's my turn now to save him back.

Even if it means being on my own.

90

Suffice to say, the letter isn't clean and smooth any more.

Two teardrops have hit the page, and are now making their slow, wobbly way downward: smudging the pen like little blue snail trails.

Which doesn't really matter, to be honest.

I know every word so off by heart they might as well be engraved there.

Patiently, I wait until the tears drop off the bottom of the paper. Then I give my letter a gentle kiss, fold it in half again and put it back in my Nick Box. Followed by the yen note, the T-rex, the Lemsip and tissue, the toy lion, the advert, the ticket. I take the planets necklace off carefully and put it on top, straightening it out so it doesn't get tangled.

Then I grab the lid.

"Harriet?"

Quick as a flash, I wipe a hand across my eyes, slam the lid on top of the box and cram it back into my satchel.

Should have locked the front door. *Idiot.*

"Mmmm?"

"Are you OK?"

I turn with wet eyes to the doorway, and through the sparkling shine in my eyes all I can see is purple.

"Absolutely," I manage, nodding. "Fine. Superb. Coolioko. Why wouldn't I be?"

India walks across the room quietly and then sits down next to me with her hair gleaming like ink.

"First of all," she says, "because that was officially the most hideous party anyone has ever thrown in the history of parties, ever. For future generations, that party will be the one parents tell their children about to dissuade them from ever throwing parties."

I nod. To say the least. "I know."

"Second of all, because you're sitting on the floor crying into a sock."

I blink at Nick's blue sock, still in my hand.

I thought I'd put it back in the box. Apparently I'm still clutching it to my face like a toddler with a tiny, faceless teddy bear.

"Ah." Flushing, I shove it back in my satchel. "And third of all I just said *coolioko* and that's a made-up word?"

"Nope," India says, pointing at the ceiling. "Indus.

Pavo. Carina. Mensa. Volans. Chamaeleon. Reticulum. Octans. They're constellations in the southern hemisphere. You've stuck the sky on the wrong way up."

91

Authenticity.

Spiritual awareness, truth, vision.

These are just a few of the psychological qualities we associate with purple, as I discovered when I was researching my immortal duck outfit.

It's also the traditional colour of royalty.

This is because the original purple dye required 250,000 individual *purpura* shellfish – hence *purple* – to extract enough to make one single ounce. By the third century BC, Tyrian purple dye cost more than gold and wearing it was a sign that you were really worth something.

As I stare at India's bright purple hair and cool but unshakeable expression, I'm starting to realise that maybe her hair colour is perfect for her in more ways than one.

"You came back."

She grabs another sandwich from the table. "I like these," she says, stuffing it in her mouth. Then she swallows. "Obviously I came back. I only left to tell

Ananya she could walk home and then push her into a bush." She points at a pink scratch glowing on the right side of her temple and another on her upper lip. "Sadly I ended up in it too. She's always been a bit scrappy."

I blink at her. "Always?"

"Yeah. Grandad was worried she'd got in with a bad crowd, so when we moved here I promised to pry her back out again."

All known mammals have tongues.

In which case I've no idea what I've just turned into: all I can do is stare at India in total silence.

"You didn't know Ananya was my cousin?" India says, black eyebrows creasing back into essay ticks. "We've got the same *surname*, Harriet. Didn't you think that was a bit of a coincidence?"

Well, obviously *now* I think it is.

But I was far too distracted by everything else over the last fortnight to make the connection.

Actually, now I'm thinking of it, I should probably have guessed anyway. They have the same dark skin, the same icy expressions: the same subtly terrifying demeanour. And I *thought* it was weird that after only six weeks India was bossing Ananya around and calling her *Banana*.

"So you're not disappointed with *me*?"

"Don't be ridiculous," India says sharply, taking

another sandwich. "I knew you weren't still with Nick straight away: nobody stares at a desk for twenty-five seconds in silence if they're still in a happy relationship. I've hated Alexa from the beginning, and I liked you as soon as I saw you chatting to Steve and helping him pick up tissue. I knew what side I wanted to be on."

My brain makes a little clicking sound.

OK, that's enough now. India, stalking coldly to my side in the rain. Icily standing up for me in the common room. Forcing Ananya and Liv to follow her.

But all the long, cold stares of disdain…

"I know," she sighs, rolling her eyes. "I have resting mean face. It's a problem." She grimaces. "Believe it or not I'm actually quite nice."

I totally and utterly believe her.

Despite the similarities, I've just noticed the key difference between India and her cousin. When Ananya smiles, it doesn't reach her eyes: with India, it's the opposite way round.

"So I'm not a let-down at all?" I just need to check. "You haven't been conned into thinking I'm cool by my fake social status and glamorous part-time job?"

"Harriet," she sighs, standing up, "I recognise the constellations of the southern hemisphere off by heart and can classify the properties of crystal. I'm not sure *cool*

is on my radar." She glares towards the door. "Sadly, I'm going to have to tell Grandad I can't get Ananya away from the bad crowd. She *is* the bad crowd."

Slowly, warmth starts to spread through me: as if I'm sitting in sunshine, coated in rainbows, curled up in the middle of a hot-water bottle.

I did it.

After everything, I made a real friend. A proper one. One who likes me for the right reasons: because I throw terrible star parties and pick up loo roll and make buddies with caretakers called Steve. (I don't know where he is, by the way. His house must be *considerably* further than twenty minutes away.)

And more importantly, I like *her*.

I always have.

"Do you want to go to my house?" I say enthusiastically, standing up. "I have a game of scrabble we can play, and there's the rest of the star quiz to do and—"

"Yeah, go on then," India says, grabbing the tray of sandwiches. "That sounds cool. Can we take the lights? It'll help me focus."

She unplugs Tabby's night-light and starts heading smoothly towards the exit, hair like a chocolate bar wrapper.

Quickly, I grab my satchel and wipe my eyes on my wrist to make them as dry as possible.

Then I start following her.

"Oh I don't *think* so," an angry voice says. "Stop right there before I rip your flaming eyes right out of your sockets and use them as ping-pong balls."

"Yeah," another voice says, not quite as angrily. "Ping-pong balls. For *mice.*"

And standing in the doorway are Nat and Toby.

92

I can only see the back of India's head, but I'm pretty sure her face hasn't altered.

I guarantee it's set in exactly the same expression as always.

"That's sweet," she says flatly, eating another sandwich. "Who are you?"

"I'm your *worst nightmare*," Nat hisses at her, folding her arms. "I'm the girl who's going to tug your toenails off and turn them into earrings and then make you *wear* them. I'm the girl who's going to pull out your eyelashes and eyebrows, hair by hair, until you're totally bald."

"*Yeah*," Toby says, scowling and folding his arms too. "And then she's going to turn them into wigs. Little tiny wigs. For *hamsters*."

"Stop talking about rodents, Toby," Nat sighs. "Seriously. Rodents have no part in this threatening process at all."

"Again," India says calmly. "Who are you?"

"Toby Pilgrim," Toby says chirpily, his face clearing abruptly. He holds his hand out and I can see he's wearing a T-shirt that says I AM A, followed by a picture of a rock next to a star. "It's very nice to meet you properly, India. I believe you're in my year at school, aren't you? I've heard you're an absolute whizz at physics."

Nat rolls her eyes. "Oh my God, Toby, you're useless."

Then she turns back, all fierce again.

"So, you're the famous *India*, are you? That makes sense. Well you can just put the sandwiches down, missy. You make Harriet cry again and I swear, I will conjure accessories out of body parts you didn't even know you had."

I've been watching this entire conversation with my hand still up to one eye, frozen in shock.

I blink and then look at it. What?

"Oh no," I say quickly, stepping forward. "I'm not crying because of India. She came back to help me, actually. She's my friend."

"*Sure* she is," Nat snarls, flicking her eyes between us. "I bet she's just *lovely*. Friends of Ananya and Alexa are friends of *ours*, right?"

"Ah," India says, nodding. "Right. Gotcha. No, I hate them too if that helps. Evil witches."

"*Well* aren't you just..." Nat stops. I can see her brain

trying to fit this into her argument. "Oh. Well. OK, then," she says slightly less fiercely. Then she rallies bravely for a last stand. "And you've not come back here just to steal snacks?"

"In fairness, they're surprisingly good." India looks at the tray of sandwiches. "Want one?"

I can see Nat evaluating the situation and assessing India. I've never seen anyone not baulk at Nat's open, transcendent fury before: it's like watching a tiger growl at a unicorn. "What are they?"

"Chicken and strawberry jam."

That does it: the last ounce of fight evaporates out of my best friend. She nods and takes one.

"We invented these. They're awesome, right? Lots of protein and carbohydrates. I'm Nat. I like your hair a lot. Did you have to bleach it first?"

"Purple is the most powerful visible wavelength of electromagnetic energy," Toby says nodding.

Then he starts rushing around the room.

"Ooh, Harriet, *well done*," he adds. "This is an *excellent* party. Although what happened to the sherbet flying saucers? Or the Magic Stars and Starmix? And there's no Star Wars stuff here at all. Nat, I *told* you we should have helped her. She's missed out *loads* of important space-based puns."

I'm still staring at both of them.

What? Just... *what*?

Did the last two weeks completely not happen? Have I been imagining all of it? First the Levaire advert magicked me out of it. Now Toby's back to being Toby again and Nat appears to have forgotten we hate each other with the heat of a trillion suns.

Is this like one of those really bad television serials where I find out I've been in a coma the entire time?

Am I awake? Am I even *alive*?

"Umm, hello?" I say as Toby grabs a camera out of his bag and starts taking photos of the ceiling. "We're not talking to each other, remember? What are you both doing here?"

"Harriet," Nat says a lot more gently. "I think there's something we need to tell you."

93

I suddenly feel a bit sick.

"Oh my God," I say, sitting abruptly on a chair. "Toby and you aren't… You're not a *couple*, are you? Theo's not just a *cover*, is he?"

It would make sense: all the weird behaviour. All the sneaking around and running away.

A gross but weirdly logical kind of sense.

"A couple of what?" Toby says, taking a photo of the tablecloth. "That's not a very specific question, Harriet. You'll never get into MI5 at this rate."

Nat's still staring at me with a blank face.

Then she abruptly looks like she's going to be sick too.

"Oh my God, no. *Ugh*. What are you *thinking*? Thanks for that visual, Harriet. I'm going to have to clean my brain with a wire pad when I get home." She pauses. "But the second bit wasn't totally wrong."

I blink at her. "Theo's… not real?"

"He is real. But I've only seen him twice in the last

two weeks. We've only just started dating, and I'm not *desperate*."

There's a silence.

"You are making no sense at all," I tell her finally. "Then what have you been doing?"

"Toby and I have been avoiding you," Nat says flatly. "Both of us. Because I told him to."

My eyes widen slightly. *I'm not allowed to see you. I'll have to check*. It was *Nat* who was forcing Toby not to see me? Not Jasper at all?

Oops. I probably owe somebody a pretty big apology.

"But... *why*?"

Nat thinks about it for a few seconds. "Harriet, do you remember what you said in the launderette?"

"Yes. I said I had made you a customised Monopoly set and you could use a sewing machine as your placer."

The corner of her mouth twists slightly. "You said we were welded, Harriet. And then you said *I've got you and Toby anyway, so what else does a sensible girl really need*?"

I hate to say it, but for just a moment Nat temporarily transforms into me. Her voice gets slightly higher and posher, her eyes get very round and she does a little toss of her head, exactly the way I do.

I blink at her again.

Nope. Still no idea what she's talking about. "So?"

"*So,* Harriet. We already had the plan, but that just confirmed for me that it was the right thing to do. What would you have done if Toby was hanging out with you at school from the beginning and I was hanging out with you afterwards? *Honestly?*"

"I'd have hung out with Toby at school and you afterwards," I say without hesitation. "My first day sucked."

"Exactly," Nat says slowly. "190 days, Harriet. 1,330 hours is a *really* long time to stop living. You're my best friend. When you're unhappy, I'm unhappy. Not being welded was the only thing I could do."

"But..." They've both been avoiding me on purpose? To force me to make friends? "Why couldn't you just tell me that?"

"Because if you *knew* then the plan would never have worked. You'd have just buried yourself in a book again and waited it out. Like you always do."

Nat's right again. Making friends is *hard.* And I'm a big fan of both books and of being in my comfort zone.

"I watched you shut down after you came home from New York," she says more gently. "I knew that if sixth form didn't start well, you were going to just keep closing unless I did something drastic. And this time I wasn't

going to be at school to stop you."

"Didn't I do *brilliantly?*" Toby says jubilantly, puffing his chest out. "I was *so* rude to you, Harriet. I really gave it some welly. You thought I didn't like you *at all,* didn't you. *Yeah.*"

He holds up a hand to high-five Nat.

"Sadly I just forgot a few things, Harriet," my best friend sighs, ignoring Toby's hand and then holding up a closed fist. "I didn't know the Yuka Ito campaign would come out or factor in the impact it would have." She holds up a finger. "You see the best in everyone, indiscriminately, all of the time, and are frequently a terrible judge of character." She holds up another one.

Then she holds the final finger up and thrusts it in Toby's face.

"And Toby is an idiot who takes everything literally. I said *give her a bit of space for a couple of weeks,* not *make her feel like a pariah,* you total pillock."

Enjoy all your new friends, Harriet.

Toby was reporting back. Nat was leaving me alone because she thought I was successfully making friends.

"Exactly," she says, nodding even though I haven't said anything. "I was *so* happy you were having a party, then we argued, but tonight Mum finally remembered to give me the invitation and I realised what was probably going

to happen. Toby and I ran here as fast as we could." She tilts her head to the side affectionately. "Night of Stars. You silly billy."

Scientists say we have different types of tears.

Basal tears, to protect our eyes. Reflex tears, to remove irritants. And emotional tears, that occur when our feelings get too much and our tear ducts can't handle it, erupt and spill over.

As my eyes start to fill up again, I think my body just can't fit my new burst of happiness in.

It needs to let some out, like steam out of a kettle.

My party can go sit on an anthill, frankly: I couldn't care less.

I've got my best friends back.

"I'm sorry," I say, abruptly lobbing myself at Nat and throwing my arms round her neck. "I'm so sorry for everything I said. I *do* need you. You *aren't* ruining my life or holding me back. I didn't mean *any* of it."

"I know," Nat grins into my neck. "I'm sorry too."

"Me too," Toby says, reaching into his bag. "Although, in my defence, Natalie was very much the mastermind of this plot and I was just the obedient slave with your well-being at the forefront of my mind."

"Thanks, Tobes," I say, grabbing him in an impulsive hug. "I've really, really missed you, you know. Please

don't do that again."

"I won't," he says, waiting patiently for me to let go. "You don't need to worry, Harriet Manners. Toby Pilgrim Is Here, TM."

He sticks a little round green sticker on my arm.

India stands quietly for a few seconds.

Then she says, "Oh what the hell," and stiffly puts her arms round all of us. "Don't hug me back. I've eaten too many sandwiches."

"See?" Nat laughs. "My plan totally worked. New friend. KABOOM. At this rate you'll have, like, twelve by the end of the year."

There's a sound from the doorway.

"*All right there, party people, DJ Earthling is back in the*... Oh, the little minxes. They've bloomin' gone and left you, haven't they."

Steve's standing in the doorway with his grey hair sticking upwards and half a pasty in his hand. That's where he was: he obviously stopped for a snack on the way back.

He looks around, shaking his head.

"I'm telling you," he says fiercely. "They'll get their comeuppance. Just mark my words. I won't be replacing the loo roll in any of the sixth form toilets for the next week."

I grin at him.

I'm starting to realise that real friendship doesn't always turn up with a bang. It creeps in quietly, without glitz and glamour, without show or fuss.

Whether it's somebody playing CDs at your party, or giving you a few minutes in the desert to watch the stars alone; whether it's leaving a new job behind to spend three days in Morocco because your stepdaughter is sad, or spending a day arranging a gift in a shed because your daughter is heartbroken.

Whether it's doing a stranger a favour, or standing by someone in the rain, or sending flowers from thousands of miles away, or a Hug Pillow when you can't give them a hug.

Whether it's reading the letters that your granddaughter doesn't know how not to write.

And – as I stand in the Guide Hut and watch everyone start packing away my party without complaint or judgement – it suddenly hits me: I had friends all along.

I was just looking for them in the wrong places, that's all.

"Don't you worry, poppet," Steve mutters crossly as he gets a broom out and starts sweeping up the bits of glitter into a plastic pan, "you're going to be OK."

"I know," I say with a bright smile.

Because I already am.

94

My parents are suspiciously unsurprised to see us.

In fact, if I didn't know better I'd think they didn't believe my party was going to be a roaring success and were prepared for catastrophe.

Which would be offensive if it wasn't… you know.

Totally spot on.

"Hello," Annabel says smoothly as I walk back into the house with Nat, Toby and India close behind me. "Would you like some dinner?"

There are six steaming pizzas in front of her.

Either my stepmother was ready for us to come home early and magically guessed how many of us there would be, or she's recently developed the appetite of a baby blue whale crossed with one of the Mario brothers.

Or…

Or Steve was reporting back and both my parents have been driving past the Guide Hut continuously all evening, keeping tabs on everything.

Of course they have.

"Hi, Mrs Manners," Nat says, flopping herself on the floor and pulling an ecstatic Tabitha on to her lap. "This is India. Please feel free to interrogate her relentlessly before we accept her into the gang."

"So far we've already discovered lack of empathy for hamsters and no respect for authority," Toby says, grabbing a slice of pepperoni. "As you can tell from the nasal piercing and general failure to bow down to the colours of nature."

"Interrogate away," India nods coolly. "The ring just stops me picking my nose and the purple makes it easier to cross roads without being run over – nobody ever misses me standing at a crossing."

Everybody laughs as my phone beeps.

"Harriet?" Annabel says gently as I grab it out of my bag. "You had some visitors, sweetheart. They left a few things, so I've put most of them in your bedroom."

I nod and look at the message I've just received.

Hannah, Levaire hated Kevin. Went a different direction. Will pay 300 for time spent. Stephanie.

I can't help noticing we're back to *Stephanie* again, and no kisses.

The science project is coming up next term.

Maybe I should focus mine on the careful subliminal analysis of text messages and use of nicknames: I think there's potentially an entire minefield of untapped psychological investigation.

Weirdly, I don't mind as much as I probably should.

I still had an amazing trip, and that quantity of money never felt very real anyway. This feels a lot more realistic. Plus, it'll still cover everything I borrowed from Annabel, so everybody kind of wins.

I watch everyone chattering happily for a few seconds, then put my phone back in my bag, climb the stairs and push open my bedroom door.

Where I abruptly stop in amazement.

There are books *everywhere*.

Heaps of books piled on my desk, on my floor, on my bed, on the fireplace, on the windowsill. Every fact book I've handed out over the last ten days is back in my room, except with one subtle difference: there is now a tiny pink sticker on the front of each of them.

I pick one up and look at it:

FACT 1: Harriet Manners is clever.

Then another:

FACT 2: Harriet Manners is funny.

And another:

FACT 3: Harriet Manners is kind.

The final one of which says:

FACT 42: Thank you for being so nice to us, Harriet Manners. Lydia, Fee, Soph and Keira xxx

I swallow a lump – even though I'm not entirely sure they're using the word *fact* accurately and we may have to discuss it. Then I pick up a photo Annabel has propped against a mug on my desk.

It's of a little brown monkey, sitting on the stump of a tree with the Atlas Mountains behind him.

Because here's the final fact of my own that I didn't tell you:

Fact 4

The last thing Annabel and I did before we left Morocco was ask Ali to take Richard (monkey, not Dad) to a monkey sanctuary a hundred miles away.

We bought him and set him free.

Then we paid for the snakes and did the same to them.

"Harriet?" Annabel calls up the stairs. "Are you coming down? The pizza's getting cold."

I nod and put the photo down. "One minute!"

There's just one thing left I have to do.

I make a space in between all the books on my bed.

Then I sit down and pull the box out of my bag.

Tokyo – June (4 months ago)

"You could stay, you know. There are multiple octopuses in Tokyo who haven't attacked you yet, Manners. You're taking so much away from so many."

I laughed. "Did you know that an anxious octopus will sometimes literally *eat* itself, Nick? I don't think it's fair to upset any more of them: it could get messy."

Then I glanced over his shoulder at Narita airport.

Bunty was doing some kind of juggling act for a security guard, but his patience was clearly running thin and the last call for our flight back to London had already been made.

"I have to go," I said, wrapping my arms round his waist and looking up. "I'm sorry."

Nick looked down with his shortened hair all ruffled and his brown eyes narrowed.

"OK. Hold out your hand." I obediently held it out, and he slotted his fingers between mine. "What kind of table joint is this, again?"

With a flash, I suddenly remembered the first time we ever met. I was so anxious: hiding under a table at The Clothes Show, trying – as always – to escape from the real world.

Nick had been so kind. So calm.

He had understood me from the beginning.

I was just looking for unusual table joints. I thought this particular table looked very… solid. In terms of construction. And I thought I'd have a closer look. You know. From… underneath.

I looked up at my boy on the Tokyo pavement and tried to memorise every detail before I left. Every black eyelash, every dark curl: the little line in the corner of his

mouth, the tiny mole on his cheek, the sharpness of his teeth.

I tried to tuck away every single piece of him somewhere safe, where I could never lose it.

"Finger joints?" I asked with a small smile.

"They're dovetail," Nick said: just like the first time. He curled his fingers round mine until they were locked together and grinned the smile that went all the way round and split me and my entire world in half. "Goodbye, Harriet Manners."

Then he leant down and kissed me until it felt like we were touching in space.

Welded permanently.

I wait for a few seconds with my eyes shut and my hand on the box, and I watch Nick's beautiful face flicker, like a bright light on a wall. It flickers and flickers, fading a little every time.

When I finally open my eyes, it's gone.

"Goodbye, Nicholas Hidaka," I say gently.

Then I smile and put the box on the floor.

I take a deep breath.

And – with all the strength I have left – I push the past under my bed.

95

Glow-worms aren't worms, they're beetles.

Koala bears aren't bears – they're marsupials – and Bombay duck is made out of dry fish. Black-eyed peas are beans, Guinea pigs are neither pigs nor from Guinea.

What I'm trying to say is: things aren't always what you think they are. You can look at something for a long, long time and still not see it properly at all.

I guess that includes me.

"Harriet?" Annabel says as I get to the bottom of the stairs. The living room has abruptly emptied, and the lights in the house have all gone off. "Did you do everything you needed to do?"

She gives me a steady look, and I know she knows.

About everything.

I've no idea *how* – magic, possibly, or hidden cameras – but she's staring at my face as if everything I have ever thought or will ever think is written there in ink.

I don't envy her: it can't be very easy reading.

"Yes," I nod. "Where is everybody?"

"In the garden, waiting for you." She pauses for a few seconds. "Harriet, I know about your list."

Of course she does. "How?"

"You left it open on your laptop just before we left for Morocco. I saw it when I was packing the suitcases."

I can feel a flush starting on my cheeks.

How embarrassing. It wasn't even grammatically *correct*.

"Harriet," Annabel says, sitting on the bottom stair and patting the bit next to her, "you're a silly billy, you know that?"

OK: that's, like, the third time I've been called that recently. Do I have another Post-it stuck on my back I'm not aware of? "I do know that, yes," I say, sitting down. "People keep telling me."

Annabel laughs.

"Harriet, you go to school even when it's hard there for you. You model, even though it scares you. Your first thought on making money was not to spend it on yourself, but to help others. You left Nat alone to be with her boyfriend when you needed her, you invited the world and its wife to your party so they didn't feel left out. You cleaned the house every time your father messed it up so

I wouldn't have to do it, and you didn't even mention it."

I open my mouth and then close it again.

Seriously. Somewhere in this house: cameras.

"I didn't realise until you were too busy today to do it," Annabel explains with a little smile. "Your father genuinely thinks he's the eponymous Shoemaker, and elves are coming in through the windows and doing it all for him."

"Oh." I shrug. Dad's mind must be a glorious place to live. "Well, you were tired. It's no biggy."

"I was, and it is." Annabel smiles again. "I'm not finished. You have a little following of fans because you remembered what it was like to be young and new, and you defend people even when they have been unkind to you."

I open my mouth again.

Oh my God: she's got them at school *too*? Is *nothing* private any more?

"What I'm saying, Harriet, is you *are* confident. You *are* brave. You have your own style, and you have always inspired everyone around you. And you know exactly who you are and stick to it when it's hard."

I can feel my cheeks getting red. She's totally memorised every line of my list and watched me working my way through it, badly.

"I do try too hard though. At literally everything."

"You really do." Annabel's mouth twitches. "It's one of my favourite things about you."

We sit in silence for a few minutes while I unsuccessfully try to swallow another lump in my throat. It's kind of annoying, sometimes: having a parent who knows everything about you.

I wouldn't give it up for anything.

Finally, Annabel stands and brushes her pinstripe suit down. "We've got a little something waiting for you in the garden. Coming?"

I nod. Then, side by side, my stepmother and I walk down the dark hallway with all the lights switched off, into a dark kitchen with the curtains inexplicably closed.

I'm just about to ask why the house has turned into the set of a horror film when my phone beeps.

Wilbur	**Every other human in the world**
My little doodlebug!	Hello!
Giant apple super zzz –	I'm bored of New York –
So this pigeon is homing.	So I'm coming back to UK
Visage you promptly.	See you soon.
Beer	XXXX

I grin with happiness and put my phone back in my cardi pocket. Then – with a sudden wave of gratitude so strong I nearly have to sit back down again – I impulsively grab my stepmother's hand.

"Thank you, Annabel. For being so kind to me."

She shakes her head.

"If people are kind to you, Harriet, it's because you're kind to them. If people are there for you, it's because you are there for them." She opens the kitchen door and points into the dark. "And if you don't need a list to make you a star, it's because you've always been one."

96

Outside are little patches of light.

They're waving around in the air with loud crackling sounds, spelling out huge letters with trailing lines of glitter.

H. R. T. I. R. E. T.

From the glow of the sparklers, I can see five of the people I love best, lit up and laughing.

Along with my number one dog.

"*Toby*," Nat snaps irritably, waving her firework in the air ferociously, "you're supposed to be making an A, you idiot. Not another T."

"Oh." Toby frowns. "So who's making the T?"

"Who *is* making the tea?" Dad asks. "I'll have one. Four sugars, just a drop of milk." I can't help noticing he has a big black moustache stuck on and is wearing a chef's hat.

Tabby's in her lobster pot, staring in awe at the lights.

Hugo races towards me: paws in my stomach before I've even closed the door.

"No offence, but I am *nailing* this letter *R,*" India says coolly. "Seriously. Step your game up, people. It's blatantly the trickiest one."

Then I glance behind them.

In the middle of the garden is an enormous, seven-foot sculpture of a white angel with gold wings. I turn in confusion to Annabel and she winks at me knowingly: it was obviously hand-delivered while I was at my so-called party.

OK, maybe she didn't have cameras at school after all.

Slowly, I walk towards it.

It's incredibly beautiful. The face is delicately shaped, the plaster is smooth and the enormous wings have been covered in tiny gold-painted feathers and attached to the sculpture with a knot of thick white string over the shoulders.

Stuck to the left wing is a little piece of paper.

It's not an angel at all, I realise, as I turn the note over.

It's Icarus.

I was wrong and I'm sorry. Friends? Jasper x

And I can feel the light starting to shine out of me, brighter than it ever has before.

Because I know a few things about space.

I know it's big and dark and lonely. I know that all stars are moving away from each other and 99.9999 per cent of the universe is made up of nothing, including us.

But I also know that there are a lot of things about it we still don't understand.

Scientists discovered very recently that ninety per cent of the universe's light source is inexplicably missing. They can see it, they can measure it, but they don't know where it's coming from.

For just a second, I think maybe I do.

As I watch the people I love, drawing my name in the sky with glitter – as I think about the people I love and miss, all over the world – I wonder briefly if some of that light is coming from us.

If with every act of kindness, we shine a little brighter and the darkness gets a little lighter. With every type of friendship, space gets a little smaller and we get a little closer.

Making our own stars so we're never really alone.

Because however fast the universe pulls apart – however much distance there is between us – these are

the ties that will hold us together.

The connections that will never break.

This is how we shine.

Acknowledgements

Thanks to my amazing editor, Ruth Alltimes, for working with me so seamlessly, valiantly and patiently, and for loving Harriet as much as I do. You have been a total champion. Thanks to Kate Shaw: my agent, my friend and my much-needed voice of reason, sense and wisdom at silly-times-o-clock. As always, I couldn't do it without you.

Thanks to the entire, incredible team at HarperCollins, who continue to work tirelessly and passionately behind the scenes as part of Team Geek: especially to Hannah, Sam, Nicola, Carla, Kate, Elorine, Georgia, Lily, Rachel and Mary. This is such a fun boat to be on, and I couldn't hope for better shipmates. Thanks also to Lizzie and Celeste, who have remained stars throughout. Your cuteness and support have been much appreciated.

As always, an infinite, heartfelt chunk of gratitude is owed to my wonderful family. Grandad, Grandma, Dad, Mum, Tig, Dan, Vero, Caro, Louise, Vincent, Judith, Lesley, Ellen, Freya, Rob, Lorraine, Mayne, Chelsea, Dixie

and Handsome. It's been a rocky year, and I am so very lucky to have – and have had – you with me; I know you always will be.

Finally, to every reader who has read Harriet, loved Harriet, cheered for Harriet and worried about Harriet over the last couple of years: you are who I write for.

Thank you. xx

First published in paperback in Great Britain
by HarperCollins *Children's Books* in 2013
HarperCollins *Children's Books* is a division of HarperCollins*Publishers* Ltd,
77–85 Fulham Palace Road, Hammersmith, London, W6 8JB.

The HarperCollins website address is: www.harpercollins.co.uk

10

ISBN 978-0-00-748946-6

Typeset in Frutiger Light 11/17.5 pt by Palimpsest Book Production Limited,
Falkirk, Stirlingshire

Printed and bound in England by Clays Ltd, St Ives plc

fit adjective

1 Appropriate or suiting

2 Proper

3 Qualified and competent

4 Prepared

5 In good physical condition

NOUN

1 Fashionable clothing

2 An onset or period of emotion

COLLOQUIAL SLANG

1 To be really, really good looking

ORIGIN from the Old English *fitt*: 'conflict or struggle'.

1

My name is Harriet Manners, and I am a model.

I know I'm a model because:

1. It's Monday morning, and I'm wearing a gold tutu, a gold jacket, gold ballet pumps and gold earrings. My face is painted gold, and a long piece of gold wire has been wrapped around my head. This is not how I normally dress on Mondays.

2. I have a bodyguard. The earrings cost so much I'm not allowed to go to the toilet without a large man checking my earlobes afterwards to make sure I haven't accidentally flushed them.

3. I haven't been allowed to smile for two hours.

4. Every time I take a bite of doughnut to keep my strength up everybody breathes in sharply

as if I've just bent down and given the floor a quick lick.

5. There's a large camera pointing at my face, and the man behind it keeps saying, "Oi, model," and clicking his fingers at me.

There are other clues – I'm pouting slightly, and making tiny movements every couple of seconds like a robot – but they're not necessarily conclusive. That's exactly how my father dances when a car advert comes on TV.

Anyway, the final reason I know I'm a model is:

6. I have become a creature of grace, elegance and style.

In fact, you could say I've really grown up since you last saw me.

Developed. *Blossomed.*

Not literally. I'm exactly the same size and shape as I was six months ago, and six months before that. As far as womanly curves go, much like the netball captain at school, puberty is making no bones about picking me last.

No, I'm talking metaphorically. I simply woke up

one day, and *BAM*: fashion and I were at one with each other. Working together, helping each other. Just like the crocodile and the little Egyptian plover bird that climbs into its mouth to pick bits of meat out of its teeth. Except obviously in a much more glamorous and less unhygienic way.

And I'm going to be totally honest with you: it's changed me. The geek is gone, and in her place is somebody glamorous. Popular. Cool.

A brand-new Harriet Manners.

2

Anyway. The really great thing about being totally *synergised* with the fashion world is that it makes shoots very smooth and focused.

"Right," Aiden the photographer says, "what are we thinking, model?"

(You see what I mean? What are *we* thinking: fashion and I are basically sharing a brain.)

"We're thinking mysterious," I tell him. "We're thinking enigmatic. We're thinking unfathomable."

"And why are we thinking that?"

"Because it says so on the side of the perfume box."

"Exactly. I'm thinking Garbo and Grable, Hepburn and Hayworth, Bacall and Bardot, but it might be best if you think reality TV show contestant and do the opposite."

"Got it," I say, shifting slightly in my position on the floor and moving my foot so that the sole is pointing towards me. Then I lean towards it gracefully. *Mysterious*. I grab the corner of my jacket and lift it slightly, like a butterfly wing, angling my face downwards. *Enigmatic*. Finally, I arch my back and poke out an arm so I'm staring at the crease of my inner elbow. *Unfathomable*.

"Got it." Aiden looks up from the camera. "Model, Yuka Ito was right. These are some very strange shapes you're pulling, but it works. Very edgy. Very high fashion."

What did I tell you? Me and fashion: I walk in and out of its mouth and it doesn't even *try* to eat me any more.

"Now point your elbow in the other direction for me." The photographer crouches down, adjusts the camera shutter and then looks back up again. "Towards the camera."

Sugar cookies.

"You know," I say without moving, "enigmatic, mysterious, unfathomable. They're tautological. Yuka could save a lot of room on the box by just picking one."

"Just move your arm."

"Umm, has she considered 'baffling'? It's from an old word used to describe a wind that buffeted sailors from all directions. It's sort of appropriate for a perfume, don't you think?"

Aiden pinches the bridge of his nose with his

fingers. "Right. How about you show me the bottom of the shoe? We should try to get the contrasting sole in the shot."

I clear my throat, mind starting to race. "Erm... but what about Saudi Arabia, China and Thailand? It's considered culturally impolite to show the bottom of your feet there..." I look around the room in a blind panic. "We don't want to risk alienating them, do we?" I sweep my arm out in a wide, persuasive gesture.

And something on my sleeve catches Aiden's eye.

Oh no. No no no.

"What's that?" he says, standing up and walking over to where I'm now scrabbling to get off the floor but my feet are caught in the enormous tutu. The photographer grabs my arm and peels a tiny gold sticker from the inside of my jacket elbow. "What's *this*?"

"Hmm?" I say, swallowing and straining to make my eyes as round as I physically can.

Aiden peers at the sticker. "$F = M \times A$?" he reads slowly. Then he pulls three more from inside the lining of the jacket. "$V = I \times R$? $Ek = \frac{1}{2} \times M \times V2$? $W = M \times G$?"

Before I can move he grabs the shoe from my foot, turns it over and pulls a sticker from the heel. Then he pulls one from my inside elbow and four from the inside folds of the tutu netting.

He blinks at the stickers a couple of times while I stare at the floor and try to look as small as humanly possible. "Harriet," he says in a slow and incredulous voice. "Harriet Manners, are you studying maths in the middle of my fashion shoot?"

I shake my head and look at the air behind the photographer's left ear. You know the crocodile and the bird? I think one of us is about to get eaten.

"No," I answer in my littlest voice. Because a) It's physics, and b) I've been doing it all the way through.

3

OK, so I *may* have stretched the truth a tiny bit.

Or – you know: a lot.

I haven't changed. In fact, I'm even more of a geek than I used to be because:

a) the grey matter in my brain is still developing extra connections on a daily basis
b) I know even more facts than I did before
c) I'm just coming to the end of exams, which means my short-term cognitive abilities are on overdrive.

I'm also not graceful, elegant or stylish, but I guess you've already worked that out for yourself.

"Unbelievable," Aiden mutters, clicking through the images as I slip behind a curtain at the back of the room to get changed into my school uniform.

"I'm so sorry, Mr Thomas," I call out. "I honestly didn't mean to disrespect you and the crocodi— erm, fashion industry. Did you get OK photos?"

"That's not the point. Do you know how many other models wanted this job?"

Yes. Last time I was at Infinity Models, two of them locked me in a cupboard so I missed a really big casting. I had to wait until the cleaner came round to let me out again.

"I'm sorry, it's just it's my final GCSE today," I try to explain as I tug off the massive tutu and smack an elbow painfully against the wall. "At 2pm, the British education system is going to decide whether I have any chance of ever becoming an award-winning physicist. My entire future is going to be shaped by today."

I pull on my school jumper, which promptly gets caught in the gold wire still wrapped around my head. There's silence while I hop in and out of the 'changing room' with my jumper over my face and my arms waving in the air like manic bunny ears.

"Hmm," Aiden agrees still clicking through images. "You're clearly a genius destined for a Nobel Prize."

"GCSE physics is not about *literal* spatial awareness," I puff, clutching blindly at my head and simultaneously smashing my knee against the wall. "It's *conceptual* spatial awareness. Two very different things."

Which is lucky, because the wire on my head now

appears to be caught on everything in a two-metre radius. I have a detailed Get To School On Time Plan in my satchel, and nowhere at all does it say: Detach Myself From A Curtain Ring.

"It's OK, Harriet," I say, spinning helplessly in little circles. "You still have an hour and eleven minutes to get to school by train. Or an hour and sixteen minutes by taxi. You've got ages."

"Erm... you know the clock on the back wall is slow. Right?"

I abruptly stop circling.

Oh my God. OH MY GOD. I *knew* there was a reason they made us study karma in religious education.

"*No*," I squeak, ripping myself free from the wire at the cost of quite a few hairs, a scratch on my cheek, a curtain ring and half a school uniform. "*How* slow?"

"An hour," Aiden says.

And – just like that – both my Get To School On Time Plan and entire life trajectory fly straight out the window.

4

This is so incredibly *typical*.

The *one* time my dad isn't at the back of a photo shoot, trying to 'liven things up a bit' by stealing bits of mannequin and pretending he has three arms and four legs, is the one time I really need him here.

But Dad's at a job interview and I now have less than fifty minutes to get to a destination over an hour away.

As the taxi driver points out cheerfully after I clamber into the back and beg him to hurry: "I can only go as fast as the traffic, Goldilocks. I'm part of it, ain't I?"

Which I would probably look at as a kind of poignant universal truth if I wasn't preoccupied by trying to make myself as light as possible, in the hope that the decreased weight would allow the car to accelerate faster.

And also with correcting his grammar.

There's nothing else I can do. Thanks to the laws of physics – and irony – the factors dictating how fast I get to my exam apparently do not include a) crying,

b) hyperventilating or c) repeating 'sugar cookies' until the taxi driver shuts the internal window and flicks the switch that stops him being able to hear me.

So I may as well use the remaining time constructively to update you on what's been happening in the past six months.

Here's a brief synopsis:

1. I've become even less popular. Geek + Model = a whole new set of graffiti on your belongings.

2. I'm trying to cry less about it. We each expel an average of 121 litres of tears in a lifetime, and I can't afford to dry up before I even hit sixth form.

3. My dad is still out of work, and Annabel is still working as a lawyer. This is worth noting, because my stepmother is now seven months pregnant, and Dad is definitely not.

4. Apparently the average person eats a ton of food a year: the weight of a fully grown elephant. Annabel is doing her best to single-handedly challenge this statistic. She is *huge*.

5. My best friend, Nat, has turned sixteen, and I have not. This means that Nat can now legally play pinball in Georgia, USA after 11pm and fly a plane solo in the UK, and I cannot.

6. I have modelled twice for Baylee, gone on a few go-sees (when not spending time productively locked in a cleaning cupboard) and that's it.

7. I've finally reached the painful conclusion that my hair is not strawberry blonde.

8. It's ginger.

And that's it. Everything else has stayed exactly the same.

My stalker, Toby, still orbits me like some kind of slightly snotty moon and my nemesis, Alexa, still inexplicably hates me.

My agent, Wilbur, still makes up words whenever he feels like it, and the fashion designer, Yuka Ito, is still totally terrifying.

My dog, Hugo, is still fond of sampling anything sticky he spots on the pavement and I still keep my textbooks lined up in alphabetical, chromatic and subject order.

Because that's how real life is: people and situations and dogs don't change that often, even when you have written *very* careful plans and tried to force them to.

And if I could leave my list there, I would. Because it's a nice list, isn't it? A lovely, positive list that looks forward to an entire summer with Nat, a brand-new graffiti-less satchel next term, and – quite soon – the legal ability to fly planes on my own whenever I feel like it.

But I can't leave it there, because one more thing happened. And – for a little while, anyway – it made all the other points seem less important:

9. Lion Boy dumped me.

5

<u>Reasons Not to Think About Nick</u>

1. He told me not to.

Don't worry. It's not as bad as it sounds.

I mean, in some ways it's *exactly* as bad as it sounds. Four months after our first kiss, Nick told me we shouldn't see each other any more and then he abruptly disappeared from my life. I haven't seen or heard from him since. Not a text. Not a phone call or a voicemail. Not an email. Not a tweet or a Facebook message. Not even a fax (even though I'm not sure who faxes these days, but the option is still sort of there, isn't it?).

But it's totally OK. You don't spend nearly sixteen years reading novels about love and scanning poetry about love and listening to songs about love and watching films about love without coming away with a pretty good idea of how love stories go.

Everybody knows the dramatic ups and downs are what make the difference between a *real* love story – the kind that people make into films – and a boring one that nobody bothers writing or singing about.

Would *Pride and Prejudice* be popular if Darcy and Lizzy hooked up at the first ball?

Would *Wuthering Heights* be a classic if Cathy chose Heathcliff?

Would *Romeo and Juliet* be studied in school if they dated for a few years and then got married and moved to the suburbs of Mantua?

Exactly.

So even if your love story involves somebody dumping you and moving back to Australia, as Shakespeare said you just have to refuse to "admit impediments", and then they'll come back to you. Everybody knows that.

And, yes, it's been more than two months so it's taking Nick a little bit longer than it probably should, but he must be on his way.

All I have to do is wait.

In the meantime, I'm trying not to think about him. I don't think about his coffee-coloured skin, or his big black lion curls, or his green smell, or his eyes that slant up at the corners. I don't think about the tilt of his nose, or the wideness of his smile, or the way he used to rub his thumb across my knuckle when we were holding hands and tap the end of my nose after I sneezed (which was very unhygienic, but for some gross and deeply disturbing reason I liked it).

I don't think about how he makes me feel like a lightning bug: as if part of me is full of fire, and the other part of me can fly.

I don't think about how I'd be with him all the time, if I possibly could.

And I absolutely never think about the fact that I'm not really enjoying this bit of my love story, and that I'd have *much* preferred the boring kind where Nick stayed and everything carried on exactly as it was before.

Even if it broke all the rules of romance straight down the middle.

The driver clears his throat.

"In love, Goldilocks?" He winks at me in the rear-view mirror, waving his hand in my direction. "That explains a lot."

I look in surprise at the anatomically correct heart I've been sketching on the window, and then blush and wipe it away. *Subtle, Harriet.*

"Nope," I say as nonchalantly as I can. "I'm just… prepping for next year's biology module."

"Course you are." The driver grins. "Anyway, thought you was in an 'urry? Some kind of exam?" He nods. "You got four minutes left."

I blink a few times. The car has stopped and we're sitting directly outside my school. I hadn't even noticed we'd stopped moving.

"But..." I say as I scrabble in my satchel for my purse, "how is that even physically possible?"

The driver shrugs. "I'm magic, ain't I," he states matter-of-factly. "Like that fat dude in *'Arry Potter*."

I glance up. He certainly looks... other-worldly. Ephemeral. Slightly over-blessed with body hair.

"And I went well over the speed limit," he adds brightly. "That's eighty quid, love. Magic is pricy these days. Now get a hop on, you got three minutes left."

6

I swear on my *Oxford English Dictionary*, I have never moved so fast in my entire life.

By the time I've slid through the closing door of the gym hall, my breathing is so strained I sound like our vacuum cleaner when Annabel's cleaning the sofa. Sweat is dripping down my neck and the only thing I have to mop it up with is the edge of my school jumper now hanging in three ripped pieces around my neck, like a piece of modern art. Or something Wilbur would wear.

I'm barely two steps into the room when Toby's fluffy head spins around. I can only assume he spotted me out of the back of it with what he calls his 'Harrietenna'.

"*Toby*," Miss Johnson says in a warning voice, and Toby immediately stops waving and starts blowing me kisses and blinking instead.

I nod hello at him, hurry past and put my little plastic bag of stationery carefully on the right-hand side of my desk. Then I sit down and close my eyes.

Only a minute left to gather my thoughts, summon The Knowledge of the Stickers and Zen my environment. Just a few precious moments to allow the stress hormones to dissipate, to regulate my breathing, stop working out what time it is in Australia and to get my mind back on physics.

Midnight. It's midnight in Sydney right now.

Somebody snorts.

Focus, Harriet. There are two types of electron: negative and positive. Like charges repel. Opposite charges attract.

Somebody snorts again, and there's a faint giggle from a few seats away.

When insulating materials are rubbed together, electrons are knocked off one atom and on to the other.

There's another laugh, and suddenly I'm vaguely aware of eyes burrowing into my forehead.

Not just Toby's, I know what they feel like.

Cautiously, I open mine and glance around the room. There are a hundred and fifty-two other students in the hall, and every single one of them is staring at me.

I have absolutely no idea why. It's not as if nobody

here has seen sweat before. Or a ripped jumper. Or a single sock and scratched face. That's how a large chunk of my year end lunch break.

I look at Toby and see he's inexplicably patting his cheeks. When I search the room for Nat and see her – a long way away – she's trying to mouth something at me.

"Go," she's saying, subtly pointing at me. "*Go.*"

I love Nat. She's my favourite person in the entire world (followed by my dad and Annabel). But I'm not going anywhere. I've only just got here.

"Go," she mouths again, and then she rolls her eyes and smacks her head with her hand.

Now *that* gesture I'm familiar with.

"Everybody *face this way,*" Miss Johnson shouts furiously, and three hundred and two eyes suddenly snap away from my face. "*Toby Pilgrim, that includes you,*" Miss Johnson yells, and the final two revert to the front. "You have thirty seconds before your exam begins."

The only person not focusing on our imminent exam is Alexa, who is sitting diagonally directly behind me. She's got a standard smug expression on her face and she's rolling something between her fingers. Before I can work out what's going on, she subtly leans down and rolls a little paper ball forward so it's positioned directly under my desk.

"Twenty seconds."

I stare at the ball in confusion, then in a flash I know: Alexa's trying to sabotage my exam. She's trying to plant revision notes on me. Yet another round of her ultimate plan – Ruin Harriet's Life.

Oh my God. If I pick it up and get caught, I'm going to be thrown out of this exam. If I don't pick up it up and it gets found under my desk afterwards, I'll get disqualified for cheating. *What do I do?*

"Ten seconds."

Pick it up or don't pick it up? Don't pick it up or pick it up?

"Five seconds."

I bend down swiftly and grab it. If I can destroy the evidence before the exam starts, I'm not cheating. I'm just… disposing of rubbish responsibly.

But, like Pandora, I need to know what's in the box. I need to know what's intended to destroy me. So I tuck the note under the desk and quietly open it:

GEEK, YOU'RE FACE IS BRIGHT GOLD.

Oh, I think.

Oh.

"Please turn your papers over," Miss Johnson announces as I shrink into my seat with my hands over my face. "You may now start."

7

I spend the rest of my final exam looking like something actresses hold once a year and cry over. According to a test I did on the internet, I have 143 IQ points. Clearly I have no idea what to do with *any* of them.

Toby isn't quite so sure.

"Harriet," he says happily as I walk out of the hall and head outside to wait for Nat. "I am honoured to stalk you. I honestly cannot think of anyone I'd rather follow obsessively around."

Somehow, Toby's gotten even more thin and stretched-out looking: as if he's a bit of melted cheese somebody's just pulled off a pizza. His hair is fluffier, he has dark shadows around his eyes, and he's bobbing along with his hands neatly by his sides, his little nose twitching slightly. He looks even more like a meerkat than he did last time you saw him.

Let's put it this way, I wouldn't be even vaguely surprised if a plane flew past and he bolted for cover.

"What are you talking about, Tobes?"

"Gold is traditionally the colour of success, achievement and triumph," Toby explains in a voice brimming over with admiration. "You're the perfect colour for the last exam. I don't know why nobody has thought of it before."

I stare at him, and then burst into an explosion of laughter. Only Toby could possibly think I painted myself gold today on purpose.

Except… *In love, Goldilocks? That explains a lot.*

I abruptly stop laughing. Oh my God: the taxi driver did too. I clearly just look like the kind of girl who goes insane and colours herself in on a regular basis.

That's not the impression I'm trying to give to the world at *all*.

As Toby starts chattering excitedly about exam questions and oscillations of light waves, I glaze over and listen to the sound of his chirpy words going up and down and round and round.

Every time I try to remember what it was like not having him around, I can't do it. Toby's like a fact: once you know him, you can't *unknow* him. Over the last few months, he's started spending a little more time where Nat and I don't have to pretend we can't see him. And we've…

Well, we've kind of let him.

He's not so bad in small doses. As long as he doesn't irritate Nat too much. She has limited interest in irrelevant facts, and I fill that quota already.

We finally get outside, blink a few times in the bright sunshine, then start wandering, half blind, towards a small patch of shade. Nat's surname is near the beginning of the alphabet, so she always gets stuck at the back of an exam room: picking at her nail varnish and making impatient huffing sounds, like a pretty, swishy-haired dragon.

By the time we spot Alexa it's too late.

She's just outside the school gates with a big group of her friends: all clad in their cunningly edited school uniforms like a fashionable army. Rolled skirts and tucked tops and pink streaks and bra-straps showing. Sprawled menacingly across the grass, as if they own the school.

And how can I put this?

In a very non-literal way, they sort of do.

8

No, by the way.

If you think a polite but firm conversation with my bully six months ago totally fixed everything between us, you've obviously never met Alexa. Or me.

Or any other teenage girl.

I want to pretend Alexa and her friends aren't waiting for me, but a quick glance at her face tells me otherwise. She's practically salivating. That's the not-so-great thing about the last day of school: no repercussions.

"Hey," she says sharply, taking a step towards me. "Manners."

I instinctively look for another exit. But, short of using Toby to hurdle the fence, there's no other way out of the school. So I duck my head and try my hardest to become completely invisible.

Thanks to not being a member of the Fantastic Four, this doesn't work.

"HEY," Alexa says again, blocking my path. She

glances briefly at Toby. He scratches at the inside of his ear and then sniffs his finger. "Did you have *fun* in that exam, geek? Bet you did. I bet it was the best fun you've had in *ages.*"

I flush slightly. She's absolutely right: it was awesome. When I got to the essay question about the life cycle of a star, I actually got a bit dizzy with excitement. "Maybe," I say with the most non-committal shrug I can muster.

"Bet you knew all the answers, didn't you, you total spod."

I shake my head. "Only about ninety-three per cent of them."

Everyone snickers – I don't know why: that's still a solid A* – and Alexa scowls at me. I try to walk away, but she blocks me again. "So you've heard about the massive house party I'm having tonight?"

The answer to this question is obviously: *yes.* There are Eskimos in Siberia who woke up this morning, fully aware of the house party Alexa is having tonight.

"No."

"*I've* heard about it," Toby interrupts eagerly. "You're having tiny jellies, aren't you? Alexa, they sound *brilliant*. I've always found normal-sized jellies unhygienic. All those different spoons. It's much more sanitary to have lots of little ones each, isn't it?"

Alexa ignores him. "A guy who used to be on TV is coming. So it's technically a *celebrity* party."

Toby nods sagely. "No green jelly then. Just awesome red and purple, right? My mum makes mine in the shape of a rocket with liquorice where the engines would be."

Years from now, historians will look back at records of these days and wonder how Toby managed to get through them alive.

"That's nice for you, Alexa," I say, finally managing to dodge round her and start walking in the opposite direction.

"So, Manners" – and she clears her throat – "Want to come?"

I stop mid-stride. Apparently when people have their heads cut off there are five or six seconds when they can hear and see and blink, but they can't move because they've already been severed in half.

That's sort of how I feel now.

Slowly, I turn back round. "*Pardon me?*"

Out of the corner of my eye, I see Nat come out of the school doors, pause and then start legging it towards us.

"Do you want to come to my party?" Alexa says,

her face totally blank. "We've got a TV star, so you'd be the perfect celebrity addition. A model."

"*Really?*"

"Yeah," she says slowly, and the smirk appears again. "And if we fancy a dance, we can tie you to the ceiling by your feet and spin you round really fast. You can be our very own human disco ball."

Then she points at my face and bursts into hysterical laughter, and a few nano-seconds later everyone starts snickering behind her.

It takes thirty minutes for a human body to produce enough heat to boil half a gallon of water. I think from the temperature of my cheeks right now I can probably cut that down to eleven or twelve, maximum.

Why didn't I just keep walking? What's *wrong* with me? Other than a gold face and an entire lack of survival instinct, obviously.

"Bite us, Hockey-legs," Nat snaps, suddenly appearing next to me. "As *if* we'd want to go to your wannabe party."

"As if I'd *want* you to want to. I'm still scrubbing the loserness off my doorstep from your last visit." Alexa sneers. "Anyway, why the hell would I want *her*," and she points at me like I'm a bit of toenail stuck in a carpet, "in my house, spreading her geekiness around? There's no level of cool that can cure *that*. I'd have an *epidemic* on my hands."

She spins round and adds, "Nobody wants that, right?" Then starts ceremoniously high-fiving her friends.

As if I'm not still standing there with my cheeks burning.

As if I don't matter.

As if I never will.

As if nothing has changed at all.

9

I count slowly to ten, and then I take a deep breath, reach into my pocket and pull out a small bit of crumpled-up paper.

I tap my still-triumphing nemesis on the back and hand it to her.

"What the hell is this?"

YOUR

GEEK, ~~YOU'RE~~ FACE IS BRIGHT GOLD.

"*You-apostrophe-r-e* is a contraction of *you are*, Alexa," I say. "If you needed help with grammar, you should've asked."

There's a stunned silence followed by a couple of desperately suppressed snorts, and I suddenly wonder whether *everyone* likes Alexa as much as they pretend they do. Or whether some of them are only here for the 'celebrity' parties and tiny jellies.

Alexa's smirk has finally gone. "I *know* the

difference," she hisses furiously. "It was a *typo*."

She scrunches the distinctly handwritten note back up and throws it hard at my face. It hits my left ear with a small *pop*.

"What do I care, anyway?" she adds. "School's over. Nobody in real life cares about that kind of rubbish."

"I do," I say quietly.

"So do I," Nat says loudly, putting her arm around my waist and giving me a quick peck on the cheek.

"Me too," Toby agrees. "Never underestimate the power of a well-placed apostrophe."

We turn to leave and Alexa suddenly loses it, as if all her anger has just exploded in one bright firework of hatred. "*Don't walk away from me*, geeks!" she screams, slamming her hand against a parking bollard. "We're not done here! You just *wait* until next year! I'm going to... I'm going to – you – you – you're..."

"Hey!" Toby says, "I think she's finally getting it, Harriet!"

"We'll look forward to hearing the rest of that sentence in sixth form, Alexa," Nat calls back. "That should give you enough time to work out something really terrifying."

We grin at each other and keep walking. Alexa's

shouting gets fainter and fainter until all I can hear is a harmless buzzing sound, like a tiny mosquito.

I look upwards.

The sky is bright blue, the trees have parted, and now there's nothing but summer stretching endlessly in front of us.

10

We don't even wait until we turn the corner to start dancing.

That's the beauty of the summer holidays. It's as if life is just a big Etch-A-Sketch, and once a year you get to shake it vigorously up and down and start again. By the time we go back to school, the whole year will be wiped clean.

Sort of.

Enough to ensure nobody remembers Toby breakdancing across the road with his satchel on his head, anyway.

"Did you see Alexa's *face*?" Nat shouts, doing a little scissor kick and punching the air. "That was *magic*."

I give a happy little hop, even though it does mean I may now have to apply to a different sixth form if I don't want to spend the rest of my teens lodged down a toilet of Alexa's choosing. (The Etch-A-Sketch isn't *that* thorough.) "Do you think I did something horrendous to Alexa when we were little that I've forgotten about, Nat?"

"Who cares if you did?" Nat yells as she does a series of excited little spins, high-fiving me on every turn. "Alexa's gone! Exams are *over*. Do you know what that means?! No more physics! No more chemistry! No more history! No more *MATHS*!"

My A Levels will be in physics, chemistry, history and maths and I fully intend to start studying for them before the week is over, but I high-five my best friend anyway.

Nat giddily grabs a calculator out of her bag and throws it on the floor. "I am *never going to use you again*," she yells at it. "Do you understand? Me and you: we're through!"

Toby bends down and picks it up. "Aren't you going to study fashion design, Natalie?"

"Yup." She tosses her shiny black hair and beams at him. "It's going to be clothes, clothes, clothes for the rest of my life."

"Then you're going to need this," Toby says, handing it back to her. "To calculate fabric measurements, body shapes, profit margins, manufacturing costs and loan repayments, not to mention pattern cutting and size differentiation."

"*What*?" Nat's face collapses. "Oh for the love of…" She looks at me. "I didn't have to know that for *months. Seriously*. Does he *have* to be here? Can't we send him back to wherever he came from?"

"Hemel Hempstead," Toby says helpfully. "I can get the 303 bus."

"We've got an entire summer ahead of us," I remind Nat jubilantly, ignoring him. I feel a bit like Neil Armstrong immediately before he boarded the *Apollo* in 1969: as if we've just been handed all the space in the universe, and we can do whatever we want with it. "In fact, I've got it all mapped out." I start rummaging in my satchel and then pull out a piece of paper with a flourish. "Ta-da!"

Nat takes it off me and frowns. "Nat and Harriet's Summer of Fun Flow Chart?"

"Exactly!"

I do a little dance and then gesture at the coloured bubbles: yellow for me, purple for Nat, and – thanks to the nature of the colour wheel – an unfortunate poo brown for everything in between. "I've got every detail planned out for maximum fun and entertainment value," I explain, pointing proudly. "Starting with Westminster Abbey, which is where Chaucer, Hardy, Tennyson and Kipling are buried, and then Highgate

Cemetery to visit George Eliot, Karl Marx and Douglas Adams. We're working our way through dead writers chronologically."

I've focused our Summer of Fun Flow Chart on London because all there is locally is a roller-skate rink and a Mill museum, and as much as I love both wheels on my feet and bread we totally exhausted both of those options before we left primary school.

"The Charles Dickens Museum?" Nat reads slowly. "Glass-blowing in Leathermarket? The Ceremony of the Keys at the Tower of London?"

She's impressed. I can tell from how quiet she is and the fact that she's not making eye contact.

"Amazing, right? They've just discovered traces of ancient blue paint on the Parthenon statues at the British Museum, scientifically proving that ancient Greece looked like Disneyland. We can go and see the new exhibition!"

Nat nods a couple of times and scratches at her neck. "Uh-huh."

I suddenly realise how selfish I sound. "Nat," I say quickly, "there's loads of stuff for you on here too. There's an exhibition on ball gowns at the V&A, and the London College of Fashion are doing a graduate show that I'm sure Wilbur can get us tickets to."

Toby nods knowingly. "Did you know the Victoria and Albert Museum employs a hawk every summer to discourage pigeons from the gardens?"

"And *tonight*... I thought we could celebrate together with *these*!" I pull DVDs of *The Devil Wears Prada* and David Attenborough's African documentary from my satchel. "And *these*!" I pull out some sparkly purple nail varnish and toe-dividers and a pack of *Game of Thrones* playing cards. "And – wait for it – *these*!" I pull out a pack of no-calorie caramel popcorn and an enormous chocolate muffin.

Then I look at Toby. "I didn't forget you," I add fondly. I hand him a *Lord of the Rings* Lego set.

"Harriet Manners," he says solemnly. "I shall begin constructing a YouTube stop-frame video sensation *immediately*."

"What do you think, Nat?" I squeak, bouncing up and down on my toes. "Are you ready to start the Most Incredible Summer Of All Time™?! I'm calling it MISOAT for short, by the way."

"Umm," Nat says, and glances at me then back into the middle distance. All signs of laughter or twirling have completely disappeared. "Toby, can you leave us alone for a second?"

"Girl stuff?" he says wisely. "Natalie, I know all about menstruation. We studied it in biology."

"*Toby*."

"Ah. Not menstruation then." Toby cocks his head to the side. "Perhaps bras?"

Nat scowls so hard her forehead looks like something out of *Star Trek*.

"Kittens?"

Just as Nat reaches out a hand to physically throttle him Toby ducks behind a tree.

I guess old stalker habits die hard.

"What's going on?" I ask nervously. "Have you already seen *The Devil Wears Prada*?"

Nat's lips twitch. "Of course I have. It's not that... I'm so sorry, Harriet. I only found out two days ago. I didn't want to upset you during exams."

My stomach tightens into a hard ball. I can already feel our trips to the Natural History Museum and the Imperial War Museum shutting down, like tiny little lights being turned off. "What's going on?"

"I'm..." and she takes a deep breath. "I'm going to France."

A couple more bulbs break. "What? For how long?"

"A whole month," Nat says miserably. "I'm leaving tomorrow."

And – just like that – my entire summer goes completely dark.

11

France? What has *France* got that my Summer of Fun Flow Chart doesn't have?

A French Home-stay Programme, apparently.

Nat's mum is making her go, as punishment for catching Nat in Boots when she should have been doing her French GCSE. Nat quickly explains this as her mum pulls up at the kerb alongside us and makes the universal gesture for Get In This Car Right Now, Young Lady.

Then she waves miserably goodbye at us from the back windscreen.

"Harriet," Toby says, when he comes out from behind the tree two minutes later. "Do you know what this *means*?"

"No," I say curtly, because obviously I do.

Don't say it, Toby, I will him silently. *Please. Just don't say it*.

But as always Toby's ability to read minds, verbal

inflections or really-quite-obvious facial expressions remains non-existent.

"It *means*," he says – staring at me with eyes like lava lamps, all liquid and glowing – "you're going to be spending the whole of summer with *me*."

OK, I'm going to bed for the next month.

I'll just spend the next six weeks under my duvet, learning how to embroider hieroglyphics by torchlight. I'll get Annabel and Dad to whizz up all my food so I can drink it through a straw from under my duvet, like an old lady's budgerigar. By the time I start A Levels I'll be the same shape as a mattress, covered in fungus and shrivelled into an even smaller and even more muscle-less mass than normal.

As Robert Burns once wrote, "The best laid schemes o' mice an' men gang aft a-gley" and the same can obviously be said for teenage girls. My plans are aft-agleying all *over* the shop.

"Harriet?" Annabel shouts downstairs as I slam the front door as hard as I can behind me. "If you're trying to break all the windows in the house simultaneously, that is an incredibly efficient way to do it."

"Hey!" I hear my dad say indignantly. "How come

Harriet gets *complimented* for slamming doors when I get in trouble? I demand a retrial."

"There hasn't been a trial, Richard," Annabel laughs, "so we can't technically 're' anything."

"Oh, fine, you win again. It's a good thing you're about to pop out a mini-me or I wouldn't be letting you triumph so easily."

"Thank you, darling. Your gallantry is, as ever, much appreciated."

I hear a loud cheerful kiss, echoing down the stairs.

"You know," Dad muses afterwards, "I *am* pretty gallant. I'm a bit like a modern-day Lancelot. Except with no horse. Why don't I have a horse, Annabel? How are we expected to be real men these days without horses?"

Yup. If you think that the prospect of creating a new human life has in any way forced my father to grow up even *slightly* over the last six months you'd be wrong.

There's a jellyfish called the *Turritopsis nutricula*, which Marine Biologists say is the only animal in the world that renders itself immortal by reverting back to adolescence every time it starts to age too much. All I'm going to say is: they obviously haven't met my dad yet.

Let's just see how long *he* sticks around.

*

Throwing my satchel into the corner of the hallway, I start a slow, stompy climb up the stairs. Six months ago they were pretty, white-painted wood; they are now covered in horrible beige, hard-wearing carpet with fiddly stair gates at either end. There used to be a space under the banister where the cat would climb the stairs and headbutt me from eye-level, as a kind of greeting. It's been blocked up.

There are also fake plug-coverings in all of the plug sockets and padding around the edges of the tables and more gates in doorways, just in case we need to be herded safely from room to room like cattle.

I reach the newly safe and sanitised landing and stare at my parents. "What are you *doing*?"

"Hello, Harriet." Annabel is wearing an enormous, elasticated, pin-stripe suit, and is calmly wiping one of my fossils with a cloth. "Sweetheart, why is your face gold? And what on earth happened to your jumper?" She looks down. "I know I'm full of pregnancy hormones, but I'm certain you were wearing two socks this morning."

"Oh *amazeballs*!" Dad cries from the study. "You coloured yourself gold! To win an exam! That is creative *genius*!"

I think my head is about to explode. "I'm serious, what are you *doing*? You can't *clean fossils,* Annabel. You are literally wiping away 230 million years of history!"

"I think this is a coating of dead skin cells and dust mites, actually. When was the last time you dusted these, Harriet?"

I grab the fossil from her. "This is an Asistoharpes! This is 395 *million years old*! Why don't you just stick it in the washing machine while you're at it?"

My stepmother raises her eyebrows in silence.

"I think if it's survived that long it can handle a bit of wet cloth, don't you?"

I ignore her and turn to Dad, who is standing on the office chair, trying to get down my collection of books about the Tudors. Every time he reaches for one he swivels slightly and has to hang on to the shelf for balance. "What are *you* doing?"

"There's a whole load of stuff here that's yours, Harriet," he explains, reaching for a biography of Anne Boleyn and swivelling again. "So we've built some more shelves in your bedroom. This is going to be the baby's room."

I grab a few of my books off the bed from where they've just been thrown, willy-nilly. "This room is called the *study*, Dad. If this was a room for a baby, it would be called something else!"

"It is, Harriet," Dad says, laughing. "We just renamed it."

I can feel every single cell in my body fizzing and bursting like those crackly sweets that pop on your tongue. First Alexa, then Nat, now this. Today isn't even making an *effort* to go to plan any more.

"There isn't *room* in my bedroom for all my stuff!"

"Then throw some of it away," Annabel suggests with a tiny smile. She's cleaning another fossil. "Or we can put it in the attic. Or maybe in the garden. I imagine these rocks would probably be very happy there."

My throat is getting tighter and tighter. "What do you mean *throw it away*? You can't just throw preserved evidence of natural evolution in the bin!"

Annabel puts her hand gently on her enormous straining belly. "Harriet, what's going on, sweetheart? Did your last exam go badly? What's the matter with you?"

"Me? What's the matter with both of *you*? Baby, baby, baby! It's all baby, baby, baby!"

"Are you about to start singing Justin Bieber?" Dad asks. Annabel snorts with laughter and then puts her hand guiltily over her mouth.

My head pops.

"*Oh my GOD*!" I yell. "I hate you, I hate this house and *THIS IS GOING TO BE THE WORST SUMMER EVER*!"

And with one grand gesture, I burst into tears, sweep every single fossil I can into my arms and storm into my bedroom.

Leaving every window in the house rattling behind me.

12

<u>Reasons Not to Think About Nick</u>

1. *He told me not to.*
2. *I've got much more important things to think about.*

OK. So maybe I didn't tell you *everything*.

I told you the stuff you might tell a teacher, or a neighbour or the old lady who works at the corner shop and won't stop asking questions. But I didn't tell you the real stuff. Not the stuff that counts.

I slide down the back of the door and stare blankly at the jumble of fossils now sitting in my lap. Here are some interesting facts I've discovered recently about the animal kingdom:

- The cuckoo is built with a small dip in its back so that it can toss out the other eggs as soon as it's born.

- Mother pandas only care for one of their cubs, and allow the other to die.
- Shark embryos fight and eat each other in the womb and only the winner is born.

Don't even get me started on what the spotted hyena does to its relations. Trust me, you really don't want to know.

What I'm trying to say is, I'm incredibly excited about having a new brother or sister. Of course I am. Babies are cute – in a baldy, screaming kind of way – and a really big part of me can't wait to meet my new sibling and buy it cute little dinosaur T-shirts and a miniature satchel and (eventually) matching crossword puzzles so that we can do them together over breakfast.

But another part of me is anxious.

Literature, history and nature repeatedly remind us that it's not always TV deals and record contracts and matching outfits when it comes to siblings. If *King Lear* and the Tudor dynasty taught us nothing else, it's that you might want to watch your back. Especially if you're a *half*-sibling like me. Because if push comes literally to shove, somebody normally ends up getting kicked out of the nest.

Over the last six months, the baby has started taking over everything:

- First breakfast streamlined into one topic: did you know that the baby's heart starts beating after twenty-two days? Did you know that by seventeen weeks it has fingerprints?
- Then random questions: do you think it'll hate mushrooms, like Annabel, or cinnamon, like Dad?
- Then it started demanding olive milkshake and ketchup on ice cream and once – to my absolute horror – a bit of the white chalk from my maths blackboard.
- People started visiting and walking straight past me to 'The Belly'.
- Annabel started looking tired all the time. Dad started looking anxious and being extraordinarily loud to make up for it.
- And the photograph of my mum on the mantelpiece mysteriously moved to the guest bedroom, as if that would help everyone forget what happened to the last person in this house who tried to have a baby.

Or the fact that the baby was me.

And – bit by bit, gate by gate – the house started changing, and my room started feeling smaller, and my parents stopped talking or thinking about anything else.

Then – without warning – Nick dumped me.

So I threw myself into the thing I'd kind of been neglecting for once: schoolwork. I studied at breakfast, lunch and dinner. I studied in the bath, and on the toilet, and on the bus, and in the shower by sketching maths equations into the steam on the glass. I even studied during modelling shoots, as you already know.

Basically, I stuffed my head with facts and formulas and dates and equations and lists and diagrams so there wouldn't be room for anything else.

But now exams are finished, and school is over.

Nat is leaving for France.

Lion Boy is still gone.

I'm less important to my parents than someone who isn't even born yet.

And all I can do is sit in my room, staring at my overcrowded new bookshelves and wondering what to do next.

Because that's the truth about people with

obsessively organised plans: we're not trying to control everything in our lives. We're trying to block out the things we can't.

But now there's nothing left.

Nothing but the baby.

13

Anyway.

By the time I wake up the next morning – owner of the world's most sparkly pillow – I feel a bit more hopeful. On the bright side, there is no *way* my life could get any worse.

Last night, everyone else in my year was getting ready to party. Sneaking out of the house in one outfit so they could change into a smaller one. Discussing in excited whispers who was going to kiss who, and who was going to wish they hadn't. Giggling and laughing and getting ready to celebrate the end of compulsory education in a way they would never, ever forget.

Meanwhile, I was sitting on my bedroom floor on my own, painted gold, crying, with a shredded school jumper pulled over my head. I think that's pretty much rock bottom, even by my own socially redundant standards.

Things always look better in the morning, though, and by the time I wake up I'm actually quite entertained to discover that I've left a trail of damp gold glitter behind me, like an enormous sparkly fairy.

Hugo's lying patiently at my feet. I give him a quick cuddle to let him know I'm mentally stable again, then hop out of bed to grab my phone and switch it on. It gets so little activity these days, sometimes I actually forget I have one.

Which is why it's a bit of a shock when it rings immediately.

"Hello?"

"Ferret-face, is that you?"

I never know what to say to questions like that.

"Hi, Wilbur. It's Harriet."

"Oh, thank holy dolphin-cakes," my agent sighs in relief. "I was starting to think you'd spontaneously combusted. I just read about a man that happened to, Kitten-cheeks. One minute he was washing up and the next minute, POOF. Just a few bubbles and a broken plate."

I blink a few times. Sometimes talking to Wilbur is like falling out of a big tree: you have to just try and catch a few branches to hang on to on the way down. "Is everything OK?"

"Not enormously, Baby-baby Panda. I've left nineteen messages on your answer machine, but you're a naughty little lamp-post and haven't answered a single bunny-jumping one of them."

Sugar cookies. I'd totally forgotten about the mess I made of the shoot yesterday. "Is this about Yuka?"

She's going to hang-draw-and-quarter me like they did in the sixteenth century. Except she's going to do it with words instead of a sword and it's probably going to hurt more.

"It most certainly is, Poodle-bottom. Time is, as they say, of the essential oils. Where have you been?"

I swallow with difficulty. "I-I-I-I'm so sorry, Wilbur."

"It might be too late now, my little Monkey-moo," Wilbur sighs. "There are forms to fill in, things to sign, governments to inform."

They're going to tell the *government*? That seems a little bit excessive, even for Baylee. "Please, Wilbur. I won't do it again."

"Once is enough, Cupcake-teeth. It normally is."

I close my eyes and sit heavily on my bed.

I don't believe this. I actually don't believe it.

It's not even eight o'clock in the morning yet; I haven't even opened the curtains. There's sleep in my eyes and the imprint of Winnie the Pooh's nose on my cheek. And it looks like I've just been fired.

14

It was only a matter of time.

I'm like the donkey in the Aesop's fable who dressed in a lion skin and got away with it until the fox heard him bray. I've been waiting for six months for the fashion industry to realise I'm their donkey and chuck me back out again.

I quickly put Wilbur on speakerphone, throw the mobile across my room and climb miserably back into bed. Then I pull a pillow over my head.

You know what? I think I *am* just going to stay here. I'm almost certain that nobody will notice. I'll be like Richard III, and in hundreds of years archaeologists will find my skeleton buried under some kind of car park, where future people keep their spaceships.

Or jet packs.

Or magnetically levitating transporters.

Or flying bubbles.

I'm just trying to work out if in 500 years they'll

have finally found a way to replace the wheels in my trainers with rockets when some of Wilbur's nonsensical words start filtering in through the pillow. "Candle-wick." "Rabbit-foot." "Potato-nose." "Tokyo."

Tokyo?

I lift the sparkly pillow so I can hear a bit better.

"...so there's going to be a lot of work to do before you go... and oh my *gigglefoot* that reminds me you need to pick up some spot cream because we do not want any dermatological disasters like last time you went abroad, do we, my little Baby-baby Unicorn? Eat some more vegetables before you get there and..."

The tiger beetle is proportionately the fastest thing on earth. If it was the size of a human, it could reach 480 mph. I'm on the other side of the room so quickly I reckon I would leave it panting and retching behind me.

"Hello?" I pick the phone up, drop it and then grab it again and start randomly whacking buttons. "Hello? Hello? Wilbur? Hello? Are you there? Hello?"

"Where else would I be, Owl-beak? This is my phone, isn't it?"

"What did you just say?"

"Love bless you, Plum-pudding. I forget your family

has a problem with earwax. I *said*, try and eat some more vegetables before you land in Tokyo, or Yuka's going to kick off again and we all know what that means."

My entire body suddenly feels like it's been electrocuted. *Before I land in Tokyo?* "I'm *not* fired?"

Wilbur shrieks with laughter. "*Au contraire*, my *petit poisson*. Yuka has a brand-new job for you in Japan, and if we get moving I should be able to get flights sorted in time."

I stare at the wall in silence.

I've been obsessed with Japan since I was six years old. It's the Land of the Rising Sun: of sumo and sushi; karaoke and kimonos; mountains and manga. Homeland of Ryuichi Sakamoto and Studio Ghibli; of Hayao Miyazaki and Haruki Murakami. Mecca for geeks and freaks and weirdos. I have dreamt about visiting Japan ever since…

Well. Ever since I realised it existed to visit.

Oh my God: this could fix *everything*. It will be my New and Infinitely More Glorious Summer Plan 2 (NAIMGS2). I can make a brand-new flow chart. It's *perfect*.

And, yes, it might only be a temporary solution, but everybody knows that if you put enough temporary solutions together you've got something that lasts a very long time indeed.

"YES!" I shout, picking Hugo up and giving him the biggest, most twinkly kiss of his life, right between his eyebrows. "When do I leave? What's the plan?"

"You leave on Saturday, my little Panda-pot. And *BOOM!*" he adds after another stunned silence. "Your fairy godmother strikes again."

15

Right. Time to initiate the New Plan.

The first and most important step to convincing your parents that you are a responsible nearly-adult, capable of foreign jaunts, is obviously not being painted gold. So I hop in the shower and scrub myself until I no longer look like the death mask of Tutankhamen.

Then I peruse my wardrobe for something that says *I am an authoritative and totally trustworthy girl on the cusp of womanhood*. Something that says *I can be sent very far away without any repercussions*.

In a moment of poetic inspiration, I put on the most expensive thing I own and grab the matching accessories. I spend a few minutes fiddling on my laptop, then stride confidently into the kitchen to face my parents.

"Zac?" Annabel's saying, pouring ketchup into an open tin of pears and mixing it up with the end of an empty biro. "For a boy or a girl?"

"Either. It's very gender neutral." Dad pauses and then adds, "Plus it's the name of a Macaw from San Jose who can slam twenty-two dunks in one minute."

"Vetoed."

"What about Zeus?"

"*Zeus?* As in the lightning-lobbing Greek father of Gods and Men?"

"As in the world's tallest dog. Great Dane. Nice eyes."

Annabel laughs. "I don't care how nice his eyes are, Richard. Vetoed."

"Archibald, the world's smallest bull?"

Annabel looks calmly at Dad. "I think it's time to give Harriet back her *Guinness Book of Records*."

Dad shakes his head. "I'm surprised at you, Annabel. Do you have no respect for the majesty of the animal kingdom?"

"I have plenty of respect for it, Richard. I just don't particularly want it coming out of my uterus."

"Liz?"

"You'd better be referring to the Queen."

"Of course I am," Dad says indignantly. "Two of them, in fact. Both fierce examples of female power, independence and majesty." He pauses. "And, you know... Hurley."

I quickly cough from the doorway before there's only one parent left alive to appeal to. Then I walk regally into the centre of the room.

"Father. Annabel." I look at Hugo who scampered down here at the first whiff of cheesy-bacon. "Dog. I would like to open this session by apologising *profusely* for my behaviour yesterday. It was an untimely display of vivaciousness due to the unexpected ruination of my Summer of Fun Flow Chart. I should have found a way to express my entirely valid opinions more reasonably."

I pause to see if this heartfelt apology has sunk in. They're both staring at me with wide eyes. Ha. I feel a bit like Atticus Finch in *To Kill a Mockingbird*. I'm totally going to nail this.

"Secondly," I say, putting my laptop down on the table and pressing a button so that it shines at the wall. "I have something very important to show you."

There are a few seconds of impressed, awed silence.

Then my parents burst into laughter so loud that Hugo steps back and starts barking at the ceiling.

"*Brilliant*," Dad gasps. "What's she wearing this time?"

"I think it's her bridesmaid dress from Margaret's

wedding," Annabel whispers, wiping her eyes. "You can still see where she sat on a candle during the after-dinner speeches."

"Oh, thank God. I thought my daughter had turned into an enormous toilet-roll holder."

I wait patiently for them both to stop giggling. I'm totally going to remember this moment when it comes time to put them in a retirement home.

"This outfit," I say, nobly deciding to rise above both of them, "may be a bridesmaid dress, but if you use your *imagination* it represents something much bigger."

I press a button on my laptop, and an image of a cygnet shines on to the wall. "I was once an ugly duckling—"

Dad puts his hand up. "With feathers all stubby and brown?"

I stick my tongue out at him and press the button again. The picture changes from cygnet to swan. "But in the last six months, I have grown up a lot. I have transformed." I click quickly through a few photos of tadpoles and frogs, caterpillars and butterflies I copied from Google. "But what happens at the end of a transformation… is that where the story ends?"

I point at the slide that says:

"Yes."

I scowl. "It's a rhetorical question, Dad. The implied answer is clearly no."

"Keep going, Harriet," Annabel says through a mouthful of ketchup pear. "I'm curious to see where this will end up."

"Does a caterpillar sit on the same leaf when it's a butterfly? No! It goes for a little fly and sees something of the world. Does the tadpole stay in the same pond once it's a frog? No! It stretches its legs, goes for a jump, explores other waters." I gesticulate energetically with my matching fake flower bouquet. "Did Cinderella go back to cleaning hearths once she married the prince?"

"Probably," Dad says. "They didn't have women's rights back then. She had to do the cooking too, and probably a bit of laundry."

"For the love of sugar cookies, Dad, *stop answering rhetorical questions*."

I take a deep breath and compose myself again.

"Transformation means moving *forwards*. If a butterfly stays on the same leaf and a frog stays in the same pond, then they may as well have stayed a caterpillar or a tadpole. There was no point in metamorphosing."

"Wrap it up now, Harriet," Annabel says gently.

I had an entire slide about a dragonfly, but maybe I'll leave that for the encore. I click to the final slide, and a picture of Mount Fuji shines on to the wall with my face hastily copied and pasted on top of it.

"So, in summary: I assert my right to go to Tokyo for a modelling job. Thank you for listening." And I plonk myself triumphantly down on a chair.

Excellent. That should do it.

Maybe I won't be a physicist after all. I'll be a lawyer, and my poetic and powerful Powerpoint presentations will be made into poignant fridge magnets for years to come.

Dad's expression reminds me of Hugo when we get takeaway pizza. "*Japan?* The agency wants Harriet to go to *Japan?* Annabel, that's where those little trees that look like big trees but smaller come from. Can I go with her, Annabel? Please?"

"Richard," Annabel says, "if you had a full-sized koala lodged in your abdomen, would you want me to stay with you?"

Dad looks horrified. "Definitely."

"Then let's assume I feel the same way, shall we?"

She turns back to me with a softer voice. "We can't take you to Japan, sweetheart. I wouldn't be able to get through the doors of the aeroplane, for starters, and I need your dad here because I could go into labour at any moment. You understand, don't you?"

I nod. Of course I understand that.

Annabel's eyes widen. "So what you're *actually* asking is to go to Tokyo, entirely on your own? At fifteen years old?"

"Yuka will be th—" I start, and Annabel looks at me sharply.

She has a point: Cruella De Vil would make a more reassuring guardian.

I clear my throat and clutch my fake flower bouquet as tight as I can. "Like Cinderella, I believe it is my turn to stop cleaning hearths."

"Harriet," Dad points out. "You don't even make your own bed."

"I'm talking *symbolically.*" Dad clearly doesn't understand the subtleties of the English language. *"Please?"*

Annabel smiles. "Come here," she says affectionately, and when I perch on the sofa next to her she nudges me with her shoulder and spikes another pear with her biro. "Listen, we know things are hard for you at the moment, Harriet. Don't think we haven't noticed."

I shrug.

"But I'm sorry, you can't go to the other side of the world on your own. You might be older than your age in some ways, but in quite a few of them you're also much, much younger."

What?

"Just because I don't have any boobs yet doesn't mean you can stop me going abroad! That's discrimination!"

Annabel laughs. "That's not even slightly what I'm talking about, Harriet."

Then I turn to Dad with my widest, most beseeching eyes. "Tell her I can go, please!"

"I'm sorry, sweetheart, but for the first time ever I'm with Annabel on this one." Dad twinkles at me but I block it with my firmest scowl.

"So what am I expected to do all summer? Just sit here and rot in a corner?"

"I don't know, Harriet," Annabel sighs. "Draw. Read. Paint. Go for walks. Build nuclear warheads. Take your dad to the zoo. Whatever you want as long as you remain within a 500-mile radius of this house."

"So what you're telling me," I shout furiously, "is

I can't go to Japan because of *that*?" and I point at Annabel's belly.

Annabel suddenly looks incredibly tired. "No, Harriet." She puts the pear tin down. "I am saying that you can't go to Japan because of *that*."

And she points directly at me.

16

Obviously the most important thing at a time like this is to remember to maintain the moral high ground. To react with dignity and self-control: noble in defeat, gallant in loss.

Which is why it's a massive disappointment when I throw the fake flower bouquet across the kitchen and yell, "Stop trying to ruin my life! This is so unfair! I wish I'd never been BOOORRRN!"

And charge over to the front door, pull it open and stomp out with as much vigour as I can muster. Leaving it hanging wide open behind me.

Before I actually run away, I'd just like to point out how incredibly unreasonable my parents are being.

I'm nearly sixteen. By this age, Isaac Asimov was at university, Eddie Murphy was doing stand-up comedy shows in New York, Louis Braille had invented raised writing, chess champion Bobby Fischer was an international grandmaster and Harry Potter was well on his way to saving the entire world of magic.

It's not that I don't appreciate having people in my life who want to be with me, every step of the way. But still.

I bet Isaac Asimov didn't get this kind of disrespect from *his* parents.

My plan is to stomp all the way to Nat's house and then stay there a) forever or b) until my parents are so prostrate with grief at my absence that they'll let me do whatever I want as long as I come home again.

Unfortunately the huge silk skirt of my bridesmaid dress gets caught on a bush at the bottom of the road, and by the time I've managed to rip myself free I don't really have any stomping energy left. I just feel like a bit of an idiot.

Nat's door swings open before I've even knocked, and – not for the first time – my brain spins slightly. When Nat's mum isn't covered in colourful miracle paste and wearing a dressing gown, she looks so much like Nat it's like having a worm-hole into the future.

"Harriet, darling!" she says, beaming at me. "What a pretty dress!" She leans forward to give me a kiss. "And I adore the tiara."

"Hello, Ms Grey," I say politely. "I've run away and I'm living here now."

"Are you, sweetie? How terribly exciting."

"Is Nat in, please?"

"She's upstairs, packing for her trip." Nat's mum pauses and sniffs. "And by the smell of it she's taking my Chanel perfume with her."

"IT'S NOT THE CHANEL ACTUALLY, MUM," Nat yells downstairs. "IT'S THE PRADA. SHOWS HOW MUCH YOU KNOW."

Nat's mum leans up the stairs. "You're being punished, Natalie. You're not taking *any* perfume, mine or otherwise. And no high heels, make-up or jewellery either. I *will* be checking."

Nat appears at the top of the stairs in about half a second, like a magic genie. "*Mum*. I can't leave the house without make-up. I'm not a *savage*."

"Maybe the next time you decide to skip an exam because you feel like testing out lipsticks, you'll think twice."

"Or maybe I'll just check first that my mum isn't testing out eyeshadow in the aisle behind me."

Nat's mum laughs. "*Touché*, Natalie. Unfortunately only one of us is Mum and it's not you."

Nat looks furious. "Fine. *Whatever*. Have it your way, *as always.*"

She looks at me and makes her Can You Believe This? face.

Then she looks at me again with her What The Hell Are You Wearing? face.

"Harriet, why do you look like something that just got kicked off the Disney Channel?"

I hold out my skirts. "Parental manipulation."

"Did it work?"

"Nope. Not even a little bit."

"I honestly don't know why we bother making an effort in the first place." Nat glares at her mum again, then beckons to me. "Anyway, come on up, Harriet. I think I might need your help."

17

Nat needs *somebody's* help, that's for sure.

I can barely open the door to her room, and – when I finally do – I realise it's because every single piece of clothing she owns is on the floor. It looks like our garden after a mole has been through it, except that instead of mounds of soil there are about fifteen hills of shoes and dresses and jumpers and handbags and scarves and vest tops and leggings, erupting from the carpet.

Nat's already crouched in the middle of her bed, holding a box of tampons.

"Hop up here," she says as I squeeze my way in, pointing at a spot on the bed with her foot.

I carefully clamber over a pile of skirts. "What on earth are you doing?"

Nat holds up a tampon with a grim face. "This." She pulls the cotton wool out of the applicator and rams a pink lipstick in. "I reckon I should be able to get five in a box, and quite a few eyeliners and lipglosses as long as they're short ones." Then she holds up a small conditioner bottle. "This is foundation." She pulls out a tiny tub of moisturiser. "This is cream blush." Finally, she pulls out a ridiculously thick copy of *Harper's Bazaar*. "I need you to cut a hole in the middle of all the pages so I've got somewhere to put my eyeshadows and mascara."

I stare at her in awe and then take the magazine off her.

"You could put a pair of strappy high heels inside a tissue box, with tissues on top? And maybe little sachets of perfume inside sanitary towels?"

Nat grins at me and holds up her hand. "Harriet Manners, what would I do without you?"

I high-five her. "Be slightly shorter and less fragrant, I'd imagine." Then I pick up the scissors and start neatly cutting through a few pages of a beautiful model with blonde waves down to her waist.

After several hours of industrious productivity, during which I tell Nat all about the awesome trip to Japan that I won't be going on, I say, "Seriously, Nat, what am I going to do without you? At least you'll be in France. I'm going to be stuck here on my own."

"And Toby. Don't forget Toby." Nat wrinkles her

nose at me so I hit her with the magazine. I said *small doses.* "I've got it worse. I'm staying on a *farm*. An actual working *farm with animals* in it and stuff. What's the prison on that island called?"

"Alcatraz?"

"Yeah. I'd rather have been sent there. At least I could have jumped out and swum to the shops in San Francisco. I'm going down in style though." She holds up a lipstick. "I'm going to look like one of the women who works behind a beauty counter in John Lewis by the time I'm finished."

"Are you going to milk cows and make butter and collect eggs?"

"I most certainly am not." Nat shudders. "You realise eggs come out of chicken's butts, right?"

"They don't, Nat," I laugh, cutting through another piece of paper. "They're actually called cloacas, and all birds and amphibians and reptiles have them. For joint reproductive and digestive purposes."

"Ew. That's actually more gross." Nat sits on the bed next to me, looking miserable. "Oh, God, Harriet. This summer is a total disaster. I bet there's going to be some disgusting boy on the farm with a little wispy moustache and a habit of accidentally walking into my bedroom while I'm getting changed."

I giggle. "And every time you take a shower he'll lurk outside so when you come out in a towel he's *right there*."

"Yeah," Nat says, starting to laugh. "And he'll ask for the salt at the dinner table with, like, *meaning*."

"And every ten minutes he'll offer to give you a massage with olive oil he stole from the kitchen."

"I bet he wears shiny green lycra cycling shorts around the house and his T-shirts are too short." We're both giggling uncontrollably now, and rolling around on the bed making vomiting sounds.

"I'm going to have to run away," Nat says decisively. "I'm going to steal a pig and ride it into Paris."

My phone beeps and I grab it out of my pocket. "Pigs can trot at up to eleven miles per hour at top speed," I say, clicking on a message from an unknown number. "It's definitely faster than walking."

"Or a tractor. I can't drive but I reckon if you're in a tractor everything else gets out of the way for you. Do you think a tractor has gears, like a car..."

Nat continues chattering but I can't really hear her any more.

The human brain consists of eighty per cent water, and for the first time in my life that's exactly what mine feels like: as if it's swishing and swirling around inside my head. My ears fill with the roaring sound you get when you sit at the bottom of a swimming pool.

Because I've just received this:

Hope you smashed your final exam. Would love to talk. Thinking of you. Nick x

18

<u>Reasons Not to Think About Nick</u>

1. He told me not to.
2. I have much more life-changing things to think about.
3. It's all I do.

January 22nd (156 days ago)

"A seagull," Nick said, leaning his head against the rope of my tyre-swing.

We were both wrapped up in big coats and scarves; I was wearing the big furry hat I got from Russia with the flaps in the sides. I leant back and looked at him, pointing at the faint scar just above his eyebrow. "A *seagull* gave you that?"

"Yeah. So I wrestled it to the ground with my bare hands. Then another seagull joined in so I fought that too. By the end there were, like, fifteen seagulls, all totally defeated. They called me Seagull Dundee after that."

I narrowed my eyes. "How old were you?"

"Four. I was a very strong little boy."

I laughed. "Now tell me the truth."

Nick's mouth curved up at the corner. "I cannot *believe* you don't trust that I wrestled fifteen seagulls with my bare hands before I was out of kindergarten. What kind of rubbish girlfriend are you?"

"The kind with quite detailed knowledge of seagulls, unfortunately for you. No knowledge of boys but it balances out."

He shouted with laughter. "I *knew* I should have gone for the girl on the Dolce & Gabbana shoot." Then he pushed my swing a few times while I stuck my tongue out at him. "OK. What actually happened is I ran away from my parents when we were collecting rocks at the beach. I was pretty tiny so I didn't get very far, but a massive seagull freaked me out and I fell over and smacked my head on a rock. When I woke up a few minutes later, it was standing on my chest."

"Were you scared?"

"No. Heroes don't get scared." Nick thought about it. "One of us definitely pooped, though. I'm pretty sure it was the seagull."

I laughed again. "I hate seagulls. Did you know that they're so smart that they hang around bridges so they can steal the heat coming off the roads, and that they tap on the ground with their feet and pretend to be rain so earthworms come out?"

"That doesn't surprise me at all. They're so sneaky."

"How big was this one?"

"The size of a tiger. Comparatively, anyway."

I tried to imagine Nick small and frightened, but I couldn't quite do it. "So what gave you the scar? The rock or the seagull?"

"The rock. Although the seagull got really close to my face too. Really, really close. Like, this close." Nick suddenly stopped the swing and put his face near mine.

I held my breath. I could see the different shades of black and brown in his eyes, and the tangle of black lashes underneath them. I could see my hat reflected in his pupils. I could see the little mole on his cheek and smell the greenness which – I had finally managed to establish – was the result of a fondness for lime shower gel combined with a tendency to constantly sit on wet grass in his jeans.

"That's pretty close," I just about managed to say as he put his hand gently on my cheek and brushed away a bit of hat fluff.

"Yup," Nick said with a smile that went up in one

corner and seemed to stretch out forever. His hand stayed where the fluff had been. "But not quite close enough to hurt me."

And he leant in and kissed me.

19

Scientists say that music can literally change the speed of a heartbeat. They failed to add:

So can a text message.

It's as if Nick is suddenly in the room with me.

I drop the phone.

"Harriet? What's going on?"

Humans are supposed to have 70,000 thoughts a day; I'm about to hit my limit in four and a half seconds.

"It's Nick," I summarise.

"*Seriously?*" Nat grabs the phone off me and reads the message. Then she chucks it back to me, jumps off the bed and starts folding a jumper messily.

I'm breathing too fast and my heart is starting to skitter around like Bambi on a frozen lake. My entire body is suddenly full of a triumphant, almost painful buzzing sensation. What did I *tell* you? It wasn't a matter of *if* he was going to change his mind. It was just a matter of *when*.

Although I'm going to be honest: he really took his time. We're not Jane Eyre and Mr Rochester, for goodness' sake. I could have set up an entire school since we last spoke.

I jump off the bed, spin around the room and start hugging my phone to my chest. "Should I ring him now, Nat?" I say breathlessly, breaking off just long enough to kiss my phone and start hugging it again. "Or should I text? What do you think he wants me to do? Do you think he's coming straight here from Australia?" My eyes widen and I fly to the window. "Oh my God, Nat. What if he's already here?"

I push the window open and then remember that I'm at Nat's house. He's very unlikely to come here first. I need to go home and get ready *right now*. I need to wash my hair. I need to clear away my chemistry kit.

I start putting my shoes on.

"How long should I wait until I reply to look cool?" I continue breathlessly. "Five minutes? Ten minutes? An hour?"

I'm so excited I can't get my shoelaces to tie up properly. "Or should I just ring now? I don't want him to get the wrong impression."

I look at the text again. The answer to these

questions must be in here somewhere. Maybe it's in code. Maybe it's a haiku. Allegory? For goodness' sake, I've studied English literature for five whole years. I can analyse the imagery in *Macbeth* and the symbolism in *Hamlet*. I should be able to work *this* out.

"You know what?" I decide. "I think I'll just ring him straight away. I can't wait any longer."

My phone abruptly disappears.

"Like hell you will," Nat snaps, and before I know it she's standing on her bed, violently waving my mobile in the air like some kind of rectangular hand grenade. "You'll have to kill me first."

I stare at my best friend. It's only now that I notice her cheeks are bright pink, and her hands are shaking. Her angry rash is starting to climb up her chest. And it's only now that I notice she's folded and unfolded the same jumper five times. "What on earth are you talking about?"

"You're not contacting Nick," she says loudly. "I'll eat this phone if I have to. And the charger."

I'm not sure that's even physically possible. "*What*? Why?"

"Because you need to wake up, Harriet."

I blink and then look down at myself. "I'm pretty sure I'm awake, Nat."

"This isn't an epic romance. It's just a boy who used you. A boy who made you forget about everything that was important to you before he came along. You've read so many books you can't even tell the difference between fiction and reality any more."

I flinch. Just because I sometimes use the words 'thou' and 'mayst' for fun does not mean I think I'm in an Austen novel. Not all the time, anyway.

"I can," I say indignantly. "I am well aware of the difference between what's real and what isn't." I'd be prettier in a book, for starters. "Give me my phone right now."

I jump for her, like some kind of killer whale trying to get a particularly nice seal.

"Harriet," Nat says urgently, moving a little further away. "Nick hasn't contacted you for *two months*. He *dumped* you weeks before the most important exams of your life and ran away. That's not what somebody who cares about you does. You have to believe me. I understand boys better than you do."

I flinch again and something in me pinches slightly. "You might know boys in general," I say defiantly. "But you don't know Nick. He cares about me. I know he does."

I jump for her again and miss.

"He doesn't," Nat says, moving until she's pressed against the wall and holding me back with a foot. "He's an idiot and I'm not letting him suck you back in with his pointy cheekbones and his pointy hipbones and his stupid pointy hair. *No*."

Fury suddenly surges through me. My best friend is acting like some kind of crazy, masterminding puppeteer. She's calling my Lion Boy an idiot. She's just reminded me about his lovely hipbones.

And – most of all – I'm furious that a very tiny part of me suspects she might be right.

"*Natalie!*" I yell. "Nat! Give me my phone NOW!"

"Don't make me do this," Nat shouts, and her cheeks get even pinker. "For once in your life just listen to me, Harriet."

"*Give me my phone!*" I shout again, and – with a lurch of my stomach – I suddenly know what Nat's going to do.

If she gets rid of that text, I will have no way of contacting him. I deleted Nick's number so I wouldn't be tempted to text him after he left. He doesn't 'do' social media. And I can't remember his email address.

He'll give up on me.

And if that happens, I'm not sure our ten-year friendship will survive. More importantly, I'm not sure

Nat will. There's a really good chance I'll just kill my best friend on the spot.

There's a red dot in the centre of each of Nat's cheeks. "I'm doing this for you," she announces, tapping the screen. "I honestly am."

"*No!*" I yell, and bundle myself at her legs in an attempt to desperately wrestle my phone out of her hands. Nat scrabbles away while I hold on to her feet, and the next thing I know she's only wearing one sock and there's yet another rip in my bridesmaid's dress.

By the time I've finally managed to claw my phone back, we're huffing and puffing and scratched and bright red all over and it's too late.

The message has gone.

My last chance with Nick has gone with it.

You really don't want to know what I say next.

Let's just put it this way: in no way do I leave my feelings about the situation open to interpretation. I am very clear about every single one of them.

I end the conversation by telling Nat I hope she doesn't get eaten by French chickens in a way that very much intimates the opposite, and then storm out of the house.

"Harriet?" Nat yells out of the window as I stomp down the road, silk dress rippling after me. "I'm *sorry.* I lost my temper! I shouldn't have done that!"

"No," I yell back, without turning round, "you shouldn't!"

Then I keep stomping. What kind of friend *does* that?

Who the sugar cookies does Nat think she *is*?

20

For the next couple of days, I simply refuse to leave my room.

There's no point. The alternative is to watch my parents take all my impeccably arranged books out of the study and pile them in a not-even-vaguely alphabetical order outside my door.

By the time it gets to Friday afternoon, I'm so sick of hearing Dad say "*another* book of random quotations? Seriously?" I decide to go for a long, cathartic walk. My ex-best friend will be in France by now, getting chased about by Mr Green Lycra Cycling Shorts.

Good. Serves her right.

I hope he doesn't even use proper virgin olive oil, and opts for low-grade cooking oil instead.

Unfortunately my stress-reducing exercise efforts are ruined within two minutes by a small, fluffy-headed figure creeping from tree to tree in front of me. I have to keep looking in the opposite direction so I don't hurt his feelings.

"Toby," I finally say as I turn back on to my road. He flattens himself behind a lamp-post considerably thinner than he is. "I can see you."

"Are you sure?"

"Pretty sure, yes."

"Oh dear," he says sadly. "My homemade camouflage stalker kit may need some more work." He points at his grey T-shirt and grey trousers. They have faint black lines drawn on them in criss-crosses.

I stare at him, and then totally give up. "What on earth are you camouflaged *as*?"

"Pavement." Toby lies down on the floor and holds himself very rigid and still. "See? It's only for urban settings, obviously. It wouldn't work in the countryside."

I laugh and carefully step over him.

"Harriet," he says, jumping up and running after me. "Are you and Natalie OK? I couldn't help overhearing a small amount of very loud fighting the other day when I was sitting in the rhododendron outside her house waiting for you to come out."

Clearly Toby hasn't moved on quite as much as I thought he had. "I've had an unexpected best-friend position open up," I say tensely. "Would you like it?"

"*Would I?*" Toby shouts, jumping up and down. "I mean, *I would*. Just to make that clear."

"Great," I say sharply. "We're now Best Friends. We can go and get some badges made up or something."

Toby bounces along next to me in contented silence, and then sighs. "I'm afraid I don't think I can take the job, Harriet," he says sadly. "You and Natalie are soulmates, except you don't kiss. It would be wrong to try to ever separate you."

I make an ambiguous snorting noise. Soulmates are usually happy for each other when supermodel ex-boyfriends text them. "Either way, now I'm not going to Tokyo, it's just you and me this summer."

"Actually, maybe not," Toby says solemnly.

I'm already thinking about my abandoned Summer of Fun Flow Chart. Maybe I can re-use it after all. I just need to find the right colour pen so I can cross out *Nat* and replace it with *Toby* and my holiday will be none the wiser. "Hmmm?"

"I think you already have a visitor."

My stomach suddenly flips and every hair on my body stands on end. *Nick?*

I look up. There's a bright pink Beetle parked outside my house.

The hairs flatten back down again. Oh no. No no. No no no no – I turn around and start walking in the opposite direction.

"Harriet?" a voice calls. "Come and give your favourite old person a nice big cuddle."

And there – standing in the doorway covered in bells and sequins, like some kind of summery Christmas tree – is my grandmother.

I just want to make something perfectly clear.

There are many, many other old people I prefer to this one. My grandad, for instance. Nat's grandad. Nat's grandma. My old piano teacher, Mr Henry. The ancient lady who works in the local newsagent and gives me free sweets without being asked.

It's not that I don't love my grandmother. I just don't really know her very well.

Or at all, actually.

"Sweetie!" she says as I approach with tiny steps, the way you might a rampaging hippopotamus. "Your hair is even redder than it used to be!" She sweeps me into her arms and all the bells on her wrists tinkle like she's an enormous cat. "From a distance it looks like your head is on fire!"

I think I'm about to get an embroidered daisy

imprinted permanently on my forehead. "It's strawberry blonde," I tell her left breast as politely as I can. She smells of wood and beetroot.

"Look how mucky you are!" she laughs, pulling back and spitting on her long wizard-like sleeve. Before I can escape she starts scrubbing it hard on my nose. "Oops. No. They're freckles, just like Richard's. Adorable! How long has it been since I saw you last? Five months? Six?"

"Three and a half years," I say, staring over her shoulder at my parents who have finally emerged. Needless to say, Annabel's eating. This time it appears to be toast with Neapolitan ice cream spread in a layer on top.

"Whoopsy," my grandmother says, beaming at us. "I took over a coconut stall in India for an afternoon and next thing I knew I was running a *roaring* backpacker trade. Good for copious amounts of diarrhoea, coconut water."

Toby races forwards with his hand out. "I am Toby Pilgrim, Harriet's stalker. Nice to meet you, Mrs Grandmother Manners."

"Bunty," she says cheerfully, shaking it.

"And on that exciting note," Toby says, wiping his nose on his finger, "I shall make my dramatic exit. I've got this new plate with a face on it and Mum's made spaghetti so I'm eager to get home while it's still hot and malleable enough to form realistic hair."

Then Toby promptly waves and scoots back out of the door. We all try to pretend that we can't see him immediately crouch down behind the hedge right outside.

"I didn't know you were coming." I look at my parents with round eyes. Does nobody tell me *anything* these days?

"Well, if somebody needs to take you abroad it might as well be somebody who spends most of her time there, right?"

I stare at her, then I stare at my parents, and then I stare at my grandmother again. *What?*

"Apparently Tokyo is the place to be this summer," she grins. "I think we should check it out, don't you?"

I suddenly don't care that I've probably met my nomadic grandmother a handful of times in my entire life. I don't care that her hair is sort of baby pink, and I don't care that she currently has what looks like a twig stuck in it.

I don't even care that the last time I saw her we had a forty-five-minute conversation about the benefits of wiping your bottom with your hand instead of a piece of toilet paper to 'save the rainforest'.

"Oh my God, I *love* you!" I yell, throwing myself around her neck. "Thank you! Thank you thank you thank you!"

"Now, *that's* the greeting I was looking for."

Then I lob myself at Dad, and then – a little bit more carefully, in case I squish my sibling – at Annabel. "Thank you! Thank you thank you! You've *saved* my summer! Totally saved it!"

Dad laughs. "How could we argue with a Powerpoint presentation of such quality, Harriet? We're not *monsters.*" He puts his hand over his mouth. "*She's* a monster," he pretends to whisper, pointing at Annabel. "But *I'm* not."

"Go upstairs and get your things packed for tomorrow, Harriet," Annabel says calmly, ignoring Dad. "I imagine your grandmother will want to help you write a brand-new Summer of Fun Flow Chart."

"What's a flow chart?" my grandmother asks. "Does it rank rivers?"

Good Lord. I'm going to have to start training her immediately. "We have new plans to make!" I shout, running up the stairs. "Itineraries! Schedules! Lists! Lists and lists and lists and—"

"Look, Harriet," my grandmother says as she follows behind me, pointing at the garden. "A squirrel!"

"Make sure she has everything she needs," Annabel calls after us.

"My darling daughter," Bunty calls down the stairs. "That's the beauty of foreign travel. You don't need anything but yourself."

"And a passport, Mum," I hear Annabel say tiredly. "And tickets. And a visa. And clean clothes and quite a few changes of underwear."

Uh-huh.

If you thought you saw a marked family resemblance between my maverick grandmother and my maverick father, you would be wrong.

Bunty isn't Dad's mum.

She's Annabel's.

21

My entire summer has just turned around.

And, as I start jubilantly packing all the important things into a suitcase – paper, dictionaries, pens, etc – I suddenly remember that I wrote Nick's email address on an old bit of paper and tucked it into an ancient copy of *Anne of Green Gables* months and months ago. *Ha.* I am so much more cunning and better organised with contact details than Nat gives me credit for.

As *if* I'd let go of Nick that easily.

Mentally high-fiving myself, I think about it carefully and then write the following email on my phone:

Dear Nick,

Got your message. Would love to talk. I've been thinking about you lots! Of course I have! Am going to Japan for a few weeks for a modelling job but taking my phone with me. Send me another message or ring me? Or ask Wilbur and he can give you my new address?

I'VE MISSED YOU SO MUCH. :)
Harriet xxxx

I look at it happily – he *definitely* can't misread or misinterpret that in any way – and then press SEND. Now it's just a matter of time before Nick tracks me down and I have the best, most romantic summer *ever*.

I spend the next twenty minutes contentedly bouncing around my room as if I'm on an enormous imaginary Spacehopper: scanning travel documents, printing them out and arranging them carefully in alphabetical order. I make a list of all the lists I need to make. I sit Bunty on my bed, and read her fascinating snippets from a Visit Japan website: "Did you know that the word *karaoke* means *empty orchestra*?" and "Can you believe it used to be customary in ancient Japan for women to blacken their teeth with dye to make them look less toothy!"

My grandmother, in the meantime, sits on the windowsill and makes comments like: "Oooh – your glasses are making a rainbow on the wall, Harriet, isn't that just *magical*?"

I'm so ridiculously happy, I don't even feel the need

to explain the difference between 'magic' and 'refraction'. I bounce around hysterically until I remember I left my laptop downstairs. I'm probably going to need it at some stage so I can look up additional facts *in situ*.

With an unprecedented degree of physical dexterity, I bound down the stairs to get it.

"Annabel?" I chirp. "Dad? Did I leave my laptop in—" Then I stop, because they're sitting at the kitchen table with their heads together, talking in low voices.

And all I can hear is the word 'Harriet'.

22

Here's the thing: my parents *never* talk in low voices.

Especially not to each other.

Now, obviously everybody knows that listening in on other people's conversations never comes to any good. You usually end up hearing something you're not supposed to hear or getting stabbed to death like Polonius in *Hamlet.* So the most sensible thing to do right now is interrupt my parents immediately, or leave before the conversation goes any further.

I have no explanation for why I duck behind the living-room wall and breathe as quietly as I can.

"I'm just so *exhausted*, Rich," Annabel continues. "It feels like I'm wading through a thick river of treacle all of the time."

"You're not," Dad says reassuringly. "Judging by the state of our cupboards, I'm pretty sure you'd have eaten that too."

Then I hear the sound of a gentle smack round the head. "Seriously," Annabel says, "I had no idea reproduction would be so much work. I would pay really good money to be a reptile or a chicken right now."

Dad laughs. "You're not doing this alone, Bels." There's a *swoosh*, which sounds like a shoulder being rubbed. "I'm not going anywhere. I'm tying myself to you like a mitten to its other mitten."

"Thank you, sweetheart."

"Through the coat sleeve of life. With the string of love."

Annabel laughs. "OK, I think that's enough of the mitten analogy."

There's the sound of a long, sloppy kiss, and I can feel myself making a *blurgh* face. According to statistics and what I overheard while waiting outside Parents' Evening, everyone else has parents that are only together For The Sake Of The Children. It makes me feel a bit awkward, knowing that mine have a relationship that is so flagrantly nothing to do with me. They could at least *pretend* to have no interest in each other.

I'm just getting ready to interrupt when Dad says, "But it still doesn't answer the question. What about Harriet?"

I abruptly stop breathing.

Annabel sighs. "I don't know, Rich. I just don't know. After today" – I can hear her tapping on the table anxiously with a biro – "She can be such hard work sometimes, you know. I don't think I can handle any more. It's my first baby, and you know I love her to pieces but…"

My whole body goes numb. But? *But?*

There isn't supposed to be a 'but'.

I poke my head around the edge of the door just in time to see Annabel put her head in her hands as Dad gently kisses the top of her head. "I just think it's best for everyone if she's not here."

23

The human brain consists of 200 billion nerve cells. In the cerebral cortex alone there are 125 trillion synapses, which is roughly the amount of stars as in 1,500 Milky Way galaxies. It feels like every single one of them is exploding simultaneously.

They're not sending me away for me. They're sending me away for *them.*

Suddenly every thought I've been pushing out of my head for six months is roaring in, the way air rushes into a vacuum. *This* is what I've been scared of. This is what has been building and building, and squashing my excitement about the baby. That the mother panda would choose, and she wouldn't choose me.

And this is just the start, isn't it?

In a year or two, it will take my room.

It will take my bed and my dog.

It will take the slice of sunshine by the window where I sit when I'm reading.

It'll take the bit at the back of the cupboard where I keep my old train set and the loose floorboard where I hide my poems and the shelf where I keep my dictionaries.

It'll take my hook in the bathroom and my time slot in the shower and the pencil lines on the side of the door that have taken nearly sixteen years to draw.

It will take my dad throwing them about in a swimming pool and messing up their hair and being an idiot.

It will take all of Annabel.

And nudge by nudge, I'll be pushed further and further away. Until I'm all on my own.

I lean against the hallway wall, breathing hard through my mouth. Then, quietly, cautiously, I open the box in my head that I haven't touched in six months.

Carefully – one by one – I start putting people inside. I put in Annabel and Dad. I put in the baby. I put in Nat. Finally, I close the lid of the box and sit on it.

It's just best for everyone if she's not here.

If that's how they feel, I'll go somewhere else. Somewhere better. Somewhere more exciting. I'll see the world, and I'll do it by myself.

Because that's the thing about a transformation: there's no stopping it. Once the tadpole has legs it jumps out of the pond. Once the caterpillar has wings, it flies away.

And once you've metamorphosed, you can't go back.

Even if you want to.

24

Agreement of Responsibility

THIS AGREEMENT is made between Annabel Manners and Bunty Brown, with reference to the guardianship of Harriet Manners as agreed to by Richard Manners, witness and father.

THEREFORE, intending to be legally bound hereby, the parties agree as follows:

- Bunty Brown will act like a mature and responsible adult, regardless of how fervently she believes that 'age is just a number'.
- Bunty Brown will acknowledge the fact that Harriet Manners is a minor and will accompany her AT ALL TIMES. She will not wander off because she sees something sparkly or rare or 'feels like it, darling'.
- Bunty Brown will not discuss with Harriet

Manners anything she did or did not do in the sixties.

- Or the seventies.
- Or the eighties.
- Bunty Brown will not attempt to convert Harriet Manners to: Druidism, Paganism, Zoroastrianism, Baha'i, Prince Philip Movement, Scientology, Buddhism, Taoism, Sikhism, Islam, Hinduism, Confucianism, Christianity, Shinto, Judaism, Wicca, or any other belief system that Bunty Brown is currently devoted to.
- Bunty Brown will not pierce, henna, tie-dye or attach flowers, feathers or sequins to any part of Harriet Manners.
- Bunty Brown will put Harriet Manners first.

Signed:

ANNABEL MANNERS

Bunty Brown

~~SpiderMan Brad Pitt~~ Richard Manners

25

The next seventeen hours can be summarised thus:

- I avoid my parents.

And that's it.

By the time Annabel and Dad have waved goodbye with the happiest facial expressions I've ever seen on adults, I'm so desperate to go I don't even care that they can't take me to the airport because of a hospital appointment.

Even though we all know that by *hospital* they mean *Harriet leaving* and by *appointment* they mean *massive party.* And by 'tidying up' they mean *blowing up balloons and turning my bedroom into an impromptu home cinema.*

I promise to ring them as soon as I arrive and then focus on:

a) Studying for the entire car journey.

b) Trying not to get knocked out by Bunty's pink dream-catcher, swinging merrily from the rear-view mirror.

By the time we reach the airport, I've managed to distract myself completely by acquiring a good ten to fifteen Japanese words *and* working out a detailed itinerary. Shrines I want to light incense at and theatres I want to visit and food I want to eat and parasitological museums I want to take photos of and show to Toby.

So when my grandmother and I walk into the airport departures lounge and there's a high-pitched squeal, I don't even turn around. That's how much I've forgotten what it is I'm actually supposed to be doing here.

"Co-eeee, my little Monster Munches!" a voice shouts. A man in a leopard-print onesie and pink wellies starts stomping enthusiastically towards us. "I've been waiting for minutes and minutes and I was spectacularly bored so I went to the Duty Free. *Smell me!* Close your eyes and I'm unwanted Christmas soap!" He wafts in a jutting, pigeon-like circular motion, and then holds his hand out to my grandmother. "*Enchanté*," he adds, curtsying deeply. "Which is French for *enchanted* because they obviously stole it from us, the naughty little Munchkins."

I stare at Wilbur in bewilderment. "Erm, they didn't," I say. "Both *enchanté* and *enchanted* come from the Latin verb *incantare*, which means *to cast spells*. Hello, Wilbur. Are you coming with us?"

I can't decide if I'm delighted or not. I love Wilbur, but in combination with my grandmother?

"Wilbur," he says, pushing me aside and kissing Bunty's hand. "That's with a *bur*, and not with an *iam*. I'm agent to this little chicken-monkey." He points at me, just in case anyone gets confused with all the other chicken-monkeys in the immediate vicinity.

"Bunty," my grandmother smiles, totally unfazed.

He points to my grandmother's pink floral dress with lace trim, beige, fringed blanket and mirrored waistcoat. "I am *loving* this. What are we calling it?"

My grandmother's eyes twinkle. "Spangled Nepalese goat-herder disco-dances by river in moonlight?"

"Oh my *holy dolphin-cakes*!" Wilbur shouts at the top of his voice. "That is superlatively *fantabulazing*! Could I borrow the waistcoat one day?"

"You can have it now, if you like," Bunty says, taking it off and handing it over. "I have dozens."

"*You!*" Wilbur squeaks, putting it on over his onesie and spinning around in little circles. "If you were liquid I would just pour you all over ice cream and sprinkle you with hundreds and thousands and gobble you up! You would be *hell* on my waistline and *laden* with calories but *I just wouldn't care.*"

See what I mean?

"Are you coming with us?" I repeat politely as my grandmother beams and then wanders towards some fluffy key rings in a nearby shop.

"No, my little Turkish delight. I'm just here to prep you."

I frown. "Wilbur—" How do I put this nicely? "At no stage at any point in my entire modelling career have you ever prepared me for anything. Ever." I pause. "Like, *ever.*"

Wilbur's eyes open wide. "I am *hurt*," he says with his hand on his chest. "Nay, *wounded*. Nay – what's another word for hurt, my little Carrier-bag?"

"Offended? Stung? Aggrieved?"

"*Précisement*. How can you say I am ever anything but one hundred per cent professional?"

"For my last photo shoot you sent me to your dentist."

"They had *very* similar business cards and I thought I'd just seen Sting walk past and it was all very confusing." Wilbur tries to look indignant, and then sighs. "OK. I'm a terrible, terrible agent. But this time it's mahoosive, Sugar-plum. Like, Calvin Klein mahoosive. Like, *mamoosive* mahoosive. Yuka's broken away from Baylee to start up her own label. It's huge, Peach-plum, and I need to make sure we're all on the same page."

I suddenly feel a bit sick. You can look at it any way you like, but last time I attempted to model I ended up covered in gold paint and attached to a curtain rod. "She's launching her new label with me?"

Wilbur starts giggling. "Oh, bunny, you *do* crack me down the middle. Can you imagine?"

I patiently wait for him to stop being so insulting.

"No: the main" – he pretends to cough – "*taller* models are being flown out today to China, Hong Kong, Macau, South Korea..."

"Mongolia and Taiwan?"

He abruptly stops laughing. "How do you know that?"

"They're the seven countries in East Asia, excluding North Korea." Wilbur's gone a strange, pale shade of mustard. "It was just a guess. Are you OK?"

Wilbur breathes out hard. "This is all top secret, Moo-noo. We need to get the campaign done before Yuka tells Baylee she's leaving. If I can just organise it" – he leans forward slightly and grabs my shoulders – "Poodle, it might be my way out of here."

"Yuka won't let you out of the *airport?*"

Wilbur starts giggling again. "Out of *agenting*, my little Nutmeg. She's *finally* going to give me a position with her new label."

I don't know why I'm so surprised. Adults almost never like doing their jobs from what I can tell.

"I like being an agent, but I'm shockingly bad at it, Muffin-top. Anyway, I didn't get a degree in fashion so I could sit at a desk, trying to talk to pretty women. If I wanted to do that, I'd have got a job in a normal office."

Wilbur straightens out the waistcoat. "This is our chance, Bunny. Yours, and mine." He pauses. "Mostly mine, because let's be honest: I'm an adult with a proper career and I'd imagine your shelf life as a teen model is almost over."

For the last twenty-four hours, I've thought about a lot of things. I've thought about how far away Japan is (5,937 miles), and how bad I am at eating with chopsticks (very) and my chances of dying in an air crash (1 in 10.46 million). I've thought about how many Hello Kittys I'm going to buy for Nat (zero: they creep her out) and how many vending machines there are for every person in Japan (23).

But it hadn't occurred to me that I might actually have to *model* when I got there. That it would be important to a lot of people. Or that I would be totally out of my depth. *Again.*

"OK," I stammer nervously. "I'll try my very hardest."

Wilbur sighs. "I know you will, Baby-baby Panda," he says, pinching my cheek. "And that is *exactly* what I'm worried about."

26

By the time we get through the security gates, I'm so excited and nervous, I feel like a shark. As if I can't stop moving or I'll die.

Or talking, for that matter.

Which is less like a shark, but does a similar job in making people try to get away from me as fast as possible.

"I'm going to Japan," I tell the man standing by the electric buggies. "I'm going to Japan," I tell the lady behind the counter at Boots. "I'm going to Japan," I tell the man who gives me a sandwich at Pret A Manger.

"I'm going on my lunch break," he replies, immediately entering into the spirit of things.

Everything is suddenly fascinating. The air-hostess uniforms. The scarily round bread rolls. The little packs with free socks and toothbrushes. The fact that you can pop the edges of the headrests out. Even the in-flight safety procedure brochure is – you guessed it – fascinating.

I think I may be over-stimulated.

"Haven't you been on a plane before?" Bunty laughs when I finish breathlessly pointing at random landmarks below us so that I can click the cup holder in and out of the seat in front of me repeatedly.

"I have, but never without—" I swallow. *My parents or Nat.* "Not long distance before. Did you know that the chances of being in a plane crash are less than 0.00001 per cent? That means that you're more likely to be killed by a donkey or to naturally conceive *identical* quadruplets."

Bunty pulls a blanket over her knees. "Is that so?"

"Uh-huh." The lights of London are starting to melt below us into a large, sparkly neon puddle. "They test plane windscreens by throwing chickens at them at five hundred miles per hour so they know they can resist errant flying birds. Once a chicken went *through* the window and smashed the pilot's chair in half. They realised afterwards they'd accidentally catapulted a frozen one."

Bunty chuckles. "You're so much like Annabel was at your age, darling. Fascinated by the little things."

I immediately look out of the window so Bunty can't see my expression. "Actually, everyone likes facts.

Apparently three million people Google the words 'interesting facts' every single month."

Bunty looks at me then twists up her nose and closes her eyes. "Funny," she says. "That's just what she would have said as well."

And before I can respond, my grandmother is fast asleep.

I fully intend to stay awake for the next fourteen hours. I have a special Flight Bag I put together to keep me entertained: maps to study and crosswords to fill in and quizzes about the flags of Asia (you never know when somebody abroad is going to test you on something like that).

But I get over-excited about the little butter tubs at dinner, peak early and pass out before we've flown over France.

And the next thing I know...

I'm in Japan.

27

Places I Want to Visit

Japan

~~Burma~~ Myanmar

~~Russia~~

I've wanted to come here for so long that when I get the list out of my satchel I can see where I struggled to join up the *a* and the *n* and there's blue glitter in the creases from when Nat threw it over everything for a term at primary school.

I'm finally here.

Within minutes of landing, it feels like I have new eyes, new ears, a new nose, a new tongue, new skin. People are talking in a language I don't understand, making gestures I've never seen before and eating food I don't recognise. There are signs I can't read, and smells I can't place, and a hum that sounds entirely different to England. Even the colours look different: there's a slightly golden glow to everything, instead of the silveriness of a summer in England. I may as well have landed on the moon.

Apart from the whole gravity element. Or I'd just be floating through the airport and it would be really hard to hang on to my suitcase.

"Enormous fun, isn't it?" Bunty says as I stand, blinking, in the middle of a tiny shop. She waves a couple of bright pink snacks with angry cartoon octopuses drawn on them at me. "Have one of these. It will blow your mind."

I've just seen a sandwich filled with whipped cream and strawberries, a drink called 'Sweat' and an entire dried squid vacuum-packed into a bag. The inside of my head has already exploded.

In a daze, I take the snack from her – it's like an enormous, fishy Wotsit – and then watch a group of schoolgirls roughly my age, standing in a little huddle in a corner. They're all wearing *exactly* the same outfit: the same skirts at the same length, the same socks, the same shirts, the same shoes, the same backpacks. They have no make-up on and one of two hairstyles: black, with a fringe in a ponytail, or black, cut short and pushed behind their ears. There's no cunning personalisation; no fashionable editing or skirt-rolling or high-heel wearing or lipgloss sneaking. It's stupidly disorientating, considering it's the precise definition of the word *uniform.*

They're all studying maps and staring, wide-eyed, around them, so I don't think they're from Tokyo. Then they spot me and their eyes get even bigger. A few start squeaking *kawwaaaaiiiiiiii* and giggling. I promptly fall over my suitcase and am met with a collection of even louder giggles, and a few squeaks of *chhhoooo kawwaaiiiii, ne*?

I have no idea what they're saying, obviously, but it doesn't feel mean.

I blush slightly and give a little shy wave. They blush and start waving shyly back. Then I notice that one of them has a little dinosaur key ring hanging off their satchel. Another has a little Winnie the Pooh, and a third a small fluffy duck.

Oh my God: is *this* where I belong? I have spent an entire lifetime struggling to fit in only to discover that all the other tidy, shy teenage girls with neat ankle socks and no make-up and a fondness for satchel accessories live on the other side of the world.

Maybe I'll ask if one of them can adopt me.

I give another shy wave and then follow Bunty outside.

We walk through a wall of intense, pulsing, dense

heat and climb into the back of a taxi.

Then we start the slow, winding drive into the heart of Tokyo.

I have literally never seen a city more *awake.*

Lights are flashing. People are everywhere. The smell of frying is coming from all directions. Everything is pushed together and jumbled up: streets and paths and roads, winding up and down and over each other like an enormous Scalextric set. The buildings get taller and taller, and – tucked away like secrets – there are tiny wooden temples and flowers and trees, peeking out like grass between pavement slabs.

Everything is moving and glowing and beeping: signs, shops, restaurants, T-shirts, pedestrian crossings, all flickering and lit up and coloured and singing.

It's as if the entire city and everything in it has just drunk eight cups of coffee and is going to spend the rest of the night shaking, feeling really sick and staring at the ceiling. (I did this with Nat a few months ago. It wasn't as much fun as we thought it would be.)

As I stare out of the window to my left, there's a shop display with a purple unicorn in it, wearing tiny orange trainers and a rhinestone saddle. A few minutes later there's a car covered in thousands of diamonds. To my right, ballerina mannequins hang from silver threads.

A group of men wearing grey suits walk past, with a man wearing red tartan in the middle.

A woman dressed as a rabbit waves at us.

And every time the taxi stops at a light, it's all I can do not to open the car door, jump out and swirl around the middle of the road with my hands stretched out, like Julie Andrews in *The Sound of Music.* Except with a much greater chance of being hit by a car and a much smaller chance of falling off the top of a mountain.

I've researched Japan for an entire decade. I've looked at photos and memorised facts and stuck maps on my wall. I've printed things off the internet and ripped pictures out of calendars. But for the first time in my life, studying has let me down. Not a single thing I've read or looked at or studied has ever come close to what it's like actually *being* here.

I stare out of the window in total silence until the car finally pulls into a smaller street with large, grey, grubby concrete blocks and stops halfway along the kerb. The windows have bars across them and there are wooden sticks strewn on the floor with bits of dried chicken still attached to them.

"Ta-da, darling," Bunty announces, flourishing her hands, as if she just pulled a grubby Tokyo suburb out of a black top hat. "Out you hop."

I go to open my door, and then pause. My grandmother looks very seated and her invitation sounds nowhere near as plural as it should do. "Me?"

"No, I'm talking to the cab driver," Bunty laughs. She playfully grabs my arm and shakes it. "Yes, *you,* silly bean."

"Where are *you* going?"

"I thought this would be so much more fun on your own, sweetie. It'll be a real, grown-up adventure. We won't tell your parents. Deal? I'd only cramp your style anyway."

The driver opens my door for me and then starts pulling my suitcase on to the pavement. I climb out with my mouth flapping in confusion. What is she *talking* about? I don't have any style *to* cramp. Does this woman know anything about me at *all*?

"B-but—" I stammer through the gap at the top of the window as the driver gets back in and the engine starts. "What about the contract you signed with Annabel?"

"What's my daughter going to do?" Bunty grins, raising an eyebrow. "Sue me?" And I'm suddenly not at all sure she knows anything about Annabel either.

The car starts moving away.

"W-wait," I shout, unsuccessfully attempting to jog after it. "I don't think that this is… this is a really big… please… I won't… I can't." I swallow. "You can't just *abandon* me on the other side of the world!"

"I'm not abandoning!" Bunty shouts through the window as the car starts driving back up the street. "I'm setting you free! Have a tremendous time, darling! Flat 6B!"

28

According to my guidebook, Tokyo is 2,187 km in area. It has 12.6 million people, twenty-three wards, sixty-two municipalities, 168 tube stations and nine train lines. There are 6,029 people for every square km, and it's the largest metropolitan area in the world. By any stretch of the imagination, it's a pretty big city.

In the last few seconds it just got a whole lot bigger.

I watch the taxi get smaller and smaller until my grandmother disappears completely. Then I take a deep breath, collect whatever enthusiasm I have left and start dragging my suitcase anxiously up the road.

The wheels keep getting stuck in the pavement, it keeps falling over, and by the time I've worked out that the sign for 6B looks like 5E I've walked past it six times and most of my excitement has been left in a sticky trail up and down the road, like a big sad snail.

Finally I clear my throat and press one of the buttons

lined up in two neat rows, like the buttons on a dinner jacket. It crackles, and a fuzzy voice says, "Yes?"

"Umm. My name is Harriet Manners. I think I'm staying here?"

"I'll be right down. Wait there." The crackling abruptly stops, and a few floors above me a door slams.

This is *ridiculous.* I've done exactly as I'm told all my life. Fifteen *years* of not taking sweets off strangers, running with scissors, playing with matches, jumping off swings, petting stray dogs or accepting lifts from people I don't know, and this is how it ends: knocking on the door of a stranger in a darkening alley on the other side of the world with nobody to hear me scream.

If I knew I was going to die like this, I could have relaxed and actually enjoyed my childhood.

I start rifling through my satchel for something to defend myself against my imminent attacker. I'm just tentatively wielding the Pocahontas pen I got from Disneyland in front of my face when the door swings open.

"Oh," the axe murderer says, inhaling sharply, and I drop my weapon.

Because standing in front of me, in black jeans and a grey vest, is the most beautiful girl I have ever seen.

29

When Nat and I were seven we realised we would never be princesses.

I had thousands of freckles and ginger hair, and everybody knew that nobody with either of those things ever got rescued from a tower. They got left there for all eternity, and thus ended their royal bloodline.

Nat had unruly black hair, dark skin and the beginnings of what her mother would later describe as a monobrow. It was generally acknowledged that princesses had complexions like fruit and two eyebrows, clearly distinct from each other. So that excluded her as well.

The tall girl standing in front of me now is precisely what we concluded princesses should look like. Huge mesmerising blue eyes, flawless skin, a pouty mouth, pale golden hair in waves down to her waist. An aura of goodness and an ability to engage in conversation with animals. A ray of sunshine, hitting her head like a halo. (I have no idea how she's found one, it's almost totally dark outside.)

Any second now, rabbits are going to start leaping around her feet in pairs and a bluebird is going to land on her shoulder.

"Hello," she says, sounding utterly delighted, and I realise that she's even more English than I am. "I'm Poppy. You're *so* not what I was expecting."

"H-Harriet Manners," I stutter, taking her hand. "It's nice to meet you, umm..." and I finish the sentence by fading into silence and staring rudely over her shoulder. Part of me is still expecting to see seven miniature men wandering around the hallway.

"I'm *so* happy to finally meet you," she says, taking my suitcase and wheeling it into the hallway. "My boyfriend's always so busy. Anyway, it's just not the same, is it? They just don't want to talk about girly things."

Oh, God. I suspect I'm about to prove an enormous disappointment.

"Umm..." I desperately start racking my brain for a subject that will make this girl like me. "Did you know that high heels for women in the West are believed to have originated with Catherine De Medici in the sixteenth century? She was about to marry King

Henry of France and wanted him to think she was taller than she actually was."

Poppy looks at me with wide eyes, and I remember why in fifteen years I have only managed to make one female friend.

"But in the Middle East," I continue nervously, "heels were used to lift the foot from the burning sand."

"How adorable!" Poppy giggles. "What else?"

What else?

That's not an answer I'm usually prepared for. I've pretty much run out of shoe-based facts. "Did you know that Neil Armstrong took his boots off and left them on the moon to compensate for the weight of the moon rocks they took?"

"Amazing!" Poppy claps a few times, and then pulls my suitcase across the hallway towards a bright green door.

She beams at me – a genuine, open, beautiful smile. I blink and look down at my battered suitcase, crumpled dinosaur T-shirt and tracksuit bottoms. I'm sticky with sweat from dragging my suitcase about, and even without lifting my arms I can tell that I smell a bit like Hugo when he's been out in the rain. This must be how Regan and Goneril felt around Cordelia in *King Lear.*

I think I'm starting to understand why they put her in prison.

"Rin?" Poppy calls, pushing the door open and manoeuvring my suitcase through the doorway with a graceful flick of her wrist. I try to hop over it and smash my ankle against the wheel. "*Harriet* is here! Come and say hello."

There's a clatter, and an incredibly pretty Japanese girl runs out of one of the rooms. Her hair is massive, waist-length and elaborately curled. She's wearing a pink flowery dress with lace trim and buttons all the way down the front, and white ankle socks with pink ribbons. A large, pink toy duck is attached on a clip to a belt covered in sequins. Her face is perfectly matt with round sparkly cheeks, huge eyelashes and glittery lipstick.

She looks exactly like one of the china dolls Granny Manners used to have on her mantelpiece, except slightly bigger and without a sign in front that says DO NOT TOUCH, HARRIET.

Rin stops in the hallway, breathless. "I go for gift, but I'm not finding it. It has gone walkabouts." She drops into a low bow. "My name is Rin. I am delight to meet you."

"Delight*ed*," Poppy corrects sweetly. "It's delight*ed*, Rin."

Rin looks bewildered. "Who is Ted? He's coming later? I have no present for Ted."

"It's... oh, never mind." Poppy gestures at me to take off my shoes and starts leading me through an incredibly narrow hallway. "We're both models too. This is a model flat, but you probably know that already."

I've suddenly realised why Poppy looks familiar: she was one of the girls I cut out of Nat's magazine. I distinctly remember putting her face in the bin.

"Me also," Rin beams, nodding happily. "Modelling sometime, then and now." She grabs my hand with her tiny, dainty fingers and starts leading me through the minuscule flat. "This is kitchen," she says, pointing to a bathroom with the smallest bathtub I have ever seen. "This is garden." She points to a kitchen. "And this is alive room." She gestures to a room with a very low table and four round cushions.

"Living room," Poppy corrects gently.

"I am very apologising," Rin says, blushing slightly and bowing again. "My English is so bad. I study super hard, but it is not sticky. I – *nandakke* – slurp."

"You don't *suck*." Poppy laughs. "Rin's obsessed with Australia so she's learning English as quickly as possible so she can move there. My boyfriend says she must have been a koala in a past life."

"One day," Rin says in a dreamy voice, "I move to Sydney and get Rip Curls and big BBQ and burn sausages. I shall be a little ropper."

"Ripper," Poppy says automatically, leading us into a teeny tiny bedroom.

Unlike the rest of the flat, it's not Japanese in style at all. There are no sliding doors and soft rush tatami mats: just a solid grey carpet, one set of bunk beds pushed against the corner and an enormous double bed with a mountain of pillows. In the middle of it is a large black cat, wearing a pink flowery dress, little white socks and a pink toy duck, attached to a sequined collar.

"My cat," Rin says unnecessarily, pointing proudly. "Kylie Minogue." The cat assesses me haughtily, licks a sock and goes back to sleep.

"She's on your bed," Poppy says, trying unsuccessfully to push her off. Kylie clearly doesn't agree: she opens one eye, glares at Poppy and tries to dig her claws through the socks into the duvet. "The big one's yours. Rin and I share the bunks."

That doesn't seem fair. I've only just got here. "I can move," I say quickly. "Or we can take turns?"

"No, Harry-chan," Rin says, shaking her head. "You have big VIP job." She says VIP as it looks: *vip.* "You stay here. Super cosy."

Rin picks Kylie up and the cat lets out an enormous disgruntled *squark*.

"I really don't care either," Poppy says, shrugging. Then she catches her reflection in the mirror behind me. "Oh my goodness, my hair. I'm going out with my boyfriend tonight, I should go and start getting ready."

I stare at one maverick gold strand, misbehaving by less than a centimetre, and then at my own rumpled reflection. There are still remnants of aeroplane gravy on my chin.

Poppy starts heading towards the bathroom, and then abruptly turns just in time to catch me surreptitiously trying to reach a splodge with my tongue stretched out.

She grabs my hand. "Harriet?" she says. "I really want to get to know you better."

I can feel my eyes open even wider. "Really?"

"Yes. You're... like a little piece of home."

"*Hai*," Rin agrees. "Home like hamster."

"Hampshire," Poppy corrects.

"Where hamsters come from," Rin says, smiling.

"Umm..." I stammer. "Th-thank you."

Poppy says, "I can tell already we're going to be inseparable."

And with that beatific smile – the kind that makes princes climb towers and fight dragons – Princess Poppy kisses my cheek and glides into the bathroom, locking the door firmly behind her.

30

OK. Something is wrong.

I blink a few times and sit heavily on my suitcase. I've just met two girls, and as of yet they haven't:

- Looked me up and down and then pretended they can't see me.
- Stood behind me, making faces.
- Said something as if they clearly mean the opposite.
- Rolled their eyes while I'm talking.
- Told me that my hair is "awfully bright for hair, isn't it?"
- Written an offensive yet painfully accurate observation about my personality on my suitcase.

They haven't pointed out sweetly that I'm quite short, for a model, or quite freckly, for a model, or quite weird-looking, for a human being. I quickly check my back with my fingers. There isn't even a sign attached. Are these girls trying to be *friends* with me?

"I search gift under bed," Rin says enthusiastically as I desperately try to orientate myself. "You will like very much, Harry-chan. It is to speak welcome to Japan." She scampers towards the bunks and then stops and turns around. "Harry-chan, where are you come from?"

"England."

"England!" Rin looks absolutely delighted, as if I've just whipped off my T-shirt and revealed multi-coloured wings. "What language is speaken in England, Harry-chan?"

"Umm." I never, ever thought I would have to answer this question. "English. Just like Poppy."

"Like in Hamster also!" Rin couldn't look more astonished. "English everywhere! Super handy!" And then she drops to her knees in her pretty dress and starts trying to fit under the bed with her bottom wagging, like an over-excited puppy.

I can feel a warmth starting in my chest: the kind I haven't felt since I crawled under the piano ten years ago and found Nat there.

You know what? This is *exactly* what I needed. Adventure. Excitement. New girlfriends, for the first time since I was five years old. A chance to start again without my parents, without Nat, and without Toby. A chance to be me, with a totally clean slate.

Plus I'm in my perfect environment, because every time I turn around there's something new to learn about. It's like being in school, except all the time and without Alexa.

I'm going to have the best summer *ever.*

There's a loud knock at the front door, and I stand up and bounce over to answer it. Honestly, I can't remember the last time I felt this happy.

And then I open the door and remember.

Because standing in the hallway is the last thing that made me feel this way.

Nick.

31

February 13th (132 days ago)

"You know," I said sleepily. "I'm not a dolphin or a duck, Nick." I had flu, and was holding the phone away from my face so my nose didn't leave little slug trails all over the glass.

"You're not?" I could hear him smiling. "Are you totally sure?"

"Hang on—" I sneezed and reached for a tissue with my eyes still shut. "Yes. And that means I don't sleep with one half of my brain still awake so that I can surface periodically for air or keep an eye out for predators, so when you ring me at" – I held the phone a little further away – "6.34am on a Saturday, I am one hundred per cent asleep."

"Gotcha." Nick laughed. "If only you were a giraffe. They only sleep for about five minutes at a time, so you'd probably be awake."

Huh. That was totally one of my facts. I couldn't

believe he was stealing them already. Did boys have no shame?

"Actually, giraffes have neither hands nor vocal cords, so I don't think that would help me much with the whole answering the phone conundrum." I smiled and sat up, rubbing my eyes. "Have you finished the Dolce & Gabbana shoot? How's Paris?"

"Cold. But not as cold as here."

I blinked. "Here? As in England?"

"As in *here*." Something hit my window.

My stomach flipped, and I bolted out of bed and pulled open the curtains. There he was: lit neon yellow in the early-morning lamplight. The only person on the entire planet who could look beautiful the same colour as a Simpson.

We beamed goofily at each other, and then he flicked his wrist and something else hit my window. "You can stop throwing pebbles, Romeo," I laughed.

"They're not pebbles," he called up. "They're mints. Something to eat on the train journey and fresh breath all in one go. A multi-purpose tactic. Or a multi-purpose Tic Tac. Catch." He grinned and lobbed another one.

(It landed in the front garden and would result in an hour of my father wandering around later, saying

"Annabel? I think the birds around here have got some *really* regularly shaped constipation.")

"Wait there," I said, and then tore around my bedroom, desperately trying to make myself look presentable. My nose was bright red and flaky, there was yellow crust in the corner of my eyes and when I licked my hand and sniffed it, there was the sick, flu-y aroma of damp curtains.

I'd have to start sleeping with a toothbrush and little bowl of rose water next to my bed, or maybe just a pre-emptive paper bag to put over my head for moments like this.

I quickly swilled a bit of cold, sugary tea around my mouth, spat it into a pot plant and sprayed some perfume in my general direction. Then I took a deep breath and flew down the stairs with my dressing gown fluttering like a superhero's cape.

"Yo," he grinned as I flung open the door. I was flushed and shaky and hot all over and it had nothing to do with my viral infection.

"Hey," I mumbled, suddenly shy.

"How are you feeling?"

"A bit snotty and gross, if I'm totally honest."

His hair was all pointy, his eyelids were sleepy, and he had his big blue army coat on: the one with pockets so big they could fit both our hands in it at the same time. He looked so handsome it took every single bit of energy I had not to dance a smug little MINE-MINE-MINE jig right in front of him on the doorstep.

"You look ridiculously cute," he said, wrinkling his nose. "Have you considered accessorising with a bug more often?" I stuck my tongue out. "On second thoughts, I wouldn't put that back in if I were you." He grinned as I play-punched his arm and pulled out a flask from behind his back.

"So, Sick Note, I've brought you a honey and lemon and paracetamol drink that shall remain unbranded for the sake of impartiality." He dipped into his huge pockets and pulled out a little box of tissues. "These, for your runny little nose." He took his stripy scarf off. "This, for your normal-length, non-giraffe neck." Then he made a little flourish and pulled out a tiny toy lion.

I went even brighter red. "Umm," I said, clearing my throat awkwardly. "I have absolutely no idea what this is referring to."

He leant forward and kissed me gently, like some kind of brave, flu-impervious Arthurian knight. "I've seen what's written all over the history exercise book that you've been sadly neglecting of late, Manners. I was going to try and bring a real one for you, but they wouldn't let both of us out of the zoo."

I kissed him back, and having the flu was suddenly the best thing that had ever, ever happened to me. I was going to look into having it forever.

"I didn't think you were in the country until Tuesday," I said when I finally caught my breath. (And sneezed into my dressing-gown collar.)

"And let you hog all these disgusting germs to yourself?" Nick brushed a strand of hair away from my face. "I needed to talk to you about something."

I tried to steady myself surreptitiously against the doorframe so my boyfriend wouldn't see that kissing him had made me dizzy. After two months, I was pretty sure that was supposed to have worn off. If anything, he was getting more and more handsome and it was getting worse. "Talk to me about what?"

"Anything," Nick grinned, tapping the end of my nose. "I just wanted to talk to you, Harriet. About anything."

And he kissed me all over again.

32

Scientists say that the earth spins on its axis at nearly 1,000 mph, and if it suddenly stopped everything would be swept away in a moment; torn from the surface and swept into oblivion. Trees. Rocks. Buildings. People.

That's exactly how it feels now. As if the world has come screeching to a halt and I'm being launched from the top of it.

"Yo," Nick says, leaning against the doorframe. "How's it going?"

His skin is darker, and his hair has been cropped. The big black curls have gone, and it's changed the proportions of his face: his cheekbones look sharper, his eyes more slanted and his lips more curved. He still looks like a lion, but now he reminds me of Aslan in *The Lion, The Witch and The Wardrobe*, just after he gets shaved and dragged to the slab. In a more modelly, less representing-Jesus kind of way, obviously.

Early Egyptians believed that the heart could literally

move around inside the body. I think they had a point: mine feels like it's lodged in my windpipe somewhere.

I blink in silence, and then realise that it's my turn to talk. I'm still looking at Nick in the blank-yet-fascinated way that Hugo stares at the television.

"H-h-hey," I finally stammer, unable to breathe. "It's g-going... erm..." *Nice one, Harriet.* That's fifteen years of studying a dictionary, totally wasted.

"*Erm*," he grins. "Not as good as *umm* or *err* but still one of my favourites."

"Actually," I say, starting to beam with my whole body. "I was trying to say erm-mazing, but you interrupted me."

"I'm umm-believable, aren't I?" He wrinkles his nose. "Awesome new T-shirt. I think I recognise that one. Diplodocus?"

"Uh-huh." I stretch it out. "Except that it's actually anatomically incorrect because this version has his head held up like a giraffe. Experts now believe it was held horizontally and they used to just *sweep* it across the foliage."

Before I can stop myself I feel my neck do a nervous little swooshing action to illustrate the point.

As if I'm a diplodocus.

*

I blush and his nostrils flare slightly.

"You should write to the T-shirt company and tell them."

"I already have," I admit, going even pinker.

Nick shouts with abrupt laughter, and – just like that – we're back to the beginning, and I have flu, and he's waking me up to kiss me all over again.

"So…" Lovely as this is, I don't really have the lung-capacity for any more small talk. A crocodile can hold its breath for up to fifteen minutes, but I am not a crocodile. If I don't start breathing soon, I'm going to pass out. "What are you doing here?"

Nick rests his head against the wall and looks at me for a few seconds through beautiful, lowered eyelids. "I'm doing a couple of modelling jobs and helping out behind the scenes of Aunty Yuka's new campaign."

"Oh." I feel a bit punctured. "But what are you doing *here*?" I point at the doorstep. "Did you get my email?"

"I did." He takes a step towards me. "And I need to talk to you about something."

Yesss! You see? I don't want to sound smug, but this is *exactly* why I wasn't worried. Nat was wrong, and I was right. All a girl really needs is a bit of faith in the romantic narrative arc that's been proven by countless films, books and TV dramas.

Nick's finally realised that the stars don't shine without me. That the sun doesn't burn, and the moon doesn't glow. (Metaphorically, obviously, or we'd all be dead.) That his world just doesn't make sense without me in it to explain everything in unnecessary detail every thirty seconds.

And OK, so he took a bit longer than I'd have liked, but if two months is what Nick needed to make a nice dramatic entrance and woo me back, then who am I to deprive him of it?

I'm *so* telling Nat that I understand boys better than she does when I get home. *She* can start taking relationship advice from *me*, henceforth.

I might even run some kind of classes.

I take the deepest breath I can find. *Stay cool, Harriet. Stay calm. Stay sophistica—*

"Oh, Nick," I blurt happily, fizzing and popping all over. "I knew I was right and you'd come ba—"

The bathroom door opens.

"Hello," Poppy says, swishing towards us with her hair pinned into a braid and bright red lipstick on.

"Hey," I smile. She looks even more ridiculously

beautiful than she did five minutes ago. "Poppy, this is—" and then all words fail me as she keeps walking and slings her golden arms loosely around Nick's neck and kisses him on the cheek.

"Hello, handsome," she says softly into his ear. "You're much earlier than we agreed." And I'm suddenly falling very slowly, like Alice through the rabbit hole.

"Am I?" Nick says stiffly. He's not looking at me. "Sorry. Are you ready to go?"

No.

No.

NO.

"With you, Nick Hidaka?" Poppy says, grabbing her handbag, beaming prettily at him and swishing into the hallway. "Any time and anywhere, baby."

I'm not falling any more.

Every part of me has just slammed into the ground.

The front door swings back behind her and Nick finally looks at me.

"Now's probably not the best time," he says quietly, as if there are other, more appropriate times for having your heart shattered into a billion pieces. "Can we talk later?"

I open my mouth to reply, but I have literally nothing to say and even fewer words with which to say it.

Nick waits patiently, and then takes a few steps backwards. "I'll see you soon?"

I open my mouth, but it's still empty.

He frowns and flushes slightly. "Have a great first night in Tokyo," he says quietly, grabbing the door handle. "Sleep well."

And then he closes the door between us.

33

Reasons Not to Think About Nick

1. He told me not to.
2. I have much more life-changing things to think about.
3. It's all I do.
4. He's an idiot.

I don't know how long I stand there for.

It could be minutes; it could be hours. It could be a thousand years and vines have started to grow up the back of my shins and moss has started to sprout out of my shoulders and squirrels and birds have set up home in my hair and I don't notice.

I have been so incredibly, unbelievably stupid.

Nick didn't want to talk to me so we could get back together. He wanted to tell me he had met somebody else. He wasn't trying to woo me.

He was trying to *warn* me.

Snippets from my happy little email are starting to bounce around inside my head, and every time a line makes contact I sink further towards the centre of the earth.

I've been thinking about you lots! Five hundred miles.

Of course I have! Another five hundred.

Send me another message or ring me? Three hundred miles down.

I'VE MISSED YOU SO MUCH. Another thousand.

Four kisses, and a needy, keen smiley face: **:)** And I'm right in the middle where there's nothing but flames and molten lava and hotness forever and ever and ever.

Oh my God. This doesn't happen in *any* of the stories I love. Except maybe in the Hans Christian Andersen version of *The Little Mermaid,* and that doesn't bode well for my immediate future.

No wonder I can't find my voice any more. I probably sold it to a Sea Witch in return for legs.

"Harry-chan?" A soft hand lands on my shoulder. "You OK, Harry-chan? You are very paling, Harry-chan. Perhaps you are lagging jet now?"

I turn and look blankly at Rin's pretty face.

"I-I-I..." I swallow. "I – umm – think I'm suddenly quite tired." I turn around and start wobbling on jelly legs into the bedroom. "It's been a really long day."

I push Kylie-cat aside, crawl into my new bed fully dressed and wrap my arms around my legs. Today is starting to feel like one of those confusing nightmares where you wake up crying and sweating and hurting and you don't quite remember why.

"Yes, you sleep," Rin says, sitting on the edge of my bed and carefully tucking me in. The cat jumps up and starts kneading my legs, but Rin picks her up. "No, Kylie Minogue. Bad cutey. No making biscuits on Harry-chan while she sleeping."

Then she follows my blank, shattered gaze to the door. "Nick is super handsome, *ne?* He is like prince or movie star or man in Abercrombie advert. One day I am hoping I will be in romantic twosome with Australian. Is it not perfect, Harry-chan? Like fairy tale?"

I can suddenly see Nick and Poppy: all cheekbones and glowing skin and perfect, magazine-approved beauty. Matching perfectly. Fitting perfectly.

"Yes," I agree. "Exactly like a fairy tale."

Just not mine.

And then I close my eyes and wish – with every part of my eternal mermaid soul – that I was at home, in England.

34

Now, I know many things.

I know that caterpillars have 4,000 muscles. I know that one in twenty people have an extra rib, and that astronomers have discovered that sometimes on Uranus it rains diamonds. I know that camels originated in North America, that killer whales breathe in unison when travelling in groups, and that there are more receptor cells in a single human eye than there are stars in the Milky Way.

But I clearly know nothing about boys.

And right now I'd trade in every single thing I've ever learnt for just the faintest idea of what it is I'm supposed to do next.

I can't sleep, so I wait until Rin is softly snoring, drag my duvet into the bathroom and curl up in the empty bathtub with my phone. It takes Nat a while to work out what's going on. This is because I'm crying so hard all she can make out for the first three minutes is "S-s-s".

"Spots?" she guesses, peering down the webcam. "Sausages? Socks?"

I shake my head. "S-s-s..."

"Sun cream? Scissors?" I can see Nat's brain scanning through her vocabulary for anything that starts with an S. "Caesar Salad?"

A little bubble of unexpected giggle-snot comes out of my nose. I try something different. "N-N-N..."

"Nipples? Nits? No offence, Harriet, but it's starting to feel like I'm trying to communicate with a penguin. Calm down and try to finish a word."

I obediently wipe my nose on the duvet (oh, come on, as if everybody in the world doesn't do that when they're heartbroken). Then I take a few deep breaths and finally manage to hiccup: "S-sorry. I'm s-s-so s-s-sorry, N-nat. Y-you w-were r-r-right and I-I was wr-wrong and N-Nick d-doesn't c-care about m-m-m-me and h-he h-has a n-n-new girlf-f-friend and sh-sh-she lives in m-my flat in T-T-Tokyo and sh-she's b-b-b-beautiful and I-I d-don't know w-what to d-do and I h-hurt a-all ov-v-ver a-and I j-just w-want to g-g-go *h-h-home*." And I promptly burst into tears again.

Nat sits bolt upright. "*What*? He's in Tokyo? *You're* in Tokyo? Are you freaking *kidding* me?"

To say that I am not in the mood for kidding anyone right now is the understatement of the century. "I j-just s-saw him."

Nat's face disappears, and somewhere in the background I can hear things being zipped. I sniffle and wipe my eyes on a separate bit of soggy bedding. "Nat? Are you listening?"

"No." Her head pops back into the screen. "I'm packing my bags and coming to get you."

I smile. Toby was right: Nat is my non-kissing soulmate. I want things to stay exactly how they always have been: like salt and pepper, strawberries and cream, cheese and Marmite. Two halves of the same teddy-bear-shaped friendship necklace.

Although Nat might be being slightly optimistic. She has no transport and no money and she's in deepest, darkest France. At 11 mph it's going to take the poor pig nearly a month to get here.

"D-don't be silly," I hiccup, feeling a little bit calmer already. "Your mum will ground you for the rest of your life and then she'll ground your ghost. I'll be OK."

Nat pauses, and then throws her passport on the

floor with a frustrated growl. "Ugh. Seriously: what is *wrong* with boys?"

We both ponder this important question. It feels like one of the ancient, unanswerable ones. You know:

Why Are We Here?

How Big Is The Universe?

Is There A God?

What Is Wrong With Boys?

"S-s-so..." I sniffle on to my hand. "What do I do, Nat? Tell me, and this time I promise I'll listen."

We sit in comfortable silence while my Best Friend thinks about it. When we were little we would do this every time one of us fell over and scraped a knee, until it didn't hurt any more. As if – just by being together – we could somehow share the pain. As if in some way we still can.

Finally, Nat makes a decision. "Pretend you don't care, Harriet. Pretend you never have."

I frown. "Nat... I didn't even have the thespian skills required to play a tree in our Year Two performance of *Snow White*, remember?"

Nat laughs. "You fell off the stage and just lay there, waving your branches around until your dad came and stood you back up again. It was hilarious."

It really was not. I couldn't look Miss Campbell in

the eye for months. She said I ruined the entire performance and maybe she would take that Drama job in Scunthorpe after all. "I don't think I can do it," I admit quietly. "It's..." How do I even put this? "It's *Nick*."

"Which is why it's even more important." I can see Nat's furious rash climbing up her neck again. "We can't let him win. He's not ruining this for you. Let me remind you, Harriet, YOU ARE MOD-EL-LING IN TOK-Y-O. You're the luckiest girl ever. EVER. You pretend, and you pretend as hard as you can."

This is all so confusing. One minute I'm being taught that lying is bad and I should never do it, and the next I'm being told to do it as convincingly as possible. Clearly when it comes to boys, every lesson I've ever learnt is supposed to be inverted. Why wasn't there a class in this at school?

I cannot believe I wasted three years of my life doing woodwork.

"Harriet, listen to me. Will you please just trust me?"

I look at the floor and nod. If I had listened to Nat in the first place I'd now be two months into getting over Nick. I'd be much, much closer to being fine. "OK," I agree. "I'll pretend."

"Good," Nat says. "I didn't want to be right, Harriet. I just didn't want *this* to happen. I didn't want him to hurt you."

I'm so glad I don't have to do this on my own.

"I miss you, Nat," I say in a tight voice. "Can we never, ever fight, ever again?"

Nat laughs. "Of course we're going to fight again. That's what we do. I'm going to kick your skinny butt for the rest of eternity." She looks at her nails. "Call whenever you need me. All I'm doing is trying not to milk cows."

"Really? What's it like? Is it all squidgy?"

"No idea. I keep telling people I'm not touching a cow's boob like a big cow lesbian so I have yet to find out." Nat grins and blows me a kiss. "This feels weird to say because it's totally broad daylight here, but: go to bed, Harriet. Things will look better in the morning. They always do."

I yawn and nod, suddenly feeling exhausted and drained. But also as if I've abruptly let go of something heavy. Or maybe something heavy has let go of me. By the time we say goodbye and I crawl back into my enormous bed – puffy but totally dry-eyed – I know exactly what my New and Infinitely More Glorious Summer Plan 3 (NAIMGS3) plan is:

Lie. Again.

This is my big adventure. I have travelled 6,000 miles and fifteen years to get here. I came to Japan to have the best summer of my life, and I am going to have it.

And no *boy* is going to ruin it for me.

35

Experts say that people with abnormally high IQs often have problems sleeping. Which is no doubt why I'm snoring within thirty-five seconds.

"Harry-chan?"

Something tiny and soft prods my face. I roll over, open my eyes and promptly shoot straight into the wall behind me. It's almost totally pitch-black, but I can vaguely see the outline of Rin's face, two centimetres from mine. She leans slightly closer and inexplicably prods me with her finger again. "Harry-chan," she says. "You are squeaking like tiny mouse. Bad dreaming?"

"Mnnneugh," I mumble. "Whatimezit?"

"Four am." Rin says this as it looks: *4am.*

"M'so sorry," I yawn, sitting up straighter. "Did I wake you up?"

"No." Rin perches on the end of my bed, picks up a still-sleeping Kylie and points to the huge earphones hanging around her neck. "I sleep super soundly. I listen to *nandakke*... Scotlands. Whales. But battery passes on and man wakes me. For you, *boom boom boom* at door."

I sleepily try to rearrange the sentences. "There's a man at the door for *me*?"

"Yes. So I came to awaken you up." Rin beams proudly and prods my face again. "I did good job, *ne*?"

Blinking, I grab my blue dolphin hoody and press the light on my Winnie-the-Pooh watch. It's just after 4am. I can't count out the possibility that I might still be dreaming. Although – if I am – I'll have to reassess what I eat before bedtime. It's certainly not one of my better ones.

In a daze I stumble through the corridor, open the front door and stare in bewilderment at the man standing there. He's wearing white gloves, a black suit and a black hat. I peer down at his little white socks. "Michael Jackson?"

"No. My name is Shinosuke. I am your chauffeur. The car is waiting outside to take you to the first photo shoot. You have five minutes to get ready."

I look at my watch again. "*Now*?"

"Not now," Shinosuke says, frowning. "I just told you. In five minutes."

OK: are they kidding me? Yuka wants me to do my first shoot at 4am? When I landed in the country nine hours ago? After a fourteen-hour flight? On four hours of sleep? With jetlag and a badly broken heart?

On second thoughts, I don't know why I'm surprised. This is the heartless world of fashion: I'm actually quite touched Yuka didn't drag me there straight from the airport by my eyebrows.

I nod briefly, race into the bedroom and grab my suitcase. I still haven't unpacked, so I drag everything into the bathroom so I don't wake up Poppy or Rin (she's already back in her bunk, snoring quietly with Kylie lying across her stomach). I quickly dress in whatever's at the top of the pile – my black and yellow stripy leggings and my Batman T-shirt – and tie my hair in a ponytail. Then I rally my inner model and glance briefly in the mirror.

Flaky skin, swollen eyes. A red dent from a pillowcase button on my cheek, an ink blob on the end of my nose and two enormous stress spots erupting by my mouth. And I still haven't cleaned the gravy off my chin.

Yet again, my inner model has clearly decided to stay there.

A couple of seconds later I'm running through the flat while brushing my teeth then out of the front door while cramming a chocolate biscuit into my mouth (I realise I got the biscuit and the toothpaste the wrong way round).

There's a huge black limousine waiting outside, and as soon as I appear it moves forward ominously by a couple of centimetres and the door swings open.

"Four minutes fifty seconds," I mumble through my mouthful, looking at my watch and clambering into the back seat. "Totally nailed it!"

"Congratulations," a cold voice says from a metre away, wiping a spray of chocolate crumbs off her face. "If only we could say the same for your personal hygiene."

A light switches on over my head.

And there – staring at me – is Yuka Ito.

36

Believe it or not, the last time I saw Yuka Ito is actually the last time you saw Yuka Ito.

After I humiliated her on national television, kissed her nephew and nearly destroyed the entire Baylee brand, I haven't run into her since. She's stayed in what I would imagine is a tower made out of fairy skulls, surrounded by molten lava and the bodies of aged models, and I've stayed buried under books in a semi-detached, three-bedroom house in Hertfordshire.

Which – I'll be totally honest – is exactly how I like it.

Swallowing my biscuit as quickly as I can, I squint upwards at the spotlight and then back at Yuka. She's so tiny, and so pale, and so completely dressed in black from head to toe that she totally disappears into the car seats, and all you can see is a small white face, hovering in the air. There's a faint iciness around her, and I'm not entirely sure it's all down to the air conditioning.

Yuka Ito looks at me, and then switches the light off. I think this might be going quite badly already.

"Harriet Manners," she says in a clipped voice, looking straight at my spots. "I thought we had agreed that you were to stop producing pus. It was part of your new contract."

I try to cover as much of my face with my fingers as I can. "I'm really sorry." The apologies have started already, and I haven't even properly sat down yet. "I don't really know where they come from."

Yuka looks pointedly at the remnants of the chocolate biscuit in my hand. "I can offer a few suggestions."

"Actually," I say, "there are numerous scientific studies that show that chocolate isn't actually a cause of acne and that it comes from hormonal—"

Yuka narrows her eyes and my survival instinct finally kicks in. I shut up, put the rest of the biscuit in my satchel and anxiously clear my throat. *Change the subject, Harriet.* "I – umm – didn't think you would be here, Yuka. I thought you would be" – *arranging your winged monkeys* – "with the other models. In one of the other countries."

"Everybody else I employ knows how to organise themselves," Yuka says, folding her hands neatly in front of her. "That's why I employ them."

I try not to notice the implication now hanging in the air. "Well, it's very nice to see you again," I lie. "How is your... umm..." *Think fashion. Think emotional connection. Think mutual interests.* "... hat feeling?"

How is your hat feeling? It's not one of the all-time great conversation starters.

"Harriet. What is a model?"

Oh, God. She's testing me already. It's a good thing I've looked it up in the dictionary quite a few times over the last few months, just to check what it is I'm supposed to be doing. "A standard or example for imitation or comparison?"

"Precisely." Yuka lowers her eyes. "The world's female population does not want to look like a crime-fighting bumblebee."

I glance down at my outfit. I look like I'm about to don a black face mask and start karate-kicking wasps and possibly grasshoppers. "I was in a hurry and it was at the top of my suitcase?"

"Then don't pack it."

In China there is a dish called 'Drunken Shrimp', which involves little shrimps being put into a hot broth of strong liquor and then eaten while still alive and wriggling. I'm starting to understand how they feel.

"Yuka," I say, taking a deep breath: "I just want

to take this opportunity to say how grateful I am to be given a chance to come to see Tokyo, and to be a part of—"

"Gratitude is not necessary," she interrupts, holding up a hand. "I want your face for my new brand. That is why I am paying you."

I flush with pleasure, even though it does sound a bit like she's about to slice it off and attach it to some kind of elaborate necklace. "What's the label called?"

Yuka looks at me as if she's already regretting her decision. "*Yuka Ito*."

"Ah."

"However," she says, leaning back in the seat slightly, "I would like to make three things clear."

I quickly scrabble in my satchel for a pen and a piece of paper. "Shoot," I squeak, and then clear my throat in embarrassment. "I mean, please go ahead, Yuka Ito. Please. Thank you very much. Please."

Yuka looks at me in silence and a line appears between her eyebrows. "Wilbur explained to you that the next few weeks require your complete discretion. Understood?"

I nod enthusiastically, and write *1. Discretion.*

"I have not flown you to Tokyo to party. This is a job, and you will be working extremely hard. Clear?"

I nod, slightly less enthusiastically, and write *2. Not a holiday.*

I guess that means I can wave goodbye to my planned trip to the Meguro Parasitological Museum, then.

Yuka narrows her eyes. "This launch campaign is a unique blend of Western and Eastern ideology. Every shoot will take stereotypical images and pull them apart: question and celebrate them. It will be powerful, fragile, feminine."

"That sounds—"

"This is not Baylee. There is no four-hundred-year heritage and enormous profit margin to fall back on. It's my designs, my name, my career. I do not have the luxury of tolerating maverick behaviour this time. Is that *perfectly clear*?"

I swallow, suitably chastened. I've never been described as a maverick before. Maybe I'm turning out more like my father than I realised.

It's a sobering thought.

"I understand," I say solemnly, and write *3. Just behave.*

"You are being paid a *lot* of money," Yuka says as I underline the last point three times for good measure and draw a series of stars next to it. "If you cannot meet those three simple expectations, there are many models who can."

I redden. Annabel made it part of my initial contract that I don't find out how much money I'm making until I'm eighteen. But – honestly – I'm a little bit intrigued now. I might be able to afford a piano, and then I can be just like Beth in *Little Women,* without the dying of typhoid part.

"OK," I agree.

"Good," Yuka says, turning to the window and making it clear that the conversation is over.

I watch the huge lights of Tokyo flash past in meek silence. You can say what you like about Yuka Ito – although obviously no one actually does – but she doesn't mince her words. She's terrifying, but at least you always know where you stand.

About four centimetres from decapitation, usually.

I clutch my new modelling list nervously in my hand until the car starts slowing down. I'm hit by a powerful salty, tangy smell that I recognise immediately. It comes from a chemical compound called *bromephenol*, which is found in algae and seawater.

I lean forward in excitement. "Ooh – are we at the seaside?"

Yuka snaps, "Tokyo is not a coastal destination."

"But the smell," I explain. "It smells like—"

"This is Tsukiji, the biggest fresh-fish market in the world."

We're pulling up outside one of the most enormous warehouses I've ever seen. It's immense, and industrial, and the fishy smell is so strong, the chocolate biscuit in my stomach is threatening to make a reappearance.

"But..." I frown. "I thought we were doing our first shoot today?"

"We are," Yuka says, opening the limousine door. "We're doing it here."

37

Whoever says that modelling is glamorous is totally fibbing.

There's blood *everywhere*. Shining at the bottom of boxes. Dripping off tables into buckets. Casually staining mounds of crushed ice, the way strawberry sauce stains a Slush Puppy. And – in the middle of all the redness – are fish. Big fish, little fish. Oysters, lobsters, squid, prawns, scallops, eels. Thousands and thousands of sea-life, piled on top of each other or laid out in rows. Whole, headless, finless or chopped into tiny pieces. Some that have already shuffled off this mortal coil, and some that are clearly in the process of desperately trying not to.

It's 4.40am and I'm standing in the middle of a Quentin Tarantino version of *Finding Nemo*.

"Problem?" Yuka says sharply.

I swallow. "Nope."

"Then find something prettier to do with your face." Yuka turns on her sharp black heels and starts clicking violently across the enormous concrete warehouse. I follow meekly behind her: smiling as hard as I can at everyone. They ignore me completely. I guess fishermen in Japan have even less interest in fashion than I do.

A corner of the warehouse has been set aside for the shoot, in the most temporary way possible. A 'changing room' has been propped against a wall with a mirror leaning next to it, and a fold-up table covered in make-up/hair accessories is standing right next to a bucket of eels. Fashion people are running around: talking loudly and plugging in hairdryers and curling tongs. It's a whirlwind of activity and noise, yet as we approach it goes strangely silent.

I'm 6,000 miles away from school, but it feels like I've just entered the classroom with the headmistress standing behind me.

"Not there," Yuka snaps at a woman who just put a chair by the wall. "Move them," she says, pointing to a pair of shoes on the floor. "Stop that," she says to a man brushing a coat with a clothes brush and wiping terrified sweat from his forehead.

Any second now she's going to demand that everyone sits up straight before she asks for their homework.

Then Yuka reaches behind a curtain and retrieves a blue plastic suit bag. Slowly, she slides it open and pulls out the contents. It's short and pale orange and frothy, made of layers and layers of delicate, transparent material: tight, rigid and wired at the top and puff-balling out at the waist into a stiff bell shape. There are tiny embroidered red circles scattered through each layer – stitched in an immaculate, intricate spiral – and at the hem and around the neck are thin tendrils of orange material, floating upwards and outwards.

It's a dress. Or perhaps I should say: it's related to a dress the way a fat ginger cat is related to a tiger, or a mural on the wall of McDonald's is related to the Sistine Chapel.

"Oh my goodness," I whisper, reaching out to touch it. "It's so beautiful."

Yuka immediately knocks my hand away. "Of course it is," she says stiffly. "I don't make things that aren't." She raises an eyebrow. "This is *haute couture*. Do you know what that means?"

I quickly scan my brain for anything I can remember from French GCSE. *Couture* = scar. *Haute* = tall.

"A huge trauma?" I guess tentatively.

"No." Yuka's lips are getting thinner by the second. "It means *high fashion*. It means there is only one. I made it, by hand, specifically for you. It is more valuable than the car we just came in. These, therefore, are your dressers." Yuka gestures to a couple of young Japanese women wearing black, who've just appeared on either side of me like twins in a creepy old horror movie.

I blink then start feeling a little bit indignant. *Dressers*? Exactly how much of a child does Yuka think I am? "I'm very nearly sixteen years old," I tell her in my most aggrieved-yet-still-respectful voice. "I think I can dress myself."

Yuka lifts her eyebrows. "This time I do not want you accessorised with stickers. Gold or otherwise."

And I think she's made her point.

38

I am a creature of maturity and elegance, maturity and elegance, maturity and elegance.

It doesn't matter how many times I say it: I'm not convincing anyone. I'm certainly not convincing Yuka. She won't let me touch anything. I'm dressed enthusiastically by strangers, with my hands stuck in the air and my feet apart like some kind of rigid, overly affectionate teddy bear.

When they've finally finished zipping and prodding and the make-up artist is done poking and colouring me in – thick white foundation, black eyeliner and red lipstick – I'm finally led over to the mirror.

It doesn't matter how many times this happens: I'm totally shocked at the transformation. My hair has been smoothed into a shiny red bob, my skin is glowing and spotless and my eyes have actual, visible eyelashes so I don't look like a rabbit. I'm totally unrecognisable. My own family couldn't pick me out of a line-up. Every single time I model, I start off as a normal schoolgirl and end up looking like somebody else. Like *somebody*.

It's like being Superman, except I only transform temporarily every few months with the help of a lot of very highly paid professionals and an enormous quantity of expensive cosmetics.

The team tweak the dress until they're happy, and then finally lead me – unable to see or walk very well – round the corner into a different part of the warehouse. Where I stop, startled.

On the floor there are fish.

Thirty or forty *enormous* dead silver fish glittering under huge temporary lights, lying nose-to-tail in perfectly straight lines like a sort of camp, aquatic military school. Faint steam is rising into the freezing air and between the fish are two men, arranging fins and spraying water to keep the fish shiny.

It's impossible to look away. Which – considering it's an advertising campaign – I'm guessing is sort of the point.

"Fresh tuna," one of the stylists whispers. "They'll go on sale in an hour to every sushi restaurant across the country. The shoot needs to be finished before the fish have to be cut up and carted off."

I nod, totally speechless. Only Yuka would shoot a fashion campaign this horribly beautiful.

Humans eat 100 million tons of fish every year and a single Brit alone consumes an average of 20kg. I can't get judgemental and weepy just because I can see their faces and they're not mixed with mayonnaise, put between two bits of bread and wrapped in a nice, bar-coded package for M&S.

A small, neat Japanese man in a dark suit with stiff, waxed hair walks over to me and bows politely. "Halloo," he says.

"Halloo to you too," I say, accidentally doing a little curtsy and then trying to turn it into a confused bow. I get sort of stuck halfway between and end up bobbing up and down as if I need the toilet.

"Halloo," he says again, a bit louder.

This is obviously some kind of Japanese custom I haven't come across yet. "*Halloo.*"

"Halloo."

We could be here all day. "Halloo. I am Harriet Manners." I quickly race through some of the phrases I've studied, and convert it to: "*Wa-ta-shi-wa Har-riet Man-ners desu.*"

"His name is Haru," a woman says from somewhere behind me. "Spelled H-A-R-U."

Ah.

I blush bright red and spin round to face a pretty Japanese lady with a straight black fringe and pouty, pillowy lips. "Oh my God, I'm so sorry." I turn back to Haru. "I didn't really get much sleep and I don't really know what I'm doing and when I get nervous I can't stop talking and I'm doing it now aren't I and I should probably shut up but this is all so exciting and—"

"He doesn't understand English," the lady adds.

"*Watashi wa kameraman desu,*" Haru says in a tone that indicates he already thinks I'm an imbecile.

"Haru is the photographer for this campaign," the lady explains, smiling. "One of the very best in Japan. I'm Naho, his translator."

I look at Yuka standing at the edge of the room, watching us with her usual expression. "Well, it's really lovely to meet you both," I say, holding out my hand nervously.

Haru looks at it. *"Kimiwa omoinohoka sega hikuine,"* he says flatly.

"You're shorter than he thought you'd be."

"Right." I can feel my cheeks getting even hotter. "Umm – sorry about that. My father's quite small as well. He claims our genes would be too overpowering for the world in larger quantities, and possibly hallucinogenic. Like nutmeg."

"*Hayaku hajimeruyo,*" the photographer says sharply, turning to his left and nodding at one of his assistants. "*Kono gaki no tameni wazawaza jikann wo saku hituyouha naikarane.*"

"Haru says—" Naho pauses just long enough for me to realise she's editing his words as well. "We don't... have time for this delightful talk. Let's begin."

She points at a small white chalk cross on the floor in a gap between two particularly shiny fish. "You stand there."

"*Isoi de,*" Haru barks.

Naho looks embarrassed. "Erm – quite soon, please?"

"Right. Sure." I start cautiously tiptoeing between enormous fish without treading on noses or fins as if I'm playing a particularly tricky game of fish-death Hopscotch. Then I stand, wobbling slightly, on top of the cross. "OK?"

"*Koitsu, baka ka?*"

"Umm..." Naho says, closing her eyes briefly. "Fine."

According to what I've gathered thus far from my epic modelling career, all I have to do is move my arms and legs occasionally with my most bored, lifeless expression on my face. How come after all the life-changing exams I've done in the past month, *this* is the one that feels the hardest?

Haru looks sternly through his camera with his eyebrows furrowed, fiddles with a few buttons and then nods.

I blink. "Did you want me to do something else?"

"*Nande gaikokujin moderu tukaunnda, nihonjin demo iijyanaika?*"

Naho frowns.

"Charlie," she says to the room in general. "Somebody grab him."

Charlie? I'm working with *another* male model?

Sugar cookies. I don't think I'm ready for this. I'm nowhere near as impervious to beautiful boys as a female model probably should be.

One of the assistants wheels an enormous tub next to me, and I blink at the very-much-alive and squiggling bright orange and red contents. I stare at the tendrils and embroidered sucker-style circles on my red and orange dress and everything slots into place. "Charlie, the *octopus*?"

"Yes," Yuka says in a clear voice from across the room. "Try not to let him outshine you."

*

I studied the domain of *Eukaryotic* for a project in biology last year. Did you know that an octopus has three hearts: two to pump blood to the lungs, and one to pump blood around the body? Or that they have special cells called 'chromatophores' that change colour so they can blend into any background?

And did you know that octopi are generally acknowledged to be the most intelligent of all invertebrates and have been known to steal cameras, defend themselves with weapons and unscrew lids to get at prey within containers?

This is my first ever encounter with a real-life octopus. I've always wanted to see one up close. They're the geeks of the sea world.

I lean forward to get a better look.

"*Furenaide kudasai,*" Haru shouts. "*Kare wa junbi ga dekite naikara.*"

"Please," Naho squeaks. "Don't touch the—"

My finger makes contact with an arm. Charlie makes a sudden thrashing motion.

And – in one swift arc – sprays dark blue ink all over my dress.

39

IQ tests on the internet can say what they like; it's not a great sign when you're outwitted by an octopus. Never mind invertebrates, Charlie's clearly smarter than at least one animal with a spine as well.

My co-model isn't ready. That's what Haru was telling me. Charlie needed a few minutes out of water first so he wouldn't panic. Nobody expected me to try grabbing him straight away; they expected me to categorically refuse to touch him, like a normal fifteen-year-old girl.

The dark ink doesn't just hit the dress: it goes everywhere. All over my face and hands and legs. All over the floor. All over the expensive tuna fish. It's like the world's biggest, most explosive, broken biro.

"*Baka!*" Haru yells as I stand there in shock, quietly dripping deep purple everywhere. "*Bakayaro!*" He throws a plastic lens cap on the floor.

"Umm…" Naho says, but this time there's no need for translation.

He's right.

I'm an idiot.

I apologise earnestly and repeatedly, but by the time they've wiped me down with half a dozen paper towels and sponged the ink off my hair, I realise the situation can't be saved. The one-off dress is ruined. The fish that aren't blue have been sold; the rest are being hosed down in a corner. The photographer is smoking outside and throwing sporadic Japanese words at me through the door. Naho is politely refusing to translate them.

And Yuka has gone.

40

For the second time in a week, I am totally the wrong colour. All I need now is a little gold lamp and a curly black beard and I'll look exactly like the genie from *Aladdin*.

What is *wrong* with me?

"For the love of dingle-bats," Wilbur sighs down the phone as I clamber back into a taxi and sit carefully on a towel. "This is exactly what I was talking about, Honeytoes. Do I need to get a portable naughty step sent with you everywhere?"

I rub my nose guiltily and then look at my finger. It's faintly purple. "I'm so sorry, Wilbur. I honestly don't know how it happens all the time."

"Really, Plum-pudding? No idea at all?" He sighs again. "I suppose I'd better ring Yuka and try to calm her down before we both get fired. But *please*, my little Carrot-cake. If we speak again this week I want it to be because you've found a sparkly pink unicorn roaming the streets of Tokyo and you'd like to gift it to me as my new steed, OK? Not because you've mucked something up again."

There's a silence.

"Are you thinking about a sparkly pink unicorn now?" Wilbur asks sternly.

"What if it's purple?"

He sighs for the third time. "I think, Kitten-shoes, this may be part of the problem. *Try and focus.*"

Nat's not as surprised about my octopus mishap as I'd like her to be either. According to the poet, Christina Rossetti, a friend is supposed to:

a) *Cheer one on the tedious way*.
b) *Fetch one if one goes astray*.
c) *Lift one if one totters down*.
d) *Strengthen whilst one stands*.

They are *not* supposed to send one a text message that says:

AHAHA u r such a plonker. xxx

While I've been busy turning everything in a ten-metre radius blue, I've also had eleven missed calls from my parents, two wrong numbers, four answer machine messages and nine text messages. Most of which want to know if I've arrived in Japan safely, and four of which want to remind me of what I'm missing:

1. **You left a multipack of Mars Bars on top of your wardrobe. Can I have one? Dad x**

2. **I had three. Hope that's OK. Dad x**

3. **I'm just going to have one more. Dad x**

4. **Harriet, your Dad's made himself sick on an entire multipack of Mars Bars again. Please don't leave sweets where he can find them. Ax**

I begin to smile, and then I remember.

Maybe it's best for everyone if she's not here.

My bottom lip sets, and I glare at my phone. They wanted me to leave: they can't get all clingy now I've actually gone.

I abruptly type:

Am fine. Stop eating my stuff. H

Then I press SEND, turn off my phone and stare miserably out of the taxi window. Tokyo is just starting to wake up: people in suits are swarming in and out of stations and music is beginning to blast out of speakers. The sunshine is bright, and the air is starting to thicken up with heat and smells.

I cannot believe I've managed to screw up already and the shops aren't even open yet. That's speedy, even by my own standards.

All I really want to do is go straight back to bed, pull the duvet over my head and wait for the day to end. Again.

So that's precisely what I do.

41

In my dreams I'm fighting octopuses and pink unicorns and Japanese-speaking seagulls, and finally one lands on my shoulder and starts screeching in my ear. I open my eyes with a start.

It's not a seagull.

A thick wave of dense black smoke is pouring under the door, and the only working fire alarm is having a loud panic attack in the living room.

"Rin?" I yell at the top of my voice, coughing hard. "Poppy?"

There's no response, so I leap out of bed and run straight into the kitchen. I switch the grill off, open a window and pull out the burning toast. Both pieces look just like Hello Kitty, except totally black and smoking. One of them has an ear on fire.

I really hope Rin never takes up arson as a hobby. They'd catch her within seconds.

"Rin?" I shout, running Hello Kitty under a cold tap until she goes soggy and her bow falls off. Then I stagger into the living room, turn off the alarm and flap my arms around to dissipate the smoke, even though I know that's not actually how smoke or arms or flapping works.

Suddenly I hear a screeching, desperate sound coming from the bathroom, and race to the door in a panic. *"Rin? Are you all right?"*

"Lalalala," somebody is singing at the top of their voice. "*No* I *won't,* be a Craig, no I-I-I-I won't be a Craig, just as l-oong as you stabby, stabby me. Lalalalalalala *me*, dddddaahly daaahly."

The bathroom door abruptly opens in a wave of steam, and a slim blonde figure pushes past me and past the girl emerging from the bathroom.

Without a word, Poppy slams the door behind her.

"*Stabby Me* is favourite Australian song," the girl states happily, drying her hair with a towel. "But who is Craig? And why does nobody want to be him?" Then she frowns and sniffs. "Are you smoking, Harry-chan? That is super bad for you. You should reassess this."

"Rin?"

The girl in front of me looks nothing like Rin. The curls have gone, and her hair is straight and in a short, ear-length crop. Her eyes are clean and shaped like a kitten and her skin is flushed pink and pearly. I look down and stare at the huge T-shirt she's wearing:

"English is magical, *ne*?" she says, beaming at my stunned expression. "Harry Potter. Cute Australian with shiny stick and glasses. Pow pow."

"Rin… I didn't even recognise you."

She looks heartbroken. "*Hai*. Yes. Pretty stuff is back in box. Models not allowed sparkliness. It's *nandakke*… non-professional." She pulls on her T-shirt and makes a vomit-face. "Now I look just like boy."

"You don't." Without all the attachments and plastic accessories, Rin gives Poppy a run for her money in the looks department. "You're so beautiful."

Rin giggles and pats me on the head, reaching up on her tiptoes because I'm considerably taller than she is.

"Foreigns are crazy, *ne*? Don't worry about Poppy, Harry-chan." She looks at the bathroom with a shake of her head. "In the morning, she is – *nandakke*. Mean like God."

"Mean like *God*?"

Rin puts two fingers up to her forehead like horns. "*Meh meh*. Eat grass."

"Goat?"

"Yes. God. Bites and booms with head." Rin taps

her forehead. "Super perfect at modelling, though. Poppy, not God."

She frowns and looks me up and down. "Harry-chan, in English is cute to look like *Avatar*?" She touches my face cautiously, looks at her finger and rubs a little blue ink experimentally on her own face.

I smile awkwardly. "Yesterday's shoot went pretty badly, to be honest."

"Then we must fix this," Rin says. She takes my hand and starts pulling me into the bedroom. "If you are unobstructed today, I will show you Tokyo."

"I think I'm free, actually." Yuka's going to need at least twenty-four hours to calm down, I reckon.

"Free? *Chotto matte.*" Rin gets a little computer out of a pocket in her T-shirt, and a few seconds later says, "Without charge? Will you normally charge me for friends, Harry-chan? Why?"

I laugh and the bathroom door opens. "Are you going out?" Poppy calls. "Can I possibly come too? Chanel's given me the day off so I'm going to be so *bored*." She wanders into the hallway and grimaces. "Sorry for queue jumping, Harriet. I was desperate for a pee and you were kind of standing in the way."

Rin makes goat horns and pretends she's eating grass behind Poppy's back.

I grin, but my stomach's starting to flip anxiously over and over. Poppy's lovely, but I'm not sure I want to spend the entire day with her. She's what Nat calls an MBF-er: a girl who refers to 'My Boyfriend' every twelve seconds, just in case anyone makes the hideous mistake of thinking she's single and unloved and unwanted. Even though people who look like Poppy never are.

I'm not sure I can cope with this. I like to think of myself as existing on the nicer end of the human spectrum, but I'm not Mother Teresa.

"Erm…" I start doubtfully.

"You come," Rin tells Poppy, promptly deciding for me. She sticks her tongue out at a pair of black jeans and a simple black vest and then pulls them on. "We will spend day together as three new BFFs." She says this *biffs*. "I shall show you the many wonders Tokyo and… *Dame! Kono itazura neko!*" She grabs Kylie, who's pouncing around a box in the corner of the room. "*Gokiburi wa tabenaino!*"

"What's that?" I bend down and pick the box up. It's a little cardboard house, with painted roof tiles, tiny drawn bricks, flowers and a little white picket fence. Out of one of the windows, between bright pink curtains, is a smiling cartoon beetle, waving happily. Over the door it says – in English – **WELCOME**.

"It's a Japanese cockroach trap," Poppy explains as I drop it on the floor. "They're huge and sooo gross." I look a little closer at it.

Under the word **WELCOME** it says – in small yellow letters – **TO YOUR DEATH**.

I guess we have to hope our cockroaches either don't speak English or have really bad eyesight.

"Cockroach climb in," Rin says perkily. "Cockroach pass out." She frowns. "*Nandakke.* Pass on." Then she looks back at me and adds, "Go shower, Harry-chan. You smell of fishes. We will begin Japan from new for you."

She pushes me gently towards the bathroom, and the warm feeling in my stomach starts to glow again. Poppy and Rin start taking photos of themselves holding up Kylie so they look like they have furry beards, and Kylie desperately tries to get back on to the bed again.

Friends, I think as I laugh and close the bathroom door behind me. After fifteen years, maybe I'm finally starting to understand how to make them.

42

I ♥ Japan.

By lunchtime, I am incoherently, head-over-heels in love with Tokyo. As my brand-new T-shirt, baseball cap, pen and pencil, and badge will tell you.

I ♥ the strangeness and the noise and the height of it.

I ♥ the politeness and how simultaneously ordered and manic it is.

I ♥ the two-storey-high televisions stuck to buildings, and the way the shop assistants bow and sing *irrashaimmaasseee*!!! (welcome!), as if you're royalty.

I ♥ the fact that you can throw coins in a ticket machine any way you like and it still counts them properly, and the way people fall asleep on the tubes against the shoulders of strangers.

I ♥ the electric toilets with warm seats that play music and spray water at your bottom and pretend to flush while you're peeing so that nobody can hear you.

I ♥ people who actually wait on the side of the road for a green light, even when there are no cars coming.

I ♥ the sense that I could never be bored, not if I lived in Japan for a billion years.

And, more than anything:

I ♥ how ignorant I am here.

I can't read, I can't write, I can't speak. All I can do is marvel with wide eyes at just how insignificant and tiny I feel.

Bunty was right: I even feel temporarily free from being me.

"Tokyo's OK," Rin concedes with a casual shrug. She's been racing us through tourist attractions as if there's a twelve-hour deadline before the entire city falls down. We've been up the enormous Tokyo Skytree; lit incense at the Asakusa Kannon Temple; wandered through Ueno Park and watched the jugglers. We've eaten bits of chicken on sticks and coffee jelly and tuna mayonnaise wrapped in rice and seaweed and bits of fried octopus in balls of batter (sorry, Charlie).

We're now in Harajuku, having crêpes on Takeshita Street, and it's taking every bit of my inner dignity not to attempt a joke that – frankly – I'm too old to be making.

I stare at Rin over the top of my strawberry, banana, ice cream and cheesecake pancake. "Rin, Tokyo is incredible."

"Not like Sydney" – Rin shakes her head – "There is no aces beach and BBQ and flaming gallahs."

I laugh. "Did you know that there are more people in this city than there are in Australia and New Zealand put together?"

Poppy sighs. She's picking off bits of strawberry, wiping cream on her napkin and then flicking it on the floor. "I find it all a bit much, really." She points at a tiny, fluffy dog walking by in a green dress with a bright green, lit-up, pulsing lead. "I mean, what exactly is the point of that?"

"But that's what's so brilliant," I say in surprise. "There isn't one."

We watch a couple of Japanese girls wander past. One has bright pink hair with blue tips, a purple tutu, green stripy tights, a camouflage-pattern jacket and yellow shoes. The other is covered – head to toe – in cuddly pink toys, as if she's doused herself in glue and run really fast through a toyshop. I turn back to Poppy with a huge smile. "How lucky are we?"

"I've been a successful international model since I was fourteen," Poppy says, pulling a bit of chocolate off her pancake, sniffing it and then wiping it on the bench. "The world gets boring pretty quickly."

I suddenly feel a pang of pity for her.

Toyshop girl and her friend notice Poppy and I, and stare at us. "*Kaaawwaaaiiiiiiii*," they squeak. Then they dissolve into giggles and skip down the street, glancing back so that they can collapse in hysterics again.

I turn to Rin. "What does *kaaawwaaaiiiiiiii* mean?"

"Cute. *Kawaii* mean cute." Rin looks with open loathing at her black jeans and vest. "You are wrong, Harry-chan. There is point. Cuteness is point."

Everything surrounding us is fluffy, or pink, or sparkly, or covered in hearts. Everything has a face: gloves, umbrellas, crisp packets, mascara. Rin's bank card is pink. Even the poles holding up the building works opposite have yellow bunnies drawn on them. "In Japan, all must be cute," Rin explains firmly, "or..."

"Or what?" Poppy suddenly says. "For goodness' sake, Rin. There are more important things in life than being *cute*."

I glance at Poppy in surprise. She's been staring at herself in every reflective surface since we left the house. A few minutes ago she was checking herself out in the pancake spoon.

Rin is appalled. "No," she says belligerently. "Cute is *most* important. Love is cute. Fashion is cute. Flowers is cute. Animals is cute. All good things is cute." She gestures at us. "Friendship is cute. We shall ask BFF questions and do answers now, *ne*?"

I beam at Rin. I *love* questions and answers. Plus, I'm not sure any girl has ever said that to me before. Even Nat tends to avoid Q&A whenever possible. She knows I get a bit too carried away.

"Brilliant," I say, trying not to notice Poppy stifling a yawn. "I'll start. Rin, where in Japan do you come from and what is it like?"

"Nichinan," she says. "It is small fishes town at bottom of Japan. Very hot. Palm trees and chicken and rice and mountains and sea. Pretty but *nandakke*… hushed." She pulls a face. "Me now. Harry-chan, have you always been wanting to be modelling?"

"No," I laugh. "It just sort of… happened."

"You enjoy model much?"

I think about this. "Sometimes. It's fun and exciting, but it can be a bit scary. And I'm a walking disaster in high heels. I guess I'm always waiting for it to end, to be honest."

Rin nods. "And you are possibly here for more Baylee, Harry-chan? I see cute jump jump picture in snow."

"Nope." I wipe cream off my jeans with a bit of pancake and then stick it in my mouth, like the Goddess of Class I am. "Actually it's for Yuka's new campaign. She's left Baylee, and she's setting up her own label. There are quite a few of us working on it in different countries. I got Tokyo, so I'm super happy." I smile at Rin. "Your turn, Poppy."

Poppy throws another strawberry on the floor. "Hit me," she says.

"Nick-kun," Rin replies, and my stomach drops as my ears go totally numb. "How long have you been in awesome twosome with perfect Australian, Poppy-chan?"

"Oh, I don't know, six weeks?" Poppy says, instantly brightening. "Seven?"

What?

He waited less than *two weeks* before moving on?

"We met on a shoot and REALLY hit it off straight away. I could tell he liked me immediately. He'd just split up with somebody else, but that was a total non-issue."

An involuntary twitch has started in the corner of my eye. *Change the subject, Harriet. Quickly. Pretend like Nat told you to.* "Who…?" I hear myself say, and then clamp my mouth together.

Yup. Whatever comes, I've totally asked for it.

"Just some girl," Poppy shrugs, throwing a bit of pancake at a passing scooter. "He must've got bored of her pretty quickly. It was no big deal."

I suddenly want to cry. The only romance of my life was *No Big Deal*?

It was a big deal to me.

No: it was a *massive* deal. Elephantine. Titanic. Megalithic; cumbersome; stupendous; monumental. I feel like I'm a tiny fly that accidentally zoomed into Nick's face: as if he's just wiped me away on a bit of tissue and carried on walking with slightly watery eyes, while I've been totally obliterated.

Boring?

I start getting all indignant and then abruptly stop. Oh, who am I kidding? I hear that insult all the time. It's currently scratched into my pencil case.

Rin is totally fascinated. "You are One for Him, Poppy-chan," she says, her eyes glittering. "I feel it here." She pats her chest. "Everything until you meet is… *nandakke.* Rehearsal."

"I guess," Poppy says, standing up gracefully and throwing the rest of the totally uneaten pancake in the bin. "When it's perfect you just know, don't you?"

No, I realise. *Clearly I do not.*

"Entirely," Rin says cheerfully, hopping off the bench. "I think we will go have *biff* photos taken now. We can ride horse and wear bunny ears together. Amazingballs?"

"Cool," Poppy says. "Can I be in the middle? I've just bought a new lipstick."

As we start making our way to a huge machine with a queue of giggling girls standing outside it, all I can think is if there's anything worse than being dumped, it's knowing that you were just a dress rehearsal.

That a Big Deal for you was just practice for somebody else.

43

Rin drags us around the rest of Tokyo until even my love affair with it starts to feel a little strained.

Finally she decides we've seen enough for one day and allows us to drag our exhausted, aching bodies back to the flat. Poppy goes straight to the bathroom to get ready to go out again.

With her MBF, I think miserably.

"Harry-chan," Rin says, patting a plastic bag containing a puffy sparkly yellow dress and matching yellow shoes. "I must go get dressed up for stay in watch TV. This trousers is making me super sad. Ooh." She bends down and picks an envelope off the mat. "Alphabet for you."

I smile and open the letter. In beautiful, curly handwriting it says:

Ring at 7am. Be ready. Yuka

On the upside: I obviously haven't been fired yet.

On the downside, I have absolutely no idea what Yuka means.

She's never been prone to particularly elaborate sentences, but this is concise even for her. There's an address written in Japanese just below that makes equal sense to me.

What am I supposed to do? Is she going to ring me? Does she want me to ring her? Are we doing a wedding shoot, or something based on horror films? Is it *Lord of the Rings* themed?

Actually, I bet this is the exact letter Frodo got before they sent him out of the Shire.

Tucking the letter into my back pocket, I go straight to the bedroom and pull an alarm clock out of my suitcase: a pretty little plastic bird that plays a genuine recording of a British skylark. I carefully set it to start dancing and flashing its eyes at 6am tomorrow morning and put it on the top of the drawers next to my bed. Then I drag out my rocket alarm clock, set it to launch at 6.10am, and put that next to the bird.

Finally, I get my target shooter clock out and put it on the other side of the room. When it goes off at 6.20am, I'll have to get out of bed, cross the room and shoot it in the middle with a laser gun to stop it beeping. And probably throw it against a wall and stamp on it as well, because even point-blank range is a bit too far for my sporting prowess.

Rin watches the entire process from her bunk bed, and then abruptly grabs Kylie (also now in a little yellow sequin dress), runs into the cupboard in the hallway and climbs inside it. After a lot of rummaging – and a bit of disgruntled yowling – she scurries back over to my bed with an armful of objects I don't recognise.

"Too-doo," she says triumphantly, dumping them on my lap.

"It's ta-da, Rin," I smile. "What's this?"

"This," she says, picking up a big white plastic ball, "shines relaxy picture on ceiling." She picks up a small plastic box. "This measure snoring." She hands me a thin sheet of plastic. "This keep pillow cold. And this" – she pulls out an umbrella – "is umbrella with lights. *Mi-teh*." She presses a button and the whole thing lights up like a Christmas tree.

I pause, trying to find a way to put this without sounding ungrateful. "Umm – what are they for?"

"For help sleep, Harry-chan. For good dream tonight." She pauses. "Not umbrella," she adds. "Umbrella for rain. Or flying, like Mary Poppins."

A lump suddenly forms in my throat. "Thank you, Rin."

"It's *nandakke*... Okily-dokily. Is that right, Harry-chan? I saw on Sampsons."

"*The Simpsons*."

"Yes. Funny yellow Australians." Rin laughs and claps her hands, at which point we both hear the sound of desperate scratching coming out of the cupboard. "Oh my goat!" Rin cries, standing up and putting her hand over her mouth. "I shut Kylie Minogue in closet!"

As she scampers out of the room, I start merrily setting my new presents up. I plug in the big round ball so it shines pictures of kittens on to the wall next to my bed, press a few buttons on the sleep analyser and stick the cooler into my pillowcase. I'm just trying to work out how I can wedge the umbrella into the corner of my bed as a kind of waterproof night-light when there's a loud knock at the door.

"Harriet?" Poppy shouts. "Can you get that for me?"

I look at the door with a sinking heart and abruptly decide: *no. Actually. Thanks, but I'd rather give myself root canal with a coat hanger.*

So I do the only thing I can think of: I whip my top off. "Sorry, but I'm not properly dressed," I shout back.

Poppy pokes her head round the door and looks at me. "Is that an Eeyore bra?"

I knew I should have listened to Nat and burnt it before something like this happened. "Kanga's on it too, actually," I say with as much dignity as I can muster. "And Roo."

"They never do silly things in my size," Poppy sighs. "It's all boring lace and silk and underwiring." She does a little twirl in a silvery dress. "How do I look?"

"Beautiful," I say, and then look down at the non-event happening on my chest.

Thanks, genetics.

"Wish me luck?" Poppy beams, grabbing her handbag and glittering out of the door in a wave of perfume and curls.

"Luck," I call and – as soon as the door shuts behind her – groan then slowly get my laptop out of my satchel.

Boring, I think as I open my computer and start playing online Snakes and Ladders with a random twelve-year-old in Indonesia.

Silly, I think as I yank my dolphin hoody on over my stupid bra.

No big deal.

44

January 17th (161 days ago)

"It's not going to rain," Nick said firmly. "They're not rain clouds. They're all fluffy and white."

"Is that the technical term?" I said, grabbing my umbrella anyway. I was *so* not taking weather advice from an Australian.

"Of course not. That's 'Clouds Which Look Like Big Sheep'. Not 'Clouds Which Make Water'."

"They're cumulonimbus," I reply. "And that out there's some stratocumulus. There's no nimbostratus but don't let that fool you. British weather is sneaky."

He leant over and kissed my nose. "I love it when you talk meteorology."

"Obviously. Meteorology is awesome. You're not *insane*."

Despite my warnings, both Nick and my dad insisted that we take a picnic. "It's not going to rain," my father said, shoving a French baguette, some cheese and a few apples into my satchel.

Nick raised his eyebrows. "I know, right? Tell that to little Miss Smarty-Pants here."

My dad shook his head sadly. "I'm afraid all the female Pants are Smarty in this house. They won't listen to rightness, and there's absolutely nothing we can do about it."

It was raining before we got to the end of my road.

Nick sighed and pulled his coat over our heads. "It's at times like this I really regret liking a girl with brains."

"At least I have an umbrella," I smiled and let him snuggle under it with me. "Did you know that 6,000 pounds of micro-meteorites hit the atmosphere every day?"

"That sounds incredibly dangerous." Nick grinned and waggled the handle. "Are you sure we're totally protected by this bit of waterproof fabric?"

"They're really tiny. They get caught in clouds and water coalesces around them so that they fall to Earth in rain."

"I should probably stop sticking my tongue out and trying to drink it then."

I laughed. "Maybe, seeing as you're catching tiny bits of shooting star that are billions of years old and have just come from outer space." I put my hand out, caught a few raindrops and showed it to him.

Nick wasn't looking at my hand. He was looking at my face. I blushed and focused on the water in my hand.

"Do you know what I think?" he said.

"Absolutely never," I said, staring at the rain. "Like, literally never. I never ever know what you think."

It was his turn to laugh.

"I think I was right," he said, closing my umbrella and tucking it away. Then he put his arm round me and continued walking us into the rain. "We don't need an umbrella after all."

45

The human body is amazing.

Did you know that the acid in our stomachs can dissolve zinc? Or that in a lifetime, we'll produce enough saliva to fill two swimming pools? Or that we're roughly one centimetre taller in the morning than in the evening?

And – most relevantly of all – did you know that in the hour before you're supposed to wake up, the anterior pituitary gland in the brain releases a polypeptide tropic hormone called *adrenocorticotropin*, which acts as a stimulant and natural alarm clock?

All of my preparation last night was a total waste of my time. After years and years of getting up early for school, my pituitary gland has been honed to perfection and is eerily accurate. It's still pitch-black and none of the alarms have gone off yet, but I'm wide-awake and perky as an otter.

If only I could start trusting my body a little bit more, I could save a huge amount of money on AA batteries.

Yawning a few times, I pull on my slippers and rub the sleep out of my eyes. Then I pad through the dark bedroom to the bathroom, then into the kitchen to get a glass of water and a couple of chocolate biscuits, and then into the sunlit living room to switch on the TV. (I love Japanese adverts. I can't understand a single word but they're so incredibly cheerful.) At which point I stop, glass frozen in my hand and a biscuit halfway to my mouth. Sunlit living room. Sunlit living room.

Sunlit living room?

It's not even dawn yet. Unless...

Oh my God.

OH MY GOD.

I run to the window, and there's the sun: emitting its massive solar energy from too high up in the sky.

I look at my watch: 9.25am.

NO.

NOOOOO.

NONONONONONONONO.

I sprint into the bedroom and fling open the curtains. The sun comes streaming in. Rin's snoring in her bunk with her headphones on, Kylie's curled against the small of her back and Poppy has gone out already. I pick up the bird alarm and shake it: its eyes are still closed. I look at the rocket: it's still in its launch pad. Then I stare at the laser alarm. The lights are dead.

None of the alarms worked.

How is that even *statistically* possible?

I need to find my mobile phone, ring Yuka and get out of here. But when I look at my bedside table, my phone isn't there.

So I grab Yuka's letter, sling a yellow cardigan over my penguin pyjamas and run straight into the streets of Tokyo.

Why didn't Yuka ring? Why didn't she send somebody to drag me out of bed by my feet? Where is my phone? Why are our bedroom curtains so thick?

Most importantly: why am I?

I ask the taxi driver all these questions, but he doesn't speak English so I just get a lot of nodding and uncomfortable glances in the rear-view mirror.

Finally – almost precisely three hours late – we pull up outside an immense, low, square building with a pale green roof. I'm so impressed I actually stop talking. The roof slopes to a gradual point in the centre, there are big glass doors at the front and the two white walls on either side of the entrance are covered in huge paintings of enormous, robust-looking men wearing bits of material around their waists, furious expressions and absolutely nothing else.

Ring.

Sumo ring.

I'm in Japan, and this is the only 'ring' that didn't occur to me?

I stare at the doors with my stomach starting to clench and squeeze. I have no idea how much trouble I'm in, but after Monday's disaster I think the answer is: quite a lot.

Focus, Harriet.

Hands shaking, I hand a pile of money to the driver, climb out of the car and start nervously running towards Yuka.

Then I stop, because:

- There's a boy sitting on the stairs.
- He's blocking my path.
- I've forgotten where I'm supposed to be going.

"It's a shame the tables in Japan are so low," Nick says, wrinkling his nose. "Where on earth are you going to hide this time?"

46

Reasons Not to Think About Nick

1. He told me not to.
2. I have much more life-changing things to think about.
3. It's all I do.
4. He's an idiot.
5. I only have finite memories, and I don't want to wear them out.

I have given my heart a number of strict instructions over the last couple of days.

Judging from what it is doing now, it has listened to precisely *none* of them.

My hands are clammy. My throat is dry. My ears are hot and my cheeks are cold; I'm breathing too fast and blinking too slow. Something has short-wired and every function in my body is in the process of swapping over.

I scowl to hide the dolphin-like leaping in my chest

and then remember I'm wearing penguin pyjamas, which sort of undermines my intended impression of fierceness and sophistication.

Pretend you don't care, Harriet. Pretend you never did.

I clear my throat and try to adopt my most nonchalant expression. "Hey! What are you doing out here on the pavement?"

Nick puts his hands to his face. "Sniffing my hands, obviously. Do you want to smell them?"

He gives me a crooked grin and holds out his hands, and I blush all over. That's what I said the second time I ever met him. He's laughing at our romance already. Isn't there supposed to be some kind of... respectful grieving period first? A minute's silence or something?

My temper flares. "Brilliant," I snap. "In that case why don't you just go—" and I promptly run out of imaginative places to send him. So I stick my nose in the air and march past.

Within seconds he's sauntering casually next to me. This is the problem with stupidly tall model-boys: they have a totally unfair stride advantage. Especially when one of us is wearing fluffy, teddy-bear slippers and their noses keep getting caught in the pavement.

I try to pick my feet up a bit, but now I just look like a little child stomping off to bed.

"Harriet…" Nick says. "Look. There's stuff I need to say but I couldn't do it at the flat. Not in front of Poppy. You understand, right? Don't be angry."

I stop walking, and my heart tips.

I don't want to hear it. I don't want to hear how guilty he feels, or how he tried to warn me. I don't want to hear that the heart just 'wants what it wants' or that some things aren't 'meant to be'.

I don't want to hear that he has inexplicably decided he prefers perfect, blonde, supermodel types over freckly, ginger schoolgirls.

I don't want to hear that he never meant to hurt me.

And – most of all – I don't want to hear that he still cares about me, *just not like that.*

As if friendship is the wooden spoon I get for being such a brave champ to give it a shot with somebody like him in the first place.

I hear Poppy's voice in my head. *Silly. Boring. No big deal.*

And I abruptly change my mind.

"Please don't say it," I say brightly, turning to him with the biggest, breeziest smile I can find.

Think mature, Harriet. Think adult. Think suave and cool.

"It's fine. It's lovely to see you, but I'd like to put the vagaries of our mutual past behind us." *Nice. Kind of Henry James-esque.* "It's totally..." *Like having my insides hacked out with an ice-cream scoop over and over and over again*? "Coolioko."

Then I flinch slightly. It's totally *coolioko*?

That's not even a word.

Nick looks stunned, and I finally realise that Nat knows exactly what she's talking about. This is the perfect way to handle the situation. I've never, ever seen a boy look more confused.

"Do you mean that?"

Not even a little bit.

"Absolutely," I say, and am rewarded with an even more shocked expression. I stick my hand out. "Friends?"

Nick stares at me.

I am so nailing this acting stuff. Take that, Miss Campbell. Maybe I shouldn't have quit GCSE drama after all.

Slowly, he takes my hand and frowns. "Are you sure?"

No.

"Definitely," I say, beaming at him and pumping

his hand up and down like a weird stranger at one of my parents' dinner parties.

Then I start quickly walking towards the building as if my insides aren't about to fall out in a heap all over the pavement.

"Right," Nick says flatly, as he catches me up. "Glad that's clear." He doesn't sound very relieved, given that I've just saved him from a really uncomfortable conversation. He should be erecting a plaque to my selflessness and bravery right now. Lighting candles next to my extremely non-confrontational portrait. "Hang on, Harriet," he says, grabbing my arm just as I reach the door.

It feels as if somebody's just stabbed me with a cattle prod. Electricity crackles down to my wrist, up to my shoulder and back again, then somehow spikes into my brain so I can't think, hear or see.

I politely tug my arm away.

Nick's staring at his hand. Then he blinks and looks back at me. "Umm…" He blinks again then shakes himself. I'm slightly worried I may have actually electrocuted him. "What I mean is… don't go through the front door. You need to go through the side entrance before Yuka sees you."

Oh, sugar cookies. I'd totally forgotten about

modelling. *Again*. Wilbur's right, I really need to learn how to focus.

"Sh-she's that angry with me?"

"I've seen her happier," Nick says, pulling a face. "We need to get into the ring pronto. That way you might survive until lunchtime."

Every romantic thought is swept away in a sudden flood of panic. "Did..." My mouth is paper dry. "Did you just say into the ring?"

"What did you think we were doing here?"

I'm going to be sick. *I'm actually doing sumo?* I didn't even have the coordination necessary to take part in last term's Year Eleven Dance. They said I wasn't 'physically equipped to move in public'. "We?"

"I'm doing the shoot too. With you. At a distance, though, I'm just in the background. A boy-shaped prop."

Oh my God. I may not know much about ex-boyfriends, but I'm pretty sure you're not supposed to throw yourself at them. Especially not physically, on a stage.

"Just me and you?" I know, shock is playing havoc with my grammar.

Nick shakes his head, and suddenly I can't breathe very well.

"Not any more," he says, opening the stadium door. "That's what you get for having a lie-in." He points to the biggest crowd that has ever existed in the history of the world, ever. "No biggy."

47

As my PE teacher will happily testify, I am not a very fast runner. But I still manage to get at least ten metres away before Nick catches me. He has to push me back into the stadium like I'm startled cattle.

Actually, I'm shaking so hard that if I *did* contain milk, I'm pretty sure it would now be butter.

"There was supposed to be nobody here," Nick explains when I've finally stopped waving my arms and legs in every direction, like an upside-down beetle. "They're here for a sumo match that starts in an hour. If you'd been here on time, it would have been empty."

I peer through the swing doors into the arena; there are chairs all the way up to the ceiling, and almost every single one is full. "I can't do it," I say almost inaudibly. "Nick, please don't make me do it."

I look desperately at the floor. If I can just find a crowbar I might be able to pull a few floorboards loose and crawl under them. I can live there forever, like a mouse or a rat. Or a really big and totally pathetic woodlouse.

"Of course you can do it," he says. "They're strangers you'll never see again. Who cares what they think of you?"

I look at the crowd again and the distant stage, and my stomach folds in half. *Nobody* can transform that much in six months. This isn't a few strangers. This is thousands of strangers. Thousands and thousands of strangers. Thousands and thousands and thousands and...

"Me," I decide. "I care."

"They're here to watch sumo, Harriet. Not us. They won't be paying any attention. We get up there, do our thing for half an hour, and then come down again. It'll be..." He twinkles at me. "Coolioko."

I glare at Nick and then sigh in resignation. This is what I signed up for: live catwalks and live television and live octopi and live sumo. Everything in modelling is *live*. There's nowhere to hide.

Plus unless I want to be disembowelled on the spot I don't think I should push Yuka's patience any further.

I nod grimly.

"Excellent," Nick says. "I'll be there, so don't worry, OK?"

That is simultaneously the best and worst sentence I've heard in the last two months. "Uh-huh."

Nick turns to a chair behind him and picks up what looks like a huge white scarf and a very large safety pin. "Here's your costume. See you out there."

And he winks at me then disappears through the doors, into the crowd.

48

I stare at the scarf in horror.

It's a traditional Japanese sumo loincloth, known as a *mawashi*. It's thirty foot long, two feet wide, made of silk and is passed repeatedly around the stomach and between the thighs and secured over the – you know. Front area. And it's worn by *men*.

But I can't afford to make Yuka any angrier, so I take a deep, professional breath as I walk into the changing room, then experimentally wind the scarf up over my penguin pyjamas and secure it with the enormous safety pin. I untie it and wrap it a little higher. Finally, I criss-cross the silk over my entire body and pin it so I'm completely mummified.

That's better.

Now I look like the world's most prudish baby.

I'm on the floor, trying to tug off my pyjamas from underneath it, when the door opens. A young Japanese woman with blue raccoon stripes in her hair walks into the room, followed by a large group of people wearing black.

People with brushes and lights and boxes and folded-up tables.

People with the serious, focused expressions of highly experienced professionals.

They stare at me, and then the woman with the stripes holds out a beautiful dark blue dress. It's floor-length and silky, with little holes punched in the bottom so that the light shines through it like stars. It has little straps, and a slit up each side. It's beautiful, my size, and exactly the sort of thing Yuka designs.

I am *so* gullible.

"Hello," I say with as much dignity as I can muster. Then I wait patiently for the floor to open up and swallow me whole.

"My name is Shion," the girl says, grinning. "I'm the new stylist." She looks me up and down. "You must be Harriet Manners."

Right.

I am going to kill Nick. That was so *not* funny.

Unfortunately, nobody else agrees with me. I spend the next ten minutes having my hair speedily gelled into a neat bun by a giggling hairdresser, my shoulders sprayed with sparkly sticky stuff by a snorting stylist and my eyes heavily painted in dark blue glitter by a shuddering make-up artist. By the time they've finished with me, I'm so embarrassed by all the giggling and snorting I've actually forgotten to be nervous.

Plus I'm far too busy working out the various forms of punishment I can wreak on my ex-boyfriend. Enormous seagulls I can train to attack him; lime-flavoured sweets I can eat without offering him any. Ominous-looking rain clouds I can get to follow him around.

That kind of thing.

Shion points me down a long corridor in the direction of the stage doors, and I'm so focused on revenge that I'm totally calm. A quick peek through the doors proves that everybody in the crowd really is just minding their own business: chatting, eating, laughing, drinking. Getting ready for the show they've actually paid to see.

Which means I can do this.

Quietly, I slip through the doors into the arena. At the bottom of the stairs leading up to the stage is a pair of amazing, bright pink, glittery high-heeled shoes with six tiny red straps. Attached to them with tape is a little note that says:

It's the shortest possible distance. x

I laugh, bend down and flick the note on to the floor. The shoes are a bit too small, but I manage to wedge my feet into them and get the straps tied.

Then I straighten up, square my shoulders and walk up the stairs on to the stage.

49

The first thing I see is Nick.

He's standing on the other side of the enormous square stage in a pair of dark blue silk trousers and a dark blue shirt buttoned all the way to the top. His head is down and facing away slightly, his skin is glowing, and for the first time I realise – with a painful pang – that even though most of his hair has gone, he still has that tiny curl at the back like a little duck tail.

Then I notice Yuka. She's partially hidden behind an enormous screen next to scowling photographer Haru: hands neatly crossed in front of her, black lace dress on, little black hat perched, face hard and white.

And then I notice the sound of my heart.

Because, as I step towards Nick and he turns and steps towards me, this is all I can hear:

The drum of my heart.

My heels against wood.
The quiver of my breath.

The entire crowd is completely silent.

50

In pretty much all of the romantic films I've ever seen, there's always a moment when the hero and heroine meet and the rest of the world becomes a blur. It doesn't matter where they are; the only thing they can see or hear is each other.

All I can say is: romantic films *lie.*

There isn't a convenient fog, misting out the audience. I see thousands and thousands of people: paused, silent and watching me intently.

Quickly, I do my best to wipe the terror from my face and walk like a model into the middle of the ring. I raise my chin and try to get my entirely rigid body to bend into a shape other than that of a stale pretzel.

None of my limbs are working properly. As I jerk awkwardly around the stage, with every movement Yuka's eyes get narrower and angrier, and Haru's hand gestures more demonstrative.

Swallowing hard, I turn away and try another pose. Then I move to the left and try again: curving forward with my hand on my hip and my right shoulder pushed back.

At which point I realise that Nick is following me.

OK, isn't this hard enough without my ex-boyfriend chasing me around the stage? He's supposed to be a *boy-shaped prop*. In the *background*.

Why is he winding me up *again*?

I flash him a dark look and hobble over to another corner of the stage. He follows, so I move again, but so does he. After a whole minute of being chased in a circle I finally accept defeat. Nick stands close enough for me to feel his breath on my neck, and every single hair on my body immediately stands up.

"What are you doing?" I hiss, bending into another pose. His hand touches my waist and an unwelcome thunderbolt shoots through the right side of my body.

"What are *you* doing?" Nick whispers. "What are you wearing on your feet?"

"Gloves," I snap, changing my pose. "What do people normally wear on their feet?"

"This is a sumo ring. You're not allowed to wear shoes. Especially not heels. The audience is furious."

It's as if the entire stadium suddenly goes dark. My brain shuts down in shock, and when I come back to my senses, I can suddenly feel where the eyes of twenty thousand people are focused: entirely on my shameful, painful, sparkling feet. "B-b-but I d-don't—"

"Take them off," Nick whispers urgently. "Now."

I bend down but my hands are shaking too hard. The red straps are too tiny and there are too many of them. All I can do is paw desperately at the buckles while my eyes fill with water and blood rushes to my head.

Suddenly Nick bends down in front of me. "I'll do it," he says. "Stay still."

He calmly takes my hand to balance me, and removes each shoe like Prince Charming in reverse, bows deeply to the crowd in every direction and dramatically throws the shoes off the stage.

"Now," Nick says with a tiny nod. "Copy me."

51

There's an animal that lives at the bottom of the ocean called a Pacific Ocean Hagfish. When it feels threatened, it oozes a defensive slime from its pores that envelops its predator in a mass of fibrous goo. It then gets trapped in its own goo and dies.

I'm so embarrassed I can't breathe properly. I can't blink. I can't move. I can't pose. I definitely can't model. Like the Hagfish, I am basically starting to suffocate on my own panic.

Rigid with humiliation, I watch Nick go back to his original starting mark on the stage, and then – to my absolute disbelief – turn around and cock his leg high in the air like a dog about to pee on an invisible lamp-post.

Before I can even blush for him – nobody is good-looking enough to get away with that kind of position – Nick looks me straight in the eye, slams his foot on the ground and yells at the top of his voice: "AAAAAARRRRRGH!!"

Then he waggles his elbows and blows a tiny raspberry, just like he did in the snow in Russia.

And I can't help laughing, just like I did on my first ever photo shoot, and everything in me suddenly starts to relax.

Trying not to look at Yuka or the photographer, I obediently lift my leg as high in the air as I can, pause and then slam my foot down with an immense "AAAAAAAARGGH!!"

Nick does the same with the other leg and shouts: "AAARRRGH AAAARGH!"

I've never felt less dignified in my entire life and – frankly – that's really saying something.

It's only when Nick hitches up his trouser legs, kicks one leg slowly out to the side and leans into a deep crouch that I suddenly understand.

Sumo. He's doing sumo.

Slowly, I pick up the sides of my dress, compose my face and kick a leg out. I bend into a squat, lift on to my toes and hold it as long as I can.

Then Nick and I stand up straight, take a few slow steps towards each other and do it all over again. And again. And again.

As we get closer and closer – as we stamp and crouch and shout and pace – something amazing starts happening. The crowd really does begin to disappear. They fade and fade until it's just the two of us.

Circling each other.

Stamping at each other.

Staring at each other, as if nothing else exists.

It's only when Nick snarls at me – and I grin and snarl back – that I finally hear a noise from the audience. A gurgling sound that gets louder and louder and louder.

And it's only when I look up that I realise the audience is laughing. When I glance at Haru and he inclines his head slightly, I know I'm going to be OK.

Which means Lion Boy has saved me.

Again.

52

Now, I have many skills.

I can recite the entire Periodic Table and six Shakespearean sonnets by heart. I can tell you every single King and Queen of England since Kenneth the Third in 997, and I can draw an almost perfect circle freehand as long as nobody's watching.

Of my many useless and untransferable skills, however, accurately interpreting subtle facial expressions is not usually one of them. But I don't think that's something I need to worry about today.

Yuka Ito is livid.

"Explain," she says quietly as we climb down the stairs and push through the stage doors. She looks like the White Witch of Narnia just after she finds the first snowdrop. "Now."

Every drop of adrenaline evaporates, and I'm suddenly so scared I feel like I'm flashing colours like a human disco ball: white, then red, pink and green, then some kind of petrified purple colour. "I'm s-sorry," I stammer quickly. "We were trying to… harness the Japanese culture creatively and—"

"I'm not talking about the poses."

No. Of course she isn't. "I…" I swallow. "It…"

"Where were you this morning?"

"I was… I set my… at least I thought I set my… my alarms didn't…" I'm too scared to complete a sentence.

"You were three hours late." Yuka doesn't need to shout. Every quiet syllable is a pointed jag of ice. "The driver waited outside your building for two hours. He rang your doorbell thirteen times. Where did you stay last night?"

My eyes widen in surprise. *What?*

"I was th… I was th…" *I was there. I was right there.*

"I rang your mobile repeatedly. It went straight to voicemail. You do not turn your phone off while you are working for me."

"I didn't—"

"I explained very clearly that you are not here to party."

My mouth opens in shock. *Party?* Has Yuka ever met me before?

"I wasn't—"

"And when you decide to grace us with your presence, you accessorise my outfit with heels of your own. On a *sumo* stage. A stage reserved for men."

"But—"

Yuka holds her hand up. "No," she says. "I don't want to hear it, Harriet. You have shown rudeness, disobedience and a total lack of respect, and you have done it in front of twenty thousand people."

I've been called a lot of names in my life, but 'rude', 'disobedient' and 'disrespectful' are not three of them. The shock finally knocks the voice back into me. "Yuka, I was at the flat, I set three alarms, I don't party – *ever* – I don't own shoes like that, I wouldn't even know where to buy any—"

"Do not compound errors with lying," Yuka interrupts. "And don't think that completing this shoot exonerates your behaviour. An ability to copy a professional is not what I have flown you halfway around the world for."

There's nothing I can say: she's absolutely right. Without Nick, I would have stood there and quietly drowned in my own panicky mucus.

"I'm so sorry," I say quietly as my eyes start to go blurry.

"If I hadn't already invested so much in you, Harriet,

you would be going home now." Every word sounds like it's been bitten off. "Do not make me regret this decision any more than I do already." And before I can say anything, Yuka turns and walks out of the building.

I stare after her, open mouthed.

"The *mawashi*," Nick says after a few seconds, raking a hand over his head. "It was a joke. I never would have—" but I've stopped listening. I'm already pushing through the doors and running back to the edge of the stage.

If I can just find the note – if I can show it to Yuka – maybe she'll believe me. She'll see that I do respect her, and that I love Japan. That I know I'm lucky to be here, and I'm trying as hard as I can.

That I'm not the person she thinks I am.

But it doesn't matter how hard I look.

The note is gone.

53

I have so many questions, I don't even know where to start.

Actually, that's not true. I totally do.

As soon as I'm back at the flat, I charge straight into the bedroom. Rin's lying on her front on the bottom bunk, reading an English dictionary with her head cocked to one side: pink lace dress on, purple-socked feet crossed behind her. Kylie's sprawled out across the small of her back in exactly the same outfit. Poppy's perched against the wall of the top bunk, carefully painting her nails pink and humming a riff from *The Sound of Music* over and over and over again.

"Why didn't you wake me up?"

They stop what they're doing and look at me.

My cheeks are hot, and my breathing is getting faster and faster. There's a tight feeling around my throat. "You left early this morning, Poppy. Why didn't you wake me up before you went?"

Poppy looks blank. "What for?"

"For my photo shoot with Yuka! You knew I had to be—"

Rin knew about the job, but Poppy didn't.

"Oh no," Poppy says, her hand flying to her mouth. "Did you have a shoot this morning? Did you miss it?"

I shake my head. "Rin – you didn't hear the alarms?"

Rin's chin is starting to wobble. "I hear no alarm, Harry-chan. I have whales on."

"What about the doorbell? It was being rung for two hours and none of us heard it?"

Poppy's eyes fly open. "Oh, Harriet, it's been crackling for ages and it finally broke. I left a note about it for you." She points at a small piece of paper duly stuck next to the bed. "And we left another one on the front door asking visitors to ring our phones."

My phone.

I crouch down and start fumbling around under my bed. After three or four seconds, I find it tucked behind a stray pillow. The battery is totally dead.

Oh my God. *What is wrong with me? What kind of person am I?*

Actually, I'd really appreciate it if nobody answers that.

Then something else in my head clicks. I run to the bird alarm, pick it up and sure enough: it's still on *British time*. All my alarms are set to go off three hours from now.

The entire morning has been my fault.

But what about the shoes? I think. Except…

Nobody actually told me to put them on, did they?

Maybe they were a gift. Maybe the note was in the wrong place, at the wrong time. Maybe they weren't even for me.

This is exactly what happens when you just blindly do what notes tell you without asking appropriate questions first. Did Lewis Carroll teach me *nothing*?

Rin and Poppy are staring at me with wide, slightly reproachful eyes, and suddenly I don't want to be here any more. I want to be far, far away, in a universe where I am not such a horrible human being. In a nicer, alternative world where I take responsibility for my own mistakes like a nearly adult, instead of stropping about, ruining things and then blaming everyone else like a spoilt little child.

It's moments like this when my unpopularity is nowhere near as much of a mystery as I'd like it to be.

"I'm so sorry," I say for the billionth time, my face getting steadily hotter. I start backing out of the room.

"I didn't mean to… I don't know what I'm… I'm" – I blush even deeper – "I'm so, so sorry."

And in a wave of shame, I grab my mobile and the charger, run into the hallway and climb into the cupboard.

54

Before you say it, no.

There is nothing weird about hiding in a cupboard. C. S. Lewis based an entire series of books on the premise that this is what normal people do on a regular basis. Anyway, I don't have any other choice. This is the only piece of furniture in Japan I can fit either into or under.

I shut the door firmly, turn on the light and slump into a large cardboard box full of towels and drying-up cloths. Then I plug my phone in and rummage around until I find one of Poppy's banished chocolate bars. I cram as much of it into my mouth as will physically fit, turn my phone on and hit speed dial.

"Hi. It's Nat. Leave a message or don't. Whatever. I've probably already been eaten by a sheep anyway and this phone is now lying in a big pile of poo, just like my life."

BEEP.

I guess Nat is still pretty angry with her mum. At

least I hope she is, or judging by that message this is going to be the beginning of a really weird and slightly depressing sixth form.

"Hey," I say. "It's me – I just needed to..."

This is not OK. I can't just steal my best friend's modelling dream and then sit in a cupboard, whining about it. A soulmate's job is to make somebody's day better, not worse.

I swiftly adopt my brightest, breeziest, happiest voice and spoil the surprise present I bought for her.

"Umm... Nat, you know you said that looking like a My Little Pony was super cool, right? Well, I found these amazing rainbow hair extensions in Harajuku. What colour would you like? Pink? Purple? Turquoise?" I pause and try to swallow a hard, distinctly unbreezy lump in my throat. "Anyway. Hope things are getting better in France. It's all amazing here and I'm having soooooo much fun." *Rein it back, Harriet.* "I miss you. Bye."

Then I hang up, shove another chocolate bar into my mouth and try a different number.

"*Hello. This is a digital recording of the electro-magnetic wave of Toby's voice, which has been encoded on to a binary system of data. Leave your own electromagnetic wave, and I will call you back when*

I've finished playing Plants versus Zombies but that could be a while because frankly it's almost impossible to get through the iron bucket on their head with a few bits of sweetcorn and a cabbag—"

BEEP.

I swallow the chocolate whole. Nat can be quite flaky in the mornings, but Toby always answers his phone. Especially when it's me. It's one of his most redeeming characteristics.

Seriously, what is the point in having a stalker if they're not at your beck and call whenever you need them?

"Toby? It's Harriet. I'm just ringing because..."

Because everything's going wrong and I want him to make me feel better? Because even though I left without saying goodbye, it's his job to be there for me regardless? Because all I'm thinking about is myself?

Again?

"Umm..." I clear my throat. "I thought you should know that if you laid all the Lego bricks sold in one year end to end they would stretch five times round the world. You can put that as a pop-up box in your *Lord of the Rings* video. You know, make it a bit more interactive." My phone makes a tiny pinging noise. I knew those facts about Lego would come in handy one day. "I hope you're having a great summer, Tobes. Speak soon."

Then I hang up miserably and click on the text that's just come through:

HARRIET STOP RING ME ASAP STOP WE NEED TO TALK STOP WILBUR KISS KISS STOP

I stare at it in confusion – my agent seems to be under the impression that his phone sends Morse code – and then close my eyes.

Did Wilbur just call me *Harriet*?

Oh my God: I am in *so* much trouble.

Eyes starting to well up again, I desperately search through my contacts for somebody else to talk to and realise I've run out of options already. Unless I want to confide my problems in one of my local bookshops or the National Trust.

Which means I'm going to have to do what no self-respecting teenager does under any circumstances.

I'll have to ring my parents.

55

It takes a good six minutes for Dad to pick up.

Predominantly because he can't work out where the phone call is coming from. I've rung the home computer from my mobile, and this complicated trick of modern technology creates total havoc. By the time Dad has run round the house, finally worked out what's going on and pressed the right button, all I can hear is him shouting upstairs: "Annabel, there's a video phone in our computer! Was that your idea?"

The webcam finally clears, but all I see is Dad's dressing gown. "Look," he adds as I hear Annabel lumbering heavily down the stairs. "Harriet hasn't died. We've still got a teenage daughter. Cancel the application for a replacement or we'll end up with two."

I scowl. "Nice to see you too, Father."

The dressing gown moves slightly. "Can she see me?" Dad's stomach asks curiously.

"You need to sit down, sweetheart," Annabel says.

There's a swift, stripy movement of dressing gown. "Is that better?"

Now all I can see is Dad's left ear. Annabel wheels him across so he's in full screen. Then she pokes her head into the corner of the screen.

"So, what delights of the fashion world have prevented you from ringing us until now?"

I shrug awkwardly. I didn't realise I'd be so happy to see them, but now I feel so homesick I just want to climb through the screen, curl up in the armchair and never ever leave again.

But I can't, can I?

It's just better if she's not here.

"Somebody wants to say hello," Dad says, handing Annabel what looks like an olive covered in peanut butter. "You're so disgusting, Bels," he tells her proudly, scruffing up her hair. The screen suddenly fills with white fluff. "Grrrr-d morning, Harriet. How are woof?"

I smile. "Hey, Hugo."

"I miss you terrier-bly, Harriet," Hugo/Dad says, licking his nose/wiggling his eyebrows. Then the camera points at Annabel's stomach. "Hello, Harriet," a squeaky voice says. "I can't wait to meet you."

"That's ridiculously creepy, Richard," I hear Annabel say. "Our child is not going to sound like a chipmunk."

"It's not my fault if it does," Dad replies. "That'll be your half. It's only fifty per cent Total Legend." He leans towards her belly, pretends to listen and then adds, "What's that? You want to be called Ralph?"

"After the world's biggest rabbit, I presume," Annabel says calmly. Then she looks back at me. "Are you actually OK, Harriet? Are you having fun?"

I swallow, hard. There's no point telling them. They only want to talk about the baby. As per usual.

"I'm great," I lie. My face is starting to hurt with all the pretend emotions. "The campaign's going great, I'm getting on great with my flatmates and Yuka's really, really... great about my incredible modelling skills."

When people lie, they look to the left because that's the part of the brain associated with the imagination. When they're telling the truth, they look to the right because that's the part of the brain linked to memory.

I look to the right as hard as I can.

Annabel frowns. "What's happening to your face, Harriet? Where's your grandmother? Let me speak to her."

Sugar cookies. I keep forgetting that Annabel is possibly related to Gandalf, Merlin and Zeus, all at the same time. "Bunty is…" I have literally no idea. "Umm…"

There's a small knock on the cupboard door next to my head.

"Harriet? Are you in here?"

"If not Harry-chan, we have big problem," I hear Rin giggle. "We have talking cupboard."

"I'm here," I call out, and then turn back to Annabel and Dad. "Oh," I say in my least wooden voice. "That's my flatmates. I should go."

"There's a strange lady at the door, Harriet. She says she wants to see you."

"Cute pink hair and sparkles," Rin adds merrily. "Like Hello Kitty."

I drop my phone.

"What?" I hear Annabel snap into the floor. "What did they just say?"

"Darling?" a familiar voice calls. "Can I stay here tonight? My friend has been hosting a party and it seems to be going on indefinitely. I haven't seen a mattress in days."

"What's going on?" Annabel shouts. "Why don't your flatmates know your grandmother? Where has she been? MOTHER, YOU PROMISED!"

Oh my God. *Do something, Harriet*. Anything.

"Oh dear," I say, picking my phone off the floor and shaking it furiously up and down. "Earthquake." Then I hang up and switch off my phone as quickly as possible.

Slowly, I open the cupboard door.

Bunty's standing there in a blue, floor-length floral dress, with white lace trailing all the way around the bottom and a blue mirrored blouse tied up in a knot at her waist. There are six or seven beaded necklaces of different colours around her neck, bells around her ankles and her pale pink hair has been piled on top of her head and appears to have been secured by a chopstick.

Not a pretty, decorative chopstick.

The kind of chopstick you get in white paper packs at convenience stores that give you mouth splinters.

"What a lovely place to hide!" Bunty says gaily, wrapping me in a hug and patting my head. One of her enormous rings bashes my forehead. "How's your adventure going, darling?"

"A-are you back for good?"

"Absolutely. I thought we could do a bit of girly catch-up. Paint our fingers, pull our eyebrows out and put bits of papaya on our eyes..."

"Nails?" Rin says. "Cucumbers?"

"I think they might be quite dangerous next to the eyes, darling. Let's go for something nice and soft."

Bunty kicks her flip-flops into the corner of the hallway, wanders into the kitchen and pulls the fridge open. "Choccy biccies?" she adds. "For the tummy," she says to Rin. "Not for the eyes. Don't worry, I'm not *insane*. Now, I've got this strange hair that grows out of my cheek and if it gets too long I feel a bit like a cat. What shall we do with it?"

She leans towards Poppy. "Darling, I don't want to be rude but I think you might have one coming too."

"I am a *top model*," Poppy says indignantly. "We don't have *whiskers*."

"How sad," my grandmother says, nodding at Rin and wandering back into the hallway. "They're awfully handy for working out whether you can fit through a small space."

And, just like that, my grandmother is back.

56

Here are a few of the things Bunty makes us do over the rest of the day:

- Mash up various foodstuffs from the fridge and put them on our faces (including soy sauce and rice, salsa and leftover tofu).
- Turn on all the hot taps and have a fully clothed 'DIY sauna'.
- Rub kitchen salt on our legs.
- Brush each other's hair at the same time.
- Moisturise with olive oil and a dash of sesame.

Clearly, my grandmother knows even less about being a girl than I do.

With great aplomb and not a little bit of scariness she powers through: dragging Rin and Poppy back into the bedroom every time they try to escape like the Year Two Class Hamster every time we left the cage door open.

As we crawl into bed, exhausted and marinated

like expensive tuna steaks, I realise I haven't had time to think about everything that's gone wrong. And that maybe I'm kind of glad to have her here, after all.

For the first time since I arrived in Japan, the next morning goes totally smoothly. My grandmother wakes me up with a cup of tea and a bowl of ready-porridge and some kind of de-stressing feather to 'stroke my cares away' (we'll forget that last bit) and I calmly get ready in my neatest, cleanest, most modelly clothes (black trousers, a white vest and some silver ballet flats).

Our taxi takes us into the centre of Tokyo. The buildings get bigger and bigger, the lights get brighter and the crowds get thicker until they look like shiny, dark-suited fish. It's the noisiest part of Tokyo I've been in yet: beeps and chirrups and music are coming from every direction, every building is flashing in different neon colours like lit-up Lego.

The majority of the people on the streets appear to be men. Apart from a pink bunny in a dress, frilly apron and high heels.

That one's probably not.

"Akihabara," Bunty says as she climbs out of the car. "This is the technology centre of Tokyo, darling.

If you want to see something crazy in Japan, you come here."

It's like being in a film set in the future, where there are barely any females and all of them look like they just fell out of an adults-only version of *Alice in Wonderland*.

"The game arcade is a popular Japanese stereotype," a voice says behind me. "Today I shall subvert it."

I spin round to face Yuka. Apparently we're not even doing greetings any more. "Brilliant," I say politely. "Umm... Yuka, this is Bunty, my step-grandmother."

"Nice to see you," Bunty says, taking Yuka's hand and pumping it unceremoniously up and down.

Yuka watches her hand in silence and then manages to extract it. "Yes," she says, and then turns back to me. "I would like to celebrate Japanese culture while also challenging Western perceptions. Every young person can relate to video games."

I'm nodding like a plastic dog in the back of a car, but my stomach is already starting to sink. Contrary to popular belief, not all geeks love *Star Trek* and gaming and fixing other people's printers. Some of us prefer dinosaur documentaries and reciting poetry at strangers while they're waiting for a bus, even after they've been asked not to.

"Fantastic," I lie enthusiastically. "I love arcade games."

"Good," Yuka says as she starts clicking towards a neon orange entrance. "Because you're going to be in one."

57

I love a good metaphor.

What Yuka actually means is that I'm going to be immersed allegorically inside the culture of modern Japanese technology. Or I'm going to be given a gun so I can fight aliens and vampires. Or I'll be scanned into a green screen so that in post-production I come out looking like a computer character. Or…

Or…

Nope. Yet again, I have literally no idea what Yuka's talking about.

Yuka, my grandmother and I walk through the immense building. The arcade is huge and heaving with people, and every square metre of it is beeping and flashing. The first floor is filled with hundreds of computer games: *boinging* and *clicking* and *peeping*. The second floor has things you can shoot and smash and bash and smack. The third floor is lit up by tiles being manically danced on and more photo booths crammed with squealing girls. The fourth is buried in soft toys. And the fifth appears to be a bowling alley.

At one stage, I see a game featuring live lobsters and a large foam bottom being smacked by a pair of teenagers. A yellow mist hangs in the air, the walls are flashing bright red, and the pale, blank gazes of gamers are everywhere, like zombies.

It's not unlike a sort of twenty-first-century high-tech version of Dante's nine levels of Hell. Except with much better refreshments and clearly marked exit signs.

By the time we make it to the sixth floor, I'm so disturbed by some of the things I've seen that I'm genuinely relieved to be pushed back into a giant cupboard. Except that this one has no chocolate in it and smells quite strongly of cleaning materials.

Bunty follows me in, then sniffs the air, pulls a face and heads straight back out.

"Sweetie pies," she says. "I'm far too old to get into a dark box voluntarily." She turns round and spies a food counter. "Ooh!" she says. "Slush Puppies! I must go dye my insides into a rainbow."

If Annabel isn't a persuasive argument for nurture versus nature, I don't know who is.

Apart from me, obviously.

"Umm, what should I do now?" I politely ask Yuka.

"Exactly what I tell you, Harriet," Yuka says, as in troops her team of stylists and hairdressers. "Do you think you can manage that?"

Here are some interesting facts:

- Manga is the Japanese word for 'whimsical picture'.
- The Manga industry in Japan is worth 420 billion yen every year, which is two and a half billion British pounds.
- It has been a style of Japanese art since the nineteenth century.
- People in Japan consume more paper as Manga than they do as toilet roll.
- Pink lace really itches.

I know this because I've just been turned into a Manga Girl. And also because I asked the stylists and the internet a lot of irritating questions.

My face has been bleached out with bright white foundation, and then given rosy cheeks and dark brown painted freckles. My eyes have been made cartoon-enormous with clever application of eyeliner and fake eyelashes and electric-green contact lenses significantly bigger than the pupil they're stuck to. I'm wearing a pale pink waist-length shiny wig with a shiny fringe that skims my eyebrows, and my dress is pale pink lace covered with hundreds of pink ruffles and bows and diamanté and ribbons and beads and feathers.

There are diamonds and pearls wrapped round my neck and wrists, and on my feet are little lacy white socks with baby blue shoes covered in sparkly silver stars. I even have frilly knickerbockers on, which reach nearly down to my knees and make me look like a Victorian lady at the seaside.

There's no doubt about it: I'm as *kawaii* as a human gets. Rin would be so proud.

Yuka makes a few last-minute tweaks, adjusts my wig and then stalks back out of the makeshift changing room to where Bunty is leaning against a wall with a laser gun in her hands. Bunty's missing every single vampire target, and when I raise my eyebrows she says, "I'm a pacifist, darling. The fact that these poor creatures do not happen to be real is neither here nor there." Then she grins. "Yuka, how lovely and talented you are. It looks like you've been having an immensely good time with a glue gun."

In fairness, I do look like a massive *Blue Peter* project. My outfit is phenomenally heavy. All I've done is walk through the door and I'm exhausted.

I really need to start doing some proper exercise. It's not a good sign when a dress wears your muscles out.

Haru and Naho are waiting in the corner, where six or seven huge lights have been set up. Everything's pointing towards a large glass and metal case, with buttons and a silver metal claw hanging from the ceiling. The whole thing has been painted bright pink, like the world's most girly Tardis. It's what Dr Who would travel in, if Dr Who was also Barbie.

As I get a little closer I realise with a start that the case is full of hundreds and hundreds of tiny dolls. Every single one has pink hair and freckles. Every single one is wearing a pink lacy dress and pale blue shoes. Every single one has massive, staring green eyes.

It's intensely creepy.

"Oh," I laugh nervously, trying not to notice that the eyes of the dolls are following me when I move. "That's me. In the arcade game. I see what you mean."

"Do you?" Yuka says. "Excellent. Now get in."

58

The word 'phobia' is a derivative of the Ancient Greek word *phobos*, which means fear.

Humans can be scared of literally anything. For instance, fear of dust is called *amathophobia*. Fear of peanut butter sticking to the roof of the mouth is called *arachibutyrophobia*. Fear of looking up is *anablephobia* and fear of space is *astrophobia*.

And that's just the As. Go on through the alphabet and there's even *phobophobia*, fear of having a phobia. Which I'd imagine then leads to a fear of irony (I'm not sure what that's called).

I'm not scared of small spaces (*claustrophobic*) or suffocating (*pnigophobic*) or glass (*crystellophobic*). I'm not scared of dolls (*pediophobic*) or things that look like humans but actually aren't (*automatonophobic*). I'm not even scared of sharp, automated metal claws hanging just above your head in a way that could feasibly pierce through your skull and kill you in a matter of seconds.

But put them all together in front of an audience? Terrified.

I barely fit into the box. Shion, Naho and Haru have to lift me in, shove me from behind and then lock the glass cabinet so I don't fall back out again. I can still breathe – there are tiny holes punctured into the top – but that's pretty much it. There's barely room to move, and certainly not enough to do more than crouch with my knees by my shoulders.

I feel like Alice when she drinks the potion in the White Rabbit's house. Except that this time there's no chimney or window to stick an arm or leg out of, no cake to eat that will make me smaller, and no lizards running around, yelling at me.

Actually, I'm quite glad about that last point. I don't think shouting lizards tend to help situations like this.

I look anxiously at the expressionless dolls, staring at me. Then at an expressionless Yuka, staring at me. I look at my expressionless grandmother, carefully studying a piece of food stuck to the front of her dress.

I take a deep breath.

Then I take an even deeper breath and remind

myself that I have to do this. Because if I don't, I'm going straight home.

And I give it everything I've got.

59

Something I've learnt over the last six months must have finally stuck.

My body and my brain are actually working together, instead of reluctantly with open hostility, like two work colleagues who secretly hate each other.

I slouch carefully against the glass sides of the box, tucking my knees in and poking my elbows out. Then I move so that one arm is over my head, pressing against the roof of the box. I draw my feet up so that they're stretched in the opposite direction and my head is at a right angle. I use the dress and the edges of the glass: leaning and pressing and bending and unwinding and bending again.

At one point, I'm actually almost upside down: legs in the air, feet on the ceiling, head on the floor, doll clutched in my hand. And – throughout – I try to keep my face as still and as wide-eyed and as expressionless as I possibly can.

Every time I move into a new position, my

grandmother pays less attention to the food on her collar. Shion starts bobbing around like a happy stripy pigeon and Naho high-fives the hairdresser. Even Haru looks mildly jolly.

"*Sugoi, jyan?*" he shouts. "*Kore wa subarashi desu! Iketeru jyan!*"

"Haru says you're doing brilliantly," Naho says straight away. "The photos are incredible."

I flash a quick grin at Naho, and then look at Yuka. With every click of the camera, something is happening to the corners of her mouth: they're starting to move almost imperceptibly upwards.

Yuka Ito is actually *smiling*. In a few clicks, the skin around her eyes might even crinkle.

I've finally done it. I've finally achieved something on my own.

Filled with a bright, hot sense of relief, I'm just shifting my position when something moves.

Something *in the box* moves.

OK. This is precisely the kind of thing that happens when you've watched *Toy Story 1, 2* and *3* too many times, and then written a letter to Pixar asking when the fourth one is due.

I crouch between the dolls with my arms out at the side, and stretch my neck upwards. I'm just reaching out a hand to lean carefully against the other side of the box when the doll nearest it does a little jiggle.

I'm going to say that again. The doll *does a little jiggle.*

I squeak and grab my hand back.

"What's going on?" Yuka snaps.

"The doll," I say before I can stop myself. "It jiggled."

My grandmother looks fascinated. "Did it say anything, sweetie? I make a point of listening to anything inanimate that tries to communicate with me."

Yuka shoots her a look of death and then turns back to me. "Dolls do not move, Harriet." The corners of her mouth are back in their normal position. "Get on with it."

I nod and go back to what I was doing before, except with one small alteration: I'm now numb with fear.

The doll moved. *I saw it.*

Apparently forty per cent of all British people believe in ghosts, and I think I'm now one of them. What if these are the trapped souls of hundreds of children? What if I'm in a haunted arcade game?

Chilled to the core and filled with visions of hundreds of tiny, cold, grasping fingers, I try to keep my face still and make my arms graceful, my legs less rigid, my movement fluid…

Something starts tickling my ankle.

Dolls don't jiggle, I start repeating under my breath as Yuka's eyes narrow until they're almost shut. *Dolls don't jiggle dolls don't jiggle dolls don't jiggle dolls don't jiggle dolls don't jiggle.*

But the tickling gets more and more pronounced, until I can't take it any more.

I look down.

A ginormous cockroach is slowly climbing up my bare leg.

Entomophobia = fear of insects.

Herpetophobia = fear of crawling things.

Fear of enormous black beetles the size of your palm creeping up your leg?

That's just called normal.

I look down, and then up again. "Oh," I say calmly to nobody in particular. "There appears to be a large semi-tropical insect of the order *Blattodea* and the subclass *Pterygota* currently meandering up my *tibialis anterior.*"

Or – you know:

GETITOFFMEGETITOFFMEGETITOFFME.

In one graceful, seamless movement, I lurch in blind panic straight into the glass side of the box.

And straight out the other side.

60

There isn't as much blood as you'd think.

That's the good news. The bad news is I don't think there's as much blood as Yuka would probably like.

I've done it again. *Again.*

There's smashed glass and dolls everywhere and, in my lunge for freedom, my dress caught on the metal side of the box and ripped all the way down the skirt. My wig has fallen off, my lipstick is smeared, my beaded necklace has snapped and I've got a metre-long scratch across my arm and tiny bits of glass lodged in my hands. Shion and Naho quickly pick me off the floor, brush me down and stick a plaster over the worst of it, but there's still enough damage to ensure I'm never allowed to get in any glass boxes again.

Not that I'd want to. Like Snow White, I think I've probably had enough of them for a while.

As soon as it's been ascertained that I'm not mortally wounded or going to sue anyone, Yuka's expression shifts from concern to fury. She thinks I'm making up excuses again.

In fact, *nobody* believes me. Once I'm out of the ruined dress, I clamber around on the floor trying to find evidence, but there's nothing there. I point out that cockroaches can move up to 80 cms per second and *fly,* but it's useless. Unless I can explain how an enormous insect could get into a sealed glass box I'm either:

a) The owner of an exceedingly overactive imagination.
b) Plain old-fashioned bonkers.

Or – worse:

c) Compulsively lying.

Again.

"*Atarashi moderu ni kaeruzo*!" Haru shouts. "*Harriet ga nayamino tane dattandayo.*"

I've studied enough Japanese since Monday to know that *moderu* means *model, atarashi* means *new* and *kaeru* means roughly: *change right now*. I'm very glad my translation skills end there.

"Well," Bunty says when the team starts packing

up again. "It's certainly never boring with you around, is it, darling?"

I look to the corner of the room, where Yuka is speaking on her phone. I don't think she's ordering a takeaway pizza.

A few minutes later, mine starts ringing. It's Wilbur. Without a second of hesitation, I swallow hard and cancel the call.

Looks like it's game over.

61

As soon as I get back into the flat, there's a flurry of activity. Rin and Poppy see the plasters and bandages and immediately want to know if I'm OK, have I hurt my head, have I seen the video already circulating the internet?

"Harry-chan," Rin says desperately when I don't respond to a cup of green tea, a rice biscuit or a 'Shouting Vase'. (I'm supposed to shout my frustrations into it to make them go away, but it just makes them go all echoey.) "Maybe you will go walk? Walk makes all person feels better."

"Yes," Poppy says, looking worried. "My boyfriend says that going outside always puts life in perspective. Especially if it's raining."

I flinch and my mood sinks a couple of metres lower.

"Actually," Bunty says wandering around, casually picking things up and putting them down again, "it's a medical fact that exercise just pushes sadness around the bloodstream faster."

That doesn't sound like a medical fact.

"I'll go," I say numbly. Not because I want to walk, but because I don't know what else to do.

"Super!" Rin cries. She jumps up. "*Chotto matteh!* I mean – wait!" She runs into the bedroom and comes back carrying a sound-asleep cat. "Maybe you take Kylie with you? Kylie love walk."

The cat abruptly opens her eyes and gives Rin a look that seriously questions that statement.

I shrug. "Sure."

"I get Kylie ready for you!" Rin stops and then says, "Are you wearing these clothes for a walk, Harry-chan?" I look down. I'm still in the black trousers, white vest and silver ballet flats from this morning. I nod.

Rin claps her hands, then disappears into the bedroom.

When she returns a few minutes later, Kylie is wearing a black jumpsuit with a white collar and little silver booties. Rin grabs a sparkly pink harness, sequined lead and wrestles her indignant cat into it. "Ready!" she says, handing the animal to me. "Enjoy!"

The cat and I look at each other, faces like thunder. For the first time, we're in total agreement.

And I slink out of the front door with the cat flopped unhappily in my arms.

*

There's an old expression: *misery likes company.*

There is *nothing* in the entire world more miserable than a cat being taken for a walk. Kylie's so wretched with despair and disgust at me and the world and everything in it, I feel slightly chirpier simply by comparison.

A walk with my dog tends to go: "Wait, Hugo. Hang on, Hugo. Stop, Hugo. Don't sniff that, Hugo. Stop licking that, Hugo. Leave her bottom alone, Hugo. *Hugo, that is not your ice cream. HUGO! DOWN! NO! HUGO, COME BACK HERE!*"

A walk with a cat goes: "Please get off the floor. *Please.*"

As soon as I put Kylie Minogue down, she defiantly spreads herself flat out on the pavement, and that's it: walk over.

I cajole. I plead. I even try a bit of mild bullying and half-hearted insults. Kylie simply glares at me.

When I tug hard on the harness, she allows herself to be dragged along the floor sideways like a wheely suitcase without wheels.

Eventually – when I've given up all hope – she stands up and walks three paces. I get over-excited, Kylie sniffs a pebble, promptly decides she's done and lies back down again.

It's only when I look up and see an old Japanese lady, dragging a ginger cat along with its eyes narrowed and its legs stiff and its claws outstretched and digging into the pavement that I start to see the funny side.

This is ridiculous. I am ridiculous. *My entire life is increasingly ridiculous.*

I get my phone out of my pocket.

"Hello. This is a digital recording of the electromagnetic wave of Toby's voice, which has been encoded on to a binary system of data. Leave your own electromagnetic wave, and I will call you back when I've finished playing Plants versus Zombies but that could be a while because frankly it's almost impossible to get through the iron bucket on their head with a few bits of sweetcorn and a cabbag—"

BEEP.

"Hi, Toby." I frown. I'm starting to get a little bit concerned. I know it's the middle of the night in England but why isn't he answering? "It's Harriet. Are you OK? I was just ringing to... umm... find out whether we need to purchase our own Bunsen burners for Chemistry A Level. Let me know. Bye."

I hang up, bite my lip and immediately try Nat's number but that goes straight to voicemail too.

"Hi," I say, desperately attempting breeziness. "It's

me. Again. I just wanted to… umm… tell you that I read somewhere that cows can be identified by their nose prints. Can you have a look for me and see if you can tell a difference between them?" I pause and breathe heavily down the phone while I search for another way to say *I need you.* "Hope you're having an OK time. Speak soon. Bye."

I'm trying to ignore the deep ache at the base of my throat. It feels as if I'm trying to swallow a whole apple without biting into it first.

Despite the fact that Kylie and I have got no further than three metres from the flat, I decide that this 'walk' is over.

I tie Kylie to a lamp-post and climb up on to the top of a high wall. Then I ignore the sullen meowing below – obviously *now* she's keen to get going – and close my eyes.

The lump in my throat is getting bigger and bigger, and there's something niggling at me; something at the base of my brain, chewing away like a mouse at a piece of cheese.

I can hear Tokyo in distant beeps and peeps, the indecipherable chatter of my next-door neighbours, an aeroplane lowering itself into Narita airport. It's still hot, but I'm getting used to the smell and the density of the city air: the flowers and the traffic fumes and the incense and the breaded pork and the slightly soapy scent coming from the laundry hanging two floors above my head.

I take a deep breath. That bit reminds me of home.

Home.

The big lump moves down to the middle of my chest. Suddenly none of this feels exciting any more.

When I was really little, Dad would tuck me into bed and turn off my bedroom light, and everything would suddenly change. Teddy bears and ornaments and books that made me happy and content during the day would abruptly become strange, unfamiliar and scary. The room and everything in it was the same, but the darkness made me different.

That's how it feels now. As if Tokyo is exactly as it was when I got here, but I'm suddenly less capable of knowing what to do with it. Because now it's just me.

I'm in one of the most populated cities in the entire world, and I have never, ever felt more alone in my life.

"My little Owl," a kind voice says. "Look at you, perched up there, just like Humpty Dumpty."

I keep my eyes tightly shut. Yuka was right: my imagination really *does* have a life of its own. Oh my God. Is this the start of madness? Is this the beginning of a downward spiral into seeing vague, shadowy shapes in the wallpaper and having my food mashed up for me before I eat it?

"Are you meditating, Baby-baby Panda?" the voice says. "I've tried to do that ever since I heard Gary Barlow was into it, but I did three sessions and didn't see him. Not even *once*. Such a waste of twenty-five pounds."

I open my eyes. "W-w-what are you doing here?"

"What do you think I'm doing here?" Wilbur says, smiling. "I'm like all the Queen's horses and all the Queen's men, my little Sugar-puff. I've come to put you back together again."

At which point I promptly throw myself off the wall, fling my arms around Wilbur's neck and burst straight into tears.

62

Wilbur takes charge immediately.

"My little Butter-crumpet," he says gently after a few minutes of relieved sobbing (mine, not his). "It's lovely to be appreciated, Mini-chickpea. But you're getting salty water all over my Hermès silk scarf."

"I can't believe you've come all this way for me," I say, ignoring his warning and weeping happily into his shoulder.

"Of course I did, my little Pineapple-chunk." Wilbur pats me on the head, the way you comfort a puppy on firework night. "Fourteen hours squished next to a woman with body odour and wandering feet. Most Fairy Godmothers can just *appear*, so if that's not commitment to a cause I don't know what is. Let me have a look at you."

Wilbur holds me at arm's length.

"Twinkle-monkey, now I *know* something's wrong. What's with the yawn-o-gear? Where has my little Munchkin gone?"

I look down at my outfit, and suddenly I feel like somebody's drained the Harriet Manners out of me.

"I don't know," I admit.

"Then let's get her back, my little Sugar-peanut," Wilbur says. He bends down and unties Kylie, who immediately starts prinking and purring like the contrary little madam she is. Then Wilbur drops a polka-dot holdall on the pavement, climbs on top of the wall and pats the spot next to him.

"I suggest you tell me exactly what the sugar-monkeys has been going on since I last saw you, Teeny-possum."

I take a deep breath and hop up next to him. "I don't even know where to start."

Wilbur nods wisely. "Then begin at the end and work your way through to the front. We can piece the story together from there."

Over the next hour, I tell Wilbur everything. I tell him about the octopus and the dress, my alarms, oversleeping, the pink shoes, the sumo shoot, smashing the arcade game. I tell him how much Haru hates me. I tell him about my new flatmates. I tell him about Bunty. I even tell him about Nick.

For the first time since I've known him, Wilbur listens without a single word.

"OK, Peach-plum-pear," he says when I finally draw to a flushed halt. "Just one question: is there *any* chance you've been abducted by aliens and that the girl in front of me is actually from a world a billion miles away?"

Exactly what kind of magazines has Wilbur started reading?

"No chance," I say reluctantly.

"Because that would make it an *awful* lot easier to get Yuka back on side."

I remember with a sickening thump that it's not just me my behaviour has consequences for.

"I'm so sorry, Wilbur. I just don't think I'm cut out for modelling."

"Baby-baby Giraffe," he says firmly, "not a single thing that's gone wrong has been anything to do with your modelling skills. I thought that you'd have figured that out for yourself by now."

I stare at him. "What do you mean?"

"Tinkle-berry," Wilbur says tying the harness back on to the cat and picking his spotty bag up. He swings it over his shoulder like a slightly podgy Huckleberry Finn. "I mean it's time to find out what the diddle cat is going on."

63

My first instinct on entering the flat is one of panic. Bunty's lying flat on the living-room floor in a shower of flashing lights. It's only when she holds up a crystal necklace that I realise I probably don't need to call an ambulance. She's lying in a small patch of sunshine, waving the necklace so that tiny rainbows bounce around the walls.

Suffice to say, Kylie immediately runs in and tries to violently kill one.

"Bunty-boo," Wilbur says, walking over and prodding my grandmother with a stripy sneaker. "May I join you?"

"Of course, darling. Take a pew."

Wilbur lies down next to her, and they both watch the rainbows in silence. Finally he says, "Any ideas?"

"Quite a few, as it happens."

"About—"

"Exactly."

"And the—"

"I thought so too. Nothing yet but it's getting there."

"What's going on?"

"Nothing to worry about, my little Paper-flip-chart," Wilbur says with a smile.

"Harriet, darling, why don't you go into the bedroom and have a little look round? See if there's anything *missing*?"

The mouse in my brain suddenly wakes up and takes another nibble. I shift uncomfortably.

"Harry-chan?" a small voice says from the doorway. "Do we have visit? Is it Ted? Do we need more presents?"

"Is it Nick?" Poppy says from behind her. "I've been calling and calling him and..."

They spot Wilbur, and there's suddenly silence. A strangely long and uncomfortable silence. The kind of silence you could drink, if you were interested in drinking silences.

"Poppy," my agent says. "Cherry-winkle, I haven't seen you since you jumped shipski to that other agency without cancelling our contract first. How's tricks, Pumpkin?" There's a slight edge to Wilbur's voice that I haven't heard before.

"Umm – hi, Wilbur," Poppy says awkwardly, tucking

her golden hair behind her ear and standing on a different foot. "Nice to see you again. How are you?"

"Fandabby, naturally, Darling-cake." Then he looks straight at Rin. "And how's my little Rin-chops?"

Wilbur knows *Rin*? How does Wilbur *know Rin*?

Then I see that Rin has gone bright red, and has immediately grabbed Kylie and buried her face in Kylie's fur. "Wilbur-San," she says, dropping into a low, formal bow. "Iamfinethankyouandyou?"

"Marvelly," Wilbur says, sitting up. "And tell me, Sheep-pudding: have you found much work since Yuka dropped you from the Baylee campaign and replaced you with Harriet?"

Rin abruptly steps backwards until she's pressed against the wall with Kylie held protectively in front of her.

What the sugar cookies is going on?

"Not so much," she says in a small voice.

"Not at all, I've heard," Wilbur says, flashing a glance my way.

I suddenly realise that although Rin said she was a model, she hasn't actually mentioned a single modelling job since I got here.

"I am OK. I enjoy the chill time." Rin's cheeks are now scarlet.

"Of course you do," Wilbur says. "Who doesn't just *adore* penniless, anonymous unemployment, Rabbit-nose?"

My head is starting to make an incomprehensible buzzing sound. *Rin* used to be the Baylee model? I replaced her? I ruined her modelling career and I didn't even *know*? I've Googled *everything in the world that has ever happened ever,* and it never occurred to me to look up the model I replaced last year?

"B-but I don't understand," I say, looking at both of my flatmates. "What are you saying—" and suddenly the mouse in my brain stops chewing.

Annabel changed the time on my alarm clocks.

While I was getting ready to leave the house for the airport, she changed my watch, my phone and all three alarm clocks. Dad had to help her screw on the back of the little bird because it was too tight.

A fraction of a second later, the mouse sighs and clonks me gently round the head.

I charged my phone the night before the sumo shoot. I *know* I did, because I had to get my six-piece adapter kit with snap-on plug out of my suitcase. And plug it in next to the doorway. *Not* under my bed.

There was no note about the doorbell next to my bed when I went to sleep.

The shoes at the sumo ring were *pink*, *glittery* and *too small*.

My brain continues making a few more whirring sounds, and – finally – the mouse stands up, rolls its eyes and punches me straight in the face.

No. No.

NO.

Feeling sick, I turn round and run to the bedroom; hoping I'm wrong, hoping I've made a mistake, hoping I've jumped to irrational conclusions. But I haven't.

The corner of the room is empty.

The cockroach trap is gone.

64

Six months ago, I had a list.

It was a list of all the people I thought hated me, and I carried it around with me everywhere. I added to it, and I studied it, and it grew and grew and grew. Eventually, I realised I was wrong and I crossed the names off and threw the list away.

Maybe I shouldn't have been so quick to do that.

I've travelled halfway around the world and fooled myself into thinking that there's a place for me here. That I fit in. That people actually want me to.

But now I'm back exactly where I started.

It looks like somebody still hates Harriet Manners after all.

65

Bunty and Wilbur don't leave my side for the next twenty-four hours. It's no longer my New and Infinitely Less Glorious Plan 3 (NAILGP3).

It's theirs too.

They take me for slightly rubbery sushi from a conveyor belt. They take me to see a Hollywood blockbuster at the Waseda Shochiku Cinema. They follow me to the Meguro Parasitological Museum, and then promptly go outside to vomit (it has the longest ever tapeworm found in a human: it's nearly nine metres long).

By the time I meet Wilbur at Tōkyō train station the next morning, I'm pretty sure that one of them is standing outside the bathroom every time I go to the toilet, just to make sure nobody's followed me in.

"Cooo-eeeee!" he screeches across the enormous, incredibly busy concourse, pushing his way to meet me. "Over here, my little Chicken McNugget!" He's wearing a bright pink suit with sparkly wings drawn on the back, and a leopard-print cap. "Back to genius attire, I'm incandescent to see." He looks me up and down. "What's the inspiration this time, Buttercup?"

I smile. "My father made it for me."

Wilbur looks carefully at my denim dungaree dress, stripy leggings, neon-green trainers and the white T-shirt with the huge word **MODEL** written on it in red marker pen.

Let's just say: Dad finally noticed my satchel.

"My Father Made It For Me," he sighs happily. "You light up my life, Sugar-lump. You really do."

Bunty nods from behind me. "Your turn," she says, pushing me gently towards him.

"Got her," he says, grabbing my arm as if we're playing Harriet Relay. "Go home and guard those two backstabbers."

"On it. Poppy's having a bath, and I may or may not have propped a chair outside the door. Rin's trying to train her cat to roll over, so that should keep her occupied for the rest of the day."

"Just don't let them leave the house," Wilbur says, and then blows my grandmother a kiss and starts leading me through the train station with his arm tucked through mine as if we're two teenage girls, not one and a slightly portly fashionista.

I assume we're going on the metro, and am already weak with relief that it's not rush hour so we won't be physically crammed into a carriage by a little man wearing little white gloves and a hat, like a really aggressive Fat Controller from *Thomas the Tank Engine*. But Wilbur steps on to the up escalator.

"The shoot isn't on the underground?"

Wilbur tinkles with laughter. "You think we'd risk making you stand up on a moving vehicle?"

OK, I asked for that. "So where are we going?"

"Think about Yuka's subverted thingummy-jiggery. You're a smart cookie, Coffee-bean, why don't you tell me?"

The butterflies in my stomach go completely bonkers.

"Mount Fuji?" I squeak, gripping his arm. "We're going to *Mount Fuji*?"

At that precise moment, we get to the top of the escalator and Wilbur points at the instantly recognisable, long, shiny white train pulling into the station.

A pointy-nosed train with a blue stripe running down the side of it.

The most famous train in the entire world. Apart from Thomas, obviously.

"We certainly are," he says, patting my head. "And we are getting there on *that*."

*

The first time Dad brought Annabel home, she brought me a book about mountains. *Everest. K2. Kanchenjunga*. But Fuji was always my favourite because – unlike the others, hanging out in the Himalayas – it didn't have any friends.

I guess I felt a certain empathy with it.

In a flash, I suddenly understand what it is Yuka's doing. She's using fashion to challenge cultural stereotypes: living fish in a dead fish market. Women on a sumo stage. People trapped inside a computer game instead of by it.

The more I know Yuka, the more I admire her.

It's just a shame the feeling is almost definitely not mutual.

Wilbur and I wait by the smooth white electronic barriers that stop people climbing on to the track. Then we clamber up the stairs on to the Shinkansen and take our seats. I'm so excited, if the windows opened I'd be like Hugo on long car journeys: head out, tongue halfway down my chin, drool hitting the unlucky person behind me.

"By 2008 these Bullet Trains had made enough trips to circle the earth 30,000 times," I tell Wilbur breathlessly.

"At top speed it takes a train three minutes and 45 seconds to stop," I inform him as the train starts gently accelerating.

"In 47 years there have been 7.1 billion trips made on the train, and never a fatal accident," I say as a beautifully dressed woman in a hat and gloves starts walking down the aisles with refreshments, like an air hostess from the 1950s.

"Ooh, peanuts," I add happily.

As we slide out of Tokyo, everything slowly changes. The buildings get smaller and smaller, and the gaps between them get bigger and bigger. Suddenly – with an almost audible pop – there are big green stretching fields and tractors and little squat houses with peacock-blue tiles on the roof and dogs barking. The ground gets very flat, the sky gets close and bright, and there are people: bent over, wearing big flat hats and picking rice. We're going so fast that I'm literally pinned to my seat: my entire body is heavy and I have to *pull* myself down the aisle to the toilet like a little tree-swinging monkey.

There's a sudden peace, and for the first time in days I feel like I can breathe.

The only thing I can't really wrap my head around is how everyone else on the train can be so *nonchalant*.

In fact, the majority of the people on here are actually fast asleep: eyes rolled back and heads lolling against the people sitting next to them.

"People can get used to anything, Possum-breath," Wilbur says quietly. "You don't go into raptures every time you see the London Eye, do you?" Then he raises an eyebrow. "Actually, my little Kidney-bean, *you* probably do."

I look at my lap. Well, it *is* the world's largest cantilevered observation wheel.

Fifty minutes and six hundred breathless observations later, the train stops and an electronic voice says in a cut-glass American accent: *"Now arriving at Shin-Fuji station."*

"Is this it?" I burst out, standing up too quickly and smacking my head hard on the overhead compartments. Ouch. "Are we here? Are we at Mount Fuji? Can I see it? Can you show it to me?"

As if it's a shy kitten, and not a volcano 3,776 metres high.

"This is us, my little Butternut-squash," Wilbur says, then he points out of the window. "And who's that?"

I turn, but even as I'm turning I know, because Wilbur's got that twinkle.

That Well-What-Do-You-Know twinkle.

That What-A-Coincidence twinkle.

That Fairy-Godmother-Before-The-Ball twinkle.

That One-Day-I'm-Going-To-Get-Shot-By-Harriet-Manners-And-It'll-Be-All-My-Own-Fault twinkle.

My eyes meet Nick's and every single one of the one hundred trillion cells in my body leaps into the air. With difficulty, I lift my hand. "Hey," I finally mouth through the glass.

"Hey," he mouths straight back.

66

One day, I'm going to be the kind of ex-girlfriend who moves in a bubble of composure and indifference, leaving former suitors sobbing in her wake.

Today is clearly not it.

Not only did Nick see me smack my head on the overhead luggage compartments, he also sees me miss my first step off the train and fall straight on to the platform floor. He immediately reaches out a hand to pick me up, but I shake it off, put my hands on my hips and thrust myself off the ground. "Exercise," I tell him imperiously, bending a couple of times to demonstrate. "It's important to practise lunges wherever possible."

"Obviously." Nick nods. "It's rule 452 in the Fashion Modelling Handbook."

What? Why has nobody given me this book yet?

He smiles. "And rule 593 is Break Everything in a Twenty-Metre Radius, so you're clearly a natural."

Oh.

I blush and pretend to look for my train ticket in my satchel, even though I know it's in my pocket.

"Come and give me a kiss, Prince C," Wilbur announces as I search fruitlessly for a suitable comeback. "I haven't seen you for yonks and diddly yonks. How's that big brute of a country treating you?"

"Fine. Freezing cold, though."

"Australia's a contrary mare, and no mistake," Wilbur agrees, shaking his head. "Sunny at Christmas, cold in summer. What does Santa wear there, I wonder?"

"Red board-shorts," Nick says as he starts leading us out of the tiny station. "He's big into surfing."

"*Well*," Wilbur exclaims triumphantly, "no *wonder* he's got such red cheeks and nose by the time he gets round to us."

"Did you know," I blurt out, "that if Santa Claus was real, in order to deliver presents to 378 million Christian children all over the world, his sleigh would have to move at 3,000 times the speed of sound with 214,200 reindeer and the air resistance and the centrifugal forces involved would cause both the reindeer and Santa to explode?" I pause. "Not that I think Santa's real," I add. "I'm just saying if he *was* real."

Oh, for the love of *sugar cookies.* Nice way to not look like a *silly* child, Harriet.

"Aaaand she's back," Wilbur says, patting me on the head as if I'm a slightly dim-witted Labrador.

"Did you bring any Polaroid with you?" Nick asks as we start walking towards a large white van with blacked-out windows. "Haru's run out."

"I'm a professional, darling. Of course I have Polaroid film." Wilbur opens a flowery bag with a rabbit printed on it. "Now, is Yuka ready for this cherub?"

"That's not exactly how she's referring to Harriet at the moment, but – yes."

"And how about the… you know?"

"Ready. It pains me to say it, but my aunt is a genius."

"That good?"

"Uh-huh."

It's like they're talking in code. To be honest, I'm not even sure I want to know what they're on about.

So far my modelling career has consisted of: jumping around in snow with bare feet; being covered in gold paint; getting attacked by an octopus; feeling humiliated in front of 20,000 people and being put in a glass box.

Judging by past experiences, I would imagine they're now planning to wrap me in clingfilm and drop me off the top of a mountain attached to an elastic band. It's for the best all round if I just don't ask.

"And any sign of..." I say to Wilbur, lifting my eyebrows. I can totally do code too. *Ha*.

"What?"

"You know."

"No, what?"

For God's sake. How come when *I* try to be all mysterious, nobody understands what I'm talking about?

I blush. "Poppy or Rin," I whisper under my breath. "Any sign of them?"

"None," Wilbur whispers back. "Your grandmother's still guarding the flat like a gloriously sparkly Pyrenean Mountain Dog. She texted me to say she's got them baking wasabi cookies. It's going to be fine this time, my little Human-firework. We've made absolutely sure of it."

My shoulders relax, but only slightly.

Over the last ten years, Alexa and her minions have shown me so many shades of hatred I could draw you an Unpopularity Rainbow.

I know the shade of hatred you get when you tell people they've used the wrong word in a sentence;

the shade when you've just had a six-page spread in *Harper's Bazaar*; the shade when you've accidentally tripped in the school canteen and thrown baked beans and chicken Kiev all over the back of the person in front of you.

I even know the shade of hatred that comes from telling people about shades of hatred, and offering to draw them an Unpopularity Rainbow.

But I'm not sure anyone has ever hated me enough before to change my alarms, wear out my phone battery, plant a pair of culturally offensive shoes on me and manhandle a cockroach, all to try and get me fired when I'm 6,000 miles from home.

Not even Alexa.

67

I've had a picture of Japan in my head for more than a decade. Skyscrapers, flashing lights, crowds, technology, sushi, girls in cute outfits and dogs in clothes and a random mountain floating in the air somewhere behind it.

In other words: Tokyo.

As we drive away from Shin-Fuji train station, I suddenly realise there's an entire country that I had ignored completely.

Huge green fields full of tiny purple flowers, dense thickets of gnarly woods with tiny roads winding through them. Huge bright blue skies, silence and rustling and birds; little restaurants with wooden chairs and paper lanterns hanging from the ceilings; regal red temples built into rocks. In between the trees and the flowers are enormous shining lakes: sometimes seasoned with tiny boats and fishermen, sometimes with windsurfers, sometimes completely empty.

And – looming behind it all, reflected perfectly – Mount Fuji.

Proud and completely alone.

The only thing that could possibly make the journey more amazing would be *not* being squidged against the van door, curled into a stiff, semi-fetal position. I'm squashed next to Nick in the front, and every time we go round a corner, his left knee brushes against my right knee, or his left elbow brushes against my right elbow, and I spring a little further into the door as if I've just been electrocuted.

And there appear to be a *lot* of corners.

Wilbur's not helping. In fact, he seems to be going out of his way to make it worse. "Nick, Sugar-pot, tell Harriet where we are now."

"This is Fuji Five Lakes."

Three minutes later: "Nick, Monkey-bum, tell Harriet where the name Fuji comes from."

"I think it translates to *without equal.*"

One minute: "Nick, Orange-pip, tell Harriet what those flowers are called."

Cue laughter. "How would I know, Wil? Purple ones?"

I'm not a naturally violent person, but after three-quarters of an hour of this I am *seconds* away from smacking Wilbur's head against the seat in front to get him to shut up. Just so that I can stop blushing scarlet and avoiding eye contact and trying to hide my sweaty palms by cramming them between my legs. Just so I can stop saying 'ah' and trying to sound all mature and indifferent.

Just so I can stop pretending I can't feel Nick's shoulder knocking sporadically against mine or his foot three centimetres from mine or that it's slightly killing me.

Finally, we pull into an enormous, muddy car park. I'm out before the engine's switched off. Next time, I am *so* sitting in the back.

I hop straight into a puddle.

Nick laughs and carefully climbs over it. "That was pretty selfless of you, Manners, protecting my jeans like that. You're like some kind of girl knight."

I blush and shake the muddy water from my leggings.

"Owl-cakes," Wilbur says, clambering out and stretching like an enormous pink sparkly cat. "Can I leave you to entertain yourselves? I'm just going to go pull the brief out of Yuka."

I glance nervously at Nick and then away again.

I'm not entirely sure that *entertain* is the right word. When a frog vomits, it ejects its entire stomach and uses its forearms to empty out the contents.

There's a small chance I may be about to do the same thing.

"Sure," I say.

"Absolutely," Nick says, and – to my distress – his nonchalance sounds totally genuine. "Take your time."

"My darlings," Wilbur sighs. "If time belonged to me I totally would."

And he skips towards a familiar big black car waiting on the other side of the car park.

68

Studies have shown it takes exactly four seconds for a silence to become awkward.

I think somebody needs to tell Nick this.

He's still standing in the car park with his hands slung nonchalantly in his pockets. There isn't a flutter of discomfort or embarrassment on his handsome face.

Five seconds: nothing. Six seconds: nope. Seven seconds: nada. Eight sec—

"Come with me," he says abruptly, looking up. I'm forced to quickly pretend I've been studying an imaginary pigeon in a tree just behind his head.

"Pardon me?"

He awkwardly scratches his head. "Please? Unless you want to spend the next ten minutes standing in a car park?"

Pretend, Harriet. Pretend as hard as you can.

"Actually," I say in a desperate attempt to sound

like I'm not bothered either way, "white vans are quite interesting. Did you know that you would need 772 of them to move one billion Cheesy Wotsits?"

Yeah. That'll work.

He'll either think I'm totally over him or inordinately obsessed with private transport. And cheese-flavoured snacks.

"Of course," Nick says, nodding seriously. "Everybody knows that. Let's go."

He turns and starts striding towards the other side of the trees. I start objecting that Wilbur won't be able to find us again, that we'll get into trouble, that we'll get lost, and then I realise that with every hesitation he's getting further away. So I set my shoulders into their most cool, unbothered position and saunter casually after him. Then – because he's so fast – I saunter a little more quickly.

Then I break into a cool, unbothered kind of jog.

I'm just about running – cool and unbothered, and breathing quite heavily through my mouth – when the trees suddenly clear.

In front of us is an enormous, sparkling lake. A few flossy white clouds are hovering in the sky, which is now starting to deepen to a faint lilac colour with a slightly pink horizon. The lake is surrounded by a grey pebble beach and tiny flowers, and directly behind it is Mount Fuji.

We are totally alone.

I suddenly feel uncomfortable. As if I'm doing something very, very wrong.

I turn around and start walking quickly back towards the car park. "Harriet?" Nick says, and I pause then turn to face him. "Are you OK?"

I half nod without saying anything.

"Here." Nick reaches into his pocket. He walks forward and hands something to me.

"What's this?" I look at the money he's just forced into my hand. "What are you *paying* me for?"

"Hold it up."

There's a picture of a man on it with big bouffant hair and a bushy moustache. "Hideyo Noguchi, the famous Japanese bacteriologist?"

Nick frowns then shouts with laughter. "Not that side. Turn it over."

On the other side of the note is a little circle: a blue picture of a mountain topped with snow, reflected in the lake below it. I must have used 1,000-yen notes at some stage in the past week but I've never noticed it. I look back at the view in front of us. "Is this—"

"Where we are now? Yes. This is the exact spot where that picture was drawn. I wanted you to see it."

There's a silence while I try to process this.

"*Why?*"

"I don't know," Nick says. "I suppose I wanted to give *you* something this time."

We both look at the floor while I fiddle with the corner of the note. Then I say quietly, "Poppy's very beautiful, isn't she?"

I sort of feel as if I need to put her name out there, like a line in the sand.

Even though it's not actually sand: it's pebbles.

But you know what I mean.

Nick glances at me sharply, and a deep line appears between his eyebrows. He pauses, then says, "Yes, she is. But I prefer you."

The awkwardness in my stomach is getting tighter and tighter, and the urge to run away is unbearable.

What the sugar cookies is Nick *doing*?

I suddenly don't want him to say anything else. I feel as if I'm about to lose the boy I knew for good. And not to someone else this time: to a different version of himself. One who is a cheat.

Which is so, so much worse.

"I think we should stop talking to each other now," I say in a brittle voice. "Frankly, I think you're being awful."

Nick flinches. "Harriet—"

"There you are, Chuckle-monkeys!" a voice cries behind us, and a hand in a twinkly pink suit lands on my arm. Wilbur beams over my shoulder. "The light's running out, Pizza-bottom. We need you to get ready now."

I glance briefly at Nick, but he's staring at the lake: profile outlined against the sky, face totally unreadable.

Whatever he was going to say has gone.

It feels like it's not the only thing.

Swallowing hard, I follow Wilbur quietly back across the car park. But not before I've folded the note in half.

And dropped it on the floor behind me.

69

I am *so* ready to be transformed.

I want the full works. I want to be primped and prodded and coloured in and brushed. I want to be preened and polished and glossed and gleamed and sprayed and beautified and augmented until I look like a proper, real model. Like somebody completely different.

Which is why it's a bit disconcerting when Shion pulls a curtain around me, ties me into a long, floaty white dress with two pockets and a bit of white ribbon round the middle, and then starts walking me back through the car park.

There's no hairdresser here. No make-up artist. No assistants. Just Shion and me.

"Umm," I say politely as she gently winds a couple of purple flowers into my hair. She nods in satisfaction then hands me a pair of rubber flip-flops. "Where's my usual... garnish?"

As if I'm some kind of fashion hamburger.

Shion smiles. "No garnish today. Yuka wants you

completely natural. I'm on strict orders not to touch you with a single product." She grimaces slightly and leans closer to my face. "Although I am *so* tempted to quickly just touch up those two zits with a bit of concealer but" – she sighs – "we'll just have to leave them for Photoshop."

What? They're sending me out *like this*? Exactly as I am?

This wasn't part of the deal.

I don't even let Nat take photos of me like this.

I'm desperately trying to pinch some colour into my cheeks and lips the way Scarlett O'Hara does in *Gone with the Wind* when a cold voice behind me says, "Can you swim?"

Yuka's standing a metre behind me. I have literally no idea how long she's been there. It's like having a shower and only seeing the massive black spider in the corner right at the end. "Sorry?"

"Can you swim?"

Fifty-four per cent of the world's population can't, but Dad ensured I was in the minority during a particularly traumatic trip to Cornwall. "Yes."

"Good." Yuka nods. "This is the most important shoot. It is absolutely pivotal that everything goes to plan. Is that perfectly clear?"

I swallow. "Yes."

"Now, I am going to do something I have never done before in my entire career."

I look at the lake nervously. "Umm… what?"

"This."

And in one smooth motion, Yuka turns and walks back to her car, then climbs in and it drives away.

70

The relief is immediate.

It's as if the Narnian winter has abruptly thawed, and everyone in a twenty-metre radius can suddenly take off their metaphorical big furry coats. Within seconds, Shion's humming under her breath; Naho taps out a tune on her notepad; Wilbur takes his sunglasses off and wipes them on his shoulder pads. Even Haru perches on a log and rubs his forehead.

Yuka has obviously realised that the best thing she can do for her own campaign is be nowhere near it.

I follow Shion towards the water and then realise that Naho, Haru and a couple of the assistants are pulling on thermals, huge, waterproof onesies, hats and thigh-high wellies.

I'm going in, aren't I. I'm actually going into the freezing cold lake. In nothing but a summer dress. And flip-flops.

Of course I am.

*

I don't want to point out the obvious, but I'm recently heartbroken. I'm wearing a long white nightie and flowers in my hair. And now I'm being sent into a large body of open water.

Has nobody read *Hamlet*?

One of the assistants shyly holds out an extra waterproof costume to Wilbur and is promptly greeted with hysterical laughter. "My little Peanut-butter-spoon," he finally wheezes at the startled girl. "I'm not wearing that: I'd vomit in my own mouth. Plus, I can't go in water, Pea-pod. I'm like sugar: I'd dissolve on the spot. I think I'll just stay here and keep a lookout for danger like a cute little meerkat."

Then Wilbur puts his mirrored sunglasses back on and gives me a knowing, wry nod.

He really *is* like a guardian angel.

Albeit one with wings stitched into the back of his suit rather than a functional part of his outfit.

I'm just trying to work out how to get into the water without ruining yet another dress when a hand lands on my elbow. "Do you need help?" Nick's now dressed entirely in yellow waterproofs, like the world's most beautiful Paddington Bear. "Because unless you're Jesus, Manners, you're going to have to get a bit wet."

Every cell in my body is now numb, apart from the area directly under Nick's hand. That's on fire.

"Actually," I say, trying to extricate myself, "that's not true. If I was a water strider with hydrophobic feet, such as a *Gigantometra gigas*, I would be able to walk on water by shedding vortex filaments into the water and simply propelling myself forward."

"What's a *Gigantrometra gigas*?"

"It's sort of like a big stick insect."

"And are you sort of like a big stick insect?"

I look at my non-hydrophobic feet. "No."

"Then you're going to get wet." Nick holds out his arm like a man in a black and white film. "Hold on to this."

No. Yes. No no no no no *no*.

"Thank you," I say with great dignity, taking a step forwards, "but I am perfectly capable of—"

The world suddenly tilts as I plunge down.

Nick grabs me before I hit the water and straightens me back up again. "Please, Harriet. That's why I'm here. I've been paid to make sure you don't knock yourself out and drown. Will you *please* let me do my job without fighting me the entire way?"

I open my mouth and then shut it again and nod.

It's only as we get deeper that I start to notice just

how beautiful this dress is. Out of water it's deceptively simple, but there are actually dozens of layers, cut at slightly different angles so that they swirl out in huge billows as the water pulls them in different directions. Despite being white, there's so much material it's not transparent at all. It's slightly mermaidy, slightly Lady of Shalott (yet another heartbroken lady who didn't fare very well in lots of water).

I slip on another rock as we reach the team, and Nick swiftly moves so that his arm is around my shoulder.

"*Yoku yatta, Harriet. Kimiwa migotoda,*" Haru says in an almost unrecognisable, low, calm voice. *"Demo, sono kakkou ha samuku naika?"*

Naho smiles at me. "Haru says you're doing brilliantly, Harriet. He also wants to know if you're too cold?"

I shake my head. All I can feel is Nick. The rest of me may as well have vanished completely.

"*Mizu no nakani suwatte moraukedo, daijyoubu kana?*"

"Is it all right if you sit down in the water?"

I try not to notice Nick's arm move and his hand rest gently on my waist. The world is starting to tilt again, even though this time I'm not actually slipping anywhere.

"*Jyaa, sorosoro hajimeyouka*?"

"Ready to start?"

Nick's hand moves and seems to slip slightly under the cloth tied around my middle. It fumbles a bit just at the small of my back and I can feel myself blushing from the roots of my hair all the way down to my toes. Apparently the sun's core is so hot that a piece of it the size of a pinhead would give off enough heat to kill a person 160 kilometres away.

The way I'm burning right now, I reckon I could obliterate everyone from here to South Korea.

But he's not mine.

There's a line between being supportive and being gropey, and he has just totally crossed it. "Nick," I snap, "what on earth do you think you're playing at? Get the hell off me."

"I'm trying to find the button," he says. "Sorry. I thought it would be easier than this."

I stare at him. That is so unbelievably rude.

"*What?!* Is that some kind of horrible metaphor for—"

But I don't finish, because Nick suddenly beams at me. My stomach promptly stands on its tiptoes then flips over backwards and everything inside me falls apart. "Got it," he says, leaning forwards.

Before I can stop him, Nick kisses me gently on the cheek.

And my entire body is covered in light.

71

For a fraction of a second, I actually think that the light is coming from me. That my emotions are so strong, I've rendered them a literal, physical, visible fact. I'm a scientific phenomenon.

Then I think, Wilbur was uncannily prescient and I've just burst into flames.

It's only when Nick pulls away and I look down that I realise the light's coming from the dress. Every single fibre of the material is a hair-thin LED, woven tightly together, and the whole dress is now shining neon white with tiny clustered knots of light around the neckline like stars.

I am glowing and glittering all over, and the light is spreading through the water and swirling around me.

Never mind metaphors. Never mind lightning bugs.

Nick has *literally* just lit me up.

Above me, the sky is starting to change colour into a dark, gold-ish pink, brightening to red at the horizon, and tiny dots of stars are forming in the blackness. In front of me, lights from the car park are bouncing off the water and an assistant is holding a soft golden light over my head. And below me, my dress is reflecting and shining through the water.

There is light everywhere. I'm surrounded by it, and covered in it, and full of it.

At some point I'm going to have to come back down to earth again. But for a few minutes, I'm going to stay exactly where I am.

Suspended somewhere a few metres above it.

"Jyunbi ha iikai?"

"Ready, Harriet?"

I nod blankly and silently lower myself into the freezing-cold water. Now that Nick's no longer touching me, it's incredibly, ridiculously cold.

And I don't care in the slightest.

"*Kirei dane?*" Haru says, gesturing around as the camera starts clicking and I stare into space somewhere over his left shoulder.

"Yes. Beautiful." Nick nods and looks at the mountain carved against the horizon behind me. "Without equal."

And then he looks directly at me.

72

Whatever Wilbur has done to protect me, it works.

The shoot goes perfectly. I sit quietly in the cold water for ten minutes, then bend into it, then lean forwards on my elbows. Finally I lie down completely so that Haru is shooting directly over me and my wet hair and glowing skirts are swirling around my head like I'm a water nymph trapped in some kind of magical, ghostly seaweed. I even manage not to inhale water into my lungs or drown.

Everyone is utterly delighted.

"*Shashin kara kannjyou ga afurete kuruyo, Harriet. Kimino kokoroga mieruyouda.*"

"There's so much *emotion* in these pictures, Harriet," Naho translates happily. "Haru says it's like he can see right into the middle of you."

Sugar cookies.

I quickly blink and try very hard to be a little less transparent.

*

Finally, Haru gives a satisfied nod, Naho wraps a towel around my freezing shoulders and we all splash and slip back out of the lake again, where Yuka is waiting for us.

I'm not even vaguely surprised. I'm going to guess she got less than three metres down the road before spying with her night-vision binoculars.

"*Umaku ittakashira*?" she asks Haru stiffly.

"*Sugoiyo*," Haru says with a nod, and I beam. That means 'excellent'. "*Honntouni sugoi noga toretayo*."

And then it happens again – Yuka's smiling. No, Yuka Ito is *grinning*.

Even Nick looks startled.

"Excellent," Yuka says, smoothing down her dress and carefully composing her face. She looks me up and down and then clicks her fingers. "What are we standing around for? I'm not paying anyone to catch pneumonia. Get my model dry."

Wilbur is going bonkers on the beach behind us. He's shouting and spinning in little circles with his pink jacket pulled over his head. "BOOM! I told you, Peaches! I told you my little Frankie-chops would knock it right out of the park!" He bends down and starts attempting Russian dancing on the pebbles.

Yuka frowns. "If you're going to be working directly

for me, William, I strongly suggest you stop that immediately."

Wilbur pauses in his crouch-jumping. "For the bajillionth time," he says indignantly: "It is Wilbur, with a bur and not an iam, and I would thank you to—" Then he stops and stands up straight. "Working for you?"

Yuka gives an almost imperceptible nod as she climbs back into her waiting car.

Wilbur's face goes all red and shaky, and then he physically explodes. "OH, MY MINI-HUMMINGBIRDS, THIS IS THE BEST DAY THAT HAS EVER BEEN BORN IF DAYS WERE BORN WHICH THEY'RE PROBABLY NOT BUT WHO CARES I MADE IT! I'M IN! I'M FINALLY IN PROPER FASSSHHHIIIOOON."

And he grabs my arm and starts swinging me round in manic giant circles. The way Nat and I used to spin years ago before I slipped and smashed into a park bench and had to be taken to hospital to get eight stitches in the back of my head.

I blush and spin, giddy and pink-cheeked.

I can't believe it: everything's going to be OK. The campaign's a success and nobody's angry with me. Wilbur's got his big job, and I've kept mine.

And Nick?

Nick *kissed* me.

Which I can't even think about until I've stopped being spun in nauseating circles. There's only so much discombobulation a brain can handle.

Wilbur finally lets go of me and I dizzily stagger a few metres into the nearly empty car park.

Nick is on the phone, facing the other way. He's talking quietly but I can still hear him.

And I really wish I couldn't.

"Poppy?" His voice sounds tight. "What are you talking about?"

There's a silence while my inner ear rebalances and the world slowly stops dipping and diving and gyrating around me. I think I'm going to be sick.

He's on the phone to her *already*?

"Of *course* I care," Nick continues impatiently. "You know I do. Don't be ridiculous."

Suddenly, all at once I'm aware of the water dripping from my hair down my nose and on to my top lip, and the icy droplets running down my arms and legs on to the floor, and the sogginess and dampness of my towel.

Apparently 300 million cells in our body die every single minute, and for the first time in my life I can actually feel them: shrinking and shrivelling all over me.

"I'm coming back now," Nick says. "Stay there."

And without even looking over his shoulder, Nick puts his phone back in his pocket, climbs on to a scooter and drives away.

Leaving me, unseen and speechless, behind him.

73

Here are a few new equations for you:

LOVE = 1 first kiss + 400 plus subsequent smaller kisses + 182 days + 278 daydreams + 186 phone calls + 2,087 texts + 1 last kiss.

LOVE = 4 nights spent crying - 2 months waiting for him to come back - 8 weeks of not being able to open a magazine or watch television in case he's in it - 63 days of getting sad every time you see a seagull or a lion or a raindrop - 11 days of pretending you're over him - a lifetime of never being able to eat lime-flavoured sweets, ever again.

LOVE = nearly ruining your GCSEs because all you're thinking about is him.

LOVE = turning into a total idiot.

I have wasted six *whole months* on Nick Hidaka.

In the space of six months, Mercury has gone round the sun *twice*. In six months, I could have walked all the way across the width of Russia, or cycled over America, or sailed to Brazil. It took Jack Kerouac three weeks to write *On the Road*, and Charles Dickens six weeks to write *A Christmas Carol*. I could have written *five classic novels* in the time I spent thinking about a boy. I could have spent 444 days on Jupiter, and 391 days on Saturn and 1.4 really luxurious days on Venus.

Instead, I filled my head with big black curls and lips that curve up at the corner; with green smell; with shouted laughter; with a boy who disappears whenever he feels like it and says whatever he wants and only ever thinks about himself.

You know what?

I am never liking a boy again, ever. When I get back to school, I'm going to invest all the extra time and brain space into learning Apalachee or Tsetsaut or Susquehannock, or some other language that has been totally dead for more than a hundred years.

And it will *still* be more productive.

"Done, my little Twinkle-bottom?" Wilbur says, tapping me on the shoulder. I take one last look at the space Nick has disappeared into the way he always does, like the proverbial genie.

Am I done? Is that it? Am I finally ready to let go?

"Yep," I say, turning to Wilbur and taking a deep breath. "This time I think I am."

I spend the rest of the journey back to Tokyo quietly staring out of the Shinkansen window at little lights scattered at random through the fields, while Wilbur lightly snores beside me.

By the time we pull back into Tokyo station, all I want is to have a hot shower, pull my penguin pyjamas back on and climb into bed with a crossword puzzle.

But it doesn't look like that's an option.

"Poppet-cakes," Wilbur says in a daze as the train pulls to a stop. He rubs his eyes. "I know I have a *super* vivid imagination, but is that who I think it is?"

I look out of the window at a small huddle of people in black. Shion, Naho, Haru and a few assistants. And – almost entirely hidden in the middle – Yuka. Like some kind of tiny, fiercely protected, Faerie Queen.

"Perhaps they're here to give us presents?"

Maybe that's how modelling works. Maybe when you do a really good job at a shoot they all rush back to greet you at the station with a surprise basket of cupcakes or kittens and maybe a few celebratory personalised banners.

Then I see Wilbur's face. It's gone very white and

very wobbly, as if all the bones have just been whipped out through his nose.

"My little Bumble-bee," he says. "Maybe I'm not such a good meerkat after all."

74

We get off the train in silence.

Wilbur and I stand as close to each other on the platform as we possibly can.

"Come here," Yuka says. "Now, please. Both of you."

I've been to the headmaster's office at school plenty of times before. In Year Seven, I was called in to receive the Biology Award and the History Essay Award and the Debate Team Award. Then I went in again in Year Eight to accept the Physics Award and another History Essay Award. In Year Nine I got the English Award, and then in Year Ten I had to go back so that he could give me quite a large book voucher and inform me tensely that I wouldn't be winning any more awards because it was upsetting the other students.

But I have never, ever been called in because I'm in trouble.

I imagine it would feel exactly like this.

Wilbur and I look at each other, and then start creeping down the platform, like two little children playing *What's The Time, Mister Wolf?* I'm so hysterical with fear and nerves, I'm quite surprised when Yuka opens her mouth and the first line out of it isn't 'Dinner Time'.

"Who gave you your first break in modelling, Harriet."

Her voice is terrifyingly gentle: in exactly the way a cat gets very slinky just before it pounces on a mouse.

I clear my throat. Technically Nick 'discovered' me, but the tiny part of me that knows how to stay alive steps in just in time to stop me saying that. "You."

"And who has given you work ever since."

"You."

"And is *this*" – Yuka gestures serenely around her – "what normally happens. Are fifteen-year-old girls normally picked out of school trips and handed highly paid international jobs for a world-class designer with no castings, no competition, and no experience?"

I can't help but feel that this is a slightly leading question. "No?" I guess weakly.

"Correct. Most models go on hundreds of castings and are rejected hundreds of times. They struggle for years against themselves and each other. Very few make any real money. Those that do have a few years, at best, before they are thrown aside. Fashion is hard work, fickle and unforgiving. It eats girls like you for breakfast."

I suddenly feel as if I'm in a Roald Dahl novel. Hasn't Wilbur said something like this before?

"I understand."

"No, Harriet. You don't understand, because I made sure of it. I gave you an exclusive contract from the beginning to ensure you would not be part of that world. And I have done everything I can since to keep you away from it."

My eyes widen. Has my entire modelling career been a sort of glamorous babysitting?

"But… why?"

"I saw qualities in you I wanted to keep. And I was worried that the industry would take them away from you."

I have literally no idea what qualities she's talking about.

"Th-thank you?" I stutter, face flaming.

"And in return," Yuka continues, "you have shown me disrespect, arrogance and disobedience. You have lied, you have been late, and you have failed to follow a single one of the basic rules I gave you."

I shut my mouth abruptly and look at Wilbur in a panic. His entire face is now a shade of mossy green.

"N-n-no, Yuka," I say, but there's so little saliva in my mouth that my tongue's starting to make a sticky, clacking sound. "I didn't… I haven't… you don't understand—"

"Yes, Harriet," Yuka says quietly, "I think I do." She reaches into her bag, pulls out a newspaper in English and hands it to me. There's a full-page spread: a large photo of a much, much younger Yuka in black lace, and the caption:

INDUSTRY ICON STEALS DESIGNS

Fashion icon Yuka Ito has broken her contract with fashion powerhouse Baylee in order to set up her own label. A source close to the fashion icon says: "A small group of us models have been flown all over Asia for the launch of her new label and it's all super top secret. I was so excited to get my shoot in Tokyo."

A spokesperson for Baylee said: "Yuka Ito is currently signed exclusively to our label. While she did design these clothes herself, until her contract

expires, they technically belong to us. We are seeking legal advice."

Yuka Ito has so far been unavailable for comment.

"I-I-It wasn't me," I say urgently, looking back at the article. '*Us models*'? That's not even grammatically correct. "Although I know it *sounds* a bit like me I didn't tell anyone about—"

But I did, didn't I?

I knew precisely how important it was to keep my mouth shut – I promised Yuka and Wilbur that I would – and I still let the secret out. Trying to make two girls like me was more important than keeping my word.

"I should have explained earlier," Wilbur says, stepping forwards while a hot, burning wave of shame knocks the wind out of me. "It's not really my little Monkey-bum's fault, there's been some unprofessional activity going on—"

"Enough," Yuka says. "I'm not interested in hearing any more stories." She turns to me and says flatly: "Do you think it was a coincidence that you were positioned in Tokyo, Harriet."

I blink. "Umm..."

"Japan is my home. You were to be the face of

the whole campaign. But that was clearly the worst decision of all. So you're fired. I trust this is one instruction you won't have a problem following."

"Now just a second—" Wilbur starts, and Yuka turns to him.

"And you're fired too, William. Please take Harriet back to the flat, collect her things and go to the airport. Your tickets will be waiting for you there."

Wilbur looks as if somebody has snatched the battery out of him. He gets visibly smaller. "It's Wilbur," he says. "With a 'bur' and not an 'iam'."

"I don't think it really matters," Yuka says. "We will not be working together again."

75

Neither of us says another word for the rest of the journey home: we're both locked in our own private miseries.

I've been waiting to come back down to earth with a bump for a while now. Wilbur, on the other hand, has almost definitely never been near it before in his life.

Finally, the taxi stops and I gently tell Wilbur to wait in the car while I get my things. He stares at me blankly, and then looks at the leather seats. "I suppose," he says, "if I'm going to cry and snot uncontrollably it may as well be somewhere wipe-clean, right?"

"Umm, yes," I say with a tentatively supportive little pat. "That's the spirit?" Then I climb out of the car and make my way over to the flat.

Nobody else appears to be at home, so I tiptoe into the bedroom as quickly and as quietly as I can.

I need to get out of here before either Rin or Poppy returns.

I'm like a feather. I'm like a mouse. I'm like a ninja of invisibility and poise and—

"Are you going?"

Sugar cookies.

I turn around, and there is Princess Poppy: leaning against the doorframe with her perfect golden hair spilling over her shoulders and her perfect shoulders tensed and her perfect arms crossed and her perfect mouth set in a totally straight and expressionless line.

I start throwing items haphazardly into my suitcase. "Uh-huh."

"That's such a shame."

I flinch and start lobbing everything faster: trousers, shoes, shirts.

"I mean, what with you sneaking around with other people's boyfriends and stuff, it's a real pain that you can't stick around."

My stomach plummets. Poppy's cheeks are pink, her blue eyes are gleaming, and I've never, ever seen anyone look more angry or more perfect. "God, no, Poppy: I didn't—"

"I know *everything* so don't lie as well."

I shut my eyes briefly. Thanks, Nick. Thanks for blaming me. "Poppy, I didn't see it coming, I wasn't prepared. I would have pushed him away, I-I didn't mean to hurt you..."

"Why can't you just LEAVE. HIM. ALONE?"

I feel sick. Is this all my fault too?

Did I want Nick back so hard that I somehow turned it into a real, physical thing? Maybe I should start focusing my magical powers on curing cancer or winning a Nobel Prize, instead of hurting people.

"I should go," I say quietly. "I'm so sorry, Poppy. If I had known all the trouble I'd cause, I wouldn't have come."

I zip my suitcase up, even though some of my belongings are still scattered around the room, and start wheeling it into the hallway. My sleeve gets caught on the door handle, and I'm now so utterly desperate to get away I strongly consider leaving my arm here and just going home without it.

"I'm glad Rin did what she did," Poppy says as I finally yank myself free and stumble into the hallway. She puts her hand on the door and my stomach goes cold. "I think maybe it's best for everyone if you're not here."

And she slams the door behind me.

76

My New and Infinitely Inglorious Plan (NIIP) is now as follows:

- *Apologise to Wilbur.*
- *Fly home.*
- *Apologise to my parents (and the bump).*
- *Apologise to Nat and Toby.*
- *Make up some kind of T-shirt that says SORRY IN ADVANCE as a cunning pre-emptive tactic.*
- *Go to bed for the rest of the summer.*

But when I come out of the flat I see Wilbur, leaning against a lamp-post, talking on his mobile phone. His voice is quiet and his shoulders are slumped. It's as if all the bright colours have been drained out of him.

And suddenly I can't face him.

I can't face anyone at all.

I'm not proud of what I'm about to do next, but I do it anyway.

I pick up my suitcase so that the wheels don't make giveaway squeaks. I tiptoe awkwardly behind Wilbur. I turn the corner of the street. I put my suitcase down.

And I run away.

All right: technically I *wheel* away.

I have no idea where I'm going. I'm just pulling my suitcase in the opposite direction to the flat.

I keep my eyes on the floor, and I walk. I walk and walk and walk in the hope that if I walk fast enough, far enough, I'll discover exactly what it is I can do to make everything slightly less terrible.

By the time I've calmed down enough to take in my surroundings, I've managed to meltdown all the way into the heart of Tokyo. There are brightly coloured lights everywhere: flashing on the streets, climbing up the enormous buildings, soaring into the sky. Ten-metre televisions are yelling from the corners, hundreds of people are swarming everywhere and every three seconds or so there's a high-pitched bird peep, followed by an answering peep from hundreds of metres away.

*

I am totally and utterly lost.

With a different type of panic setting in, I desperately try to find my bearings. There's a Starbucks, some kind of enormous train station and the biggest zebra crossing I have ever seen running across five different roads. It's so big that everyone has to wait on the pavement, and – when the peeps start – simultaneously scramble across the road in a vicious star shape: criss-crossing and bumping and shoving.

It's like a huge computer game testing coordination and timing, and I know from harsh experience that I have precisely neither of those things.

I wait six entire crossing cycles before I can find the courage to step out and then take my deepest breath and start pulling my suitcase across. There isn't much time: when the beeps start speeding up, you have ten seconds to reach the other side before the cars start again. And they *will* start. I've already witnessed at least two people put their hands out and physically *push* against car bonnets to stop themselves getting run over.

Getting hotter and hotter, I desperately try to manoeuvre my way across but my suitcase keeps getting stuck, people keep pushing me, blocking me, physically holding my arm so that they can go in front.

By the time the beeps start speeding up, I'm only halfway there. And I can't turn back because that would take longer and then I'll just have to do it all over again. Somebody shouts something in Japanese at me, and I realise – to my horror – that I've stopped, frozen on the road like a terrified rabbit.

My heart is hammering, my eyes are starting to fill up.

I've managed to take a bad situation and make it a hundred times worse, all on my own.

Well, me and the Tokyo road planners.

I've just begun to start running to catch up with the people ahead of me when I hear a *whoosh*.

The world spins around.

And the road jumps up to meet me.

77

Thankfully I don't die.

The bicycle just clips me, and the only real damage is a bloody knee and elbow and quite a large hole in my leggings, pride and mental stability. A tiny lady swoops down to pick me up and guides me gently across the road. By the time I've stopped shaking enough to thank her, she's gone.

Rocking my suitcase on its side, I ignore the dubious glances from the crowds and sit heavily on the floor next to it.

I want to go home.

I want to go home more than I have ever wanted anything before in my entire life.

I want to be in my tiny stupid bedroom, putting fossils on overcrowded shelves and trying to stop my dog from eating talcum powder. I want to be studying Shakespeare and Milton and star constellations; I want to be worrying about chemistry formulas and physics equations instead of dresses and poses and octopuses and kisses. I want to see my dad dancing around the living room and I want to see Annabel laughing at him and Hugo getting all over-excited. I want to see Nat roll her eyes at me and Toby wipe his nose on his jumper. I even want to see Alexa. Nice, predictable Alexa. Who hates me with the least amount of effort and national newspaper coverage possible.

I just want everything to be exactly how it was.

Maybe this is what happens to the butterfly and the frog. Maybe they go to so much effort to grow wings and legs and run away, and when they see a little bit of the world they just feel sad and lonely and end up hopping straight back home again. Where they belong.

I pick my phone up and ring Dad. There's no answer.

I try Annabel: her phone is off.

Then I try Bunty: engaged.

I call Nat and get her voicemail again, then try Toby. It rings a few times before suddenly switching off.

Did Toby just *hang up* on me? Am I now so pathetic that my own stalker just cancelled my call?

That does it.

I pull my jumper tightly over my head. And I start crying.

78

I don't know how long I cry for.

In fairness, people don't normally time themselves. All I know is that I cry long enough for my face to get all swollen and weird-shaped, and not quite long enough to forget what it is I'm crying about.

Not one person stops to ask if I'm OK. Not a single stranger asks if they can help. Not a human soul interrupts to offer poignant words of wisdom and kindness and—

"Are you OK?"

I sniffle and wipe my nose on my jumper. All right. Maybe I should have been a bit more patient before I attacked the entire human race. I nod.

"Are you sure?"

The voice is muffled and indistinct. "Yes. Thank you."

"Because," it continues, "for somebody who thinks they're OK, you spend a hell of a lot of time rolling around on pavements."

Slowly I remove the jumper and wipe my eyes.

"Hey," Lion Boy says with a small smile. "There's my girl."

I look at Nick, with his beautiful face and his beautiful hair and his beautiful cheekbones. I look at the way he's slouched, and the way his lips curve as if the world is permanently, irresistibly funny.

To summarise, I look at how incredibly beautiful and perfect he is.

"Go to hell," I say, pulling my jumper back over my head.

I hear Nick sit down next to me. I immediately whip my head out again like the furious tortoise I am. "I'm not sure your geographical knowledge of the afterlife is very strong," I say through my teeth. "Do I need to draw you a map?"

"I didn't realise this was your pavement."

"*Actually*," I snap, and then stop. Stupid Japanese laws about public pavements. "Leave me alone, Nick. I mean it. *Now*."

He opens his mouth to respond, and then sees the blood on my hands and knee. "God, Harriet. What happened? Are you hurt?"

I jerk away from his hand. "No," I snap, struggling to stand up. "I am not hurt."

I'm suddenly so angry it feels like the contents of my chest are about to rush out of my ears like the magma inside Mount Tambora in 1815 (the biggest ever recorded volcanic eruption). "Get lost, please. Go away. Go on, *shoo*."

Nick's lips twitch and his nostrils flare. "Did you just *shoo* me, Harriet Manners?"

And my head bursts.

"*WHO THE SUGAR COOKIES DO YOU THINK YOU ARE, NICK*? You may be a supermodel and you may be beautiful and charming and cute and funny but you're also just a *boy*! You're just a boy, and I am a girl, and every time I breathe in there is a molecule that used to be part of a dinosaur in it which I assimilate into my body which means that I AM PART DINOSAUR, POSSIBLY T-REX, AND YOU DO NOT GET TO TREAT ME LIKE THIS."

I'm so swept up in a torrent of blind fury that I am making little claws at random passers-by. Nick blinks and then grabs one of my T-Rex hands. "Hang on a second, Harriet—"

"And OK," I continue fiercely, shaking him off, "you're probably part dinosaur too, but you're probably a Dilophosaurus with a rubbish frilly neck or a Linhenykus which only had a little pointed finger where an arm should be like this." I hold my forefingers out by my armpits and wave them around uselessly.

Nick snorts and I take a cross little hoppy step towards him.

"Oh, *that's* it. Am I not *mature* enough for you? Not *interesting* enough for you? Too *silly* for your epic adultness? Well *you're* the problem, Nick. Not me. Don't you *ever* try and make me want to be someone else again. I am just *fine* the way I am." I grab the handle of my suitcase. "And this time *you* can sit and watch while *I* disappear."

I turn to sweep elegantly away, but Nick holds on to my suitcase. I cannot *believe* that on top of everything he has now totally ruined my dramatic exit.

"Can I say something now?" he says, lifting an eyebrow. "Or do you have more second-rate dinosaurs you'd like to compare me to?"

I scowl and stick my nose in the air. "Whatever."

"Great. First of all, it turns out somebody has been sabotaging the campaign. I only found out at the lake. I had no idea before. We thought you were just being clumsy as usual."

OH MY GOD HOW DARE HE—

Oh, OK. I suppose that's a reasonable assumption to make. "I already figured *that* out yesterday, genius," I say, rolling my eyes. "Poppy and Rin."

"No," Nick says, frowning. "Not Rin. She actually helped us sort everything out."

I abruptly sit down on top of my suitcase. "Oh."

"Harriet, Rin hasn't got a bad bone in her body – plus she adores you. She's getting a T-shirt made with both your faces on it. She wanted to make your friendship 'official'."

I'm so relieved I feel like crying. Of all the girls I've ever thought might be my friend – other than Nat – Rin's my absolute favourite. I'm suddenly filled with so much happiness I have to desperately claw back a few remaining strands of anger to finish what I need to say. "So it was Poppy. *Big* surprise."

"It was to me."

"I bet," I say in my most sarcastic voice. "Don't you know your own *girlfriend* very well?"

"Usually," Nick says, raising his eyebrows. "But Poppy's not my girlfriend. She never has been."

79

There's always this excellent moment in really good action films where everybody's kicking and fighting and there are legs and arms and bodies everywhere, and suddenly somebody leaps into the air and it all goes very slow, and very quiet, and you just *know* that the end is somehow coming.

As if we're all hanging in the air, waiting for somebody to pull the move that changes everything.

"*Uh?*" I say.

"I have never dated Poppy," Nick repeats, and there it is: the metaphorical boot in my face. "*Ever*. She's just a model I worked with on that D&G shoot in Paris. I had absolutely no idea she'd told you we were together until Rin called me at the lake."

I suddenly hear that overheard phone call again. '*Poppy?*'

He wasn't talking *to* her: he was talking *about* her.

"But—" I try to swallow but it's not really working. "You came to the flat... she said—"

"Exactly. *She* said. I didn't. We were doing another shoot that evening, but the reason I'd raced over was to see you. I was waiting for you at the airport, but you looked so happy and excited to be in Tokyo... I guess I didn't want to confuse things. So I decided to turn up at your flat instead and do it properly."

My mind makes a little whirring rewind motion.

He *did* turn up a few minutes after I did.

And at no stage did Poppy *ever* refer to Nick as My Boyfriend in front of Nick. She kissed his *cheek*.

"B-but what about the sumo match?"

"I waited for you." The corner of Nick's top lip twitches. "For *three hours,* Manners. But then you made it brutally clear you were over me."

I suddenly remember his white, punctured face on the steps.

He wasn't confused, he was *hurt.*

I feel abruptly guilty, and also a tiny bit pleased with myself. *Ha!* I am an excellent, excellent actor. Nat is going to be *delighted* when I tell her.

"So at the lake..."

"I had to give it one last shot. But you gunned me down again, so the kiss" – he shrugs and looks pained – "I guess I was kind of saying goodbye."

It's a good thing I'm sitting down, because if I wasn't

standing would be a bit of a problem. You know how my bedroom always looked strange and unfamiliar once the lights went off? Now it's the other way round. The lights have gone back on, and everything looks completely different. Unexpected. Brilliant.

"But..." I pause and blush.

The sumo. The lake.

Nick's been totally innocent the entire time.

Oh my God, I have been *so horrible* to him. I said he was part Linhenykus. Nobody deserves that. Except maybe for—

I blink. "Why would Poppy pretend like this? And how did she even know about me?"

He shrugs. "Poppy's the kind of girl who gets exactly what she wants. I think she kind of lost control when it didn't work this time. I suppose she thought if she believed in it enough, and if she got rid of you, I'd end up with her. Which I wouldn't, because she's a nightmare and also" – he twists his finger up to his head in a way that politely suggests *bat-poop crazy* – "and... and I talked about you in Paris. *A lot*. She basically had an entire character-assassination arsenal at her disposal. Sorry about that."

I look at Nick's beautiful face, all screwed up and flushed and anxious, and suddenly know *exactly* why

Poppy put in so much effort. "But… Nick, you *dumped* me, remember?"

"No, Harriet," Nick sighs. "I told you *really* clearly that I was gonna leave you alone for a couple of months while you did your exams. I should've realised you'd zone out and stop listening – you *always* do that when you panic. I should've sent a supporting document or an email afterwards or recorded a message or something."

And the last piece of the puzzle slots into place with a click, like an enormous, romantic Rubik's Cube.

All I actually remember from that conversation over two and a half months ago is 'we shouldn't see or speak to each other any more' before I went into internal meltdown mode.

And, though I'll obviously never admit it to the Nobel Prize committee judges, there *was* quite a lot of time spent with Nick when I should've been revising.

Like, almost all of it.

Who wants to revise biology when you're going out with a supermodel? Even *I'm* not that much of a geek.

Oh my God. I am *such an idiot.*

Nick smiles awkwardly. "I said I'd be back when

your exams finished. But you made me think I'd left it too late."

The text. It arrived the day after the end of my exams.

"So… you still like me then?"

"Don't you get it yet, Harriet?" Nick says in total exasperation. "I *like* that you know about the stars in rain and the shape of clouds and the heartbeat rate of a hummingbird. I like that you know that giraffes don't have vocal cords and sharks can't stop moving. I like the way you stick your little nose in the air and stomp your feet and frown just before you laugh. I like how your ears go red when you're embarrassed and your freckles get darker when you're angry. I like that little crumpled paper ball your chin makes before you cry. I like that when you're shouting at me you physically pretend you're a T-Rex. I like *you,* Harriet. Why is that the only thing in the universe you find so hard to wrap your big fat brain around?"

I suddenly feel like I'm at the lake again: as if I'm covered from head to toe in lights. I have absolutely no idea what to say to any of that.

"My brain isn't big and fat. It has a totally normal fat quantity, which is roughly half of its dry mass."

Oh. Apparently I do.

Nick grins. "My point exactly."

It feels like two strings have been attached to the corners of my mouth and somebody is pulling them upwards. "And is this all because of you?" I gesture around me. "Am I in Tokyo because you made it happen?"

"Nope." Nick shakes his head. "This time I'm here because of you. I actually begged Yuka for this job. I had to organise *dresses* and stuff. It nearly killed me."

Nick pulls a face, but underneath the usual calmness is something I haven't seen before: uncertainty. And I suddenly realise with a pang that all of this has been for me.

Nick found me, seven months ago. For me, he left. For me, he came back again. He made me laugh when I needed to; he annoyed me when it helped me; he saved me when I couldn't save myself.

For me, he tries to keep it simple.

There are 7,123,024,873 people in the world, and Nick keeps choosing me.

I look at him – sitting on the pavement, pulling at the holes in his jeans – and he suddenly looks so earnest, and so worried, and so nervous, and so totally *un-Nick*, that there are only two possible things I can do.

So I do both of them at the same time.

I leap up from my suitcase and I lob myself at him so quickly he falls over slightly and has to steady himself on his elbow. "Thank you," I say into his ear. "Thank you for liking me."

And I kiss him as hard as I can.

80

Reasons to Think About Nick

1. *He always thinks about me.*

I don't know how long we kiss for.

Let's just say it's long enough to make the entire world and everybody in it melt and turn to vapour, and not quite long enough to get us arrested.

Which is good. My urge to see the inside of a Japanese prison is only a very small and transient one.

"OK, I just have one more question," I say when I finally pull away, flushed and beaming with my lips all tingly and my heart all swoopy and my hair all sticky-outy, like a small dog who's just been harassed with a hairdryer.

"Of course you do." I'm pleased to note that Nick looks exactly the same as me, if not a bit beamier and more rumpled.

"How did you find this all out? Poppy didn't confess all, did she?"

"Obviously not. FYI she's currently on her way back to England. Yuka is absolutely furious and she's made sure Poppy's agent knows it. I think Poppy's next modelling job will be staring vacantly out from a kitchenware catalogue with her hands on her hips," Nick says. "Rin, Bunty and Wilbur helped, but most of it came from somebody else."

"Who?"

Nick points into the distance. "Him."

I follow his finger and stare at the huge crowd of people walking across the zebra crossing, dodging the bicycles. Then I stare a little bit harder. Because walking through the middle of them – wearing a T-shirt with a guitar drawn on it and a bright purple velvet jacket – is Toby.

Right, I give up.

I clearly know nothing about people at all.

Slowly, I stand up and wait for Toby to reach me. He starts playing *Three Blind Mice* on his T-shirt. After a few wrong notes he shrugs. "It's so very important to make an entrance, isn't it, Harriet? Although in hindsight, I wish I'd worn the drum-kit

T-shirt. It's a bit easier to play under pressure."

I stare at him, too startled to speak.

"Hey, Nick," he adds chirpily, waving with his spare hand. "I liked the wellies you were wearing earlier. Do you think they'd go with this outfit, or would it get a bit sweaty around the knee area?"

"*Toby*," I finally manage. "What are you *doing* here?"

"I'm your stalker, Harriet. I've been here the whole time. What kind of terrible stalker would I be if I wasn't?"

"But—"

"I'm getting really good at it, right? I don't think you knew I was here *at all.*"

"But *how* are you here? You're not even sixteen yet."

"Oh, I'm here with my parents. They said we could go on holiday anywhere I liked to celebrate the end of my exams, but I just couldn't decide where to go. That is until some information came to my attention last week." And he actually winks at me. "They think I've been *really* busy with a school project."

Toby looks extremely chuffed with himself. "I mean, you're at my school, right? And this was a *fascinating* project. I found all sorts of incriminating evidence."

He pulls out photos and crumpled bits of paper and audio recordings and maps and drawings.

All this time I thought I was alone. But really I was surrounded constantly by people who cared about me: Toby, Nick, Wilbur, Bunty, Rin. I just couldn't see them.

I don't know whether to be incredibly touched or slightly creeped out.

"Toby – why on earth would you follow somebody *6,000 miles*?"

"5,937 miles, to be precise." He points behind me. "Do you know what that is, Harriet?"

Oh dear. I patiently follow the direction of Toby's finger. "It's a statue of a dog."

"Not just any dog, Harriet. That's a dog called Hachiko. He was a brown Akita dog and he was adopted in 1924 by a Tokyo professor called Hidesaburo Ueno."

"Ah." I nod politely. After everything he's done, the least I can do is listen to one of his random facts. I make people do this for me all the time.

"Every day for a year Hachiko would come and greet Hidesaburo after work here, at this exact spot at Shibuya station. In 1925 the professor suffered a stroke at work and died, but Hachiko returned to the same spot every single day for nine years waiting for him to come back."

Tears suddenly spring to my eyes.

"The dog waited for the rest of his life, and when he eventually died the people of Tokyo built a statue in the place he used to wait to commemorate his loyalty, and the fact that he never, ever gave up."

I bite my lip. That's one of the most beautiful stories I've ever heard.

It's also exactly why I love dogs. Kylie Minogue would have waited about thirty seconds before going home with the next person who had food in their handbag.

"But it still doesn't explain what you're doing here."

"Yes, it does, Harriet. I'm your Hachiko."

And before I realise what's about to happen, Toby darts forward and kisses me.

81

OK:

- Two kisses with two different boys in five minutes is not something I want to encourage.
- Ever.
- All kisses are not the same.
- *Ewwwwwww*.

Toby really goes for it.

I mean: he really, *really* goes for it. He twists his head from left to right as if he's trying to unscrew a light bulb from my mouth, and then attempts to lick my top lip, and then sort of opens and shuts his mouth like a baby bird trying desperately to get fed.

He tangles my hair in his fingers so I can't get away without physically pushing him with both of my hands and losing quite a few strands in the process.

Which I do, obviously.

"*Toby*," I snap, wiping my mouth on my hand.

"*Seriously*. You have to wait for a *signal* before you kiss a girl. I did not give you any kind of signal *at all.*"

Toby looks completely undisturbed. "Did you not? I thought I saw one."

"*What* signal did I give you?"

"You were looking very pretty, Harriet. And kind of boggle-eyed, like a little owl."

I sigh. "That's very nice of you, Toby, but a) that's just my face and b) *prettiness* is not and never will be a kissing signal. It's important that you realise that as soon as possible."

I glance anxiously at Nick who looks – if anything – slightly amused. Isn't he supposed to be fighting for my precious honour round about now? Isn't he supposed to be throwing Toby against a wall and telling him not to touch His Woman again?

What kind of rubbish love triangle *is* this?

"That was my very first ever kiss," Toby tells Nick. "How do you think it looked from there, buddy?"

Nick grins as I blink at both of them. "I think maybe you went in a bit too fast," he says. "She looks a bit shocked."

"Right." Toby gets a little notepad out of his velvet jacket which – I've just realised – was his Charlie and the Chocolate Factory costume from two Halloweens ago. He scribbles something and then frowns. "Perhaps a simple customer announcement would be best? *I am about to launch a kiss.* That kind of thing?"

Nick shouts with laughter.

For God's sake. Bella never had to put up with this kind of friendly, bonding nonsense in *Twilight*.

"You realise I'm still here, right?"

"Kissing is important stuff, Harriet," Toby says solemnly. "We boys need to discuss it just as much as girls do, you know. And we can't just read *Cosmopolitan*." He pauses. "Actually, we *can* but when our mums find it under our beds we have to have really long and confusing conversations about it."

"Tobes, I really think maybe we should look into getting you a hobby other than me."

"Actually I don't want to be rude, Harriet," he says thoughtfully, "but you're not quite as good at this whole kissing thing as I had hoped. You just kind of stood there, smacking me quite briskly with your hands. It was a bit of a disappointment, if I'm being perfectly honest."

My eyes widen, and Nick quickly stands up and puts his arm around me. He kisses my forehead. "I'll volunteer for now," he laughs.

Then he holds up his other arm. A taxi stops

immediately and Nick pokes his head through the window. "*Sumimasen*," he says flawlessly. "*Tokyo-eki made dekirudake hayaku onegai shimasu*."

I keep forgetting Nick's half Japanese. I may have to ask him to speak in other languages all the time. I had never realised bilinguality could be so attractive. "Where are we going?"

"Back to the beginning," Nick says with a grin, opening the car door for Toby and me.

I'm just not sure which one.

82

Here is my absolute favourite fact of all time:

99.99999999999999999 per cent of every atom consists of empty space.

It sounds simple, but do you know what that means? It means that every single thing in front of you *right now* – the chair you're sitting on, the shoes on your feet, the glasses on your nose, the chocolate in your mouth – is mostly not there.

And *that includes you*.

I know: mind-blowing, right? It doesn't matter how many times I'm told this fact, it's almost entirely impossible to process. And when it finally sinks in, it's hard not to find it a bit overwhelming.

As I open the door to the flat I'm hit by a waft of sequins and lace and beetroot and perfume as Bunty, Rin and Wilbur all launch themselves at me. Within seconds a glitter-covered Rin is wrapped around my neck. There appear to be pink feathers in her hair. And some in Wilbur's too.

I *knew* I shouldn't have left them alone with my grandmother.

"Oh, Harry-chan!" Rin says into my T-shirt collar. "We are so very mistakable about Poppy! Kylie found cockroach box in her handbag! She is a naughty, naughty pretty girl!"

I notice the distinctly missing affectionate 'chan' from Poppy's name. I think that's as harsh as Rin is going to get. "I'm sorry," I say, patting her on the back. Then I say what I haven't said for ten years: "Umm – would you like to be friends?"

"Ooooh!" Rin says, clapping her hands in delight. "Yes please! I will come to seeing you in London! I will see Big Ben and Wheel and wear Top Hat and we shall be spoiling for choice and shall have BIG BLAST!" I laugh and Rin suddenly spots Toby. "It is nice to finally meet you," she says, bowing slightly. "I am Rin. You must be Ted."

"I'm not Ted, I'm Toby. Did you know that teddy bears have killed more people than real bears have?"

Rin's eyes widen and she turns to me. "*Harry-chan!* He is just like you!"

I nod and grin at him fondly. "Yup."

Toby's eyebrows raise. "Are you going to try and kiss me again, Harriet? Because I strongly suggest you check your emails first in case I blow your mind and reading is rendered physically impossible. I think there might be something important."

I frown at him and immediately turn and head straight to the bedroom to get my laptop. Seriously. Do I have to change all my passwords *again*?

Through the thin paper walls I can hear Wilbur's high-pitched voice in the bathroom. With every second it's sounding more and more like the agent I know and love.

"Really?" (Pause.) "For diddling?" (Pause.) "For *shiddling, diddling*?" (Pause.) "For *shiddling diddling middling piddling*?" (Pause.) "*NEW YORK?* OH MY DONKEY-CAKES! Are you McKidding me? I am the *King* of interested!"

There's another pause and then Wilbur's head pops round the bedroom door. He puts his hand over the receiver. "Yuka's not the only designer in the world, my little Caramel-macchiato," he whispers with a wink. "Let's not forget that." And his head disappears again.

I blink at the door, and then back at my computer.

For the attention of Harriet Manners
From the office of Yuka Ito

It would seem that new information has come to light. As a result, I would like to apologise and am withdrawing my offer of redundancy, effective immediately.

Yuka Ito

And, just like that, my adventure has come full circle. Things are back exactly as they were at the beginning. As if I'm still the geek hiding under a table at The Clothes Show Live, just about to be thrown haphazardly into the world of fashion. As if I'm still a girl who doesn't know who she is or who she's supposed to be.

As if nothing has changed at all.

Except it has.

I take the deepest breath I can find, and then type:

Dear Yuka,

I would like you to release me from my exclusive contract with you. I will not be accepting my job back.

I really appreciate everything you have done for me, but whatever those qualities you see in

me are, they're not going anywhere. This is me, and I'm stronger than I look.

I want you to give me the freedom to grow up, even if it's scary. I want that adventure.

Thank you for everything you have taught me.

Goodbye.

Harriet

I'm just about to press SEND when Bunty wafts into the room.

"Did you get an apology, sweetie? I'll give that to Yuka, at least. She always knows when she's backed into a corner."

I blink at my grandmother for a few seconds, and then my brain clicks. *Nice to see you.* When she saw Yuka outside the Arcade Hall, she said *nice to see you.* Not *nice to meet you.*

"Do you *know* Yuka?"

"Of course I do, sweetie. We've run in the same circles for years. I've been trying to tell her what's been going on this whole time, but she just refused to listen. Typical Yuka. All talent, no ears."

I stare at Bunty in amazement.

I don't want to sound ungrateful, but can people *please* start telling me stuff?

"AND BOOOOOOM!" I hear Wilbur shout at the top of his voice. "LONDON CAN KISS MY GUCCI BOOTIES. AMERICA, HERE I COME."

"Now, darling," my grandmother says as I send the email and shut my laptop. Without warning she slams me into her embroidered breasts again. "It's been lovely spending some proper, quality time with you, but it's time to get going."

I blink in disappointment. I was really starting to like her. I was kind of hoping we could spend a few weeks getting to know each other properly, and that it might be the start of a proper granddaughter-grandmother relationship of the non-Little Red Riding Hood/Wolf variety. "*Now?*" I ask her boob sadly.

"I'm afraid so, darling. We have a plane to catch."

"*We?*"

"Yes, sweetheart."

Bunty pulls back and I suddenly notice the bright expression on her face. She looks exactly as I felt earlier at the lake.

"Annabel has just gone into labour."

83

OK.

I don't want to point out the obvious, but Annabel has gone into labour an entire *month* early. My new sibling is clearly a maverick with no respect at all for plans, schedules, appointments, or other people's itineraries.

Just like my father.

Fifteen hours later, Bunty and I emerge at Heathrow only to be hit by a whirlwind of shiny hair and handbag and scarf and perfume, like a kind of girl-bomb.

"You're *home*!" Nat shouts, almost knocking me over. "*Finally!*"

I look over her shoulder at the trolley she just hurdled. I have never seen her run that fast for anything, ever. Maybe she shouldn't have given up PE for A Level after all.

"What are you doing here?" I laugh as she covers

my cheek in little hard bird-pecks. "I thought you'd still be in France."

Nat flushes and manages to look cheeky and delighted all at the same time. "Erm, well…"

I narrow my eyes at her. My best friend looks totally incandescent. She's also wearing a lot less make-up than normal and her hair hasn't been straightened. Her natural scraggy curls are back and her fringe is slightly sticking out on the left-hand side. It's *very* un-Nat-like. "Nat, what's going on?"

"Hmm?" My Best Friend picks a bit of fluff off my hoody. "So – how was it? Did you see any dogs in dresses? Did people talk Japanese at you?"

"Excuse me," Bunty says, smiling and handing me a little carton of coconut water. "Stay hydrated, darling. Air conditioner is a killer. I'm just going to go and find us a taxi outside."

And she scoots off, her flip-flops making a *clack clack clack* sound on the floor. I turn back to Nat. "Right," I say. "What's happened?"

"Well, umm…" She clears her throat, looks at the ceiling and then looks at the floor. "Ooh – I like your shoes. Are they new?"

"Of course my shoes aren't new, Nat. My shoes

are never new. Stop changing the subject."

Two red spots appear on her cheeks. "I *may* have…" she starts. "I mean, it's *possible* that… I *could* have…"

"No offence, Nat, but this is like trying to talk to a dolphin. Try to get a whole sentence out."

"I met a boy."

The coconut water I'm sipping gets spat all over her.

"The guy with the *green lycra*?" I shout. "The guy with the *olive oil*? The guy with the *meaningful salt*?"

"It's not like that," Nat says indignantly. "He's… lovely. And sweet. And *super hot*." She goes a bit dreamy. "And he has this way of cracking his knuckles when he's nervous that's *so cute.* And he can *totally* kill it at Guitar Hero. And he has this amazing lilting accent like his voice is… on a boat or something."

Like his voice is on a boat?

"Oh my God, Nat. You've got it really bad."

She blushes even deeper. "I know. That's kind of why I'm here. Mum found out and dragged me home again. She said falling in love was enough punishment for anyone so we were quits."

I laugh. "Is that why you disappeared?"

"Not really. Oh, Harriet, I feel so embarrassed. I

gave you such a hard time about Nick. I don't think I quite realised until I met François that it's not really like that. You can't protect yourself from it. Nothing exists but them."

"François?" I laugh. "He's French and his name is François?"

"Some French people are called François, Harriet," Nat says crossly. "It's a thing. It happens."

I smile and we start heading outside the airport. "You were wrong about Nick, by the way. I'll tell you all about it in the taxi."

"You know what?" Nat sighs. "Maybe I don't know anywhere near as much about boys as I thought I did. They're quite complicated, aren't they? I think this might be the start of a lifetime of confusion."

She links her arm in mine. "So, did you have a good time? Did it live up to the epic Flow Chart? You know we've still got loads of time left to do that stuff together."

I think back to the bright lights, and the booming televisions, and the beautiful shrines, and the madness of Harajuku. I think about Mount Fuji, and the Shinkansen, and Tsukiji and the video arcade and the sumo hall; about my lit-up dress and Charlie and Kylie Minogue and the cockroach. I think about Yuka and

Bunty and Toby and Haru and Naho and Shion; about Rin, who waved us off at the airport wearing a pink tutu and gave me the friendship bracelet I'm wearing now.

I think about Nick, who kissed me again before I got on the plane and had to literally push me into check-in because I decided last minute I wasn't going anywhere.

Then I think about how different I feel to the way I did when I went there. As if I'm still me, but stronger. As if I've found my wings, and I finally know what to do with them.

"Yes," I say with a grin as Bunty opens a taxi door and we climb in. "As far as adventures go, I'd say Tokyo was pretty coolioko."

84

I don't like hospitals.

Let's be honest: nobody actually does. Ostensibly they're about making people better, but they're not. They're about reminding us that at some stage we all get sick, and we all hurt, and we all get lonely, and sometimes there's nothing anybody can do about any of it.

The only thing on my mind as we walk through the big metal doors into the waiting room is that the last time I was in this exact hospital, I had a mum. And when I left three days later, I didn't.

I suddenly feel horribly sick – right through to the middle – and it hits me just how much my feelings towards this baby are about the fact that it might take Annabel away from me. Because that's what babies do, isn't it? Babies change everything.

As we walk across the big green floors, I try to focus on the rhythm of my breathing and the beating of my heart and the tap of my trainers. Then I feel Nat gently grab my hand. "It's going to be OK, Harriet. Look."

I glance up and there's Dad doing some kind of Riverdance in the hospital corridors. Every time a nurse or doctor walks past, he grabs them and spins them in a little triumphant circle.

This must happen more often than you'd think, because they just wait patiently until he lets them go and then continue with a slight smile down the corridor.

Nat kisses my cheek. "I'll go and get a cup of tea. See you in a few minutes?"

"Offspring Number One!" Dad shouts across the hospital as my non-kissing soulmate disappears through the doors. He immediately wrestles me into a bear hug and tries to whirl me in another circle. "You're back! That's your name henceforth, by the way. Or maybe 'Good' and I shall call your sibling 'Bad' and we'll have an entire set of Manners."

He lets go and I steady myself. "Is..." I swallow. "Does that mean Annabel's OK?"

Dad looks at my face and then wraps me up even tighter. "Of course she's OK, sweetheart. She was always going to be OK."

I can feel my chin starting to do the crumpled-up paper-ball wobble. Dad kisses the top of my head and pulls away. I finally notice his T-shirt. In big letters in red marker pen it says **MY DAUGHTER'S A SUPERMODEL**, and underneath, in little letters, it says: **THE OTHER'S JUST SUPER**.

"It's a girl? I have a baby sister?"

"You certainly do," Dad says with a grin that almost cracks his face in half. He ruffles my hair, and for the first time in my entire life I don't scowl and try to smooth it back again. "I think it's time you met her."

85

The room is totally quiet.

Sunshine is streaming through a window, and there's a small, comforting beeping sound. Annabel's sitting calmly in bed in a clean white nightgown. Her blonde hair is smoothed into its normal impeccable bun, her face is peaceful and her cheeks are rosy. If it wasn't for the fact that she isn't wearing a suit and there's a small, snuffling bundle of material in her arms, you wouldn't know anything had changed at all.

Except it has.

I lurk nervously in the doorway while Dad bounds straight into the room like an excited Labrador. "WIFE-FACE!" he says loudly, and then claps his hand over his mouth. "Sorry," he says in a fake whisper. "I meant wife-face, lower caps." He leans over the bed and peers at the lump in Annabel's arms. "When do her eyes open?"

"I didn't give birth to a kitten, Richard. Her eyes have already opened. She's asleep."

"Don't be so sure, Annabel," Dad says firmly. "They're smarter than they look. Harriet used to have this trick of pretending to be asleep when actually she was listening and storing it all up and getting ready to spout it all back out again just when you least expect it. We need to be prepared. This one looks wily too."

"Good," Annabel says, affectionately rearranging a few of the blankets. "The wilier the better." Then she looks up to the doorway. "Mum? Can I have a word?"

Bunty nods and jingles into the hospital room. She's surprisingly quiet.

"I'm sorry, Mum," Annabel continues. "I've been far too harsh. You've done an amazing job taking care of Harriet. We couldn't have done it without you."

There's a pause and I see Annabel searching for the right words, which is something I have literally never seen before.

"I've changed my mind about your kind offer. We'd love to have you stay with us for the first month or two." There's a pause. "*I* would love you to stay."

Bunty kisses Annabel on the forehead.

"Thank you, darling. I know I haven't been around in the past as much as I should, but I'd really like to change that."

She can be such hard work sometimes, you know.

I don't think I can handle any more.

It's my first baby, and you know I love her to pieces but…

I just think it's best for everyone if she's not here.

They weren't talking about me.

They were talking about Bunty.

A tiny squeak escapes from my throat, and Annabel looks up. She stares at me for a split second and then twists towards Dad.

"Take Tabitha, please," she says, gently thrusting the bundle at him.

"*Tabitha?*" Dad says. It's only when he takes the baby and fits her swiftly into the crook of his arm that I remember he's actually done this before. "Tabitha Manners? As in Tabitha from *Bewitched*?"

Annabel laughs. "It's also Aramaic for *gazelle* and the cat in Beatrix Potter so it should keep us all happy. I'm sure if we do enough research we can find a few record-breaking owls and koalas too." Then she turns back to me. "Come here, Harriet."

I walk towards her and sit gently on the bed. With a slight wince, Annabel bends down and gets a piece of paper out of her handbag. She hands it to me.

On it, written in perfectly neat handwriting, double underlined, it says:

THE MANNERS FAMILY

- HARRIET
- TABITHA
- RICHARD
- ANNABEL
- BUNTY

"You see that?" she says quietly, pointing to it. "You're still at the top of my list, Harriet."

She nudges me with her shoulder, and my world suddenly falls straight back together as if it never exploded in the first place.

"Oh, *what*?" Dad moans, leaning over us. "Are you *kidding* me? I'm *third*? It's my surname in the first place: I gave it to you little name-stealers." He looks at the bundle and gently prods it with a finger. "I've got your card marked, Missy, and I know where you live."

"Can I see her?" I ask nervously. "My sister?"

Dad grins and carefully hands me the bundle, and I stare down at Tabitha.

I don't believe it. I actually do not believe it.

Not only is my new sister a maverick with no respect at all for timetables and plans, apparently she has no interest in statistics either. Less than two per cent of the world has red hair and it's a recessive gene.

She's even more ginger than I am.

"Another top model in the making," Dad says proudly, looking at both of us. "Annabel, you are so incredibly lucky I'm genetically such a hotty."

At that precise moment, Tabitha opens huge blue eyes and looks at Dad with a calm, unimpressed expression that says: *Seriously? Billions of fathers in the world and I got landed with this plonker?*

And I am suddenly absolutely certain that I'm going to love her more than I've ever loved anything, ever. Even maths. Even English. Even history.

Even more than *physics*.

My phone beeps. I quickly give my tiny, adorable sister a gentle kiss on the head and then hand her back to Dad.

Coming back to England tomorrow. ;)
Nick. xxxx

I grin happily and then look over at Bunty, who's vaguely sniffing some flowers next to the bed. Then at Tabitha, yawning and wrinkling her little red nose. Then at Dad, humming under his breath and trying to get Tabitha to high-five him with her tiny palm. Then I look at Annabel, still gazing calmly at me.

She wrinkles her nose and I wrinkle mine back, and I suddenly realise that it doesn't matter how far I go, or how lost I am, or how lonely I feel. I fit in here. I always will.

That's how I know I'm home.

Acknowledgements

Thanks to my wonderful editor, Lizzie Clifford, for helping me discover 'the statue in the stone', and to my agent Kate Shaw, whose patience and kindness gave me the time to find it. Thanks to the whole team at HarperCollins, who have supported both Harriet and myself with passion and tireless creativity from the start, and to Pippa Le Quesne, whose guidance is always illuminating.

Thanks to my family: to my amazing Mum and Dad, always proud of me whether I deserve it or not, and my grandparents, for the world's best cuddles, advice and jam tarts. Thanks to Flossy, for trying so hard to kill my keyboard, and to my little sister, Tara: my best friend, and the only person I'd give up my giant teddy-bear with the blue bow for.

Enormous thanks to Julian and Naho for their incredible generosity, and for re-translating my terrible Japanese without mocking me too heartily. Thanks also to Kristin, Laura and Sarah, for years of support and friendship. You have made many dramas so much smaller.

Finally, to everyone who has read and loved Harriet: you have brought her alive, and I couldn't have done it without you.

Thank you. x